Humanitarianism in the Modern W[

This is a history of famine relief and humanitarianism. The authors apply a moral economy approach to shed new light on the forces and ideas that motivated and shaped humanitarian aid during the Great Irish Famine, the famine of 1921–2 in Soviet Russia, and the 1980s Ethiopian Famine. They place these episodes within a distinctive periodisation of humanitarianism which emphasises the correlations with politico-economic regimes: the time of elitist laissez-faire liberalism in the nineteenth century as one of ad hoc humanitarianism; that of Taylorism and mass society from c. 1900–70 as one of organised humanitarianism; and the blend of individualised post-material lifestyles and neo-liberal public management since 1970 as one of expressive humanitarianism. The book as a whole shifts the focus of the history of humanitarianism from the imperatives of crisis management to the pragmatic mechanisms of fundraising, logistics on the ground, and accounting.

NORBERT GÖTZ is a professor at the Institute of Contemporary History at Södertörn University, Sweden. He is the author of *Ungleiche Geschwister* (2001), for which he has been awarded the Hans Rosenberg Memorial Prize, and *Deliberative Diplomacy* (2011).

GEORGINA BREWIS is an associate professor at University College London. Her previous publications include *A Social History of Student Volunteering* (2014), *English Teachers in a Postwar Democracy* (2014), and *The World of UCL* (2018).

STEFFEN WERTHER is an associate professor at the Institute of Contemporary History at Södertörn University, Sweden. He is the author of *SS-Vision und Grenzland-Realität* (2012).

Humanitarianism in the Modern World
The Moral Economy of Famine Relief

Norbert Götz
Södertörn University

Georgina Brewis
University College London

Steffen Werther
Södertörn University

CAMBRIDGE
UNIVERSITY PRESS

Shaftesbury Road, Cambridge CB2 8EA, United Kingdom

One Liberty Plaza, 20th Floor, New York, NY 10006, USA

477 Williamstown Road, Port Melbourne, VIC 3207, Australia

314–321, 3rd Floor, Plot 3, Splendor Forum, Jasola District Centre, New Delhi – 110025, India

103 Penang Road, #05–06/07, Visioncrest Commercial, Singapore 238467

Cambridge University Press is part of Cambridge University Press & Assessment, a department of the University of Cambridge.

We share the University's mission to contribute to society through the pursuit of education, learning and research at the highest international levels of excellence.

www.cambridge.org
Information on this title: www.cambridge.org/9781108737371

DOI: 10.1017/9781108655903

First published 2020
First paperback edition 2022

A catalogue record for this publication is available from the British Library

Library of Congress Cataloging-in-Publication data
Names: Götz, Norbert, 1965– author. | Brewis, Georgina, author. | Werther, Steffen, 1976– author.
Title: Humanitarianism in the modern world : the moral economy of famine relief / Norbert Götz, Georgina Brewis, Steffen Werther.
Description: 1 Edition. | New York : Cambridge University Press, 2020. | Includes bibliographical references and index.
Identifiers: LCCN 2020009071 (print) | LCCN 2020009072 (ebook) | ISBN 9781108493529 (hardback) | ISBN 9781108737371 (paperback) | ISBN 9781108655903 (epub)
Subjects: LCSH: International relief. | Fund raising. | Humanitarianism–History.
Classification: LCC HV553 .G657 2020 (print) | LCC HV553 (ebook) | DDC 363.8/526–dc23
LC record available at https://lccn.loc.gov/2020009071
LC ebook record available at https://lccn.loc.gov/2020009072

ISBN   978-1-108-49352-9   Hardback
ISBN   978-1-108-73737-1   Paperback

Additional resources for this publication at www.cambridge.org/Humanitarianism.

Contents

Figures

Tables

Acknowledgements

This book is the result of a research project entitled 'The Moral Economy of Global Civil Society: A History of Voluntary Food Aid' conducted from 2013 to 2019. The study was an international partnership between scholars based at the Institute of Contemporary History, Södertörn University, Stockholm, and the UCL Institute of Education, University College London. We thank our respective institutions and extend our gratitude to the project's funders, the Swedish Research Council, for enabling this fruitful collaboration under grant no. 2012-614.

Our particular thanks go to those who, in various ways, have been affiliated with the project. Katarina Friberg was one of the original team members and contributed significantly in bringing the project to focus on economic and other practices of humanitarianism, and on rethinking the concept of moral economy. Francesco Zavatti and Julia Lindström have published detailed studies of Italian relief efforts during the Great Irish Famine and on Swedish fundraising for the famine in Somalia 2011–12 that have informed our work. Franziska Kols briefly served as a research assistant. Teddy Primack has provided help with the editing of the manuscript.

We would also like to thank all those who participated in our international workshops and conference sessions for their contributions. Our research benefitted greatly from the insights of many scholars, especially Maria Framke, Daniel Laqua, Andrew Newby, and Pamala Wiepking. Dominique Marshall and Bertrand Taithe, who commented on early drafts of this manuscript, deserve particular mention and special thanks for their inspiring critique and invaluable advice on the book's proposed structure.

We are also greatly indebted to the many archivists and librarians around the world who made our research possible, as well as two anonymous readers for Cambridge University Press for their rigorous comments. We thank the Foundation for Baltic and East European Studies, Södertörn University's Publication Committee, University College London, and Roma Tre University for additional financial aid in the research, writing, and publication stages.

Our deepest and warmest thanks go to our families. They have supported us with patience and love through the frequent travels for research and the countless hours of writing over the past six years: Alexandra, Alma, Felix, Hattie, Iain, Joella, Linus, Lorena, Philine, and Toby, can you believe it – *it's done!*

Abbreviations

AFSC	American Friends Service Committee
AICF	Action International Contre la Faim
AMR	American Mennonite Relief
ARA	American Relief Administration/ARA Archives
ARC	American Red Cross
BBC	British Broadcasting Corporation
BRA	British Association for the Relief of Extreme Distress in the Remote Parishes of Ireland and Scotland
CA	Christian Aid/CA Archives
Can	Canadian
CARE	Cooperative for Assistance and Relief Everywhere
CDAA	Churches Drought Action for Africa/Ethiopia
CIA	Central Intelligence Agency
CIDA	Canadian International Development Agency
CRC	Central Relief Committee of the Society of Friends (Ireland)
CRDA	Christian Relief and Development Association
CRS	Catholic Relief Services
DAC	Diocesan Archives, Cashel
DAD	Diocesean Archives, Dublin
DEC	Disasters Emergency Committee (UK)
DM	German marks (currency)
ECA	Economic Commission on Africa (UN)
EEC	European Economic Community
EPLF	Eritrean People's Liberation Front
ERA	Eritrean Relief Association
ERC/Eurelcon	European Relief Council
ERD	Emergency Relief Desk
FAI	Fondo Aiuti Italani
FAO	Food and Agriculture Organisation
FCO	Foreign and Commonwealth Office
FEWVRC	Friends' Emergency and War Victims Relief Committee

FSR	Friends of Soviet Russia
FUJ	Federation of Ukrainian Jews
FY	fiscal year
GCRC	General Central Relief Committee for all Ireland
GNP	gross national product
GPU	State Political Directorate (Russia/Soviet Union)
HAC	Historical Archives of the Congregation for the Evangelisation of Peoples
HO	Home Office
IAH	Internationale Arbeiterhilfe
ICRC	International Committee of the Red Cross
ICRR	International Committee for Russian Relief
IIED	International Institute for Environment and Development
IRA	Irish Relief Association for the Destitute Peasantry
ISCU	International Save the Children Union
IWRF	Imperial War Relief Fund
JDC	Joint Distribution Committee
JRO	Joint Relief Operation (Ethiopian Red Cross)
MAD	multiple accountabilities disorder
MP	Member of Parliament (general)
	Monteagle Papers (NLI)
	Murray Papers (DAD)
NCWC	National Catholic Welfare Council
NEP	New Economic Policy
NER	Near East Relief
NGO	non-governmental organisation
NLI	National Library of Ireland
OD	overseas development
ODI	Overseas Development Institute
OEOE	Office for Emergency Operations in Ethiopia (UN)
PIC	Pontifical Irish College
PR	public relations
PRONI	Public Records Office of Northern Ireland
R2P	responsibility to protect
REST	Relief Society of Tigray
RFRF	Russian Famine Relief Fund (UK)
RLN	The Robinson Library, Newcastle University
RRC	Relief and Rehabilitation Commission (Ethiopia)
SC	documents referred to in the weekly meetings
SCF	Save the Children Fund/SCF Archives
SEK	Swedish kronor (currency)
SF	Swiss francs (currency)

SOAS	School of Oriental and African Studies, University of London
SoF	Society of Friends
SoS	Secretary of State (Vatican)
SP	Slattery Papers
SRC	Swedish Red Cross
SVP	Society St Vincent de Paul
t	(metric) tonnes
T	Treasury
TNA(IRL)	The National Archives of Ireland
TNA(UK)	The National Archives (UK)
TP	Trevelyan Papers
TPLF	Tigray People's Liberation Front
UK	United Kingdom (of Great Britain and Ireland)
UN	United Nations
UNICEF	United Nations Children's Fund
URA	United Relief Association
US	adjective form of USA
USA	United States of America
USAID	United States Agency for International Development
UshCL	Ushaw College Library
VSA	Vatican Secret Archives
VRS	Volga Relief Society
WFP	World Food Programme
WIR	Workers' International Relief
WOW	War on Want/WOW Archives
YMCA	Young Men's Christian Association
YWCA	Young Women's Christian Association

Introduction

In a much-cited essay on the occasion of the 1971 famine in East Bengal (today's Bangladesh), moral philosopher Peter Singer claimed that the UK government valued the development of the supersonic Concorde airplane thirty times as highly as the lives of nine million refugees. The Sydney Opera House – then still under construction – served as a benchmark for a similar Australian calculation. Singer sidestepped the more common trope of making comparisons between military and humanitarian spending, perhaps to avoid a tedious discussion of the appropriate level of national security expenses. With regard to individuals, he noted that 'people do not feel in any way ashamed or guilty about spending money on new clothes or a new car instead of giving it to famine relief'. Thus, according to him, while charity may be praised, its lack is not condemned. Singer decried the inadequate reaction to famine on the part of those living in relatively affluent countries as totally unacceptable. For him, the way we look at moral issues and our way of life needs to change.[1] Singer himself donated 10 per cent of his income to Oxfam at the time.[2]

Drawing on scholar-activists such as Singer, as well as Amartya Sen and E. P. Thompson, among others, this book is a call for us to rethink humanitarianism. The history of distant responses to humanitarian crises is full of compelling appeals, remarkable efforts on the ground, and accounts of encouraging achievements. It is a record that is longer than commonly assumed and, as we see it, not adequately known. We have attempted to take a fresh look at humanitarian action through the concept of moral economy.

In Thompson's classic exposition of the concept, moral economy is tied to food riots as the key to understanding how disadvantaged groups confront the rich within agrarian society.[3] Subsequent research across the humanities and

---

[1] Peter Singer, 'Famine, Affluence, and Morality', *Philosophy and Public Affairs* 1, no. 3 (1972): 229–30, 235 (quotation).

[2] Peter Singer, 'Preface', in *Famine, Affluence, and Morality* (Oxford: Oxford University Press, 2016), xi.

[3] E. P. Thompson, 'The Moral Economy of the English Crowd in the Eighteenth Century', *Past and Present*, no. 50 (1971): 76–136. See also E. P. Thompson, 'The Moral Economy Reviewed', in *Customs in Common* (London: Merlin, 1991), 259–351.

1

social sciences has proven the fruitfulness of this Marxist approach, while at the same time monopolising and infusing a term that has a much broader appeal and potential with specific normative presumptions.[4] Whereas the self-interested crowd has found approval as a moral force and inspired researchers, few have engaged in an exploration of the more complex 'paternalistic model' of moral economy, to which Thompson ascribed both 'an ideal existence, and also a fragmentary real existence' in eighteenth-century England.[5] As we see it, such a model still exists today, in both ideal and practice. The present book applies a reframed moral economy approach that focuses on the wealthy and others in generally affluent countries with regard to their provision of food aid in studying three cases of famine relief in different periods, geographical locations, and political circumstances: the Great Irish Famine of the 1840s, the famine in Soviet Russia in 1921–3, and the famine in Ethiopia in the mid-1980s. Our analysis shows that the construction of altruistic meaning is pivotal to understanding the background, practice, and documentation of relief efforts.

The motivation for charitable giving, while often ascribed to universal philanthropy, in fact often reveals impulses and blind spots that result from the specific interests and preferences of donors.[6] As a result, the allocation of limited resources across borders depends on the success of appeals in attracting funds for particular causes, on appropriate ways of providing relief, and on the accountability of aid brokers. Around these key elements of humanitarian reason, a web of moral arguments and choices emerges. By analysing them, one may gain new insight into relief operations, which have been in most cases the traditional focus of research.

Our approach emphasises what are often under-investigated topics, namely, aid appeals, and relief accounts in their narrative and statistical form. Thus, unlike the frequently criticised 'presentism' of relief agents and humanitarian studies, our moral economy approach allows a detached analytical perspective that looks at the future and the past on a par with the present. At the same time, we also suggest a fresh periodisation of humanitarianism, based on the socio-cultural and economic preconditions under which aid efforts operate. In contrast to what has been criticised as a myopic tendency of humanitarian studies in general,[7] the nineteenth century is treated as part of a larger history of emergency aid.

---

[4] Norbert Götz, '"Moral Economy": Its Conceptual History and Analytical Prospects', *Journal of Global Ethics* 11, no. 2 (2015): 147–62.
[5] Thompson, 'Moral Economy of the English Crowd', 88.
[6] Tony Vaux, *The Selfish Altruist: Relief Work in Famine and War* (London: Earthscan, 2001).
[7] Bertrand Taithe, 'Humanitarian History?', in *The Routledge Companion to Humanitarian Action*, eds Roger Mac Ginty and Jenny H. Peterson (London: Routledge, 2015), 70. On various aspects of presentism, see John Borton, 'Improving the Use of History in the International

Although transnational charity predates the twentieth century and the Red Cross, early humanitarianism has left few sources and remains under-researched. The rise of humanitarian action is correlated to Western modernisation and expansion, with its improved communication, widened frames of reference and material, and logistical capabilities. Singer's call for famine relief argued that the progression from a world of face-to-face contacts to a global village with an awareness of faraway places and the power to make a difference has brought distant strangers into a sphere of moral obligation.[8] The increasingly interconnected world that has emerged over the past two-and-a-half centuries has had its bearing on the evolution of thinking along such lines – whatever privileges and biases may inform the morality of current world citizens.

Our analysis of aid organisations thus includes contributions from English and non-English speaking countries in today's Global North and the world-at-large. We employ a theoretical outlook that reflects the emerging academic interest in histories of morality, the cross-disciplinary rise of a 'moral economy' discourse beyond the confines of Thompson's framing, and the growing field of humanitarian studies, with a history of the humanitarian movement. Our original research is based on a rereading or first-time examination of a wide range of published and unpublished sources. Three unique aspects distinguish this book.

First, its integrated moral economy perspective draws on philosophical, humanitarian, and medical ethics, especially the problems of triage. This allows a balanced assessment of humanitarian action that goes beyond endorsing idealistic efforts or denouncing power politics. In avoiding both naïveté and cynicism, we have sought a nuanced understanding of the mechanisms and dilemmas of humanitarian action by examining how donors and relief agencies endow aid choices with altruistic meaning in mounting appeals, allocating, and accounting for aid. Our moral economy perspective is built on an understanding of humanitarianism as voluntary emergency aid. At the same time, we point out the correlation between humanitarian efforts and human rights advocacy, actions taken by governments, and development assistance. Other significant discussions to which the moral economy approach contributes insights concern religious stimuli; the motivation of aid between the poles of altruism and social control; market affinity; the connection between domestic and foreign philanthropy; imperialism and neo-colonialism; gender and class relations; and the types of humanitarian agencies and endeavours that characterise different epochs.

Humanitarian Sector', *European Review of History* 23, nos 1–2 (2016): 193–209; Maria Framke and Joël Glasman, 'Editorial', *Werkstatt Geschichte*, no. 68 (2015): 3–12; Peter Stamatov, *The Origins of Global Humanitarianism: Religion, Empires, and Advocacy* (New York: Cambridge University Press, 2013), 8; Jean-Hervé Bradol and Jacky Mamou, 'La commémoration amnésique des humanitaires', *Humanitaire*, no. 10 (2004): 12–28.

[8] Singer, 'Famine, Affluence, and Morality', 232–3. See also Singer, 'Preface', xxvi.

Second, the book's contextualised case studies provide instructive narratives of how humanitarianism developed over the past two centuries. We propose a periodisation of humanitarianism by analogy to politico-economic regimes, rather than the geopolitical sequencing that has dominated academic analyses in this field up to now. In the view taken by our moral economy approach, the time of elitist laissez-faire liberalism was one of *ad hoc humanitarianism* (c. 1800–1900); that of Taylorism and mass society was one of *organised humanitarianism* (c. 1900–70); and the blend of individualised post-material lifestyles, flexible production and communication regimes, and neo-liberal public management in our own time is what we call *expressive humanitarianism* (since c. 1970). We thereby shift the principal question regarding humanitarian efforts from 'what?' to 'how?', moving the focus of the history of humanitarianism from the imperatives of crisis management in the outside world to the pragmatic mechanisms of fundraising, relief efforts on the ground, and accounting, thus correlating their history with that of voluntary action and broader societal trends.[9]

Third, the empirical studies provide insights into the history of three humanitarian causes. The study of Irish famine relief in the 1840s, for example, redetermines the origins of the major British relief campaign. It is also singular in acknowledging the role of the Society of St Vincent de Paul, and in drawing on material from the Vatican-based Sacred Congregation for the Propagation of the Faith and diocesan archives across the Western Hemisphere. The study on Soviet famine relief in the 1920s provides a broader perspective than previous organisation-based studies and identifies similarities among competing ethnic, religious, political, and national relief cultures. Another feature is the analysis of letters of appeal written by individuals and groups in Russia facing starvation, addressed to private individuals and groups in the USA – a rare documentary source in the context of famine studies. Our analysis of the famine in Ethiopia of the 1980s is one of the few historical examinations of transnational food aid during that disaster that draws on newly available archival sources. Historical research to date has generally focused on Anglo-American fundraising and the geopolitics of aid for Ethiopia, rather than on issues of allocation and accounting. Likewise, scholars have concentrated more on the cultural impact of the Band Aid and Live Aid phenomena than on the changes they wrought in the humanitarian industry, which is what we studied.

* * *

---

[9] See also Norbert Götz, Georgina Brewis, and Steffen Werther, 'Humanitäre Hilfe: Eine Braudel'sche Perspektive', *Freiwilligenarbeit und gemeinnützige Organisationen im Wandel: Neue Perspektiven auf das 19. und 20. Jahrhundert*, eds Nicole Kramer and Christine G. Krüger (Berlin: DeGruyter, 2019), 89–119.

Revisiting his article 'Famine, Affluence, and Morality' after more than forty years, Singer corrected two points. He had drawn an analogy between pulling a drowning child out of a pond and donating money to save the life of a Bengali. Implicit in the argument that distance did not matter was that the cost of replacing muddy clothes would be equivalent to the amount that could save a life in the Global South. In a later essay, Singer also referred to a calculation that donating US$200 would be enough to enable a two-year-old in a country like Pakistan or Nigeria to reach the age of six, giving it a high likelihood of survival until adulthood. Based on further research into charity effectiveness that put the figure at closer to US$5,000, Singer now acknowledged that life-saving was a more expensive business than he had previously assumed.[10] However, citing the middle class in affluent countries, Singer did not think that this undermined his moral argument that 'instead of spending our available income on new clothes, cars, dinners in expensive restaurants, or other items that cannot be compared, in moral importance, to saving someone from starving to death, we ought to give our money to those who can most effectively use it to prevent starvation'.[11]

Singer's second revision is a tacit but sweeping reformulation of what he had written previously. Apparently uncomfortable with his infantilisation of the 'Bengali', he now reformulated the analogy as pertaining to two children, one drowning in a pond nearby and another 'in a developing country dying from poverty-related causes'.[12] Earlier, Singer had explained that his use of the example of children is not grounded on the belief they are more worth saving than adults, but rather to simplify the issue, since children cannot be assumed to have brought poverty upon themselves.[13] Seen in this light, the imbalance in the original analogy appears to be not so much a postcolonial faux pas as a well-intentioned rhetorical move assigning a moral state of innocence to a broader circle of people suffering from famine in the South. However, in singling out a particular group to make his analogy vivid, Singer surrendered that impartiality which he himself esteems, and which is generally considered a core value of humanitarian action.[14]

The present book focuses on related dilemmas, contradictions, and unintended consequences in an asymmetrical world. Human agents in different

---

[10] Singer, 'Famine, Affluence, and Morality', 231–2; Singer, 'Preface', xix–xx; Peter Singer, 'The Singer Solution to World Poverty', *New York Times Magazine* (5 Sept. 1999).

[11] Peter Singer, 'Reconsidering the Famine Relief Argument', in *Food Policy: The Responsibility of the United States in the Life and Death Choices*, eds Peter G. Brown and Henry Shue (New York: Free Press, 1977), 37.

[12] Singer, 'Preface', xvii.   [13] Singer, 'Singer Solution'.

[14] Singer, 'Famine, Affluence, and Morality', 232; Singer, 'Reconsidering', 42–3; Peter Singer, 'Outsiders: Our Obligations to Those beyond Our Borders', in *The Ethics of Assistance: Morality and the Distant Needy*, ed. Deen K. Chatterjee (Cambridge: Cambridge University Press, 2004), 14.

official positions act according to their socially embedded preferences, drawing on fragmented information, insufficient material resources, and the limited trust they have in others. We have arranged these topics thematically according to our moral economy approach. We analyse appeals for aid, the allocation of relief, and accounting documents as three characteristic dimensions. These main chapters treat the cases of relief in Ireland, Soviet Russia, and Ethiopia in chronological order. However, those interested in a single case can follow its thread across the three central chapters.

Chapter 1 draws on literature that addresses dilemmas of humanitarian aid, exploring the social origins of famine and outlining our moral economic perspective on humanitarian aid. Chapter 2 presents an overview of humanitarian history as seen according to our periodisation scheme, followed by background information on the context of the three case studies. Chapter 3 discusses aid appeals as measures of humanitarian sensibility and as instruments for securing donations. Chapter 4 examines relief operations, showing the difficulties humanitarian workers face from headquarters or encounter in the field as their efforts are either facilitated or constrained by economic, moral, or political considerations. Chapter 5 shows how humanitarian agencies account for the aid they provide, acknowledging donors, creating aid narratives, and seeking to legitimise their allocation decisions. The Conclusion brings together our findings and recommendations for future histories of humanitarian aid and for research on humanitarianism in general.

1   Famine Relief in Perspective

1.1   Social Origins of Famine

An undercurrent of popular resistance in rich countries tends to curtail development aid to the Global South. Nevertheless, the sums the humanitarian sector raised after the 2004 tsunami catastrophe – so considerable that there were difficulties effectively deploying them – illustrate the public's greater willingness to alleviate suffering in times of acute emergency.[1] The resulting discrepancy between transnational approaches to development, on the one hand, and disaster relief, on the other, emerges from moral assumptions about causality and economic ones about terminability. The sympathy for those affected by exceptional catastrophes is paralleled in domestic politics, where governments tend to make greater efforts to combat famine than they do in dealing with everyday hunger and malnutrition.[2] However, compared to eruptive disasters like earthquakes, famine is an insidious slow-onset emergency that tends to evolve incrementally in a succession of calamities with a variety of intersecting causes. Famine is, therefore, a complex crisis of subsistence and survival that reveals vulnerabilities in the social order.[3]

The processes of famine are triggered by external and sometimes internal shocks rather than arising by 'spontaneous combustion'. At the same time, its

---

[1] Cormac Ó Gráda, *Eating People Is Wrong, and Other Essays on Famine, Its Past, and Its Future* (Princeton, NJ: Princeton University Press, 2015), 196; Keith Epstein, 'Crisis Mentality', *Stanford Social Innovation Review* 4, no. 1 (2006): 48–57; Rony Brauman, 'Global Media and the Myths of Humanitarian Relief: The Case of the 2004 Tsunami', in *Humanitarianism and Suffering: The Mobilization of Empathy*, eds Richard Ashby Wilson and Richard D. Brown (Cambridge: Cambridge University Press, 2009), 108–17; Carolina Holgersson Ivarsson, 'Moral Economy Reconfigured: Philanthropic Engagement in Post-tsunami Sri Lanka', *Journal of Global Ethics* 11, no. 2 (2015): 233–45.
[2] Amartya Sen, *Development as Freedom* (Oxford: Oxford University Press, 1999), 156; Dan Banik, 'Is Democracy the Answer? Famine Prevention in Two Indian States', in *The New Famines: Why Famines Persist in an Era of Globalization*, ed. Stephen Devereux (London: Routledge, 2007), 290–311; Judith Lichtenberg, 'Absence and the Unfond Heart: Why People Are Less Giving than They Might Be', in *The Ethics of Assistance: Morality and the Distant Needy*, ed. Deen K. Chatterjee (Cambridge: Cambridge University Press, 2004), 87.
[3] David Arnold, *Famine: Social Crisis and Historical Change* (Oxford: Blackwell, 1988), 7, 19, 26, 29, 75.

causes are embedded in the economic, social, and political fabric of a society.[4] Socio-economic indicators are therefore more reliable than satellite technology or hydrological instruments for the assessment of famine, although artificial intelligence may combine such indicators in powerful ways in the future.[5] Consequently, natural anomalies such as exceptional droughts or floods need not result in widespread mortality. They may have disastrous and at times global effects on food production and vulnerable populations, but afflicted societies may nonetheless be resilient enough to absorb shocks, cope, and recover without major demographic effects. Thus, the tens of millions who have perished from famine in centuries past may have represented a largely avoidable tragedy caused by the inadequate performance of public institutions and markets.[6]

Amartya Sen's ground-breaking economic studies have contributed insights into the social conditionality of famine in regard to modern exchange economies. According to Sen, mass starvation is not 'the last and most dreadful mode by which nature represses a redundant population', as Malthus believed.[7] Rather, starvation results from the failure of governance or from purposeful decisions, whatever hardships nature may impose on livelihoods. As Sen has demonstrated, there need not even be an overall 'food availability decline' in order for a famine to emerge. The lack of financial or legal entitlement to vital amounts of food suffices to cause starvation in certain groups.[8]

In this perspective, public action or inaction that results in people dying from epidemics of hunger or famine may be a consequence of (a) adherence to inappropriate entitlement patterns; (b) questionable economic doctrines;

---

[4] Arnold, *Famine*, 6–7; Martin Ravallion, 'Famines and Economics', *Journal of Economic Literature* 35, no. 3 (1997): 1207; Gilles Carbonnier, *Humanitarian Economics: War, Disaster and the Global Aid Market* (London: Hurst, 2015), 128. See also Kathleen Tierney, *The Social Roots of Risk: Producing Disasters, Promoting Resilience* (Stanford, CA: Standford University Press, 2014).

[5] Randolph C. Kent, *Anatomy of Disaster Relief: The International Network in Action* (London: Pinter, 1987), 22–3; Ben Parker, 'Famine and the Machine: Can Big Money and Big Data Make Famine a Thing of the Past?' (Geneva: New Humanitarian, 2018), available at www.thenewhumanitarian.org/analysis/2018/10/12/famine-and-machine-funding-prevention-data (accessed 29 June 2019).

[6] Mike Davis, *Late Victorian Holocausts: El Nino Famines and the Making of the Third World* (London: Verso, 2001), 8; Ravallion, 'Famines and Economics', 1219, 1236.

[7] Thomas Robert Malthus, *An Essay on the Principle of Population, as It Affects the Future Improvement of Society: With Remarks on the Speculations of W. Godwin, M. Condorcet and Other Writers* (London: Johnson, 1798), iv.

[8] Amartya Sen, *Poverty and Famines: An Essay on Entitlements and Deprivation* (Oxford: Clarendon, 1981), 154. See also Guido Alfani and Cormac Ó Gráda, 'Famines in Europe: An Overview', in *Famine in European History*, eds Guido Alfani and Cormac Ó Gráda (Cambridge: Cambridge University Press, 2017), 3, 21; Haris Gazdar, 'Pre-modern, Modern and Post-modern Famine in Iraq, 1990–2003', in *The New Famines: Why Famines Persist in an Era of Globalization*, ed. Stephen Devereux (London: Routledge, 2007), 129.

(c) irresponsibility; or (d) corruption. It may also be a side effect or a weapon of war. Whether famine is due to systemic malfunction or intentional abuse, officials tend to gloss over it or blame nature. However, Sen argues that democracy and famine are incompatible. According to him, a free press and a pluralistic political system are 'the best early-warning system a country threatened by famines can have'.[9] Democratic governments cannot afford to ignore such warnings without incurring political repercussions, and so they engage the apparatus and resources of the state to prevent large-scale starvation.

Sen's argument combines a rational theory of government with an assumption derived from natural law that there exists a commonly shared understanding of general needs and rights.[10] Although the extent to which popular consensus on the unacceptability of famine may impact democratic politics varies, depending on the organisation of the political system, the dynamics of the public sphere, and the nature of historical experience, such impact is generally believed to have a preventative effect. Even under repressive regimes, the activism of opposition groups or the government's attempt to maintain popular support may entail a similar tendency.[11] From this perspective, famine results from stunted patterns of reciprocity or their absence, namely, from the relative insensitivity of authoritarian or colonial regimes to popular acclaim as opposed to the 'moral economy of democracy'.[12] The decreasing significance of poor harvests for the emergence of famine in the twentieth century and the increasing likelihood that starvation is a consequence of war or ideological projects are attributable – apart from technological and material factors – to the spread of democracy.[13]

In the case of India, Sen points out that dedicated public policy has averted the threat of famine since independence, whereas under the British, famine had been endemic. Acknowledging the immediate pull effect on food that a cash flow to affected populations has, as through public employment programmes

---

[9] Sen, *Development as Freedom*, 181.
[10] Ibid., 150–1; Hans Agné, 'Does Global Democracy Matter? Hypotheses on Famine and War', in *Transnational Actors in Global Governance: Patterns, Explanations, and Implications*, eds Christer Jönsson and Jonas Tallberg (Basingstoke: Palgrave Macmillan, 2010), 182–3.
[11] Sen, *Development as Freedom*, 152–6. The Nazis were highly attentive to the sustenance of the German population. See Gustavo Corni and Horst Gies, *Brot – Butter – Kanonen: Die Ernährungswirtschaft in Deutschland unter der Diktatur Hitlers* (Berlin: Akademie, 1997).
[12] Parama Roy, *Alimentary Tracts: Appetites, Aversions, and the Postcolonial* (Durham, NC: Duke University Press, 2010), 22. Against the belief in the 'moral economy of democracy', which Roy ascribes to Sen, she herself highlights the persistence of alimentary inequality and violence in democratic India.
[13] Cormac Ó Gráda, *Famine: A Short History* (Princeton, NJ: Princeton University Press, 2009), 10–11, 36; Alex de Waal, *Mass Starvation: The History and Future of Famine* (Cambridge: Polity, 2018), 94. See also the essays in Stephen Devereux, ed. *The New Famines: Why Famines Persist in an Era of Globalization* (London: Routledge, 2007).

or direct disbursals, Sen remains ambiguous about relief-in-kind. The provision of food may compensate for malfunctioning markets, but administrative and logistic capacity is presupposed. However, where markets fail, governments also tend to be dysfunctional.[14]

Ultimately, Sen's approach faces the dilemma that undemocratic governments do exist. Intergovernmental bodies and voluntary agencies[15] from abroad may be more committed to saving lives than authoritarian governments, although they lack a formal mandate to act on behalf of those starving. Outsiders may also be engaged in hegemonic projects for which their humanitarian ideas and practices offer a partial remedy. From a practical point of view, therefore, international relief organisations, with their ability to draw attention to emergencies and their capacity for material intervention on the supply-side, remain crucial to the alleviation of suffering.[16]

Sen has been accused of representing an agenda along Keynesian lines by proposing public works projects in times of crisis. The economic and legal (rather than political) understanding suggested by the entitlement approach, and its neglect of public relief and charity, has been cited as failing to adequately take human responsibility into account. Some authors have contrasted the legalistic view of entitlements with the assertion of provisions through active negotiation of societal rules. In accordance with E. P. Thompson's moral economy of the 'crowd', this includes collective action and unruly behaviour. Sen's analysis disregards 'extra-entitlement transfers', such as looting, that leave those who are well-off particularly vulnerable.[17]

---

[14] Amartya Sen, 'Food Entitlements and Economic Chains', in *Hunger in History: Food Shortage, Poverty, and Deprivation*, ed. Lucile F. Newman (Oxford: Blackwell, 1990), 380–1. The claim that famines have been averted in independent India is questionable, as 130,000 people died in a drought-induced famine in 1972–3. See Ó Gráda, *Famine*, 231, 276.

[15] We avoid the term 'non-governmental organisations' (NGOs) throughout this book, not only because it would be anachronistic to apply it before the second half of the twentieth century but also since it has a highly problematic history, is a negative epithet, and is rejected by parts of the voluntary sector. See Norbert Götz, 'Reframing NGOs: The Identity of an International Relations Non-starter', *European Journal of International Relations* 14, no. 2 (2008): 231–58.

[16] Mark Duffield, 'NGOs, Disaster Relief and Asset Transfer in the Horn: Political Survival in a Permanent Emergency', *Development and Change* 24, no. 1 (1993): 132; Ravallion, 'Famines and Economics', 1227; Giorgio Agamben, *Homo Sacer: Sovereign Power and Bare Life* (Stanford, CA: Stanford University Press, 1998), 133; Agné, 'Does Global Democracy Matter?'.

[17] Sen, *Poverty and Famines*, 49; Jenny Edkins, *Whose Hunger? Concepts of Famine, Practices of Aid* (Minneapolis: University of Minnesota Press, 2000), 44, 48–9; David Keen, *The Benefits of Famine: A Political Economy of Famine and Relief in Southwestern Sudan, 1983–1989* (Princeton, NJ: Princeton University Press, 1994), 4–5; Arnold, *Famine*, 83–6; Charles Gore, 'Entitlement Relations and "Unruly" Social Practices: A Comment on the Work of Amartya Sen', *Journal of Development Studies* 29, no. 3 (1993): 448; Stephen Devereux, 'Sen's Entitlement Approach: Critiques and Counter-critiques', in *The New Famines: Why Famines Persist in an Era of Globalization*, ed. Stephen Devereux (London: Routledge, 2007), 77; Thompson, 'Moral Economy of the English Crowd'.

Building on Sen, Alex de Waal has introduced the idea of a political anti-famine contract that he links to a popular movement's assertion of rights vis-à-vis a reluctant government. It is similar to the notion of a 'moral economy', although it excludes law-breaking and violent behaviour from consideration as a legitimate means of protest. While such analytical perspectives yield a more nuanced picture, the 'political voice' of the underprivileged is inherent in 'Sen's law' of a nexus between democracy and the prevention of famine, even though the resulting administrative measures for subsistence may appear managerial.[18]

Another criticism accuses Sen of failing to regard organised violence and intentional starvation.[19] Ever since antiquity blockades, scorched earth policies, and other 'faminogenic actions' have been deliberately used as instruments to subdue and kill.[20] The emergence in modern times of 'total war' has aggravated these practices. For example, the 'Hunger Plan' of the German occupiers and their withdrawal of food from the Russian population caused four to seven million people to starve to death in the Soviet Union between 1941 and 1944.[21] Warlords in our times continue to deliberately create food shortages in order to starve target populations as part of the repertoire of genocide.[22] Democracies have also routinely used the withholding of food as a tool of warfare or part of sanctions imposed on what they considered 'rogue states', and continue to do so.[23] While the purposeful starving of civilians was

---

[18] See Alex de Waal, *Famine Crimes: Politics and the Disaster Relief Industry in Africa* (Oxford: Currey, 1997), 11–12, 214; Edkins, *Whose Hunger?*, 54, 62.

[19] Amrita Rangasami, '"Failure of Exchange Entitlements" Theory of Famine: A Response', *Economic and Political Weekly* 20, nos 41–2 (1985): 1747–52, 1797–801; Alex de Waal, 'A Re-assessment of Entitlement Theory in the Light of the Recent Famines in Africa', *Development and Change* 21, no. 3 (1990): 486–8; Keen, *Benefits of Famine*, 5.

[20] de Waal, *Mass Starvation*, 30 (quotation); Ó Gráda, *Famine*, 229; Arnold, *Famine*, 97.

[21] Lizzie Collingham, *The Taste of War: World War Two and the Battle for Food* (London: Allen Lane, 2011); Wigbert Benz, *Der Hungerplan im 'Unternehmen Barbarossa' 1941* (Berlin: Wissenschaftlicher Verlag, 2011), 77–80; Alex J. Kay, 'Germany's Staatssekretäre, Mass Starvation and the Meeting of 2 May 1941', *Journal of Contemporary History* 41, no. 4 (2006): 685–700. See also Tatjana Tönsmeyer, Peter Haslinger, and Agnes Laba, eds, *Coping with Hunger and Shortage under German Occupation in World War II* (London: Palgrave Macmillan, 2018).

[22] de Waal, *Mass Starvation*; Jenny Edkins, 'The Criminalization of Mass Starvation: From Natural Disaster to Crime against Humanity', in *The New Famines: Why Famines Persist in an Era of Globalization*, ed. Stephen Devereux (London: Routledge, 2007), 50–65.

[23] Ó Gráda, *Famine*, 229–30; Mary Elisabeth Cox, 'Hunger Games: Or How the Allied Blockade in the First World War Deprived German Children of Nutrition, and Allied Food Aid Subsequently Saved Them', *Economic History Review* 68, no. 2 (2015): 600–31; C. Paul Vincent, *The Politics of Hunger: The Allied Blockade of Germany, 1915–1919* (Athens: Ohio University Press, 1985); Joan Beaumont, 'Starving for Democracy: Britain's Blockade of and Relief for Occupied Europe, 1939–1945', *War & Society* 8, no. 2 (1990): 57–82. For a contemporary example, see Gazdar, 'Pre-modern, Modern and Post-modern Famine'.

ruled a war crime by the end of the twentieth century,[24] there continue to be instances of war, civil strife, and economic blockade that raise the issue of food supply, which Sen does not seem to find problematical. Moreover, Sen does not systematically discuss the reverse situation, where food may be used as a tool in power struggles by providing nourishment to select populations. Instead, he sees this as a positive force in democratic competition. However, the provision of food is routinely used in different ways: it may serve a country's interests abroad, or it may be co-opted by authoritarian regimes and unholy alliances. The US 'Food for Peace' programme was a policy instrument that created loyalty throughout the Cold War and continues to serve US foreign interests today, while recipient authorities, for example in Sudan, have a long record of appropriating food aid for their own purposes. The distribution of aid may be correctly or incorrectly attributed to foreign leaders like Reagan or Gaddafi; or elites in recipient countries may not acknowledge the source of the aid and try to take control of it themselves. As a Sudanese official lamented: 'Rather than the family seeing me as the main breadwinner, now they see another important person coming in at the time of my inability to play that role.'[25] It is a neglected aspect of Thompson's work that, apart from demands from below, the moral economy encompasses a dimension through which the provider of food symbolically assumes a parental role. As a manifestation of an asymmetrical power relationship, the origin of relief supplies is highly significant for both the feeder and the fed. At the same time, the source of the gift may be understood in different ways and may be subject to power struggles. The control of the 'last mile' in the aid chain is decisive for whose stomach will be relieved, and it allows for a strong claim of paternalistic credit vis-à-vis the final recipients.

Sen does not treat mass atrocities or the deliberate use of power, for example, in the negotiation of rules or through violent actions, nor does he consider how paternal food providers wield power. However, all these scenarios may be understood as the manipulation of entitlement patterns.[26] Moreover, entitlement to food, even when it is contested, remains significant for individual chances of survival under varying conditions. Thus, food deliveries may be perceived as charitable aid alongside the notion of entitlement, thereby creating a moral economy of provision.

Objection has been made to Sen's supposed failure to capture essential triggers of contemporary famines. Stephen Devereux argues that 'new

---

[24] Jean-Marie Henckaerts and Louise Doswald-Beck, *Customary International Humanitarian Law, vol. 1: Rules* (Cambridge: University Press, 2005), 186.

[25] Susanne Jaspars, *Food Aid in Sudan: A History of Power, Politics and Profit* (London: Zed, 2018), 160 (quotation), 172–3, 179.

[26] See Helinä Melkas, *Humanitarian Emergencies: Indicators, Measurements, and Data Considerations* (Helsinki: UNU/WIDER, 1996), 24.

famines' (i.e., since the 1980s) may originate from unconventional factors such as epidemic diseases (HIV/AIDS), flawed political liberalisation and economic reform processes, tensions between governments and donors, or international sanctions. He suggests that the paradigm shift in famine studies from Malthusian food production failure over to Sen's entitlement and market failure should be complemented by another shift that would encompass failures of accountability and lapses in humanitarian responses. This would switch the focus from natural and economic factors to a political orientation that recognises 'complex emergencies'.[27]

Since famines today are less widespread and severe than in the past, there are controversies over which cases should actually be classified as famines. Devereux concedes that, while the entitlement approach refers primarily to access to food through market mechanisms, it may also be applied to the spheres of production and transfer (the latter with particular affinity to politics and 'new famines').[28] However, his suggestion disregards the coping strategies of the starving, the significance of which is encapsulated in the observation that 'relief is generally merely a footnote to the story of how people survive famine'.[29] In addition, the shift towards failures of response and the raising of questions such as 'who allowed the famine to happen?' ignores Sen's analysis of the significance of different political regimes for the emergence and prevention of famine, and his transfer-oriented recommendation for public policy.[30]

Sen's approach may be more robust than some of his critics like to believe. A weakness of his perspective remains an entrenchment in the paradigm of the nation-state, since it fails to take international conflicts and capabilities into account. The weight of these factors may increase in a globalising world, although they have already been significant in the past and are certain to remain so in times of a re-emergence of nationalism. While Devereux's suggestions may stimulate further research, his model seems to unduly endogenise the provision of foreign aid, making any absence of humanitarian action appear as a trigger of famine, rather than as a failure of its remedy.[31] Despite the advancement of a permanent 'aid industry' and the rise of 'global

[27] See Stephen Devereux, 'Introduction: From "Old Famines" to "New Famines"', in *The New Famines: Why Famines Persist in an Era of Globalization*, ed. Stephen Devereux (London: Routledge, 2007), 2, 7, 9–11, 22–3. For an account of recent famines, including so-called new variant famines correlated to HIV/AIDS, see Ó Gráda, *Eating People*; de Waal, *Mass Starvation*.

[28] Stephen Devereux and Zoltan Tiba, 'Malawi's First Famine, 2001–2002', in *The New Famines: Why Famines Persist in an Era of Globalization*, ed. Stephen Devereux (London: Routledge, 2007), 144; Devereux, 'Sen's Entitlement Approach', 67.

[29] de Waal, *Famine Crimes*, 1. See also Mark Duffield, 'From Protection to Disaster Resilience', in *The Routledge Companion to Humanitarian Action*, eds Roger Mac Ginty and Jenny H. Peterson (London: Routledge, 2015), 28–9.

[30] See Devereux, 'Introduction', 10.   [31] Devereux, 'Introduction', 6, 8–9, 13, 23.

governance' as a buzzword of international relations, humanitarian assistance may still be best understood as the response to an external crisis, not a safety net to be taken for granted. The realisation that certain emergency structures such as relief camps and distribution centres disrupt social life should encourage the critical examination of humanitarian efforts.[32]

1.2   The Moral Economy of Aid

Humanity and impartiality are the main principles of humanitarianism. They were formally established by the Red Cross and Red Crescent movements and have long since been adopted by the humanitarian sector as a whole. Together they form the backbone of the imperative of assistance, whereas other values, such as neutrality, unity, and independence, address operational means to achieve those two ends.[33] While humanity and impartiality may emanate from a specific tradition, as with the Red Cross, or a particular consequentialist utilitarian ethic, as in the case of Singer, they also mirror the human condition more broadly and constitute 'the precepts of many religions and moral codes'.[34] Both as ideas and in practice, these principles preceded the establishment of the Red Cross, although they have not always been standards of humanitarian efforts.[35] Together humanity and impartiality suggest an active, needs-based, universal approach to the provision of relief and the prevention of suffering. This is also made clear by the fact that the Red Cross, and the codifier of its principles, Jean Pictet, define impartiality as encompassing the dimensions of non-discrimination and proportionality.

Providing aid to distant strangers has emerged from this broader ethical pedigree as the vaunted ideal of humanitarianism over the past 250 years.

---

[32] See Amartya Sen, 'Human Rights and Development', in *Development as a Human Right: Legal, Political, and Economic Dimensions*, eds Bård A. Andreassen and Stephen P. Marks (Cambridge, MA: Harvard School of Public Health, 2006), 1–8.

[33] Jean Pictet, *The Fundamental Principles of the Red Cross Proclaimed by the Twentieth International Conference of the Red Cross, Vienna, 1965: Commentary* (Geneva: Henry Dunant Institute, 1979), 12–13, 48. See also Vaux, *Selfish Altruist*, 5. Regarding the significance of the principles of humanity and impartiality for humanitarian actors in general, see Hugo Slim, *Humanitarian Ethics: A Guide to the Morality of Aid in War and Disaster* (London: Hurst, 2015), 39–64.

[34] Pictet, *Fundamental Principles*, 34; Don Johnston, 'An Examination of the Principles-based Ethics by which Red Cross Personnel Evaluate Private Donor Suitability', in *Conscience, Leadership and the Problem of 'Dirty Hands'*, eds Matthew Beard and Sandra Lynch (Bingley: Emerald, 2015), 125.

[35] Jean Pictet, *Development and Principles of International Humanitarian Law* (Dordrecht: Nijhoff, 1985), 21–2; Jean Guillermand, 'The Historical Foundations of Humanitarian Action, vol. 1: The Religious Influence, vol. 2: Humanism and Philosophical Thought', *International Review of the Red Cross* 34, nos 298–9 (1994): 42–55, 194–216. On the lack of significance that these principles have had for some early humanitarian groups, see Michael Barnett, *Empire of Humanity: A History of Humanitarianism* (Ithaca, NY: Cornell University Press, 2011), 5.

The same ideal is also prominent in the hagiographic narratives that sometimes displace accounts of actual practice. However, the extent to which the ideal is pursued and its significance for the provision of aid is controversial. A recent study of the 'projectification' of the humanitarian field urges us 'to look beyond the content of ideas towards the way they are interpreted in practice and implemented, and the way resources associated with them are allocated'.[36] In fact, the historical record of humanitarian efforts is one of both inclusion and exclusion. Even professional aid workers tend to feel greater attachment to specific individuals, such as their colleagues or patients, rather than being able to cherish generic humanity.[37] In practice, 'no one can feel all the suffering in the world with equal force', and humanitarianism is characterised by its 'selective patterns'.[38] Even Singer admits the proposition that distance ought not matter for the obligation to help may be counter-intuitive. He therefore calls for a new reflective morality to supersede evolutionary-bred community ethics.[39] At the same time, humanity is also an abstraction that glosses over existing racial and other prejudices, and prevalent gender norms, all of which frequently have a bearing on how aid causes are presented and addressed.

The discrepancy between theoretical outlines and practices can be seen from the approaches taken by aid providers themselves. In-group solidarity and special relationships have always been significant motivations, which under conditions of distress tend to morph into humanitarian assistance. Partly overlapping this phenomenon is the uncoordinated division of labour – or even competition – between humanitarian initiatives that leaves the needs of different groups of people addressed unevenly. In addition to avowed divergence from basic humanitarian norms, there are more or less subtle, unconscious departures as a consequence of personal and institutionalised biases. These issues all ensue from the conditionality of human compassion, for which universal humanity frequently serves as a grand narrative, while active sympathy draws on a recipient's credibility, reputation, or similitude, and on strategic expectations of the donor.

Apart from the varying extent to which humanitarian efforts embrace the ideals of serving humanity and impartiality, their application is necessarily subject to external constraints. Humanitarian agents constantly struggle with insufficient means, with the logistic difficulties of reaching those suffering

---

[36] Monika Krause, *The Good Project: Humanitarian Relief NGOs and the Fragmentation of Reason* (Chicago: University of Chicago Press, 2014), 171.

[37] Liisa H. Malkki, *The Need to Help: The Domestic Arts of International Humanitarianism* (Durham, NC: Duke University Press, 2015), 33.

[38] Brauman, 'Global Media', 108; Laura Suski, 'Children, Suffering, and the Humanitarian Appeal', in *Humanitarianism and Suffering: The Mobilization of Empathy*, eds Richard Ashby Wilson and Richard D. Brown (Cambridge: Cambridge University Press, 2009), 211.

[39] Singer, 'Preface', xxi–xxviii; Singer, 'Reconsidering', 42.

most, and with vested public and private interests seeking to manipulate aid. Such difficulties make the practice of humanitarian ethics 'profoundly interpretive rather than enactive'.[40] Humanitarian ideals can be translated into meaningful precepts only when directed towards 'a second-best world based on hard-headed assessments of needs and options'.[41]

Attempts to act under the banner of humanity and impartiality are therefore compromised by the concrete political and economic circumstances surrounding them. The humanitarian sector must seek to ward off political influences in order to safeguard a 'humanitarian space' (both virtual and actual) in which its own principled logic of humanity and impartiality can prevail. As such space depends on a ruler's circumscription and on donors who may impose restrictive agendas, humanitarian action is caught in an insoluble dilemma.[42] The political exploitation of aid, rather than being an anomaly, is its 'principal condition of existence': it necessitates agreements with which all players can live.[43]

The economic challenge humanitarian efforts face is two-fold. They must (a) generate adequate resources for any aid emergency and (b) apportion these resources in a fair manner to fulfil the needs of individuals. However, the economic means provided by the voluntary and public sector for humanitarian responses are invariably insufficient for saving all the lives that could be preserved and reducing all the suffering that could be ameliorated. Due to these limitations, therefore, as well as delays in response, earmarking, and logistical bottlenecks, the distribution of aid tends to be uneven and sporadic, often failing to adequately supply all those who are in need. In practice, the economic constraints under which humanitarian efforts operate require choices across emergencies and among the people affected in any given crisis.

The process by which a relief agent adjusts a particular aid approach to the political and financial predicaments on the ground is key to understanding humanitarianism. We call the mechanisms of facilitating the supply of aid and aligning it with demand along such lines the *moral economy*. This concept exhibits many parallels to the market economy, including its dependence on

---

[40] Hugo Slim, 'Wonderful Work: Globalizing the Ethics of Humanitarian Action', in *The Routledge Companion to Humanitarian Action*, eds Roger Mac Ginty and Jenny H. Peterson (London: Routledge, 2015), 19. See also Claire Magone, Michaël Neuman, and Fabrice Weissman, eds, *Humanitarian Negotiations Revealed: The MSF Experience* (London: Hurst, 2011).

[41] Fiona Terry, *Condemned to Repeat? The Paradox of Humanitarian Action* (Ithaca, NY: Cornell University Press, 2002), 216–17.

[42] Vaux, *Selfish Altruist*, 2–3, 17–42; Terry, *Condemned to Repeat?*, 23; Slim, *Humanitarian Ethics*, 15.

[43] Marie-Pierre Allié, 'Introduction: Acting at Any Price?', in *Humanitarian Negotiations Revealed: The MSF Experience*, eds Claire Magone, Michaël Neuman, and Fabrice Weissman (London: Hurst, 2011), 3. This insight is lost when the categories themselves are jumbled and states are made to appear as humanitarian actors proper. See Andrea Paras, *Moral Obligations and Sovereignty in International Relations: A Genealogy of Humanitarianism* (Abingdon: Routledge, 2019).

preferences, its political embeddedness, and the risk of failure. However, unlike the marketplace and its material incentives, the moral economy of humanitarian efforts is determined by alternative ways of '"utility maximisation" through the construction of altruistic meaning for economic transactions'.[44] The 'moral' component is thereby not something that is uneconomic or laudable in itself. Rather, what is assumed as moral may find approval; on the other hand it may appear naive, parochial, or patently unethical as it reaches out to the wider world. The 'moral' may impose the ideas of the powerful on others, or it may emerge from a dialogue among stakeholders. Morality and the emotional forces that support it will vary according to what individuals and groups believe is required of them and what they can afford. Such a subjective understanding of socially situated morals underlies the conversion of material resources into 'moral capital' through philanthropic acts.[45]

Compassion, as an emotional sentiment that yields moral agency, involves both heart and mind. 'A sharp, skeptical intelligence', according to a major work on moral imagination, has been seen as 'required to ensure the proper exercise of that sentiment'.[46] In the moral economy, supply and demand are thus variables that proceed through a 'dispassionate and cold calculation which alone can be efficient enough to be real compassion', that is, through the filter of humanitarian donors and agents.[47] Supply draws on the economic sphere, demand on an assessment of legitimate needs and the feasibility of providing relief. Both dimensions are characterised by radically unequal access to resources, and both depend on the recognition of moral claims. Supply is contingent on the response of a donor who voluntarily shares assets and may feel rewarded for giving by a 'warm glow' of self-satisfaction, or, in accordance with Marcel Mauss' pivotal analysis, might benefit in various ways from a demonstration of power.[48] Likewise, effective demand is donor-driven.[49]

---

[44] Götz, 'Moral Economy', 158.
[45] Thomas Adam, *Buying Respectability: Philanthropy and Urban Society in Transnational Perspective, 1840s to 1930s* (Bloomington: Indiana University Press, 2009); John Kane, *The Politics of Moral Capital* (Cambridge: Cambridge University Press, 2001).
[46] Gertrude Himmelfarb, *Poverty and Compassion: The Moral Imagination of the Late Victorians* (New York: Knopf, 1991). For current discussions, see Heidi L. Maibom, ed. *Empathy and Morality* (Oxford: Oxford University Press, 2014), and Paul Bloom, *Against Empathy: The Case for Rational Compassion* (New York: Ecco, 2016).
[47] Bertrand Taithe, '"Cold Calculation in the Face of Horrors?" Pity, Compassion and the Making of Humanitarian Protocols', in *Medicine, Emotion and Disease, 1700–1950*, ed. Fay Bound Alberti (New York: Palgrave Macmillan, 2006), 93.
[48] Marcel Mauss, *The Gift: Forms and Functions of Exchange in Archaic Societies* (London: Cohen & West, 1954). See also Charles Harvey, Mairi Maclean, and Suddaby Roy, 'Historical Perspectives on Entrepreneurship and Philanthropy', *Business History Review* 93, no. 3 (2019): 443–71. On the concept of 'warm glow', see James Andreoni, 'Philanthropy', in *Handbook of the Economics of Giving, Altruism and Reciprocity, vol. 2: Applications*, eds Serge-Christophe Kolm and Jean Mercier Ythier (Amsterdam: North Holland, 2006), 1220.
[49] de Waal, *Mass Starvation*, 116, 119.

It involves means testing or acknowledging entitlement, rather than being based on unfiltered requests by the needy. While responses to need may emerge from a dialogue with beneficiaries, they may also be founded on assumptions sustained by the 'monologue' of an external donor or relief agency.[50]

From a philosophical point of view, the stringent obligation to save people's lives appears proportional to the effectiveness of the means available.[51] This amounts to a call for historical investigation. At the same time, the finite quantity of relief supplies requires an examination of the mechanisms by which precedence among aid causes is established. Luc Boltanski outlines the general predicament as follows: 'The central problem confronted by a politics of pity is actually the excess of unfortunates. There are too many of them. Not only self-evidently within the domain of action (which requires a ranking and the definition of priorities), but also in the domain of representation: media space is not unlimited and cannot be entirely given over to showing misfortune.'[52]

The connotation of the term pity is problematic, but it is not as easily distinguished from compassion as may be assumed. In our context, pity indicates the painful emotion aroused by contemplating the undeserved misfortune of another being. The issue of justice implicit in this assessment is something philosophers seek to retain in the modern framing of compassion.[53] In practice, voluntary organisations and governments need to deal with the moral economies of those who donate or pay taxes under certain assumptions and who have limited patience with objects of compassion. As a consequence, relief organisations sometimes downplay their altruistic motivations and emphasise self-interest to generarate a greater response.

The ways in which universal, in-group, or self-interested arguments and practices create moral reciprocity under particular historical circumstances (or fail to do so) helps explain the driving forces of humanitarianism. The strength of moral commitment may not ultimately be 'a matter of physical distance per se, but rather of relationships that are strongly although contingently connected to it: relationships of family, community, country, and the like'.[54] The advance of transnational patterns of interaction owes much to

---

[50] Kent, *Anatomy*, 16.

[51] William Aiken, 'The Right to Be Saved from Starvation', in *World Hunger and Moral Obligation*, eds William Aiken and Hugh La Follette (Englewood Cliffs, NJ: Prentice-Hall, 1977), 97.

[52] Luc Boltanski, *Distant Suffering: Morality, Media and Politics* (Cambridge: Cambridge University Press, 1999 [1993]), 155.

[53] Martha C. Nussbaum, *Upheavals of Thought: The Intelligence of Emotions* (Cambridge: Cambridge University Press, 2001), 301. See also Juha Käpylä and Denis Kennedy, 'Cruel to Care? Investigating the Governance of Compassion in the Humanitarian Imaginary', *International Theory* 6, no. 2 (2014): 264, 277.

[54] Lichtenberg, 'Absence and the Unfond Heart', 86–7.

such relations. Thus, although expats living abroad might appear to act transnationally in dealings with their home country, their motivation may be entirely national.

According to conventional wisdom, charity begins at home. In the nineteenth century, Dickens denounced humanitarianism across borders and oceans as a self-celebratory 'telescopic philanthropy', driven by the elite's imperial and cosmopolitan interest.[55] Whatever their rationale, to provide aid remotely may conflict with notions of moral economy that are held by the 'crowd' at home. The linkage of relief causes to pre-existing interests across borders presents an alternative to both abstract universalism and tangible communitarianism. Such a middle way can sustain action and offer the possibility of eventually recasting aid to include wider groups.[56] On the other hand, there is evidence of a humanitarianism that transcends both spatial and social divisions, although the logic it follows depends on the responding philanthropist or humanitarian intermediary. Hence, the moral economy approach acknowledges that aid to strangers will often yield gratifying outcomes for donors, irrespective of distance. This challenges ideas of universality and self-interest.

Likewise, individual needs are not easily weighed against one another. Their transformation into effective aid demands requires 'priority regimes', that is, the concerns privileged in specific humanitarian settings.[57] The traditional ideal of humanitarianism is to respond to needs, and so its first priority is not cost-effectiveness. The ideal has been compared with Thompson's moral economy of provision for displaying an 'egalitarian sense of prioritization' grounded in feelings about human suffering, rather than material advantage.[58] The 'ethics of refusal' practiced by Médecins Sans Frontières (MSF) is even more reluctant to accept market rationality, engaging instead in outspoken political action against the logic of producing the most good with limited means.[59] Nevertheless, there remains the constant 'problem of picking without discriminating' that cannot be circumvented by principled rejection of utilitarian economics.[60] Patient compliance with the humanitarian regime, according

---

[55] Charles Dickens, *Bleak House* (London: Bradbury and Evans, 1853), 24.

[56] Boltanski, *Distant Suffering*, 190.

[57] Kent, *Anatomy*, 13; Paul Howe, 'Priority Regimes and Famine', in *The New Famines: Why Famines Persist in an Era of Globalization*, ed. Stephen Devereux (London: Routledge, 2007), 342.

[58] Peter Redfield, 'Doctors without Borders and the Moral Economy of Pharmaceuticals', in *Human Rights in Crisis*, ed. Alice Bullard (Aldershot: Ashgate, 2008), 132.

[59] James Orbinski, 'Médecins Sans Frontières: Nobel Lecture', Nobelprize.org (10 Dec. 1999), available at www.nobelprize.org/prizes/peace/1999/msf/lecture/ (accessed 29 June 2019); Jennifer C. Rubenstein, *Between Samaritans and States: The Political Ethics of Humanitarian INGOs* (Oxford: Oxford University Press, 2015), 13, 144–5.

[60] Peter Redfield, *Life in Crisis: The Ethical Journey of Doctors without Borders* (Berkeley: University of California Press, 2013), 167 (quotation), 169.

to Didier Fassin, has become a controversial, barely conceded selection criterion for MSF, incorporating economic rationality through 'moral judgments (about who were the "good patients" to be trusted)'.[61]

While Singer and Pictet represent the different ethical stances of maximising doing good, as opposed to responding to individual needs, they both point to the difficulty of applying humanitarian principles where resources are limited. This raises issues of non-discrimination and proportionality, and ultimately of triage, that is, the appropriate selection of aid recipients.[62] Singer suggests prioritising 'younger, healthier people', as they need less assistance and greater numbers can be helped; directing aid to food producers may also multiply the benefits of aid. The exclusion of other groups facing starvation, in Singer's view, would not pose a genuine ethical dilemma as long as the relief effort observes the goal of preventing as many people as possible from starving. At the same time, he endorses the conditioning of aid by tying it to population control.[63] Pictet, in speaking of the frequent exceptions made by medical workers who cannot cure all those in need of treatment, suggests that priority be given in accordance with prevailing cultural standards, for example 'to those who have family responsibilities rather than to those who do not; to the young instead of to the old; to women instead of men'.[64]

Pursuing the ideal of humanity, vulnerability becomes a dominant norm in accordance with which agencies target their aid. They apply shifting principles and procedures to determine eligible groups, quantities, modalities, timing, and specific purposes of aid, and seek to 'minimize "exclusion errors" while keeping "inclusion errors" within reasonable limits'.[65] However, societal norms and power structures may clash, as when recipient communities prioritise

---

[61] Didier Fassin, 'Heart of Humaneness: The Moral Economy of Humanitarian Intervention', in *Contemporary States of Emergency: Anthropology of Military and Humanitarian Intervention*, eds Didier Fassin and Mariella Pandolfi (New York: Zone, 2010), 292 n. 47.

[62] Redfield, *Life in Crisis*, 167–75; Peter Redfield, 'Sacrifice, Triage, and Global Humanitarianism', in *Humanitarianism in Question: Politics, Power, Ethics*, eds Michael Barnett and Thomas G. Weiss (Ithaca, NY: Cornell University Press, 2008), 196–214; Kenneth V. Iserson and John C. Moskop, 'Triage in Medicine, Part I: Concept, History, and Types, Part II: Underlying Values and Principles', *Annals of Emergency Medicine* 49, no. 3 (2007): 275–87; Robert Baker and Martin Strosberg, 'Triage and Equality: An Historical Reassessment of Utilitarian Analyses of Triage', *Kennedy Institute of Ethics Journal* 2, no. 2 (1992): 103–23; Stuart W. Hinds, 'On the Relations of Medical Triage to World Famine: An Historical Survey', in *Lifeboat Ethics: The Moral Dilemmas of World Hunger*, eds George R. Lucas and Thomas W. Ogletree (New York: Harper & Row, 1976), 29–51; Richard Rorty, 'Who Are We? Moral Universalism and Economic Triage', *Diogenes* 44, no. 173 (1996): 5–15.

[63] Singer, 'Reconsidering', 45–7.

[64] Pictet, *Fundamental Principles*, 39–40. For a discussion of preferring women and children, see Slim, *Humanitarian Ethics*, 62–3.

[65] Ron Ockwell, *Recurring Challenges in the Provision of Food Assistance in Complex Emergencies: The Problems and Dilemmas Faced by WFP and Its Partners* (Rome: World Food Programme, 1999), 32; Jaspars, *Food Aid*, 6, 189.

feeding their elders over the children targeted by aid programmes.[66] Based on its practical experience, the United Nations World Food Programme recommends an approach that balances a concern for the poorest with a broader territorial or community-orientation by involving recipients, relying on efficient transfer methods, and avoiding expensive or unfeasible targeting strategies.[67] Since the beginning of the twenty-first century, there has also been a 'new model of moral triage based on human rights and good governance' that has exerted considerable influence on aid agencies.[68]

Thus, choices determine aid eligibility across humanitarian platforms, based on different relief agents' priority regimes and pragmatic considerations: their templates of suffering, victimhood, reproductive value, and gender, on the one hand, and their perceived options under economic and cultural constraints, on the other. The prevalent utilitarian public health approach seeks to minimise excess mortality, giving preference to sufferers with higher chances of survival if they receive relief, and neglecting those requiring extensive treatment.[69] Some moral philosophers suggest that decisions be made by dividing expected aggregate moral value by expected aggregate cost.[70] A current training manual for aid workers acknowledges the moral quagmire: 'When weighing numerous considerations – including the feasibility, maximum opportunity benefit, minimum opportunity cost, maximum effectiveness, maximum cost-effectiveness, and timeliness of various intervention options – technical questions can quickly morph into major ethical dilemmas.'[71]

Fassin, the humanitarian scholar who has used the term moral economy extensively, has anticipated our suggestion that moral economy refers to the allocation of scarce aid resources. However, his definition and predominant use of the concept assumes 'economy' to be an organising principle in general, which he then applies to morality and its constituent emotions and values, without further regard to economy as the sphere of production and distribution

[66] Redfield, *Life in Crisis*, 174.
[67] D. John Shaw, *The World's Largest Humanitarian Agency: The Transformation of the UN World Food Programme and of Food Aid* (Houndmills: Palgrave Macmillan, 2011), 149–50.
[68] David Rieff, *A Bed for the Night: Humanitarianism in Crisis* (New York: Simon and Schuster, 2002), 317.
[69] Terry, *Condemned to Repeat?*, 225; Onora O'Neill, 'Lifeboat Earth', *Philosophy and Public Affairs* 4, no. 3 (1975): 273–92; Iserson and Moskop, 'Triage in Medicine', 277.
[70] Thomas Pogge, 'Moral Priorities for International Human Rights NGOs', in *Ethics in Action: The Ethical Challenges of International Human Rights Nongovernmental Organizations*, eds Daniel Bell and Jean-Marc Coicaud (Cambridge: Cambridge University Press, 2007), 241. For a critique, see Lisa Fuller, 'Priority-setting in International Non-governmental Organizations: It Is Not as Easy as ABCD', *Journal of Global Ethics* 8, no. 1 (2012): 5–17.
[71] 'Humanitarian Assistance Webcast 10: Public Health and Humanitarian Crisis' (30 Aug. 2012), cited from www.hpcrresearch.org/events/humanitarian-assistance-webcast-10-public-health-and-humanitarian-crisis/ (accessed 4 Feb. 2020).

of goods and services.[72] Such a view has been criticised as confusing and redundant, making moral economy akin to the wider notion of culture.[73] In contrast to Fassin's vague conception, we see moral economy as a tool able to clarify the motivation behind a particular allotment of resources for humanitarian purposes. Three dimensions of the aid process characterise this concern: calls for aid, practical arrangements for allocation, and accounting for what has been achieved.[74] Research has tended to neglect appeals and accounting in favour of broad narratives of humanitarian ideals and action in the field, whether in (conventional) heroic terms, or in (rarer) critical fashion.[75]

The present study updates and reconfigures moral economy as a tool for understanding transnational charity between the poles of the ideals held and the practices applied, that is, its system of triage. It stresses the choices and rationale used by aid providers in appealing to donors, deploying their resources, and documenting their efforts. This approach concerns both the 'macro triage' of identifying a larger aid cause and triage in its established sense of assessing priorities among the needy on the ground.[76] We also reference two alternative, although not mutually exclusive, ways of understanding moral economy, despite the fact that the term itself does not appear in our primary sources.

First, with regard to the religious dimensions of humanitarian action, we examine instances reminiscent of the predominantly faith-based conceptualisation of 'moral œconomy' in the eighteenth and nineteenth centuries. It was presupposed at the time that there was a divine order given to the world, including the notion that there would be 'an exact recompence for the virtuous, and a suitable vengeance for the wicked'.[77] Echoing biblical notions of reward and punishment, the grace bestowed for acts of dutiful or

---

[72] Didier Fassin, *Humanitarian Reason: A Moral History of the Present* (Berkeley: University of California Press, 2012), 12, 266 n. 22; Fassin, 'Heart of Humaneness', 283, 292 n. 47; Didier Fassin, 'Les économies morales revisitées', *Annales: Histoire, Sciences sociales* 64, no. 6 (2009): 1237–66.

[73] Johanna Siméant, 'Three Bodies of Moral Economy: The Diffusion of a Concept', *Journal of Global Ethics* 11, no. 2 (2015): 163–75; Götz, 'Moral Economy', 156–7, 159 n. 8.

[74] See also Katarina Friberg, 'Accounts along the Aid Chain: Administering a Moral Economy', *Journal of Global Ethics* 11, no. 2 (2015): 246–56.

[75] On the lack of research into fundraising and accountability practices, see Sarah Roddy, Julie-Marie Strange, and Bertrand Taithe, 'The Charity-Mongers of Modern Babylon: Bureaucracy, Scandal, and the Transformation of the Philanthropic Marketplace, c. 1870–1912', *Journal of British Studies* 54, no. 1 (2015): 119. The same authors' new book proposes a remedy for this: Sarah Roddy, Julie-Marie Strange, and Bertrand Taithe, *The Charity Market and Humanitarianism in Britain, 1870–1912* (London: Bloomsbury, 2019).

[76] Henk ten Have, 'Macro-triage in Disaster Planning', in *Disaster Bioethics: Normative Issues When Nothing Is Normal*, eds Dónal P. O'Mathúna, Bert Gordijn, and Mike Clarke (Dordrecht: Springer, 2014), 13–32.

[77] Götz, 'Moral Economy', 149–50; quotation from the apocryphal *Athenian Letters, or, The Epistolary Correspondence of an Agent of the King of Persia, Residing at Athens during the Peloponnesian War*, vol. 2 (Dublin: Archer, 1792), 459.

supererogatory beneficence was often believed to be higher than the normal return. Aspects of this approach continue to resound behind certain twentieth-century secular variants.

Second, one of the prominent themes throughout this volume is the moral economic view that entitlement to subsistence is a natural law and human right.[78] Singer postulates this as an imperative for anyone with financial means to act. Sen problematises the same notion with regard to the materialisation of entitlements under different political regimes. Thompson has traced entitlements in British customary law, citing the riots that took place when such entitlements were denied (particularly against the backdrop of the modern market economy).[79] In the sphere of humanitarianism, the view that suffering people are entitled to aid is ubiquitous, although it is usually unclear what that means. On the other hand, the notion that they are entitled to riot is not widespread. In fact, elites far removed from a humanitarian disaster have often accepted their obligation to provide relief assistance, not only because they felt that it was the right thing to do for the distressed, but because it would maintain order and prevent social upheaval.[80]

---

[78] See Sandra Raponi, 'A Defense of the Human Right to Adequate Food', *Res Publica* 23, no. 1 (2017): 99–115; Sebastian Thieme, *Das Subsistenzrecht: Begriff, ökonomische Traditionen und Konsequenzen* (Marburg: Metropolis, 2012).

[79] Sen, *Poverty and Famines*; Thompson, 'Moral Economy of the English Crowd'.

[80] See also Judith Lichtenberg, 'Altruism', in *The Routledge Companion to Humanitarian Action*, eds Roger Mac Ginty and Jenny H. Peterson (London: Routledge, 2015), 139.

2 Case Studies

2.1 Three Ages of Humanitarianism

Relief efforts during the Great Irish Famine of the 1840s, the famine that ravaged Soviet Russia in 1921–3, and the devastating famine in Ethiopia in the mid-1980s are characterised by widely different societal and international circumstances. They represent three distinct phases of humanitarian engagement: the *ad hoc humanitarianism* of elitist nineteenth-century laissez-faire liberalism, the *organised humanitarianism* associated with Taylorism and mass society (c. 1900–70), and the *expressive humanitarianism* brought forth by a mix of post-material values and neo-liberal public–private entrepreneurship that is characteristic of the half century from 1968 to the present.[1] The years surrounding 1900 and 1970 were incubators of the second and third industrial revolutions; they saw the first and second wave of women's liberation; and they have been identified as two phases of the twentieth century's pronounced internationalisation that contributed to the rapid dissemination of new models and practices.[2]

Our cultural and socio-economical approach goes along with the call for a new history of humanitarianism, with greater consideration of economic developments.[3] It challenges the dominant paradigm of humanitarian studies that selects historical turning points from geopolitical landmarks. We do not claim that all emergency relief follows a dominant pattern of traditional, bureaucratic, or charismatic agency. Ad hoc, organised, and expressive elements of humanitarianism coexist and interact with each other at all times. While not mutually exclusive, time-bound humanitarian models set standards and exert pressure on the sector as a whole.

---

[1] The following discussion on periodisation draws on Götz, Brewis, and Werther, 'Humanitäre Hilfe'.
[2] Glenda Sluga, *Internationalism in the Age of Nationalism* (Philadelphia: University of Pennsylvania Press, 2013).
[3] Enrico Dal Lago and Kevin O'Sullivan, 'Introduction: Toward a New History of Humanitarianism', *Moving the Social* no. 57 (2017): 7, 19.

The characterisation of our first two periods as ad hoc humanitarianism and organised humanitarianism is derived from Merle Curti's classic study *American Philanthropy Abroad*, although Curti did not give these names to the eras he described.[4] The term organised humanitarianism also reflects the proliferation of 'organisation' as a dominant principle in the early twentieth century. This surfaces in contemporary social democratic theorist Rudolf Hilferding's notion of 'organised capitalism' and in the aspirations of the internationalist movement of the time.[5] The concept of 'expressive humanitarianism' that we propose pertains to post-material self-expressiveness and to an increasing fusion of relief with advocacy strategies and the notion of rights, media-driven spectacle, commercial branding, popular involvement and populism, 'projectification', and the aggressive pursuit of humanitarian intervention. These tendencies emerge from what leading sociologists, economic analysts, and contemporary historians have identified as a caesura around 1970 that was formative for the society of our time.[6] In contrast to the beginning of the twentieth century, when 'organisation' was a prominent term in humanitarian discourse, the terms 'ad hoc' and 'expressive' are solely analytical rather than being directly derived from our sources.

Our outline of humanitarianism seeks to address levels of transatlantic history that are deeper than such eventful years as 1918, 1945, and 1989, on which contemporary observers have tended to focus. We also deviate from such geopolitically determined perspectives as that of Michael Barnett's *Empire of Humanity*, the most comprehensive historical synthesis to date of humanitarian action. Barnett's study, while representing a mature judgement, is characterised by a US bias and lacks historical perspective.[7] Moreover, it utilises a highly problematic periodisation and several terminological idiosyncrasies (development becomes 'alchemy', for example). In our view, the epoch Barnett describes as 'imperial humanitarianism' is an inadequate catch-all characterisation of the field prior to decolonisation in 1945. His subsequent 'neo-humanitarianism' is an offshoot of neocolonialism with a tautological

---

[4] Merle Curti, *American Philanthropy Abroad: A History* (New Brunswick, NJ: Rutgers University Press, 1963), 619–23.

[5] Heinrich August Winkler, ed. *Organisierter Kapitalismus: Voraussetzungen und Anfänge* (Göttingen: Vandenhoeck & Ruprecht, 1974); Guido Grünewald, ed. *'Organisiert die Welt!': Der Friedensnobelpreisträger Alfred Hermann Fried (1864–1921) – Leben, Werk und bleibende Impulse* (Bremen: Donat, 2016).

[6] See, e.g., Luc Boltanski and Eve Chiapello, *The New Spirit of Capitalism* (London: Verso, 2005); Thomas Borstelmann, *The 1970s: A New Global History from Civil Rights to Economic Inequality* (Princeton, NJ: Princeton University Press, 2012); Anselm Doering-Manteuffel and Lutz Raphael, *Nach dem Boom: Perspektiven auf die Zeitgeschichte seit 1970* (Göttingen: Vandenhoeck & Ruprecht, 2010).

[7] Barnett, *Empire of Humanity*. The author, a political scientist, draws exclusively on secondary literature and shows little knowledge of nineteenth-century disaster relief.

ring, and 'liberal humanitarianism' conveys a misleading picture of developments after the Cold War.[8] Barnett's three categories further imply a progressive trajectory of voluntary action, when in fact many practitioners and observers oppose the increasing exploitation and manipulation of humanitarian efforts by governments and quasi-imperial coalitions. Moreover, the author's belief that only after the Cold War could humanitarianism overcome a 'quaintly and stubbornly pre-modern' condition in favour of a bureaucratised and professionalised approach underestimates the rationalisation of this sector in the first half of the twentieth century, the dysfunctional tendencies of current media- and donor-driven efforts, and the enduring parochialism of US agency in world affairs.[9]

Silvia Salvatici's recently published *A History of Humanitarianism* is a valuable overview. She does not attempt to identify an 'age of origins', adopting instead what she calls an archaeological approach to investigate the evolution of humanitarianism from the Lisbon earthquake of 1755 until the mid-ninteeeth century. This is followed by a war-related period that lasts for a hundred years, 1854–1951. However, her Third World–oriented period from the 1950s to 1989 was also a time of war and blends official development aid and emergency relief. An epilogue describing the complex emergencies and growth of the humanitarian sector after 1989 follows the dominant political science narrative without adding insights from empirical research.[10]

Chronology of Humanitarianism

Charity is part of a global heritage that acquired a new quality following the social, religious, and economic transformations in Britain during the late eighteenth and early nineteenth centuries. A crucial factor in this reshaping was the Protestant revival with its activism and incorporation of benevolent traditions like those of the Quakers.[11] Domestic charity, advocacy and reform of prisons and the slave trade, and aid to foreign countries were closely intertwined.[12] All this was preconditioned by the rise of capitalism

---

[8] Barnett, *Empire of Humanity*.

[9] Michael Barnett, 'Humanitarianism as a Scholarly Vocation', in *Humanitarianism in Question: Politics, Power, Ethics*, eds Michael Barnett and Thomas G. Weiss (Ithaca, NY: Cornell University Press, 2008), 253. For dysfunctionalities, see Brauman, 'Global Media'; Paul Farmer, *Haiti after the Earthquake* (New York: Public Affairs, 2011).

[10] Silvia Salvatici, *A History of Humanitarianism, 1755–1989: In the Name of Others* (Manchester: Manchester University Press, 2019 [2015]).

[11] Frank Prochaska, *The Voluntary Impulse: Philanthropy in Modern Britain* (London: Faber and Faber, 1988), 21; Ormerod John Greenwood, *Quaker Encounters, vol. 1: Friends and Relief* (York: Sessions, 1975), 5.

[12] Stephen Tomkins, *The Clapham Sect: How Wilberforce's Circle Transformed Britain* (Oxford: Lion, 2010), 12; Ford K. Brown, *Fathers of the Victorians: The Age of Wilberforce*

and was shaped, in Thomas L. Haskell's analysis, by 'the power of market discipline to inculcate altered perceptions of causation in human affairs', which yielded a new scope of agency upon others.[13] Distant charity likewise emerged from the bonds forged alongside European colonial expansion. While local efforts dominated disaster relief in the seventeenth- and eighteenth-century Atlantic world, religious groups in particular would sometimes raise money for distressed coreligionists abroad. By the second half of the eighteenth century, voluntary overseas aid began to play an increasing role in disaster recovery in the Anglo-Atlantic space. This development was facilitated by the introduction of private subscriptions as fundraising instruments. Rather than relying on government approval or religious edict, these depended on the work of an engaged committee, a media-oriented campaign, and public meetings in coffeehouses and taverns.[14] Although imperial direction shaped humanitarian efforts, the claim that eighteenth-century donors of transnational relief generally 'sought to further hegemonic aims' and that 'they offered aid paternalistically in order to strengthen their grip on a devastated region and its people' overlooks the great variety of motivations and anticipated returns.[15]

The US declaration of independence from Britain unsettled prevailing charitable practices, but it also contributed to expanding the imperial horizon of relief efforts.[16] By the beginning of the nineteenth century, relief campaigns in support of foreign lands in distress became more common. Driven by well-integrated immigrant groups and the evangelical circles that were also engaged in the struggle against the slave trade, Britain during the Napoleonic wars conducted a non-military aid campaign that benefitted various German and Austrian lands as well as Sweden. The fundraising was in response to reports of distress caused by the war and word of an anticipated or actual famine. Suffering populations in enemy states as well as allies were aided.[17]

(Cambridge: Cambridge University Press, 1961), 374–5. See also Norbert Götz, 'Rationales of Humanitarianism: The Case of British Relief to Germany, 1805–1815', *Journal of Modern European History* 12, no. 2 (2014): 186–99; Norbert Götz, 'The Good Plumpuddings' Belief: British Voluntary Aid to Sweden during the Napoleonic Wars', *International History Review* 37, no. 3 (2015): 519–39.

[13] Thomas L. Haskell, 'Capitalism and the Origins of the Humanitarian Sensibility, Part 1', *American Historical Review* 90, no. 2 (1985): 342.

[14] Matthew Mulcahy, *Hurricanes and Society in the British Greater Caribbean, 1624–1783* (Baltimore: Johns Hopkins University Press, 2006), 142, 146–9.

[15] See Alessa Johns, 'Introduction', in *Dreadful Visitations: Confronting Natural Catastrophe in the Age of Enlightenment*, ed. Alessa Johns (New York: Routledge, 1999), xxi.

[16] Amanda B. Moniz, *From Empire to Humanity: The American Revolution and the Origins of Humanitarianism* (New York: Oxford University Press, 2016), 4.

[17] Götz, 'Rationales of Humanitarianism'; Götz, 'Good Plumpuddings'; Norbert Götz and Frank Palmowski, 'Humanitäre Hilfe im Zeitalter Napoleons: Bürgerliche Gesellschaft und transnationale Ressourcen am Beispiel Erfurts', *Historische Zeitschrift* 305, no. 2 (2017): 362–92.

A striking feature of nineteenth-century humanitarian relief was the ad hoc nature of its organisation and perspective. While relief committees responded to specific crises in accordance with established patterns, the same committees dissolved when they considered their work done, but sometimes reconvened when a similar crisis arose.[18] Relief consisted of taking emergency measures on top of those by local donors and governments, rather than creating structural interventions that would improve the long-term resilience of beneficiaries. Foreign countries were seen as responsible for the maintenance of their own charitable institutions and economic development, while transnational relief was reserved for the selective alleviation of extraordinary disasters. This led to tension between donors calling for an immediate appropriation of funds and recipient committees abroad who wanted to preside over long-term charitable investments.[19] However, early transitional groups laid the foundation for more enduring organisations such as the Society of St Vincent de Paul (SVP) in the 1840s and the Red Cross in the 1860s.[20]

The 1890s have been identified as a 'fruitful time for the development of humanitarian practices'.[21] It was the beginning of a decades-long transformation in an era described as 'progressive' in US history, and it involved physicians, social workers, engineers, and later public relations specialists and accountants, all of whom promoted scientific and technological innovations, new media, and modern business practices. An expansive humanitarian vigour surfaced for what may have been the first time in the merging of Protestant missionary zeal and liberal civilisational aspirations during the Russian Famine of 1890–1, when a reluctant US government agreed to lend logistical support to relief efforts. In the USA, the last decade of the nineteenth century is widely seen as a period of transition from a 'non-interventionist tradition' to 'missionary humanitarianism'.[22]

Curti's periodisation emphasises the correlation of voluntary and government action and the institutionalisation of relief, both of which became manifest in the run-up to the Spanish–American War of 1898. According to Curti, the bureaucratic-rational and semi-official approach of the American Red Cross (ARC) marginalised earlier voluntary relief efforts. The advancement of organisational structures, mass appeals, and government intervention

---

[18] Curti, *American Philanthropy Abroad*, 619–21.

[19] Götz, 'Good Plumpuddings'; Götz and Palmowski, 'Humanitäre Hilfe'.

[20] Norbert Götz, 'The Emergence of NGOs as Actors on the World Stage', in *Routledge Handbook of NGOs and International Relations*, ed. Thomas Davies (London: Routledge, 2019), 19–31; Thomas Davies, *NGOs: A New History of Transnational Civil Society* (London: Hurst, 2013), 4.

[21] Luke Kelly, 'British Humanitarianism and the Russian Famine, 1891–2', *Historical Research* 89, no. 246 (2016): 824.

[22] Jeff Bloodworth, 'A Complicated Kindness: The Iowa Famine Relief Movement and the Myth of Midwestern (and American) Isolationism', *Historian* 73, no. 3 (2011): 482–5.

revolutionised humanitarian action.[23] Over the following decade, the ARC was transformed into the professional operation it is today.[24]

Ian Tyrrell calls attention to the networked culture of humanitarianism that emerged 'through the historical experience of organized giving' in response to the remote calamities of the 1890s. He also points to the gradual displacement of idiosyncratic human interest endeavours by the more systematic work of foundations, which contributed greatly to the emergence of philanthropy as a coherent epistemic field and community in the decade after 1900.[25] For British India, Georgina Brewis has traced the transition from religious philanthropy to organised social service in famine relief efforts during the closing years of the nineteenth century.[26] Pre-war imperialism, as a recent study concludes, had a profound impact on British humanitarianism after the First World War. It affected the entire humanitarian sector, from the 'ethics of relief' to aid practice and staffing. Administrators and relief workers with experience from colonial institutions, missionary groups, or the Society of Friends remained an essential part of the 'mixed economy' of voluntary and official aid during the interwar years. Thus, newly established organisations like the Save the Children Fund (SCF) or the American Relief Administration (ARA) 'utilized the expert knowledge and techniques of famine relief first elaborated by the liberal imperialism of the late nineteenth century'.[27]

Such developments coincided with the first wave of women's liberation, leading to the 'feminisation of relief work' in the first two decades of the twentieth century.[28] However, despite this new feminised public image of aid work (such as in Red Cross advertisements), and despite the emergence of 'feminine' organisations like the SCF and the prominent role of female

---

[23] Curti, *American Philanthropy Abroad*, 199–223, 258, 621–2. For similar observations regarding the UK at the time, see Rebecca Gill, *Calculating Compassion: Humanity and Relief in War, Britain 1870–1914* (Manchester: Manchester University Press, 2013), 179.

[24] Marian Moser Jones, *The American Red Cross from Clara Barton to the New Deal* (Baltimore: Johns Hopkins University Press, 2013), 80–136.

[25] Ian Tyrrell, *Reforming the World: The Creation of America's Moral Empire* (Princeton, NJ: Princeton University Press, 2010), 98, 118. On the role of contemporary foundations and 'scientific philanthropy', see Craig Calhoun, 'The Imperative to Reduce Suffering: Charity, Progress, and Emergencies in the Field of Humanitarian Action', in *Humanitarianism in Question: Politics, Power, Ethics*, eds Michael Barnett and Thomas G. Weiss (Ithaca, NY: Cornell University Press, 2008), 79; Katharina Rietzler, 'From Peace Advocacy to International Relations Research: The Transformation of Transatlantic Philanthropic Networks, 1900–1930', in *Shaping the Transnational Sphere: Experts, Networks, Issues, 1850–1930*, eds Davide Rodogno, Bernhard Struck, and Jakob Vogel (New York: Berghahn, 2015), 173–95.

[26] Georgina Brewis, '"Fill Full the Mouth of Famine": Voluntary Action in Famine Relief in India 1896–1901', *Modern Asian Studies* 44, no. 4 (2010): 887–918.

[27] Tehila Sasson, 'From Empire to Humanity: The Russian Famine and the Imperial Origins of International Humanitarianism', *Journal of British Studies* 53, no. 3 (2016): 522 (quotation), 519–37.

[28] Gill, *Calculating Compassion*, 186.

fieldworkers in Quaker relief, men still dominated the humanitarian arena, and in some cases denied access to women and disputed their capability of conducting humanitarian field work.[29] At the same time, as victims, women continued to benefit from idealised notions of motherhood or paternalistic chivalry towards the 'fair sex'. While we know about the contributions of women in the early ad hoc campaigns (including the anti-slavery movement and philhellenism), much remains to be learned about female leadership, mobilisation, activism,[30] and negative and positive discrimination in humanitarian efforts.

Photographs came into wider use in the fundraising campaigns for India (1896–7) and the Second Boer War (1899–1902) and onwards, creating an enhanced sense of the authenticity of aid causes in an unholy alliance 'with the sensationalistic mass culture that intensified after the turn of the century'.[31] While children had played a special role in philanthropic campaigns since the Enlightenment, the twentieth century placed increased emphasis on the suffering of children.[32] As a group, children required extensive relief administration because self-help programmes were inappropriate for them. Since the South African War of 1899–1902, sympathy towards enemy children has also served as a way to oppose war.[33] The First World War and the period of political and economic instability that followed, with its collapsing empires, civil and border hostilities, expulsions, and waves of refugees, created a vast humanitarian crisis. The war became a node for organised humanitarianism

---

[29] Bertrand M. Patenaude, *Big Show in Bololand: The American Relief Expedition to Soviet Russia in the Famine of 1921* (Stanford, CA: Stanford University Press, 2002), 50; Rickard to Lovejoy, 25 Oct. 1921, ARA, reel 502.

[30] Abigail Green, 'Humanitarianism in Nineteenth Century Context: Religious, Gendered, National', *Historical Journal* 57, no. 4 (2014): 1167.

[31] Heather Curtis, 'Depicting Distant Suffering: Evangelicals and the Politics of Pictorial Humanitarianism in the Age of American Empire', *Material Religion* 8, no. 2 (2012): 155; Valérie Gorin, 'L'enfance comme figure compassionnelle: Étude transversale de l'iconographie de la famine aux dix-neuvième et vingtième siècles', *European Review of History* 2, no. 6 (2015): 944. For more background, see Heide Fehrenbach and Davide Rodogno, 'Introduction: The Morality of Sight: Humanitarian Photography in History', in *Humanitarian Photography: A History*, eds Heide Fehrenbach and Davide Rodogno (Cambridge: Cambridge University Press, 2015), 1–21.

[32] Dominik Collet, 'Mitleid machen: Die Nutzung von Emotionen in der Hungersnot 1770–1772', *Historische Anthropologie* 23, no. 1 (2015): 67; Gill, *Calculating Compassion*, 201, 210; Heike Fehrenbach, 'Children and Other Civilians: Photography and the Politics of Humanitarian Image-Making', in *Humanitarian Photography: A History*, eds Heide Fehrenbach and Davide Rodogno (Cambridge: Cambridge University Press, 2015), 181; Dominique Marshall, 'Children's Rights from Below: Canadian and Transnational Actions, Beliefs, and Discourses, 1900–1989', in *Taking Liberties: A History of Human Rights in Canada*, eds David Goutor and Stephen Heathorn (Oxford: Oxford University Press, 2013), 189–212.

[33] Dominique Marshall, 'International Child Saving', in *The Routledge History of Childhood in the Western World*, ed. Paula Fass (London: Routledge, 2013), 474.

that displaced ad hoc charity efforts.[34] However, the rise of international and humanitarian organisations after 1918 only resumed an ongoing trend that the war had interrupted.[35]

The present study concurs with Johannes Paulmann's claim that the Second World War was not the watershed in the history of humanitarian action that it is proclaimed to be by Curti, Barnett, and many others, since the ideas and procedures that marked this period drew strongly on previous developments.[36] Paulmann proposes the late 1960s and early 1970s as a turning point, and some academics agree.[37] At that time, decolonisation had decoupled 'caring' from direct forms of 'ruling',[38] and modern identity politics, including the second generation of feminists, had its breakthrough. The international relief effort for Biafra (1967–70) is widely recognised as a rupture in the history of humanitarianism. It effected a split in the Red Cross movement with the formation of Médecins Sans Frontières (MSF), moulded a generation of relief workers, and brought civil society organisations to centre stage as mediators between Western audiences and the 'Third World'.[39]

The truism that the end of the Cold War transformed the world has led many to assume that a new period of humanitarianism began after 1989. Researchers

---

[34] Branden Little, 'An Explosion of New Endeavours: Global Humanitarian Responses to Industrialized Warfare in the First World War Era', *First World War Studies* 5, no. 1 (2014): 1; Barnett, *Empire of Humanity*, 86; Johannes Paulmann, 'Conjunctures in the History of International Humanitarian Aid during the Twentieth Century', *Humanity* 4, no. 2 (2013): 225–6.

[35] Akira Iriye, *Global Community: The Role of International Organizations in the Making of the Contemporary World* (Berkeley: University of California Press, 2002), 20; Curti, *American Philanthropy Abroad*, 621–2.

[36] Paulmann, 'Conjunctures', 226.

[37] Kevin O'Sullivan, Matthew Hilton, and Juliano Fiori, 'Humanitarianism in Context', *European Review of History* 23, no. 1–2 (2016): 1–15; Eleanor Davey, *Idealism beyond Borders: The French Revolutionary Left and the Rise of Humanitarianism, 1954–1988* (Cambridge: Cambridge University Press, 2015), 3, 21; Matthias Kuhnert, *Humanitäre Kommunikation: Entwicklung und Emotionen bei britischen NGOs 1945–1990* (Berlin: de Gruyter, 2017), 23–4; Salvatici, *History of Humanitarianism*, 142.

[38] Anna Bocking-Welch, *British Civic Society at the End of Empire: Decolonisation, Globalisation, and International Responsibility* (Manchester: Manchester University Press, 2019), 5.

[39] de Waal, *Famine Crimes*, 72–7; Paulmann, 'Conjunctures'; Barnett, *Empire of Humanity*, 133; Rieff, *Bed for the Night*, 108–9, 331; Philippe Ryfman, *Une Histoire de l'humanitaire*, 2nd ed. (Paris: La Découverte, 2016); Marie-Luce Desgrandchamps, '"Organising the Unpredictable": The Nigeria–Biafra War and Its Impact on the ICRC', *International Review of the Red Cross* 94, no. 888 (2012): 1409–32; Kevin O'Sullivan, 'Humanitarian Encounters: Biafra, NGOs and Imaginings of the Third World in Britain and Ireland, 1967–1970', *Journal of Genocide Research* 16, no. 2/3 (2014): 299–315; Arua Oko Omaka, *The Biafran Humanitarian Crisis, 1967–1970: International Human Rights and Joint Church Aid* (Madison: Fairleigh Dickinson University Press, 2016); Florian Hannig, 'The Biafra Crisis and the Establishment of Humanitarian Aid in West Germany as a New Philanthropic Field', in *German Philanthropy in Transatlantic Perspective: Perceptions, Exchanges and Transfers since the Early Twentieth Century*, eds Gregory R. Witkowski and Arnd Bauerkämper (Cham: Springer, 2016), 205–25; Lasse Heerten, *The Biafran War and Postcolonial Humanitarianism: Spectacles of Suffering* (Cambridge: Cambridge University Press, 2017).

do not conceive the new global order as a consequence of previous developments in Western society with which the Soviet bloc was unable to compete. However, there is little evidence of a major shift in the culture of humanitarianism that parallels the geopolitical change. Paulmann does not answer the question of whether we have witnessed 'a new departure', or merely an emphasis on emergency aid in places where sovereignty has broken down and aid has been implemented to contain conflicts at low cost. With reference to our time, Paulmann cites satellite transmissions and the BBC report on famine in Ethiopia that resulted in the Live Aid benefit concert in 1985 – events predating the end of the Cold War.[40] He also questions the significance of the geopolitical shift of 1989 for humanitarian 'so-called complexities'.[41] Similarly, Monika Krause emphasises a major shift in terms of symbolic differentiation in the humanitarian sector with the founding of MSF in 1971 and suggests another shift by the end of the Cold War. However, her account makes MSF appear to be the creator of contemporary humanitarianism, while the period commencing in 1989 is mainly characterised by expansion of the basic trend.[42]

Lilie Chouliaraki, who contrasts examples from the 1970s and 1980s with those of recent years, labels the entire period from the 1970s forwards as an 'age of global spectacle' typified by three transformations: (a) the market-compliant instrumentalisation of aid, (b) the decline of the grand narrative of solidarity, and (c) the technologically fuelled rise of self-expressive spectatorship. Taken together, she suggests that they effect an epistemic shift towards an emotional, subjective humanitarianism correlated to narcissistic morality and an emergent 'neoliberal lifestyle of "feel good" altruism'.[43] Similarly, Mark Duffield contrasts the 1970s and the present, but ultimately suggests that the decline of modern humanitarianism and the 'anthropocentric turn' brought about by its postmodern variant can be traced to the Biafran War.[44] At the same time, powerful tools of results-based management were introduced in the humanitarian sector that shifted the emphasis from overarching societal to project-specific goals.[45] Our concept of expressive humanitarianism encapsulates these trends, which are also summarised in Alain Finkielkraut's formula of the 'sentimental alienation' that has characterised humanitarian efforts in the past half-century.[46]

---

[40] Paulmann, 'Conjunctures', 229 (quotation), 221, 230.
[41] Johannes Paulmann, 'The Dilemmas of Humanitarian Aid: Historical Perspectives', in *Dilemmas of Humanitarian Aid in the Twentieth Century*, ed. Johannes Paulmann (Oxford: Oxford University Press, 2016), 3.
[42] Krause, *Good Project*, 104–10, 124.
[43] Lilie Chouliaraki, *The Ironic Spectator: Solidarity in the Age of Post-Humanitarianism* (Cambridge: Polity, 2013), 52, 4 (quotations), 1–21.
[44] Duffield, 'From Protection', 29 (quotation), 27.   [45] Krause, *Good Project*, 87.
[46] Alain Finkielkraut, *In the Name of Humanity: Reflections on the Twentieth Century* (New York: Columbia University Press, 2000), 93.

A focus on major emergencies with established systems of humanitarian response, rather than key turning points, has guided the selection of our three case studies. Our interest concerns humanitarian action, not the disaster as such. For example, the death toll of the Soviet Famine of the 1920s was exceeded by that of the Ukrainian Holodomor of the 1930s and the famine accompanying China's 'Great Leap Forward' (1959–61); but while the disaster of the 1920s became a major instance of transnational aid, in the Holdomor and the Chinese cases, there was domestic neglect of the emergency and they failed to attract much international attention.[47]

In order to examine how the relief efforts of governmental, intergovernmental, and voluntary groups unfolded in the context of their time, we turn to overviews of the Great Irish Famine of the 1840s, the Soviet Famine of 1921–3, and the famine in Ethiopia of 1984–6.

2.2   The Great Irish Famine and Ad Hoc Humanitarianism

The characteristics cited in Curti's identification of nineteenth-century ad hoc humanitarianism were (a) the lack of formal and institutional connections between different relief efforts; (b) the marked stress on voluntary initiatives; and (c) the reliance on a fundraising repertoire that in the USA had emerged from the philhellenic movement of the 1820s. Included in these were the formation of committees for the collection of money and the transportation of foodstuffs (often linked to economic boards), public meetings, church fund drives, charity events, ladies' bazaars, and ultimately newspaper campaigns.[48] In the UK, building upon the long-distance imperial charity of the eighteenth century, ad hoc humanitarianism had already emerged during the Napoleonic era. Despite the war context, foreign relief was an entirely civilian endeavour at the time, with links to the British and Foreign Bible Society, the evangelical and anti-slavery movement, and domestic charity.[49] In the 1820s, engagement with the Greek struggle for independence from the Ottoman Empire became an exemplary international aid campaign based in several countries, although military emphasis prevailed in this early instance of 'humanitarian intervention', and providing relief to distressed civilians remained a subordinate goal.[50] In addition to Curti's points, the repertoire of ad hoc humanitarianism included committee rules and procedures for the

---

[47] Andrea Graziosi, 'Political Famines in the USSR and China: A Comparative Analysis', *Journal of Cold War Studies* 19, no. 3 (2017): 42–103; Ó Gráda, *Eating People*, 130–73; Nicolas Werth, 'Déni, connaissance, responsabilité: Le régime stalinien et la grande famine ukrainienne de 1932–3', *European Review of History* 22, no. 6 (2015): 900–16.

[48] Curti, *American Philanthropy Abroad*, 619–21.   [49] Götz, 'Rationales of Humanitarianism'.

[50] Natalie Klein, '*L'humanité, le christianisme, et la liberté?' Die internationale philhellenische Vereinsbewegung der 1820er Jahre* (Mainz: Zabern, 2000); Gary J. Bass, *Freedom's Battle:*

documentation of subscriptions and disbursements. However, there were no agencies active in monitoring food insecurity or other disasters, nor was there any permanent infrastructure for fundraising or aid distribution. Governments were also unprepared to manage foreign aid.

In Ireland, where famines had occurred periodically, the first significant British relief effort took place in 1822, when funds for that country were solicited by a London Tavern Committee. Collections from other British cities soon followed, and the Dublin relief committee even expressed its thanks for North American and French aid. The Irish cause included a Catholic newspaper in Paris among its supporters in 1831.[51] Some activists and donors from those years, even philhellenic veterans, later participated in relief efforts during the Great Irish Famine of the 1840s. Donors of the 1840s in turn subscribed in later years to similar campaigns, such as the Finnish famines of 1856/7 and 1867/8.[52]

Despite these compassionate forces, the 'hungry forties' represented a difficult time for transnational relief. Europe was experiencing bad harvests, an economic downturn, and political unrest.[53] In such an environment, individual and collective action typically parted ways, as local moral economies easily clashed with larger ones. Thus, although Pope Pius IX and Sultan Abdulmejid I contributed to the Irish plight in 1847, both the Vatican State and the Ottoman Empire banned the export of grain in the face of domestic scarcity and disturbances.[54] During Easter of that year, the pope spent three times the

---

The Origins of Humanitarian Intervention (New York: Knopf, 2008), 45–151; John Bew, "'From an Umpire to a Competitor': Castlereagh, Canning and the Issue of International Intervention in the Wake of the Napoleonic Wars', in Humanitarian Intervention: A History, eds Brendan Simms and D. J. B. Trim (Cambridge: Cambridge University Press, 2011), 117–38.

[51] For 1822, see Ó Gráda, Famine, 218; Patrick Hickey, Famine in West Cork: The Mizen Peninsula Land and People, 1800–1852: A Local Study of Pre-famine and Famine Ireland (Cork: Mercier, 2002), 47. For 1831, see Donal A. Kerr, A Nation of Beggars? Priests, People, and Politics in Famine Ireland, 1846–1852 (Oxford: Clarendon, 1994), 54. For a broader background, see Cormac Ó Gráda, 'Ireland', in Famine in European History, eds Guido Alfani and Cormac Ó Gráda (Cambridge: Cambridge University Press, 2017), 166–84.

[52] Andrew G. Newby, 'The Society of Friends and Famine in Ireland and Finland, c. 1845–68', in Irish Hunger and Migration Myth, Memory and Memoralization, eds Christine Kinealy, Patrick Fitzgerald, and Gerard Moran (Quinnipiac: Quinnipiac University Press, 2015), 112. For philhellenic connections, see Measures Adopted in Boston, Massachusetts, for the Relief of the Suffering Scotch and Irish (Boston: Eastburn, 1847), 14–15.

[53] Eric Vanhaute, Richard Paping, and Cormac Ó Gráda, 'The European Subsistence Crisis of 1845–1850: A Comparative Perspective', in When the Potato Failed: Causes and Effects of the 'Last' European Subsistence Crisis, 1845–1850, eds Cormac Ó Gráda, Richard Paping, and Eric Vanhaute (Turnhout: Brepols, 2007), 15–40.

[54] 'Intelligence of the Week', Roman Advertiser, 9 Jan. 1847; Semih Çelik, 'Between History of Humanitarianism and Humanitarianization of History: A Discussion on Ottoman Help for the Victims of the Great Irish Famine, 1845–1852', Werkstatt Geschichte, no. 68 (2015): 25.

amount he had given towards Irish relief to buy bread for poor families in Rome.[55] In France, relief efforts for Ireland only took on significant proportions when the winter was over and there was no longer fear of domestic food hardship, despite the knowledge that 'while one suffers in France, one dies in Ireland'.[56] Disaffection with the Age of Metternich, culminating in the revolutions of 1848 (among the consequences of which were an exiled pope and a crushed Irish rebellion), minimised the concern of European elites with the Irish disaster.

In contrast to the view presented by earlier research, Ireland experienced the greatest surge of food riots in its history during the Great Famine. While they coincided with agrarian protests and hunger-induced crime more than previously, and while the authorities treated them as an 'outrage' and an act of 'plundering provisions' that had to be countered by force, a distinct Irish moral economy, similar to the English equivalent described by Thompson, was still at work.[57]

Meanwhile, conditions for providing famine relief were good in the USA in 1847. A populous Irish community that was in close touch with their homeland already existed. Irish-American organisations became the nucleus for broader civic engagement and a nationwide campaign. At the same time, plentiful US harvests enabled great profits in undersupplied European markets, facilitating generosity and giving rise to the notion of a moral obligation to compensate those who suffered most under the anomalous terms of trade. Moreover, concurrent opposition to US aggression against Mexico inclined many people towards humanitarian action. The provision of famine relief for Ireland was a show of peaceful intent that allowed concerned US citizens to maintain their moral self-respect. By contrast, nativist resentment and anxiety over the prospect of paupers immigrating to the USA eventually constrained charitable giving.

UK Relief

Conditions within the UK played a special role in Irish relief. This was true from the beginning of the famine in autumn 1845, when Ireland lost nearly half its potato crop, through peaks after the nearly complete potato failures of 1846 and 1848, until its gradual diminution between 1850 and 1852.[58]

---

[55] 'Intelligence of the Week', *Roman Advertiser*, 17 Apr. 1847.
[56] Appeal (27 May), in *L'Ami de la religion*, 10 June 1847.
[57] James Kelly, *Food Rioting in Ireland in the Eighteenth and Nineteenth Centuries: The 'Moral Economy' and the Irish Crowd* (Dublin: Four Courts, 2017), 237–41.
[58] William J. Smyth, 'The Story of the Great Irish Famine 1845–52: A Geographical Perspective', in *Atlas of the Great Irish Famine*, eds John Crowley, William J. Smyth, and Mike Murphy (New York: New York University Press, 2012), 5–6.

The dramatic catastrophe resulted from exclusive reliance on a new food crop.[59] The famine ravaged Ireland in absolute and relative terms. The death toll amounted to approximately one million people, and it caused the emigration of more than a million more men, women, and children out of a population of slightly more than eight million. As a result, the population of Ireland shrank by a quarter in just a few years. However, this does not take regional aggravation, averted births, and long-term physical and psychological damage into account.[60]

Ireland at the time was a formally integrated part of the UK which was the wealthiest polity in the world (despite an economic downturn from 1847 to 1849). The British government was generally considered responsible for safeguarding the welfare of Ireland's population, although this meant something different in Britain and abroad. The UK administration pursued a hands-off policy, passing financial responsibility on to overtaxed local Irish authorities. As the result of a fierce market logic that did not recognise a country's inalienable right to subsistence, Ireland was made to export foodstuffs to England while parts of its own population starved to death.[61] This lack of compassion was primarily due to British resentment towards the Irish and the influence of the evangelically inspired 'moralist' faction within the ruling Whig party after 1846. These ultra-liberal moralists, with their strong grip on the treasury and support from the metropolitan press, appropriated a 'heaven-sent "opportunity" of famine to deconstruct Irish society and rebuild it anew' along modern capitalist lines.[62] Ironically, the austere development approach was designed by the heirs of the same evangelical movement that had made up the humanitarian avantgarde at the time of the Napoleonic Wars. While moral rigidity and anxiety lest there be abuse of benevolence were not unique to the Victorian age, the second generation of evangelicals had 'degenerated into doctrinaire pedantries' at such a

---

[59] William Crossgove, David Egilman, Peter Heywood, et al., 'Colonialism, International Trade, and the Nation-state', in *Hunger in History: Food Shortage, Poverty, and Deprivation*, ed. Lucile F. Newman (Oxford: Blackwell, 1990), 229. See also Christine Kinealy, *The Great Irish Famine: Impact, Ideology and Rebellion* (Basingstoke: Palgrave Macmillan, 2002), 10.

[60] Cormac Ó Gráda, 'Mortality and the Great Famine', in *Atlas of the Great Irish Famine*, eds John Crowley, William J. Smyth, and Mike Murphy (New York: New York University Press, 2012), 170–1.

[61] Cecil Woodham-Smith, *The Great Hunger: Ireland 1845–9* (London: Hamish Hamilton, 1962), 75. However, Irish food imports exceeded exports from 1847 onwards, see Cormac Ó Gráda, 'Ireland's Great Famine: An Overview', in *When the Potato Failed: Causes and Effects of the 'Last' European Subsistence Crisis, 1845–1850*, eds Cormac Ó Gráda, Richard Paping, and Eric Vanhaute (Turnhout: Brepols, 2007), 53.

[62] Peter Gray, *Famine, Land and Politics: British Government and Irish Society, 1843–50* (Dublin: Irish Academic Press, 1999), 331 (quotation), 233; Peter Gray, 'The European Food Crisis and the Relief of Irish Famine, 1845–1850', in *When the Potato Failed: Causes and Effects of the 'Last' European Subsistence Crisis, 1845–1850*, eds Cormac Ó Gráda, Richard Paping, and Eric Vanhaute (Turnhout: Brepols, 2007), 99.

rate that a historian of the movement suggests 'Frankenstein's giant creation had got out of all control'.[63]

In hindsight, the Irish famine compromises political economy along the lines of Smith, Malthus, and Mill, as well as confidence in the project of modernity and in the civilisational standard of the British Empire. Ireland represented the 'other',[64] and was routinely addressed as 'that country' in the correspondence of British officials at the time. Ireland was treated differently than other parts of the UK, giving Irish–British relations a transnational and colonial character, despite formal participation in the same polity.[65] Few would go so far as to characterise the British government's conduct during the famine as genocide, but it is evident that British notions of the inferiority of an Irish 'surplus population' let them turn their backs while an unseen hand took the lives of the starving.[66]

The first Irish voluntary organisation for relief, the Mansion House Committee, was established in Dublin in October 1845.[67] The initial response of the UK government was to accommodate relief appeals, although it adhered to free trade principles and tied relief to the repeal of the Corn Laws. Based on experience with previous food crises, the government installed a relief commission that coordinated and subsidised local committees and voluntary collections, and financed public works. It also secretly purchased maize in the USA to regulate market prices, distributing it to depots throughout Ireland, and eventually selling it to the people. These measures saved the poor from starving to death during the first year of the crisis, but they were decried in the public debate as overly generous and in part regarded as one-time interventions. In Ireland, popular unrest and opposition to its coercive suppression spread, forcing the conservative government of the UK, headed by Sir Robert Peel, to resign in June 1846.[68]

---

[63] Brown, *Fathers of the Victorians*, 6.   [64] Kinealy, *Great Irish Famine*, 30.

[65] Oliver Macdonagh, 'Introduction: Ireland and the Union, 1801–70', in *A New History of Ireland, vol. 5: Ireland under the Union, 1801–70*, ed. W. E. Vaughan (Oxford: Clarendon, 1989), lii; David Nally, 'The Colonial Dimensions of the Great Irish Famine', in *Atlas of the Great Irish Famine*, eds John Crowley, William J. Smyth, and Mike Murphy (New York: New York University Press, 2012), 64–74.

[66] Charles Edward Trevelyan, *The Irish Crisis* (London: Longman, Brown, Green & Longmans, 1848), 32 (quotation); James Vernon, *Hunger: A Modern History* (Cambridge, MA: Belknap, 2007), 42, 45; David Nally, *Human Encumbrances: Political Violence and the Great Famine* (Notre Dame, IN: University of Notre Dame Press, 2011), 14, 20, 82–4. For the genocide hypothesis, see A. J. P. Taylor, 'Genocide', in *From Napoleon to the Second International: Essays on Nineteenth-Century Europe* (London: Hamish Hamilton, 1993 [1962]), 152–7; Richard L. Rubenstein, *The Age of Triage: Fear and Hope in an Overcrowded World* (Boston: Beacon, 1983), 11, 124; Tim Pat Coogan, *The Famine Plot: England's Role in Ireland's Greatest Tragedy* (New York: Palgrave Macmillan, 2012).

[67] Christine Kinealy, *Charity and the Great Hunger in Ireland: The Kindness of Strangers* (London: Bloomsbury, 2013), 54.

[68] Peter Gray, 'British Relief Measures', in *Atlas of the Great Irish Famine*, eds John Crowley, William J. Smyth, and Mike Murphy (New York: New York University Press, 2012), 75–8.

Lord John Russell's succeeding Whig administration was a weak minority government that was pressured to take a less interventionist course. Despite gravely rising food prices, it refrained from market interference and included penal elements in the public works scheme. This countered benefits to landowners from work projects and introduced performance-based remuneration that pushed the sick and the elderly below the subsistence level. After the almost complete potato failure of 1846, destitution made the number of those engaged in public relief works rise from 114,000 in October 1846 to 714,390 in March 1847. An increasing number of malnourished labourers died on the job. Notwithstanding harsh conditions and the huge number of enrollees, demand for employment in the relief scheme far exceeded availability.[69]

The government abandoned its public works programme by spring 1847. It was apparently ineffective and had become prohibitively expensive. Instead, the government sponsored a network of soup kitchens for the needy in conjunction with the aid being provided by the Quakers. This was a comparatively cheap entitlement-based approach that was intended to operate as a government programme only throughout the summer of 1847. By July, the soup kitchens were feeding three million people on a daily basis. In autumn, the burden of famine relief was written into an extended poor law. From then on, taxpayers in the distressed unions (i.e., 'poor law' districts) of Ireland had to bear the cost of the relief they received. A relative improvement in food availability during the second half of 1847 gave the illusion that the famine was over, occasioning the permanent withdrawal of means by the central government.[70] However, in 1848, blight again destroyed most of the potato crop. In 1848 and 1849, more than one million people were given relief through the extended poor law.[71] However, inmates of workhouses – the core institution of the Irish Poor Law – made up almost one-third of the victims of the Irish famine.[72] In all, public expenditures for Irish famine relief was about £10 million, mostly intended as loans.[73] Figure 2.1 depicts an official, single-copy map drawn in 1849 that uses three colours to highlight different degrees of distress. It shows that the western half of Ireland was affected most and that the government was aware of the suffering.[74]

The voluntary fundraisers during the Great Irish Famine came from varied backgrounds and their inclination to help differed considerably. Their level of

---

[69] Gray, 'British Relief Measures', 78–9. Regarding the demand for public relief employment exceeding the supply, see Christine Kinealy, 'The Operation of the Poor Law during the Famine', in *Atlas of the Great Irish Famine*, eds John Crowley, William J. Smyth, and Mike Murphy (New York: New York University Press, 2012), 90.

[70] Gray, 'British Relief Measures', 80–4.   [71] Kinealy, 'The Operation of the Poor Law', 92–3.

[72] William J. Smyth, 'The Creation of the Workhouse System', in *Atlas of the Great Irish Famine*, eds John Crowley, William J. Smyth, and Mike Murphy (New York: New York University Press, 2012), 127.

[73] Ó Gráda, 'Ireland', 180.   [74] See Section 5.2 for a further discussion of the map.

Figure 2.1 Map of Ireland accompanying Colonel Jones's report to Sir C. Trevelyan, 21 Dec. 1849, with 'distressed counties' coloured. Courtesy of the National Archives, UK. For the colour version, refer to the Cambridge University Press website, www.cambridge.org/Humanitarianism.

activity fluctuated, although in grossly inadequate proportions, with the severity of the distress, efforts by others, and press coverage, and it decreased over time. The first faraway group to provide relief at the end of 1845 was the Irish community of Boston. In early 1846, the British imperial forces in Bengal, which included many Irish soldiers, initiated another long-distance effort. When the famine intensified at the end of that year, some Catholic parishes and proselytising societies in England, as well as Irish organisations in the USA and transnational Quaker networks, began raising funds. The SVP expanded its model of soliciting local Catholic charity in major Irish cities, and also gave some subsidies.[75]

However, before the founding on 1 January 1847 of the British Association for the Relief of Extreme Distress in the Remote Parishes of Ireland and Scotland (or British Relief Association, BRA), transnational activity was low. While this new British initiative was controlled by the financial elite of London, it was directed by the same officials who had previously been responsible for inadequate government relief to Ireland – in particular, Charles Trevelyan, the permanent secretary of the treasury (and second-generation evangelical). In contrast to the communications of the Quakers and various relief efforts abroad, the BRA, following the official language policy, avoided the word 'famine' altogether.[76] Their campaign raised £470,000, mainly in the first months of 1847. More than two-fifths of that sum was the result of the reading of two letters by Queen Victoria in Anglican churches throughout England.[77] One-sixth of the total fund was reserved for Scotland, where some districts had also suffered from a poor harvest. The £390,000 collected for Ireland, which included donations from various parts of the empire and the wider world, was depicted as a success, although it barely exceeded funds raised during the minor famine of 1822.

Catholic and Foreign Relief

The appearance of a major British campaign encouraged the nascent relief efforts of Irish communities in the USA and Catholics around the world. Thus, a considerable, although short-lived, international voluntary effort came about in 1847, and for some time alleviated Irish distress.

British vicars apostolic (as Catholic bishops were then called) began to issue aid appeals in late 1846, perhaps challenged by the preparations being made to establish the BRA. The Catholic weekly, *The Tablet*, became the truest trusted conduit of news from Ireland to the British public. It continued to serve famine

---

[75] *First Annual Report of the Society of Saint Vincent de Paul, Cork* (Cork: O'Brien, 1846).

[76] John O'Rourke, *The History of the Great Irish Famine of 1847, with Notices of Earlier Irish Famines* (Dublin: McGlashan and Gill, 1875), 371.

[77] *Report of the British Association for the Relief of the Extreme Distress in Ireland and Scotland* (London: Clay, 1849), 50.

relief when that cause was no longer fashionable, illustrating the durative power of institutions, even journalistic ones, over individual efforts in raising aid. Catholic bishops as well as other Catholic collectors and donors in Britain generally forwarded gifts to their sister clergy, who constituted the spiritual authority for four-fifths of the Irish population, but they also contributed significant sums to the BRA.[78]

Prompted by Paul Cullen, rector of the Pontifical Irish College, the newly inaugurated Pope Pius IX made a personal donation to the cause of Irish relief and, assimilating an interdenominational relief committee formed by UK citizens in Rome, mandated collections for Ireland in mid-January 1847. By means of an encyclical, he extended the call for famine relief to the greater Catholic world in March 1847. Its impact was most evident in France and Italy, although the encyclical was widely circulated and resulted in contributions from other places as well. Prelates from Italy and elsewhere forwarded offertories of their districts to the Vatican's Sacred Congregation for the Propagation of the Faith, which distributed the sums totalling upwards of £10,000 among two dozen Irish bishops and archbishops. French fundraising was also carried out by dioceses, but was ultimately coordinated by the voluntary Comité de secours pour l'Irlande, which conveyed the proceeds of roughly £20,000 to the Irish clergy. The committee's first action, taken at a time when the pope's sphere of activity was still limited to Rome, was to ask him to address the world-at-large.[79]

The key figure behind the French petition was Jules Gossin, the president of the SVP, whose role has gone unrecognised in previous research. Gossin's circular, issued to SVP chapters in February 1847, resulted in funds that helped establish new branches in various Irish cities. These groups and their transnational network transcended the ad hoc humanitarianism of the nineteenth century, although the amount they raised abroad barely exceeded £6,000, and their raison d'être was local charity.[80] SVP branches continued their work throughout the years of famine, even after external funding had dried up; they are still flourishing today.

The isolated relief initiatives that emerged in the USA by the end of 1846 were coordinated and expanded by a national fundraising meeting that took place in Washington, DC, in February 1847. Contemporary discourse framed US relief efforts as a national enterprise of doing good that transcended ethnic, religious, and party divisions. Researchers have corroborated those claims.[81] However,

---

[78] On confessional demography, see *First Report of the Commissioners of Public Instruction, Ireland* (London: Clowes and Sons, 1835), 7.

[79] *Comité de secours pour l'Irlande* (Paris: A. Sirou et Desquers, 1847).

[80] Eugène Gossin, *Vie de M. Jules Gossin* (Paris: Oudin, 1907).

[81] Apart from Kinealy, *Charity and the Great Hunger*, see a dozen articles by Harvey Strum describing famine relief from different US localities, e.g., 'South Carolina and Irish Famine Relief, 1846–47', *South Carolina Historical Magazine* 103, no. 2 (2002): 130–52; 'Famine

individuals and organisations with an Irish background played a crucial role in the relief committees – something that was downplayed at the time in order to appeal to a wider circle of donors. The role of personal ties is also evident when one considers that remittances from Irish people abroad dwarfed humanitarian efforts, even at the height of voluntary action. Such remittances continued to increase in the following years, whereas transnational charity as a manifestation of sympathy ebbed after a few months.[82] Since the USA was construed as a 'nation of joiners', most Catholic fundraisers forwarded their collection to general committees in major cities like Boston, New York, Philadelphia, Charleston, and New Orleans.[83]

These committees and some of their smaller counterparts chartered ships with relief goods that they sent to Ireland – most famously, Boston's iconic *Jamestown*, with a cargo bound for Cork. The UK government reimbursed freight costs across the Atlantic, a subtle move that gave England moral credit in the eyes of the world and co-opted critical opinion in the USA. Nevertheless, US committees maintained their distance from UK authorities and principally relied for the distribution of their foodstuffs on Irish Quakers, who had a sterling reputation of providing impartial relief, rather than entrusting the US cargo to the quasi-governmental BRA. Contributions from the USA totalled approximately £200,000.

Ad Hoc Voluntarism

When in 1847 relief for Ireland was on the global agenda, collections were initiated worldwide. Most significant was the imperial context, in which British, Irish, and confessional backgrounds joined forces. Substantial sums from India, Canada, and Australia were given to the BRA, to Irish relief committees, or to the clergy in Ireland. Catholics in third countries such as the Netherlands, Belgium, and Germany tended to donate through church channels, whereas the BRA administered most other subscriptions and donations, including Sultan Abdulmejid I's much-cited contribution of £1,000. Overviews of relief are frequently inflated by sums being counted twice,

Relief from an Ancient Dutch City', *Hudson River Valley Review* 22, no. 2 (2006): 54–78; 'A Jersey Ship for Ireland', in *Ireland's Great Hunger: Relief, Representation, and Remembrance, vol. 2*, ed. David Valone (Lanham, MD: University Press of America, 2010), 3–20; 'Pennsylvania and Irish Famine Relief, 1846–1847', *Pennsylvania History* 81, no. 3 (2014): 277–99.

[82] For statistics, see 'Thirteenth General Report of the Colonial Land and Emigration Commissioners', *Justice of the Peace, and County, Borough, Poor Law Union, and Parish Law Recorder* 17 (1853): 582.

[83] See Arthur M. Schlesinger, 'Biography of a Nation of Joiners', *American Historical Review* 50, no. 1 (1944): 1–25.

among other flaws.[84] The present study estimates that voluntary relief to Ireland during the Great Famine totalled £1.4–1.5 million, of which almost £1 million came from abroad.[85]

By the end of 1846, the British Empire had to demonstrate its goodwill by providing famine relief in the sphere of voluntary action. Meanwhile, the Catholic world could not passively watch as the dominant Protestant society spread its benevolence over the Irish people. In the USA, people of Irish ancestry were crucial in stimulating relief efforts for Ireland, although nationality was often de-emphasised for improved outreach to US citizens who had no prior commitment to Ireland. For the same reason, Catholic churches in the USA, rather than making aid a confessional matter, joined local campaigns that principally channelled donations through Quaker intermediaries. English Catholics similarly maintained a cautious profile, trying to avoid causing their Anglican counterparts to develop a negative attitude towards Irish relief. The SVP chapter in Kilrush, which also distributed aid for the BRA and the Society of Friends, illustrates the local entanglement of foreign aid.[86]

Thus, the Irish Famine of 1847 saw a broad, well-coordinated network of fundraising bodies, aid providers, and local distributors working together on a hitherto unknown scale. Nevertheless, there was no preparedness for a sustained effort. By the summer of 1847, relief committees in the USA and elsewhere began to disband, church bodies turned their attention to other issues, and volunteers who had distributed aid on the ground were exhausted. Famine raged for another three years (five years in some parts of Ireland) with no significant voluntary or official relief efforts. Few people abroad could have imagined that a powerful government as the UK would remain largely passive in view of such an ongoing domestic calamity. When in the autumn of 1847 civil servants declared the situation in Ireland under control, it was widely assumed that this was in fact the case. Thus, almost all efforts ceased after a single season, showing that ad hoc humanitarianism was a weak and unreliable source of aid.

By the mid-nineteenth century, despite the trust in public authorities, a European, trans-Atlantic, imperial disposition to engage in far-reaching humanitarian projects emerged. It qualitatively surpassed the bilateral

---

[84] See fig. 2 in Grace Neville, '"Le pays classique de la faim": France and the Great Irish Famine', in *Atlas of the Great Irish Famine*, eds John Crowley, William J. Smyth, and Mike Murphy (New York: University Press, 2012), 489. This chart is mainly based on Donal A. Kerr, *The Catholic Church and the Famine* (Blackrock: Columba, 1996).

[85] This confirms the contemporary estimation by the Society of Friends. See *Transactions of the Central Relief Committee of the Society of Friends during the Famine in Ireland in 1846 and 1847* (Dublin: Hodges and Smith, 1852), 45.

[86] *Report of the Proceedings of the Society of St. Vincent de Paul, in Ireland, during the Year 1848* [SVP 1848] (Dublin: Wyer, 1849), 18.

endeavours of the Napoleonic era and the limited multilateral (chiefly military) philhellenic activism of the 1820s. Anticipating the 'glocal' civil society of the twentieth century, the SVP illustrates the potential of charitable structures that are more enduring than the temporary committees of the nineteenth century. While other relief initiatives slackened, the SVP extended its network of auxiliaries throughout Ireland in the latter half of the 1840s. This infrastructure allowed the local middle class to engage with their suffering compatriots and provide a maximum of aid with a minimum of resources.

2.3   The Russian Famine of 1921–3 and Organised Humanitarianism

The famine that began in parts of Soviet Russia in 1921 was preceded by bad harvests, a harsh winter, and a subsequent drought – especially in the Volga Valley (see Figure 2.2). The post-revolutionary country had been ravaged by war and by then had endured seven years of chaos. The methods of war communism, including confiscation and collectivisation, had weakened rural communities, while the White armies were still active in some parts of the country. The New Economic Policy (NEP) adopted in March 1921 did not relieve conditions immediately, and the lack of emergency planning coupled with mismanagement aggravated the situation. Twenty million people were threatened by starvation; an estimated two million eventually died.[87] Neverthe-less, the Bolshevik government would not officially acknowledge the famine or solicit foreign assistance until mid-1921. At that point, the author Maxim Gorky dramatically appealed for aid. His call immediately triggered an inter-national relief campaign for Russia.[88]

Organised Humanitarianism

Historians and contemporary witnesses cite the Russian Famine of 1921–3 as a defining moment in the history of humanitarian aid.[89] The extensive

---

[87] Bruno Cabanes, *The Great War and the Origins of Humanitarianism, 1918–1924* (Cambridge: Cambridge University Press, 2014), 239–40; Patenaude, *Big Show*, 197.

[88] An English translation of Gorky's appeal may be found in *ARA Bulletin* 2, no. 16 (1 Sept. 1921), 2.

[89] League of Nations, *Report on Economic Conditions in Russia: With Special Reference to the Famine of 1921–1922 and the State of Agriculture* (Geneva, League of Nations, 1922), 1; Marguerite E. Bienz, ed. *Für unsere kleinen russischen Brüder! Gaben westeuropäischer Schriftsteller und Künstler für die notleidenden Kinder in den Hungersnotdistrikten Russlands* (Geneva: Hohes Kommissariat, 1922), 9; C. E. Bechhofer, *Through Starving Russia, Being a Record of a Journey to Moscow and the Volga Provinces, in August and September, 1921* (London: Menthuen, 1921), xii; Sasson, 'From Empire to Humanity', 520; Fuyuki Kurasawa, 'The Making of Humanitarian Visual Icons: On the 1921–1923 Russian Famine as Founda-tional Event', in *Iconic Power: Materiality and Meaning in Social Life*, eds Jeffrey Alexander, Dominik Bartmanski, and Bernhard Giesen (New York: Palgrave Macmillan, 2012), 68.

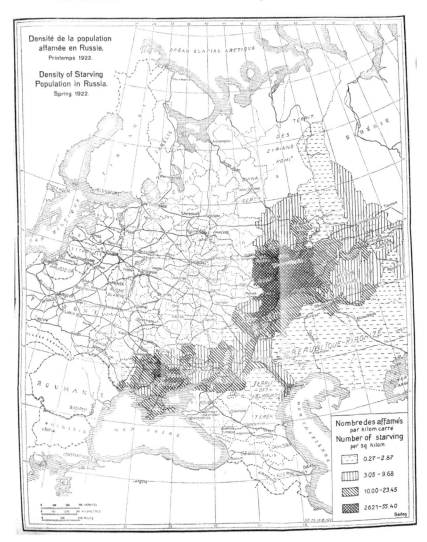

Figure 2.2 Map of famine regions illustrating the 'Density of Starving Population in Russia' in spring 1922, published by the League of Nations, *Report*, 165.
Image reproduced courtesy of the University of Warwick Library Collections, Reference HK 317.L3

international relief effort it called forth reflects trends that originated in the years around 1900 and were reinforced, refined, and sometimes redirected during and after the First World War. Those efforts provide a paradigm for what we term organised humanitarianism. The era which saw an increased focus on children, was characterised by (a) the institutionalisation and professionalisation of humanitarian practice, including businesslike fundraising, purchasing, and accounting procedures; (b) the active engagement of experts and the impact of science; (c) a 'mixed economy' of voluntary and state efforts; and (d) the systematic use of photographs and motion pictures in fundraising campaigns.

With origins in the late nineteenth century, the model of organised humanitarianism gained considerable momentum at the beginning of the First World War when Herbert Hoover created the Commission for Relief in Belgium (CRB), which would also serve as the blueprint for US relief efforts after the war. Between 1914 and 1919, the CRB managed an aid operation on an unprecedented scale, sustaining an entire nation suffering under German occupation and an allied blockade. A contemporary observer described the CRB as a hybrid 'piratical state organized for benevolence'.[90]

Hoover's accomplishment was achieved by skilful diplomacy and recourse to his business and engineering expertise. Commission offices purchased raw materials on the global food market, convoys shipped them across the Atlantic, and thousands of warehouses aided in the distribution. Overhead costs were kept low as the majority of the staff was made up of volunteers; and shipping, insurance, and other companies agreed to offer charitable discounts. Moreover, individual recipients or relief committees were asked to pay for provisions wherever they could. About 80 per cent of the US$900 million at Hoover's disposal came from governmental sources, primarily via loans from the USA and the UK, and only 6 per cent came in private donations.[91]

After the war, Hoover continued his work with the ARA, first in Central Europe and then during the famine in Soviet Russia. Mainly a government sponsored organisation, the ARA was also supported by tens of thousands of private donors. It spent US$5 billion between the armistice of 1918 and 1924.[92] The ARA Food Remittance Program, which allowed individuals to purchase food packages worth US$10 for relatives and friends in certain European countries, was a successful creation of the period, and it was also deployed during the Russian Famine.[93]

---

[90] George I. Gay and H. H. Fisher, eds, *Public Relations of the Commission for Relief in Belgium: Documents, vol. 1* (Stanford, CA: Stanford University Press, 1929), v.

[91] The remaining 15 per cent (US$135 million) came from an enormous 'operating surplus'. For statistics, documents, and contemporary analysis, see George I. Gay, *The Commission for Relief in Belgium: Statistical Review of Relief Operations* (Stanford, CA: Stanford University Press, 1925).

[92] Charles E. Noyes, 'American Relief of Famine in Europe', in *Editorial Research Reports, vol. 2* (Washington, DC: CQ Press, 1940), 53–68.

[93] Patenaude, *Big Show*, 92.

Motivated more by pragmatic considerations than compassion, the principal post-war US goals were unloading an agricultural surplus, boosting the US economy, and securing future markets. In addition, the ARA and affiliated organisations like the ARC were tools to contain communism and influence the nation- and institution-building process in Central Europe.[94] More than leaders of relief efforts in former times, the new humanitarians aimed to shape the governance structures of the societies that they were targeting.[95]

The Near East Relief (NER), which emerged in 1919 out of the American Committee for Armenian and Syrian Relief (founded in 1915), was equally ambitious in its goal of reshaping societies in the Eastern Mediterranean by providing both emergency aid and long-term relief in the form of educational programmes. Its Protestant missionary background caused it to choose Christian children, especially Armenian orphans, as its main beneficiary group.[96] Limiting its services to a marginalised minority group contrasted with the NER's intention of raising a generation of decision makers. The NER had close governmental ties, but depended far more than the ARA on private donations and it embraced modern fundraising techniques. Over a period of ten years it spent more than US$100 million to provide relief and 'help to self-help' through education and training. As did other representatives of organised humanitarianism, the NER emphasised its own professionalism and efficiency. However, while 'tales of perfectly executed plans' dominate its official publications, its work was in many cases based on improvisation.[97]

Whereas the CRB and the ARA were examples of twentieth-century relief efforts that were largely state-financed and partially state-led, the British SCF represented an alternative format of organised voluntary action. It combined humanitarian service with advocacy, and it functioned as a corrective to government policy. Eglantyne Jebb, who co-founded the SCF in 1919, saw her organisation's role as a counterforce to nationalist politics and consciously chose 'enemy children' (first German and Austrian, then Russian) as primary beneficiaries.[98] Although child-focused charity was familiar in

---

[94] Friederike Kind-Kovács, 'The Great War, the Child's Body and the American Red Cross', *European Review of History* 23, nos 1–2 (2016): 41; Patenaude, *Big Show*, 335–8.

[95] Little, 'An Explosion', 5; Davide Rodogno, Francesca Piana, and Shaloma Gauthier, 'Shaping Poland: Relief and Rehabilitation Programs by Foreign Organizations 1918–1922', in *Shaping the Transnational Sphere: Experts, Networks, and Issues from the 1840s to the 1930s*, eds David Rodogno, Bernhard Struck, and Jakob Vogel (Oxford: Berghahn, 2014), 259–78.

[96] Keith David Watenpaugh, *Bread from Stones: The Middle East and the Making of Modern Humanitarianism* (Oakland: University of California Press, 2015), 97–8.

[97] Davide Rodogno, 'Beyond Relief: A Sketch of the Near East Relief's Humanitarian Operations, 1918–1929', *monde(s)* 6, no. 2 (2014): 53.

[98] Linda Mahood and Vic Satzewich, 'The Save the Children Fund and the Russian Famine of 1921–23: Claims and Counter-claims about Feeding "Bolshevik" Children', *Journal of Historical Sociology* 22, no. 1 (2009): 55–83; Rodney Breen, 'Saving Enemy Children: Save the Children's Russian Relief Operation, 1921–1923', *Disasters* 18, no. 3 (1994): 221–38.

1919, even greater attention shifted from wounded soldiers to children after the war.[99] The ARA and affiliated organisations also focused on minors, and the innocent child became an international icon closely linked to appeals for humanitarian relief.[100]

By contrast to the ARA, but like the Quakers, the outspoken SCF goal was 'to foster a new generation of peace-loving internationalists'.[101] The SCF's transnational ambitions were further emphasised by the foundation of the International Save the Children Union (ISCU) in Geneva in 1920. Thus, the SCF combined fundraising and relief with the championing of children's causes more generally, and by 1924 had brought about the adoption of the Declaration of the Rights of the Child by the League of Nations.

The SCF addressed its appeals to the entire population and, despite a generally progressive tendency, it actively recruited patrons and members representing a wide range of political views. In December 1919, Pope Benedict XV announced his support for the SCF, and religious leaders in Great Britain followed. Through its adoption of business methods, the SCF contributed significantly to the professionalisation of the humanitarian sector in the UK. Public relation experts from private firms, hired on a commission basis, designed nationwide advertising campaigns, and Jebb understood the 'efficiency of controversy' for voluntary organisations.[102] The magazine *The Record*, which began publication in October 1920, functioned as a mouthpiece. The SCF established, or at least popularised, an innovative scheme by which donors symbolically 'adopted' children in Austria, Serbia, Germany, Hungary, and other countries, creating long-term bonds. Rooted in the Christian tradition of caretaking godparents, child sponsorship has remained a popular method of humanitarian aid that has special appeal to contributors.[103]

In comparison with the ARA, however, the SCF was a small-scale player. It relied almost entirely on private donations, only addressed children's issues, and (at least during its early years) passed funding on to other groups rather than organising relief on its own. Despite its relative inexperience and a

---

[99] Rebecca Gill, 'The Rational Administration of Compassion: The Origins of British Relief in War', *Le mouvement social* 227, no. 1 (2009): 26.

[100] Kind-Kovács, 'The Great War', 38. See also Dominique Marshall, 'The Construction of Children as an Object of International Relations: The Declaration of Children's Rights and the Child Welfare Committee of League of Nations, 1900–1924', *International Journal of Children's Rights* 7, no. 2 (1999): 103–47; Paul Weidling, 'From Sentiment to Science: Children's Relief Organisations and the Problem of Malnutrition in Inter-war Europe', *Disasters* 18, no. 3 (1994): 203–12.

[101] Gill, 'Rational Administration', 26.

[102] Linda Mahood, *Feminism and Voluntary Action: Eglantyne Jebb and Save the Children, 1876–1928* (Basingstoke: Palgrave, 2009), 168 (quotation), 171–3.

[103] Brad Watson, 'Origins of Child Sponsorship: Save the Children Fund in the 1920s', in *Child Sponsorship: Exploring Pathways to a Brighter Future*, eds Brad Watson and Matthew Clarke (New York: Palgrave Macmillan, 2014), 18–40.

difficult political environment ('feeding enemy children' was far from a popular cause in post-war Britain), its fundraising methods enabled the SCF to collect about £1 million during the first two years of its existence.[104]

American and British Quakers were other groups that played a significant role during the Russian Famine. They had previously set up humanitarian missions during the Russian Famine of the 1890s in the city of Buzuluk, to which they returned in 1916 and 1917, and which became the centre of their famine relief five years later. They were then engaged by both the ARA and the international Red Cross movement to channel relief.[105] During the First World War, transnational Quaker relief work was professionalised. The British Friends' Emergency and War Victims Relief Committee (FEWVRC) and the American Friends Service Committee (AFSC) were established in 1914 and 1917, respectively. Initially, both organisations cooperated closely.[106]

The Nationalisation of Universal Causes

The growing awareness of global interconnectedness led to the 'heyday of a vigorous internationalism' in the early twentieth century that benefitted the humanitarian sector considerably.[107] However, the war experience also led to the nationalisation of transnational aid. Governments started to coordinate, seek control over, and channel humanitarian efforts from their territory, resulting in limited room for internationalist and pacifist organisations to manoeuvre.[108] As a consequence, transnational humanitarian efforts were often organised along national, rather than international, lines.[109] In the case of the Red Cross, the outcome was the juxtaposition of the International

[104] 'A Calendar of Principle Events', *The Record* 3, no. 1 (1922); Balance sheet notes, Cadbury Research Library, University of Birmingham, Save the Children Fund Archives (SCF), reel 33.

[105] David McFadden and Claire Gorfinkel, *Constructive Spirit: Quakers in Revolutionary Russia* (Pasadena, CA: International Productions, 2004), 9, 27.

[106] James E. Miles and Meaburn Tatham, *The Ambulance Unit, 1914–1919: A Record* (London: Swarthmore Press, 1919); Daniel Maul, 'American Quakers, the Emergence of International Humanitarianism, and the Foundation of the American Friends Service Committee, 1890–1920', in *Dilemmas of Humanitarian Aid in the Twentieth Century*, ed. Johannes Paulmann (Oxford: Oxford University Press, 2016), 63–87.

[107] Andrew Arsan, Su Lin Lewis, and Anne-Isabelle Richard, 'Editorial: The Roots of Global Civil Society and the Interwar Moment', *Journal of Global History* 7, no. 2 (2012): 163; Cabanes, *Great War*, 5; Mahood, *Feminism and Voluntary Action*, 174.

[108] Daniel Maul, 'Appell an das Gewissen: Fridtjof Nansen und die Russische Hungerhilfe 1921–23', *Themenportal Europäische Geschichte* (Berlin: Humboldt Universität, 2011): 3, available at www.europa.clio-online.de/essay/id/artikel-3604 (accessed 29 June 2019); Paulmann, 'Conjunctures in the History'. Humanitarian commitment could also provide a patriotic, but pacifist, alternative to military service, the Quaker ambulance corps being one example.

[109] Daniel Laqua, 'Inside the Humanitarian Cloud: Causes and Motivations to Help Friends and Strangers', *Journal of Modern European History* 12, no. 2 (2014): 182.

Committee of the Red Cross (ICRC), which had little means but great moral authority, against the financially better-situated national Red Cross societies.[110] The relationship between the British SCF and its Geneva-based international counterpart, the ISCU, developed in a similar way. In contrast to the conservative Imperial War Relief Fund (IWRF), which emphasised the British and imperial character of its mission and shunned international cooperation, the SCF had encouraged the establishment of national chapters in other countries, a dozen of which emerged by 1921. Competing with the IWRF, the SCF also received substantial donations from the British dominions, principally New Zealand and Canada, where new chapters were forming. However, during the Russian Famine, the SCF put increasing emphasis on the nationalisation of relief and joined forces with the IWRF in an 'All British Appeal'. Aware that the bulk of their donations came from Britain, the SCF urged that national chapters within the ISCU receive full credit for their generosity.[111]

The shift in the global power balance towards the USA and the emergence of the first communist state in Russia further politicised the question of humanitarian aid. With Hoover as its leading promoter, humanitarian aid was increasingly treated as diplomacy – if not war – by other means, explicitly aimed at winning the hearts and minds of distressed populations and fighting the spread of communism in Europe.[112] Hoover was convinced that food aid would 'win the post war', and for that goal strict national control and administration appeared indispensable.[113] A unified national front was supposed to 'preserve American prestige' and ensure that beneficiaries knew and appreciated that the help they received came from the USA, something assumed to enhance political, social, and economic influence.[114]

The establishment of the US European Relief Council (ERC) in 1920 was a major step in this direction. Like many other organisations, it concentrated on relief for children and in addition to the ARA, it embraced the AFSC, the ARC, the Federal Council of Churches, the Jewish Joint Distribution Committee (JDC), the Knights of Columbus, the National Catholic Welfare Council (NCWC), and the Young Men's and Women's Christian Associations (YMCA and YWCA).[115] Within a few months, an appeal to save the

---

[110] Maul, 'Appell an das Gewissen, 3–4; Gill, Calculating Compassion, 198–9.

[111] Mahood, Feminism and Voluntary Action, 178, 193; Emily Baughan, 'The Imperial War Relief Fund and the All British Appeal: Commonwealth, Conflict and Conservatism within the British Humanitarian Movement, 1920–25', Journal of Imperial and Commonwealth History 40, no. 5 (2012): 845–61; 'Co-operation True and False', The Record 2, no. 3 (1921).

[112] Patenaude, Big Show, 635.   [113] Cabanes, Great War, 212–14.

[114] Richard Gribble, 'Cooperation and Conflict between Church and State: The Russian Famine of 1921–1923', Journal of Church and State 51, no. 4 (2009): 649.

[115] Interim Report of European Relief Council, Including Statement of Contributions by States, and Auditors' Preliminary Report on Accounts (New York: Brown, 1921).

children of Europe addressed to the US public resulted in US\$29 million in donations in late 1920, with Hoover prominently leading the campaign.[116] The organisational collaboration continued during the Russian Famine, with some changes in membership.

The difficulty of coordinating international relief during the Russian campaign is well illustrated by the example of the Society of Friends. Despite a long tradition of close cooperation between British and American Quakers, first during the Russian Famine of the 1890s, and later during the First World War, the AFSC decided to sever ties with their British counterparts in 1921.[117] Setting aside concerns about principles such as pacifism, neutrality, and impartiality, the AFSC chose to join Hoover's US relief efforts under the protection and with the ample resources of the ARA, rather than continuing its transnational approach on a more modest scale. As Daniel Maul argues, two recurrent conflicting ideas of humanitarianism are symbolised in this decision: national versus international, and professional versus 'ethical'.[118] The Catholic Church was also subject to similar tensions. While the NCWC regarded its inclusion under Hoover's ARA umbrella a victory for Catholicism in the USA, some clerics decried it as a loss of episcopal autonomy.[119] For practical reasons, the NCWC and the Papal Relief Mission were later affiliated with the ARA. However, Vatican representatives continually struggled for their independence, wanting to provide aid not in the name of the USA, but as the Catholic Church.[120]

Russian Famine Relief

The devastation caused by the Russian Famine, and the extent and international dimensions of the relief efforts, were exceptional. Ideological and political factors complicated the situation, as the Bolshevik regime was still fragile and unrecognised by most Western governments. As a result, any bilateral arrangement was difficult and left humanitarian operations in private hands. Both exiled Russians and conservative foreign politicians were sceptical or openly hostile to the idea of supporting Soviet Russia with food,

---

[116] Kendrick Alling Clements, *The Life of Herbert Hoover, vol. 4: Imperfect Visionary 1918–1928* (New York: Palgrave Macmillan, 2010), 79–84.

[117] McFadden and Gorfinkel, *Contructive Spirit*, 27; Maul, 'American Quakers, the Emergence of International Humanitarianism', 63–87; Thomas C. Kennedy, *British Quakerism 1860–1920: The Transformation of a Religious Community* (Oxford: Oxford University Press, 2001).

[118] Daniel Maul, 'American Quakers and Famine Relief in the Soviet Union 1921–1923', paper presented at the workshop 'Brokers of Aid: Humanitarian Organizations between Donors and Recipients', Södertörn University, Stockholm, 12 June 2014.

[119] Gribble, 'Cooperation and Conflict'.

[120] Marisa Patulli Trythall, '"Russia's Misfortune Offers Humanitarians a Splendid Opportunity": Jesuits, Communism, and the Russian Famine', *Journal of Jesuit Studies* 5, no. 1 (2018), 86–7.

warning that this would stabilise the tottering regime. Others saw the famine as an opportunity, either for coming to terms with the new regime or for eliciting pro-Western attitudes among Russians and increasing the chance of a regime change. In fact, almost all relief help came from parties who were opposed to the ideology represented by Lenin, which in part explains why communist leaders deeply mistrusted foreign organisations and feared a counter-revolution in humanitarian disguise.[121] Nevertheless, they realised the benefit of accepting Western aid.

In the end, some 900,000 tonnes of relief goods were brought into the famine regions between late 1921 and early 1923. More than eleven million people were receiving food aid through foreign organisations by the time operations peaked in August 1922.[122] Relief was mainly delivered by two umbrella agencies, both of which signed treaties with the Bolshevik government: Hoover's ARA and the International Committee for Russian Relief (ICRR), led by Norwegian explorer Fridtjof Nansen. The ARA drew on the experience of its vast relief efforts in post-war Europe and provided more than four-fifths of all foreign aid. The ICRR was a creation of the ICRC, in cooperation with the Secretariat of the League of Nations. By 1921, both Hoover and Nansen were already internationally cele-brated humanitarians.[123]

Most US relief agencies, including the ARC, worked under the ARA auspices, while Nansen represented a number of organisations from two dozen primarily European countries. The majority of humanitarian committees and organisations dealt with fundraising only. The ARA was the main agency responsible for distributing US relief, but even the AFSC in Buzuluk and, at a later point, the JDC in Ukraine worked in the field, although on a much smaller scale. Nansen depended to a great extent on the SCF and the British Quakers, who established their own distribution systems in the provinces of Saratov and

---

[121] See, e.g., 'The Famine and the International Situation, Material for Agitators by the Central Agitation Comission to Combat the Famine of the Central Committee of the Russian Comunist Party', undated translation by the ARA (probably Sept. 1921), Hoover Institution Library and Archives, Stanford University, ARA Russian operational records (hereafter ARA), reel 14.

[122] See 'Russian Feeding Progress: Number of Persons Fed on the First of Each Month', undated (after Apr. 1923), ARA, reel 568 and 'Feeding of the Starving Russian Population on August 1st 1922: Organisations Working under the Nansen Agreement', *International Committee for Russian Relief – Information* 30 (30 Aug. 1922), 20.

[123] The standard work on the ARA operation is Patenaude, *Big Show*. See also Benjamin M. Weissman, *Herbert Hoover and Famine Relief to Soviet Russia, 1921–1923* (Stanford, CA: Stanford University Press, 1974). The official ARA history was written by Harold Henry Fisher, *The Famine in Soviet Russia, 1919–1923: The Operations of the American Relief Administration* (New York: Macmillan, 1927). For the ICRR, see Carl Emil Vogt, *Nansens Kamp mot Hungersnøden i Russland 1921–23* (Oslo: Aschehoug, 2007); Carl Emil Vogt, 'Fridtjof Nansen and European Food Aid to Russia and the Ukraine 1921–1923', *Dvacáté století* 1, no. 2 (2009): 40–50; Maul, 'Appell an das Gewissen'. For British relief, see Luke Kelly, *British Humanitarian Activity in Russia, 1890–1923* (Cham: Springer, 2018), 159–211.

Buzuluk. Some national Red Cross chapters, including Italian, Swiss, and Swedish groups, also sought to direct relief work, but due to their limited resources, their efforts were often contingent on other players.[124]

Despite conflicts among organisations, few relief agencies remained outside the Nansen and Hoover spheres, although some like the SCF and the Quakers later signed their own aid treaties with the Soviet government. The most relevant exceptions were communists, such as the Berlin-based Workers' International Relief (WIR), and its US branch, the Friends of Soviet Russia (FSR).[125] There were also competing socialist and social democratic initiatives, such as one by the Amsterdam-based International Federation of Trade Unions, (IFTU), which mirrored ideological conflicts within the international workers' movement. In Denmark, for example, three nationwide campaigns were organised: one by the Danish Red Cross, one by the Social Democratic Union, and one by the communist Committee for Aid to Russia – the Danish auxiliary of the WIR, led by author Martin Andersen Nexø.[126] Labour movement organisations followed an agenda that differed from that of Hoover and Nansen. They saw their efforts as part of an international class struggle, rather than as a humanitarian initiative, and regarded ARA relief in particular as 'one part Trojan Horse, one part opiate'.[127] The WIR was also an exception in making extensive use of world-renowned artists and intellectuals, such as Käthe Kollwitz, George Bernard Shaw, and Albert Einstein, in their fundraising campaigns.[128]

About a month after Gorky's appeal, the ICRC organised a conference in Geneva on 15 and 16 August 1921 that brought together representatives from more than twenty humanitarian organisations and some governments.[129] The objective was to join forces and coordinate famine relief in Russia. The most tangible result was the establishment of the ICRR as an umbrella organisation.

---

[124] For a detailed account of this, see 'Work of the International Russian Relief Committee', *International Committee for Russian Relief – Information* no. 26 (10 July 1922), 26–32 (Swedish Red Cross), and 44–50 (Italian and Swiss Red Cross).

[125] Kasper Braskén, *The International Workers' Relief, Communism, and Transnational Solidarity: Willi Münzenberg in Weimar Germany* (Basingstoke: Palgrave Macmillan, 2015); Efrain M. Diaz, 'Friends of Soviet Russia: The Friendly Front Survives the Famine', *Perspectives* 34 (2007/8): 41–58. The original German name of the WIR was Internationale Arbeiterhilfe (IAH). In the following, the acronym WIR will be used, although some documents speak of International Workers' Relief, IAH, or refer more concretely to the Workers' International Russian Famine Relief Committee (WIRFRC).

[126] Kim Fredrichsen and Asger Pedersen, 'Dansk-Russisk Forenings tidlige historie', in *Dansk-russiske mellemfolkelige kontakter før og nu* (s.l.: Dansk-Russisk Forening, 2015), 3.

[127] Barnett, *Empire of Humanity*, 6. See also Braskén, *International Workers' Relief*, 39.

[128] Braskén, *International Workers' Relief*, 41–3.

[129] For lists of participants and detailed minutes of the meetings, see SCF, reel 33; Library of the Society of Friends, London, Friends Emergency and War Victims Relief Committee (FEWVRC) Archive, Relief Mission to Russia, 7/5/2/1–2.

The initial plan of a dual European–US chairmanship failed, as Hoover, whose European representative had already negotiated terms for ARA relief with Russian authorities, declined the nomination. Therefore, Nansen became the sole high commissioner, and the ICRR remained a predominantly European body.

Apart from being a celebrity, Nansen was already an experienced humanitarian worker. His commitment to the repatriation of prisoners of war on behalf of the League of Nations had gained him international respect. In September 1921, he also became the League's high commissioner for refugees, parallel to his engagement for famine relief in Russia.

However, the preconditions for Nansen's work were difficult, as initially no government, except for his home country, Norway, supported the ICRR, nor would the participating humanitarian organisations financially commit themselves. Only the SCF pledged in advance to feed 10,000 children. While Hoover drew on the well-functioning machinery of the ARA and had ample financial means at his disposal when bargaining with suspicious Russian authorities in Riga, Nansen's position was weak as he negotiated the conditions under which relief would be provided. When Nansen arrived on 20 August, Hoover's representative had already successfully secured far-reaching US control over distribution and had even obliged the Russian government to fund part of the relief work with its gold reserves.[130]

Nansen's agreement was less favourable, particularly with regard to distribution. However, his major problem remained funding.[131] European governments were generally unwilling to invest in the enterprise, either by donations or with loans, which according to the Riga treaty, Nansen was bound to negotiate on behalf of the Soviet government. Back in Geneva, Nansen delivered two acclaimed speeches before the Assembly of the League of Nations. In the first, on 9 September, he appealed to European governments for help, pointing out that private relief alone was insufficient.[132] Two weeks later, he presented an emotional sketch of the absurdity of the situation: ships and a surplus of food were available, while twenty million people in Russia were starving and Western governments remained indifferent.[133]

Nansen received applause for his speech, but little money. The ICRR continued its work, depending on private charity and supported by minor sums from a few governments such as Norway, Sweden, and the Baltic

---

[130] The complete agreement as an appendix may be found in Patenaude, *Big Show*, 745–8.
[131] Vogt, 'Fridtjof Nansen and European Food Aid', 43; Vogt, *Nansens kamp*, 145–69.
[132] 'Dr Nansen at the League of Nations', *The Record* 2, no. 1 (1921).
[133] 'Fridtjof Nansens Rede vor dem Völkerbund (24 Sept. 1921)' (in English), *Themenportal Europäische Geschichte* (Berlin: Humboldt University, 2011), available at www.europa.clio-online.de/quelle/id/artikel-3535 (accessed 29 June 2019).

states. The principal affiliated organisations like the SCF, the British Quakers, and the Swedish Red Cross acted largely on their own in their fundraising and relief work, but in many cases served as distribution agencies for ICRR provisions.

Culmination

The development of humanitarianism after 1900 culminated in the relief efforts during the Russian Famine. Foreshadowing our designation of this humanitarian era, the SCF proclaimed during the Russian Famine that 'whatever is not organised is dead'.[134] While ARA officials praised the centralised relief work under a national umbrella, they showed little understanding for the wishes of affiliated organisations to preserve independent operations or their own culture of altruism. With regard to efficiency, the ARA suggested that 'all these organizations would be greatly benefitted if their funds were donated outright to the ARA'.[135] The SCF adopted a similar position, suggesting that there was no longer room for amateur philanthropy.[136] Professionalisation also meant that experts would handle the logistics of relief, procurement of food and other supplies, and accounting, as well as marketing and public relations – the latter an area that especially created conflicts.[137] During the Russian Famine, various organisations produced at least five films.[138] The SCF appropriated the slogan 'Seeing Is Believing' and attempted to settle public controversies by claiming their documentaries irrefutably proved the reality of famine.[139]

A symbiotic mixed economy, with private relief organisations on the one hand, and the goverment on the other, was a necessity if comprehensive relief was to be provided for millions threatened by starvation in Russia, as the success of the ARA illustrates. It was possible because Hoover's goals and those of Washington generally coincided. Hoover led the ARA as a private citizen, but was also secretary of commerce in the Harding administration. Nansen and the SCF were equally quick to declare governmental support indispensable, and put great effort into lobbying for state-financed relief

---

[134] 'The New Charity', *The Record* 2, no. 8 (1922).
[135] Haskell to London, 20 Mar. 1922, ARA, reel 115.
[136] 'Of Giving Way to Others: A Word to Workers and Friends', *The Record* 2, no. 4 (1921).
[137] Breen, 'Saving Enemy Children'.
[138] Produced by the SCF, ARA, ICRR, British Quakers, and FSR. See also Sasson, 'From Empire to Humanity', 531; Christina Twomey, 'Framing Atrocity: Photography and Humanitarianism', *History of Photography* 36, no. 3 (2012): 255–64; Heide Fehrenbach and Davide Rodogno, eds, *Humanitarian Photography: A History* (New York: Cambridge University Press, 2015).
[139] 'Seeing Is Believing', *The Record* 2, no. 10 (1922).

missions. Other than symbolic success, however, they failed because they were unable to persuade European governments that their common interest justified a joint commitment. Although the SFC saw itself as a government corrective, its attempts to gain state support show the inevitability of a humanitarian mixed economy. Even the Quakers, with their storied incorruptible relief philosophy, considered it necessary to adapt to the new development during the Russian Famine, and so the AFSC reluctantly engaged in a pragmatic relationship with the ARA, not least because of Hoover's access to government funding.

In the wake of Gorky's appeal, lingering conflicts between the ICRC and major national Red Cross societies surfaced, and the ICRC tried to regain the ground it had lost by setting up Nansen's high commissariat. At the same time, the ambitions of the League of Nations created new, sometimes painful discrepancies, as Nansen's unsuccessful appeals in Geneva demonstrate. Similarly, the SCF experienced difficulties when they began to extend their activities beyond fundraising to launching their own transport and distribution systems. The AFSC, which had a working relationship with the ARA, also had such problems, and ended up fearing for the loss of their identity.

Hoover and the ARA were confronted with the question of how practical economically and politically their endeavour had been. Could both humanitarian and political success be repeated as supposedly achieved in Central and Eastern Europe? In the end, while the huge relief apparatus significantly alleviated the suffering of the Russian people, saving many lives and winning over many hearts and minds, the operation failed to destabilise the Bolshevik regime.

2.4   Famine in Ethiopia 1984–6 and Expressive Humanitarianism

By late 1984, famine was affecting wide swaths of Sahelian Africa. The catastrophe had been developing since December 1982. Starvation acutely threatened more than seven million people in the northern and south-eastern regions of Ethiopia or approximately one-fifth of the total population. Warnings from aid organisations had been ignored by the international community and the government downplayed the scale of the crisis. In the 1980s, Ethiopia was ruled by a committee of military officers known as the Derg, headed by President Mengistu Haile Mariam.[140] These Marxists had assumed power after

---

[140] 'Derg' or 'Dergue' is the Amharic word for 'committee', an abbreviation of the government's full title, 'Provisional Military Administrative Committee'.

a 1974 coup d'etat which overthrew Emperor Haile Selassie. They consolidated their rule through a reign of terror. The long civil war the military government engaged in against the secessionist Eritrean People's Liberation Front (EPLF) and Tigray People's Liberation Front (TPLF) escalated in 1985 (see Figure 2.3).[141] In 1982, the World Bank ranked Ethiopia as the second poorest country in the world in terms of GNP per capita. Owing to its socialist ideology, the country could not attract significant foreign investment or development aid.[142]

The causes of the famine are complex and disputed, but civil war, years of drought across the Sahel region, compulsory land reform, and forced collective farming policies all played a part. In addition, food aid was late in coming, and when it did arrive, problems supplying relief to rebel-held areas as well as the regime's programme of forced resettlement for famine-affected people added to the death toll. Meanwhile, the Derg diverted food from rural areas to urban markets in an attempt to stifle political dissent in the cities. Estimates vary, but between 400,000 and 1 million people are believed to have died between 1984 and 1986.[143]

An Age of Expressive Humanitarianism

The famine in Ethiopia has been cited as a landmark in the history of humanitarianism, both by those who participated in the relief operations and by others who have later written about it.[144] It signified an age of expressive humanitarianism, marked by the Band Aid and Live Aid

---

[141] Alex de Waal, *Evil Days: 30 Years of War and Famine* (New York: Human Rights Watch, 1991), 177–84, 197–203.

[142] Richard Pankhurst, 'The Ethiopian Famine: Cultural Survival's New Report', *Anthropology Today* 2, no. 3 (1986): 4–5; John Clarke, *Resettlement and Rehabilitation: Ethiopia's Campaign against Famine* (London: Harney and Jones, 1987), 17.

[143] de Waal, *Famine Crimes*, 115; Paul C. Hébert, 'Feed the World: Food, Development, Aid and Hunger in Africa, 1984–1985', unpublished MA thesis, Corcordia University, Canada, 2008; de Waal, *Evil Days*, 173–6; Peter Gill, *Famine and Foreigners: Ethiopia since Live Aid* (Oxford: Oxford University Press, 2010), 43.

[144] Eleanor Davey, John Borton, and Matthew Foley, *A History of the Humanitarian System: Western Origins and Foundations* (London: Overseas Development Institute, 2013); Barnett, *Empire of Humanity*, 133; Alexander Poster, 'The Gentle War: Famine Relief, Politics and Privatization in Ethiopia, 1938–86', *Diplomatic History* 26, no. 2 (2012): 399–425; Matthew Hilton, James McKay, Nicholas Crowson, and Jean-Francois Mouhot, *The Politics of Expertise: How NGOs Shaped Modern Britain* (Oxford: Oxford University Press, 2013); Kurt Jansson, 'The Emergency Relief Operation: An Inside View', in *The Ethiopian Famine: The Story of the Emergency Relief Operation*, eds Kurt Jansson, Michael Harris, and Angela Penrose (London: Zed Books, 1987), 1–77; Alula Pankhurst, *Resettlement and Famine in Ethiopia: The Villagers' Experience* (Manchester: Manchester University Press, 1992).

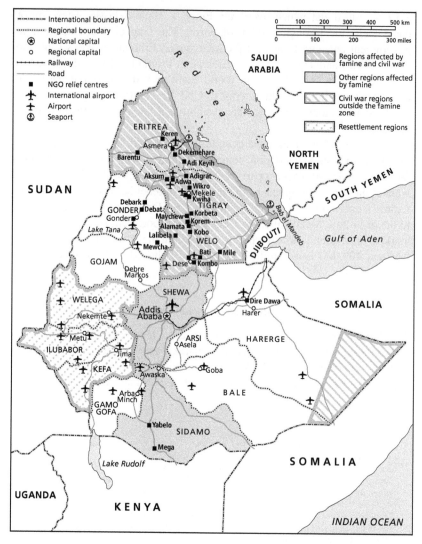

Figure 2.3 Map showing famine-affected regions of Ethiopia, Eritrea, and Tigray, 1985.
Adopted from Lafayette Barnes, 'Ethiopian Food Situation: International Response', Congressional Research Service, Issue Brief, 28 June 1985

movements, and including other phenomena that engaged the world-at-large. The relief effort saw the culmination of several trends that had their origins in the late 1960s and became prominent in the response to the humanitarian crisis in Biafra of 1968–70. These included (a) a media-driven understanding of disasters and relief efforts, as Biafra was the first time a famine was televised;[145] (b) an emphasis on celebrity, spectacle, and mass participation in relief, described as a 'revolution in giving' in which aid and development became attributes of an enlightened lifestyle and attracted formerly uninterested donors;[146] (c) the transformation of voluntary giving beyond established agencies to new organisations such as Band Aid, which received large sums of money and became conduits between donor governments, the charitable public, and recipients of relief, as well as voicing a commitment to 'people-to-people' aid;[147] and (d) an increased humanitarian concern for witnessing and reporting on misdeeds and perceived manipulations of aid.[148]

The period between the 1960s and the famine in Ethiopia saw the 'rise and rise' of humanitarian organisations.[149] The formation of a global aid regime in the Cold War was in part facilitated by the Soviet boycott of many of the international organisations through which this system operated. It created the context for Western powers to treat development problems and humanitarian emergencies from a security point of view, employing their aid 'to contain communism, delegitimate national liberation movements, and reproduce neo-colonial rule'.[150] The Biafran crisis clearly revealed these tendencies, at the same time, it was a post-colonial conflict and domestic power struggle in West Africa that instrumentalised suffering for political ends, provoking new responses, but also rendering those offering relief complicit.[151]

In May 1967, the eastern region of Nigeria declared its independence under the name Republic of Biafra. The subsequent blockade imposed by the Nigerian government led to widespread starvation, with eight million people

---

[145] Susanne Franks, *Reporting Disasters: Famine, Aid, Politics and the Media* (London: Hurst, 2013); Prochaska, *Voluntary Impulse*, 2.

[146] The term 'revolution in giving' is from Franks, *Reporting Disasters*, 71.

[147] Kevin O'Sullivan, 'Biafra's Legacy: NGO Humanitarianism and the Nigerian Civil War', in *Learning from the Past to Shape the Future: Lessons from the History of Humanitarian Action in Africa* (London: Overseas Development Institute, 2016), 5–13; Tanja R. Müller, '"The Ethiopian Famine" Revisited: Band Aid and the Antipolitics of Celebrity Humanitarian Action', *Disasters* 37, no. 1 (2013): 61–79; Ami V. Shah, Bruce Hall, and Edward R. Carr, 'Bono, Band Aid, and Before: Celebrity Humanitarianism, Music and the Objects of Its Action', in *Soundscapes of Wellbeing in Popular Music*, eds Gavin Andrews, Paul Kingsbury, and Robin Kearns (Farnham: Ashgate, 2014), 269–88.

[148] Franks, *Reporting Disasters*; O'Sullivan, 'Biafra's Legacy'; Ryfman, *Une Histoire*; Eleanor Davey, 'Famine, Aid, and Ideology: The Political Activism of Médicins sans Frontières in the 1980s', *French Historical Studies* 34, no. 3 (2011): 531–58.

[149] Kevin O'Sullivan, 'A "Global Nervous System": The Rise and Rise of European Humanitarian NGOs, 1945–1985', in *International Organisations and Development, 1945–1990*, eds Marc Frey, Sönke Kunkel, and Corinna R. Unger (New York: Macmillan, 2014), 196–219; Davies, *NGOs*, 123.

[150] Young-Sun Hong, *Cold War Germany, the Third World, and the Global Humanitarian Regime* (Cambridge: Cambridge University Press, 2015), 4.

[151] de Waal, *Famine Crimes*, 72–7.

considered in danger. The famine came to media attention around the globe in early 1968 through the efforts of Christian missionaries. The televised images of starving children pushed aid agencies and governments to take a stand, despite the complex political situation. The response signalled a break with humanitarian traditions and the emergence of a more politically engaged humanitarianism, most evident in the creation of MSF, but also seen in less well-known groups such as the Oxfam spin-off Third World First.[152] In 1968, a group of French doctors led by Bernard Kouchner publicly denounced the Red Cross principles of silence and neutrality in Biafra. On returning home, they organised marches and media events to raise awareness of Nigerian atrocities against civilians. Their activism, followed by similar experiences in Bangladesh, led to the formation of MSF in 1971.[153] Kouchner and his followers were part of a new generation of humanitarian individuals who cultivated close links with the media. Kouchner developed humanitarian action as a form of theatre or carnival.[154] MSF cherished the idea of *témoignage* (speaking out), although how and when this should be put into practice was subject to internal dispute. Following a split in 1979, Kouchner went on to found Médecins du Monde. By the early 1980s, MSF had become a 'brand' with a privileged place in French politics, but was also known for its increasingly anti-communist stance and critical view of Third Worldism.[155]

The role played by voluntary organisations in disaster relief had a greater impact in attracting public attention than long-term development efforts. In the final quarter of the twentieth century, it became increasingly evident that for many organisations 'association with high profile disasters was good for business'.[156] After Biafra, voluntary agencies acquired a reputation for efficiency, in part based on a perceived ability to work with grass-roots communities. With each major relief operation (including Bangladesh in 1970–1, the Sahel region in 1973, and work on the Thai–Cambodian border after the fall of the Khmer Rouge in 1979), the 'humanitarian international' appeared as 'more powerful and more privileged'.[157] Musicians and pop stars also became increasingly engaged in humanitarian activities, a development seen in George Harrison and Ravi Shankar's 1971 Concert for Bangladesh and the

---

[152] Georgina Brewis, *A Social History of Student Volunteering: Britain and Beyond, 1880–1980* (New York: Palgrave Macmillan, 2014), 184–5.

[153] Davey, *Idealism beyond Borders*, 31–6.

[154] Alex de Waal, 'The Humanitarian Carnival: A Celebrity Vogue', *World Affairs* 171, no. 2 (2008): 54.

[155] Bertrand Taithe, 'Reinventing (French) Universalism: Religion, Humanitarianism and the "French doctors"', *Modern & Contemporary France* 12, no. 2 (2004): 147–58.

[156] Barnett, *Empire of Humanity*, 132.

[157] de Waal, *Famine Crimes*, 85 (quotation), 78; Luther Banga, *Reducing People's Vulnerability to Famine: An Evaluation of Band Aid and Live Aid Financed Projects in Africa Final Report* (Douala: PAID, 1991), 1.

1979 Concerts for the People of Kampuchea (Cambodia).[158] Although modest in comparison, such events paved the way for Irish singer Bob Geldof's global success with Band Aid and Live Aid during the 1980s.

Ethiopia, Famine, and Media-Driven Humanitarianism

In Ethiopia, recurrent famines had been met by indifference to suffering under the rule of Haile Selassie, but in 1973, the media spotlight shone on the region with the documentary 'The Unknown Famine' by British broadcaster Jonathan Dimbleby. It led to a global response and precipitated the emperor's downfall.[159] The new military government set up a Relief and Rehabilitation Commission (RRC) to oversee aid work. While this institution built a reputation as one of the most effective famine relief agencies in Africa in the 1970s, with 12,000 staff across Ethiopia, by the early 1980s it had become compromised as an arm of the Mengistu regime.[160] The RRC was widely distrusted and its communications treated with scepticism by international donors. The result was that an urgent appeal for food aid in March 1984, after the failure of the short rains, was largely ignored by relief agencies.[161] A second organisation to emerge from the 1973 famine which played a key role a decade later was the Christian Relief and Development Association (CRDA). Formed mainly of Catholic charities, along with other religious groups, some secular agencies, transnational organisations, and domestic groups, CRDA's creation was the first organised cooperation in Ethiopia between the government and voluntary organisations.[162]

Initially, the mounting disaster in Ethiopia was covered only to a limited extent by the international media. In early 1983, appeals for food aid led to some news coverage and donations in the USA and Europe – particularly from the UK, Germany, and Sweden. In July 1984, a public appeal was made by the

---

[158] Shah, Hall, and Carr, 'Bono, Band Aid and Before', 277.

[159] Angela Penrose, 'Before and After', in *The Ethiopian Famine*, eds Kurt Jansson, Michael Harris, and Angela Penrose (London: Zed Books, 1987), 100; Andrew Jones, 'The Unknown Famine: Television and the Politics of British Humanitarianism', in *Global Humanitarianism and Media Culture*, eds Michael Lawrence and Rachel Tavernor (Manchester: Manchester University Press, 2019), 122–44.

[160] Ethiopians are properly referred to by the first name.

[161] de Waal, *Famine Crimes*, 107; Mark Duffield and John Prendergast, *Without Troops and Tanks: Humanitarian Intervention in Ethiopia and Eritrea* (Lawrenceville, NJ: Red Sea Press, 1994), 42–3; Tony Vaux, 'The Ethiopian Famine 1984: Oxfam's Early Involvement', Feb. 1985, MS Oxfam PGR 2/3/10/8, 10 (Bodleian Library, Oxford University, Oxfam Archive); Peter Gill, *A Year in the Death of Africa: Politics, Bureaucracy and the Famine* (London: Palladin, 1986), 30–2.

[162] Jeffrey Clark, *Civil Society, NGOs, and Development in Ethiopia: A Snapshot View* (Washington, DC: World Bank, 2000), 5.

UK Disasters Emergency Committee (DEC) to accompany a television documentary.[163] In retrospect, the delay in relief efforts has been attributed to a de facto alliance between top officials in the Reagan administration and the Mengistu regime, neither of which wanted a large-scale response. Approaching its tenth anniversary in power in August 1984, the Ethiopian government did not wish to draw attention to either famine or civil war. It exerted tight control of travel visas for journalists and aid workers during the summer of 1984. The USA, for its part, had suspended development assistance to Ethiopia in 1979 and was reluctant to participate in a relief effort for a Soviet-aligned country until increased publicity forced a change in attitude.[164] United Nations (UN) agencies and voluntary organisations themselves were also partly responsible for the delay. Scepticism over RRC figures was compounded by inaccurate and misleading data on food aid requirements from the World Food Programme (WFP) and the Food and Agriculture Organisation (FAO) during 1984.[165] At the time, many donors regarded the RRC's invocation of the international community's moral responsibility as offensive.[166]

By September 1984, its anniversary celebrations over, the Mengistu regime shifted from a policy of denial to one of blaming the international community for the famine, notably the US government. The Ethiopian regime was not so much reluctant to accept aid, as it was to receive it on its own terms. It had traditionally preferred development assistance to emergency relief.[167] The CRDA telexed an urgent appeal calling for 'immediate, massive, and coordinated' action.[168] Film-maker Peter Gill, who had long been seeking access to the famine-affected regions, proposed making a documentary that would contrast overproduction of food in Europe with hunger in Ethiopia, and this met with approval, enabling him to get the necessary travel permits. Other journalists

[163] Dawit Wolde Giorgis, *Red Tears: War, Famine and Revolution in Ethiopia* (Trenton, NJ: Red Sea Press, 1989), 187; Christian Aid Memo, 11 Oct. 1984, CA 4/A/16 (School of Oritental and African Studies (SOAS), University of London, Christian Aid Archive, hereafter CA); Vaux, 'Ethiopian Famine 1984', 21.

[164] Poster, 'Gentle War', 404; Gill, *Year in the Death*, 4–6; Harold G. Marcus, *A History of Ethiopia*, 3rd ed. (Berkeley: University of California Press, 2002), 205–7; US General Accounting Office, 'The United States Response to the Ethiopian Food Crisis', Apr. 1985, 2–3, available at http://pdf.usaid.gov/pdf_docs/Pcaaa061.pdf (accessed 29 June 2019).

[165] Minutes of DEC Operational Meeting, 10 May 1984, 1, CA 4/A/16; Vaux, 'Ethiopian Famine 1984', 14–15.

[166] Ann Wilkens, 'Katastrofbiståndsutredningen: Fallstudie Etiopien. Svältkatastrofen i Etiopien 1984/85, en dokumentation av nödhjälpsoperationen', in *Katastrofbistånd för utveckling: Några fakta och synpunkter. Fallstudier av Etiopien och Bangladesh*, ed. Sture Linnér (Stockholm: SIDA, 1986), 11.

[167] Edward Kissi, 'Beneath International Famine Relief in Ethiopia: The United States, Ethiopia, and the Debate over Relief Aid, Development Assistance, and Human Rights', *African Studies Review* 48, no. 2 (2005): 113.

[168] CRDA to Renshaw, 26 Sept. 1984, CA 5/5/358; Christian Relief and Development Association Relief Programme 1986, 1, CA 5/A/358.

were granted access to the afflicted area. On 23 October 1984, in a now famous BBC television newscast, reporter Michael Buerk and video journalist Mohamed Amin drew the world's attention to a 'biblical famine' affecting large tracts of Ethiopia. In the days that followed, their film was rebroadcast by 425 stations, reaching a global audience of 470 million, and finally sparking a major international response.[169] The famine in Ethiopia became '*the* story, and *the* cause'.[170] The moral outrage it raised was heightened because news of the famine came immediately after a widely reported abundant harvest in Europe, which further swelled the European Economic Community's (EEC) notorious 'grain mountain'.[171] As the head of the RRC put it, his country had been forgotten 'by a world glutted with a surplus of grain'.[172]

International Response

The BBC announcement triggered a flood of cash donations to voluntary organisations around the world. Donor governments also began to mobilise in earnest and establish a new apparatus to oversee relief. Finnish diplomat Kurt Jansson was appointed UN assistant secretary general for emergency operations in Ethiopia. The Office for Emergency Operations in Ethiopia enabled the UN to make a fresh start in relief administration and to renew relationships with the RRC.[173] The EEC development ministers met and immediately pledged millions in aid.[174] Recalling the approach in Soviet Russia more than sixty years earlier, food aid was to be a means to win the 'hearts and minds' of a demoralised recipient population. The director of USAID visited Ethiopia, followed by legislators who helped secure support for relief in the US Congress. In early November, an emergency airlift began that transcended the Cold War and the North–South divide. It was a cooperative effort of the USA, UK, France, Poland, Libya, and both German states.[175]

---

[169] Greg Philo, 'From Buerk to Band Aid: The Media and the 1984 Ethiopian Famine', in *Getting the Message: News, Truth and Power*, ed. John Eldridge (London: Routledge, 1993), 108–9, 121; Penrose, 'Before and After', 154. See Franks, *Reporting Disasters*, ch. 1 for background.

[170] Barnett, *Empire of Humanity*, 156.

[171] Paul Keleman, *The Politics of the Famine in Ethiopia and Eritrea* (Manchester: Manchester University Press, 1985), 156.

[172] Gill, *Year in the Death*, 40.

[173] Jansson, 'Emergency Relief', 1; IIED, *Report on the African Emergency Relief Operation 1984–1986 with Particular Reference to the Contributions of Non Governmental Organisations, and at the Request of the UN Office for Emergency Operations in Africa* (London, International Institute for Environment and Development, 1986), 35.

[174] EEC press release, Dec. 1985, available at https://europa.eu/rapid/press-release_P-86-6_en.htm (accessed 21 Sept. 2019).

[175] USAID, *Final Disaster Report Ethiopia Drought/Famine FY 1985 1986* (Washington, DC: USAID, 1987), 5, 11, available at http://pdf.usaid.gov/pdf_docs/PNABG233.pdf (accessed 29 June 2019).

While reluctant to provide additional aid, Moscow did not object to Ethiopia seeking food aid from the West, although they considered this assistance to be 'subversive' and designed to discredit socialism.[176] In addition to ongoing military support, the Soviet Union's main contribution during the famine was providing transportation for the Derg's controversial resettlement programme.[177] Alongside measures such as the famine tax imposed to support the RRC, resettlement was framed as Ethiopia's major domestic relief measure, and one that was part of a strategy of reducing reliance on external aid; its aim was to relocate 1.5 million people from the north to the south-west of Ethiopia (see Figure 2.3).[178] The programme was halted in early 1986, by which time 600,000 people had been moved, and it resumed in 1987 when famine again threatened Ethiopia.

In all, about 1.5 million tonnes of emergency food aid reached Ethiopia. The food and non-food aid provided from 1984 to 1986 was valued at US$1.5–2 billion. The US government became the largest single donor, contributing more than US$500 million to a USAID programme under the slogan 'a hungry child knows no politics'. The second most significant contribution came from the EEC and its ten member nations, where since the 1970s, food aid had been used in part as a measure to deal with surplus production. Other donors included Canada, Australia, the Scandinavian countries, Japan, China, and Zimbabwe.[179] Sweden had a long history of missionary work in Ethiopia and Eritrea, and since the mid-1970s, had employed relief assistance as a way to maintain and strengthen those connections. Voluntary groups used this history to describe the Swedish obligation to help in terms of 'trusteeship'.[180] The creation of the Fondo Aiuti Italiani (Italian Aid Fund) illustrates the stimulus the famine had on aid policy in Italy, where socialist Prime Minister Bettino Craxi developed one of the largest aid programmes in the horn of Africa, although it was marred by corruption and misallocation. The Italian effort reflected both historical ties – Italy was the former colonial ruler in

---

[176] Radoslav A. Yordanov, *The Soviet Union and the Horn of Africa during the Cold War: Between Ideology and Pragmatism* (Lanham, MD: Lexington Books, 2016), 224–5.

[177] CIA, *Ethiopia: Political and Security Impact of the Drought – An Intelligence Assessment*, Apr. 1985, iv, available at www.cia.gov/library/readingroom/docs/CIA-RDP86T00589R0002 00160004-5.pdf (accessed 29 June 2019); de Waal, *Evil Days*, 211.

[178] Pankhurst, *Resettlement and Famine*, 52–3; Article 19, *Starving in Silence: Report on Famine and Censorship* (London: Article 19, 1990), 110–13.

[179] Banga, *Reducing People's Vulnerability to Famine*, 7; USAID, *Final Disaster Report*, 36, 38; Poster, 'Gentle War', 399; Gill, *Year in the Death*, 69; D. R. Morrison, *Aid and Ebb Tide: A History of CIDA and Canadian Development Assistance* (Waterloo: Wilfrid Laurier University Press, 2011), 234–5; Patrick Kilby, *NGOs and Political Change: History of the Australian Council for International Development* (Canberra: Australian National University Press, 2015), 103.

[180] Cecilia Steen-Johnsson, 'Lutherhjälpen: Ökad insats, dyr transport', *Dagens Nyheter*, 10 Nov. 1984, 7; Duffield and Prendergast, *Without Troops*, 46.

Somalia, Eritrea, and briefly in Ethiopia – as well as ongoing sympathies with the region's Marxist regimes.[181] Between 1984 and 1986, Italy became the largest single donor of non-food aid to the RRC (including trucks and trailers), valued at US$17 million.[182]

In January 1985, Geldof, whose Irish roots increased his sensitivity to famine,[183] launched a new UK charity, The Band Aid Trust, to disperse funds raised by the charity single 'Do They Know It's Christmas?'. The trust also arranged additional participatory fundraising efforts, of which the Live Aid concerts were by far the most significant. The unexpected success of the original recording encouraged the production of the US song 'We Are the World' and at least twenty other charity singles in many languages.[184] This novel approach transformed fundraising around the globe. For example, for the first time in Germany, eighteen voluntary organisations held a joint television benefit, a spectacular known as the 'Day for Africa', in January 1985.[185] Celebrity activism has deep roots, and for over two centuries reformers, fundraisers, and campaigners have sought to maximise public attention by enlisting well-known public figures to aid their cause, a tendency that grew significantly in the late twentieth century.[186]

Jansson judged that the role played by voluntary organisations in Ethiopia was greater than in earlier emergency relief programmes. Although some agencies, including the Red Cross, SCF, and Catholic Relief Services (CRS), had long been active in Ethiopia, there was a rush to get into the country following the heavy media coverage.[187] Organisations working on the ground increased in number from twenty-one at the beginning of 1984 to forty-eight by the middle of 1985, and in the end involved some 600 expatriate staff and 2,000 Ethiopian employees.[188] An organisation's presence during a disaster had become an essential aspect of the humanitarian system by the mid-1980s.[189]

---

[181] Paola Bollina and Michael R. Reich, 'The Italian Fight against World Hunger: A Critical Analysis of Italian Aid for Development in the 1980s', *Social Science of Medicine* 39, no, 5 (1994): 607–20; Wolfgang Achtner, 'The Italian Connection: How Rome Helped Ruin Somalia', *Washington Post*, 24 Jan. 1993; Carol Lancaster, *Aid to Africa: So Much to Do, So Little Done* (Chicago: University of Chicago Press, 1999), 160–4.

[182] USAID, *Final Disaster Report*, 39, 85.

[183] 'Bob Geldof Says 1916 Rising Was "Nonsense" and Great Famine Was True Birth of the Irish Nation', *Irish Post*, 18 Oct. 2018.

[184] Food and Trucks and Rock 'n' Roll: The Band Aid Story, directed by Ian McMillan (London: Band Aid, 1985).

[185] Heinrich von Nussbaum, 'Das Medienspektakel: "Ein Tag für Afrika"', *Medium*, no. 2 (1985): 5–7.

[186] Shah, Hall, and Carr, 'Bono, Band Aid'; Lucy Robinson, 'Putting the Charity Back into Charity Singles: Charity Singles in Britain 1984–1995', *Contemporary British History* 26, no.3 (2012): 405–25.

[187] Jansson, 'Emergency Relief', 22.   [188] Giorgis, *Red Tears*, 228.

[189] de Waal, *Famine Crimes*, 80; de Waal, 'Humanitarian Carnival'.

In addition, new aid consortia were put together to ease the delivery of relief, while the famine accelerated trends towards a long-standing, often unfilled, desire for greater coordination and information-sharing among agencies. Most of the organisations working in government-controlled Ethiopia were members of the CRDA umbrella body, which expanded considerably during the crisis and by December 1986 had forty-six members.[190] The CRDA held monthly meetings in Addis Ababa, providing the main forum for the exchange of information between aid agencies, the UN, and the RRC.[191] The reluctance of some donor nations to work with the RRC strengthened the position of the voluntary agencies, so that they distributed 95 per cent of the food aid that the USA provided. The EEC was more willing to work with the Ethiopian government, although 29 per cent of its food aid was still given out via voluntary organisations in 1985. Many smaller donor countries like Japan, Finland, and Switzerland directed all their relief through channels in civil society.[192]

Food distribution was complicated by the fact that many of those affected by famine were living in areas outside of the control of the Ethiopian government, such as Eritrea, Tigray, and northern Wollo (see Figure 2.3). The respect officially accorded to sovereignty during the Cold War – even to unpalatable regimes like the Derg – meant that Western governments were slow to provide aid to rebel-held areas. There, quasi-autonomous relief organisations linked to rebel forces worked with supportive organisations and diasporic communities abroad. Large donors, reluctant to associate themselves with the rebels, relied heavily on voluntary organisations in the regions controlled by the liberation fronts.[193]

Both the Ethiopian government and the rebel groups tried to manipulate Western aid for their own ends. MSF was the only aid agency to publicly criticise the Ethiopian authorities and their resettlement programme, and was ultimately expelled for doing so. MSF's refusal to 'renounce our moral responsibilities or cooperate blindly in a perversion of the very meaning of international aid' is a hallmark of the expressive humanitarianism that developed after the Biafran crisis, and was driven by the belief that the

---

[190] *CRDA Biannual Review 1985–6*, 20–3, CA 5/5/358.

[191] John Borton, *The Changing Role of NGOs in the Provision of Relief and Rehabilitation Assistance: Case Study 3 – Northern Ethiopia and Eritrea* (London: Overseas Development Institute, 1994), 70.

[192] Poster, 'Gentle War', 415; Jansson, 'Emergency Relief', 47; USAID, *Final Disaster Report*, 38.

[193] Duffield and Prendergast, *Without Troops*, 3; de Waal, *Famine Crimes*, 129; Max Peberdy, *Tigray: Ethiopia's Untold Story* (London: Relief Society of Tigray UK Support Committee, 1985); Borton, *Changing Role*, 85.

donating public needed to be made aware of how their contributions were being used.[194] However, this position was rejected by other organisations who were critical of a stance which to them appeared to put vulnerable famine-survivors at greater risk.

The famine in Ethiopia accelerated the formation of aid structures embodying expressive humanitarianism, namely, the involvement of high-profile figures, large-scale televised spectaculars, and the emotional engagement of the general public (particularly young people). Musicians and celebrities across the world initiated numerous fundraising activities. Aid organisations raised significant sums and also benefitted from unsolicited donations from individuals outside of their traditional support base.[195] Things reached their height when Band Aid and other groups capitalised on this participatory enthusiasm. Moreover, while the Ethiopian crisis in some ways marked the continuation of the professionalisation of voluntary humanitarian action,[196] the Band Aid Trust, as a self-styled newcomer, represented an innovative moral economy that stood in opposition to the professional aid industry, with its high overhead and salaries. Geldof later suggested that the legacy of Band Aid was as much in mobilising the public to believe that anything was possible, contrary to experts telling them 'it is hopeless', as in delivering on its relief and rehabilitation projects.[197] However, the price for the wide-scale mobilisation was 'anything goes!', as the celebrated performance of superstar Farrokh Bulsara (better known as Queen's frontman, Freddie Mercury) at the Live Aid concert in 1985 illustrates. While performing the rock anthem 'We Are the Champions', he cried out 'No time for losers!'.

---

[194] Bertrand Desmoulins and Michael Fiszbin, 'An Open Letter to NGOs in Ethiopia', 13 Dec. 1985, CARE 1220, File 17 (New York Public Library, CARE Archives).

[195] Robert Dodd, 'Oxfam's Response to Disasters in Ethiopia and the Sudan', June 1986, MS Oxfam PGR 5/5/1, 37.

[196] Andrew Jones, 'Band Aid Revisited: Humanitarianism, Consumption and Philanthropy in the 1980s', *Contemporary British History* 31, no. 2 (2017): 195.

[197] Band Aid, *With Love from Band Aid: Report of 7 Years Work* (London: Band Aid Trust, 1992), 3.

3   Appeals

3.1   The Humanitarian Appeal

Research into contemporary philanthropy corroborates the importance of direct solicitations for raising charitable contributions.[1] How successful relief organisations are in generating capital and gathering resources depends largely on their appeals and fundraising activities. Other beneficial factors for fundraising, such as trust in the organisation or commitment to particular aid schemes, are often also the result of direct appeals or pleas for assistance in documents such as organisation flyers or annual reports.[2]

During the representation of needs and agency on behalf of others, humanitarian paradoxes may arise.[3] Calls for aid try to maximise philanthropic success by narratives and visuals that typically express the moral views of those making the appeal and what they presume may motivate potential donors. On the one hand, humanitarian agents point to need, worthiness, and entitlement, and on the other, they cite compassion, obligation, and interest, thus tailoring their message to different audiences and media formats. Scholars have proposed a variety of classifications for these aid schemes, based on ideal types, general patterns, or genres of appeals.[4] Analyses tend to overlap with

---

[1] René Bekkers and Pamala Wiepking, 'A Literature Review of Empirical Studies of Philanthropy: Eight Mechanisms That Drive Charitable Giving', *Nonprofit and Voluntary Sector Quarterly* 40, no. 5 (2011): 928, 931; Beth Breeze and Wendy A. Scaife, 'Encouraging Generosity: The Practice and Organization of Fundraising across Nations', in *Palgrave Handbook of Global Philanthropy*, eds Pamala Wiepking and Femida Handy (Houndmills: Palgrave Macmillan, 2015), 570–96. On trust and commitment, see Adrian Sargeant and Stephen Lee, 'Trust and Relationship Commitment in the United Kingdom Voluntary Sector: Determinants of Donor Behavior', *Psychology & Marketing* 21, no. 8 (2004): 613–35.

[2] Per-Anders Forstorp, 'Fundraising Discourse and the Commodification of the Other', *Business Ethics* 16, no. 3 (2007): 286–301; Vijay K. Bhatia, 'Generic Patterns in Fundraising Discourse', *New Direction for Philanthropic Fundraising* 22 (1998): 101.

[3] Chouliaraki, *Ironic Spectator*, 54.

[4] Anne Vestergaard, 'Humanitarian Appeal and the Paradox of Power', *Critical Discourse Studies* 10, no. 4 (2013): 445; Bhatia, 'Generic Patterns', 100; Jeffrey Flynn, 'Philosophers, Historians, and Suffering Strangers', *Moving the Social* no. 57 (2017): 139; Forstorp, 'Fundraising Discourse', 292–4.

regard to the content and underlying strategy.[5] Key features of appeals during the last 200 years have been 'reductivist messages' and visually based emotional representations.[6] They use 'incitement' (or diagnostic frames), employing facts, definitions, and legitimation of the cause; and 'enticement' (or motivational frames), stirring up emotions, marshalling reasons to take action, and evoking images of deserving recipients.[7]

Jeffrey Flynn has proposed two ideal types that may be useful in analysing the moral economy of food aid. The first, which he calls the 'suffering stranger appeal', imposes a causal relation on distant suffering by telling donors that they have the *means* to alleviate misery. The responsibility to help derives here in a Singerian sense from the ability to help. By contrast, the less frequently deployed 'causal contribution appeal' confronts donors with their complicity and creates a moral obligation for reparation (rather than aid) by disclosing a *causal* responsibility for distant suffering. Thus, the former approach motivates 'those who are capable', while the latter addresses 'those who are culpable'.[8]

Irrational Donors and Rational Fundraisers

Economic theories have not been good at explaining why people would make voluntary contributions for the well-being of strangers. The presumption that rational individuals make purposeful choices does not seem to apply to the humanitarian sector. It is an area where individual donors may not actively seek out charitable causes, but do tend to respond to appeals for aid.

Extensive research on donor behaviour shows that the decision to contribute, the amount, the cause, and the organisation chosen are seldom based on rational economic considerations, such as 'How can one save as many lives as possible with as little money as possible?'. Rather than pondering ideas of effective altruism, donors tend to be influenced by psychological numbing, such as the proportion dominance effect. When asked, people usually say they prefer to save 90 per cent of 1,000 endangered people, rather than 0.1 per cent of 1,000,000 – although 100 more would survive in the latter case.[9] They also

---

[5] However, those analyses generally rely on empirical material from the recent past. Some exceptions are Fehrenbach, 'Children and Other Civilians', and Dal Lago and O'Sullivan, 'Introduction'.

[6] Mervi Pantti and Minttu Tikka, 'Cosmopolitan Empathy and User-Generated Disaster Appeal Videos on YouTube', in *Internet and Emotions*, eds Tova Benski and Eran Fisher (New York: Routledge, 2014), 178–92; Dal Lago and O'Sullivan, 'Introduction', 6.

[7] Vestergaard, 'Humanitarian Appeal', 447; Mahood and Satzewich, 'Save the Children Fund', 56–7.

[8] Flynn, 'Philosophers, Historians, and Suffering Strangers', 151 (quotations), 139.

[9] David Fetherstonhaugh, Paul Slovic, Stephen Johnson, and James Friedrich, 'Insensitivity to the Value of Human Life: A Study of Psychophysical Numbing', *Journal of Risk and Uncertainty* 14, no. 3 (1997): 285.

favour actions helping a single individual rather than intervening on behalf of a group, and they prefer a known beneficiary over an anonymous one – the so-called identifiable victim effect.[10] This effect occurs following minor de-anonymisation and is especially important if the person in need belongs to a potentially adversarial group.[11]

Some patterns are especially evident from an analysis of famine relief. First, it is easier to raise money for sudden emergencies.[12] The initial days and weeks after the news of a disaster reaches the general public are usually the most successful. However, donations decrease as a relief situation becomes chronic. The amount of publicity given to crises and the donor expectations aroused also shape aid choices of emergency agencies.[13] Second, the identification of alleged perpetrators and the suspicion that a catastrophe is man-made reduces the willingness of donors to contribute, compared to disasters conceived of as 'natural'.[14] It is, therefore, in the interest of humanitarian organisations and their beneficiaries to conceal possible human causes of famine.[15] Third, research shows that perceived distance correlates negatively with donations. The slogan 'charity begins at home' not only expresses parochial or national sentiments regarding who has a greater claim to assistance, but also reflects the widespread expectation that charitable donations will have a greater impact on nearby recipients.[16] However, humanitarian organisations can

---

[10] Paul Slovic, 'If I Look at the Mass I Will Never Act: Psychic Numbing and Genocide', in *Emotions and Risky Technologies,* ed. Sabine Roeser (Dordrecht: Springer, 2010), 37–59; Dorina Hysenbelli, Enrico Rubaltelli, and Rino Rumiati, 'Others' Opinions Count, but Not All of Them: Anchoring to Ingroup versus Outgroup Members' Behavior in Charitable Giving', *Judgment and Decision Making* 8, no. 6 (2013): 678–90; Seyoung Lee and Thomas Hugh Feeley, 'The Identifiable Victim Effect: A Meta-analytic Review', *Social Influence* 11, no. 3 (2016): 199–215.

[11] Deborah Small and George Loewenstein, 'Helping a Victim or Helping the Victim: Altruism and Identifiability', *Journal of Risk and Uncertainty* 26 (2003): 5–16; Ilana Ritov and Tehila Kogut, 'Ally or Adversary: The Effect of Identifiability in Inter-group Conflict Situations', *Organizational Behavior and Human Decision Processes* 116, no. 1 (2011): 96–103. See also Tehila Kogut and Ilana Ritov, 'The "Identified Victim Effect": An Identified Group, or Just a Single Individual?', *Journal of Behavioral Decision Making* 18, no. 3 (2005): 157–67.

[12] Epstein, 'Crisis Mentality'; Hanna Zagefka and Trevor James, 'The Psychology of Charitable Donations to Disaster Victims and Beyond', *Social Issues and Policy Review* 9, no. 1 (2015): 168–9. Relief organisations have addressed this problem long ago. See Eglantyne Jebb, 'A History of the Save the Children Fund', *The Record* 3, no. 1 (1922).

[13] Redfield, *Life in Crisis,* 172.

[14] Trevor James and Hanna Zagefka, 'The Effects of Group Memberships of Victims and Perpetrators in Humanly Caused Disasters on Charitable Donations to Victims', *Journal Applied Social Psychology* 47, no. 8 (2017): 448.

[15] Zagefka and James, 'The Psychology of Charitable Donations', 163; de Waal, *Mass Starvation,* 124.

[16] Maferima Touré-Tillery and Aleyet Fishbach, 'Too Far to Help: The Effect of Perceived Distance on the Expected Impact and Likelihood of Charitable Action', *Journal of Personality and Social Psychology* 112, no. 6 (2017): 860. The authors term this 'closeness-equals-strength-of-effect' metaphor.

counter the latter view by mounting customised appeals.[17] This is especially important as the willingness to rely on a charitable organisation's discretion increases with the distance from the population in need; that is, the further away a sufferer is, the greater the acceptance of a humanitarian broker, who otherwise might be deemed unnecessary, to supply aid.[18] Fourth, there is an in-group effect that prioritises helping members of one's own social, ethnic, religious, or national group.[19] Nevertheless, the primacy of the in-group depends on perceptions. Thus, humanitarian organisations may try to create or enlarge in-groups (e.g., children, coreligionists, or people with regional ties), aligning them with the respective cause. In this way, those who formerly were outsiders are admitted to the donor's in-group through the back door.[20] By making the self-interest of donors or their in-groups central to a campaign, an organisation can exploit the in-group effect indirectly, even where direct beneficiaries are perceived as outsiders.

As a consequence of these factors, not all disasters result in calls for aid, while other emergencies may result in donations that exceed the basic needs on the ground. Aid supplies depend on funding raised by the effective communication of a humanitarian cause to the public. Ideally, this is done in ways that not only evoke personal emotions, but also result in social concern and a sense of financial obligation.[21] In order to accomplish such a goal, relief organisations and fundraisers must incorporate strategies identified by research and experience.[22] Thus, fundraising is an activity that aligns moral and economic rationales: human suffering and the 'intentions and actions of the donor are commodified', and the altruistic act of giving is 'imbued with

---

[17] Touré-Tillery and Fishbach, 'Too Far to Help', 861.

[18] Danit Ein-Gar and Liat Levontin, 'Giving from a Distance: Putting the Charitable Organization at the Center of the Donation Appeal', *Journal of Consumer Psychology* 23, no. 2 (2013): 197–211.

[19] Zagefka and James, 'The Psychology of Charitable Donations', 173. This preference has recently been explained by feelings of responsibility, rather than empathy. See Arvid Erlandsson, Frederik Björklund, and Martin Bäckström, 'Emotional Reactions, Perceived Impact and Perceived Responsibility Mediate the Identifiable Victim Effect, Proportion Dominance Effect and In-Group Effect, Respectively', *Organizational Behavior and Human Decision Processes* 127 (2015): 1–14.

[20] Mika Aaltola, 'Theoretical Departures to Disasters and Emergencies', in *The Politics and Policies of Relief, Aid and Reconstruction: Contrasting Approaches to Disasters and Emergencies*, ed. Fulvio Attina (Houndmills: Palgrave, 2012), 75.

[21] Taithe, 'Cold Calculation', 88. See also Jonathan Benthall, *Disasters, Relief and the Media* (London: Tauris, 1993), 27.

[22] Contemporary non-profit organisations use scientific guidebooks to adapt to these psychological mechanisms. For a recent example, see Evan C. Parker, *Altruism, Empathy and Efficacy: The Science behind Engaging Your Supporters* (Washington, DC: Georgetown University, 2018), available at http://csic.georgetown.edu/wp-content/uploads/2018/01/Altruism-Empathy-and-Efficacy-The-Science-Behind-Engaging-Supporters-1.29.18.pdf (accessed 29 June 2019).

innovative business models'.[23] The discrete logic of 'the good project', by which aid organisations link donor publics with selected groups of recipients, gains ascendancy, and determines the formatting and merchandising of particular humanitarian causes.[24] This leads to conflicts within the moral economy. It also entails criticism, as the resulting fundraising practices may collide with changing humanitarian principles, especially idealistic notions of how and where humanitarian work should be done.

Moral Economy Dilemmas

It is a troublesome dilemma that successful fundraising strategies may be ethically problematic and imperil the moral integrity of the organisation and its beneficiaries. The imaginary presented in some humanitarian campaigns, however effective it might be, has been accused of being founded on a 'pornography of pain'.[25] The trade-off between emotional appeals with a high financial return and adhering to high moral standards has also been described as a conflict of aesthetics and ethics.[26] It mirrors the general humanitarian schism between the stereotyped figure of the cold-blooded calculating professional and the compassionate but inefficient grass-roots activist.

Reductionist and paternalistic practices, such as the use of heart-rending images of a woeful child to stimulate compassion, raise the issue of the dignity of would-be beneficiaries upon the conscience of humanitarians who seek to link distressed populations with donors in a manner that is both ethical and efficacious.[27] While the use of certain essentialising images that contrast with Western plenty may serve the immediate goal of generating donations, it can inhibit the formation of deeper commitments and sustained patterns of collective action.[28] When celebrities speak on behalf of humanitarian causes, there is a similar risk that they may 'steal the show' from those who need help. In this way, some strategies that raise large sums for the most dire situations may hamper long-term change and increase the likelihood that aid will be needed again in the future.

A paradox of the moral economy is that often the most pressing calls for donations are those proclaiming a beneficiary's entitlement and the obligation of the benefactor to provide aid, factors that appear inconsistent with the

---

[23] Forstorp, 'Fundraising Discourse', 299, 286.   [24] Krause, *Good Project*.

[25] Karen Halttunen, 'Humanitarianism and the Pornography of Pain in Anglo-American Culture', *American Historical Review* 100, no. 2 (1995): 303–34; Janice Nathanson, 'The Pornography of Poverty: Reframing the Discourse of International Aid's Representations of Starving Children', *Canadian Journal of Communication* 38, no. 1 (2013): 103–20.

[26] Vestergaard, 'Humanitarian Appeal', 445.

[27] Rubenstein, *Between Samaritans and States*, 86; Käpylä and Kennedy, 'Cruel to Care?', 259, 267, 272, 277.

[28] Boltanski, *Distant Suffering*, 189.

voluntarist character of humanitarianism.[29] Such moral commitment appeals seek to create correlates with the request for government intervention, and therefore entail a measure of charitable self-abrogation. However, the dividing line for the individual donor and public agencies remains that between de facto choice and legal obligation. As long as moral judgement precedes compulsory legislation, the concept of humanitarianism continues to make sense. Michael Walzer has argued that humanitarianism is a 'two-in-one enterprise', based on both charity and justice – on the supererogatory kindness that acknowledges a moral duty to strangers.[30] From the point of view of social psychology, charitable giving resembles the medieval purchase of indulgences, 'paying taxes to God'.[31] Today many humanitarian organisations have adopted a vocabulary of justice and entitlements that symbolically empowers beneficiaries.[32] However, rather than seeking to establish global justice by the redistribution of the necessities of life among the world's citizens, this practice shows that from their non-governmental perspective, such organisations find utility in drawing on a strong aid narrative.[33]

3.2   Empire, Faith, and Kinship: Ireland

In the closing days of 1846, newspapers across England published a Cork magistrate's eyewitness account of famine in Ireland that was a revelation for the public. The open letter was addressed to the duke of Wellington and described the horror of hundreds of living skeletons in Skibbereen, a small town west of Cork that became notorious for its plight (see Figure 3.1). Even the *Times*, an organ with little sympathy for Irish suffering and critical towards voluntary contributions, printed the piece in its Christmas Eve edition. The letter included an indirect aid appeal to those who could send relief by urging that ignoring the desperate situation of the Irish would see them fail before 'the Judge of all the earth'. Moreover, calling upon Wellington to help rescue the land of his birth and not abandon his compatriots who had lost their lives for the empire, the magistrate urged him to bring Ireland's plight before Queen Victoria and thus secure for himself the inscription 'Servata Hibernia' upon his

[29] See Henry Shue, 'Morality, Politics, and Humanitarian Assistance', in *The Moral Nation: Humanitarianism and U.S. Foreign Policy Today*, eds Bruce Nichols and Gil Loescher (Notre Dame, IN: University of Notre Dame Press, 1989), 14–16; Michael Walzer, 'On Humanitarianism: Is Helping Others Charity, or Duty, or Both?', *Foreign Affairs* 90, no. 4 (2011): 69.

[30] Walzer, 'On Humanitarianism', 80.

[31] Memo by marketing psychologist Ernest Dichter in 1955, quoted in Heike Wieters, *The NGO CARE and Food Aid from America, 1945–80: 'Showered with Kindness'?* (Manchester: Manchester University Press, 2017), 116. See also Bekkers and Wiepking, 'Literature Review', 939.

[32] Vestergaard, 'Humanitarian Appeal', 464.

[33] Julia Lindström, *The Moral Economy of Aid: Discourse Analysis of Swedish Fundraising for the Somalia Famine of 2011–2012* (Huddinge: Södertörn University, 2016).

Figure 3.1 Funeral at Skibbereen, *London Illustrated News*, 30 Jan. 1847.
Engraving from a sketch by H. Smyth. This image is reproduced courtesy of the
National Library of Ireland

tomb. Wellington was to invoke the queen's female sense of decency, and let
the published letter's account of destitution and nakedness encourage her to
command that aid no longer be withheld.[34] The letter illustrates that the
gendered perception of emergencies and the addressees of calls for aid has
not changed over time. Other direct appeals to the queen petitioned her 'as a
woman' and 'a mother'.[35] They all mirrored the widespread notion in Ireland of
being entitled to aid from Britain, and minor sums were immediately sent to the
Cork magistrate for distribution.[36] However, according to one Irish calculation,
their country was entitled to thirty million pounds, a sum greater than that spent
for ending slavery, as Irish distress was said to exceed that of the blacks.[37]

Imperial Relief

The comparatively broad acknowledgement of Irish suffering in the press
at the time of the open letter coincided with the preparation of the major

---

[34] Open letter by Nicholas Cummins to the duke of Wellington, 17 Dec. 1846, first printed in the
Cork Examiner, 21 Dec., reprinted in London by the *Standard*, 22 Dec., and by the *Times*, 24
Dec.; subsequently reprinted many times in the UK and abroad. See also Woodham-Smith,
Great Hunger, 162–3.

[35] E.g., 'Skibbereen', the *Cork Examiner*, 18 Jan. 1847.

[36] The *Cork Examiner*, 30 Dec. 1846.

[37] 'Appalling State of West Carbery', *Southern Reporter and Cork Commercial Courier* [hereafter
Southern Reporter], 19 Jan. 1847. For another strong claim of entitlement, see 'Verdict of
Wilful Murder against Lord John Russell [Prime Minister of England], and Sir Randolph
Routh', *Southern Reporter*, 23 Jan. 1847.

extra-governmental aid effort, the creation of the British Relief Association (BRA).[38] The BRA was a voluntary effort closely related to the government, but its origin and the deliberate exclusion of its beneficiaries from the aid narrative have not been examined. A deputation of the interdenominational Relief Committee of Skibbereen, sent to London in December 1846, took the first initiative, rather than English residents.[39] The Irish representatives consisted of protestant ministers Richard B. Townsend and Charles Caulfield, who were granted a meeting with the home secretary and with Charles Trevelyan, the permanent secretary of the treasury and the principal figure in government relief to Ireland. At their first meeting, the Irish deputies felt that they were treated as 'insignificant individuals'; they were then granted a second meeting. Nevertheless, the letter they received a few days later declared that their request for a queen's letter was premature and suggested the alternative of private Irish, as well as English, charity.[40]

Such a response was not simply an abdication of responsibility: Trevelyan's evangelical morals, while hostile to state intervention, were more receptive to voluntary efforts. Three days after the first meeting with the deputies, he recommended a general English subscription supervised by officials to supplement what he believed were 'the necessary deficiencies of our Government Relief'.[41] Another motivation was the desire to pass the verdict of God and history, despite alleged Irish misbehaviour.[42] This dutiful attitude is indicative of the widespread contempt for what was perceived as 'Irish apathy and abuse'. Trevelyan's belief that 'further horrifying accounts' were needed to promote the subscription indicates the dismissive attitude towards reports from Ireland of which there was no lack.[43] At another meeting, the deputies were

---

[38] On the comparatively favourable public opinion at the time, see Peter Gray, '"The Great British Famine of 1845 to 1850"? Ireland, the UK and Peripherality in Famine Relief and Philanthropy', in *Famines in European Economic History: The Last Great European Famines Reconsidered*, eds Declan Curran, Lubomyr Luciuk, and Andrew G. Newby (Abingdon: Routledge, 2015), 90–1.

[39] Some authors have mentioned the deputation in passing. See Gray, *Famine, Land and Politics*, 257; Peter Gray, 'National Humiliation and the Great Hunger: Fast and Famine in 1847', *Irish Historical Studies* 32, no. 126 (2000): 197; Terri Kearney and Philip O'Regan, *Skibbereen: The Famine Story* (Skibbereen: Macalla, 2015).

[40] 'Skibbereen Relief Committee: The Deputation to England', *Southern Reporter*, 2 Jan. 1847; Grey to deputies, 9 Dec. 1846, The National Archives, London (hereafter TNA(UK)), Home Office (hereafter HO) 122/19. The letter was printed in the *Standard*, 21 Dec. 1846, and elsewhere.

[41] Trevelyan to Routh, 5 Dec. 1846, *Correspondence from July, 1846, to January, 1847, Relating to the Measures Adopted for the Relief of Distress in Ireland* (hereafter *Correspondence I*) (London: Clowes and Sons, 1847), 332. On Trevelyan's principal affinity to voluntary action, see Gray, *Famine, Land and Politics*, 257.

[42] Trevelyan to Labouchere, 15 Dec. 1846, The Robinson Library, Newcastle University (hereafter RLN), Trevelyan Papers (hereafter TP), CET 18, vol. X.

[43] Trevelyan to Labouchere, 19 Dec. 1846, RLN, TP, CET 18, vol. X.

made to feel 'as if they were the first men in the land' and were advised how to go about raising private charity.[44]

Townsend and Caulfield favoured a public fundraising event that would also rebut English misconceptions about Ireland. Although they were now treated respectfully, they could not obtain the backing of individuals needed for such an undertaking. This outcome was influenced by the deputies' contact officer, who thwarted their call for support behind their backs.[45] In their report they state 'it was by little and little the real nature of our position as a deputation opened upon us'. The contact officer ultimately made it clear that a public meeting was 'utterly impracticable', as it was likely to engender political controversy and damage the Irish cause. He promised that the addressees of the deputation 'would work the matter themselves' and would raise a subscription far exceeding the expectations of the two representatives. Thus, committing their 'begging-box into hands most influential at present in the Kingdom', Townsend and Caulfield returned to Ireland.[46] The *Times* explained the deputation's failure by maintaining that, rather than robbing their own deserving poor and supporting conspiracy, agitation, and possibly arms and secession, the English people preferred 'to bestow their charity where they can direct its application' and 'secure both benefit to the recipient, and something like gratitude to the giver'.[47]

Thus, the London establishment designed its own fundraising campaign. The queen's offer of £1,000 (an amount equal to that already pledged by several financial magnates) was refused as 'it wasn't enough'.[48] Scotland, where people in some areas were also suffering, was added to the cause in a last-minute manoeuvre to provide a rationale for the queen to double her contribution.[49] This boosted the legitimacy of the humanitarian enterprise, although, according to a later allotment formula, it implied that one-sixth of the funds collected were diverted from Ireland.[50] A prominent committee ran the relief effort as an all-British campaign, primarily by means of repeated advertisements in major newspapers and two queen's letters issued in January and October 1847.

The campaign's first appeal to the public included a statement on objectives and a list of donors, headed by the queen, and also noted a contribution by the 'Children and Servants of a Family in the Country'. As customary in

[44] 'Skibbereen Relief Committee'.

[45] Stephen Spring Rice to Lionel de Rothschild, 17 Dec. 1846, Rothschild Archive, London, Private Correspondence Sundray, 1814–1913, XI/109/58B.

[46] 'Skibbereen Relief Committee'.   [47] Editorial, *Times*, 8 Jan. 1847.

[48] Prime Minister Russell to Spring Rice, 1 Jan. 1847, with annotation, National Library of Ireland (hereafter NLI), Monteagle Papers (hereafter MP), 13, 397/5.

[49] Grey to Wood, 4 Jan. 1847, Borthwick Institute, University of York, Halifax/A4/58.

[50] British Relief Association, Minute Book, 61 (16 Jan. 1847), NLI, MS 2022.

nineteenth-century fundraising, accounting elements were prominent through the documentation of subscriptions, but the appeal also indicated restrictions in the appropriation of aid. It was to consist only of provisions, not cash, targeted at individuals with no employable male relative, and was to entail some work by the recipient in return, wherever practicable. The appeal was based on 'the strong conviction that there are a large number of benevolent persons fully acquainted with the distress, and ready to bestow their bounty whenever a channel is presented to them through which it may be applied, and secured as far as possible from the danger of being abused'. In addition to the BRA's passive self-image as a strictly controlled channel, it was announced that donors were able to contribute in kind and that earmarking for any particular district would be strictly observed.[51]

Subsequent advertisements were commonly accounting summaries, with indirect appeals in the form of a list of subscribing social peers. The BRA prominently cited the chairman of the East India Company and the governor of the Bank of England as auditors; itemised provisions shipped to various Irish ports; explained the principles of distribution and monitoring procedures; and listed exceptional instances in which small sums of money were granted for further distribution.[52] Later advertisements included mention of the extreme distress witnessed by agents of the BRA, or limited themselves to printing lists of subscribers and the names of committee members and auditors.[53] More explicit appeals also continued. In a typical one, the committee expressed its hope that the liberality of the British people would enable them 'in some degree' to continue mitigating 'the horrors of a calamity, the extent and severity of which … it is hardly possible to over-picture'.[54]

Another framework for appeals was provided by a queen's letter authorising church collections in support of the BRA's fundraising. It was directed to Anglican bishops in their provinces, thereby prompting them to 'effectually excite their parishioners to a liberal contribution'.[55] The letter was read from the pulpit in the first months of 1847, accompanied by sermons promoting the cause of relief. The government also declared 24 March a national day of fasting and 'humiliation'. A number of sermons were published and raised additional funds by offering arguments to encourage giving. Following the royal proclamation of a national fast day, many 'famine' sermons were delivered urging the nation to atone for its collective sins. However, the sense that Ireland, although part of the UK, was a peculiar country suppressed British

---

[51] *Times*, 6 Jan. 1847; *Daily News*, 6 Jan. 1847; *Morning Post*, 6 Jan. 1847.
[52] *Times*, 4 Feb. 1847.
[53] *Daily News*, 16 Feb. 1847; *Daily News*, 21 Apr. 1847; *Times*, 3 June 1847.
[54] *Daily News*, 5 Mar. 1847; *Times*, 6 Mar. 1847.
[55] 'The Queen's Letter', *Times*, 22 Jan. 1847.

contributions. The paltry, somewhat hostile response to the queen's second letter, issued in connection with an improvised national day of thanksgiving, made this especially obvious.[56]

The Irish and English affiliation could be clearly seen in the armed forces. The Irish Relief Fund in Calcutta had been the first attempt of its kind in the British Empire, outside of Ireland itself. At a time of heavy losses in the conquest of India, the fund's secretary declared that the Irish were those 'who "clear the road" in the battle' – that is, comrades-in-arms whose hearts should be comforted by care for their families and friends at home.[57] A newspaper article cautioned that recent battlefield casualties would mean that fewer remittances would be flowing to Ireland, something that a community effort could mitigate.[58]

At the first public meeting of the fund on 2 January 1846, the Catholic archbishop of Calcutta, despite propaganda for cohesion, took it upon himself to refute the condescending remarks of other committee members by pointing to centuries of English injustice and maladministration that had reduced Ireland 'habitually to the condition of a pauper' (see Figure 3.2). He reminded those present that the gospel said donors should make recipients feel that they were receiving charity from 'equals before God', and that gratitude was a pre-eminent trait of the Irish character. Apart from addressing bilateral relations, the meeting represented the subscription as an opportunity – in response to the British administration of relief in India – 'for the wealthy natives of this country to show that they were not behind Europeans in this exercise of beneficence'.[59] The Calcutta Relief fund continued its work in the following years by sending substantial sums to the BRA and other relief organisations.

The activism in their homeland at the time prompted UK citizens in a number of cities abroad to organise collections among themselves and within the society that they lived in, with varying success. In Hamburg, six individuals called for the support of Europe-at-large for their campaign, suggesting a particular duty was owed to their compatriots, and expressing confidence that the local public would join their effort. The collection raised £450, but a German newspaper derided the call from a different moral economy perspective: 'Do the wealthy Brits also want to burden us with their country's destitution? They have instigated it; let them remedy it.'[60] A charity concert

[56] Gray, 'National Humiliation', 198, 203–5, 211–12.
[57] 'Public Meeting: Distress in Ireland', *Bengal Catholic Herald*, 10 Jan. 1846.
[58] 'The Late Battles near the Sutledge, and the Irish Relief Fund', *Bengal Catholic Herald*, 17 Jan. 1846.
[59] 'Public Meeting: Distress in Ireland', *Bengal Catholic Herald*, 10 Jan. 1846.
[60] Quotation from *Kölnische Zeitung*, dated 15 Jan., in 'Freie Städte', *Fränkischer Merkur*, 23 Jan. 1847. Collection results from *Report of the Proceedings of the General Central Relief*

UNION IS STRENGTH.

John Bull. "HERE ARE A FEW THINGS TO GO ON WITH, BROTHER, AND I 'LL SOON PUT YOU IN A WAY TO EARN YOUR OWN LIVING."

Figure 3.2 English benevolence for Ireland, *Punch*, 17 Oct. 1846.
Drawing by Richard Doyle. Photo by Rischgitz, Hulton Archive, courtesy of
Getty Images

organised in the English church in Hamburg did not attract many people and
received a very poor review.[61] Meanwhile, at a public concert in London,
Jenny Lind's fee for an opera season was said to be £12,000 plus travel and
lodging, something that made another German newspaper exclaim with moral
economic indignation, 'And all this, while Ireland starves!'[62]

---

*Committee for All Ireland from Its Formation on the 29th December, 1846, to the 31st
December, 1847* (Dublin: Browne, 1848), 10.
[61] 'Nachrichten', *Allgemeine Musikalische Zeitung*, 7 Apr. 1847.
[62] 'Auswärtiges', *Augsburger Anzeigenblatt*, 10 May 1847.

Catholic Relief

In Catholic circles, Ireland was referred to as the Islands of Saints. It was seen as having provided invaluable historical services to religion, literature, and the advancement of England.[63] The priest of a Liverpool church, whose background included ties to Ireland, proposed a more aggressive request for relief. He declared that England owed Ireland a great deal for the misery brought about by centuries of tyranny and oppression, and that the Irish had a claim on the gratitude of English Catholics for their successful battle for religious emancipation – something that lifted their coreligionists in the UK up from being 'a proscribed and degraded class'.[64] Moreover, Catholic charity was aroused in opposition to what they saw as the 'black charity' of the proselytising Special Fund for the Spiritual Exigencies of Ireland. This fund provided relief for those willing to undergo religious conversion, appealing for donations by suggesting that 'the Gospel is, more readily than heretofore, now received from hands which have willingly administered relief to ... temporal necessities'.[65] In view of its timing in mid-October 1846, the first explicitly Protestant relief activity seems to have come about in reaction to Catholic efforts.[66]

Catholic fundraising in England was generally conciliatory, ecumenical, and careful not to alienate the Protestant majority. At the beginning of October 1846, Irish expatriates in London created a network of district committees for Irish relief that also lobbied the government to compel Irish landlords to be more loyal to their homeland. While the network's central committee passed all proceeds on to the four archbishops of Ireland, a Catholic magazine emphasised that Protestants, Jews, and Englishmen were among the donors and activists.[67] Catholic clergymen from Ireland became speakers at fundraising events, such as one held at the City Lecture Theatre in London.[68] Another preacher from Ireland delivered charity sermons in churches at Leamington Priors and London. Speaking in Christian rather than Catholic terms, he warned that the 'distressed fellow-creatures in the Sister Country' might be the 'future selves' of his audience, depending on the extent of others' goodwill. He claimed that charity was 'blessed in proportion as it blesses' and that the duty of giving was advocated by nature, reason, and God, the neglect of which

---

[63] 'State of the Country', *Tablet*, 17 Apr. 1847.

[64] 'Collection at St. Joseph's', *Liverpool Mercury*, 5 Feb. 1847.

[65] 'The New Reformation', *Tablet*, 9 Jan. 1847; 'Ireland – An Appeal', *Morning Herald*, 4 Jan. 1847; 'Ireland – An Appeal', *Times*, 5 Jan. 1847. For religiously motivated counter-charity, see 'English Subscriptions for the Relief of Irish Distress', *Tablet*, 17 July 1847.

[66] 'National Club – Famine in Ireland', *Standard*, 17 Oct. 1846; Letter to the Editor, *Evening Mail*, 19 Oct. 1846.

[67] 'Distress in Ireland', *Morning Advertiser*, 6 Oct. 1846; 'London Relief of Irish Famine', *New Weekly Catholic Magazine*, 14 Nov. 1846.

[68] 'Distress in Ireland', *Morning Post*, 12 Oct. 1846.

would be 'the forerunner of eternal damnation'. On the Day of Judgement, he declared, benevolent works would insure generous donors 'a portion of that same mercy which they were that day called upon to exercise towards their famishing fellow-creatures'.[69] A later newspaper advertisement asked all to 'remember that Salvation is denied to those who do not feed the Starving according to their ability'.[70]

Around the time that the BRA was set up, Fredric Lucas, editor of the *Tablet*, in an article entitled 'The National Christmas Famine', asked what he and his readers could do about the starvation in Ireland. Being a Quaker convert, Lucas suggested that the Society of Friends had 'borrowed from the Catholics of other days an example which we ought to be ashamed not to follow'. As he put it, Christ was perishing for want in Irish cabins, and the Catholic code of morality entailed an obligation of charity at the same time that the 'penalty of hell' awaited those who failed to perform their appointed task.[71] From then on, the *Tablet* became 'the repository of Irish grievances and of Irish sufferings' in England – that is, the primary outlet for aid appeals from the Irish clergy.[72]

By the end of 1846, the vicar apostolic (bishop) of London issued a pastoral epistle with instructions for celebrating the jubilee of the commencing papacy of Pius IX. He ordered that an appeal be made in London chapels for the purpose of relieving distress in Ireland as well as in the respective congregation – the collection to be divided into equal portions.[73] Criticism of the bishop's coupling of charity abroad and at home made him revise his instructions so that the sum raised was solely devoted to Irish relief.[74]

Episcopal collections were held throughout England and Wales, often on a weekly basis until Easter to enable poor parishioners to contribute greater aggregate sums. One pastoral made it clear that the present Irish suffering 'has never been equalled in the memory of any one of our generation', and called for 'generous sacrifices for its alleviation'.[75] The bishop of Yorkshire had personally witnessed the distress in Ireland and urged the claims of 'our famishing Brethren' upon the charity of his flock, asking rhetorically where those not sufficiently attentive to the cries of the hungry expected to stand 'on the great accounting day'.[76] In a subsequent call, he pleaded for additional alms, warning that God was fully capable of afflicting England in the same

---

[69] 'Famine in Ireland', *Leamington Spa Courier*, 31 Oct. 1846.
[70] 'Famishing Irish and Scotch', *Bristol Mercury*, 30 Jan. 1847.
[71] 'The National Christmas Famine', *Tablet*, 26 Dec. 1846.
[72] Letter to the Editor, *Tablet*, 17 Apr. 1847.   [73] 'The Famine in Ireland', *Times*, 4 Jan. 1847.
[74] 'The Famine', *Tablet*, 9 Jan. 1847.
[75] Francis Mostyn, 19 Jan. 1847, Ushaw College Library (hereafter UshCL), Durham, Vicariate/Diocesan Papers, UC/P32/231b.
[76] 'Pastoral of the Bishop of Trachis', 12 Jan., *Tablet*, 23 Jan. 1847.

manner as Ireland.[77] In a like manner, another bishop's pastoral cautioned that the time had come 'for each one to measure out with that measure wherewith he desires that it be meted to him again'. It emphasised that those affected by the famine deserved aid not merely as fellow creatures and subjects of the same empire, but also as parishioners 'closely knit together with us in religious communion'.[78]

Descriptions of the distress in Skibbereen, and the British home secretary's letter endorsing private charity in England to the deputies of that town, were reprinted in France and Italy.[79] As a result, philosopher Antonio Rosmini, an early advocate of 'social justice' and founder of the Institute of Charity, was spurred into action. Even before the general British campaign started, he requested one of his missionaries in England to initiate a collection for Irish relief, citing God's recompensing moral economy. He himself issued an appeal in Northern Italy that raised £556 by the end of 1847.[80]

The first transnational call from a Catholic institution was issued by the Society of St Vincent de Paul (SVP) through its president, Jules Gossin (see Figure 3.3). Upon receipt of various letters and documents from Ireland, the SVP council general had ordered its local branches (conferences) to raise funds for the clients of the ten Irish conferences. The appeal declared that the principle of self-subsistence for local chapters was untenable in view of the extraordinary calamity, and urged the society's members to give generously and quickly as 'death does not wait'.[81] The Dutch national council began its ensuing appeal by reminding members of the Irish saints who had evangelised the Netherlands, suggesting there was a 'religious debt to pay'.[82]

The most authoritative call for Irish relief came from the newly inaugurated Pope Pius IX in his second encyclical, issued on 25 March 1847. Addressing prelates all over the world, he invoked the Catholic tradition of alms-giving for Christians in need, quoting the moral economy of church

---

[77] 'English Subscriptions for Irish Distress', *Tablet*, 27 Feb. 1847.

[78] 'Pastoral Letter of the Right Rev. Thomas Bishop of Combysopolis', *Tablet*, 23 Jan. 1847.

[79] 'Irlande', *L'Ami de la religion*, 26 Dec. 1846; 'Le notizie che si ricevono dall' Irlanda', *Gazzetta Piemontese*, 29 Dec. 1846; Grey to deputies, 9 Dec. 1846, in *Journal des débats*, 24 Dec. 1846; *La Presse*, 24 Dec. 1846; *Gazzetta Piemontese*, 30 Dec. 1846.

[80] Rosmini to Giambattista Pagani, 31 Dec. 1846, in Antonio Rosmini-Serbati, *Opere: Epistolario, part 1, vol. 2* (Turin: Paravia, 1857), 273–4. The first appeal was published in *Gazzetta Piemontese*, 19 Jan. 1847. We are indebted to Francesco Zavatti's forthcoming article 'Charity as Social Justice: Antonio Rosmini and the Great Irish Famine'.

[81] SVP appeal, 2 Feb. 1847, Vatican Secret Archives (hereafter VSA), Rome, Secretary of State (hereafter SoS), 1848, rubr. 241, fasc. 2, 87v. For letters from Ireland, see 'Extraits de divers renseignements', ibid., 88r–90r. For further background, see *The Circular of the President General of the 21st November, 1846, to which is appended the Letter of the President of the Council of Ireland of 9th February, 1847* (Dublin: Clarke, 1847), 22–3.

[82] 'N°. 40', *De Tijd*, 20 Feb. 1847.

Figure 3.3 Jules Gossin (1789–1855). Daguerreotype, 1844.
Image reproduced courtesy of National Library of Sweden

father St Ambrose: 'Christians should learn to use money in looking not for their own goods but for Christ's, so that Christ in turn may look after them.' Pius IX mentioned his own Irish relief efforts, warned of the worsening calamity, and suggested that Ireland particularly deserved aid for its loyalty to Rome and its missionary engagement around the world. He proclaimed a triduum (three days) of public prayer for suffering Ireland, with an indulgence of seven years granted as a reward for attendees, and exhorted all Catholics to give alms for relief.[83]

A total of 30,000 copies of the encyclical were printed and within a month distributed all over the world by the Sacred Congregation for the Propagation of the Faith.[84] It was further reproduced by the Catholic press and hierarchy. For example, the Central district (the future Diocese of Birmingham) made 150 copies of the encyclical, which was to be read at all churches together with a pastoral epistle from the bishop.[85] When it was sent to the Irish bishops, the encyclical was accompanied by a letter that in general terms complied with the wish of Prime Minister Russell that the pope praise the

---

[83] Pius IX, 'Praedecessores nostros', in *The Papal Encyclicals, vol. 1: 1740–1878*, ed. Claudia Carlen (Raleigh: Pierian, 1990), 285–6.

[84] 'Rom', *Schweizerische Kirchenzeitung*, 30 Apr. 1847.

[85] Cash Book (1843–7), 15 Apr. 1847, Diocesan Archives, Birmingham, DF3; Pastoral, 3 May 1847, ibid., B1027.

Irish clergy for their conduct during the famine and ask them to trust the government and its relief efforts.[86]

While the encyclical was heeded in many places, it was ignored or depreciated in others. The Austrian emperor, for example, decreed that only the sections on prayer and indulgences be communicated to the faithful, not allowing systematic collections that benefitted foreigners. When the issue was discussed in autumn 1847, the time for relief was considered past, and the extent of American contributions served as a further argument against the need to solicit funds.[87] In the diocese of Brixen, church collections were made nevertheless, but they were announced incidentally and were only conducted on a voluntary basis.[88]

In St Gallen, a Swiss town named after an Irish monk, where distress in the local bishop's own parish caused him to leave it to the discretion of the wealthy to contribute to Irish relief, the sum of 4,325 francs (£170) was collected.[89] The prevailing opinion among Catholics abroad was expressed by a Swiss newspaper, which stated that 'England has a very heavy – and the primary – duty of Irish relief.' However, the paper, continued, 'we may not now ask what duties England has to Ireland, but rather the duties we Catholic Christians from Switzerland must fulfil to aid that unfortunate country'. As in the case of the Dutch, obligations to Ireland were acknowledged for its role in Christianising Germany and Switzerland.[90]

An Irish bishop thanked the pope for his initiative as 'well calculated to inspire the people with hope and to fill the Clergy with confidence'.[91] Pius IX had been drawn to the issue of Irish relief when Paul Cullen, rector of the Pontifical Irish College, urged Catholics not to fall behind the generosity of Protestants in Rome.[92] UK residents of the Holy City held a fundraising meeting on 13 January 1847, at which the rector was represented by a deputy who suggested that 'the collection [be made] general through the city'; Cullen

---

[86] Pius IX to Murray, 10 Apr. 1847, in Peadar MacSuibhne, *Paul Cullen and His Contemporaries, vol. 1* (Naas: Leinster Leader, 1961), 296–7. For background, see Viale-Prelà to Gizzi, 14 Mar. 1847, VSA, SoS, 1848, rub. 241, fasc 2, 37–41; James P. Flint, *Great Britain and the Holy See: The Diplomatic Relations Question 1846–1852* (Washington, DC: Catholic University of America Press, 2003), 27–30.

[87] Provincial government for Tyrol and Vorarlberg to Diocese of Brixen, 17 Sept. 1847, Diocesan Archives, Brixen, Consistorial Records 1847/no. 22599/3710 Geistlich.

[88] Diocese of Brixen to provincial government for Tyrol and Vorarlberg, 24 Sept. 1847, ibid., no. 2752; Diocese of Brixen to deanary of Brixen, 29 Oct. 1847, ibid. (no number).

[89] 'St. Gallen', *Schweizerische Kirchenzeitung*, 12 June 1847; 'L'année dernière', *L'Ami de la religion*, 5 Feb. 1848.

[90] 'Was kann und soll die Schweiz für Irland thun?', *Schweizerische Kirchenzeitung*, 15 May 1847.

[91] Cantwell to Pius IX, 8 June 1847, Pontifical Irish College (hereafter PIC), Archive, Rome, Cullen Papers (hereafter CUL), CUL/NC/4/1847/34.

[92] Undated draft Cullen to Fransoni, PIC, CUL/NC/3/1/7.

was also elected to the committee.[93] It was announced that the pope would contribute 1,000 Scudi (£213), and that he ordered a solemn triduum in one of the local churches from 24 to 26 January, with sermons in Italian, English, and French, to elicit donations for relief. Pius IX expressed 'the deep pain which it had given him to hear of the suffering state of Ireland' and 'regretted that his power of contributing to her relief was not more in proportion to his good wishes'.[94] Cullen, who was eager that Rome distinguish herself and show the world 'that she is not only the centre of faith, but also the soul of charity', explained that the papal donation was 'a very large sum for one who has so many calls to respond to' and suggested that a thousand dollars from the pope was 'more than a hundred thousand from the queen of England'.[95] In a fundraising pamphlet in the Italian language that appears to have been published on behalf of the Rome committee of UK citizens, Cullen claimed it was general knowledge that the English government had failed to provide sufficient relief.[96] He later described the underlying significance of the pope's encyclical as 'a standing testimony against the misrule of England'.[97] A contemporary witness commended Cullen's sermon during the triduum as impressive.[98]

Acclaimed pulpit orator Gioacchino Ventura held the triduum's main sermon in Italian. He suggested that the spirit of charity was the bond uniting all Catholics, but that the Irish people also had particular merits, had suffered extraordinarily, and had conducted themselves admirably, making them deserving of his audience's best sympathies. Hence, he

conjured all his hearers in the name of humanity, virtue, love of country, and above all of religion, to aid by their contributions, and by their most fervent prayers to rescue from starvation a people, which was a model to all the countries in the world, for their social virtues, their patriotism, their fidelity to constituted authority, and above all for their attachment to the Catholic Faith, their practice of its holy duties, and their zeal in propagating it.[99]

---

[93] Correspondence from Rome, 14 Jan., *Daily News*, 29 Jan. 1847; 'Destitute Irish', *Roman Advertiser*, 16 Jan. 1847. For a more complicated, but opaque, account of developments in Rome, see 'Subscriptions for Irish Destitution in Rome', *Dublin Evening Post*, 16 Feb. 1847.

[94] Journal of John Scandrett Harford, Bristol Record Office (quotations); Cullen to Murray, 14 Jan. 1847, Diocesan Archives, Dublin (hereafter DAD), Murray Papers (hereafter MP), 34/9/229; Kirby to Murray, 18 Jan. 1847, ibid., 34/9/230. In Jan. 1847, 4.7 scudi was equivalent to £1. See Fransoni to Murray, 30 Jan. 1847, ibid., 32/3/159.

[95] Cullen to Murray, 14 Jan. 1847, DAD, MP, 34/9/229; Cullen to Slattery, 14 Jan. 1847, Slattery Papers (hereafter SP), Diocesan Archives, Cashel (hereafter DAC), 1847/10 (all documents from this collection on NLI microfilm); Cullen to Murray, 30 Jan. 1847, DAD, MP, 34/9/231.

[96] *Breve notizia dell' attuale carestia in Irlanda* (Rome: Menicanti, 1847), 4. From the context, it appears that Cullen was the mastermind behind the pamphlet, although this was not the Vatican publication that previous research has assumed.

[97] Cullen to Slattery, 28 Apr. 1847, SP, DAC, 1847/35.

[98] John Minter Morgan, *A Tour through Switzerland and Italy in the Years 1846–47: In Letters to a Clergyman* (London: Longman, 1851), 112.

[99] 'Italy – Rome', *Tablet*, 20 Feb. 1847.

Ventura framed the welcome contributions by English and Irish Protestants in Rome as 'an emanation of Catholic charity', inherited from the spirit of their forefathers or inspired by the surrounding Catholic atmosphere. He hoped that what appeared to be Irish acquiesce in starving to death in union with the disposition of Christ would 'ascend as a holocaust of reconciliation to the throne of the Most High, to draw down on England not the justice and indignation which liar crimes deserve, but conversion to the true faith, grace, mercy, and salvation'. The colourful report on the effects of the sermon, with its surrounding choreography of church rituals for a time of famine and an appeal by alumni of the Pontefical Irish College, included the observation that 'the very beggars with tears in their eyes emptied the contents of their poor purses into the hands of the collectors'.[100]

Rome's example was followed in some Italian bishoprics even before the pope's encyclical was issued. Thus, a pastoral letter from the town of Jesi argued that Christian charity being universal, the obligation towards brothers of faith was all the more stringent; that the modern principle of association was a force for good; and that the rational and enlightened spirit embodied in public opinion contributed to the denouncement of selfish behaviour. The Jesi pastoral underscored the possibility that the local populace might some day find themselves in need of such aid, and so charity shown to Ireland might be insurance against such a calamity befalling their own selves. It also claimed that God rewarded 'good works with great interest, giving eternal glory as the recompense of the most trifling acts of beneficence'.[101]

Apart from church collections, committees in Rome and Florence launched fundraising events such as society balls and an aid concert. One socially conscious woman even organised a lottery for a valuable painting.[102] The pope himself provided an autograph letter and a rosary of agates that were exhibited at a bank in London and raffled off for the relief of Irish famine hungry. However, the £61 realised fell short of the £100 that the organisers had hoped for, and critics accused the event of 'dispensing the spiritual graces, of which the Pope claims to be the depositary'.[103]

The idea of famine relief as an undertaking for the entire Catholic world originated with Gossin at a point in time before the SVP's general

---

[100] Ibid. See also 'Foreign and Colonial Intelligence', *Tablet*, 13 Feb. 1847; on the Irish alumni's appeal, see 'Kirchenstaat', *Katholische Blätter aus Tirol*, 15 Feb. 1847.
[101] 'Colonial and Foreign Intelligence', *Tablet*, 13 Mar. 1847.
[102] *Roman Advertiser*, 13 Feb. & 13 Mar. 1847.
[103] 'Foreign and Colonial Intelligence', *English Review* 8, no. 15, 233–56, 252, n. 1. Regarding expected and realised sums, see 'Pope Pius IX. and the Irish', *Times*, 14 June 1847; Fitzmaurice to Murray (no date), DAD, MP, 33/6/42.

appeal, and the Holy See acknowledged the SVP's role in bringing the encyclical about.[104] Gossin was the driving force behind a petition signed by 197 prominent Frenchmen, including mathematician Augustin-Louis Cauchy, publisher and politician Count Charles de Montalembert, and political analyst Alexis de Tocqueville. Dated 6 January 1847, it called on the pope to launch a 'new crusade, although a completely peaceful crusade, a crusade of charity, of prayer, and of good deeds' for suffering Ireland and for persecuted Christians of the Lebanon as well. By May, when the archbishop of Paris implemented the famine encyclical, a subscription was opened under his auspices.[105] The committee's public appeal described it as 'a truly national and French enterprise' that would attract everyone, without distinction of party or creed. The appeal stated that high food prices were responsible for the campaign's slow start, but insisted that French economic hardship could not compare with the suffering of the Irish.[106] However, the minister of justice protested against unauthorised publication of the encyclical and reminded the French clergy of the requirement of obtaining permission to do so.[107]

The bishop of Marseilles had already issued a pastoral epistle on 24 February that drew an analogy between the Irish and the early Christians, who, during the Roman Empire, adhered to their faith even under torture. He also argued that Catholic beneficence was particularly called for in light of the active proselytism in Ireland; and, as in the pastoral from Jesi, he suggested that a universal plea for charity was even more incumbent on his coreligionists when those who were suffering belonged to 'the great Catholic family'.[108] Following the encyclical, at least twenty-one French bishops published pastoral letters. Despite differences in form and content, their message was one: 'The Irish are starving and need your help.' An analysis sees a deliberate choice of shocking examples, but also notes the 'almost throwaway fashion' in which the famine is presented. The arguments put forward were similar to those of English and Italian clerics, but some French pastorals also suggested that famine relief

---

[104] Bruno Belhoste, *Augustin-Louis Cauchy: A Biography* (New York: Springer, 1991), 189; James Gerard Martin, 'The Society of St. Vincent de Paul as an Emerging Social Phenomenon in Mid-nineteenth Century Ireland' (MA thesis, National College of Industrial Relations, 1993), 135; Copy of letter from Cardinal Gizzi to Gossin, 15 Apr. 1847, DAD, MP, 32/3/ 164 (reprinted in the *Cork Examiner*, 19 May 1847, and other newspapers).

[105] Petition, 6 Jan. 1847, VSA, SoS, 1848, rubr. 241, fasc. 2, 25–9 (missing the last seventy-three signatures). The printed version of the appeal (with all signatures) was dated 17 Jan. and published together with the pope's encyclical and a pastoral letter by the archbishop. See *Comité de secours*. On Gossin's role, see Martin, 'The Society of St. Vincent De Paul', 143.

[106] Appeal of 27 May, in *L'Ami de la religion*, 10 June 1847.

[107] 'Paris', *L'Ami de la religion*, 1 July 1847.

[108] 'France: French Sympathy for Ireland', *Tablet*, 20 Mar. 1847.

offered a high moral ground vis-à-vis the English, or that it otherwise served the self-image of France as *le grande nation*.[109]

Despite the fact that French collections for Ireland were generally church organised, they were ultimately coordinated by the voluntary Comité de secours pour l'Irlande. Laymen took a prominent role in the effort because of the contemporary distress prevailing in France. It was regarded as 'a matter of Prudence not to expose the clergy to be reproached by the people of neglecting their fellow Country men, and of manifesting their solicitude for strangers'.[110] However, the Irish were no strangers to the French Catholic elite – they were their idealised model of Catholic spirituality.[111]

US Relief

Catholic appeals in the New World resembled those of the Old, but at times had clearer political references and more compelling language. For example, John Bernard Fitzpatrick, bishop of Boston, stated in a pastoral that Ireland no longer lamented her lost liberties nor the union with Great Britain, bewailing instead the dying of her children. According to him, 'our own home; or at least … the home of our loved fathers and friends' required extraordinary charity, something that made any discussion of responsibilities of the UK parliament or Irish landlords immaterial. This engendered the bishop's conviction that 'not one will fail to act nobly and generously his part, or to fulfil to the extent of his means what we do not hesitate to call a sacred duty'.[112]

Irish communities were the driving force for famine relief in North America. In addition to Catholics, those communities included Protestants and had much to gain by reaching out to a wider public. The resulting fundraising rhetoric outlined an impartial, national campaign that resembled the one in France. North American society, however, was more diverse. It was made up of large groups of Irish immigrants with a vested interest in their country of origin, alongside a Protestant majority with no particular religious affinity to Ireland. The situation in Canada was akin to that of the USA, but contained a stronger Catholic element and had the British Empire as an additional bond.

---

[109] Grace Neville, '"Il y a des larmes dans leurs chiffres": French Famine Relief for Ireland, 1847–84', *Revue Française de Civilisation Britannique* 19, no. 2 (2014): 69, 71–2. The analysis refers to the seventeen pastorals archived in the NLI. For an analysis of the Italian pastorals, see Francesco Zavatti, 'Appealing Locally for Transnational Humanitarian Aid: Italian Bishops and the Great Irish Famine', *Quellen und Forschungen aus italienischen Archiven und Bibliotheken* 99 (2019): 313–39.

[110] Abbé Moriarty to Murray, 27 Feb. 1847, DAD, MP, 32/3/88.

[111] Seamus Deane, 'Catholicism, Republicanism and Race: Ireland in Nineteenth-century French Thought', in *Paris – Capital of Irish Culture: France, Ireland and the Republic, 1798–1916*, eds Pierre Joannon and Kevin Whelan (Dublin: Four Courts, 2017), 110–29.

[112] 'Relief for Ireland', *Boston Pilot*, 13 Feb. 1847.

Nonetheless, a satirical journal in Montreal derided the Irish predominance in relief committees by publishing a fictional list of miniscule contributions, all coming from members of one family clan.[113]

It has hitherto been accepted that Irish relief was a national US effort, without scrutinising who was involved. It has not been considered that downplaying social disparities between donors is a common humanitarian propaganda strategy, although the emphasis on particularly deserving beneficiaries frequently surfaces amid an overall universalist rhetoric. For example, a speech that Henry Clay delivered at a New Orleans town meeting in 1847 invoked a humanitarian imperative irrespective of colour, religion, and civilisation. After a tribute to universalism, Clay explained at length that the meeting did not concern any distant country, but a nation 'which is so identified with our own, as to be almost part and parcel of ours, bone of our bone and flesh of our flesh'.[114]

President Polk's threat to veto US government aid to Ireland for constitutional reasons thwarted a plan that had been developed with reference to Americans being an 'offspring' of the Irish.[115] However, civil society responded positively to a convention in Washington on 9 February 1847, chaired by Polk's vice-president. A member of Congress from each of the twenty-nine states was appointed an honorary vice-president of the meeting, which recommended that fundraising committees be set up throughout the USA. A lengthy appeal was issued to the public, cautiously mentioning that there were hundreds of famine victims, explaining the hardships in Europe, and the efforts made by the British. The Cork magistrate's letter to Wellington was cited, as well as correspondence from the West Cork region addressed to the 'Ladies of America'.

Although the Washington appeal spoke of 'a sister nation' to which one of the speakers suggested the USA owed 'a deep debt of gratitude', and which according to another was well blended into the American 'blood', the overall approach and message were universal. Robert Dale Owen, congressman and son of the British social reformer, exemplifies this with an appeal that anticipated Singer's argument on the insignificance of distance whenever there is knowledge of need. Other voices suggested that the financial boom in the USA at the time (which was in stark contrast to bad harvests and economic depression across Europe), and the demand for labour and settlers, facilitated the framing of Irish relief as a broader cause. The meeting concluded with the

---

[113] 'The Pattypans of Gaspe', *Satirist* 1, no. 2 (1847): 8.
[114] Henry Clay, 'Appeal for Ireland', in *The American Common-School Reader and Speaker*, eds John Goldsbury and William Russell (Boston: Tappan, Whittemore, and Mason, 1850), 350–1.
[115] Ann Mary Chapman Coleman, ed. *The Life of John J. Crittenden, with Selections from His Correspondence and Speeches*, vol. *1* (Philadelphia: Lippincott, 1871), 288. For background, see Curti, *American Philanthropy Abroad*, 43–50.

adoption of a resolution moved by an Irishman, thanking those involved in the gathering and, by extension, the American nation, and indicating an elaborate humanitarian choreography.[116]

Despite the advancement of famine relief as a national cause, the case of the Philadelphia Irish Relief Committee, which, according to a recent study, typified "'universal America" where class, ethnicity, and religious denomination did not matter',[117] indicates the need for critical review. The first relief committee in November 1846 was practically an organ of the Hibernian Society for the Relief of Emigrants from Ireland, although it figured as a group of 'gentlemen' who addressed 'fellow citizens' in Philadelphia and the southwestern region of the USA. By February 1847, in order to extend its reach beyond the ethnic ghetto in more than words, the committee broadened its membership. However, the majority of members of the executive committee for the city of Philadelphia still belonged to the Hibernian Society. Others bore Irish names. Yet another called attention to 'the claim of the Irish people upon us, from blood association, and the influence of the many domestic ties'. The committee resolved that its papers be placed in charge of the Hibernian Society and, in its final report, noted that its relief efforts had not been confined to people of Irish descent – a truism that downplayed the centrality of the ethnic community in the campaign.[118]

The Philadelphia Committee, with its published report and the extensive documentation of its networking within the city's Irish community's elite, is easily verifiable with regard to its social basis. It suggests that the case of the similarly named Irish Relief Committee, which was organised by the Hibernian Society of Charleston, was not the exception researchers have claimed, but may rather have been typical of relief initiatives for Ireland.[119]

The first foreign effort mounted in the USA to assist Ireland was initiated by John W. James, the president of the Boston Repeal Association, on 25 November 1845. He proposed a subscription among members of the organisation 'for their suffering brethren, which would, when sent forward, not only do much to relieve their distress, but also redound to their own credit'.[120] The resulting Irish 'community effort' was based on collections in churches, at a public meeting, and private subscriptions. However, since it was linked to the

---

[116] 'Public Meeting for the Relief of the Suffering Poor in Ireland', *National Era*, 18 Feb. 1847.

[117] Strum, 'Pennsylvania', 295.

[118] *Report of the General Executive Committee of the City and County of Philadelphia ... to Provide Means to Relieve the Sufferings in Ireland* (Philadelphia: Crissy and Markley, 1847), 5–10, 16, 18, 23–4, 34; John H. Campbell, *History of the Friendly Sons of St. Patrick and of the Hibernian Society for the Relief of Emigrants from Ireland* (Philadelphia: Hibernian Society, 1892).

[119] Strum, 'South Carolina', 151.

[120] T. Mooney, 'Enthusiastic Meeting of the Boston Appeal Association', *Boston Pilot*, 29 Nov. 1845.

movement for the repeal of the Act of Union between Great Britain and Ireland, this aid effort and its association with the demand for Irish autonomy came into conflict with political priorities.[121] In the years that followed, the Boston Repeal Association continued to collect funds for Ireland, but it combined providing food aid and the shipment of arms for the insurgency of 'Young Ireland'.[122] The repeal movement had branches throughout the USA that it also mobilised for famine relief in other areas.[123]

By 7 February 1847, after the Catholic clergy of Boston had established a committee that became the Relief Association for Ireland, a broad circle of sponsors from that city disseminated an address on Irish relief by means of the newly introduced electric telegraph. It reportedly made a strong impression on the country.[124] Various calls led to the formation of the broader New England Relief Committee one week later. The appeals urged the public to provide relief regardless of the causes of famine. They emphasised suspicions that the reports from Ireland may have been exaggerated were untrue.[125] During a time of US aggression against Mexico, a Protestant minister declared that the sight of relief ships 'under the white flag of peace and mercy' would be a 'nobler spectacle' than that of battleships, and said that aiding Ireland would make war with the UK psychologically unlikely.[126] An examination of contemporary speech acts shows that they highlighted notions of Christian duty, idealistic humanitarianism (sometimes from an internationalist perspective), and a belief in the obligation of sharing America's abundance. Some voiced uneasiness over profitting from the European food shortage or the Mexican War, seeing an opportunity to improve British–American relations. An instance of Irish aid for New England in the seventeenth century was recalled. As in the case of other US relief efforts, it appears that the sense of common purpose that was evoked had a value of its own for a much divided community.[127] At the same time, the strong Irish presence in Boston, despite being poorly integrated, was a significant factor. A major facilitator of the Boston civic effort was of the opinion that the Great Irish Famine represented a unique charitable cause because its stories

---

[121] Henry A. Crosby Forbes and Henry Lee, *Massachusetts Help to Ireland during the Great Famine* (Milton: Captain Robert Bennet Forbes House, 1967), 1–5.

[122] Luther S. Cushing, ed. 'Patrick Murray & Another vs. Terence McHugh [etc.]', in *Reports of Cases Argued and Determined in the Supreme Judicial Court of Massachusetts, vol. 9* (Boston: Little, Brown, 1858), 158–63. See also Anelise Hanson Shrout, '"Distressing News from Ireland": The Famine, the News and International Philanthropy' (PhD dissertation, New York University, 2013), 168.

[123] Strum, 'Jersey Ship', 5.

[124] George Potter, *To the Golden Door: The Story of the Irish in Ireland and America* (Boston: Little, Brown, 1960), 457.

[125] Forbes and Lee, *Massachusetts Help*, 11–17.

[126] 'Relief for Ireland', *Boston Daily Advertiser*, 16 Feb. 1847.

[127] Forbes and Lee, *Massachusetts Help*, 22–5.

came 'so directly from the Irish around us, who themselves contributed all they could to relieve their relations in the old country'.[128]

In New York, where people of Irish descent made up a quarter of the population, the first Irish relief committee was formed in December 1846, mostly by members of the ethnic community with affinities to the Democratic party. A broader General Relief Committee coalesced by February 1847. It included, among others of Irish background, the Quaker Jacob Harvey, who conducted public relations that raised famine awareness throughout the USA and resulted in funds that were generally forwarded to the Society of Friends in Dublin. The Irish-born Catholic bishop of New York joined forces with the general committee, serving as a speaker and, in an ecumenical gesture, transferring the collections from his diocese to the Society of Friends as well. Despite a considerable Irish presence among the committee members, its founder and chairman, Myndert van Schaick, did not have a family connection to Ireland. Ultimately, the committee represented a broad group of businessmen and prominent individuals with links to shipping interests and to the Commissioners of Emigration (i.e., immigration) of the State of New York.[129]

During the 1840s, a period of rising food prices and mounting freight rates, the transportation of emigrants was a business that lowered the overall cost of conveying American goods to European markets. One of the most active members of the New York committee was the treasurer of the Irish Emigrant Society of that city. Harvey, who was among the commissioners of emigration, envisioned a solution to the Irish subsistence crisis through populating the American West: 'The more people we can bring over, the better for all parties.'[130] Van Schaick concluded a public speech somewhat obscurely with the hope that 'the Irish people would adopt the American system of Common School education, or something similar to it, which would enable them to take care of themselves in future'.[131] The committee's appeal to the public distilled the economic fundamentals down to a single line 'What is death to Ireland is but augmented fortune to America; and we are actually fattening on the starvation of another people.' The appeal raised the cry that four million people were on the verge of starvation resulting from a famine that was not caused by improvidence or vice. A triad of charity, civilisation, and Christianity was

---

[128] Sarah Forbes Hughes, ed. *Letters and Recollections of John Murray Forbes, vol. 1* (Boston: Houghton, Mifflin, 1899), 121. On the lack of integration, see Thomas H. O'Connor, *Fitzpatrick's Boston 1846–1866* (Boston: Northeastern University Press, 1984), 83.

[129] See also John Ridge, 'The Great Hunger in New York', *New York Irish History* 9 (1995): 7–8; Enda Delaney, 'Ireland's Great Famine: A Transnational History', in *Transnational Perspectives in Modern Irish History*, ed. Niall Whelehan (New York: Routledge, 2015), 111.

[130] *Transactions*, 256.   [131] 'Relief for Ireland', *New York Herald*, 16 Feb. 1847.

invoked, along with the plea that 'Every dollar that you give, may save a human being from starvation!'[132]

US celebrity peace crusader Elihu Burritt made a similar appeal in one of his 'Olive Leaf' broadsheets to the American people. Reprinted by US newspapers, it claimed that 'A penny a day will save a human life.' (For his audience at home, he translated the phrase as 'two cents' worth of Indian meal'.)[133] Burritt also travelled to the scenes of misery, reporting on what he found in another 'Olive Leaf' that circulated across the USA and England.[134] He described people in the terminal stages of starvation, and added political observations comparing the dire labour situation in Ireland with 'the curse of slavery'.[135] For his British audience, he published a pamphlet detailing three days of horror he experienced in Skibbereen in February 1847. A prominent Quaker wrote the pamphlet's foreword and called for a moral economy for Ireland equivalent to that of England. He based his appeal on the Irish people's entitlement to 'support from the land and other fixed property' which entitlement, in times of distress, superseded any landlord's or creditor's demand for rent or interest.[136] However, he did not go so far as to suggest that there was a moral economy that included Ireland as an equal among the other members of the UK.

3.3   Altruism, Self-interest, and Solidarity: Soviet Russia

Although it was known for months that a famine threatened parts of Soviet Russia in 1921, it was Maxim Gorky's appeal in July of that year that first brought the famine to the world's attention. In contrast to many other famines, relief was triggered by a representative of the afflicted country requesting help for himself and his compatriots. It was a 'deputy appeal' in the sense that Gorky lent his voice to the Bolshevik government, which after long reluctance had decided to accept foreign aid. To make the call more acceptable to the West (and perhaps also to avoid humiliation), the Russian leadership signalled their 'surrender' through a non-communist international celebrity. Lenin and the People's Commissar for Foreign Affairs, Chicherin, only launched their

---

[132] *Aid to Ireland: Report of the General Relief Committee of the City of New York Organized February 10th, 1847* (New York: General Irish Relief Committee, 1848), 147–8.

[133] Elihu Buritt, 'An Olive Leaf for the American People', Feb. 1847; reprinted in the *Boston Daily Advertiser*, 25 Feb. 1847. On his celebrity status, see Melissa Fegan, *Literature and the Irish Famine 1845–1919* (Oxford: Clarendon, 2002), 93, n. 68.

[134] Elihu Burritt, 'An Olive Leaf for the American People: One Word More for Poor Ireland', *Christian Citizen*, 20 Mar. 1847.

[135] Neil Hogan, *The Cry of the Famishing: Ireland, Connecticut and the Potato Famine* (East Haven: Connecticut Irish-American Historical Society, 1998), 42, 44.

[136] Joseph Sturge in Elihu Burritt, *A Journal of a Visit of Three Days to Skibbereen, and Its Neighbourhood* (London: Gilpin, 1847), iv.

own, somewhat different, appeals weeks later. Accordingly, Gorky did not speak in the name of the government, but rather for the Russian people. Stressing their cultural significance, he wrote 'Gloomy days have come for the country of Tolstoy, Dostoyevsky, Meneleyev, Pavlov, Mussergsky, Glinka and other world-prized men and I venture to trust that the cultured European and American people, understanding the tragedy of the Russian people, will immediately succor with bread and medicines.'[137]

While initially stating that the famine was caused by nature, thereby relieving the government of responsibility, Gorky also blamed 'the damnable war and its victors' vengeance' for the conditions, thus suggesting an unsettled debt on the side of the West. Gorky developed this thought further by demanding aid especially from 'those who, during the ignominious war, so passionately preached fratricidal hatred', although he did not point to a specific country or group. Finally, when he characterised the famine to Western philanthropists as a 'splendid opportunity to demonstrate the vitality of humanitarianism', it was with a tinge of sarcasm, although he apologised immediately for his 'involuntary bitterness'. He concluded by asking 'all honest European and American people for prompt aid to the Russian people'.

During the following months, Gorky's appeal was reprinted in newspapers abroad and used in the campaigns of various relief organisations. It was the starting point of an international relief campaign. For example, while the Save the Children Fund (SCF) magazine *The Record* had barely mentioned conditions in Russia until then, the famine dominated its headlines and those of other relief organisations' publications, such as the *Bulletin* of the American Relief Administration (ARA), for the next one and a half years. Dozens of smaller aid agencies, committees, and individuals, along with journalists, did their best to keep the Russian famine in the public eye.

Funding Approaches

After the ARA and Nansen's International Committee for Russian Relief (ICRR) had signed treaties with the Soviet government, their affiliated organisations promulgated appeals in a multitude of leaflets, letters, and newspaper advertisements. There was some cooperation among them, such as the All-British Appeal, but often they competed for donations. The SCF addressed people from all walks of life through advertisements placed in mass media, whereas other organisations focused on specific groups. Thus, the Joint Distribution Committee (JDC) called upon American Jews, the Volga Relief Society (VRS) solicited Americans of Russian-German origin, the Berlin-based

---

[137] 'Maxim Gorky's Appeal to the American People', *ARA Bulletin* 2, no. 16, Sept. 1921, 2.

Workers' Relief International (WIR) and their US auxiliary, the Friends of Soviet Russia (FSR), appealed to the working class, and religious groups solicited their own members. In addition, a great number of individuals founded voluntary committees that collected donations from acquaintances or colleagues.

The ARA, as a US umbrella organisation, never made any public appeals. Before the Riga treaties were signed, Hoover was already determined to oppose appealing to the public, as had been done in relief work for Central Europe in 1920.[138] He was convinced that US citizens should not be asked for help again, as their charitable generosity was exhausted. The slogan 'charity begins at home' gained momentum, especially as relief for 'Red Russia' was the object.[139] As an ARA staff member put it, Hoover 'has dreaded seeking, or encouraging others to seek, financial support for people outside our own country during a period when so many of our own people are unemployed'.[140] Another reason for the ARA not launching a public appeal was to avoid discussions and counter claims that they feared might endanger the whole operation.[141]

These considerations were paralleled by doubts concerning the profitability and practicality of public appeals.[142] In contrast to other organisations, the ARA aimed to fight the famine in its entirety. From the start, Hoover was certain that the Russian operation was 'entirely beyond the resources of all the available private charity' and needed substantial governmental support.[143] He considered it a better strategy to ask Congress for a larger sum than to hope for thousands of small donations. However, while rejecting a public appeal, the ARA turned to long-standing supporters and primarily solicited their major donors.[144] The ARA also established its own press department, which supplied journalists in the USA and correspondents in Russia with press material, instead of paying for advertisments.[145]

The fundraising campaigns of organisations affiliated with the ARA felt the impact of this strategy.[146] After Congress had granted US$20 million to the ARA, other relief organisations were asked why the public was still being appealed to for donations, and whether the government contribution would not

---

[138] 'The European Relief Council Is Recalled, Mr. Hoover's Statement', *ARA Bulletin* 2, no. 16, 1 Sept. 1921, 11.

[139] Patenaude, *Big Show*, 142.   [140] ARA to Morris Gest, 31 Mar. 1922, ARA, reel 500.

[141] Hoover to Burns, 29 Jan. 1923, in Fisher, *The Famine in Soviet Russia*, 533–7, and Hoover to Burns, 6 Feb. 1923, ibid., 539. On 'counter claims', see Mahood and Satzewich, 'Save the Children Fund', 68–78.

[142] Draft to Mitchel, unsigned (London), 27 Apr. 1922, ARA, reel 499.

[143] Hoover to Ador (IRC), 9 Aug. 1921, *ARA Bulletin* 2, no. 16, 1 Sept. 1921, 5–7.

[144] See Hoover to Baker, 16 Nov. 1921, ARA, reel 11. The database contained 200,000–300,000 names. See Page to Herter, 20 Sept. 1922, ARA, reel 389.

[145] Baker to Hoover, 8 July 1922, ARA, reel 549.   [146] Fisher, *Famine in Soviet Russia*, 165

be 'sufficient for the necessary work'.[147] For smaller organisations that did not receive governmental funding, the crowding out tendency of public funding and Hoover's reservations posed a serious problem.[148] Hoover had not only refused to back an appeal, but at the turn of 1921/2, publicly announced that there was hardly any need for additional grain donations, as the Russian infrastructure could not cope with more than the ARA was already supplying. Some Quakers regarded this as conscious sabotage, and the American Friends Service Committee (AFSC) sought to make Hoover retract his statement.[149]

Morally Worthy Recipients

Advocating and justifying relief for the population of a foreign country was far from uncontroversial after the Great War, but in the case of Russia, nearly all organisations (apart from some pro-communist groups) faced an even greater challenge: raising money for a foreign power with a hostile ideology. After all, during the Russian civil war, most Western states had openly supported the Whites in their fight against the Reds.[150] Many saw communism not merely as an alternative political system, but as a disease spreading chaos and threatening civilisation, especially as Western media had provided their readers with sensationalistic stories about Bolshevik horrors.[151]

Many politicians, some members of the press, and Russian emigrant organisations criticised relief efforts as aiding the Soviet government.[152] In order to create 'morally worthy victims', aid organisations tried to draw a distinction between Russian citizens and the Bolshevik government.[153] They had to 'make people realise that these Russian children, starving and dying, are essentially the same as our own', as *The Record* put it.[154] Accordingly, ordinary Russians were portrayed as 'brave, simple, splendid folk' who carried out relief work as best they could and were no Bolsheviks.[155] Hoover himself stated on several occasions that the Russian people could not be blamed, nor should they suffer, for the mistakes of their government.[156]

---

[147] White to Baker, 28 Oct. 1921, ARA, reel 500. See also Rickard to Hoover, 16 Dec. 1921, ARA, reel 115, and Tapley to Hoover, 9 Dec. 1921, ARA, reel 504.
[148] Patenaude, *Big Show*, 140–1.   [149] McFadden and Gorfinkel, *Constructive Spirit*, 73.
[150] Vogt, *Nansens Kamp*, 56–8.   [151] Patenaude, *Big Show*, 8.
[152] For opposition to the ARA, see e.g., Fisher, *Famine in Soviet Russia*, 149. For the SCF, Mahood and Satzewich, 'Save the Children Fund', and Breen, 'Saving Enemy Children'. For a similar Norwegian case, see Carl Emil Vogt, '"Først vore egne!" Da Aftenposten saboterte Nansens nødhjelp til Russland', *Historisk Tidsskrift* 108, no. 1 (2008): 29–59.
[153] Mahood and Satzewich, 'Save the Children Fund', 64.
[154] F. A. Mc Kenzie, 'Little Mother – The Heart of a Russian Child', *The Record* 2, no. 15 (1922).
[155] Philip Gibbs, 'Russia's Hungry Christmas', *The Record* 2, no. 7 (1921).
[156] Hoover to Rickard, 14 Nov. 1922; Telegram, draft by Hoover, 16 Nov. 1922. Both ARA, reel 389.

However, even if those starving were Bolsheviks, many humanitarians were convinced that political considerations must not play a role in alleviating a famine. Nansen rhetorically asked his critics whether it would be worth letting twenty million people starve to death in order to avoid strengthening the Soviet regime.[157] SCF co-founder Jebb even admitted that relief tended to benefit the Soviet government because the 'indirect result of relief is to ... stabilise the existing order', but like Nansen she asked whether this would be reason enough to let millions of Russian children die.[158] An article in *The Record* at the time argued that 'it is a detestable and frigid charity that refuses to stretch out a hand to save those who differ in politics or religion from itself'. Nevertheless, the criticism had an effect, and many appeals concentrated initially on the least controversial group, Russian children. As the article stated, those children are 'no more Bolshevik than you and I are'.[159] Both the SCF and the ARA kept emphasising that all food would reach the children, that no Red Army soldier would profit thereby, and that those on the ground providing relief would immediately leave the country if the smallest part of the aid was diverted from the children.[160]

In addition, relief organisations, except for communist ones, largely avoided speculation about the causes of the famine. If reasons for the famine were discussed at all, it was described as a natural catastrophe that came to the Russian people 'not through their fault or the fault of others'.[161] Possible human factors, such as Soviet policies or the blockade imposed by the Western Powers, were brushed aside to avoid controversy.[162] In one of the few cases where the question of guilt was mentioned in *The Record*, the author tried to create a balanced picture in which both sides were to blame:

While it may be true that misgovernment has aggravated the effects of the famine, it must be remembered that it is primarily due to the war, the blockade and the drought of last year, for which the Russian people are in no way responsible, and in any case this furnishes no ground for allowing the population to die while we carefully apportion the blame for their death.[163]

This narrative absolving the Russian government of blame was necessary as co-operation with Russian authorities was essential for relief work to succeed. In order to describe the Russians – even communists – as deserving benefi- ciaries, Russian institutions were praised for their willingness to co-operate

---

[157] Nansen, cited in Cabanes, *Great War*, 194.
[158] Cited in Clare Mulley, *The Woman Who Saved the Children: A Biography of Eglantyne Jebb, Founder of Save the Children* (Oxford: Oneworld, 2009), 291.
[159] Mc Kenzie, 'Little Mother'.
[160] 'Politics and Charity', *The Record* 2, no. 2 (1921); Philip Gibbs, 'Russia's Hungry Christmas', *The Record* 2, no. 7 (1921); Telegram, draft by Hoover, 16. Nov. 1922, ARA, reel 389.
[161] Mc Kenzie, 'Little Mother'.   [162] Mahood and Satzewich, 'Save the Children Fund', 60.
[163] 'The Fruit of the Tree', *The Record* 2, no. 17 (1922).

and conflicts were downplayed. In addition, it was underlined that the Russians had not passively submitted to their fate, but that the government and the population heroically fought the famine. ARA, SCF, the Quakers, and especially the WIR emphasised Russian relief efforts and their co-operative spirit in articles and appeals. Well-organised children's hospitals, the exemplary work of Russian volunteers and employees, domestic fundraising efforts, the distribution of crop seeds by the government, and similar Russian initiatives were highlighted to Western audiences.[164] Internally, however, criticisms about the lack of Russian assistance, their inadequate work ethic, and a cumbersome bureaucracy were widespread, especially within the ARA.[165]

Mixed Emotions: Children, Horrors, and Holidays

By 1920, children had become the 'quintessential humanitarian subject' and 'descriptions and depictions of children's bodies were closely linked to humanitarian appeals' (see Figures 3.4, and 3.5).[166] The innocent child as a victim had become a humanitarian means to an end, as it exemplified both the horrors of wars and catastrophes as well as the hope for a better future.[167] Consequently, not only the SCF, but the ARA and affiliated organisations, as well as several Red Cross societies, spoke exclusively about children in their first public commitments and appeals. A European campaign by artists and writers, supported by the WIR and Nansen, ran under the slogan 'For Our Little Russian Brothers', and even the FSR asked its audience to answer 'the cry of children whose fathers died by bullets supplied to the counter-revolutionary ... by American, British and French imperialists'.[168]

To evoke maximum feelings of pity, descriptions of needy children were often embellished with hyperbole. For example, children were said to have 'hands like claws' and 'only their big dark, wondering eyes give any indication of the childish beauty gone forever'.[169] An early SCF report depicted the

---

[164] Mahood and Satzewich, 'Save the Children Fund', 64–5; Edward Fuller, 'Real Life in Russia (part 2, Saratov)', *The Record* 2, no. 5 (1921); 'How Russia Helps Herself', *The Record* 2, no. 4 (1921); 'The Russian Famine – Mr. Laurence Webster's experience', *The Record* 2, no. 3 (1921); 'Work of the International Russian Relief Committee', 4; 'The ARA Russian Operation at Glance', paper by Communication Division, 9 May 1923, ARA, reel 548; Hoover to Harding, 9 Feb. 1922, in Fisher, *Famine in Soviet Russia*, 543–7, 545.

[165] See, e.g., Quinn to New York, 28 Dec. 1922, ARA, reel 496; Brown to Rickard, 14 Mar. 1922, ARA, reel 548; ARA report titled 'Troubles', undated (probably late 1922), signed HHF, ARA, reel 496; Patenaude, *Big Show*, 565–7.

[166] Gill, 'Rational Administration', 26; Kind-Kovács, 'Great War', 38.

[167] Kind-Kovács, 'Great War'; Marshall, 'Construction of Children'; Weidling, 'From Sentiment to Science'.

[168] Bienz, *Für unsere Kleinen Russischen Brüder* (in French: *Pour nos petits frères russes*); FSR pamphlet 'They Are Knocking at Your Door', ARA, reel 115.

[169] 'News from Relief Areas', *The Record* 2, no. 5 (1921).

Figure 3.4 *Russia Restituenda* (Russia Must Recover), 1922.
Poster by Czech artist Alfons Maria Mucha. Used as a plea to help starving Russian children. Courtesy of Buyenlarge/Getty Images

situation in a children's home as follows: 'Little cots each containing a little shrivelled form, its eyes staring out of a head which seemed nothing more than skin stretched tightly over a skull, with a little mouth that gasped out a mute appeal for help, as a fish gasps for breath when taken out of water.'[170]

Texts like these led to criticism that the SCF was making 'capital out of popular emotions'. However, an article in *The Record* readily conceded that this was the intention. Helping others, the author claimed, was a primitive instinct and charities in general, and the SCF especially, capitalised on this instinct.[171] Individuals and groups from Russia used this strategy as well, and thrust themselves upon their Western addressees with descriptions of cannibalism, suicide, and murder, hoping this would open their hearts and purses.[172]

---

[170] Edward Fuller, 'Real Life in Russia (part 2, Saratov)', *The Record* 2, no. 5 (1921).
[171] 'The New Charity', *The Record* 2, no. 8 (1922).
[172] Tzaritzin Union of School Teachers to ARA, undated, ARA, reel 499.

Figure 3.5 Screenshot of the pamphlet *Jewish Life Here and There – Some Pictures and a Few Facts* by the Federation of Ukrainian Jews, London, 1922.
American Relief Administration Russian operational records, Box 92, Folder 3, Hoover Institution Archives

Photos and postcards, often depicting children in dire need, were widely circulated, mostly with a calculated shock effect.[173] In articles and pamphlets, pictures of children were also used to illustrate a before–after development, a humanitarian strategy that was already some decades old, showing the effects of the feeding programme, as well as providing a here–there contrast between children in the West and in Russia (see Figure 3.5).[174] For the SCF, campaigning and propaganda were embedded in public relations programmes and often designed by mass media experts. The cornerstones of effective communication were 'originality in announcements, designs, speeches', 'simplicity and clearness', and constant repetition. As in the advertising industry, it was considered

[173] For an example, see 'Les deux étapes de la faim', a postcard photograph of two starving children, probably taken by Nansen himself, part of a larger set issued to raise funds, available at upload.wikimedia.org/wikipedia/commons/0/05/Fridtjof_Nansen%2C_Les_deux_étapes_de_la_faim_%281922%29.jpg (accessed 29 July 2019). Other examples are in Patenaude, *Big Show*, 324–7. The FSR also used Nansen's pictures. See *The Russian Famine [Pictures – Appeals]* (New York: FSR, c. 1922, hereafter cited as FSR, *Pictures – Appeals*) and *Matrix Service* (New York: FSR, c. 1922).

[174] For the history of this visual strategy, see Fehrenbach, 'Children and Other Civilians', 179.

'necessary to strike the same nail and to strike for a long time in order to drive it in deeply into the consciousness of the unknowing crowd'.[175] However, it was realised at the time that the adoption of business methods could raise ethical problems. An article by the noted author and playwright Israel Zangwill ridiculed this development by presenting charity slogans like 'Try our cheap charity – Certified pyre', 'Ten thousand war orphans – guaranteed genuine', and 'Good deeds at a unique discount'.[176] Ruth Fry, head of the Friends' Emergency and War Victims Relief Committee (FEWVRC), viewed the increasing influence of public relations techniques on the humanitarian sector sceptically. For Quakers, she suggested, 'relief is propaganda'. However, as this propaganda was a reflection of fieldwork rather than a public relations effort, it remained 'free from the sting and stigma it would have had, had it been undertaken of set purpose'.[177] Fry's moral concerns seem to have had little practical impact: like the SCF, the FEWVRC hired publicity staff and acknowledged the correlation between advertising expenditures and income.[178]

Like the SCF, the ARA knew that providing businesslike relief was not enough to win public goodwill, and that propaganda had to deal with 'human suffering ... as emotional arguments have greater carrying power ... than scientific or statistical analysis'.[179] The ARA press department was, therefore, eager to receive usable information from the famine front.[180]

The medium of film became part of the campaign, and the SCF, ARA, ICRR, Quakers, and FSR produced films or documentary clips that were shown to a broader public and during fundraising events.[181] However, it seems that the SCF alone was wholeheartedly convinced by the medium. They

---

[175] 'The International Movement', *The Record* 1, no. 10 (1921). The article originally appeared in the ISCU journal *Feuilles de Propagande*, no. 3, 30 Mar. 1921.
[176] Israel Zangwill, 'Bargains in Beneficence', *The Record* 1, no. 14 (1921).
[177] Ruth Fry, 'The Relation of Relief to Propaganda', *Friends' Quarterly Examiner* 57 (1923): 322–35.
[178] Kelly, *British Humanitarian Activity*, 194–5.
[179] Fisher to Rickard, 1 July 1922, ARA, reel 549.
[180] Mayer to Wilkinson, 9 May 1922, ARA, reel 549.
[181] Both the ARA and the Red Cross had some experience with this medium by the 1920s. See Cabanes, *Great War*, 220; Daniel Palmieri, 'Humanitarianism on the Screen: The ICRC Films, 1921–1965', in *Humanitarianism & Media, 1900 to the Present*, ed. Johannes Paulmann (New York: Berghahn, 2019), 90–106. The SCF film was called *Famine: A Glimpse of the Misery in the Province of Saratov,* or in other versions simply *The Russian Famine of 1921*. See Leaflet for Famine Movie, undated, SCF, reel 33, and Cabanes, *Great War*, 221. The material was also modified and used by the ICRR and Soviet authorities. The film is partially available at https:// avarchives.icrc.org/Film/5449 (accessed 29 June 2019). For the Quaker film *New Worlds for the Old: Quaker Relief in Stricken Europe*, see Minutes of meeting of executive, Buzuluk, 27 Oct.1922, FEWVRC 7/3/1/1. The FSR film was entitled *Russia through the Shadows*. See Charles Evan Hughes to Hoover, 7 Feb. 1923, and FSR to Department of Education, Ohio, 3 Jan. 1923; both ARA, reel 115.

adopted the motto 'Seeing Is Believing' and put great efforts into promoting their famine movie. An article in *The Record* suggested that the film aroused 'emotions akin to those engendered by an autopsy' among members of the audience. Moreover, the camera provided 'incontrovertible evidence of the ravages of the famine' and proved all those who had denied its death toll and criticised the work of the SCF wrong. Those who nevertheless still doubted were said to be 'deliberately condemning them [the children] to death'.[182] However, the direct financial return of the famine film was disappointing, and the SCF admitted that at many screenings only a handful of viewers were present.[183] The ARA, on the other hand, remained sceptical regarding the effectiveness of films as a fundraising tool. Its director general, Edgar Rickard, pointed out that 'the history of our film ventures, starting with Belgium relief, have as far as I know produced nothing but anxiety'.[184]

The coverage of the famine was especially evident during Christmas and Easter, when headlines full of pathos dominated the newspapers.[185] Holiday drives often included here-and-there comparisons, contrasting Western abundance with Russian deprivation (see also Figure 3.5): 'As I look into the crowded shops [in London] I think of thousands of villages, very silent in a snow-covered land, where there will be no Christmas feast but only the moaning of the peasant families sitting at empty boards or lying down to die. Some of these I saw a week or two ago must now be dead.'[186] Even the ARA, otherwise reluctant to issue any kind of appeal, took the opportunity to encourage US citizens to buy food remittances as Christmas gifts. The organisers hoped doing so would widen the donor community, as 'the actual saving of lives at Christmas will appeal to many charitable Americans having no relatives or friends in Russia'.[187]

In the end, not even the communist FSR could afford to refrain from mounting an appeal. Among other things, it organised a 'Nation-Wide Holiday Drive',[188] sold Christmas stamps, and organised a campaign called 'A Million Meals for a Million Russian Orphans This Christmas' to collect one million

---

[182] 'Seeing Is Believing'. See also Kurasawa, 'Making of Humanitarian Visual Icons', 79.

[183] 'The Famine Film and the Future of Europe', *The Record* 2, no. 12 (1922).

[184] Rickard to Herter, 7 Apr. 1922, ARA, reel 549. See also Bertrand Patenaude, 'Shooting the Bolsheviks', *Hoover's Digest*, no. 2 (2012), available at www.hoover.org/research/shooting-bolsheviks (accessed 29 June 2019).

[185] Breen, 'Saving Enemy Children', 227; 'Can You Listen Unmoved to the Easter Death Dirge of Starving Children?', *Glasgow Herald*, 13 Apr. 1922.

[186] 'Russia's Hungry Christmas', *The Record* 2, no. 7 (1921).

[187] Cablegram from Haskell to Head Office, 8 Dec. 1921, ARA, reel 389. See also redraft of letter to contributors to the ARA by Hoover, undated (probably mid-Dec. 1921), ARA, reel 389, and Hoover's Appeal to the Federal Council of the Churches of Christ in America, 2 Dec. 1921, ARA, reel 11.

[188] FSR, 'Nation-Wide Holiday Drive for the Famine Stricken of Soviet Russia, 15 Dec. 1921 – 1 Jan. 1922', ARA, reel 115.

dimes, representing an equal number of meals, for which every donor received a 'handsome certificate'.[189] Despite many similarities, the slogans used by communist organisations sometimes differed from those of other agencies. Even during holiday campaigns, they did not fail to refer to the international class struggle: 'At Christmas, profiteers buy pearl necklaces for their mistresses, but the class conscious worker makes a gift of food for his starving Russian comrades.'[190] In addition, socialist holidays, like the anniversary of the October Revolution, were used to advantage for fundraising purposes.[191]

Self-interest as a Fundraising Strategy

Another way of coping with the 'helping the enemy' dilemma was to minimise the altruistic dimension of relief and stress that national and individual self-interest was served by helping Soviet Russia. Nansen justified Norway's governmental aid in a statement to the Assembly of the League of Nations in Geneva by suggesting Russian relief would contribute to the economic stabilisation of war-ridden Europe. In the end, he alleged, it was not 'humanitarian sentiment' but 'cold economic importance' that determined the Norwegian government's actions in this question.[192] A conference organised by the International Committee of the Red Cross in Berlin in December 1921 passed a resolution embodying a similar notion, namely, that the world economy depended on the restoration of Russian markets and production.[193]

Hoover was an outspoken anti-Bolshevik, but since the ARA relied on public funding, he emphasised US self-interest as being served by famine relief, which he described as an 'act of economic soundness'.[194] When lobbying for congressional funding, he argued that buying grain would stabilise the market and thereby help US farmers. 'Helping ourselves helps others' was President Warren Harding's summary of this idea in a speech on Russian relief in December 1921.[195] However, this strategy allowed Russian leaders to understate the altruistic dimension of Western help and their own debt of

---

[189] 'FSR Activities', *Soviet Russia* 7, no. 11 (1922).
[190] 'Famine Relief by the Workers', *Soviet Russia* 6, no. 4 (1922).
[191] FSR, *The Russian Famine: Forty Facts* (New York: FSR, c. 1922), 4.
[192] *League of Nations, Official Journal*, Aug. 1922, Annex 385. Statement presented to the Council 22 July 1922 by Representative of Norwegian Government.
[193] 'Un appel de la conférence international de Berlin, 4 Dec. 1921', *Société Russe de la Croix-Rouge Bulletin*, no. 5, 15 Dec. 1921.
[194] Hoover's testimony before the Senate Foreign Relation Committee, Dec. 1922, as cited by Patenaude, *Big Show*, 638.
[195] 'President Talks to Restore Normal Basis', *Wall Street Journal*, 7 Dec. 1921. On the debate in Congress see Barry Riley, *The Political History of American Food Aid: An Uneasy Benevolance* (Oxford: Oxford University Press, 2017), 63–7.

gratitude, depicting food aid as a capitalist endeavour.[196] When the humanitarian enterprise in Soviet Russia reached its peak in 1922, Leon Trotsky stated that 'philanthropy is tied to business, to enterprises, to interests – if not today, then tomorrow'.[197] Trotsky's depiction of humanitarian aid as donor driven is shared by many modern commentators.[198]

Even relief organisations with a more cosmopolitan and altruistic profile, like the SCF, used economic reasoning in their campaign, arguing that if Russia were to enter world markets again, unemployment at home would be reduced.[199] Relief for Russia therefore appeared as 'an investment rather than an expenditure', and it was further claimed that 'no [other] investment would bring so great a return'.[200] Although pursuing spiritual aims, the Papal Relief Mission was in a way also investment-oriented. Current research confirms the claims of contemporary critics that its efforts were guided by the hope of reclaiming ground it had lost to the Orthodox Church, rather than simply by benevolence as such.[201]

To critics wary of stabilising an enemy regime, Hoover replied that the ARA campaign was not about helping a Bolshevik country, but about helping a country that anticipated a regime change in the near future. The relief campaign would contribute to this by securing the good will of the Russian people. Hoover believed that relief for Soviet Russia was the most effective way to halt the 'Bolshevik disease' from spreading into Europe, and perhaps even heal Russia herself of it. US relief would enhance democracy and give the USA an advantage over Europe in future competition for untouched Russian markets.[202] For Hoover, in the long run, gratitude and the resulting moral credit was a political means to an end, which is why the ARA took measures to ensure that recipients knew their food came from the USA.

The rhetoric urging the West to counter the spread of a disease was also meant literally. Labour MP George Nicoll Barnes, in a parliamentary debate about British governmental aid, warned that 'disease stalked behind hunger and cold', it being the government's responsibility 'to stop that westward march'.[203] The SCF reminded its compatriots that ignoring the famine was not an option, as 'even Britain's geographical insularity would not preserve her

---

[196] 'The Famine and the International Situation, Material for Agitators by the Central Agitation Comission to Combat the Famine of the Central Committee of the Russian Comunist Party', undated translation by the ARA (probably Sept. 1921), ARA, reel 14; 'On the Volga', translation of an article in *Izvestia*, 11 Aug. 1922, ibid.
[197] As cited by Patenaude, *Big Show*, 639.
[198] Vaux, *Selfish Altruist*; de Waal, *Famine Crimes*.
[199] 'British Unemployed and Starving Russians', *The Record* 2, no. 19 (1922).
[200] 'Work and Doles', *The Record* 2, no. 19 (1922) (first quotation); 'In Parliament', *The Record* 2, no. 14 (1922) (second quotation). See also Meredith Atkinson, 'Impressions that Remain – A Glimpse of Russia's Agony', *The Record* 2, no. 13 (1922).
[201] Gribble, 'Cooperation and Conflict', 652; Trythall, 'Russia's Misfortune', 79–80.
[202] Gribble, 'Cooperation and Conflict', 341.   [203] 'In Parliament'.

from the possibility of a scourge analogous to the Black Death of the four-teenth century'.[204] The German Red Cross likewise justified providing relief to Soviet Russia so that a cholera epidemic might not spread to German territory. Consequently, its efforts were concentrated on medical relief.[205]

Motivating and legitimising famine relief on the basis of self-interest caused a sense of unease, especially in the SCF and among the Quakers. Hoover was also warned by a US senator to 'not dilute our generosity with any selfish purposes'.[206] A major article in *The Record* stated that it was depressing to read constant appeals to economic self-interest. It might well be 'that men are unemployed in England because Saratov is starving', but if we let the Russians perish, the author argued, we will suffer greater losses than potential economic markets: 'then we shall be killing our own humanity within us, and we shall soon show the signs of it in increasing brutality, in social misery and in personal desolation'. Such reasoning downplayed empathy for the hungry and stressed psychological well-being of the donors. The crucial issue was no longer that millions were dying, but that 'others are willing to let them die'. A people who would let this happen were seen as 'morally doomed'.[207] The images of starving Russians, a fundraiser warned, would pursue those unwilling to give 'like a remorse' for the rest of their lives.[208]

This change of perspective towards the donor also prevailed when relief agencies invoked a nation's reputation. Some organisations, like the Imperial War Relief Fund (IWRF), employed a nationalist rhetoric in which altruism was presented as a genuinely British trait. In such a context, even donations benefitting former enemies could be exalted as acts of true patriotism, demonstrating the nobility of the British race.[209] Similarly, the ARA suggested to its donors that their aid was carrying 'American ideals' to the Russians.[210]

For smaller nations, participation in international relief offered an opportunity to demonstrate their sovereignty and gain foreign prestige.[211] Lord Robert Cecil of the IWRF considered it humiliating that Britain was being surpassed, not only by the USA, but by her former colonies, Canada and New Zealand, when it came to providing government funds for Russian relief. In like manner, the German Red Cross observed that Germany could hardly stand by while the whole civilised world was sending relief.[212] Afterwards,

[204] 'Eyes ... but See Not', *The Record* 2, no. 9 (1922).
[205] Braskén, *International Workers' Relief*, 35; Wolfgang U. Eckart, 'Nach bestem Vermögen tatkräftige Hilfe leisten', *Ruperto Carola* 3 (1999).
[206] As cited by Patenaude, *Big Show*, 638.
[207] 'The Famine Film and the Future of Europe', *The Record* 2, no. 12 (1922). See also 'Russia's Hungry Christmas', *The Record* 2, no. 7 (1921).
[208] Cited in Kurasawa, 'Making of Humanitarian Visual Icons', 69.
[209] Baughan, 'Imperial War Relief Fund'.
[210] Stutesman to Sutter, 1 June 1922, ARA, reel 502; Stutesman to Rev. George Batt, 31 Aug. 1922, ARA, reel 502.
[211] Baughan, 'Imperial War Relief Fund'.   [212] Braskén, *International Workers' Relief*, 35.

that country's commitment would be praised as illustrative of the 'German willingness to make sacrifices'.[213]

The SCF showed that an impartial and international agenda did not rule out patriotic orientation, and it agreed with the IWRF that voluntary relief organisations had taken the lead for Britain in Russia. A visitor to the famine region stated in *The Record* that the SCF was upholding British esteem while the government did nothing. Viewing SCF's accomplishments filled him 'with pride in the British race'. The same spirit that made the British people such great colonisers of Australia, Canada, and New Zealand, he continued, was now enabling them 'to colonize in another sense the frozen steppes of Russia'.[214] Liberal MP Isaac Foot even invoked a military analogy by referring to SCF and the Quakers as quasi-imperial troops: 'I understand that in time of war the first concern is for the outposts. I ask the Government to consider whether we have not in Saratov an outpost, which ought to be assisted, and it will be a shameful humiliation if we withdraw our forces.'[215] Accordingly, the All-British Appeal, in which the SCF, the FEWVRC, and the IWRF participated, claimed that donating was a 'national duty' as 'our honour as a nation is involved'.[216] Even the FSR responded to what amounted to a contest over a nation's reputation. In a letter appealing for donations to support children's homes in Russia, the FSR urged that since similar homes were already being financed by Dutch and German workers, American labourers, with their higher salaries, should be able to do the same.[217]

In general, relief organisations attempted to blend altruistic and pragmatic motivation in order to draw in large groups of potential donors. Helping children was teaching them how 'to love Britain', the claim went. Someday, *The Record* suggested, when these children become grown-ups with political influence, they will remember that it was the British people who helped them.[218] Lord Weardale, chairman of the Executive Committee of the SCF, cited individual suffering and drew a still broader picture: 'Children are the raw material of the League of Nations and while we care for the individual sufferer ... it is rather as a potential father of the race, a citizen of the future, that we seek to save him.' For Weardale, SCF's work was 'constructive as well as palliative'.[219]

[213] Peter Mühlens, *Die Russische Hunger- und Seuchenkatastrophe in den Jahren 1921–22* (Springer: Berlin, 1923), iv.
[214] 'Angliski kuchnia', *The Record* 2, no. 14 (1922).   [215] 'In Parliament'.
[216] Benjamin Robertson, *The Famine in Russia: Report* (London: The Russian Famine Relief Fund, 1922), 14.
[217] 'Soviet Russia Calls', FSR, s.a., ARA, reel 115.
[218] 'Politics and Charity', *The Record* 2, no. 2 (1921); Mahood and Satzewich, 'Save the Children Fund', 8.
[219] Lord Weardale, 'The To-Morrow of Society', *The Record* 1, no. 3 (1920).

The JDC had similar ideas about influencing societal developments and earmarked a portion of their aid for Russian doctors. Lewis Strauss, who had previously worked for Hoover, insisted in a letter to the ARA that recipients should be informed that aid came from a Jewish organisation, as 'it may create a certain amount of good will among a cultured and intelligent group of Russians toward their Jewish fellow citizens'.[220]

Sometimes the narrative anticipating a positive future if aid were provided was complemented by dystopian horror scenarios of help denied. Matching Hoover's argument that communism was caused by desperation and famine, Weardale pointed out to a critic that hunger promotes hatred, and that letting enemy children starve and degenerate would only harm British interests in the long run.[221] A Jewish-American relief organisation asked rhetorically whether famine survivors should be 'left to grow into a race of demoniac men and women, burning with hatred, replete with the instinct of savagery, cherishing only revenge, rebellion and fear'.[222] Thus, feeding Russian children, the SCF argued, was 'warding off the otherwise inevitable revenge'.[223]

Obligation to Give

'You must give!! Thousands will freeze and starve to death unless you help right now!!'[224] This appeal launched by the FSR, with its deadly alternative, entails a strong obligation. The line between requesting and demanding donations is blurred. Relief organisations have often stretched such limits. Suggesting a moral obligation to give while simultaneously making people feel guilty has always been a fundraising technique. Detailed descriptions of harm, misery, disease, and individual suffering, combined with the insinuation of direct or indirect responsibility, seek to morally force potential donors to act and make it hard for them to remain passive.

Even before the Russian operation began, Zangwill had pointed out that 'charity is a cloak to cover sins' – a cloak bitterly needed, as Western actions and inactions had doomed millions of children to die. The money being donated at the time, he wrote, was for that reason 'not so much alms as blood money', similar to the restitution that archaic religious codes required for murder. However, as this modern form of blood money was paid voluntarily, it might erase the crimes of the past and lead to the reconciliation of peoples.[225]

---

[220] Strauss, JDC, to Page, 16 Dec. 1921, ARA, reel 500.
[221] Lord Weardale, undated (probably autumn 1920), SCF, reel 30.
[222] 'Some Pictures and a Few Facts', undated, ARA, reel 115.
[223] Zangwill, 'Bargains in Beneficence'.   [224] FSR, 'Nation-Wide Holiday Drive'.
[225] Zangwill, 'Bargains in Beneficence'.

The purported obligation to give arose in many cases from religious or ethnic kinship between donors and beneficiaries. The London-based Federation of Ukrainian Jews (FUJ) urged its members to donate (successfully, as the ARA noted) by stressing 'These are *your* people, bound to you by the sacred bonds of blood and faith, and you must assume the responsibility of helping them!'[226] Swedish collections for compatriots in Ukrainian Gammalsvenskby, Mennonite relief for coreligionists in Russia, German Red Cross campaigns for Volga German settlements, and Turkish donations for Crimean Muslims were motivated by similar arguments.[227] However, exploiting the in-group mechanism was not limited to ethnic and religious communities. For example, in March 1922, Russian Boy Scouts urged their US counterparts 'to demonstrate their fidelity to the Boy Scouts law' by sending food.[228] Many group appeals from Russia were similarly based on solidarity and directed towards foreigners with the same occupation.

Obligations could also be created in other ways. The SCF's kitchen system, which was the instrumentality of their food provision in Russia, was in part developed to ensure the continuous influx of money. The maintenance of their own distribution structure was supposed to bind donors to a concrete aid project over a longer period and thereby generate more permanent funding.[229] Individuals, groups, local SCF committees, private companies, and schools who contributed £100 or more had feeding kitchens in Russia named after them. In addition, donor's names and amounts were published in *The Record* under the banner 'The Hundred Pound Roll of Honour'.[230] Donors received information from *their* kitchen, such as photos, numbers of children fed, the amount and kinds of food distributed, and individual stories. The system created personal bonds and the feeling that a particular kitchen depended on a specific donor, rather than on general relief. Advertisements stated that 100 children could be fed for twenty weeks on £100. A letter was generally sent to donors before the period covered by their contribution was about to

---

[226] FUJ appeal 'Spare Them a Garment', ARA, reel 115.

[227] Documents regarding Gammalsvenskby are available at www.gammalsvenskby.se/NSoderblom1932.htm (accessed 29 June 2018); P.C. Hiebert and Orie O. Miller, *Feeding the Hungry: Russian Famine 1919–1925, American Mennonite Relief Operations under the Auspices of Mennonite Central Committee* (Scottdale, PA: Mennonite Central Committee, 1929); Paul Weindling, *Epidemics and Genocide in Eastern Europe, 1890–1945* (Oxford: Oxford University Press, 2000), 173–8; Hakan Kirimli, 'The Famine of 1921–22 in the Crimea and the Volga Basin and the Relief from Turkey', *Middle Eastern Studies* 39, no. 1 (2003): 37–88.

[228] Beloretzk Boy Scouts to Boy Scouts of America, 9 Mar. 1922, ARA, reel 498.

[229] 'Cheap Publicity', *The Record* 2, no. 5 (1921).

[230] See for example, 'Links with Saratov – The Hundred Pound Roll of Honour', *The Record* 2, no. 8 (1922), and *The Record* 2, no. 10 (1922). Installment plans were also offered (see 'A Suggestion to Public Schools', *The Record* 2, no. 9 (1922), and 'SCF Kitchen Contact Scheme', *Daily Telegraph*, 25 Nov. 1921).

end. A draft of this letter (which was probably not used) literally put children's lives in the donor's hands:

The amount you subscribed for the maintenance of a kitchen in Saratov has now run out. For twenty weeks 100 children have received a nourishing meal daily by your gift. . . . I am writing to ask whether you would find it possible to keep your kitchen open for a further period. If we cannot continue to feed the children preserved so far from an otherwise inevitable death from starvation they will certainly die.[231]

The addressee was not left with much choice. In a later internal document, an SCF fundraiser confined that she had told donors 'the money they have previously spent will have been wasted, unless they can make a further effort', an argument that was also used during campaigns in mid- and late 1922.[232] Hence, an initial donation was nurtured into a moral obligation to give more, suddenly placing someone who had previously donated under greater moral pressure to contribute than a person who had given nothing. However, the SCF soon realised that this was a problematic approach. The formulation was modified in a second draft in which the donor was invited to renew the commitment, but also assured that, in any case, the SCF would do its 'utmost to find new supporters who will carry on your kitchen'.[233]

Professional fundraising entailed costs, a fact that was often withheld from the public, although it sometimes became part of the appeal itself. An FSR solicitation opened with the declaration that the cost of writing and sending this letter was the equivalent of two meals for a Russian child. If they ignored the letter, addressees were chided for having 'taken away from a tattered little hungry orphan two nourishing meals'. Consequently, the least one could do was to reimburse the FSR for its costs, that is, make a small donation, for 'surely it shall not be said that you deprive any starving child of food'.[234]

Individuals used similar tactics in appealing for aid. In April 1922, a Russian teacher wrote to the ARA, asking for a loan or donation. Among other things, he offered to pay in collectible Russian stamps, some of which he enclosed. He probably hoped that ignoring the letter would be difficult for the addressee, who would feel a certain obligation upon receiving it. He wrote that he knew the ARA could not deal with individuals when millions were starving, but nevertheless expressed hope for 'a small exception'.[235] The sender, who had made every effort to prevent his letter from getting lost in the flood of appeals,

---

[231] Draft of a form letter, undated, SCF, reel 30.
[232] SCF, reel 30; 'To-day and To-morrow in Russia', *The Record* 2, no. 20 (1922).
[233] 'Draft letter for expiring kitchens (2nd edition), 24 Apr. 1922', SCF, reel 30.
[234] FSR, appeal letter, undated, ARA reel 115.
[235] Konovaloff to ARA, Apr. 1922, ARA, reel 500.

was successful, as a member of the ARA staff personally paid for five food parcels that were sent to him.[236]

The moral obligation to give could also be inferred from prior actions. When unsuccessfully lobbying for £500,000 in government aid, MP Isaac Foot reminded his colleagues that Britain had spent £100 million for war in Russia, but was now refusing to supply 'one two-hundredth part of that sum to sustain these people, most of them whom are frail women and weak children'.[237] The communist FSR used a similar approach when calculating that the 'exploiting class' invested the 'stupendous sum of $260,680,000,000 to kill fifteen million men, to cripple twenty million more, and to ruin Europe industrially', equalling '2,606 times the amount of money required to save the 20,000,000 famine stricken Russians'.[238] Previous deeds could also work in a positive way, as when in February 1922 the Polish government wanted to show Hoover its 'deep gratitude' for ARA relief in previous years by opening up the port of Gdansk and transporting up to 15,000 t of relief goods per month from there to the Russian border free of charge.[239]

Solidarity, Not Charity

The situation for communist organisations like the WIR and the FSR differed from that of other relief organisations, as it implied an unprecedented interplay of humanitarianism and international class politics.[240] As a result, it was Lenin's 'Appeal to the International Proletariat' of 6 August 1921, rather than Gorky's letter to the American and European people three weeks earlier, that initiated relief efforts and led directly to the establishment of the WIR and its national chapters. Lenin blamed Western states for having caused the famine and accused them of 'planning a fresh campaign, intervention, and counter-revolutionary conspiracies'.[241]

For this reason, he only asked industrial workers and small farmers for help. WIR appeals consequently invoked workers' solidarity (see Figure 3.6) and were framed as part of an international class struggle. A campaign in France, for example, ran under the slogan 'We have worked all our life for our capitalist masters. Let us work one day [per month] for the benefit of our brothers dying on the Volga.'[242]

---

[236] 'I am willing to risk 50 dollars on this correspondent.' Julius H. Barnes to Dailey, 28 Apr. 1922, ARA, reel 500.
[237] 'In Parliament'.   [238] FSR, *Pictures – Appeals*, 11.
[239] ARA press release, 8 Feb. 1922, ARA, reel 548.
[240] Braskén, *International Workers' Relief*, 39.
[241] Lenin's appeal is reproduced at www.marxists.org/archive/lenin/works/1921/aug/02.htm (accessed 29 June 2019).
[242] 'Famine Relief by the Workers'.

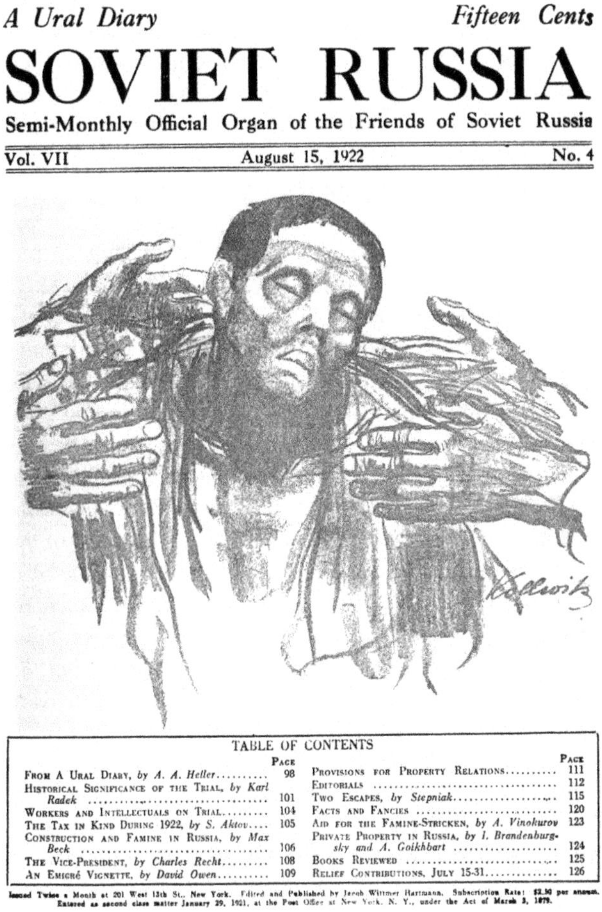

A Ural Diary   *Fifteen Cents*

SOVIET RUSSIA

Semi-Monthly Official Organ of the Friends of Soviet Russia

Vol. VII	August 15, 1922	No. 4

Issued Twice a Month at 201 West 13th St., New York. Edited and Published by Jacob Wittmer Hartmann. Subscription Rate: $2.50 per annum. Entered as second class matter January 29, 1921, at the Post Office at New York, N. Y., under the Act of March 3, 1879.

Figure 3.6 Cover of Friends of Soviet Russia publication with lithograph *Helft Russland* (Help Russia) by Käthe Kollwitz, *Soviet Russia*, 15 Aug. 1922.
Original from University of California, Google-digitised, public domain

Nevertheless, although they differed in content and vocabulary, appeals by the FSR and WIR show many similarities regarding general motivational techniques to those of non-socialist organisations. Their campaigns suggested that workers' donations would serve their own self-interest, because Soviet Russia was not an ethnic nation, but a state based on class affiliation. In this context, class was equated with kinship and Russians were described as 'blood of your blood because they belong to your class'.[243] Fighting the famine would not only help Russians, but would destroy the hopes of the global bourgeoisie. FSR appeals suggested that whatever US workers would do for their Russian comrades today, the latter would reciprocate tomorrow. Moreover, as Russian workers had fought and died in the October Revolution for the 'ultimate freedom of all workers from wage-slavery', an unpaid debt existed that created an obligation to give on the side of workers elsewhere, and a claim to solidarity on the side of Russian workers.[244]

Like the SCF, the FSR encouraged activists to launch fundraising collections on their own, and detailed instructions were given on how to proceed when approaching potential donors.[245] Similarly, the mainstream slogan in such solicitation was that 'The future is built upon children.' In the case of the FSR, however, donations were sought to make sure that the coming generations would defend the world's first communist state against its enemies. Thus, the FSR was dealing far less diplomatically with the guilt question than other aid agencies; it openly blamed the West for exploiting the calamity, if not for causing it, by refusing Russia credit. Moreover, in accordance with the ideology of class struggle, it was stated that famine orphans 'suffer today because famine-relief was withheld by the greedy billionaires and millionaires of the world'.[246]

The focus on children was believed to attract donors outside of the realm of communist organisations.[247] Those organisations also copied bourgeois fundraising innovations, like the adoption scheme of the SCF. Clubs, associations, or employees of a factory could take a specific child under their wing. As in the case of the SCF, lasting bonds between donors and children were envisioned through an exchange of letters and photographs.[248] A special feature of the WIR campaigns was the participation of artists and celebrities, who supported fundraising activities in different ways. Among them were Käthe Kollwitz (who contributed a famous lithograph, see Figure 3.6), Selma Lagerlöf, Albert Einstein, Henri Barbusse, George Bernard Shaw, Anatole France, and Martin Andersen Nexø.

Campaigning in WIR publications shifted in spring 1922 from soliciting emergency relief to a development approach (see Figure 4.6).[249] A first step of reconstruction aid was the delivery of machines and tools, partly purchased with donations, partly collected in kind, as during the International Tool Collection Week in May 1922. Appeals claimed that 'the cry for bread, the struggle for bare existence is being drowned in the cry for production, for

[243] FSR, 'Nation-Wide Holiday Drive'.
[244] FSR, *Pictures – Appeals*, 9. See also Braskén, *International Workers' Relief*, 45 and Eugene V. Debs, 'An Appeal for Contributions for Russian Famine Relief', *Soviet Russia* 6, no. 6 (1922).
[245] FSR letter to 'comrades', 5 Dec. 1921, ARA, reel 115.   [246] 'Soviet Russia Calls'.
[247] Braskén, *International Workers' Relief*, 51.
[248] 'Help Children of Soviet Russia', *Soviet Russia* 7, no. 7 (1922); 'FSR activities'.
[249] Braskén, *International Workers' Relief*, 60.

working capacity, for labor!'.[250] It was argued that 'food and clothing can only alleviate the suffering engendered by the famine, but they cannot exterminate the roots of famine in Russia'.[251]

The FSR regarded 'capitalist charity' as a counter-revolutionary means to 'smother Soviet Russia and re-establish the reign of the over-lords'.[252] As Braskén points out, from a communist relief organisation's point of view, it was essential to describe Western efforts as inadequate or as a Trojan horse (or both) in order to make the international proletariat consider its own sacrifices justified.[253]

Direct Appeals from Russians

When in October 1921 the ARA introduced its food remittance programme (see Figure 4.4), which allowed donors to supply friends and relatives in Russia with food parcels worth US$10, relief workers in Russia immediately began distributing appeal forms to be filled in and sent to addressees in the West. This created a situation in which prospective beneficiaries were given the opportunity to contact potential donors directly, thus giving them a chance to affect their own destiny. It contrasted greatly with other famines, where the famine-affected often appear voiceless. Thus, the machinery of organised humanitarianism was supplemented by an ad hoc element of recipient expression.

The first-hand appeals of Soviet citizens to the West vary in form and style, as well as in the background and strategies of their authors. Among the applicants were desperate individuals with starving families asking strangers for help, representatives of villages begging for food rations, and ethnic and religious groups (such as communities of Volga Germans or Orthodox parishes) that specifically applied to their brothers and sisters in blood and faith.[254] Most appeals, however, flowed between those linked by occupation. For example, teachers of a school, members of an orchestra, or staff of a hospital wrote to their counterparts in the USA directly or asked the ARA to assume the role of 'philanthropic matchmaker' and pass their appeals on to suitable parties.

However, successful match-ups between groups who made appeals and donors were the exception rather than the rule. The report of a successful pairing between a Russian training school for nurses and the Nurses' Home of the Presbyterian Hospital in New York came about after 'passing many

---

[250] 'International Tool Collection Week', *Soviet Russia* 6, no. 9 (1922). See also Braskén, *International Workers' Relief*, 61. The original appeal was drafted by WIR chief Willi Münzenberg, *International Press Correspondence* 2, no. 13, 17 Feb. 1922, 96.

[251] FSR, *The Russian Famine: One Year of Relief Work* (New York, FSR, c. 1922).

[252] FSR, 'Nation-Wide Holiday Drive'.   [253] Braskén, *International Workers' Relief*, 45.

[254] Shapishnikov to ARA, 6 Mar. 1922 (original in Russian), ARA, reel 11; Eutemeier on behalf of Basilev Volost (peasant community) to ARA, 9 Jan. 1922, ARA, reel 499; Kummerl on behalf of 1,500 Volga Germans to the editor of the *New York Herald*, 20 Jan. 1922, ARA, reel 498.

hundreds of such supplications to prospective benefactors in the USA with no apparent result'. For an ARA official in London, it was therefore 'a distinct pleasure to learn, that out of the multitudinous appeals dispatched from Europe ... one, at least, has awakened the sympathies'.[255]

In New York, ARA secretary Page was less enthusiastic and complained that the 'great number of pathetic appeals' that came in every day were bound to result in 'the establishment of hundreds of little campaigns' that neither served the ARA nor the starving people. The mere fact that the appeals arrived in New York created 'a certain obligation' towards the senders, he bemoaned.[256] But the flood of appeals could not be stemmed. By the end of May 1922, Page's attitude had turned fatalistic: 'I wish we had a plan for clearing up these appeals from Russia, but we haven't.'[257] Half a year later, he admitted that while few of the appeals could be used for publicity, the majority were simply filed. With resignation he added, 'I hate to be quite as cold-blooded as that.'[258]

Academics were the principal applicants because they had the skills to write and submit appeals, something that farmers and workers rarely were capable of doing. In many cases, private appeals were the last resort for teachers, librarians, and scientists, as they had limited access to the general feeding programme. Moreover, the ARA considered the Russian intelligentsia, in a broad sense, as particularly worth support, because they could help spread a positive image of the USA and articulate Russian gratitude. Haskell, the ARA director in Moscow, reported that this group was encouraged to send appeals to the USA with the hope of facilitating relief that was outside of Soviet control. Some major donations, for example by the Commonwealth Fund and the Laura Spelman Rockefeller Memorial Fund, were earmarked for the Russian intelligentsia. However, these attempts were slowed down or forestalled when Soviet officials objected to such a specific distribution.[259]

Group appeals usually created or referred to alleged common ground. Attempts to establish a relationship with distant strangers were primarily based on similar educations or professions. References to universal humanity – often applied in individual letters – were of minor importance. Consequently, recipients were addressed as colleagues and told about working conditions and

[255] Dailey to Supervisor Nurses Home Presbyterian Hospital, 2 May 1922; Dailey to London office, 15 June 1922; Myers to New York, 17 July 1922, all ARA, reel 500. In this specific case, US$772 was collected for the Russian colleagues, an outcome far beyond expectations.

[256] Page to Herter, 12 Apr. 1922, ARA, reel 498. See also Draft to Mitchel, unsigned (London), 27 Apr. 1922, ARA, reel 499.

[257] Page to Colton, 24 May 1922, ARA, reel 499.

[258] Page to Rickards, 18 Oct. 1922, ARA, reel 498.

[259] Haskell and Quinn to London, 3 Apr. 1922, ARA, reel 499. See Patenaude, *Big Show*, 178–9, and Rickard to Herter, 28 Aug. 1922, ARA, reel 500. The food remittance programme offered an alternative.

supplies. Doctors depicted the situation of the local health service, academics described the state of affairs in their university, and so on.

Despite the variety of such appeals, certain patterns and elements frequently recurred. A common feature was the promise to repay what was given at some future time, whether with money, by working for the ARA (with obvious motives), or at least with eternal gratitude. A group of Volga Germans made 'the sacred promise' to pay back any debt as soon as possible by assisting other victims, and the Corporation of Dentists from Ufa, who had sent an appeal to colleagues in Chicago, considered it their 'moral duty to refund the value of the food packages' at a later date.[260] Others offered a factual, often intellectual, quid pro quo. For example, a biologist from Moscow sent two scientific articles as payment for a food draft, while two mineralogists from Petrograd offered their research results on building stone materials from the Onega Lake region in exchange.[261]

Perhaps applicants hoped to increase their chances of success by offering to settle their debt, although their use of such phrasing may be understood as a symbolic act. At the same time, this approach was important for the applicants' self-image. No matter how desperate they may have been, they often showed strong aversion to being seen as beggars or recipients of charity. A teacher from Tarsk wrote that he expected 'least of all to be an object of philanthropy', and a group of scholars from Kazan University would only accept help 'as long as they could hope of repaying it'.[262] An applicant from Odessa confronted his humiliation directly: 'You see, Gentlemen, it is very hard to get used to be a pauper... After a life full of work, of initiative, I am a beggar.'[263]

The applicants themselves, as well as ARA officials, saw such expressions as indicative of a particular form of Russian pride. For example, in their appeal to colleagues in New York, a group of typists from Ufa explained that the intelligentsia of Russia does not have the habit of begging for help – something only the existential threat of starvation made them do.[264] An ARA memorandum noted that Russian academics rarely asked for help from abroad and

---

[260] Kummerl to the editor of the *New York Herald*, 20 Jan. 1922 (original in German), ARA, reel 498; Corporation of Ufa dentists to the dentists of Chicago, 2 Feb. 1922, ARA, reel 498.

[261] Efimoff, Moscow University, to ARA, 17 July 1922, ARA, reel 500; Niskovsky to ARA, undated (summer 1922), ARA, reel 11.

[262] Shapishnikov to ARA, 6 Mar. 1922 (original in Russian), ARA, reel 11; Oriental Academy, Kasan University to 'Scholars of the USA', undated (probably Jan./Feb. 1922), ARA, reel 500. Similar formulations occurred in many other appeals, see, e.g., Members of Legal Profession in Odessa to New York Law Association, 24 Apr. 1922, ARA, reel 11; Telephone Workers of Viasniki to ARA, 8 Mar. 1922, ibid.

[263] Fabrikant to ARA Odessa, 24 Mar. 1923, ARA, reel 12.

[264] The typewriter girls of the ARA Ufa to the typewriter girls and women of New York, 13 Oct. 1922, ARA, reel 11.

would generally rather suffer than beg for assistance.[265] In letters accompanying Russian appeals, potential donors were asked to imagine how much pride it cost the writers to beg for help.[266] When the Boy Scouts of Theodosia (Crimea) asked the Boy Scouts of America for 'literature of scoutism' and used uniforms, their timidity was deciphered by the ARA, and it was pointed out to the US recipients of their request that 'these boys were likely in great need of food'.[267]

3.4   Television, Shame, and Global Humanity: Ethiopia

A BBC television news report on 23 October 1984 was the appeal that launched the large-scale international aid mobilisation for those afflicted by famine in Ethiopia. In the media-driven humanitarianism of the late twentieth century, 'an emergency begins and ends when the BBC says so', noted one commentator.[268] The public's response had been muted as a result of poor television and press coverage earlier that year, and by October a UK Disasters Emergency Committee (DEC) appeal that had raised some £9 million was on the point of closing down.[269] At a time when charitable appeals on European radio and television were highly regulated, collaborating with media outlets provided valuable opportunities for voluntary organisations to communicate news of disasters to a wider public.[270] As a result, many aid agencies had come to depend on the 6 o'clock news as a major fund raiser.[271]

Michael Buerk and Mohamed Amin produced the BBC's report that day with the assistance of Oxfam and World Vision (see Figure 3.7). The seven-minute piece – unusually long for a single news item – primarily focused on the Korem relief camp in northern Ethiopia. Save the Children had established a supplementary feeding programme there in March 1984, financially supported by the European Economic Community (EEC), and Médecins Sans Frontières (MSF) was providing health care. A graphic film by Amin showed bodies being laid out for burial, malnourished babies being weighed, and in one segment a three-year-old dying while being filmed. Panoramic shots followed people running across the plain when rumours of a grain shipment

---

[265] Memorandum: Special Funds for Relief of Individual Cases of Suffering among the Professionals in Russia, undated, ARA, reel 500.

[266] John Ellingston to the members of Yale University, 30 Mar. 1922, ARA, reel 499.

[267] George B. Baker to Boy Scouts of America, 20 July 1922, ARA, reel 498.

[268] IIED, *African Emergency*, 39.

[269] DEC Famine in Africa Sitrep 1, 13 July 1984, CA 4/A/16.

[270] In the UK, for example, charities were not allowed to purchase advertising space on commercial television until 1989. See Andrew Jones, 'The Disasters Emergency Committee (DEC) and the Humanitarian Industry in Britain, 1963–85', *Twentieth Century British History* 26, no. 4 (2015): 573–601.

[271] IIED, *African Emergency*, 272–3; de Waal, *Famine Crimes*, 84.

Figure 3.7 Mohamed Amin (wearing hat) and Michael Buerk (in white suit) with their news team and Ethiopian children, 26 Oct. 1984.
Courtesy of Camerapix/Mohamed Amin Archive

triggered a stampede. Buerk's voice-over spoke of a 'biblical famine, now, in the twentieth century'. The broadcast highlighted the discrepancy between the aid that was needed (food) and the only relief the camp could offer (medical care and clothing). The camera zoomed in as a starving Ethiopian put on a donated suit jacket, many times too big for him, highlighting the absurdity of distributing cast-offs of well-fed Westerners instead of food. In a direct appeal from the camp, Brigitte Vasset of MSF lamented, 'I don't know what we are doing here. If there is no food, the medical treatment is a nonsense.'[272]

As a result of Amin's compelling footage and Buerk's powerful narration, set against a background of abundant harvests in Europe, the film had a global impact, whereas earlier coverage had been largely ignored.[273] It was shown worldwide by 425 broadcasting stations, unlike the much smaller number to which the BBC's famine reports in July had been syndicated.[274] In the USA, the NBC network broadcast a three-minute version using Amin's footage, which was still lengthy coverage of a foreign news story so close to a US

---

[272] Vasset on BBC News, 23 Oct. 1984; Médecins Sans Frontières, *Rapport D'Activite 1984*, May 1985, 9.

[273] For a more detailed discussion, see Franks, *Reporting Disasters*, ch. 1.

[274] Penrose, 'Before and After', 154; Philo, 'From Buerk to Band Aid', 121.

presidential election. A second report by Buerk, which provided greater detail on the ongoing civil war, was shown by the BBC on 24 October, but by then the story had been picked up by other broadcasters and the print media, and the connections between the civil war and the famine were largely lost in the ensuing coverage.[275] Renewed attacks by the Ethiopian government on central Tigray in late October 1984 became known as the 'Silent Offensive' because of the lack of attention in both the Ethiopian and international media.[276]

Then, on 25 October, Peter Gill's film *Bitter Harvest* was televised across the UK.[277] The documentary exposed the contrast between the famine and the European harvest more explicitly than Buerk's report. It opened with scenes showing mountainous piles of grain and posed the straightforward question: 'Why don't we give our unwanted food to save the lives of those who need it?' The film interspersed footage of autumn harvest festivals being celebrated in churches throughout Europe with video of Ethiopian relief camps, and featured interviews with staff at MSF, Oxfam, and Save the Children. A British farmer observed on camera that allocating excess grain to famine relief was not only the morally right thing to do, but that 'in longer-term self-interest, [there is] a real value in making sure that people who are hungry are fed'.[278] Such moral and economic incentives became topics of public debate in Europe and the USA.[279] A War on Want report summed up the incredulity of the public in the late twentieth century when it asked, 'How is it possible to *film* people dying and send the pictures back by satellite, yet still [be] impossible to bring them the food and the medicines to keep them alive?'[280]

Television news and documentaries conveyed updated appeals for aid in late 1984, reigniting waning interest in the famine and sparking an influx of unsolicited charitable donations. The US-based relief organisation CARE suggested it was the BBC footage that finally legitimised the claims of Ethiopia on the American public.[281] Buerk, who saw his reports on the famine as appeals for aid, later confirmed that he downplayed the impact of the civil war over fears that he might prevent people 'from coughing up

[275] Franks, *Reporting Disasters*, 101.   [276] Article 19, *Starving in Silence*, 111.

[277] The film's release by Thames Television had been delayed by a technicians' strike, some of whom nevertheless worked for free to finish the editing. Advertising revenue from the broadcast was donated to Oxfam and Save the Children. 'Strikers Call It off Just to Show Disaster Film', *Daily Mail*, 25 Oct. 1984, 24; Oxfam, 'Ethiopia Bulletin No. 13', 29 Oct. 1984, 3, MS Oxfam COM2/6/11.

[278] Thames Television, TV EYE 'Bitter Harvest', 25 Oct. 1984.

[279] Oxfam, Newsletter, Nov. 1984, MS Oxfam APL/3/5/3; Mark Luetchford and Peter Burns, *Waging the War on Want* (London: War on Want, 2003), 127; 'Bröd och Bensin', *Dagens Nyheter*, 13 Oct. 1984.

[280] George Galloway, 'General Secretary's Report', in *War on Want Annual Report 1984–5* (London: War on Want, 1985), 1.

[281] IIED, *African Emergency*, 272.

their money'.[282] The film's immediate impact can be seen by looking at Oxfam UK's income. Oxfam had raised a respectable £51,149 from its appeal for 'Famine in Ethiopia' through September 1984. However, this sum was dwarfed by the £600,000 in unsolicited public donations it received in the five days after the film was aired on the BBC.[283] In Canada, a similar response to the newscast about famine in Ethiopia led one commentator to note, 'People in High River [in Alberta, Canada] don't read FAO reports. They do watch television.'[284] Other broadcasters were encouraged to explore the famine in a series of documentaries and news reports.[285]

In several instances, the Ethiopian government criticised aid appeals that showed conditions in their country, but did not earmark the resulting funds specifically for Ethiopian relief.[286] On the other hand, voluntary organisations recognised that media attention concentrating only on Ethiopia might detract from other severely affected African nations. As CARE noted, 'the challenge is to utilize current media awareness, but not to have our fundraising efforts be dictated by its emphasis'.[287] In the UK, the unanticipated influx of donations resulted in some conflict among voluntary organisations. The five members of the DEC were accused by others of unfairly monopolising airtime. Although War on Want (a DEC founder member) left the alliance in 1979, it and other groups continued to seek an allocation of funds for famine relief in Africa through 1984, although this attempt was rebuffed.[288]

The television broadcasts brought about an increase in media coverage across all platforms. In the UK, the popular press increasingly took the lead from television, and tabloid newspaper column inches devoted to the famine increased from 50 in the first three weeks of October to 1,200 in the last ten days of that month.[289] Newspaper editorials urged an international response, while feature stories detailed relief work and provided instructions on how to donate.[290]

---

[282] Michael Buerk, as cited in Daniel Wolf, 'What Happened to the F***ing Money?', *The Spectator*, 23 Oct. 2004, 12–13.

[283] Oxfam, 'Ethiopia Bulletin No. 13', 29 Oct. 1984, 3. MS Oxfam COM2/6/11.

[284] Morrison, *Aid and Ebb Tide*, 234.

[285] See, for example, Food and Trucks and Rock 'n' Roll; Alter Ciné, *Songs of the Next Harvest*, directed by Yvan Patry.

[286] Vaux, 'Ethiopian Famine 1984', 21.

[287] 'Care: The Campaign for Africa: Memo to Regional Directors 903', 15 Nov. 1984, CARE 1120/17.

[288] Galloway to Pouncey, 17 Jul. 1984, CA 4/A/16; DEC Secretariat Telex, 17 Jan. 1985, CA 4/A/ 16. Despite mounting criticism, it was not until 1997 that the DEC was reformed and its membership expanded.

[289] Figures from Magistad, in Philo, 'From Buerk to Band Aid', 109.

[290] Comment, *Daily Mail*, 25 Oct. 1984; 'Where to Contribute to Aid the Ethiopians', *New York Times*, 27 Oct. 1984; 'Famine in Ethiopia – How You Can Help', *Daily Mail*, 25 Oct. 1984; Monica Almgren, 'Organisationer som söker hjälpa de svältande', *Svenska Dagbladet*, 27 Oct. 1984.

The Stockholm newspaper, *Aftonbladet*, for example, included the story of an Ethiopian girl saved by Rädda Barnen (Save the Children, Sweden), followed by a listing of the bank account details for three voluntary organisations.[291] British tabloid rivalries helped to promote the story of the famine.[292] The *Daily Mirror* launched its own appeal and by 5 November had raised over £600,000 to fund its own 'mercy flights' to Ethiopia.[293] Some Western media outlets also alerted readers to the blatant hypocrisy of the Ethiopian Marxist government that would let its people starve while ordering a 'boat-load of booze' – half a million bottles of Scottish whisky – to celebrate its ten years in power.[294] This notorious episode also found its way into generally pro-Ethiopian English-language newspapers in Ghana, Kenya, Nigeria, and Tanzania.[295]

The public response to the famine included thousands of letters from private individuals to voluntary organisations, the Relief and Rehabilitation Commission, United Nation (UN) agencies, and newsrooms in the days and weeks following the broadcasts.[296] Letters received by the BBC, including many from children, were read out on air or posted in the television studios. In much of this correspondence, themes of shame and guilt dominate, with the looming food mountains of Europe an ever-present backdrop.[297] The invidious contrast between the commodities of everyday Western life – abundant food, alcohol, cigarettes, and consumer goods – and the situation faced by people in Ethiopia was drawn out by many, who often described their own personal sacrifices.[298] One woman from the USA wrote to say that seeing the scenes on television 'left a big lump in my throat, sitting down to a big Thanksgiving meal, knowing there are many starving'. Another reported that the famine had finally led her to quit smoking and to direct the money to relief: 'I think of that starving child who needs the money a lot worse than I need those cigarettes.'[299]

After October 1984, media coverage of the famine focused as much on such individual acts of giving as on questions of relief.[300] A *New York Times* article included stories of two little girls each pledging their US$5 allowance, a

[291] Maria Torshall, 'Räddad från svälten', *Aftonbladet*, 23 Nov. 1984.

[292] Nick Cater, 'The Hungry Media', *Ten·8*, no. 10 (1985): 2–4.

[293] 'How You Can Help', *Daily Mirror*, 25 Oct. 1984; 'Your Goodwill – Their Grief', *Daily Mirror*, 5 Nov. 1984; Alistair Campbell, 'Mirror to the Rescue', *Daily Mirror*, 27 Oct. 1984.

[294] Robert Porter and Andrew McEwen, 'Storm over Ethiopian Whisky Ship', *Daily Mail*, 27 Oct. 1984; 'Comment: The Famine and the Folly', *Daily Mail*, 27 Oct. 1984.

[295] Hébert, 'Feed the World', 37.   [296] Giorgis, *Red Tears*, 205.

[297] 'Ethiopia: We Must Act Now: Letters', *Daily Mail*, 30 Oct. 1984; David Nattrass, 'Letters to the Editor', *Guardian*, 26 Oct. 1984.

[298] Oxfam, 'Ethiopia Bulletin No. 14', 6 Nov. 1984, 3. MS Oxfam COM2/6/11.

[299] Giorgis, *Red Tears*, 205.

[300] Cheryl Lousley, '"With Love from Band Aid": Sentimental Exchange, Affective Economies, and Popular Globalism', *Emotion, Space, and Society* 10 (2014): 10.

Vietnamese man who wanted to repay UNICEF for helping resettle him in the USA, and a baker who arrived at an organisation's office with a large box of coins collected by his children.[301] These sentimental giving narratives involved ordinary, relatively powerless people. The point in circulating such stories, as cultural theorist Cheryl Lousley suggests, was not only to celebrate the pleasure of acting as a benefactor, but to 'reveal and perpetuate a tremendous affective investment in famine relief'.[302] Such emotional investment, characteristic of expressive humanitarianism, helps explain the popular enthusiasm behind the new, more participatory forms of famine relief that peaked in the mid-1980s, and that are in some ways at odds with the long-standing fundraising techniques utilised by many agencies.

Voluntary Organisations' Appeals

Although the immediate public response to the television news footage from Ethiopia was unanticipated, the fundraising sections of relief organisations around the world moved quickly to capitalise on it through press and billboard advertising, direct mail campaigns, and other appeals. However, after the high level of spontaneous donations for famine relief in October, some agencies cut back on public appeals because they already had more money than they could responsibly spend.[303]

Reviewing the fundraising advertisements placed in newspapers and magazines in the USA, UK, Italy, and Sweden, along with the campaigns of selected aid agencies, reveals common strategies.[304] The most prevalent technique in 1984–5 seems to have been to emphasise the magnitude of the crisis in Ethiopia and stress its unprecedented nature.[305] Hyperbolic language was routinely deployed in press advertisements. World Vision referred to the 'most devastating human crisis of our time' and the American Red Cross (ARC) to 'the worst drought in history'.[306] Similarly, an Oxfam direct mailing piece in

---

[301] Joseph Berger, 'Offers of Aid for Stricken Ethiopia Are Pouring into Relief Agencies', *New York Times*, 28 Oct. 1984.

[302] Lousley, 'With Love from Band Aid', 12.   [303] IIED, *African Emergency*, 271.

[304] In the UK, the archives of the following national newspapers (daily or Sunday) were examined: *Daily Telegraph, Daily Mail, Guardian, Observer, Times, Sunday Times, Listener*. The tabloids *Daily Mirror, Daily Express*, and *Daily Star* did not carry fundraising advertisements from famine relief charities. Sweden's two largest daily papers, *Dagens Nyheter* and *Svenska Dagbladet*, and the two main evening papers, *Aftonbladet* and *Expressen*, were analysed. For Italy, the main national papers reviewed were *Corriere della sera, La Repubblica, La Stampa, L'Unità*, and *il Manifesto*. For the USA, searches were conducted using ProQuest Historical Newspapers.

[305] Oxfam advertisement, 'Emergency in Ethiopia S.O.S', *Daily Telegraph*, 27 Oct. 1984; 'Famine in Africa Appeal', DEC advertisement, *Times*, 20 July 1984.

[306] 'Ethiopia', World Vision advertisement, *Washington Post*, 25 Nov. 1984; 'I'm Picking up the Tab', ARC advertisement, *Boston Globe*, 20 Jan. 1985; Ethiopian organisations' advertisement in *Expressen*, 3 Nov. 1984.

November 1984 stated that 'Ethiopia is the largest disaster situation we have ever faced'.[307]

For the most part, aid agencies avoided confronting the Cold War complexities of the famine, including Ethiopia's civil war and concerns over sending aid to a Soviet-backed regime. Many advertisements followed Buerk's depoliticised description of a 'biblical famine', emphasising the failure of rains and crops.[308] By the mid-1980s, relief organisations were well-practiced in using discretion in choosing what they would stress in fundraising appeals; they had become adept at uncoupling the humanitarian relief of suffering from the geopolitical realities.[309] However, some organisations, including Oxfam and War on Want, did mention the conflict, and sought to draw attention to the failure of many Western governments to commit aid. War on Want hired a well-known advertising agency with links to the Labour party to develop a hard-hitting campaign on famine in Ethiopia, alongside South Africa, Nicaragua, and the 'Third World' debt crisis. The Ethiopia poster stated that crops 'are being destroyed by another plague' and showed Derg military jets, depicted as a swarm of locusts, above a war-torn landscape.[310]

As in previous campaigns, aid agencies tried to distinguish between the innocent victims of famine and the unpalatable Marxist regime in Ethiopia by emphasising that aid was mainly targeted at women (specifically mothers) and children. Although relatively few advertisements appearing in print media contained images, those that did generally depicted a group of children or a mother and child.[311] The images of vulnerable children reinforced the televised pictures of the famine that were replayed throughout the October and November of 1984.[312] Save the Children's press advertisements suggested that it would be far less painful for readers to reach for their cheque books than to watch children starve on television.[313] By autumn 1985, a year after the famine story first appeared, Oxfam addressed potential donors as ironic spectators, asking them if they were 'fed up with pictures of famine on television?'.[314]

[307] Direct mail letter, 26 Nov. 1984, MS Ox APL3/6/6.

[308] 'Ethiopia Famine Disaster', Help the Aged, advertisement, *Times*, 31 Oct. 1984; 'Du har väl inte glömt att vattna blommorna älskling', *Dagens Nyheter*, 1 Dec. 1984.

[309] Maggie Black, *A Cause for Our Times: Oxfam: The First 50 Years* (Oxford: Oxfam, 1992), 245.

[310] Luetchford and Burns, *Waging the War on Want*, 142–3.

[311] Oxfam Posters, MS Oxfam COM1/8/75/1–2; 'It's Not just Ethiopia that's Drying up', Unicef UK advertisement, *Daily Telegraph*, 2 Nov. 1984.

[312] 'Ethiopia: Please Help Us Now!', Oxfam advertisement, *Daily Telegraph*, 2 Nov. 1984; World Vision, *Times*, 25 Oct. 1984.

[313] 'Which Is More Painful?', Save the Children advertisement, *Daily Telegraph*, 27 Oct. 1984; 'Christmas Appeal', Save the Children advertisement, *Daily Mail*, 1 Dec. 1984; War on Want advertisement, *Daily Mail*, 5 Nov. 1985; 'Emergency in Ethiopia S.O.S', Oxfam advertisement, *Daily Telegraph*, 27 Oct. 1984.

[314] 'Fed up with Pictures of Famine on Television?', *Times*, 12 Nov. 1985.

The use of photographs was frequently discussed internally by aid agencies. War on Want was among the few organisations to publicly criticise the spreading of such 'helpless and powerless' images, and instead published a series of positive scenes from Eritrea in its own newsletter.[315]

Another technique in press appeals was to stress the aid agency's record of service to Ethiopia and its ability to provide immediate famine relief. The organisation's accomplishments in Ethiopia were emphasised in direct mail appeals and advertisements that included extensive data on relief camps, numbers of nurses and aid workers, and quantities of food already shipped.[316] Such accounting-oriented advertising implied that not all relief organisations could draw on the same knowledge and expertise.[317] The US-based Catholic Relief Services (CRS), for example, boasted it had already been working in Ethiopia for ten years, and with the famine emergency for sixteen months.[318] Oxfam America, while it could claim no such history in Ethiopia, proudly stated that it could draw on similar experiences of relief work in Bangladesh and Kampuchea.[319] These claims were part of a process of establishing trust between the aid agency and potential donors, assuring the latter that their money would directly go where it was most needed, and would be adminis- trated by competent teams.

The need to foster trust was sometimes higher in the case of umbrella organisations or coalitions of voluntary agencies that were often less familiar to ordinary donors. In November 1984, the US-based coalition InterAction, placed a full-page advertisement in twelve major newspapers, seeking dona- tions that would 'end hunger' in Africa.[320] The ads made much of the importance of collaborative work, declaring 'The experts are ready – For the first time ever, America's private voluntary organizations have joined in a powerful coalition, 60 of which are already working in Africa.'[321] This was a common strategy worldwide, but especially in Canada, Australia, and Western Europe. In Sweden, a joint appeal by six 'Ethiopia organisations' referred to their 'necessary connections and many years of experience' in relief work.[322]

---

[315] 'Images of the Poor', *War on Want News*, winter 1984/5, 7.

[316] 'Christian Aid Christmas Appeal', *Daily Telegraph*, 24 Dec. 1984; Action Aid advertisement, *Daily Mail*, 15 Nov. 1984; Oxfam America advertisement, 'To Save a People', *New York Times*, 2 Dec. 1984; Oxfam direct mail letter, 26 Nov. 1984, MS Oxfam APL3/6/6.

[317] British Red Cross advertisement, 'Ethiopia: A Great Human Tragedy', *Daily Telegraph*, 27 Oct. 1984; Swedish Red Cross, 'Leylas och Alis alla kor har dött. Men de har tre barn kvar', *Aftonbladet*, 30 Nov. 1984.

[318] 'Thank You', Catholic Relief Services advertisement, *Los Angeles Times*, 4 Nov. 1984.

[319] Oxfam America advertisement, *New York Times*, 2 Dec. 1984.

[320] *Monday Developments*, 19 Nov. 1984, vol. 2, no. 24.

[321] Interaction advertisement, *New York Times*, 18 Nov. 1984.

[322] Ethiopia organisations advertisement in *Expressen*, 3 Nov. 1984. The partcipating organisa- tions included the Swedish Red Cross, Rädda Barnen, Lutherhjälpen, Evangeliska Fosterlands- stiftelsen, Svenska Kyrkans Mission, and the Swedish Pentecostal Movement.

Since the late 1970s, aid organisations working on behalf of their own secessionist liberation fronts had sought to make direct appeals to the West. They did this in an attempt to avoid widespread reluctance on the part of most donor governments to provide aid to areas outside of the control of the government of Ethiopia. The Eritrean Relief Association (ERA), established in 1975, and the Relief Society of Tigray (REST), founded in 1978, believed that public opinion could be mobilised with the help of a network of overseas support committees to counter Western government policy.[323] Advertisements placed by these groups in late 1984 alerted prospective donors that two million people living outside government-controlled areas were facing famine.[324] REST's support committee in the UK, for example, stated its credentials as 'the only indigenous humanitarian agency' working in Tigray during a decade of war and four years of drought, and the only group that could guarantee aid would reach starving Tigrayans.[325] Emphasising the humanitarian record of REST and ERA, while simultaneously downplaying connections with their respective military forces, was an attempt to legitimise these organisations through their association with various intermediaries, including the Sudan-based Emergency Relief Desk (ERD), an ecumenical consortium engaged in cross-border relief operations, that channelled aid to rebel-held areas.[326] There was also significant fundraising among global Jewish communities, particularly in the USA, in support of Operation Moses, the secret airlift of thousands of Ethiopian Jews to Israel.[327]

At the end of 1984, many appeals were explicitly linked to Christmas, with donors being urged to spread a little goodwill.[328] This followed long-established patterns of linking fundraising to religious holidays. Christmas had been a key date on the fundraising calendar in the USA and Europe since at least the 1860s. Such appeals were especially lucrative for Christian Aid, whose headquarters was processing £70,000 a day in donations around Christmas 1984.[329] The holiday prompted a diverse range of appeals that went beyond references to the biblical story and the need to think of others. Solicitations for Ethiopia at this time were framed in morally provocative and challenging terms. In the UK, Help the Aged ran a mock 'shopping days' til Christmas' countdown in a number of newspapers throughout

---

[323] Duffield and Prendergast, *Without Troops*, 25–6.

[324] 'Classified Ad 128', *Guardian*, 31 Oct. 1984.

[325] REST UK Support Committee advertisement, 'The Famine in Tigray', *Times*, 9 Nov. 1984, 30; 'Help Tigrayans', *Guardian*, 6 Feb. 1985.

[326] Duffield and Prendergast, *Without Troops*, 6.

[327] Tudor Parfitt, *Operation Moses: The Story of the Exodus of the Falasha Jews from Ethiopia* (London: Wiedenfield and Nicolson, 1985), 103–4.

[328] Save the Children advertisement, 'Christmas Appeal', *Daily Mail*, 1 Dec. 1984.

[329] *Christian Aid Information*, 2 Nov. 1984, CA 4/A/32/1; 'What Ethiopia Has Meant to the Africa Section', CA 4/A/32/1. See 'Christian Aid Christmas Appeal', *Daily Telegraph*, 24 Dec. 1984.

December, marking '15 dying days' til Christmas', and so on.[330] YCare International printed a picture of an emaciated child with a spoof four-course Christmas menu listing grass, weeds, berries, and dirty water.[331] An ARC campaign asked people to stop and think the next time they paid for a restaurant meal, and to 'pick up the tab' for someone who really needed it this Christmas.[332]

The strategy of 'praising the donor' reflects the notion that aid is essentially donor-driven. As David Williams writes, 'Aid to Africa is about "us", not "them."'[333] Advertisements and articles repeatedly referred to the generous, concerned, caring public in Sweden, Britain, or the USA, and thanked donors while urging them to give again.[334] Help the Aged's November 1984 appeal for Ethiopia was placed in all the major UK newspapers as an advance 'thank you letter' to the generous readers of each paper.[335] The strategy wanted to make donors feel part of a special group and increase the likelihood that they would donate more. The ARC described Americans as 'the most generous people in the history of mankind'.[336] Similarly, CARE's direct mail campaign for famine in Africa addressed supporters as 'caring Americans' who 'share a belief in the value of human beings, whoever and wherever they are'.[337] This marketing approach was in contrast to CARE's newspaper ads, where emotive language was avoided in favour of recounting the organisation's track record in relief work.[338] The relatively few appeals that were made to the general public in Italy praised the country's generosity as resulting in part from the recent memory of poverty at home.[339]

Oxfam thanked its supporters for having contributed earlier, but also pleaded for more and it chastised undecided potential donors: 'None of us has the excuse that a small contribution will achieve nothing.' However, the organisation expressed its concern that long-term development work would suffer as a result of diverting attention to emergency relief unless some donors

[330] Help the Aged advertisement, '15 Dying Days to Christmas', *Daily Mail*, 10 Dec. 1985.
[331] YCare International, 'His Four-Course Christmas Lunch', *Times*, 24 Dec. 1984.
[332] 'I'm Picking up the Tab', American Red Cross advertisement, *Boston Globe*, 20 Jan. 1985.
[333] David Williams, 'Review Article: Aid as Autobiography', *Journal of the International African Institute* 72, no. 1 (2002): 150–63.
[334] Oxfam advertisement, 'Emergency in Ethiopia S.O.S', *Daily Telegraph*, 27 Oct. 1984; Oxfam advertisement, 'The Two Things You Can Do for Ethiopia', *Daily Telegraph*, 20 Dec. 1984; Catholic Relief Services advertisement, 'Thank You', *Los Angeles Times*, 4 Nov. 1984; Maria Torshall, 'Räddad från svälten', *Aftonbladet*, 23 Nov. 1984.
[335] Help the Aged advertisement, 'A Thank You to the Readers', *Daily Mail*, 3 Nov. 1984.
[336] Joyce Gemperlein, '$70 Million Sought for Famine Aid', *Philadelphia Inquirer,* 11 Dec. 1984.
[337] CARE direct mail letter, CARE 199, Folder 'Ethiopia Drought Famine Relief 1984–5'.
[338] CARE advertisements, 'Campaign for Africa', *Boston Globe*, 9 Dec. 1984; 'Campaign for Africa: The Need Continues', *New York Times*, 10 Feb. 1985.
[339] G. Barbiellini Amidei, 'Una tassa per la vita', *Corriere della sera*, 31 Dec. 1984.

gave unrestricted funds, in addition to the famine appeals.[340] The Swedish Red Cross likewise urged people to share their wealth, deploying moral economic language by stating 'It is not a matter of buying yourself free from a bad conscience. You are investing in life.'[341] A billboard advertising campaign in Sweden asked passers-by to remember 'Ethiopia is starving. What are you doing?'[342]

Another strategy was to try to engage potential donors in wider campaigning and advocacy work on hunger, aid, and development.[343] War on Want, for example, mounted an effort to secure 'safe passage' for relief supplies to Eritrea and Tigray, and used its newspaper advertisements to encourage readers to lobby politicians on this issue. In direct mailings and newspaper ads, Oxfam asked supporters to join its 'Hungry for Change' campaign, launched in October 1984 by a cross-party line-up of politicians, journalists, church leaders, and celebrities. Two hundred 'Hungry for Change' local groups were formed, and thousands took part in a weekend fast in November 1984.[344] In the same month, Oxfam led a group of other organisations in promoting a 'Famine in Africa' petition directed at the British government.[345] People were encouraged to cut the petition from the newspaper and solicit signatures from family and friends. When it was submitted to UK Prime Minister Margaret Thatcher in March 1985, over 760,000 had signed it.[346] The group of six 'Ethiopia organsiations' in Sweden published a similar appeal demanding government action.[347]

In the competitive charity marketplace, the primary purpose of newspaper advertisements was to convince would-be donors that they should choose one particular organisation over another. In the UK, charity shops located on almost every high street were significant local sites from which direct appeals were made to the British public in the days before television or Internet advertising.[348] Leading overseas aid charities like Oxfam and Save the Children had hundreds of shops each – an important network of collection points for revenue ranging from children's pocket money to the proceeds of local

---

[340] Direct mail letter, 26 Nov. 1984, MS Ox APL3/6/6.
[341] Swedish Red Cross, 'Leylas och Alis'.
[342] Svenska röda korsets Årsbok 1984 (Stockholm: Svenska röda korset, 1985), 48.
[343] Oxfam advertisement, 'The Two Things You Can Do for Ethiopia', Daily Telegraph, 20 Dec. 1984; War on Want advertisement, Daily Mail, 5 Nov. 1985; Oxfam advertisement, 'Can You Give Thirst Aid?', Times, 23 May 1985; Swedish Red Cross, 'Leylas och Alis'.
[344] Black, Cause for Our Times, 261–2.
[345] 'Africa Famine Petition', Guardian, 16 Nov. 1984; 'Famine in Africa Petition', Oxfam PRG 2/3/1/8.
[346] Michael Simmons, 'Cash Flow Turns into a Torrent', Guardian, 22 Mar. 1985.
[347] Björn Erik Rosin, '1000 dör varje dag av svält i Etiopien', Svenska Dagbladet, 26 Oct. 1984.
[348] Jessica Field, 'Consumption in lieu of Membership: Reconfiguring Popular Charitable Action in Post–World War II Britain', Voluntas 27, no. 2 (2016): 979–97.

events. Large appeal posters produced by Oxfam for display in shop windows used arresting red-black-and-white images of women and children to urge passers-by to enter the shop and 'give £1 or more TODAY' to the famine fund.[349] 'Keep the change for Ethiopia' became a common catchphrase in Save the Children's shops.[350]

Voluntary organisations adopted a different approach when using direct mail campaigns to address supporters or lists of 'warm' contacts. Such appeals were generally longer in format and in language directed at individuals. As relief appeals continued throughout 1985 and into 1986, advertisers had to contact donors repeatedly and persuade them to give again and again, while also trying to recruit new donors. For example, a UNICEF UK advertisement in July 1985 urged those who read it, 'Don't stop caring now – we are so close.'[351]

Are We the World? Celebrities and Participative Fundraising

Although celebrity activism had played a role during earlier relief efforts, it assumed increased significance at the time of expressive humanitarianism. It reached its peak in 1984–5 when Band Aid managed to capitalise on popular enthusiasm and inspire imitators around the world. Musicians and celebrities began to initiate fundraising activities in October 1984. In Sweden, musician David Bradish rapidly put together a televised fundraising gala for November 1984 under the banner 'People Who Care', raising half a million Swedish kronor, which he followed up with a series of initiatives throughout 1985.[352] Similarly, Bob Geldof set out to raise a few hundred thousand pounds by writing and recording a charity single. Geldof later justified his personal response to the news in moral economic terms: sending money did not seem enough of a response to the pictures he had seen because to 'expiate yourself truly of any complicity in this evil meant you had to give something of yourself'.[353] Band Aid was, therefore, 'never a charitable impulse, it was a moral imperative'.[354] Geldof's approach was to translate his emotion into popular music, attracting a large audience and a powerful support base.[355]

Celebrity humanitarians like Geldof and Bradish have been seen as bridges between Western audiences and distant tragedies; the celebrity is 'a focus for

---

[349] Oxfam Posters, MS COM 1/8/75/1–2.
[350] *Save the Children Annual Report, 1984–1985* (London: Save the Children, 1985), 24.
[351] UNICEF UK advertisement, 'Africa's Fast Food Problem', *Times*, 13 July 1985.
[352] Arne Söderlund, 'Jag hamnade på . . .', *Dagens Nyheter*, 6 Nov. 1984; Gunnar Berghcrantz, 'Lill och Hasse drog in halv miljon till svältoffren', *Aftonbladet*, 6 Nov. 1984; Sofie Rolf, 'Nu finns det svensk musik för Etiopien', *Aftonbladet*, 11 Feb. 1985.
[353] Bob Geldof with Paul Vallely, *Is That It?* (London: Sidgwick and Jackson, 1986), 215–17.
[354] Banga, *Reducing People's Vulnerability*, 1.
[355] Frances Westley, 'Bob Geldof and Live Aid: The Affective Side of Global Social Innovation', *Human Relations* 40, no. 10 (1991): 1020.

empathy, an emotional interpreter'.[356] Further, the celebrity personifies 'an altruistic disposition' in which all can share.[357] Although there had been earlier charity singles – notably the 1971 song 'Bangladesh' by George Harrison – none had experienced such success. At the time, therefore, the explosive rise of the song written by Geldof and Midge Ure and recorded by a super-group in November 1984 took everyone by surprise.[358] 'Do They Know It's Christmas?' became the fastest selling single of all time in the UK and went straight to number one on the charts. By January six million copies had been sold and the song had raised £8 million. The record became a focus for public outrage at the international community's inaction at a time of abundant harvests.[359]

Like many of the aid agencies' fundraising appeals, the song spread a compelling message of common humanity, and its repeated chorus of 'Feed the world/Let them know it's Christmas time' contained a simple but seemingly irresistable call to action.[360] The name Band Aid reflected the idea that this effort 'would be like putting a tiny plaster on a wound that required twelve stiches'.[361] The success of the recording reflected widespread desire on the part of many sections of the British public to do something that would put a halt to the pictures of children dying on television. The contrast of 'us' and 'them', so evident in letters from individuals, was central to the emotive lyrics of the song, which reminded the public that they should 'thank God it's them instead of you'. Reflecting on the organisation's slogan, 'With Love from Band Aid', Lousley observes that Geldof's project can be understood as part of a 'popular culture of sentimental exchange' in which donating to famine relief is positioned as a gesture of love, and famine relief images, stories, tears, gifts, and money are exchanged and circulated.[362]

Band Aid's success was followed by the ambitious Live Aid concerts held on both sides of the Atlantic and elsewhere on 13 July 1985. They were watched by over 1.5 billion people on television and raised US$80 million for the Band Aid Trust.[363] Of this total, US$25 million came from the USA, where the independent Live Aid Foundation was established to allocate funds. Apart from ticket and merchandise sales, sponsorship, television rights, and mailed contributions, new banking technology enabled credit card donations to be made by telephone during the show in certain countries.[364] Geldof infamously interrupted the announcer, who was in the midst of giving details for

[356] de Waal, 'Humanitarian Carnival', 44.

[357] Lilie Chouliaraki, 'The Theatricality of Humanitarianism: A Critique of Celebrity Advocacy', *Communication and Critical/Cultural Studies* 9, no. 1 (2012): 1–21.

[358] Caroline Moorehead, 'Geldof and the Givers', *New Society*, 18 Oct. 1985, 99–101.

[359] Banga, *Reducing People's Vulnerability*, 1.

[360] Bel Mooney, 'Why Did We Give So Much?', *Listener*, 19 Dec. 1985, 42.

[361] Banga, *Reducing People's Vulnerability*, 1.   [362] Lousley, 'With Love from Band Aid'.

[363] Band Aid, *With Love*, 4.   [364] IIED, *African Emergency Relief*, 211.

postal donations, to exclaim 'Let's fuck the address, let's get the [phone] numbers, for that's how we're gonna get it [money].'[365] Swedish public television broadcast sixteen hours of Live Aid but was criticised for not organising a call centre to accept telephone donations.[366] Funds raised by the telethon in various countries were generally remitted to local organisations, including MSF in France and the Red Cross in Thailand.

It was said that Live Aid 'conveyed a sense of political action without recourse to politicians'.[367] In one memorable segment, the news footage of the Korem relief camps was used as background to the performance of a rock song by The Cars, the suffering of those projected onto the screens 'sublimated' for the audience. Geldof argued at the time that anything he did was morally justified because the horrors of the famine had made it immune to political argument. In subsequent years, the apparent universal solidarity of Live Aid has been widely critiqued as a depoliticising response to the catastrophe that has defined the ways in which the West has conceptualised Africa ever since.[368] The Band Aid Trust did seek to make political capital out of the concerts, however, citing the decision of the UK development minister that the emergency airlift in Ethiopia would continue as a direct result of Live Aid.[369]

Although the scale and marketing success of Band Aid and Live Aid has tended to overshadow smaller scale initiatives outside the Anglo-American world, celebrity involvement in fundraising in 1984–5 was more diverse and international than retrospective analyses have suggested. There were expressive, emotionally laden initiatives by celebrities, politicians, and public individuals in many countries. In Sweden, figures from the world of sports and fine arts became involved. Athlete Ricky Bruch, for example, organised a series of events, held a fast over Christmas 1984, and lobbied the government for tax relief on charity.[370] In Italy, seventy members of the Radical party threatened to go on hunger strike until Christmas if the government refused to pass a law giving aid to Ethiopia.[371]

Across Europe, several celebrity-endorsed spectacles were held, with widespread television and media coverage and sales of merchandise. A 'One for Africa' day of action organised by the national television and radio networks in the Netherlands in November 1984 raised the equivalent of US$24 million; a

---

[365] Geldof's words have passed into legend as 'Give us your fucking money!', although this is not what he said.

[366] Eva Häggman, 'Varför fick inte vi också ge pengar?', *Aftonbladet*, 14 July 1985; Sakari Pitkänen, 'Hela Sverige ville hjälpa', *Expressen*, 14 July 1985.

[367] Franks, *Reporting Disasters*, 76.   [368] Chouliaraki, *Ironic Spectator*, 122–4.

[369] Food and Trucks and Rock 'n' Roll.

[370] Anders Medin, 'Ricky spolar julen – startar jätteinsamling för Etiopien', *Aftonbladet*, 23 Dec. 1984, 9.

[371] Giovanni Negri, 'Noi dibattiamo e l'Etiopia muore', *Corriere della sera*, 11 Dec. 1984.

survey found that the television broadcast had been watched by two-thirds of the population over the age of 15 years. However, there was also criticism of an apparent disconnect between some of the performances and the subject of famine.[372] On 23 January 1985, the Federal Republic of Germany held a fundraising marathon known as Ein Tag für Afrika (A Day for Africa) that raised 125 million marks (around US$40 million) to be shared by more than a dozen German voluntary agencies (see Figure 3.8).[373] After Italian media complained about the absence of their country's artists at Live Aid, noting sarcastically that Italy had been outperformed 'even by Yugoslavia', a benefit concert for Ethiopia was held in Verona in August 1985.[374] However, involvement in star-studded events could also backfire. In August 1985, the secretary general of the Swedish Red Cross categorised as 'grotesque' a charity gala that sought to raise money through a luxury dinner linked to the opening of a new nightclub.[375]

By the summer of 1985, the success of the Band Aid single had inspired the production of at least twenty other charity singles around the world.[376] Unlike Band Aid, most of these identified specific aid agencies from the outset as beneficiaries. 'We Are the World' was put together by US music impresarios Harry Belafonte and Ken Kragen, influenced both by Band Aid and the memory of singer and hunger activist Harry Chapin. The single, written by Michael Jackson and Lionel Ritchie, was released in April 1985 and was quickly followed by an album.[377] Its sponsor, the United Support of Artists for Africa organisation (USA for Africa), was incorporated in January 1985, and by December 1987 had raised US$58 million for famine relief and long-term development work in Africa. Like the British recording, this song's lyrics drew on the theme of common humanity, urging that this was a time 'when the world must come together as one'. The song also contained the notion of empowerment, that ordinary Americans could make a difference by donating, and that by so doing they would be 'saving their own lives', as the chorus maintained. A film made about the recording emphasised the 'choice we're

---

[372] Letter to Lady Marre, 17 Jan. 1985; BBC Written Archives; Richard W. Solberg, *Miracle in Ethiopia: A Partnership Response to Famine* (New York: Freindship Press, 1991), 72. Additional information provided by Pamala Wiepking.

[373] 'Stau und Rückstau', *Der Spiegel*, 8 Apr. 1985, 28–9; 'Hungerhilfe: Schokolade für Zuckerkranke?', *Der Spiegel*, 21 Jan. 1985, 88–99. Agencies included Caritas, Misereor (German Catholic Bishops' Organisation for Development Cooperation), Diakonisches Werk, Brot für die Welt, Welthungerhilfe, German Red Cross, and fourteen smaller agencies.

[374] Gino Castaldo, 'Il Mondo e un Villaggio', *La Repubblica*, 14 July 1985; 'Nell'Arena di Verona un Concerto per l'Etiopia', *La Repubblica*, 4 Aug. 1985.

[375] Stefan Bokström and Otto Sjöberg, 'Högsta basen tar avstånd från gala för Röda Korset', *Expressen*, 13 Aug. 1985.

[376] Food and Trucks and Rock 'n' Roll.

[377] USA for Africa, *Memories and Reflections: USA for Africa's Experiences and Practice: The First 20 Years* (s.l.: USA for Africa, [2005]).

Figure 3.8 Danish singer Gitte Haenning (left) with German actress Edith
Hancke at the recording of the Ein Tag für Afrika television fundraiser, 23
Jan. 1985.
Photo by Peter Bischoff, reproduced courtesey of Getty Images

making' and contained direct appeals from Jane Fonda and Lionel Ritchie. The
song inspired further participatory activities on a number of fronts. It was
played on 8,000 radio stations in twenty-five countries on Good Friday 1985,
and was said to have made the world 'momentarily a neighbourhood of
concern'.[378]

The double French A-side single 'Starvation' and 'Tam Tam pour
l'Ethiope', which had been in the planning before the Band Aid song, raised
money directly for MSF, Oxfam, and War on Want (see Figure 3.9). In
contrast to 'Do They Know It's Christmas?', the recording included many
Black artists – some from African countries singing in French and a number of
African languages. It was less commercially successful than either its British or
US counterparts.[379] Many of the other singles allocated a small proportion of
the funds that they generated to domestic charities dealing with hunger and
poverty. In France, a group known as Chanteurs sans Frontières recorded a
song entitled 'Ethiopie' that raised 23 million francs, 90 per cent of which
went to MSF and the rest to the charity Restos du Coeur. The Canadian song

---

[378] 'We Are the World: The Story Behind the Song', directed by Tom Trbovich, 1985.
[379] Robinson, 'Putting the Charity'.

Figure 3.9 'Ethiopie Meurt' (Ethiopia is dying), MSF fundriaising
campaign, 1985.
Photo by Patrick Aventurier. Courtesy of Getty Images

'Tears Are Not Enough' raised Can\$3.2 million for the Red Cross, UNICEF,
and CARE, with 10 per cent going to food banks in Canada.[380] Other singles
included the Spanish-language Cantaré, cantarás, which featured a group of
Latin American stars known collectively as 'Hermanos'.

Celebrity activism also sought to channel and shape public sentiment about
disaster relief. For example, the chorus of the Austria für Afrika song 'Why'
(*Warum*) provided an ironic commentary on the Western response to the
famine: 'We're sending money so we don't feel so bad' (*wir schicken Göd –
damit's uns besser geht*). Compared to the West German 'Naked in the Wind'
(*Nackt im Wind*), which addressed the gravity of the situation and the lack of
political consciousness in the West, the Austrian song was political on a deeper
level. It referenced the Ethiopian regime's use of famine as a weapon and
alluded to its support from 'Big Brother' – the Soviet Union. An Ethiopian folk
song was included along with some Ethiopian students based in Vienna.[381] In
communist Yugoslavia, YU Rock Misija contributed to the global famine
relief effort through a charity single 'For a Million Years' (*Za milion godina*)

---

[380] 'Tears Are Still Not Enough: 30 Years Later', available at www.cbc.ca/news/politics/tears-
still-are-not-enough-30-years-later-1.2949836 (accessed 29 June 2019).

[381] Rudi Dolezal, *Die Geschichte des Austropop in 20 Songs* (Salzburg: Servus, 2016), 160–7.

and a rock concert that raised over US$400,000. All three songs, alongside other national efforts, were performed and broadcast as part of the Live Aid concerts. An analysis of English-language African newspapers shows that both official and popular responses to celebrity fundraising in 1984–5 were overwhelmingly favourable.[382]

A key difference between earlier forms of celebrity humanitarianism and Band Aid was Geldof's insistence on retaining control over the disbursement of funds – perhaps alarmed by the financial problems that had plagued Harrison's 1971 Concert for Bangladesh.[383] A deep-rooted suspicion of aid agencies as 'pickpockets' shaped Geldof's approach to relief.[384] Of his single's £1.35 selling price, 96p went to the Band Aid Trust set up by him and officially registered as a British charity in January 1985.[385] Although the record industry waived most of the costs of production, the UK government took 18p of the cover price in taxes, which it initially refused to remit despite a public outcry, although it did later quietly allocate an equivalent sum to famine relief. More money was raised through a series of spin-off campaigns, including Fashion Aid, Classical Aid, Food Aid, Visual Aid, Sport Aid, and School Aid, and a series of local initiatives.[386] Like Band Aid, USA for Africa rejected the 'traditional foundation game'; both sought to develop models of allocating aid that reflected their self-made origins.[387]

Expressive humanitarianism was evident in other participatory fundraising activities aimed at children and young people. In the UK, this included the 1984 Blue Peter Appeal in which millions of people collected stamps, postcards, and buttons that could be turned into cash for Ethiopia. The appeal built on a growing relationship between the children's television show Blue Peter and Oxfam, a partnership which the charity was keen to continue. The programmers had responded to pressure from audience members who wrote in the thousands asking 'Please, please, please can we have an appeal this year for the starving people in Ethiopia? They need the food much more than we do.'[388]

---

[382] Hébert, 'Feed the World', 103–5.
[383] The 1971 concert raised US$240,000, but it took over a decade to distribute the additional sum of US$8.8 million that came from album and film sales for UNICEF. Andrew Lycett, 'Songs for Africa with Another Tune', *Times* 12 July 1985; Richard Williams, 'Grains of Hope from the Gods of Pop', *Times* 15 July 1985; de Waal, 'Humanitarian Carnival', 51.
[384] Vaux, *Selfish Altruist*, 53.
[385] The first trustees included co-writer Midge Ure; theatrical manager Chris Morrison; Lord Gowre, Conservative minister for the arts; solicitor John Kennedy; controller of the BBC Michael Grade; promoter Harvey Goldsmith; Lord Harlech; and Maurice Oberstein, chairman of the British Phonographic Institute.
[386] Food and Trucks and Rock 'n' Roll; Tony Samstag, 'Charities', the *Times*, 16 Dec. 1985; News in Brief, *Times*, 18 Nov. 1985; 'Entertainments', *Times*, 6 Mar. 1985; Advertisement, *Listener*, 10 July 1986, 29.
[387] USA for Africa, *Memories and Reflections*, 8.
[388] Letter from Amy and Katherine Hawthorn to Blue Peter, BBC Written Archives.

The same kind of enthusiasm in their own countries caused voluntary organisations across the world to create a range of appeals through link-ups with young people's magazines, television programmes, schools, youth organisations, and student unions.[389] Save the Children (UK), for example, reported that donations from children and young people in 1984/5 were 476 per cent higher than the previous year.[390] In Sweden, Lutherhjälpen's annual fast, in which three million households took part, used a series of daily reminders and simple tasks to motivate children's giving.[391] However, War on Want cautioned against 'cashing in on compassion' without offering an accompanying educational programme on the political context of aid.[392] Nonetheless, even War on Want echoed Band Aid's rhetoric in its 1985 membership recruitment leaflets, noting that 'If you've helped feed the world, then help change the world' by joining War on Want.[393]

In summer 1985, a Band Aid spin-off programme in the UK called 'Schools for Africa' – also known as School Aid – followed a well-established pattern of asking for gifts-in-kind rather than cash contributions from children (see Figure 5.8). The scheme invited schools to apply for special sacks that pupils would fill with sugar, flour, and dried peas or lentils, and would then be shipped to Africa, arriving at ports for free via British Rail's parcel delivery service. The appeal was 'on the basis that one more cheap item added onto the shopping list of every family could save thousands of people'.[394] The Schools for Africa scheme was a success in terms of the numbers participating: even though it was August, the middle of the UK holidays, 200 schools a day were applying to join.[395] In all, six million school children were enrolled.[396] School Aid had a French counterpart called 'Action Ecole' that raised 4.6 million francs for projects in Mali.[397]

Many commentators agree that Band Aid succeeded in stimulating interest in famine relief and wider development issues among groups previously unreached by overseas aid charities – notably young people and blue collar

---

[389] 'Fundraising', *War on Want News* 1 (1986), Box 249, War on Want Collection; 'Television', BBC 1, *Times*, 11 Aug. 1986; *Save the Children Annual Report 1986* (London: Save the Children, 1986), 22, 25; 'Blue Peter Appeal 1984', Memo from John Clark, 29 Oct. 1984, MS Oxfam, PGR2/3/1/8; Martin Nilsson, 'Svensk nödhjälp', in *Svälten på Afrikas horn,* eds Lars Adaktusson and Allan Hofgren (Uppsala: EFS-förlaget, 1986), 72–9.
[390] *Save the Children Annual Report 1986*, 22.
[391] Lutherhjälpen, *I God Jord: Lutherhjälpens årsbok 1984* (Uppsala: Lutherhjälpen, 1984), 58.
[392] 'Fundraising', *War on Want News* 1 (1986).
[393] Luetchford and Burns, *Waging the War on Want*, 138.
[394] 'Together This Year Let's Make Sure They Know It's Christmas', Band Aid Press Release, July 1985, CARE Archive.
[395] 'Band Aid Meeting, 7 Aug. 1985', CA 4/A/16.
[396] Band Aid, 'Minutes of a Meeting with Coordinating Agencies on 23 Sept. 1985', 2, CA 4/01/130.
[397] Band Aid, *With Love*, 5.

workers. Humanitarian organisations recognised Band Aid's pivotal role in heightening public awareness of famine and poverty abroad, leading to discussions on how to tap into this newly awakened interest. Christian Aid conducted a survey that concluded the Band Aid constituency was 'not ours', while research commissioned by Oxfam suggested that younger people responded to Band Aid, Live Aid, and Sport Aid because these campaigns offered 'something more participatory and emotive rather than rational', unlike Oxfam's usual messages.[398] From early on, Oxfam's campaign manager was eager for the charity to develop strong ties with Band Aid in order to 'freshen' its image among young people and to publicise their support in its annual report.[399]

This all had long-term consequences for future fundraising, for it made aid agencies more receptive to novel ideas that they might earlier have dismissed. Notably among these was the 'Joke Aid' aid concept proposed to Oxfam and SCF after Live Aid by the comedy writer Richard Curtis. It eventually evolved into a regular UK fundraising telethon known as Comic Relief that featured comedians and entertainers.[400]

There was also soul-searching on the Left. The cultural theorist Stuart Hall argued that the Band Aid and Live Aid movement had mobilised a new, youthful constituency that put international aid onto the political agenda in Britain and created a 'famine movement'.[401] Other critics identified this phenomenon as a manifestation of hedonistic 1980s consumer culture.[402]

The UK Ambassador to Ethiopia, Sir Brian Barder, credited Geldof with awakening the conscience of people and keeping that awareness alive.[403] Backed by what he called 'a constituency of compassion', Geldof had prime ministers, presidents, and the EEC in his sights, as his new-found mobilisation force made 'Western politicians rush for cover'.[404] Geldof used his unique position to confront those in power with concerns that few aid workers or diplomats dared to raise for fear of jeopardising long-term relations.[405] The main Sport Aid event, held in May 1986, was a sponsored run called the 'Race Against Time' held in eighty-nine countries to coincide with the opening of the

---

[398] 'What Ethiopia Has Meant to the Africa Section', CA 4/A/32/1; BJM Research Partners Group, 'Oxfam and the Charity Market in Britain: A Report of Survey Findings', 1987, MS Oxfam APL/2/2/4, 8; IIED, *African Emergency*, 218.

[399] John Clark, 'Band Aid', 2 Jan. 1984. MS Oxfam, PGR 2/3/1/8.

[400] Hinton to Judd, 15 Aug. 1985, MS Oxfam PGR 2/3/10/8.

[401] Stuart Hall with Martin Jacques, 'People Aid: A New Politics Sweeps the Land', in *The Hard Road to Renewal: Thatcherism and the Crisis of the Left*, ed. Stuart Hall (London: Verso, 1988), 251–8.

[402] See Franks, *Reporting Disasters*, 85.

[403] Sir Brian Barder interviewed by Malcolm McBain, 6 Mar. 1997, British Diplomatic Oral History Programme, Churchill College, Cambridge.

[404] de Waal, 'Humanitarian Carnival', 51.   [405] Geldof with Vallely, *Is That It?*, 249.

UN General Assembly's first session on Africa and the food crisis. The funds raised were split between Band Aid and UNICEF.[406]

USA for Africa was not involved in organising Live Aid (although the song was performed in Philadelphia). However, in May 1986, it staged its own spin-off mass participation event, 'Hands across America', a human chain of 6.5 million people headed by celebrities, politicians, and religious leaders. It raised US$34 million, which largely went to combat hunger in the USA, rather than overseas.[407] Such initiatives kept the issue of hunger in the public eye far longer than it might otherwise have been, and succeeded in generating substantial funds that were eventually deployed for rehabilitation and development programmes in Africa. Manifestations of celebrity humanitarianism held one idea in common: issues of hunger and poverty in Africa require prominent interpreters or 'intermediaries' in order to make them meaningful – even enticing – to Western audiences.[408] Expressive humanitarianism built on a long-standing tradition of popular engagement with charity in the form of consumption – that is, through sales of ancillary merchandise.[409] Thus, through tie-ins with McDonalds and other commercial companies, Hands across America and Live Aid also influenced the development of cause-related marketing in the 1980s, more recently conceptualised as 'Brand Aid'.[410]

The celebrity-endorsed, media-driven fundraising extravaganzas from 1984 to 1986, particularly Live Aid, have assumed iconic status in how the period is remembered in many countries, and have since been widely duplicated. As highly successful instances of a 'marketised philanthropy', these one-off, immersive, participatory experiences largely succeeded because they were not seeking any long-term engagement with the underlying issues of global inequalities.[411] Self-declared 'band-aids', they proposed only temporary amelioration of hunger. Nonetheless, such participatory appeals worked not by duping 'audiences mesmerised by spectacle', but by tapping into a genuine desire for emotional investment in feeding the world – if it might be achieved without paying too high a price financially and emotionally.[412]

3.5   Arousing Compassion: A Long View on Calls for Famine Relief

Our three case studies take a long view of the evolution of appeals for emergency aid. Stretching over a period of almost 150 years and drawing on

---

[406] Sport Aid activities raised approximately US$30 million.
[407] USA for Africa, *Memories and Reflections*; Buck Wolf, 'Great Shakes: Hands across America: 20 Years On', ABC.com, 23 May 2006.
[408] Franks, *Reporting Disasters*, 83.   [409] Field, 'Consumption *in lieu* of Membership'.
[410] Stefano Ponte and Lisa Ann Richey, 'Buying into Development? Brand Aid Forms of Cause-Related Marketing', *Third World Quarterly* 35, no. 1 (2014): 65–87.
[411] Jones, 'Band Aid Revisited', 190.   [412] Lousley, 'With Love from Band Aid', 16.

source material from a range of donor countries, the cases presented illustrate the trajectory of humanitarian fundraising over time. We identify distinctions between the three examples, noting the differing historical contexts in which relief funds were raised, as well as the similarities and continuities in discourse and practice.

In all three cases, famine conditions had been developing for some time. However, transnational aid mobilisation first gained momentum as a consequence of media events after the crisis had escalated. For Ireland, it was the report from the Skibbereen neighbourhood in December 1846; in the case of Russia, the circulation of Gorky's appeal in July 1921; and for relief to Ethiopia, the screening of Buerk's and Amin's BBC report in October 1984. Once a broader public had become aware of the famine, fundraising, organisations, and the media deployed hyperbolic language to vivify conditions in the afflicted areas. In each of our examples, aid agencies depicted as unprecedented the scale of the crisis, the number of people affected, and the horrors of starvation.

While Irish and Russian representatives appealed directly to donors abroad, Ethiopian recipients depended on brokers in Europe and the USA. Those intermediaries shared images rather than transmitting the voices of those suffering, thereby depriving them of their own voice in the catastrophe. In all three countries, diaspora communities were engaged in fundraising, but their importance for the overall relief effort decreased over time. During the 1840s, Irish communities in the British Empire and the USA played a pivotal role in relief activities, and entreaties originating from Ireland are well documented in publications concerning relief efforts. Still, the largest British campaign calculated that they would receive a greater return in donations by citing officials and humanitarian workers, rather than beneficiaries. A similar strategy can be observed in the 1920s regarding Russia. Even though fundraising campaigns were triggered by Gorky's appeal, in the two years that followed, aid organisations relied mainly on reports and graphics provided by foreign visitors to the famine region. Russian voices, mostly in the form of letters, were occasionally heard in communications of gratitude or requests for small-scale relief. The role of Russian communities abroad, however, was ambivalent, as some members were active adversaries of the Bolshevik regime. Still, many supported the relief efforts financially and organised collections that were often directed at specific groups. With regard to Ethiopia, individuals were only depicted as famine victims to illustrate the horrors of starvation. The fact that they were given no other identity contributed to a distorted picture of Africans in the Global North that had lasting consequences. Exiled groups allied to the Tigrayan and Eritrean liberation fronts tried to create awareness of the fate of the population in areas outside governmental control, but their overall influence was limited.

Historically, the waning voices of famine victims might appear surprising. It can partially be explained by the increasing spatial and emotional distance between donors and beneficiaries in our three cases. During the Irish Famine, many donors felt closely connected to beneficiaries, either as UK citizens, through their Irish kinship, or as Catholic coreligionists. At the time of organised humanitarianism, appeals on behalf of more distant populations became possible, even for enemies and former enemies, if other bonds appeared meaningful. Accordingly, Gorky described Russians as members of a European family of cultivated nations, and appeals often focused on children as a group presumably untainted by ethnic, religious, or political divisions. Many organisations called on the entire population of their home countries, or even beyond, with appeals in the name of humanity, Christianity, and the idea of reconciliation. Others continued to rely on more narrowly defined religious and ethnic bonds, and the obligations and entitlements they entailed.

By contrast, relief for ethnic was mainly provided by 'distant strangers' in a geographical, ethnical, and cultural sense, although the rapid coverage provided by the media gave donors a sense of participating in real time. Appeals relied almost exclusively on notions of urgency and the broader ties of humanity or Christianity, again focusing on children. The role of celebrities as mediators between the donating public in the West and starving Africans, while it had earlier roots (such as the engagement of Gorky and other writers and artists in the early 1920s), is generally seen as a hallmark of modern-day humanitarianism. However, Live Aid is also reminiscent of earlier engagements, such as the Anti-Corn-Law League Bazaar in 1845, which raised an enormous sum of money while politicising the middle classes.[413] The notion that there can be reconciliation after political rupture, prominently advocated after the First World War, did not play a role in the Ethiopian case.

Worthy Victims and Guilty Governments

Doubts regarding the entitlement of famine victims were handled in various ways. At the time of the Great Irish Famine, the Anglo-Saxon discourse was not only characterised by prejudice against the Irish, but also by a Malthusian logic that considered starving populations at least partly responsible for their own fate. Thus, many appeals suggested a 'quid quo pro' moral economy regarding a beneficiary's entitlement, adjusted to the targeted donor group: Catholic efforts and US campaigns tended to stress historical justifications, such as a debt owed to Ireland for being a stronghold of Catholicism or a nucleus of North American society, while appeals in the British Empire

---

[413] Prochaska, *Voluntary Impulse*, 14.

recalled Ireland's military contributions to imperial expansion. In the case of Russia, a future requital was occasionally promised, if only indirectly, by suggesting that relief to Russia would serve the donors' economic self-interests in the long run. Only communist relief organisations argued explicitly for reciprocity by referring to Russians as a revolutionary avant-garde who had bled for workers all over the world. During the famine in Ethiopia, notions of reciprocity no longer played a substantial role, even in the abstract; instead, appeals to a common humanity dominated, alongside a vague sense of responsibility to the 'Third World'.

In the 1840s, many fundraisers presented aid to the Irish as either ethnic, religious, or imperial in-group relief. The breakthrough of the principle of impartiality that followed – anticipated in numerous campaigns during the Great Famine – was a humanitarian milestone. However, it also led to the counterclaim that charity should begin at home, a position that was especially strong when nationalist or ideological tensions were high. Humanitarian appeals, therefore, had to stress that true altruism could not be limited to certain groups, but must be founded on an objective evaluation of need. The existence of deserving people at home was never denied, either during the Russian or the Ethiopian Famine, although humanitarian organisations tried to explain that their own compatriots were far better off than the victims of famine. Descriptive and visual here–there comparisons translated this argument into fundraising appeals. Nevertheless, in many cases, humanitarian agencies were forced to accompany their actions in support of distant sufferers with ancillary campaigns for the local charity market. For example, relief to Ireland was paralleled by relief to Scotland, and during the Russian Famine, the SCF ran a simultaneous fundraising drive for domestic relief. Likewise, USA for Africa and similar Canadian and French celebrity fundraising activities in the 1980s earmarked part of their donations for domestic charities.

While the necessity of objective evaluation and impartiality was promulgated early on, so was the modern criticism heard that such an approach might reduce relief 'from a moral enterprise to a merely technocratic one'.[414] Fundraisers realised that solely functional appeals would not result in the desired outcome, as donors rather 'react to people who have problems than to statistics about people with problems'.[415] In the case of all three countries

---

[414] Jacqueline Pfeffer Merrill, 'Peter Singer's Advice: No Charity at Home', *Philanthropy Daily*, 14 Aug. 2013, available at www.philanthropydaily.com/peter-singers-advice-no-charity-at-home/ (accessed 29 June 2019).

[415] Deborah A. Small, George Loewenstein, and Paul Slovic, 'Sympathy and Callousness: The Impact of Deliberative Thought on Donations to Identifiable and Statistical Victims', *Organizational Behavior and Human Decision Processes* 102, no. 2 (2007): 146.

examined, appeals sought to individualise suffering by describing or portraying specific outcomes – preferably focusing on children and mothers. Another common campaign feature was engaging holidays, especially Christmas, to inspire giving, while repeating the claim that the scale of the famine was unprecedented.

During the Irish Famine, such strategies tended to move the public away from Malthusian reasoning. At the beginning of the appeals for starving Russia, however, many fundraisers were worried about a possibly desensitised post-war audience. They assumed that more powerful emotional triggers were needed and acted accordingly. Fundraisers for Ethiopia in the 1980s also presumed donor fatigue after the high-profile crises of the 1970s. The three campaigns we analysed confirm modern studies of media responsibility. Such studies claim that the presumption of 'compassion fatigue' not only reinforces simplistic press coverage, but also sets the sensationalism bar higher for coming emergencies, which in each case must then be described as 'more dramatic or more lethal than their predecessors'.[416]

The inclination to blame victims gave way to a modern humanitarian narrative during the late nineteenth century, although the old tendency seems to have reappeared in recent times. However, doubts regarding natural causes of famines – especially claims concerning the responsibility of governments – still hinder relief efforts. The situation in the three settings we examined differed, as Russia and Ethiopia were ruled by regimes hostile to the West, making transnational aid a delicate matter, while Ireland was part of the British Empire. Many Irish people, joined by some Germans and French, spoke out against the failure of the British government. In opposition, UK relief tended to frame the famine as a calamity limited to a discrete area with a problematic population, rather than concede that it was a domestic crisis. Hence, imperial calls for aid during the Irish Famine were careful to explain the safeguards put in place to prevent donations from being abused, as did Western organisations in Russia and Ethiopia.

Contemporary fundraisers understood that the perception of an emergency as a product of human agency might damage otherwise successful campaigns. They denounced any such claim of human causality, despite often knowing better, and attempted to depoliticise the context, either by concealing human causes or by rhetorically separating innocent suffering populations from their leaders. During the 1920s, relief organisations avoided any discussion of communism's failure and the adverse effects of Western engagement in the Russian Civil War, highlighting instead their co-operation

---

[416] Susan D. Moeller, *Compassion Fatigue: How the Media Sell Disease, Famine, War and Death* (New York: Routledge, 1999), 2.

with the Russian population and governmental authorities. Similarly, the well-known broadcaster Buerk admitted he downplayed the civil war in Ethiopia in order not to compromise relief efforts. Another fundraising strategy was to assure donors that aid would not strengthen a country's hostile ideological order, but that they would rather weaken it by winning the 'hearts and minds' of the starving masses.

Despite transnational ambitions and appeals invoking humanity and universal siblinghood, one striking continuity across our three case studies is the framing of campaigns as a national relief effort. During the Irish Famine, many fundraisers abroad drew on feelings of national pride and competition when trying to encourage donors. This partitioning of transnational relief became more prevalent during the Russian Famine, and by the 1980s, most practical and effective campaigns were organised within the framework of the nation-state, such as the various celebrity-endorsed national television rallies during the Ethiopian Famine. However, the success of national campaigns for wider impartial relief efforts cannot only be explained by nationalist feelings, practicalities, or the expectations of higher donations and an economisation of expenditures for logistics. It also has to do with the role charity plays in religious, political, and social power relations. During the Irish Famine, charity was already being used as a means of influencing affected populations, or, alternatively, to counter the attempts of others to do so. In Ireland, the conflict between Catholics and Protestants was most important in this regard, while during the Russian Famine, ideological and political antagonism was decisive. Similar mechanisms were at work in Ethiopia, where a Cold War narrative contributed to national forms of organising aid campaigns.

Ethics, Effectiveness, and Efficiency

Reductionist and paternalistic attitudes during the Ethiopian Famine characterised ongoing discussions about the moral agency of beneficiaries and Northern 'pornography of pain' in a fundraising context. The humanitarian organisations of the 1920s were aware of the ethical tensions that resulted from the dependence of relief work on professional advertising agencies and public relations techniques. The SCF had to face the reproach of exploiting the public's emotions, while the ARA was accused of abusing famine relief for political purposes.

Fundraisers struggled to find a balance between the objective of running an efficient aid operation and the necessity of creating compassion and generating donations. During the Irish Famine, the utilitarian recommendation that relief should 'give the greatest amount of needful help, with the smallest encouragement to undue reliance on it' was implicitly part of appeals.[417] This Victorian approach remained a guiding principle for some organisations during the Russian Famine. However, appeals now followed a business logic, vowing to save as many people as possible with the smallest means possible. More often than in the case of Ireland, Russian appeals put a price tag on human lives – '£1 saves one child' – thereby encouraging people to translate everyday expenditures into rescuing children from starvation – something Singer later did more systematically. During the famine in Ethiopia, such arguments were already well-established and are evident in various calls for aid.

Throughout the whole period, there were appeals that incorporated the three-fold goal of not only feeding the starving, but also fighting the origins of famine and providing long-term aid. The 'help them to help themselves' credo was highly regarded at the time of the Irish Famine. During the 1920s, both the FSR and the Quakers anticipated later forms of 'development assistance' by sending agricultural equipment and tools as well as instructors to Russia. In Ethiopia, too, some appeals promised to address broader questions of long-term rehabilitation, while continuing to provide aid in the present.

Regarding Flynn's ideal types of the 'suffering stranger appeal' and the 'causal contribution appeal', it becomes clear that while the latter remains an exception, it is not a modern phenomenon. Already during the 1840s, the colonial exploitation under English rule was considered a major cause of famine by some Irish commentators. Similarly, US appeals sometimes related Ireland's agony to profiteering caused by the discrepancy between poor harvests in Europe and New World abundance. During the Russian Famine, Nansen and Hoover pointed in like manner to the large surplus of grain in the Americas. The SCF further called donations 'blood money' and an atonement for previous deeds and Gorky's appeal hinted in a similar direction. That a donor's capability and culpability often go hand in hand is illustrated by the feelings of shame and guilt many Europeans expressed over the notorious 'butter mountains' and 'milk lakes' they were taunted with during the Ethiopian Famine. Thus, the moral economy topic of overflow versus need was significant in all three cases, although neither one of the pair was necessarily described as conditioning the other.

The critical observation that relief is often 'about us, not them' gained broad recognition towards the end of the twentieth century, having already been noted by commentators on the Irish and Russian famines. Several appeals could be cited that focused on the well-being of the donor rather than the beneficiary by promising salvation for those who gave – a promise meant in a literal, religious sense during the Irish Famine. Fundraisers in the 1920s also

---

[417] John Stuart Mill, *Principles of Political Economy: With Some of Their Applications to Social Philosophy*, vol. 2 (London: Parker, 1848), 536.

invoked spiritual salvation, but sometimes also economic salvation and the promise of a better future in the here and now. The USA for Africa song, 'We Are the World', exemplifies this utopian longing for a just global community, its lyrics suggesting that donors would be saving their own lives by contributing to a good cause. Donor-centredness is also apparent in the expressive mixture of consumerism and appeals typified by charity concerts and the sale of recordings.

4   Allocation

4.1   Allocating Gifts

The humanitarian sector facilitates the flow of money, goods, or services to people in dire need and tries 'to be as fair as possible in an unfair world'.[1] In neoclassical economics – the doctrine that has conditioned humanitarianism for more than a century – the key concern is the allocation of resources with maximum efficiency, based on information, including prices, transmitted by markets. This tends to reinforce the prevailing pattern of distribution, which is seen as an 'equilibrium' in accordance with the common good. Such a pattern does not address inequalities and needs, and is indifferent to an individual's claim to a right of subsistence.[2] Donor decisions, on the other hand, are driven less by notions of efficiency and more by an emotional response to aid appeals; political, religious, or communal affiliations; or what they consider to be appropriate and fair. Humanitarian organisations are bound to consider such preferences in any given crisis, while at the same time recognising what impact allocation decisions have as moral statement and what they might mean for future donor behaviour.[3]

The sphere of charity is thus a subsidiary market that lacks a price mechanism which would facilitate basic transactions, and that is only loosely linked to the final destination of relief goods. The market for donations, which calibrates sponsor motivation and information provided by aid organisations and the media, depends generally on discretionary sums. This volatile market for contributions is not supported by a comparably efficient mechanism informing aid organisations about which needs to address. On the contrary, a prevailing disaster tends to prevent recipients from being able to offer money in exchange

[1] Samia A. Hurst, Nathalie Mezger, and Alex Mauron, 'Allocating Resources in Humanitarian Medicine', *Public Health Ethics* 2, no. 1 (2009): 92.
[2] Stanley Reiter, 'Efficient Allocation', in *The New Palgrave: A Dictionary of Economics, vol. 2: E to J*, eds John Eatwell, Murray Milgate, and Peter Newman (London: Macmillan, 1987), 107–20.
[3] Scott Wisor, 'How Should INGOs Allocate Resources?', *Ethics & Global Politics* 5, no. 1 (2012): 43.

for provisions (and thus from sending the usual signals that a market needs to function). The relief effort lacks the clearing mechanism of regular markets and depends primarily on reports from activists and the press.

Donors generally find it difficult to assess and compare the effectiveness and efficiency of voluntary organisations in allocating relief, although low over-heads, presence on the ground, and the ability to elicit further funding are seen as important 'selling points'. At the same time, while working on emergencies, aid agencies confront uncertainties far exceeding those of ordinary markets. Organisations may have to 'second-guess the needs of the beneficiaries',[4] rely primarily on trust, and establish their own targeting priorities. This includes attempts to internalise human suffering into economic calculations as a 'deprivation cost'; utilising planning and controlling instruments (such as the 'Public Equitable Allocation of Resources Log') and individual needs assess-ment tools (such as the mid-upper arm circumference tape); and the creation of other relief metrics and algorithms.[5]

Efficient versus Engaging Allocation

The basic problem of humanitarianism resembles that of economics-at-large, namely, the differential of scarce resources and the wants that exceed them. However, while the economy proper is construed as settling down to a relative equilibrium, humanitarianism suffers from an overall mismatch between inelastic, morally charged subsistence requirements, and the means to satisfy them. As a result, many needs remain unaddressed, resulting in suffering and death. Under such circumstances, any effort by donors or humanitarian organ-isations carries with it an 'awesome responsibility' in view of the 'moral opportunity costs' that arise when some people are privileged as beneficiaries over others with similar needs.[6]

Although choices are inevitable, the only aspect that surfaces is usually the positive allocation decision. A large body of research suggests that the

---

[4] Peter Tatham and Martin Christopher, 'Introduction', in *Humanitarian Logistics: Meeting the Challenges of Preparing for and Responding to Disasters*, 3rd ed. (London: Kogan Page, 2018), 4.

[5] José Holguín-Veras, Noel Pérez, Miguel Jaller, Luk N. van Wassenhove, and Felipe Aros-Vera, 'On the Appropriate Objective Function for Post-Disaster Humanitarian Logistics Models', *Journal of Operations Management* 31, no. 5 (2013): 262–80; Claire Elizabeth Carlson, Paul A. Isihara, Roger Sandberg, et al., 'Introducing PEARL: A Gini-like Index and Reporting Tool for Public Accountability and Equity in Disaster Response', *Journal of Humanitarian Logistics and Supply Chain Management* 6, no. 2 (2016): 202–21; Joël Glasman, 'Measuring Malnutri-tion: The History of the MUAC Tape and the Commensurability of Human Needs', *Humanity* 9, no. 1 (2018): 19–44.

[6] Pogge, 'Moral Priorities', 220; Wisor, 'How Should INGOs', 27. See also Carbonnier, *Humani-tarian Economics*, 4.

actual severity of a humanitarian cause is a secondary criterion. More significant are media attention, the perceived merits of potential recipients, and even more so the self-interest and herd behaviour of donors. A project idea that appears appropriate and manageable for a particular organisation tends to outweigh the concern of that organisation over beneficiaries.[7] Practices of screening affected people and identifying potential recipients vary widely, although vulnerable children and mothers are frequently among those chosen. At the same time, aid agencies throughout history have sometimes misinterpreted the needs of recipients and delivered inappropriate goods. Similarly, donors have burdened relief transactions with complicated demands and unsolicited items.

Against such tendencies, a recently developed 'Greatest Good Donation Calculator' seeks to educate contributors about the advantages of giving cash over gifts-in-kind.[8] In addition, an 'effective altruism' movement, based on a consequentialist utilitarian theory of ethics, has called for recasting humanitarian aid with a focus on (1) how many people benefit from an initiative and to what extent; (2) best practices; (3) everyday calamities, underserved places, and most needy causes, rather than simply major disasters; (4) genuine contributions and avoidance of bandwagon effects; and (5) weighing risks and potential gains.[9] However, these strategies are not new and are typical of the organised humanitarianism of the early and mid-twentieth century.

A study of how Médecins Sans Frontières (MSF) justifies the opening, closing, or restructuring of projects illustrates different contemporary approaches. Three types of legitimation were found to prevail. The first was based on statistical comparison and resembles the mass-oriented perspective taken by organised humanitarianism and the effective altruism movement. However, it was found to be of limited applicability. The other two are reference to one's organisational mission and identity, and solidarity with and advocacy on behalf of destitute communities. Both are self-centred or relational, founded on a deontological (i.e., rule-based) understanding of ethics. They can be traced back to earlier humanitarian campaigns, but are particularly reflective of present-day expressive humanitarianism. As both identity and solidarity entail bias towards a status quo orientation of humanitarian commitments, a balanced approach has been advocated in which the inclination of

---

[7] Jónína Einarsdóttir and Geir Gunnlaugsson, 'Applied Ethics and Allocation of Foreign Aid: Disparity in Pretensions and Practice', *Development Policy Review* 34, no. 3 (2016): 345–63; Krause, *Good Project*.

[8] Koray Özpolat, Juanita Rilling, Nezih Altay, and Eric Chavez, 'Engaging Donors in Smart Compassion: USAID CIDI's Greatest Good Donation Calculator', *Journal of Humanitarian Logistics and Supply Chain Management* 5, no. 1 (2015): 95–112.

[9] William MacAskill, *Doing Good Better: How Effective Altruism Can Help You Make a Difference* (New York: Gotham, 2015).

fieldworkers to 'go native' is regularly challenged by the distanced attitude of headquarters of aid organisations.[10]

The logic of fieldwork and disaster response correlates with the 'rule of rescue', namely, focusing on identifiable individuals rather than maximising abstract aid. The rule stresses the agility and effectiveness of concrete humanitarian efforts over their cost and efficiency in the long view. From a situational perspective, the question of alternative resource allocation may appear as a 'lack of moral concern'. However, humanitarian organisations generally need to find a balance between deontological and consequential approaches when planning relief efforts.[11] Famines hold an intermediate position on the urgency continuum. They are usually attributed in part to natural causes, but tend to have a more complex character than such sudden-onset disasters as earthquakes, storms, or floods.

Humanitarian Logistics, Nutrition, and Their Pull-Effect

Prompted by failures after the 2004 Indian Ocean tsunami, humanitarian logistics has become a field of increased research and social engineering. Issues discussed include inter-agency trust and product-centred cluster formation; lessons that may be learned from commercial logistics and humanitarian–private partnerships; the integration of relief and development programmes; examples of good practice; the seamless transition between in-kind and cash modalities of relief (turning beneficiaries into customers); return of investment for emergency preparedness (i.e., conserving money through a well-planned relief infrastructure); and providing services in a businesslike manner.[12] This agenda correlates with the displacement of social nutrition approaches by apolitical and medicalising ones over the past two decades. There has been a shift from providing ordinary foodstuffs to delivering therapeutical nutrition (such as high-energy biscuits) for malnourished people. Feeding programmes are no longer based on patronage, but on anthropometric indicators.[13]

---

[10] Lisa Fuller, 'Justified Commitments? Considering Resource Allocation and Fairness in Médecins Sans Frontières-Holland', *Developing World Bioethics* 6, no. 2 (2006): 59–70.

[11] Hurst, Mezger, and Mauron, 'Allocating Resources', 89; Daniel M. Bartels, 'Principled Moral Sentiment and the Flexibility of Moral Judgment and Decision Making', *Cognition* 108, no. 2 (2008): 381–417.

[12] Rebecca Lewin, Maria Besiou, Jean-Baptiste Lamarche, Stephen Cahill, and Sara Guerrero-Garcia, 'Delivering in a Moving World … : Looking to Our Supply Chains to Meet the Increasing Scale, Cost and Complexity of Humanitarian Needs', *Journal of Humanitarian Logistics and Supply Chain Management* 8, no. 4 (2018): 518–32; Graham Heaslip, Gyöngyi Kovács, and David B. Grant, 'Servitization as a Competitive Difference in Humanitarian Logistics', *Journal of Humanitarian Logistics and Supply Chain Management* 8, no. 4 (2018): 497–517.

[13] Susanne Jaspars, Tom Scott-Smith, and Elizabeth Hull, *Contested Evolution of Nutrition for Humanitarian and Development Ends: Report of an International Workshop* (Oxford: Refugee

Logistics research frequently points out that 60–80 per cent of the budget of aid organisations is consumed by logistics.[14] However, these figures include not only delivery costs, but also the purchase of relief goods. Recent studies have found that among logistics expenses, procurement costs ranged from 84 per cent for the Red Cross to 28 per cent for Action Contre la Faim, reflecting different organisational structures, mission profiles, and procurement sources.[15]

Apart from the asymmetry of its gift economy, famine relief presents a unique logistical challenge as it tends to operate in peripheral areas where there is inadequate infrastructure and a lack of time and opportunity for systematic capacity-building. Therefore, it is frequently based on a combination of commercial models with rapid, less cost-sensitive military contingency management and needs-based approaches. Critical factors for an effective response are structural flexibility, coordination, and the management of disparate information, particularly the utilisation of local knowledge and resources.[16]

Material supplies are generally provided to recipients at delivery nodes (including distribution points, soup kitchens, feeding centres, etc.). Arranging for pick-up, beyond what supply chain management regards as the 'last mile', is left to the ultimate beneficiary, who needs to retrieve provisions at the aid organisation's chosen distribution site. The confusion of delivery stations with 'demand points' is indicative of the prevailing moral economy and of the technocratic leanness of certain logistics frames.[17] Market-based solutions, cash transfer programmes, or the availability of individual delivery services influence distribution, but still presuppose a functioning infrastructure and efforts by recipients, sometimes considerable, to obtain the goods needed. Little discussed is how the improvement of food security, something evident as one moves up the aid chain, exerts a pull-effect on recipients. Thus, the last mile for aid agencies is frequently the second mile to the source of supplies for those in need, and can take them across their homeland, to neighbouring countries, and across the sea (directly and as a domino effect).

The moral dilemmas thereby created are a trade-off between logistic costs and the proportionality of relief, or efficiency and fairness. There is a bias

Studies Centre, 2018); Tom Scott-Smith, *On an Empty Stomach: The Humanitarian Approach to Hunger* (Ithaca, NY: Cornell University Press, forthcoming 2020).

[14] E.g., Tatham and Christopher, 'Introduction', 3; Luk N. van Wassenhove, 'Humanitarian Aid Logistics: Supply Chain Management in High Gear', *Journal of the Operational Research Society* 57, no. 5 (2006): 475–89.

[15] Email by Jonas Stumpf, 12 Apr. 2019. See also, Lea Stegemann and Jonas Stumpf, *Supply Chain Expenditure and Preparedness Investment Opportunities* (Schindellegi: HELP Logistics, 2018).

[16] Douglas C. Long and Donald F. Wood, 'The Logistics of Famine Relief', *Journal of Business Logistics* 16, no. 1 (1995): 213–29.

[17] E.g., Burcu Balcik, Benita M. Beamon, and Karen Smilowitz, 'Last Mile Distribution in Humanitarian Relief', *Journal of Intelligent Transportation Systems* 12, no. 2 (2008): 51–63.

towards depreciating material standards with distance from the centre, and the 'creative' disruption caused by the pull of relief and the imagination of a better life may go along with both voluntary and forced migration. Aid organisations also need to consider the impact of their allocations on donor behaviour, such as the request for speedy disbursal or demands for privileging certain groups of recipients. The history of 'humanitarian practices *as* practices' in the field is one that includes the complicity of humanitarian efforts with acts of 'systemic violence'.[18]

4.2   Fostering Local Efforts: Ireland

The partial Irish potato failure of autumn 1845 marked the beginning of the Great Famine. Although the catastrophe had been alleviated by local charity (supplemented by a few overseas donations), public works programmes, and the government purchase and sale of Indian corn, there was worse to come. In the following season, the new Whig government was unwilling to interfere with the almost complete failure of the potato crop. Not only did officials refuse to interfere with the food market, but they also tightened the rules governing public works. While the public works scheme expanded rapidly in the winter of 1846/7, it proved to be ineffective, demoralising, and tremendously expensive. Offsetting those costs through local taxation remained a treasury pipe dream.

Voluntary soup relief preceded the soup provision programme that Westminster later adopted. It was a stop-gap during a period of policy adjustment in the spring of 1847, when neither food nor wages were forthcoming from the government. While different forms of charity – partly collaborative and partly antagonistic – coexisted, the largest of such organisations, the British Relief Association (BRA), was in fact a proxy of the government responsible for stimulating local Irish relief committees by assisting them in the acquisition of foodstuffs. Quaker and independent committees also attempted to sell tickets for meals to local benefactors, or to the hungry themselves, but they saw the need for gratuitous relief as well. Money that was collected and sent to Ireland underpinned this economy of provision. However, the Catholic Church and private donors also forwarded cash to parish priests and others in the stricken area, and sometimes directly to the starving poor. Concrete relief allocation caused shifts in the population and, in turn, shaped demands for aid. The search for food, other relief, and ultimately improved living conditions either in England or North America also increased the pressure on donors to provide shelter for displaced people, even if it were under their own roofs.

---

[18] Bertrand Taithe and John Borton, 'History, Memory and "Lessons Learnt" for Humanitarian Practitioners', *European Review of History* 23, nos 1–2 (2016): 219, 211.

Aid for Sale: The BRA

In February 1847, James Crawford Caffin, captain of one of the first relief ships the BRA sent to Ireland, presented the admiralty with graphic accounts of distress on the country's south-western headland. The captain concluded by noting that autopsies of people who had starved to death revealed that 'the inner membrane of the stomach turns into a white mucus, as if nature had supported herself upon herself, until exhaustion of all the humours of the system has taken place'. He only parenthetically mentioned his own cargo of foodstuffs and did not say that he was engaged by a humanitarian organisation that was prepared to do work on the ground. Instead, he simply requested gratuitous relief for the distressed people.[19]

When a London newspaper published the captain's letter, the BRA reacted immediately. In a Letter to the Editor, its chairman pointed out in defense of the BRA that the captain's ship had been laden with goods from a committee advised by the BRA. Additional cargoes, he asserted, had been placed under the management of their agent on site. He explained it in this way in order to do 'justice to the efforts of the British Association, and for the satisfaction of the humane feelings of the public'.[20] On a later occasion, when the captain delivered a different cargo, a newspaper published another letter of his in which he thanked the head of the tiny London-based United Relief Association (URA) for supplying him with £10 in cash, 'for really the demands upon my own purse were so many and great, that I should soon be a beggar, or else have to steel my heart against the misery and woe around me'. Once again, Caffin urged the provision of gratuitous relief, a practice to which the URA, but not the BRA, was committed.[21]

The BRA was assigned the relief of remote parishes in western and southern Ireland in collaboration with local committees. It utilised existing administrative and logistic structures, and generally duplicated government standards. Treasury instructions 'to consider the operations of the [BRA] Committee as identical ... with the Government operations' reveal its semi-official character.[22] The BRA's mission was not saving lives as such, but correcting market failures and developing commercial structures in remote areas in ways that would not 'come into competition with our merchants and

---

[19] 'A Distressing Picture', *Daily News*, 19 Feb. 1847. Caffin's letter, dated 15 Feb., was frequently reprinted. See also David McLean, 'Famine on the Coast: The Royal Navy and the Relief of Ireland, 1846–1847', *English Historical Review* 134, no. 566 (2019): 103.

[20] Jones Loyd, Letter to the Editor, *Daily News*, 20 Feb. 1847.

[21] 'Distress in Ireland', *Standard*, 15 Mar. 1847. For the amount, see the URA advertisement in *Shipping and Mercantile Gazette*, 13 Mar. 1847.

[22] Treasury minute, 14 Jan. 1847, *Correspondence* I, 497.

Figure 4.1 Government sale of Indian corn at Cork, *London Illustrated News*, 4 Apr. 1846.
Engraving from a sketch by James Mahony. This image is reproduced courtesy of the National Library of Ireland

upset all their calculations'.[23] The means to achieve this were two-fold: supply side intervention in shipping foodstuffs to Ireland and their distribution through a network of depots; and stabilisation of the demand on the market for food by facilitating local charitable action (Figure 4.1). In fact, what the BRA did was sell provisions at cost to local relief committees which, in turn, allocated these for gratis distribution to families in distress who lacked a breadwinner.[24]

In this way, British aid utilised Irish charities to bridge the gap that remained between the demand of people who could afford to pay for food, and those whose vital need for sustenance still existed, regardless of market 'equilibrium'. Such an arrangement was intended to multiply the resources available to relieve distress, thereby maximising their impact as follows: revenues from the sale of food would enable the purchase of further relief goods, while at the same time local charities, who knew the deserving poor, would handle the distribution of relief, thus putting donations to work in the most efficient way.

---

[23] Trevelyan to Routh, 18 Dec. 1846, *Correspondence* I, 382.
[24] 'Conditions of the Grant', *Report of the British Association*, 175.

These goals were all achieved. The proceeds from the sale of food (and, on a much smaller scale, seed) by the BRA in Ireland were spent for additional relief, while reports of abuse were rare.[25]

However, this approach was not without difficulties. When the BRA sent their first fieldworker, Henry Cooke Harston, then on leave from the Royal Navy, to the area west of Cork in January 1847, their instructions cautioned that 'in the present excited state of men's minds exaggeration and misrepresentation must prevail to an unusual extent'.[26] Thus, even after the harrowing report of the two deputies from Skibbereen that led to the establishment of the BRA, the organisation still gravely underestimated the famine.[27] While Harston's communication in the following months concerned technical matters regarding the campaign, he noted in dismay that half the population in his area was beyond recovery and doomed to die.[28] Another fieldworker informed headquarters that the distress had 'reached such degree of lamentable extremes, that it becomes above the power of exaggeration and misrepresentation', adding that 'you may now believe anything which you hear and read, because what I actually see surpasses what I ever read of past and present calamities'.[29] Although its agents provided the BRA committee with a more realistic understanding of the famine, there was no revision of the approach. Instead, the BRA gave fieldworkers the following striking instructions:

The funds ... being thus insufficient to secure the result which would be wished, it is most desirable to economize them as far as practicable. Urgent cases, of necessity must, it is true, be provided for at all hazards; but it must be always remembered that caution to economy ... will be the best security against the general spread of famine throughout the country. The object of your mission being the early relief of distress[.][30]

BRA personnel on the ground were told that finite resources were not to be expended on those whose prospects of survival were uncertain. The instructions pointed out that while the 'essential duty of an agent' was to sell provisions to local committees at cost, the BRA also authorised them to make gifts of aid up to the value of one-tenth of local subscriptions. Should any 'extraordinary' additional grant be advisable, the agent was to justify his recommendation in a letter to London.[31] These new guidelines were liberal

[25] *Report of the British Association*, 50–1.
[26] Minute Book, 39 (12 Jan. 1847), NLI, MS 2022.
[27] See 'Statement relative to the distress in Skibbereen / By Deputation from Relief Committee', 2 Dec. 1846, TNA(UK), HO 45/1080A.
[28] Harston to BRA, 5 Feb. 1847, *Report of the British Association*, 60.
[29] Strzelecki to BRA, 15 Mar. 1847, *Report of the British Association*, 970.
[30] Spring Rice to Loney, 14 Apr. 1847, Loney letter book, available at www.pdavis.nl/Famine3 .htm (accessed 29 June 2019).
[31] Ibid.

compared to those given to the first agent, which limited him to selling provisions to relief committees 'for cash only'.[32]

Despite the sales philosophy, grants became the dominant form of relief distributed by the BRA. While information on unsettled purchases is lacking, it seems such cases were retrospectively treated as grants. The UK government provided infrastructural support, including reimbursement of freight charges. Since other overhead costs were low, the £391,700 in donations that the BRA received for Ireland largely corresponded to the prime cost of aid. Provisions for more than two-thirds of this amount were distributed free of charge. Food and seed sold in Ireland yielded approximately £125,000. Moreover, since Irish relief committees defrayed only two-fifths of the costs of foodstuffs sold, the UK government paid for the rest, showing the discrepancy between on-site sales projections and receipts. Due to the dire conditions in Ireland, the BRA became more generous and instituted alternative procedures. However, despite the failure of the plan to sell provisions to the affected communities, the income generated allowed the BRA to mount the final phase of its relief effort. Beginning in autumn 1847, the organisation spent more than £123,000 to feed and clothe school children in the most distressed areas of Ireland.[33]

Initially, the BRA was determined never to distribute money to 'parties relieved', assuming that cash could easily be abused and that it would have an inflationary tendency, whereas supplying food would have the opposite effect.[34] The BRA's earliest instructions reformulated this as pertaining to 'applicants for relief'. Agents were ordered to find places where cash grants might be appropriate and identify trustworthy people for the administration of the funds.[35] Subsequently, £7,250 in cash was transferred to certain national Irish relief organisations, along with another £10,000 in conjunction with a request by the government for allocation of the Queen's Letter Fund to the General Central Relief Committee for All Ireland (GCRC). Small grants of money to local relief committees and their representatives amounted to £3,692.[36]

A striking example of how important voluntary contributions were to official agencies, and the cynicism of the prevailing policy, may be seen in a request Treasury Secretary Trevelyan made to the BRA. Recounting the

---

[32] Minute Book, 38 (12 Jan 1847), NLI, MS 2022. Underlined phrase in minutes.

[33] 'Statement of the Receipts and Expenditures', *Report of the British Association*, 50–1. On government reimbursements, see 18; for the inception of the school feeding and clothing programme, see 40.

[34] Minute Book, 3 (1 Jan. 1847), NLI, MS 2022. See Memorandum by Spring Rice, 24 Jan. 1847, NLI, MP, 13, 397/10.

[35] Minute Book, 39 (12 Jan. 1847), NLI, MS 2022.

[36] 'Statement of the Receipts and Expenditures', *Report of the British Association*, 51. On the transfer to the GCRC, see Minute Book, 253 (26 Mar. 1847), NLI, MS 2022; on the payment to individuals on behalf of committees, see 122 (3 Feb. 1847).

mental and physical suffering of officers involved in relief work (and anticipating Captain Caffin's second letter), he suggested the following:

It would be a great act of charity, not only to the people themselves, but to our officers, who often have to witness the dreadful distress of the people without being able to afford them any immediate relief, if you would place at the absolute disposal of such of our Inspecting Officers as you have entire confidence in, moderate sums of money (say £100 at a time), to be employed by them entirely at their discretion.[37]

Despite the BRA's close interaction with Trevelyan and its customary compliance with government directives, the request was initially dismissed. When it was brought up again after a few weeks, the BRA granted £50 worth of provisions to each government inspector and the same to its own agents.[38]

Earmarking for particular localities proved complicated for the BRA, but it had the potential of attracting more donors. The organisation's distribution key, according to which one-sixth of the collection went to Scotland and five-sixths to Ireland, was not to everyone's satisfaction: some asked for a different ratio or preferred to give money to only one cause. Keeping track of such matters in accounting and reporting to the public would have been an intricate task. Instead, the BRA acknowledged individual contributors and the designated recipients of their gifts in advertised lists of donors, but they made sure that Scotland's one-sixth share included any amounts specifically contributed for that country.[39]

Narrower earmarking was not very common. While the BRA stated that contributions for certain districts would strictly be observed,[40] the organisation did not live up to its own standard. This is illustrated by an anonymous Irish landlord's gift of £1,000 to the poor of Skibbereen.[41] When the Skibbereen Relief Committee requested that the sum be dispersed, they were told that the BRA had shipped provisions to neighbouring ports, the distribution of which was delayed, but underway. In addition, they were informed that the BRA had 'no power to transmit to you the sums of money you ask for'.[42]

Richard B. Townsend, one of the former Skibbereen deputies to London, made the affair public and demanded to know by what right the BRA had withheld the money, diverting it for general purposes while continuing to sell provisions in Skibbereen. He listed the ways in which this action was disastrous: relief was delayed; the cash sum would have made the Skibbereen Relief

---

[37] Trevelyan to Jones Loyd, 1 Feb. 1847, *Correspondence from January to March, 1847, Relating to the Measures Adopted for the Relief of Distress in Ireland* (hereafter *Correspondence* II) (London: Clowes and Sons, 1847), 49.

[38] Minute Book, 120 (3 Feb. 1847), 273 (7 Apr. 1847), 282 (13 Apr. 1847), NLI, MS 2022. On Trevelyan's influence, see Gray, *Famine, Land and Politics*, 258.

[39] Minute Book, 61 (16 Jan. 1847), NLI, MS 2022.   [40] E.g., *Times*, 6 Jan. 1847.

[41] *Times*, 9 Jan. 1847; *Times*, 14 Jan. 1847.

[42] 'Skibbereen – British Association, &c.', *Cork Examiner*, 12 Feb. 1847.

Committee eligible for a government grant doubling the amount; the public announcement of the gift most likely caused donations to be sent to other places, which, at the same time, might be recipients 'of that which ought to be ours!' – all with potentially fatal consequences for Skibbereen.[43] In fact, mortality in the Skibbereen workhouse was the highest in Ireland at the time, reflecting the destitution of the surrounding area.[44] In a subsequent letter, Townsend appealed to his correspondent's 'own sense of Justice', while asserting that the Skibbereeners' belief in their entitlement was unimpaired by the distress that they endured. While Townsend realised that the BRA had the advantage, he claimed the moral high ground for not letting philanthropic wrong-doing pass without reproach. 'We have right', he insisted, and requested the £1,000 for Skibbereen.[45]

The letter caused the BRA to ascertain the intention of the donor and explain to him the chosen mode of allocation. However, while this was happening, the committee ordered the allotment of £1,000 in weekly instalments of £100 worth of provisions, half of which was to be given to the Skibbereen Relief Committee, and the other half to neighbouring parishes that were selected because of their historical attachment to Skibbereen.[46] The Skibbereeners acquiesced and passed a vote of gratitude, although one of their members criticised the arrangement for 'justice but by halves'.[47] The identity of the donor was not revealed at the time, despite Townsend's awareness that it was the young Lord Dufferin, author of a pamphlet about the famine in Skibbereen.[48] However, through a British bank, the BRA consulted Frederick Pigou, a confidant of Dufferin. On being informed that the chairman of the Skibbereen union had approved the BRA model, Pigou declared his perfect satisfaction.[49]

---

[43] Ibid. According to a newspaper account, the only thing Skibbereen had received from the BRA by the end of February was the privilege to obtain £90 worth of rice and peas at cost ('Skibbereen', *Southern Reporter*, 25 Feb. 1847). For the policy of matching voluntary personal contributions, see 'Instructions for the Formation and Guidance of Committees for Relief of Distress in Ireland, Consequent on the Failure of the Potato Crop in 1846', *Correspondence* I, 492.

[44] Patrick Hickey, 'The Famine in the Skibbereen Union (1845–51)', in *The Great Irish Famine*, ed. Cathal Póirtéir (Cork: Mercier, 1995), 187, 193. Mortality in the vicinity of Skibbereen peaked in Mar. 1847. See Hickey, *Famine in West Cork*, 214–15.

[45] Townsend to Spring Rice, 20 Feb. 1847, NLI, MP, 13, 397/6; printed with revisions in *Southern Reporter*, 25 Feb. 1847.

[46] Minute Book, 171–2 (22 Feb. 1847), 174–5 (23 Feb. 1847), NLI, MS 2022.

[47] McCarthy Downing, Letter to the Editor, *Southern Reporter*, 18 Mar. 1847 (quotation); Harston to BRA, 14 Mar. 1847, *Report of the British Association*, 65.

[48] Townsend to Dufferin, 1 May 1847, Public Record Office of Northern Ireland (PRONI), Belfast, Dufferin and Ava Papers, D1071/H/B/T/252; Frederick Dufferin and George Boyle, *Narrative of a Journey from Oxford to Skibbereen during the Year of the Irish Famine* (Oxford: Parker, 1847).

[49] Minute Book, 174 (23 Feb. 1847); 179 (24 Feb. 1847), 213 (8 Mar. 1847), 217–18 (9 Mar. 1847), NLI, MS 2022.

Soup Kitchens

During the Irish Famine, a well-known charity body determined it would strive 'to exercise great caution in furnishing gratuitous supplies of food; to endeavour to call forth and assist local exertions ... and to seek to economise the consumption of bread-stuffs, by promoting the establishment of soup shops.'[50] What sounds like a government declaration was in fact a mission statement by the Society of Friends. Soup kitchens set up in times of distress were a Quaker hallmark deployed at the end of 1846 along with other local groups.[51] A Quaker kitchen opened on 7 November of that year in the city of Clonmel, and on the same day an independent soup kitchen began operating in Skibbereen.[52] These may have been the first large establishments of their kind. Earlier examples include a soup kitchen in Kilcoe parish, not far from the Skibbereen neighbourhood, which was already operating in September 1846.[53]

In the official relief work documentation of the period, the word 'soup' first appears in the description of a meeting the home secretary and Trevelyan had with the two deputies from Skibbereen.[54] At the time, a request for permission to open soup shops with local taxpayer's money by their poor-law union was declined.[55] Instead, by the end of December 1846, a government agent had incorporated the local soup committee into a public–private partnership that set a precedent for Ireland. The arrangement doubled local subscriptions, included officials, and used the services of a policeman to fortify a humanitarian space to ensure that 'the articles purchased for the soup are actually put into it, that it is distributed at twelve o'clock precisely'.[56]

At the beginning of 1847, the Central Relief Committee (CRC), which had been formed as a Quaker umbrella organisation for Ireland, opened a model kitchen in Dublin that sold an average of 1,000 bowls of soup daily until the end of July, when complimentary government provisions had curbed the

---

[50] *Transactions*, 35.

[51] Helen E. Hatton, *The Largest Amount of Good: Quaker Relief in Ireland, 1654–1921* (Kingston: McGill-Queen's University Press, 1993), 42–3, 84; James S. Donnelly, 'The Soup Kitchens', in *A New History of Ireland, vol. 5: Ireland under the Union, 1801–70*, ed. W. E. Vaughan (Oxford: Clarendon, 1989), 307. For background on the soup kitchen movement, see Scott-Smith, *Empty Stomach*.

[52] Skibbereen Committee of Gratuitous Relief, 'Statement of the Present Condition of the Skibbereen Poor Law Union District', 1 Feb. 1847, The National Archives of Ireland, Dublin (TNA (IRL)), Relief Commission, RLFC3/2/6/55; 'Charity Souphouse at Skibbereen, 1846', *Journal of the Cork Historical and Archaeological Society* 51, no. 174 (1946): 189–90.

[53] Bishop to Routh, 27 Jan. 1847, *Correspondence* II, 40.

[54] Trevelyan to Routh, 3 Dec. 1846, *Correspondence* I, 327.

[55] Minutes of the Board of Guardians of the Skibbereen Union, 5 Dec. 1846, TNA(UK), HO, 45/1080A; Reply by the Poor Law Commission Office, Dublin, 10 Dec. 1846, TNA(UK), HO, 45/1080A.

[56] Routh to Hewetson, 30 Dec. 1846, *Correspondence* I, 438. See also 420–2, 426–7, 442, 475–7.

Figure 4.2 Famine tokens, 1846/7.
Courtesy of the National Famine Museum, Strokestown

demand. In the Quaker shop, one penny gave the poor a quart of soup, and another halfpenny added bread. Nearly 50 per cent of the rations 'sold' were purchased with coupons from benefactors who distributed them among the poor at their own discretion (see Figure 4.2). The CRC supported in its efforts by a local collection covered more than one-third of the expenses. They reported frequent visits by observers from similar establishments across the country who wanted to study their operation.[57]

The CRC helped in the establishment of such soup facilities by others, assisting with boilers and money, and importing provisions. They emphasised the many grants that they had given to women, whom they regarded as their most efficient social workers, and regretted their want of proper stores and reliable agents. The storage problem and the trouble of arranging transportation within Ireland were solved in connection with the goods sent to the CRC from the USA throughout the spring and summer of 1847. Modelled on an arrangement with the BRA, the government allowed the CRC to transfer incoming supplies to the nearest commissariat depot (at public expense), crediting these shipments at their current market value. The sum could then be used to pick up foodstuffs from any other government depot. This system, based on a substructure of escorted food transports along waterways and major roads (railways were still in their infancy), lasted until late summer, by which time the depots were empty. The CRC then sold aid supplies that continued to arrive and used the proceeds as discretionary funds.[58]

The government itself turned to soup kitchens as the cheapest way of feeding people and as 'economising our meal', in the sense of offering the best possible nourishment with limited funds.[59] Medical experts provided

---

[57] *Transactions*, 53–4, 358–60.
[58] *Transactions*, 55–8, 67, 335–46. See also Trevelyan to Routh, 6 Apr. 1847, ibid.
[59] Routh to Trevelyan, 30 Dec. 1846, *Correspondence* I, 437. See also Routh to Hewetson, 30 Dec. 1846, ibid., 437; Grey to Bessborough, 28 Jan. 1847, TNA(UK), HO 122/19.

advice regarding the comparative nutritional value of different foodstuffs (which was to be considered when comparing prices) and the necessity of a varied diet.[60] Soup kitchens also solved the problem of sweetcorn consumption, with which the Irish were unfamiliar. Another major advantage of a soup facility was that a simple 'indulgent' administration sufficed, as a person presenting themself for a meal which they receive in their own mug served as a means test to ensure the neediest were being served.[61] According to a contemporary assessment, serving cooked food, compared to handing out staples for home preparation, reduced the number of claimants by more than one-third, suggesting issues of pride and accessibility.[62] In addition, soup kitchens provided jobs for women.[63] However, according to one report, preparing so much soup brought about a 'great slaughter amongst the poor people's cows'. Thus, adding meat to the soup, due to the urgency of the moment, unfortunately deprived the same people of milk and butter.[64]

The government wanted to have the 'soup system' run by relief committees operating across Ireland by the beginning of 1847. However, officials realised that any scheme depending on voluntary contributions would be inadequate to sustain the starving population.[65] Nevertheless, as the public works programme became increasingly dysfunctional and threatened to interfere with the sowing season, soup kitchens were seen as a viable alternative. In February, Parliament adopted them as a way to feed up to three million people on a daily basis. Thus, between May and September 1847, the self-defined 'night watchman state' demonstrated its logistic capacity.[66] According to the analysis of Skibbereen's physician, Daniel Donovan, not only had the public soup act provided people with essential nourishment, but it had also proved to be 'the best cure for Irish fever', as the often deadly famine diseases were then called.[67] The soup programme was not only appreciated in Ireland at the time; today there is widespread agreement that it provided the most effective transfer of entitlements. It is also believed that had it been implemented over a longer period, it would have significantly lowered mortality. However, the provision of soup, offering subsistence without requiring any return in labour, and with only the minor discomfort of having to consume one's meal in a public place, was incompatible

---

[60] Erichsen to Trevelyan, 9 Mar. 1847, *Correspondence* II, 228.
[61] Trevelyan to Routh, 23 Jan. 1847, *Correspondence* II, 39.
[62] Donnelly, 'Soup Kitchens', 312.
[63] Routh to Trevelyan, 14 Jan. 1847, *Correspondence* I, 480.
[64] Bishop to Trevelyan, 29 Jan. 1847, *Correspondence* II, 30.   [65] Trevelyan, *Irish Crisis*, 83.
[66] See Gray, 'British Relief Measures', 80, 83; James S. Donnelly, 'The Administration of Relief, 1846–7', in *A New History of Ireland, vol. 5: Ireland under the Union, 1801–70*, ed. W. E. Vaughan (Oxford: Clarendon, 1989), 299; Donnelly, 'Soup Kitchens', 308–9, 314.
[67] Daniel Donovan, 'Observations on the Peculiar Diseases to which the Famine of Last Year Gave Origin, and on the Morbid Effects of Insufficient Nourishment', *Dublin Medical Press* 19 (1848): 131.

with the austere moral economy of UK elites. It was, therefore, restricted to a seasonal measure that was to terminate with the upcoming harvest.[68] The BRA's role in this connection was to prepare for the policy shift from public works to the government-sponsored feeding programme. They were to make foodstuffs available in the remote south and west, particularly in kitchens set up by local committees. With the implementation of the government soup act in May 1847, voluntary aid was shut down.[69] As the BRA only accepted as partners relief bodies that adhered to official guidelines and submitted their applications through government officers, it reinforced state control of local charities, which was also based on the match-funding of voluntary collections with public grants (after mid-December 1846, such grants had been doubled, occasionally tripled).[70]

Fundraising for Ireland at the beginning of 1847 inspired Alexis Soyer, Victorian London's celebrated French chef, to create a soup based on food science to provide maximum nutrition at minimal cost, and to raise funds for a model kitchen. The government was interested in Soyer's plan and provided him with a soup house in Dublin that had been designed for mass feeding. It incorporated calculated flows of people, spoons chained to the tables, and a rigorous time regime – anticipating later shop floor management.[71]

Some of the local press described the opening ceremony, at which high society congregated with the suffering poor, as an imperial spectacle that subjected the latter to a 'pitiless gaze', outraging 'every principle of human-ity'.[72] For a five shilling admission fee, one could watch charitable ladies serve paupers food. Although the proceeds were put to good use, a newspaper condemned the procedure as akin to the inspection of animals in a zoo at feeding time. Nevertheless, it was hoped that the fees collected would be of some benefit to those 'beggar-actors' whose humiliating performance had raised them.[73] Whatever one may think of Soyer's moral balance or his recipes

---

[68] Donnelly, 'Soup Kitchens', 307, 314. See 312 on the violation of a sense of dignity; Gray, *Famine, Land and Politics*, 264, 332. For an early example of applying the concept of 'moral economy' to the Russel cabinet's policy, see David C. Sheehy, 'Archbishop Murray of Dublin and the Great Famine in Mayo', *Cathair na Mart* 11 (1991): 121.

[69] BRA, Minute Book (Finance Committee), 70 (26 May 1847), NLI, MS5218.

[70] Minute Book, 191 (27 Feb. 1847), NLI, MS 2022; 'Instructions for the Formation', 490–2.

[71] Alexis Soyer, *Soyer's Charitable Cookery, or the Poor Man's Regenerator* (Dublin: Hodges and Smith, 1847). Soyer was not without his critics. See Julian Strang and Joyce Toomre, 'Alexis Soyer and the Irish Famine: "Splendid Promises and Abortive Measures"', in *The Great Famine and the Irish Diaspora in America*, ed. Arthur Gribben (Amherst: University of Massachusetts Press, 1999), 66–84; Ian Miller, 'The Chemistry of Famine: Nutritional Contro-versies and the Irish Famine, c.1845–7', *Medical History* 56, no. 4 (2012): 444–62.

[72] 'Extraordinary Fete: The Blessings of Provincialism', *Freeman's Journal*, 6 Apr. 1847; 'The Soup Kitchen Insult', *Dublin Evening Packet*, 6 Apr. 1847.

[73] 'Finale of a Cook's Triumph', *Dublin Evening Packet*, 13 Apr. 1847; 'The Soup Kitchen Insult Again', *Dublin Evening Packet*, 20 Apr. 1847 (quotation).

(which included oysters, a cheap food at the time), his combination of applied science, personal showmanship, and spectacle for donors transcended nineteenth-century philanthropy and perhaps the Irish context. A British officer in Dublin commented at the time that, while Soyer would be successful anywhere in the world, his success was impossible to foresee, as the Irish were 'a strange nation, they hate every thing new, and they must have any change thro' their own people and in their own way'.[74]

The Quakers created a soup distinguished by a high proportion of meat – six-fold that which was called for in Soyer's recipe.[75] However, like government aid, most Quaker relief ceased by late summer 1847, or took on other forms. When faced in early 1848 with the question of whether to reopen their soup shops, the Quakers found that people in the surrounding area were too exhausted to serve as organisers and workers in such a project. Despite the Quakers' charitable tradition, the CRC emphasised that they had no experience in the humanitarian undertaking upon which they had embarked, and that the underdevelopment of Ireland posed its greatest problem: the country lacked a middle class able to administer relief and a commercial infrastructure for the distribution of food. The organisation eventually spent some of its funds for development projects, conceding that using money raised for emergency relief to fund a permanent object posed an ethical dilemma.[76]

Money and Aid-in-Kind

British charity in the 1840s favoured the distribution of aid-in-kind. In the USA, the abundance of grain resulted in the adoption of a similar policy, making a virtue – providing humanitarian aid – out of a necessity – getting rid of agricultural surplus. Both countries shipped much needed provisions to Ireland. Staple foodstuffs were sometimes sent directly by their producers.[77] Collections, particularly in religious communities, resulted in donations of jewellery, clocks, a marble statue of the blessed virgin, and other such items, although they were not always readily convertible to cash. After a few weeks of such collection, the Irish College in Rome estimated it had received up to £300 worth of precious objects.[78] However, a diamond ring that was said to cost £100 in England could only be sold for £20 in Rome, and so (like the marble statue) was forwarded to Dublin in expectation of a better price.[79] It is

---

[74] Routh to Trevelyan, 22 Feb. 1847, TNA(UK), Treasury (T) 64/362A. The section of the letter cited here was excluded from government print.
[75] Hatton, *Largest Amount of Good*, 140.   [76] *Transactions*, 68, 100, 105.
[77] *Aid to Ireland*, 62–5.
[78] Cullen to Meyler, 13 Feb. 1847, DAD, MP, 32/3/144; 'Subscriptions for Ireland for the Present Week', *Tablet*, 3 Apr. 1847.
[79] Cullen to Murray, 25 Mar. 1847, DAD, MP, 34/9/232.

unclear whether the offer of 2,000 cubic palms (37 m³) of fine breccia Gregoriana marble, to be sold in Italy or Ireland, ever was accepted.[80] At the same time, worthless devotional items were forwarded to the Vatican, since they were believed to 'demonstrate great charity'.[81]

Most importantly, there were separate collections of clothing. Alongside money, second-hand apparel played a large role in charitable drives, although some of it was likely to join the original clothing of the beneficiaries in a pawn shop. With reference to such divestment, an Irish landlady suggested that 'whatever clothing is sent, ought to be of a *very peculiar* pattern or colour, and marked in a very conspicuous way, so as to be unsaleable'.[82] Necessity also led to the reuse of empty food sacks as material for making clothes.[83]

Most inedible gifts had to be converted into cash to be of any use. The provision of aid was thus dependent on financial transactions and frequently on valuta exchange. Sometimes this involved consecutive operations, such as when the Vatican gathered funds in various currencies and sent the proceeds to Ireland. At the same time, the notion of round sums or specific collection results clashed with the market principle, where fixed wholesale quantities of foodstuffs were traded at constantly fluctuating prices.[84]

While most relief monies were used for the purchase of supplies, cash was occasionally given directly to recipients in distressed Irish localities in order to strengthen their buying power, as Sen would later also recommend. Although these sums were too small to have any significant effect on the importation of food, the entitlements enabled individuals to meet their own needs for sustenance or help some of those around them. Money was a decentralised and flexible form of relief, flowing through a variety of direct and indirect channels.

Such relief typified how churches in the Irish homeland forwarded domestic and foreign donations. Aid arrived at all levels of the hierarchy, although larger amounts and contributions from distant lands were often received at the highest level. Thus, the Catholic prelates of Ireland became recipients of funds conveyed to them for use either at their own discretion, or as earmarked sums. Church officials are also said to have significantly contributed from their own pockets.[85] Generally, the four archbishops of Ireland divided the money they

---

[80] Mauri and Alimonda to Brunelli, 4 Feb. 1847, PIC, CUL/1324a; Cullen to Murray, 26 Feb. 1847, DAD, MP, 34/9/232.

[81] Paracciani to Fransoni, 30 May 1847, Historical Archives of the Congregation for the Evangelisation of Peoples (HAC), Rome, Documents referred to in the weekly meetings (SC), First series (I), Ireland, vol. 29, 989.

[82] Sligo to Spring Rice, 13 Apr. 1847, NLI, MP, 13, 397/6 (emphasis in original).

[83] 'State of West Skull', *Southern Reporter*, 5 June 1847.

[84] Routh to Trevelyan, 22 Feb. 1847, in *Correspondence* II, 168.

[85] Sheehy, 'Archbishop Murray', 126; Edward Alfred D'Alton, *History of the Archdiocese of Tuam, vol. 2* (Dublin: Phoenix, 1928), 34.

received among the country's twenty-four bishops, who passed it on to more than 1,000 parish priests and heads of church institutions. For more rapid dissemination, the archbishops also provided aid directly to the local clergy.[86]

Vertical distribution was complemented by a horizontal plan. Daniel Murray, archbishop of Dublin, and William Crolly, primate of all Ireland and archbishop of Armagh, were often charged with distributing Catholic welfare across the country. Both transferred funds designated for Catholic distribution to Michael Slattery and John MacHale, their colleagues in the most afflicted sees of Cashel and Tuam in the south and west of Ireland. They were praised for the fairness with which they shared incoming aid.[87] However, both Murray and Crolly were politically conservative, prioritising interdenominational co-operation in their approach to famine relief. They feared that targeting aid towards Catholics 'would seem to the public as too exclusive, and as having but little of the spirit of the good Samaritan in it; and perhaps even cramp the benevolence of protestants to us', or, even worse, serve as a model for 'other influential persons, who will refuse to give relief to the Catholic poor'.[88] They, therefore, tended to forward those donations that were not explicitly designated for Catholic distribution through broader relief channels.[89]

Although such diversion of 'Catholic money' was internally controversial and at times criticised in the press,[90] no open dispute arose. Murray had handed over the collection of London Catholics to the GCRC, where he was a key figure.[91] He hoped the same distribution would be done in the case of Vatican collections, but ultimately yielded to Slattery and MacHale, who challenged the 'great tendency to set aside the bishops in favour of mixed boards and government officials'.[92] Cullen later asserted from Rome that the Vatican had hoped for distribution through the Church and that they were glad the donation had not been allowed to pass into 'government management'.[93] However, some bishops did forward money to local relief committees, rather than to their priests.[94] Parish priests were the customary recipients of money

---

[86] Crolly to Murray, 31 Mar. 1847, DAD, MP, 34/12/130. On the number of parish priests, see Peter O'Dwyer, 'John Francis Spratt, O.Carm., 1796–1871' unpublished PhD dissertation, Pontificia Universita Gregoriana, 1968.

[87] Sheehy, 'Archbishop Murray', 125–6.

[88] Murray to Slattery, 20 Feb. 1847, DAC, SP, 1847/10 (the second quotation cites a letter by Crolly to Murray).

[89] Bob Cullen, *Thomas L. Synnott: The Career of a Dublin Catholic 1830–70* (Dublin: Irish Academic Press, 1997), 45.

[90] Letter to the Editor by 'An Irish Priest, for Several Years on the English Mission', *Tablet*, 6 Mar. 1847 (quotation); MacHale to Slattery, Feb. 1847, DAC, SP, 1847/10.

[91] Receipt for the London collection, 21 Jan. 1847, DAD, MP, 34/12/15.

[92] Slattery to Cullen, 9 Apr. 1847, PIC, CUL/1368.

[93] Cullen to Slattery, 28 Apr. 1847, DAC, SP, 1847/35.

[94] See, e.g., the note of thanks by John Murphy, bishop of Cork, in *Southern Reporter*, 2 Feb. 1847.

grants by the GCRC, but were expected to see that distribution took place across denominational lines. In many instances, the channels that were used are unclear, since the secretary of the GCRC was simultaneously involved in distribution through the Catholic hierarchy.[95]

Parish priests gave the alms that they received to the poor of their flocks and to other sufferers at their own discretion. The extent to which they did this by means of money, food coupons, and material aid such as foodstuffs, clothes, and even coffins is unknown. In any case, the cash flow did sometimes reach those suffering from hunger. At the same time, there are many reports that people stopped using coffins during the famine, or adopted a frugal variation with a hinged bottom that made it reusable, illustrating the descent into a moral economy of survival.[96]

Whereas Vatican instructions generally took a needs-based approach to relief,[97] its own disbursement among Irish prelates went from providing centralised aid to dealing personally with bishops and certain monastic and ecclesiastical institutions. Although the intention of aiding the most distressed areas remained, the actual distribution showed moral support for all of Ireland and reflected regional differences in suffering to a lesser extent. For example, the money the Holy See sent between April and July 1847 benefitted each of the Irish bishops and archbishops, the former in the amount of £50–150, the latter ranging from £150 to £300.[98]

The Comité de secours pour l'Irlande had a more targeted approach, initially focusing on the most afflicted sees of Cashel and Tuam. However, on recommendation of Redmund O'Carroll, president of the Irish branch of the Society of St Vincent de Paul (SVP), the Comité included five northern dioceses to their list of beneficiaries, applying a formula according to which 40 per cent of their funds went to the south, 30 per cent to the west, and another 30 per cent to the north of Ireland.[99] Thus, they took into account the fact that the provinces around Dublin to the east were not a major famine area, but they did distribute aid to the less affected north of Ireland. The French reliance on a single informant illustrates the problem of making rational allocation decisions from a distance.

By contrast, SVP donations supported existing and newly established branch organisations that were mainly in Dublin and the south of Ireland.

---

[95] Cullen, *Thomas L. Synnott*, 30, 44, 46; Sheehy, 'Archbishop Murray', 126; *Proceedings of the General Central Relief Committee*, 5.

[96] 'Crookhaven', *Cork Examiner*, 11 Dec. 1846; 'Skibbereen', *Saunders's News Letter*, 29 Dec. 1846; 'Employment for the Labouring Population of Skibbereen', *Cork Examiner*, 6 Jan. 1847.

[97] Fransoni to Murray, 30 Jan. 1847, DAD, MP, 32/3/159; Cullen to Murray, 30 Jan. 1847, ibid. 34/9/231; Cullen to Slattery, 8 June 1847, DAC, SP, 1847/47.

[98] 'Distribuzione', HAC, SC, I, Ireland, vol. 29, 224–6.

[99] O'Carroll to Murray, 27 May & 20 July 1847, DAD, MP, 32/3/138 and 139.

They were part of an effort at the time to roll back the 'New Reformation' in Ireland. The choice of certain rural locations for SVP expansion, like Dingle and West Schull, was geared to counter the evangelical 'traffickers in human souls' there, as was claimed.[100] In Schull, the Congregation of the Mission encouraged the establishment of an SVP chapter 'with a promise of pecuniary aid' from SVP headquarters in Dublin.[101] Dingle also received regular allotments from the Vatican.[102] Catholic donors showed particular interest in places where there was religious rivalry and the presence of 'Soupers', as Protestant proselytes or proselytisers were called because of their alledged trade in faith and food. However, even the Catholic Church began to use food as a tool for securing its flock and winning back 'perverts'.[103] Such food conflicts tended to arise in impoverished locations, although sectarian competition in a country strongly divided along religious lines and with a dominant Protestant minority culture was a factor.

Efficient and safe ways of forwarding donations was a frequently discussed issue. Sometimes, cash was simply carried from one place to another. For example, the Irish College in Rome recruited a student who was returning home, to carry thirty-four silver medals back to Ireland.[104] In general, funds were conveyed across borders by bills of exchange (see Figure 4.3). However, this well-established method had its drawbacks. Bills of exchange presupposed brokers, trustworthy networks, and maturity periods that delayed the disbursal of relief funds.[105] As financial institutions abroad often had no commercial relations with Ireland, transactions were frequently conducted through London banks.[106] This roundabout method occasioned additional costs and time delays. Bills of exchange also depended on the proper working of two financial systems. A recipient of French aid via a bill of exchange had to postpone cashing a voucher for two weeks because the 'pressure for money' was so great in Dublin that the face amount could not be obtained on its stated due date without incurring a substantial bank fee.[107] That the recipient in this case chose to wait two weeks for the full amount shows that the larger sum was of more value to him than receiving less money immediately, despite the high mortality rate at the time.

[100] SVP 1848, 21 (quotation), 7; Hickey, *Famine in West Cork*, 243.
[101] Minutes of the Provincial Council, 10 Aug. 1848, Vincentian Archives, Raheny.
[102] See various thank you letters in PIC, CUL.
[103] Hickey, *Famine in West Cork*, 244; for the quotation, see Egan to Cullen, 16 Feb. 1848, PIC, CUL/1537.
[104] Cullen to Murray, 26 Feb. 1847, DAD, MP, 34/9/331.
[105] For background, see Markus A. Denzel, *Handbook of World Exchange Rates, 1590–1914* (Farnham: Ashgate, 2010), xxiv–lii.
[106] E.g., Richarz (bishop of Augsburg) to Murray, 25 Dec. 1847, DAD, MP, 32/3/98.
[107] O'Carroll to Murray, 27 May 1847, DAD, MP, 32/3/138.

Figure 4.3 Bill of exchange for £421.1.10 from Father Anthony Fahey, Buenos Aires, 1847.
Courtesy of Dublin Diocesan Archives, MP, 33/13/10

Within Ireland, relief funds were often transferred by postal or bank money order, a system that apparently worked well. Complaints, like a rector's grievance that the Skibbereen post office was out of cash for a period, or the Dingle Presentation Convent's problems with receiving the donations sent to them, were exceptions.[108]

While foreign banks generally profitted from transactions involving relief funds, the BRA was governed by a 'cabinet of bankers' based in London who offered their services gratis.[109] English Catholics used the Commercial Bank, which also appears to have provided its assistance at no charge.[110] The same was true of the Paris-based bank of Luc Callaghan, used by the Comité de secours pour l'Irlande, and of the SVP's bank, which charged neither commission nor exchange fees.[111] There were also banks in Ireland that transferred money for the relief of the poor at no cost.[112] The trustees of the Indian Relief Fund thanked the directors of the Bank of Ireland for cashing their bills without charge, 'although at six months date'.[113] Thus, in many cases, transaction costs for aid agencies were minimal due to the free provision of bank services. This is in agreement with attempts to keep overheads low. Examples

---

[108] Richard Francis Webb, Letter to the Editor, *Southern Reporter*, 22 Dec. 1846; Mahony, Letter to the Editor, *Tablet*, 5 June 1847.

[109] Editorial, *Times*, 9 Jan. 1847.

[110] 'To the Recipients of English Subscriptions', *Tablet*, 8 May 1847.

[111] 'Comité de secours pour l'Irlande', *L'Ami de la religion*, 11 Nov. 1847; SVP circular letter, c. 28 Feb. 1847, VSA, SoS, 1848, rubr. 241, fasc. 2, 80r.

[112] Editorial Note, *Southern Reporter*, 22 Dec. 1846.

[113] *Distress in Ireland: Report of the Trustees of the Indian Relief Fund, Shewing the Distribution of the Sum of £13, 919 14s. 2d., Commencing the 24th April, and Ending the 31st December, 1846* (Dublin: Browne, 1847), 23.

of private support are free rent for relief organisations, not charging for labour,[114] no commissions, and not seeking profit, while government subsidies were generally reimbursement for transportation costs. In addition, the government contributed to reduced transaction costs by making its food depot infrastructure available to private charities.

Domestic and Overseas Migration

Aid efforts, whether public or private, set people in motion, with both desired and unintended consequences. Some soup kitchens distributed food by cart in their neighbourhood. Invalid's diets were sent to the homes of the sick, anticipating modern 'meals-on-wheels', although finding volunteers who dared to go near the sick was a challenge.[115] Despite such services, the soup kitchen model generally required people to line up and sometimes walk long distances for a daily meal, which presupposes greater mobility than a monetary distribution system.

The conviction that 'people for distances round will come in to partake of the benefit' functioned as a means test, but also caused an uprooted population to resettle wherever aid was available.[116] Thus, whereas the overall population of Ireland sharply declined during the Great Famine, the four largest cities continued to grow.[117] Even a '"relief" town' – as a contemporary journalist called it – like Skibbereen experienced a continuous influx from the countryside that stabilised the total number of inhabitants in the winter of 1847, despite exceptional mortality.[118] Locals complained that the misery of their town was multiplied by the paupers who flocked in from surrounding areas.[119] Similarly, benevolent circles in Cork were alarmed by Skibbereen sending its poor over to their city. The suspicion that charitable funds were misappropriated in hiring carriages to dispose of the destitute caused particular indignation. It made a newspaper demand (and receive) a 'strong and unequivocal contradiction' of such an 'ungrateful return' by a people who owed much to Cork

---

[114] For example, the relief ship *Jamestown* was loaded by unpaid labour. See Robert Bennet Forbes, *Personal Reminiscences* (Boston: Little, Brown, 1878), 188.

[115] Patrick Cleary and Philip O'Regan, eds, *Dear Old Skibbereen* (Skibbereen: Skibbereen Printers Ltd, 1995), 22. See also McCarthy Downing, Letter to the Editor, *Southern Reporter*, 18 Mar. 1847. On difficulties, see Richard B. Townsend, Letter to the Editor, *Cork Examiner*, 26 Mar. 1847.

[116] Mann to Hewetson, 22 Jan. 1847, *Correspondence* II, 54.

[117] Kevin Hourihan, 'The Cities and Towns of Ireland, 1841–51', in *Atlas of the Great Irish Famine*, eds John Crowley, William J. Smyth, and Mike Murphy (New York: New York University Press, 2012), 228–39.

[118] 'The State of West Carbery', *Southern Reporter*, 20 May 1847.

[119] Richard B. Townsend, Letter to the Editor, *Cork Examiner*, 3 Feb. 1847; John Fitzpatrick, Letters to the Editor, *Tablet*, 13 Feb. and 20 Mar. 1847.

and the regional press.[120] Further up the aid chain, British philanthropists also felt 'ungratefully treated' when they learned that Irish relief committees were shipping their destitute to them.[121]

Skibbereen played a conspicuous role in the exportation of misery, with an elaborate scheme reflective of their moral economy. The three target groups for their emigration programme were healthy men seeking work, women and children who had someone in England who could maintain them, and elderly people of Irish background unjustly returned by British authorities 'for support on a people who never derived any benefit from their labour'.[122] In a Letter to the Editor, accounting for the donations entrusted to him, Townsend declared that he was to give £5 'towards helping a few heads of families to go over to England to shew the *Times* that Paddy loves his good English fare too well not to go there when he can, and earn for his poor, empty, hungry stomach some of his bread and cheese, and take a crotchet out of his gamut'.[123]

Some Skibbereen emigrants were sent by coach via Cork to a steamer headed for London, but most embarked directly at the local County Cork harbour of Baltimore. Two individuals established the emigration scheme by the end of November 1846: Donovan, who used the income from his work-house vaccination contract to redeem indispensable clothing from pawn and buy biscuits for the journey, and a ship and mill owner who provided free passage to Newport, South Wales. Adverse winds, a captain who fell ill, and provisions that were only enough for seven days made one of the first ships, carrying 113 paupers, strand near Cork. After a five weeks journey, the 'floating pest-house' reached its destination, five of its passengers dying upon arrival. The journey also generated one of the few reports hinting at sexual exploitation by relief workers during the Great Irish Famine. The mate and the sailors on the ship, while otherwise treating passengers unkindly, were said to have 'become familiar with some of the girls, whom they took with them to the forecastle'. Sustaining the newcomers became an additional task for the Newport Irish Relief Fund.[124] Such problems were not reported from other

---

[120] 'Skibbereen', *Southern Reporter*, 11 Mar. 1847 (quotations); 'Health Committee – Expulsion of County Paupers', *Southern Reporter*, 22 Apr. 1847. See also James S. Donnelly, *The Land and the People of Nineteenth-Century Cork: The Rural Economy and the Land Question* (London: Routledge, 1975), 86–7.

[121] 'Overwhelming Immigration of the Irish Poor to Newport', *Monmouthshire Merlin*, 20 Feb. 1847.

[122] 'Emigration of Paupers from Skibbereen', *Southern Reporter*, 24 Apr. 1847.

[123] Letter to the Editor, *Southern Reporter*, 23 Jan. 1847.

[124] 'Coroner's Inquest', *Monmouthshire Merlin*, 27 Feb. 1847 (quotation); 'Distress in West Carbery', *Southern Reporter*, 3 Dec. 1846;'Wretched Condition of Emigrants', *Monmouthshire Merlin*, 6 Feb. 1847; 'Overwhelming Immigration of the Irish Poor to Newport', *Monmouthshire Merlin*, 20 Feb. 1847 (quotation). For the British context, see Frank Neal, *Black'47: Britain and the Famine Irish* (Houndmills: Palgrave Macmillan, 1998), 69–71, 109–15. Another case of sexual misconduct is that of an officer in the Skibbereen workhouse

Skibbereen ship passages, but the misery of Irish emigrant ships in the North Atlantic during the late 1840s was notorious.

When the steady flow of emigrants became known to the administrator of the Skibbereen food depot, he reported that funds designated for poor relief were being diverted for the shipment of 'wretched naked creatures' to England and Wales.[125] While landlords in many cases were glad to defray the emigration expenses of their tenants, and although there was a general suspicion that relief committees were shipping their clients off to Liverpool, the account from Skibbereen was exceptional in suggesting an actual misappropriation of funds.[126] A later investigation into the 'deportation of paupers' from Skibbereen to England concluded that public monies had not been applied.[127] However, the police report on the matter reveals a local enterprise with semi-official traits: Donovan had privately received £10 from the poor law guardians, which he used together with money of his own to send 500 paupers from Skibbereen and its surrounding areas to England. A private shipowner had gratuitously supplied two vessels for this purpose, and the government commissary provided a supply of biscuits for the passage at cost.[128] The fact that Donovan was a prominent, well-thought-of relief worker, whose diaries with glimpses of the distress in Skibbereen were circulated widely in the press, may have caused objections to how the exodus was financed to be dropped.

The migration of paupers and others from Ireland affected England, the British dominions (particularly Canada), and the USA. The influx of famine refugees launched relief operations wherever they disembarked. It also resulted in criss-cross migration, as poor-law unions in England deported Irish paupers back to their origin. The GCRC, which otherwise disregarded Dublin, made a special £400 grant to the lord mayor of Dublin on their behalf.[129]

Liverpool was greatly affected, as large numbers of famine refugees poured into the city until 1853. In 1847 alone, more than 116,000 paupers arrived from Ireland, in addition to more than 180,000 transmigrants to North America (the cost of passage to the New World being a maximum of £4). It is estimated

---

who was accused of 'improper liberties with some of the female paupers'. See 'Skibbereen Union', *Cork Examiner*, 30 Apr. 1849.

[125] Hughes to Routh, 12 Feb.1847, *Correspondence* II, 130.

[126] Commissioners of Colonial Land and Emigration to Stephens, 10 Feb. 1847, *Correspondence* II, 159; Routh to Trevelyan, 20 Feb. 1847, ibid. 160.

[127] Redington to McGregor, 10 May 1847 (quotation), TNA(UK), HO 45/2054; Burgoyne to Trevelyan(?), 24 May 1847, ibid.

[128] Report by County Inspector Kingston Fox, 15 May 1847, TNA(UK), HO 45/2054. Another account, which tends to downplay the incident, speaks of 580 paupers. See Report by Prendergast, 13 May 1847, ibid.

[129] Lewis Darwen, Donald Macraild, Brian Gurrin, and Liam Kennedy, '"Unhappy and Wretched Creatures": Charity, Poor Relief and Pauper Removal in Britain and Ireland during the Great Famine', *The English Historical Review* 134, no. 568 (2019): 589–619; Cullen, *Thomas L. Synnott*, 41. For context, see Neal, *Black'47*, 217–23.

that 5,500 famine refugees died of typhus, dysentery, and diarrhoea in Liverpool that year, making the city known as the 'cemetery of Ireland'. The epidemics spread by disease also raised the mortality rate among other sectors of the population.[130] Estimates of deaths in Great Britain brought about by the Irish Famine range from 10,000 to 15,000 for the year 1847 alone, to 150,000 for the late 1840s.[131] A Cork newspaper recognised the generally kind reception that refugees received in English towns, which it interpreted as a gesture of appreciation: 'The Famine that has driven swarms of our people to Liverpool for instance has enriched its merchants; their [export] profits upon food consumed in Ireland might be reckoned by the million.'[132] Even in inland cities such as Birmingham, collections for those back in Ireland competed with the needs of Irish newcomers in English towns – something that especially affected the Catholic communities. Thus, in the beginning of February 1847, 200 refugees were being cared for daily at the bishop's house, and many others at the convent.[133] The poor families aided at the time by English branches of the SVP were mainly Irish.[134]

In North America, famine migration also caused donors to open their doors to the new arrivals. As fares were lowest to Canada (as little as £1½), ships bound there were greatly overcrowded and wretched.[135] In Quebec, approximately one-sixth of all passengers who came ashore from Ireland in 1847 died shortly after arrival. Many more had already perished at sea. Grosse Île, the quarantine station for those entering Canada, was unprepared for the mass influx of migrants and became a symbol for the plight of the famine refugees.[136] Charitable Irish societies assisted the newcomers in many places, and new societies such as the Hibernian Benevolent Emigrant Society of Chicago or the Irish Emigrant Society of Detroit were founded in response to the famine migration.[137] However, the social and medical problems caused by this influx also called forth an estrangement between the refugees and their host population that contributed to the drying up of transatlantic charity during the latter

---

[130] Neal, *Black'47*, 61–2, 153. On the cost of passage, see letter from Hodder, 8 Feb. 1847, *Correspondence* II, 159.

[131] Ó Gráda, 'Ireland', 182.   [132] 'Skibbereen', *Southern Reporter*, 24 Apr. 1847.

[133] 'The London Catholic Collections', *Tablet*, 6 Feb. 1847. On the simultaneous relief for Ireland and for famine refugees, see also Neal, *Black'47*, 277–8.

[134] 'Rapport géneral pour l'année 1847: Suite et fin', *Bulletin de la Société de Saint-Vincent de Paul* 1, no. 4 (1848), 89.

[135] Hickey, *Famine in West Cork*, 223.

[136] Mark McGowan, 'Grosse Île, Quebec', in *Atlas of the Great Irish Famine*, eds John Crowley, William J. Smyth, and Mike Murphy (New York: New York University Press, 2012), 532–5; André Charbonneau and Doris Drolet-Dubé, *A Register of Deceased Persons at Sea and on Grosse Île in 1847* (Ottawa: Canadian Heritage, 1997).

[137] 'Hibernian Benevolent Emigrant Society (Chicago)', in *Irish American Voluntary Organizations*, ed. Michael F. Funchion (Westport, CT: Greenwood Press, 1983), 135–6; JoEllen McNergney Vinyard, 'Irish Emigrant Society (Detroit)', ibid., 168–71.

part of 1847 and to tightened immigration policies.[138] Strum suggests that, in hindsight, various leaders of Irish famine relief appear to have developed hostile attitudes and turned into nativists.[139] In many ways, nineteenth-century society in the UK, Europe, and the world at large was unprepared for the sustained relief effort that would have been needed to significantly mitigate the Great Irish Famine, thus illustrating the limits of ad hoc humanitarian efforts.

4.3   Live and Let Die: Soviet Russia

Providing famine relief in Soviet Russia between 1921 and 1923 posed a multitude of challenges to foreign organisations. Concerns about the misuse of aid, paralleled by the inevitable necessity of collaborating with Soviet agencies, made more difficult a situation that was already financially and logistically complicated. Continuous negotiations with Soviet authorities were necessary during the whole operation to keep things running smoothly. This often led to conflicts, especially on a local level, partly because of personal and ideological animosities and mistrust, and partly because details of the 1921 Riga agreement were unknown in the Russian provinces.[140]

Apart from control of distribution, a major concern of organisations providing foreign relief to Russia was logistical questions. There was hardly enough capacity in the Baltic ports to unload large cargoes. Moreover, they were blocked by ice all winter, so that Black Sea ports had to be used instead. The Russian railway network was in disrepair. A transport from Riga to the famine region of Saratov was estimated to take fifteen days, but in December 1921 took thirty days. In February 1922, travel came to a complete standstill due to weather conditions and fuel shortages.[141] The train system proved to be a bottleneck in relief operations, no matter how well planned, and conflicts arose between different organisations about cargo space.[142] During the winter season, many areas most severely affected by the famine could only be reached with sleighs drawn by horses or camels. A trip of under 300 km could take up to seven days. In many famine regions, more than 90 per cent of the livestock had died, so that even this outmoded form of transportation was often unavailable.[143]

---

[138] Laurence M. Geary, "'The Noblest Offering That Nation Ever Made to Nation": American Philanthropy and the Great Famine in Ireland', *Éire-Ireland* 48, nos 3–4 (2013): 128; Hidetaka Hirota, *Expelling the Poor: Atlantic Seaboard States and the Nineteenth-Century Origins of American Immigration Policy* (New York: Oxford University Press, 2017), 42, 71.

[139] Strum, 'Famine Relief', 62.

[140] Brown to Rickard, 14 Mar. 1922, ARA, reel 548; report 'Troubles', ARA, reel 496; Patenaude, *Big Show*, 385.

[141] Laurence Webster, Report on relief by International Save the Children Union in Russia 1921–23, 8 May 1924, SCF, reel 30. See also Patenaude, *Big Show*, 75.

[142] ISCU report, 31 Jan. 1922, SCF, reel 29. See also Vogt, *Nansens kamp*, 221.

[143] Webster, Report; Benjamin Robertson, 'Descriptive notes on tour in Saratov and Samara provinces', Jan. 1922, SCF, reel 30. See also Cabanes, *Great War*, 231.

As organisations sought to keep the number of their staffers as low as possible, each fieldworker – mostly young and often unprepared for the job – had to shoulder an enormous workload and great responsibility. A number of the men (only Quakers accepted female relief workers) experienced what was referred to as 'famine shock' when facing the horrors of starvation. Several cases of nervous breakdowns and alcohol abuse ensued.[144] In addition, poor hygienic conditions – trains, for example, were described as 'lice-infested death traps' – impeded operations and threatened aid workers' lives.[145]

Those who were responsible for planning and coordination went through a similar collision with reality. Their previous work in Central and Eastern Europe made them profoundly underestimate the gravity of the situation in Russia. What had been planned often proved unrealistic and inadequate. The idea of concentrating the distribution of food in big cities – presupposing that refugees would flock there – was revised after representatives of the organisations began operating from the country and sent in their reports from the Volga area (see Figure 2.2).[146] When Hoover, in answer to Gorky's appeal, committed to feeding one million children, he assumed that each Soviet citizen was receiving a daily, state-financed meal, so that a supplementary ration would suffice. It was only during the Riga negotiations that this misunderstanding was corrected.[147] The Save the Children Fund (SCF) also realised that the portion distributed was often the only food people would eat that day. Their general plan of systematic feeding had to be adjusted when they learned this and other facts on the ground.[148] Attempts were made to take current research into account and prepare meals constituting a balanced diet. However, it was practically impossible to arrange such things as individual nutrition cards and customised diets. Methods of assessing the degree of malnutrition, like the Pelidisi table that had been tried in Central Europe, could seldom be applied under Russian conditions: there were too many victims, too few doctors, and a lack of time.[149]

Organising Famine Relief

When planning and distributing aid to Russia, organisations drew on their prior experience in European relief operations after the Great War, and on British imperial expertise battling famines in India. Hoover continued to support the European Relief Council (ERC) that had united major US aid agencies during post-war operations under the banner of the American Relief Administration

[144] Cabanes, *Great War*, 234–5; Patenaude, *Big Show*, 225.
[145] Webster, Report. See also Vogt, *Nansens kamp*, 235–6, and Cabanes, *Great War*, 229–31.
[146] Patenaude, *Big Show*, 53; Cabanes, *Great War*, 233.   [147] Patenaude, *Big Show*, 43–4.
[148] Webster, Report.   [149] Cabanes, *Great War*, 228; Patenaude, *Big Show*, 87.

(ARA) as the main distribution entity. He favoured forms of allocation that were tested and proven, including a warehouse and kitchen system, the establishment of local committees to provide assistance, and the food remittance programme. The British colonial system of famine relief helped coordinate various agencies across large territories and the spatial organisation of relief centres, both of which were effective under Russian conditions.[150] The British also took a 'Victorian approach' to aid that was similar to ARA relief ideals and can be summarised as 'keep[ing] people alive without making them dependent'. Accordingly, former colonial administrators, like Sir Benjamin Robertson and Lord George Curzon, as widely respected famine experts, influenced not only the work of British agencies, but also that of the ARA and Nansen's International Committee for Russian Relief (ICRR).[151]

The famine region was divided early on in order to avoid under- and over-supply. The ARA appointed more than a dozen district supervisors, each responsible for a specific area. Organisations like the SCF and the Quakers worked in the same manner, but on a much smaller scale. For example, SCF established ten sub-bases, headed by British supervisors, in villages and small towns around its headquarters in Saratov.[152] Communication between districts and headquarters took place via cables and letters. The ARA set up its own carrier service, paralleling the Russian postal service, and would transmit more than 50,000 telegrams during the relief operation.[153]

Distributing agencies further divided the afflicted area into spheres of influence. This forestalled conflicts and enabled smaller organisations to retain a certain independence, something that was valuable in their fundraising and public relations campaigns. Thus, the Saratov province was divided between the ARA, on the one hand, and the SCF and the International Save the Children Union (ISCU), on the other, giving the USA responsibility for the zone east of the Volga, while the Europeans took the western part. The Quakers proceeded in a similar way in their assigned territory in the Samara province: after a split backed by Hoover, British Friends covered the western part of the Buzuluk District, while the American Friends Service Committee (AFSC) took over the eastern part, receiving their supplies from the ARA.[154]

Such zones of influence had to be adjusted to new conditions from time to time. When British Quakers extended their adult feeding programme in 1922, the ARA supported them and concentrated resources accordingly. Similarly, when a Swedish Red Cross (SRC) team arrived in Samara in December 1921,

---

[150] Tehila Sasson and James Vernon, 'Practising the British Way of Famine: Technologies of Relief, 1770–1985', *European Review of History* 22, no. 6 (2015), 864.

[151] Sasson, 'From Empire to Humanity', 527, 532–6.   [152] Robertson, 'Descriptive notes'.

[153] 'The ARA Russian Operation at Glance', paper by Communication Division, 9 May 1923, ARA, reel 548.

[154] Robertson, 'Descriptive notes'.

the ARA, which was already present, assigned them a specific field of operation, extending it in the months that followed as Swedish resources increased.[155] For the ARA, in its role as the main distributing agency, such co-operative agreements meant that resources could be saved. However, moral dilemmas also arose, when smaller actors fuelled expectations, which they were not able to meet. For example, when the Volga Relief Society (VRS) withdrew from the Saratov province in September 1922, an ARA officer reported that he now felt 'morally bound to continue support to the German colonists' whom the VRS had aided before.[156]

A decentralised system of distribution, as well as the establishment and provisioning of camps and hospitals for refugees, was also meant to forestall, arrest, and reverse migration from villages to towns, and from the Volga region to Ukraine and Siberia. The 'imperial anxieties' of 'famine wanderers' were evident in the recommendations of former colonial administrators,[157] but a cover of the journal *Soviet Russia* showed similar concerns. Beneath a poster depicting hungry peasants heading westwards, a caption explained that the Friends of Soviet Russia (FSR) sent food and tractors 'in order to maintain these masses at their post'.[158]

A widespread net of warehouse and food depots also proved necessary, since any interruption of supply was generally due to transportation difficulties. In fact, transport was the biggest problem at the beginning of the relief operation, and it prevented an early extension of the feeding programme. The distribution of reduced rations to a greater number of people had been considered, but it proved infeasible, as the ration being provided already constituted an 'irreducible minimum'. The chief of the SCF operation in Saratov described how warehouses in Riga were stocked to full capacity in late 1921 'as far as financial means were available' because it was expected that the port would be inaccessible during the winter months. In the Volga region, winter threatened to cut off the supply to the most affected areas, where the population depended on river transport since they were far away from railheads. Depots there were stocked as much as possible in order to guarantee an uninterrupted supply of food. It was equally important that provisions be balanced, that is, 'the correct proportion one to another of different foodstuffs required for our menus'.[159]

The ARA food remittance programme, a further development of its popular and successful food remittance programme that had been used in Central

[155] Ibid. For specific areas assigned to smaller organisations, see 'Work of the International Russian Relief Committee'. Concerning the SRC's dependence on the ARA, see Haskell to Brown, 29 Nov. 1921, ARA, reel 115.
[156] Rickard to Page, 15 Sept. 1922, ARA, reel 115.
[157] Sasson, 'From Empire to Humanity', 524, 527, 534.   [158] *Soviet Russia* 6, no. 5 (1922).
[159] Webster, Report.

Figure 4.4 Packing ARA food remittances in Moscow, 1922. In contrast to
previous remittance programmes, food parcels were now packed in the
affected country.
American Relief Administration, Russian operational records, Box 400, Folder 4,
Hoover Institution Archives

Europe, was introduced in October 1921 as an alternative instrument of famine
relief. People outside Russia could donate a food package with a US$10
remittance at any ARA office (see Figure 4.4). Needy individuals or groups
in Russia could then collect the parcels from a local ARA warehouse.[160]

Initially, Soviet officials mistrusted this form of relief, as they had little
control over the beneficiaries. They feared that people with relatives or friends
abroad (who were already suspect for that reason) would profit, whereas
committed communists may be left empty-handed. In addition, parcels might
be used for speculative transactions. To prevent that, a limit of five parcels for
individuals and fifty for groups was imposed, and each addressee had to sign a
form stating that they would not sell any of the contents.[161] Donors were told
that the estimated US$2.25 per package profit from the food remittance

---

[160] Patenaude, *Big Show*, 91–4.
[161] Information Flyer 'Food Remittance to Russia', 15 Jan. 1922, ARA, reel 499; Patenaude, *Big
Show*, 95–6.

programme would be invested in a child relief campaign. Another positive argument was that the availability of more food – whether or not it was received by a needy person – would lead to an easing of the local market.

However, critics voiced moral concerns that such a programme might result in an unjust distribution of relief. For example, Jewish organisations and individuals were over-represented on the private donor side, which meant that regions in Ukraine and Belarus with large Jewish minorities would receive a substantial share of the packages.[162] In order to organise the distribution, the ARA had to build up delivery stations in these regions, although some were technically outside the famine zones.[163] ARA supervisors in districts where few people had emigrated to Europe or the USA in the decades before complained that inhabitants received no food parcels simply because they had no kinship connections beyond Russia. Thus, the ARA was forced to supply these areas with more general food aid.[164]

While organised robberies and large-scale embezzling were exceptions, internal reports and anecdotal evidence reveal many incidents of diversion.[165] These included thefts by harbour and transport workers, desk clerks demanding illegal charges for releasing remittances, Russians claiming the rations of dead relatives, attempts to obtain parcels with falsified documents, local committee members giving family and friends advantages, kitchen personnel eating food intended to feed children, and the seed grain being consumed as food.[166]

Some relief workers were also operating for personal gain. Already in December 1921, an ARA officer noted that employees were 'purchasing furs, diamonds and other things, evidently with an idea that they will personally profit by these investments'.[167] In February 1922, Soviet authorities thwarted an ARA employee's attempt to smuggle several kilos of gold and twenty-six carats of diamonds out of the country. While an incident involving goods of such high value was exceptional, this was not an isolated case.[168] In view of the widespread habit of relief workers using their salary to buy valuable goods at bargain prices, a pro-communist US journalist questioned 'whether the millions of loot they are taking out of the country isn't more than their relief'.[169]

---

[162] The Jewish Joint Distribution Committee claimed to have sold food remittances worth US$2 million (Experience of the Joint Distribution Committee in Food and Clothing Remittance Service under the American Relief Administration Nov. 1921–Mar. 1923, JDC (American Joint Distribution Committee) Archives, New York, AR192132/2/3/92).

[163] Patenaude, *Big Show*, 96.   [164] Bell to Burland, 22 Feb. 1923, ARA, reel 57.

[165] Patenaude, *Big Show*, 617.

[166] Vogt, *Nansens kamp*, 234–5; Patenaude, *Big Show*, 169, 617–23; Howard (ARA Odessa) to Moscow, 25 Dec. 1922, ARA, reel 566.

[167] Cited in Patenaude, *Big Show*, 671.   [168] Ibid., 667–90.

[169] Anna Louise Strong, cited in ibid., 676.

Having a privileged position also brought social advantages to foreign relief workers. In Moscow and Petrograd, 'plebeian Americans of no importance at home' gained the status of celebrities, as an ARA observer noted.[170] Numerous relief workers carried on intimate affairs with local women, relations that could entail sexual exploitation. An older ARA man commented prosaically that 'one does not have to pay much for women who are starving and some of our boys are making the most of the market'.[171] No less than thirty ARA men married during their service, most of them bringing their 'famine bride' back to the USA.[172] Nansen's representative in Ukraine, the later Norwegian Nazi leader Vidkun Quisling, married two women during his tour of humanitarian service, one of them only 17 years old.[173]

Kitchens and Food

In urban centres like Saratov, warehouses and a basic kitchen infrastructure were already in place when the foreign aid workers arrived. It was reminiscent of earlier years when parts of the population were fed in public kitchens.[174] However, the situation in the cities was not as devastating as in the surrounding rural areas. Robertson, after his inspection of the SCF feeding programme, observed that 35,000 of the 250,000 children being supported were city residents. He proposed that this number be reduced and the resources be better used in the countryside.[175]

The kitchens run by ARA, SCF, the Quakers, and other organisations including Soviet authorities varied in size. They were feeding between two dozen children per day in some villages, and several thousand in larger cities. In the Saratov region, the SCF had approximately 400 kitchens by January 1921, serving an average of 500 children.[176] The staff in many kitchens, was compensated in part on a commission basis, receiving a stipulated number of rations for themselves after they had fed a specific number of children. Other Russians employed by foreign organisations often received parts of their salary in the form of food as well, a so-called *paiok*.[177]

When provisions finally reached the famine regions, often far behind schedule, 'much ground [still had] to be covered before the food could enter the children's mouth'.[178] As feeding everybody was impossible, lists dividing famine victims into different categories were made, a practice adopted from colonial experience.[179] ARA, SCF, and the Quakers co-operated with local

---

[170] Cited in ibid., 298.   [171] Cited in ibid., 305.   [172] Ibid., 304.
[173] Vogt, *Nansens kamp*, 225, 268–9.   [174] Webster, Report.
[175] Robertson, 'Descriptive notes'.   [176] Ibid.
[177] Webster, Report; Patenaude, *Big Show*, 610.   [178] Webster, Report.
[179] Sasson and Vernon, 'Practising the British Way of Famine', 865.

committees for that purpose, but recruiting reliable agents in Russia was sometimes difficult. A considerable number of the local elites had vanished in the social upheavals of the revolution or because of the famine; others suffered greatly from hunger themselves. Unlike in Poland and Hungary, it was difficult to find individuals in whom the population, the relief organisations, and the authorities would place their trust.[180]

The ARA sought to influence the make-up of these committees, a right they had fought hard for during the Riga negotiations, where Soviet representatives vehemently opposed this request.[181] Determining who was on the committees was important to prevent abuse and make sure that relief goods were targeted 'without regards to politics, race and religion', and to silence critics at home. The SCF, however, assumed that the compilation of detailed lists and the organisation of single food kitchens were 'of course ... done by the local authorities'.[182] Robertson indicated in his report that the Russian recommendations regarding those who should be fed must be verified, 'but the numbers are so large that Mr. Webster [Laurence Webster, head of the SCF operation] has practically to take it on trust that the Committee recommends the most deserving cases'.[183] Meanwhile, SCF officials limited themselves to functioning as a 'court of appeal' in cases of complaints.[184] A regular inspection of all kitchens was impossible due to a lack of personnel; both the SCF and the ARA employed Russians for this task. Unannounced inspections and the threat to immediately close any institution that was badly run proved to be 'the most effective weapon of control'.[185]

In the case of SCF relief, each child selected was given a ticket for two months, with numbers representing a daily ration that were cut off when entering the kitchen. If ticketed children did not show up and food remained, others without a ticket who were waiting outside received the leftovers. The ARA implemented a similar system. British Quakers based their child feeding programme on a division of the villages in their relief area into four categories. Depending on the estimated need, either 30, 20, 15, or 10 per cent of the children were fed. In contrast to both the ARA and the SCF, the British Friends' Emergency and War Victims Relief Committee (FEWVRC) did not use their own forms to gather information about the children chosen by local committees, but relied completely on Russian authorities to do this, at least in some villages. Even Nansen, often criticised as gullible, was apparently uneasy about such an arrangement.[186]

---

[180] Patenaude, *Big Show*, 82.   [181] Vogt, *Nansens kamp*, 124   [182] Webster, Report.
[183] Robertson, 'Descriptive notes'.   [184] Webster, Report.
[185] Robertson, 'Descriptive notes'. See also Patenaude, *Big Show*, 88, 618.
[186] Robertson, 'Descriptive notes'. On Nansen, see Sund to Gorvin, 6 June 1922, FEWVRC 7/5/1/5.

The SRC used slightly different geographical targeting methods when planning for the allocation of food in the limited area for which they were responsible. With the help of Soviet statistics, the current economic conditions in different villages were compared with their state in 1914, generally by measuring numbers of livestock. If wealth had declined by 75 per cent, three out of four inhabitants were to receive food. Accordingly, in the village of Voskresenska, where wealth had declined by 70 per cent, the proposed food entitlement comprised seven out of ten. However, Robertson's report from the famine region suggested instead that a local moral economy prevailed, according to which the food was shared in such a way that the whole population received a 70 per cent ration.[187]

Some feared that a focus on the neediest could be counterproductive or even unethical. A Mennonite relief worker pointed out that because of inadequate supply and a lack of means testing, his organisation was 'feeding all of the thieves, vagabonds, the shiftless, the lazy poor, while the good people who had struggled and saved and put themselves on rations, had to go on eating their black bread'. He questioned whether it would not be wiser to support those who knew how to help themselves, not the least because this group 'must ultimately take care of the poor'.[188]

Gifts from government stores to SCF, the British Quakers, and Nansen 'complicate[d] the work of distribution', as Robertson pointed out. He referred especially to the delivery of large amounts of herring from Norway, but also cited 200 t of lime juice from British government stores that took up valuable cargo space when transported to Saratov. Robertson considered it obvious that something of this nature should be distributed in Moscow or Petrograd instead. Other deliveries, like chilled meat from Australia, had to be consumed before the frost was gone, requiring changes to be made in the standard rations.[189] The Nansen mission received a variety of food donations at different times, all of which had to be integrated in the menus. This made the development of standardised feeding plans, something most organisations tried to achieve, a difficult task.

When the SCF opened its first kitchen at the end of October 1921, local authorities were invited to test three types of soup that were to be offered in rotation. Each ration contained 720 calories and was prepared with regard to nutritional value as well as cost, transportation, and shelf-life.[190] These dishes were served in the form of a half-litre bowl of soup based on flour and either rice or beans, and served with bread. The Russian officials present made several suggestions for changes, mostly based on the assumption that Russian

---

[187] Robertson, 'Descriptive notes'.   [188] Hiebert and Miller, *Feeding the Hungry*, 219–20.
[189] Robertson, *The Famine in Russia*, 11–12. See also Vogt, *Nansens kamp*, 232.
[190] Webster, Report.

children would neither accept the soup nor the unfamiliar white bread. Webster rejected any changes as 'not practical' and claimed later a broad acceptance of the foreign meals by the children.[191]

Nevertheless, the lack of dark bread in the rations was a constant source of complaint. A Soviet functionary commented to an ARA relief worker that while he understood that the rations were composed according to scientific standards, the peasants simply wanted their black bread.[192] On the other hand, exotic products like condensed milk and cacao became symbols not only of foreign relief, but of the unknown Western world, and were dearly missed when the organisations withdrew from Russia.[193]

The ARA's main export was corn in its raw state and Hoover argued that 'nearly double the food values can be delivered in corn as could be delivered in wheat for the same money'.[194] Critics suggested that corn would provide inadequate relief, as Russian peasants were neither used to it nor able to prepare it properly. As was the case in Ireland in 1845, corn was unknown in Russia at the time, and so instructions on how to use it had to be conveyed in supplementary information campaigns.[195] Despite the lack of grain mills, the consummation of raw corn only led to a few cases of discomfort, as Russians improvised and found ways to prepare it. In the end, even former critics acknowledged the success of the 'corn campaign'.[196]

To Feed or Not to Feed

Partly out of conviction, but also as a concession to potential donors and political enemies, the ARA, the SCF, and other organisations originally limited their relief mission to children, even though exceptions were made in the field for pregnant women, nursing mothers, and patients in hospital.[197] At the beginning of the relief mission, when the ARA was requested to help adults, their standard reply was that they were 'authorized to feed and clothe only children'.[198] In Russia, however, this caused unexpected dilemmas, both with respect to morals and to effectiveness.

From the start, British and US Quakers opposed the 'children only' policy. Even though they, too, prioritised children, they felt that targeting only this group was a fatal error.[199] They feared the situation would deteriorate 'if we allow the farming population ... either to die or to run away', and they reported that 'where children are being fed ... the families from contiguous

---

[191] Ibid.   [192] Haskell to Herter, 6 Mar. 1923, ARA, reel 496.
[193] Patenaude, *Big Show*, 511–12.   [194] Cited in Patenaude, *Big Show*, 146.
[195] ARA press release, 3 Mar. 1922, ARA, reel 548.   [196] Patenaude, *Big Show*, 169–70.
[197] Robertson, 'Descriptive notes'.   [198] Shafroth to Friedman, 6 Nov. 1921, ARA, reel 11.
[199] Kelly, *British Humanitarian Activity*, 201.

neighbourhoods emigrate into those cities and desert their children'.[200] British experts considered feeding adults essential to prevent further migration and secure the manpower to plant and bring in the next harvest. *The Spectator* criticised limiting the aid clientele to children early on, maintaining that a child saved, with its parents lost, was but 'a lonely atom in the world'.[201] Around the same time, ARA representatives in Russia came to the same conclusion and recommended feeding both children and adults.[202]

The food remittance programme that was introduced soon afterwards could not solve this problem completely, as it did not always support the neediest people. For this reason, the ARA initiated an adult feeding programme, mainly financed with funds the Congress had granted and by Soviet gold. While in March 1922, fewer than 10,000 adults were being supported, by June the number had risen to 4.5 million. More adults than children were already being provided for in April. Adult feeding reached a peak of 6.3 million recipients in August, then quickly dropped to less than 100,000 in October. One reason for the decline was a conflict between the ARA and the Soviet government over the export of grain.[203]

The SCF, although children were its eponymous target, could not avoid dealing with the question after Robertson's report on the famine region stated that 'a most serious problem was being presented by the keeping alive of children, whilst the adult population was being allowed to dwindle from starvation to death'.[204] Robertson also drew attention to the questionable practise that, according to the standardised system, the same amount of nourishment was provided to a young person of 14 as to a four-year-old child, and that 15-year-olds were considered adults and received nothing.[205]

While the statutes of the SCF did not permit feeding adults with its own financial resources, the 'vital necessity' for this was acknowledged early on.[206] The dilemma was addressed indirectly, but with a moral undertone. For example, an SCF press release told of a little girl who tried to smuggle food out of a feeding centre. When caught, she exclaimed, 'How can you expect me to eat all this when mother at home has not had a bite for two days?'[207] Reports like this prepared SCF supporters for a compromise. Beginning in January 1922, the SCF carried out an adult feeding programme in Saratov on behalf of Britain's Russian Famine Relief Fund (RFRF). In addition, the SCF served as a distribution agency for relief goods donated to the Nansen organisation, such as cod liver oil and the

---

[200] Haines (AFSC), quotations cited by McFadden and Gorfinkel, *Constructive Spirit*, 51.
[201] 'How to Help in the Russian Famine?', *The Spectator*, 16 Sept. 1921.
[202] Patenaude, *Big Show*, 70–1.
[203] 'Russian Feeding Progress: Number of Persons Fed on the First of Each Month' (undated, but after Apr. 1923), ARA, reel 568.
[204] Robertson, *Famine in Russia*, 9.   [205] Robertson, 'Descriptive notes'.
[206] Webster, Report.   [207] SCF Report from the Press Department, 9 Nov. 1921, SCF, reel 29.

herring from Norway. In contrast to the child feeding programme, adult provisions, often consisting of corn, were generally distributed as fortnightly or monthly rations. In mid-1922, the SCF also took over some of the ARA food aid clients in the Saratov region, so that it was feeding approximately 250,000 adults and the same number of children. By July 1922, for the first time, the SCF was supporting more adults (375,000) than children (300,000), before the programme was dropped that autumn. As Webster admitted, adult feeding was especially necessary 'during the arduous time of harvesting'.[208]

According to one crucial rule in the child feeding programmes of ARA and SCF, meals had to be consumed in the kitchens (see Figure 4.5). Robertson regarded this principle as indispensable because, on the one hand, misuse had to be avoided, and, on the other, the caloric requirements that medical research considered basic had to be met. If rations were split, a child might die, and previously donated food would have been wasted.[209] However, the SCF soon granted exceptions for home consumption if it was very cold or wet, or if a child was ill or had no adequate clothing.[210]

While the SCF promised that exceptions to the eating-on-premises rule would only affect one-tenth of the children, the British Quakers rejected Robertson's kitchen doctrine as 'a practical impossibility', admitting that, contrary to their original plan, most children did not eat in the kitchen. Arthur Watts, who organised FEWVRC relief in Buzuluk, enumerated the disadvantages of the kitchens: personnel consumed a large part of the food, theft caused provisions to dwindle, and the soup distributed 'was generally speaking too thin'.[211] In reaction, the Quakers abandoned the kitchen strategy and concentrated on the distribution of dry rations instead – also because 'many of the most needy could not possibly come to kitchens'.[212]

Local circumstances prevented other rules aimed at efficiency from being adopted. When an ARA inspector criticised the uncoordinated opening hours of a kitchen and recommended the introduction of shifts for different groups of children, the local staff replied that this would be impossible, as in their remote area most of the families did not own watches or clocks, but relied instead on the sun.[213]

By contrast to previous relief operations in Central Europe, feeding programmes in Russia were accompanied by medical services. This proved necessary, as people did not only die from starvation, but also from hunger-related diseases like typhus, dysentery, and cholera. In addition, existing

---

[208] Webster, Report.   [209] Robertson, 'Descriptive notes'.
[210] Press release from the SCF, 9 Nov. 1921, SCF, reel 29.
[211] Watts to Fry, 10 June 1922, FEWVRC 7/3/6/1.
[212] Watts to Fry, 28 June 1922, FEWVRC 7/3/6/1.
[213] ARA press release, exclusive for the *New York World Sunday Magazine*, undated (Mar. 1922), ARA, reel 548.

Figure 4.5 ARA feeding station for children in a former palace, 1922. Note the ARA posters in the background.
American Relief Administration, Russian operational records, Box 397, Folder 3, Envelope 1 'Childfeeding', Hoover Institution Archives

hospitals lacked basic equipment, and many nurses and doctors were themselves struggling for survival. The ARA, therefore, assigned a chief physician to each district. In addition, a medical division, well-equipped with funds and supplies from the American Red Cross (ARC) and the US War Department, began operations in November 1921. Feeding programmes for hospital staff complemented these efforts.[214] In the case of SCF, the Quakers, and other agencies, medical relief depended on donations that often consisted of army surplus; their programmes were not as well established as those of the ARA and ARC. A welcome contribution was soap, handed out to children in SCF kitchens and in hospitals.[215] The German Red Cross, for its part, focused solely on providing medical assistance, as a 'defence against the danger of epidemics from the east' (*Abwehr der Seuchengefahr aus dem Osten* – the title of the government fund that financed the mission).[216]

---

[214] Vogt, *Nansens kamp*, 219; Patenaude, *Big Show*, 90–1.   [215] Webster, Report.
[216] Wolfgang U. Eckart, *Von Kommissaren und Kamelen: Heinrich Zeiss – Arzt und Kundschafter in der Sowjetunion 1921–1931* (Paderborn: Schöningh, 2016); Eckart, 'Nach bestem Vermögen'; Mühlens, *Die Russische Hunger- und Seuchenkatastrophe*.

Efficiency and Compassion

In the age of organised humanitarianism, dilemmas caused by the tension between a businesslike relief philosophy, on the one hand, and humanitarian compassion and moral considerations, on the other, were inevitable, both on an agency and an individual level. To implement such a gigantic operation as providing relief to starving Russia, rules had to be strictly observed, since any deviation from an established routine would cost time, money, and ultimately human lives. Efficiency had to be given top priority when organising relief for millions of people; individual fates could not be taken into consideration.

For this reason, a large organisation like the ARA was ambivalent about collaborating with organisations that worked on a smaller scale, and towards the many individuals who offered their help in the form of donations, campaigns, or services. ARA staff repeatedly deplored the waste of resources that they believed little campaigns and donations entailed, considering them only symbolic gestures measured against the enormity of the famine.[217] Well-meaning donors with special wishes took time and consideration from the ARA staff. However, ARA archives reveal a willingness to process even odd requests and suggestions (e.g., a proposal to drive herds of Siberian reindeer to the famine region).[218] The service attitude of the ARA staff was particularly evident in the beginning, exhibiting a strong wish not to offend anyone. When an exiled Russian professor requested that ARA convey sugar worth US$250 to his colleagues in Russia (instead of the regular remittance parcels), it created an enormous paper trail in which Hoover and other key officers became involved until it was declared that 'we must not under any circumstances attempt to vary our food remittance program'.[219]

Donations in kind were also routinely refused, as 'the expense of handling and collecting same for shipping is too expensive'.[220] However, the risk of this policy was that some potential donors might feel offended when their offer was not accepted. Such individuals received a form letter in which the ARA, 'though not unmindful of the generosity which prompted it', recommended that they sell the items and contribute the proceeds in the form of food remittances.[221] Alternatively, they were advised to donate the goods to the AFSC or other organisations. It was not always understood that such a policy made sense from an economic point of view, and some donors may have felt deprived of the 'warm glow' they thought that they deserved.

---

[217] Draft to Mitchel, unsigned (London), 27 Apr. 1922, ARA, reel 499.
[218] (Illegible) to Hoover, 6 Jan. 1922, ARA, reel 550.
[219] Rickard to Page, 31 Oct. 1921, ARA, reel 500.
[220] Barringer to Refield, 31 Jan. 1922, ARA, reel 501.
[221] E.g., Barringer to Troper & Company, 26 Jan. 1922; Barringer to Bose, 6 Feb. 1922; Barringer to Giedt, 16 Feb. 1922, all ARA, reel 501.

Unlike the ARA, both the FEWVRC and the AFSC gratefully accepted all sorts of gifts in kind. The ARA saw this as intentional 'amateurism', whose consequences 'professional' organisations would have to suffer in the end. As an ARA staff member, not without a tinge of irony, put it:

> I greatly fear that when the various radical groups and the Quakers have failed to secure much more than enough to pay the freight on a shipload of grain, we will have to come to the front, as usual, and find them the money to go on with, thus exhibiting a Christian spirit which they will neither understand nor acknowledge.[222]

Regarding the FEWVRC, Nansen's supervisors criticised the 'Quaker way' in the field as too lax and gullible.[223] In replying to this accusation, Ruth Fry explained that 'our plan of believing the people and giving them to understand that we expect them to be entirely upright and honest has been rewarded by their behaving very well'.[224] The Quakers, for their part, were critical of other relief agencies for preferring ex-militaries as relief workers. When one of this group was assigned to the FEWVRC unit, complaints were raised that it was difficult to 'fit a militarist' who did not understand and appreciate their approach into the Friends' work. 'So long as people do not mind being sworn at the whole day and driven like slaves he could do excellent work, but this is not our way.'[225] Similar judgements were voiced about nurses who had received their training in the military.[226]

Despite different relief cultures, most fieldworkers saw no alternative to a rational structuring of humanitarian aid and the ensuing disregard of individual fate.[227] However, in practice, this principle caused moral conflicts and psychological problems. Like many others, a Mennonite relief worker recounted how 'distasteful' the necessary selection of the 'most needy' was.[228]

At headquarters, it was realised that it was difficult for relief workers to be confronted with 'destitute cases which do not come under the classification of the relief work they are doing'.[229] When they were forced to turn down people who were obviously in need, the idea that they were doing good was often extinguished. Many of them 'spent a considerable amount of money from their private incomes' on remittance parcels, so that they could at least support Russian acquaintances or colleagues.[230] Even small amounts that they could use as they saw fit had 'the result of distinctly strengthening their morale', as

---

[222] Baker to Brown, 10 Oct. 1921, ARA, reel 549.
[223] Vogt, *Nansens kamp*, 232–4; Sund to Gorvin, 6 June 1921, FEWVRC 7/5/1/3.
[224] Fry to Nansen, 22 July 1922, FEWVRC 7/5/1/5.
[225] Watts to Fry, 2 June 1922, FEWVRC 7/3/6/1.
[226] Watts to Fry, 20 June 1922, FEWVRC 7/3/6/1.
[227] McFadden and Gorfinkel, *Constructive Spirit*, 71; Patenaude, *Big Show*, 141.
[228] Hiebert and Miller, *Feeding the Hungry*, 262.
[229] Page to Strauss, 8 Nov. 1922, JDC Archives, NY AR192132/4/30/3/489.
[230] Bell to Burland, 22 Feb. 1923, ARA, reel 57.

an ARA official wrote in a letter of thanks to the Jewish Joint Distribution Committee (JDC), which had just conveyed such discretionary funds to two ARA supervisors.[231] Similarly, when an ARA district office received 500 packages to distribute at will, a relief worker described the excitement it caused: 'Every man with whom I came into contact urged (some pleaded) for permission to use a portion of these remittances.'[232]

Despite their cultivated image as businesslike administrators, sources reveal numerous cases of ARA staff members acting contrary to any organisational logic and following their own moral convictions. The criteria for those exceptions appear arbitrary, although heart-wrenching letters from children had a good chance of succeeding.[233] In other cases, exceptions were made less due to individual moral considerations than because ARA's reputation might be at stake. For example, creating the small Special Funds for the Relief of Individual Cases of Suffering was a way to reply to appeals from scientists of worldwide renown. It was worried that turning down such requests would put 'the ARA in the light of cold-bloodedness'.[234]

More than Food: Communist Relief

The Workers' International Relief (WIR) and its national affiliates differed from other agencies in their approach, as they aimed not only to support distressed people, but the Soviet system itself.[235] In contrast to 'bourgeois philanthropic societies', the WIR combined delivering food and clothing with aid for reconstruction (i.e., development, in today's terms), thereby targeting the root causes of famine.[236]

The implementation of communist relief from abroad went through different phases. A major part of cash donations during the first months was used to purchase food that was shipped to Russia and delivered to local WIR administrators, who co-operated closely with Soviet authorities. Already by December 1921 the WIR claimed to be feeding more than 200,000 people, having collected US$900,000 via national affiliates worldwide, with at least

---

[231] Page to Lewis Strauss, 8 Nov. 1922, JDC Archives, NY AR192132/4/30/3/489.

[232] Cable to Rickard: Food Remittances to Intellectuals, 20 Feb. 1922, ARA, reel 500.

[233] E.g., Galoschka to ARA, undated (early autumn 1922); Lee to 'Miss Galoschka', 6 Oct. 1922; Lee to London office, 6 Oct. 1922; Haskell to ARA London, 16 Nov. 1922, all ARA, reel 11.

[234] Memorandum: Special Funds for the Relief of Individual Cases of Suffering among the Professionals in Russia, undated, ARA, reel 500.

[235] Braskén, *International Workers' Relief*, 42. An FSR pamphlet claimed that more than twenty national chapters existed, not only in Europe, but also in Argentine, Brazil, Japan, Korea, and South Africa. See FSR, *One Year of Relief Work*, 1–2.

[236] 'Eighteenth Session', *Bulletin of the IV Congress of the Communist International*, 28 Nov. 1922; 'Program of the FSR', *Soviet Russia* 7, no. 11 (1922). See also Braskén, *International Workers' Relief*, 60.

one-third coming from its US branch, namely, the FSR.[237] As in the case of other organisations, relief was centred in specific geographic areas.[238]

After the first wave of food aid, efforts concentrated on children, and national branches collected money for orphans' homes. The quarters provided for this purpose by the Soviet government were often said to be estates of former noble families. Staff, food, and maintenance were financed by donations.[239] By the end of 1922, the FSR alone claimed to have funded ten such homes, each supporting at least 100 orphans.[240] The focus on children was believed to attract donors outside the reach of communist organisations. However, it was emphasised that the WIR – in contrast to other organisations – offered a long-term solution for the welfare of the children in the programme, rather than temporarily feeding a large number.[241] Other forms of aid were already being discussed by the end of 1921, including 'productive assistance' in the form of agricultural machinery and expertise, as well as innovative business ventures that combined famine relief with the reconstruction of local economies.[242] It was argued that 'food and clothing can only alleviate the suffering engendered by the famine, but they cannot exterminate the roots of famine in Russia'.[243]

For that reason, the FSR established an Agricultural Relief Unit, which in May 1922 sent twenty tractors and other material to Russia (see Figure 4.6).[244] The shipment was accompanied by a team of agricultural workers and a doctor, along with food and medicine for half a year. While the main task was the 'actual production of food on a large scale', an educational aspect was also built into the programme. Qualified Russians should be taught 'American methods' of modern machine farming, not only through learning by doing, but also via 'several thousand feet of educational moving picture films' that the US comrades brought with them.[245]

At the Third World Congress of the WIR, held in summer 1922 in Berlin, delegates from more than a dozen countries decided that they would overcome

---

[237] FSR, *Forty Facts*, 3. The FSR contribution to WIR relief was most likely more than half by the end of the operation. See 'Famine Relief by the Workers'.

[238] Kazan, Samara, Saratov, Tsaritsin, Orenburg, and Chebliabinsk, FSR, *One Year of Relief Work*, 1.

[239] Braskén, *International Workers' Relief*, 51; Workers' International Relief, British Joint Labor Aid Committee, undated pamphlet (probably 1925), available at https://cdm21047.contentdm.oclc.org/digital/collection/russian/id/2896 (accessed 29 June 2018).

[240] 'FSR activities'.

[241] Braskén, *International Workers' Relief*, 51, 'Help Children of Soviet Russia', *Soviet Russia* 7, no. 7 (1922); 'FSR activities'.

[242] Braskén, *International Workers' Relief*, 60–1; 'International Tool Collection Week', *Soviet Russia* 6, no. 9 (1922).

[243] FSR, *One Year of Relief Work*, 6.

[244] 'FSR Relief Shipments, From American Workers to Russian Workers', FSR (New York, 1922).

[245] 'Our Agricultural Relief Unit', *Soviet Russia* 6, no. 10 (1922).

Figure 4.6 Cover of Friends of Soviet Russia publication: 'Machinery for Russia' by Lydia Gibson. *Soviet Russia*, 15 Sep. 1922.
Original from Princeton University, Google-digitized, public domain.

'superficial, philanthropic means of relief' by 'reviving the productive forces of Soviet Russia'.[246] During the coming months, the WIR received concessions for several agricultural and industrial ventures in Soviet Russia, including a fishery in Volgograd, a number of agricultural holdings (the biggest one run by the US tractor team), and factories. Officially non-profit companies, these businesses worked under the direction of WIR according to capitalist methods, the expected surplus to be used for famine relief.[247]

---

[246] FSR, *Productive Relief for Soviet Russia* (New York: FSR, c. 1922).
[247] Braskén, *International Workers' Relief*, 67–8; 'Eighteenth Session'.

In the spirit of Lenin's New Economic Policy, Western workers were invited to invest in this relief project by buying Workers' Bonds, which were advertised as 'furthering reconstruction in the famine areas'.[248] Most of these ventures had limited success: the surplus of the farms run by WIR was feeding a few hundred people at the most. Mismanagement on the part of WIR administrators in Russia made the situation worse and led to the termination of the programme in 1923.[249] Most shares of the Workers' Bond remained unsold, and only one similar initiative to help rebuild Russia's garment industry saw moderate success.[250]

Don't Mourn: Organise

On an organisational level, the inequalities of power and financial means within humanitarian alliances led to friction, something that was intensified by the diversity of relief cultures and interests. These conflicts concerned economic resources, fundraising, and an agency's influence on the management and distribution of relief. A more general source of disagreement was the extent to which a provider would adapt to organised humanitarianism and modern forms of fundraising and relief work. Organisations that were progressive in this regard, like the ARA and the SCF, felt that they had to drag their more old-fashioned collaborating partners along with them.[251]

In the USA, the difference between major and minor players was particularly striking. Despite assuring others that they had no desire 'to monopolize Russian relief', ARA officials were openly in favour of centralising aid work under one national roof and showed little understanding for affiliated organisations wishing to preserve independent relief operations, cultures, and goals.[252] This resulted in conflicts with the AFSC and the JDC, the only two affiliated organisations that operated their own relief programmes in Russia and Ukraine, respectively. While many Quakers criticised the decision to work under the ARA as a sell-out of their ideals, the JDC was dissatisfied with the mode of distribution and the lack of public acknowledgement of relief financed

---

[248] Braskén, *International Workers' Relief*, 65–7; Robert Minor, 'A Splendid Opportunity', *Soviet Russia* 7, no. 11 (1922); 'Our Workers Investing in Russia', *Literary Digest* 74, no. 2 (1922).

[249] 'Eighteenth Session'; Braskén, *International Workers' Relief*, 69.

[250] The Russian-American Industrial Corporation, *For Aid in the Economic Reconstruction of Russia: Prospectus* (1922); 'Our Workers Investing'; Report of the Directors and Financial Statement Submitted to Second Annual Meeting of Stockholders of the Russian-American Industrial Corporation, 26 Feb. 1924.

[251] For conflicts between SCF and IWRF, see Baughan, 'Imperial War Relief Fund', 851; also Weardale in an undated letter to a critic (probably autumn 1921), SCF, reel 30. For ARA's reservations regarding other organisations, see Haskell to London, 20 Mar. 1922, ARA, reel 115.

[252] Hoover to Payne, ARC, 8 Mar. 1922, ARA, reel 289.

by the Jewish community.[253] The ARA denounced the JDC for wanting to impose 'a religious discrimination in the delivery of relief', and argued further that feeding predominately Jews with JDC money would 'reflect adversely' upon this group in Russia and Ukraine, bringing on them the 'displeasure of the government' and the hate of the population, 'with possible resulting pogroms'.[254] The ARA was so concerned about this that it excluded Jews when staffing its Russian unit.[255] As a compromise, an urban orientation for JDC aid was later agreed upon, since the Jewish population was concentrated in cities and towns.[256]

The fact that some affiliated organisations had their own well-defined groups of donors and recipients caused difficulties for the ARA because Hoover was obliged to administer impartial relief – independent of ethnic, religious, or social background. In addition, attempting to fulfil earmarked conditions meant an increased workload. Accordingly, the ARA complained that 'the superimposing of details by other organizations outside of the ARA puts a strain upon our staff'. Instead, they recommended that funds collected be given directly to the ARA without conditions.[257]

Arguments against sectarian targeting were supported by the experience of American Mennonite Relief (AMR). They initially used so-called bulk sales from the ARA to support their brethren in Russia, so that food worth US$500 or more was to be distributed according to the wishes of the purchaser, but under the condition that one-quarter was to be retained by the ARA for general relief. In hindsight, the AMR criticised this programme:

Local problems soon showed that one could not distribute any large quantity of food to one group of people in a village, ignoring the other groups, without getting into serious trouble. There had always been considerable race feeling, and the local officials would never have tolerated any relief program which was limited to helping the Mennonites. Several of the other relief organizations were very much handicapped in their attempts to do effective relief work, largely because they ignored political and racial problems.[258]

While the conflict with the JDC and the example of the AMR illustrate the tension between the principle of impartial relief and sectarian commitments,

---

[253] Patenaude, *Big Show*, 47, 139–42, 181; McFadden and Gorfinkel, *Constructive Spirit*, 71–5; Maul, 'American Quakers and Famine Relief'; Wilkinson to Herter, 19 Apr. 1922; JDC Cable, Rosenberg to Strauss, 26 May 1922; Galpin to Mullendore, 29 May 1922; Herter to Page, 15 Jan. 1923, all ARA, reel 404.

[254] ARA draft to Strauss, undated (probably May 1922), ARA, reel 404 (first quotation); Herter to Page, 15 Jan. 1923, ibid. (following quotations).

[255] Patenaude, *Big Show*, 50.

[256] Rosenberg to Brown, 14 Sep. 1922, JDC Archives, NY AR192132/4/30/3/489.

[257] Page to Haskell, 16 Jan. 1922, ARA, reel 115 (quotation); Haskell to London, 20 Mar. 1922, ibid.

[258] Hiebert and Miller, *Feeding the Hungry*, 209.

relations between the ARA and AFSC were marred by other issues as well. Hoover had aspired to a 'united national relief front'. Thus, he commanded the AFSC to terminate its co-operation with the British Quakers, a request that was met with resistance. Another disagreement arose over the question of how to deal with 'red-minded' fundraising groups. Hoover reproached them for 'using the Quakers as a cloak' in an attempt to 'undermine' the ARA.[259] In the end, the AFSC reluctantly agreed to submit to the ARA and the Riga agreement. In compensation, they were given their own relief area. In this way, a certain amount of independence was preserved and ensued no open quarrel with Hoover or his critics.

While in the USA, the existence of an umbrella organisation such as the ARA was considered 'a hindrance to the smaller agencies',[260] in Europe, Nansen's ICRR, despite its original ambitions, was almost at an end. Due to a lack of resources, they could hardly claim leadership or wield the power to coordinate affiliated organisations, depending rather on the money of financially strong British organisations to keep running the operation. The same donor organisations began to question the efficiency of the ICRR in early 1922 and a few months later considered it a burden.[261]

In March 1922, L. B. Golden, SCF representative, inspected the office of the Nansen mission in Geneva. He was accompanied by a professor of economic history who had recently returned from a visit to Russia. The latter's verdict was scathing, describing the main office as 'at least as worthy of condemnation' as the 'utterly inefficient' branch in Moscow, and suggested 'a speedy conclusion'. This harsh judgement culminated in the allegation that a 'great wastage of human life must certainly result from such a state of things'.[262] Golden's report was equally critical. He described Nansen's organisation as 'perfectly hopeless' and 'ridiculous' and recommended that not only the SCF, but the Quakers and the RFRF, should also 'stop any further subsidies'.[263] However, criticism of the ICRR was to be kept from the public in order not to hurt the relief campaign or Nansen himself, who was held in high regard personally and offered an honorary position.[264] This shows striking similarity to the ARA staff's criticism of the ICRR as inadequate and internally derided it as 'Nansen Promissory Relief Operation', while at the same time expressing

---

[259] Hoover to Jones, 10 Sept. 1921, and Confidential Memorandum of ERC meeting discussion by Norton for the AFSC, 24 Aug. 1921, both cited in McFadden and Gorfinkel, *Constructive Spirit*, 70, 72.

[260] Fisher, *Famine in Soviet Russia*, 165.

[261] See, for example, Minutes of Russian Famine Relief Fund meeting (confidential), 12 July 1922, SCF, reel 29.

[262] Atkinson to Robertson (confidential), 22 Mar. 1922, SCF, reel 29.

[263] Strictly confidential report, 23 Mar. 1922, SCF, reel 29.

[264] Golden to Clouzot, 11 Sept. 1922; Confidential meeting minutes, 12 July 1922. See also Minutes of informal meeting, 14 July 1922, all SCF, reel 29.

their respect for its leader as a person.[265] To avoid a public break, the British organisations granted financial support for a gradual liquidation of the Nansen mission, which was to cease operations by the end of 1922, and signed new agreements with the Soviet government.[266]

4.4 Relief, Rehabilitation, and Resettlement: Ethiopia

The process of deploying famine relief in Ethiopia in the mid-1980s was shaped by geo-political factors. Both the Ethiopian government and the liberation movements in Tigray and Eritrea sought to use international aid for political and military advantage. In general, aid was monitored by the government Relief and Rehabilitation Commission (RRC), while the Eritrean Relief Association (ERA) and Relief Society of Tigray (REST) oversaw distribution in the insurgent regions. Concerns about the possible misappropriation of aid on all sides influenced the allocation practices of donors during the famine. Reluctance on the part of foreign governments to work directly with the RRC meant that approximately two-thirds of all international aid was earmarked for distribution to specific beneficiaries by voluntary agencies, despite objections from the RRC.[267] Sidestepping the Mengistu regime in this fashion was a way for foreign governments to assure their own taxpayers that money was reaching those who needed it, and not being diverted for military purposes. Similarly, support from large donors for cross-border feeding operations in Eritrea and Tigray was only forthcoming because such support was channelled through consortia like the Emergency Relief Desk (ERD), which served as a 'neutral screen'.[268]

Logistical problems of getting supplies to affected areas was a key consideration for all involved in the relief effort. Most food aid entered Ethiopia via the Assab docks, although Massawa and Djibouti also played a role. Offloading at the Port of Assab was a recurrent source of tension between donors and the Mengistu regime. In 1985, an international airlift was begun. It transported nearly 15 per cent of all food aid, but trucking was the main method of in-country distribution (see Figure 4.7). Building up a reliable transportation fleet – including maintenance and repair teams – was therefore central to relief operations. The distribution of an increasing proportion of food aid through voluntary channels from early 1985 on led many organisations to establish or rapidly expand their own trucking operations, resulting in a total of more than 600 trucks on the road.[269] From December 1984 until May 1985, food aid was

---

[265] Haskell to Brown, 19 Feb. 1923, ARA, reel 112; Patenaude, *Big Show*, 652–3.
[266] Minutes of meeting between Nansen and British representatives, 17 July 1922, SCF, reel 29.
[267] Poster, 'Gentle War', 415; Jansson, 'Emergency Relief', 47.
[268] Duffield and Prendergast, *Without Troops*, 53.
[269] Borton, *Changing Role*, 28, 50; IIED, *African Emergency*, 28.

Figure 4.7 Trucks are loaded with grain at Addis Ababa airport, Jan. 1985.
Photo by Joel Robine, reproduced courtesy of Getty Images

distributed at the rate of 45,000 t per month – four times what the UN had previously estimated was possible.[270] In Eritrea and Tigray, a trucking consortium created in 1983 with War on Want as the lead agency complemented the cross-border work of the ERD.[271]

Earmarking aid to voluntary organisations or to different regions of the country was the customary practice of donor governments, much to the displeasure of UN representative Jansson.[272] The voluntary agencies then divided the country into spheres of influence. The UK Save the Children, for example, was dominant in Korem and the adjacent area of Wollo, while Oxfam UK covered other parts of Wollo, and the Lutherans worked mostly in the southwest. The US organisation Catholic Relief Services (CRS) led relief work in the northern regions of Eritrea and Tigray.[273] There were major coordination problems as a result of such earmarking and, according to one evaluation, it 'probably contributed to the undersupply of some of the worst affected areas during 1985'.[274] A major challenge was to ensure that adequate supplies

[270] Penrose, 'Before and After', 155.
[271] Duffield and Prendergast, *Without Troops*, 57; Borton, *Changing Role*, 28.
[272] Jansson, 'Emergency Relief', 23.   [273] Poster, *Gentle War*, 402.
[274] Borton, *Changing Role*, 50.

reached areas beyond government control because the Ethiopian government sought to use starvation as a weapon in its conflict with the liberation fronts. The crisis led large numbers of refugees to flee across the border to Sudan.

Working in Government-Controlled Ethiopia

The scale of the crisis in 1984–5 placed a great strain on the capacity of voluntary agencies as they tried to manage aid in Ethiopia. Many of their programmes went from specialised intensive feeding, health care, or development schemes to large-scale general food ration distribution, something that previously had been the RRC's responsibility.[275] Oxfam, for example, earmarked £21.7 million for emergency relief in Ethiopia and Sudan in a twelve-month period, beginning in late 1984, a 'scale of activity completely unprecedented' in its history.[276] Organisations hurried to increase the number of expatriate and locally recruited staff. From October, the usually half-empty Hilton Hotel in Addis Ababa found itself fully booked by relief workers, government officials, and journalists; its swimming pool, cocktail lounge, and burger bar providing a stark contrast to work in the field.[277]

The RRC, headed by Dawit Wolde Giorgis from 1983 until his defection to the USA in December 1985, had a complex relationship with international donors. Although relief was earmarked for distribution by voluntary agencies, donors could not entirely avoid RRC control, as every organisation engaging in relief or rehabilitation had to adhere to a lengthy set of rules and monitoring arrangements.[278] Dealing with the scores of international agencies who wanted to work in Ethiopia was difficult for the RRC leadership, who perceived many foreign aid ground personnel as having 'condescending' and 'self-righteous' attitudes. Overall, the Mengistu regime distrusted Western organisations, looking upon them – in Dawit's words – as 'imperialist agencies or religious organisations that dampened the militant spirit of the people'.[279] Throughout the famine, the Ethiopian government remained reluctant to publicly acknowledge international aid, particularly that coming from the USA.[280] It did,

---

[275] Ibid., 86.   [276] Black, *Cause for Our Times*, 263.

[277] Robert D. Kaplan, *Surrender or Starve: The Wars behind the Famine* (London: Westview Press, 1988), 24; Midge Ure, *If I Was . . . : The Autobiography* (London: Virgin Books, 2005), 147.

[278] Dawit Wolde Giorgis, 'Mode of Operation and Staffing of the Non-governmental Organisations Operating in Ethiopia', circular letter from RRC, CARE 1248/10; 'General Agreement for Undertaking Relief and/or Rehabilitation Activities in Ethiopia by Non-governmental Organisations', Nov. 1984, CARE 1220/16; IIED, *African Emergency*, 30.

[279] Giorgis, *Red Tears*, 241.

[280] William Shawcross, 'Report from Ethiopia: An Update on the African Nation's Catastrophic Famine', *Rolling Stone*, 15 Aug. 1985, available at www.rollingstone.com/politics/politics-news/report-from-ethiopia-2-63303/ (accessed 29 June 2019).

however, station an RRC representative in New York to connect with donors and to try to improve relationships with voluntary aid agencies. RRC staff in the field also earned the respect of foreign aid workers, despite chronic budgetary and administrative problems. CARE, for example, stated that the RRC had been 'cooperative, responsive, and genuinely helpful in removing bottlenecks and solving problems'.[281]

Increased pressure to accelerate the distribution of funds contributed to 'genuine moral and management problems' for already overburdened voluntary organisations. They discussed the 'terrible temptation to be expedient rather than effective' presented by such an influx of money, admitting that by radically modifying their operations, they would be at risk of ending up over their heads.[282] The complex nature of the crisis encouraged the formation and growth of aid consortia or 'super agencies'. For example, the Joint Relief Operation (JRO) of the Ethiopian Red Cross and the International Committee of the Red Cross (ICRC) had been operating since 1980, but their work scaled up enormously when, in 1985, they supported 720,000 people. Similarly, in October 1984, the Churches Drought Action for Africa/Ethiopia (CDAA) was formed as an ecumenical consortium of Lutheran and Roman Catholic organisations working in collaboration with their counterparts in Ethiopia. In 1985 and 1986, this consortium, headed by CRS, distributed over one-fifth of all food aid in government-controlled Ethiopia, reaching an estimated two million people.[283] Four organisations acted as lead agencies in different parts of the country, delivering relief directly or subcontracting its distribution with other groups. The consortium comprised twenty-six organisations in total.[284] As it was not an agency, CDAA declined to register with the RRC. However, its close connection with the US government (which supplied most of its funding) and its large central secretariat was a source of ongoing tension with the Ethiopian government.[285]

A further development was the arrival of some twenty-five aid agencies that were either previously unknown in Ethiopia (including CARE) or entirely new to the relief business (such as Band Aid and USA for Africa). After October 1984, having a programme in Ethiopia appeared to be 'a prerequisite for any respectable international aid agency'.[286] As part of this trend, some agencies that had previously limited themselves to coordinating tasks became operational. For example, the umbrella organisation Christian Relief and Development

---

[281] 'Care Programs in Ethiopia', CARE 1217/3, 2. See also Vaux, 'Ethiopian Famine 1984', 36; Poster, *Gentle War*, 402.

[282] IIED, *African Emergency*, 270 (quotations); Vaux, 'Ethiopian Famine 1984', 37. See also Jansson, 'Emergency Relief', 24.

[283] Solberg, *Miracle in Ethiopia*. The CDAA was later renamed the Joint Relief Programme (JRP).

[284] IIED, *African Emergency*, 31.   [285] Solberg, *Miracle in Ethiopia*, 112–13.

[286] Article 19, *Starving in Silence*, 109.

Association (CRDA), established during the famine of 1974, set up seventeen emergency feeding shelters and appealed successfully to the international donor community to fund a fleet of sixty-five trucks.[287] By February 1985, the CRDA had more than doubled its staff from twelve to twenty-eight.[288] This change of direction attracted criticism from some of the larger consortium members, who felt that the CRDA was encroaching on their territory. Oxfam was particularly critical.[289] In December 1985, the CRDA was forced to shut down all programmes, except for its trucking activities, after agencies including Save the Children and the Irish aid organisation Concern threatened to leave the network.[290]

Band Aid, which began as a fundraising venture, quickly moved into the provision of relief because its founder, activist Bob Geldof, was reluctant to transfer funds to existing aid agencies (see Figure 4.8). He visited Ethiopia and Sudan in January 1985 to compile a shopping list of relief supplies that his new organisation could source and ship from the UK.[291] However, in order to reach those who needed help, Geldof had little choice but to tap into the established network of aid agencies already working on the ground. In Addis Ababa, Gus O'Keefe, head of the CRDA, became an important go-between. The CRDA worked with its members to identify high-priority supplies; over US$5 million of Band Aid money was eventually channelled through the CRDA.[292]

Key to the evolving Band Aid operation was a group of volunteers with little experience in relief work. They were led by Kevin and Penny Jenden, whose professional background was in architecture and anthropology. Band Aid spent an initial £8 million directly on supplies. The first plane containing Land Rovers, high-protein biscuits, tents, and dried milk in bags marked 'Love from Band Aid' arrived in Ethiopia in March 1985.[293] Frustrated by the high cost of shipping, Band Aid leased a fleet of vessels to carry goods to Africa and transported approximately 100,000 t of food, tents, medical equipment, and vehicles over the course of an eighteen-month operation.[294] Such action was part of Band Aid's 'gung-ho attitude, which meant we suggested a lot of stuff that regular charities couldn't – or wouldn't – do'.[295] A number of other organisations, ranging from Oxfam to small voluntary and church groups, benefitted from the free shipping Band Aid offered.[296]

---

[287] *CRDA Biannual Review 1985–6*, 9, CA 5/5/358; CRDA Rehabilitation Programme, 1 Aug. 1985, ibid.

[288] Visit from O'Keefe, 14 Feb. 1985, CA 5/5/358.   [289] Vaux, 'Ethiopian Famine 1984', 34.

[290] Borden to Phipps, 'Christian Relief and Development Association', 23 Feb. 1986, CA 5/5/358.

[291] Geldof with Vallely, *Is That It?*, 335.

[292] Band Aid, *With Love*, 11; Geldof with Vallely, *Is That It?*, 248–9.

[293] Ure, *If I Was*, 147; Midge Ure, 'My Live Aid Nightmare', *Daily Mail*, 9 Oct. 2004.

[294] Band Aid, *With Love*, 6.   [295] Ure, *If I Was*, 157.

[296] Vaux, *Selfish Altruist*, 54; MS Oxfam, PGR2/3/1/8.

Figure 4.8 Bob Geldof in Ethiopia, 1985.
Photo by Mirrorpix/Brendan Monks, reproduced courtesty of Getty Images

Despite some criticism about the contents of the shipments, Band Aid generally avoided the pitfalls faced by other inexperienced donor efforts, such as the *Daily Mirror* 'Mercy Flights', which became notorious for sending inappropriate goods.[297] Although the amateur status of Geldof's team was well-known and drew the scorn of aid circles, Geldof defended it vigorously, stating that it 'is really quite simple. Rank amateurs can grasp things quickly.'[298] Critics, including Jansson, felt that Band Aid should have concentrated on fundraising and left distribution to established agencies.[299]

The creation of the UN Office of Emergency Operations in Ethiopia (OEOE) was an important step for the West in regaining the confidence of Ethiopian authorities. Jansson appointed an NGO officer and the OEOE took on the role of mediating between the RRC and foreign organisations. As Jansson saw it, both sides 'sometimes needed reminding that each needed the other just as much'.[300] However, critics accused the office of being too close to the Ethiopian government to be able to challenge it effectively. The OEOE held the RRC in far greater esteem than USAID officials would

[297] Paul Vallely, 'Bureaucrats, Take Note', *Times*, 24 July 1985.
[298] Geldof with Vallely, *Is That It?*, 320.   [299] Jansson, 'Emergency Relief', 27.
[300] IIED, *African Emergency*, 38.

have liked.[301] Restrictions on aid organisations were strengthened during 1985, and the number of expatriate relief workers allowed into the country remained a major point of contention.[302]

Concerns over possible misallocation of aid were paramount for many organisations, even if there was muted criticism of the Ethiopian government. In December 1984, War on Want publicly aired its apprehensions that food aid was being diverted to feed the Ethiopian military, and that the Derg was seeking to use starvation in rebel-held areas as a tactic of the ongoing civil war. George Galloway, the general secretary of the War on Want was aware that other agencies saw his radical development organisation as 'rocking the boat', but he justified this stance, saying 'I think there comes a time, when to pretend that the famine relief effort is going well is to do a disservice to those people in Ethiopia who are in most need.'[303] The ICRC, protected in part by a status agreement with the Ethiopian government and its links to the Ethiopian Red Cross, was also more outspoken than many organisations about aid being diverted to the army or forced resettlement programmes.[304] In February 1985, the ICRC director for operational activities warned donors, 'Either you just want to send a lot of food to the country, or you really want to help the starving. In the second case, what is happening is unacceptable.'[305]

Allocating Aid to Rebel-Held Areas

A central moral challenge for humanitarian agencies was how to ensure that people living outside government-controlled areas received relief, without also compromising those agencies' ability to work in Ethiopia proper. Estimates varied widely, but some organisations suggested that 60–80 per cent of those affected by the famine in 1984–5 were living in regions controlled by the liberation fronts, while Christian Aid, a more cautious organisation, calculated that the figure was more likely less than half.[306] The failure to make adequate provisions for Tigray and Eritrea saw growing numbers of refugees flee to Sudan. Beginning in late 1984, at least 200,000 Tigrayans crossed the Sudanese border, their movements organised by REST. This included 80,000 during October and November 1984 alone.[307] As major donors were persuaded of the humanitarian needs of the areas under the insurgency, supplies began flowing

---

[301] Vaux, 'Ethiopian Famine 1984', 36; Poster, *Gentle War*, 402.
[302] Poster, 'Gentle War', 417; Giorgis, 'Mode of Operation and Staffing'.
[303] Tomson Prentice, 'British Charity Rocks Boat: Ethiopia Accused of Misusing Famine Aid', *Times*, 3 Dec. 1984.
[304] Gill, *Year in the Death*, 140.
[305] Jean-Pierre Hocké, as cited in Gill, *Year in the Death*, 141.
[306] Christian Aid, 'Eritrea and Tigray: Drought, War, and Aid in Northern Ethiopia', CA J/5.
[307] Duffield and Prendergast, *Without Troops*, 62; Keleman, *Politics of the Famine*, 20.

to the contested regions through Sudan, and later also from areas controlled by the Ethiopian government via the new 'Food for the North' initiative.[308]

Throughout 1983 and 1984, a group of church-based Western agencies – notably Christian Aid, Norwegian Interchurch Aid, and Dutch Interchurch Aid – called for relief assistance to Tigray and Eritrea through REST and ERA.[309] In 1983, Dutch Interchurch Aid led a five-agency consortium that secured a one-time allocation of the European Economic Community (EEC) emergency grain for Eritrea; however, applications for additional grants in the following year were repeatedly rejected. Supporting the rebel-held areas was deemed 'too political' for many donors.[310] In Britain, for example, Foreign Office members suggested that their country had to keep its distance from such groups in public, even if the UK gave some aid in secret via partners.[311] Likewise, UN agencies and officials in Ethiopia avoided direct contact with the liberation fronts and their aid organisations. Relief assistance was vital to the relationship between the liberation fronts and the population in the areas they controlled, and because of this, both fronts pursued a policy of ensuring that ERA and REST maintained oversight over relief distributions.[312]

Non-operational consortia had less to lose from speaking out about the famine in Eritrea and Tigray than agencies on the ground did. European church organisations and the liberation fronts were not natural allies, but the consortium did hold together, apparently through the strong moral convictions of its partners.[313] Christian Aid, for example, identified a moral imperative to provide relief to Eritrea and Tigray because 'as the Government of Ethiopia has no intention of reaching these people, we feel we have to try'.[314] The organisation criticised the EEC for stressing the difficulties of providing aid more than it did the needs of the population. Between April 1983 and February 1985, Christian Aid directed over 90 per cent of the approximately £5 million it raised for the Ethiopian famine to the disputed regions of Eritrea and Tigray.[315] ERD members kept up the pressure on donor governments, the UN, and the EEC to increase aid to Eritrea and Tigray, or at least to support the safe passage of provisions from Sudan into the rebel-held areas.[316] Christian Aid threatened the UK aid minister that if there was no change in EEC policy, they would go public with the story of delays, noting 'we have a responsibility

[308] Borton, *Changing Role*, 85.
[309] Paul Keleman and Hilary Nelson, 'The Long Shadow of a Famine', *Guardian*, 20 Jan. 1984.
[310] Christian Aid, 'Eritrea and Tigray'.
[311] Memo from Mure, 'Eritrean Relief Association', 23 Aug. 1985, TNA(UK), Foreign and Commonwealth Office (FCO) 31/4614.
[312] Borton, *Changing Role*, 87, 50.   [313] Duffield and Prendergast, *Without Troops*, xi.
[314] Elliot to Mr and Mrs Allen, 3 May 1984, Christian Aid Archive, SOAS 4/A/26/3.
[315] Bax to Raison, 4 Feb. 1985, CA 4/A/26/3; de Waal, *Famine Crimes*, 131.
[316] *War on Want Annual Report 1984–85*, 2, WOW Archive, SOAS.

not only to the people dying but also to our supporters who have given so much to our appeals'.[317]

While ERD faced pressure to be a more 'vocal solidarity movement' than most of its members were comfortable with, War on Want was an open supporter of the two liberation fronts, the Tigray People's Liberation Front (TPLF) and Eritrean People's Liberation Front (EPLF).[318] War on Want engaged in high-level diplomacy around the issue of safe passage, suggesting the formation of an international commission headed by Willy Brandt to mediate between the Mengistu regime and the liberation fronts. Such calls were ignored because of the Ethiopian government's refusal to recognise the rebel movements, which it regarded as 'bandits' and 'terrorists'.[319] Moreover, War on Want's close connection to the rebel forces cost the scheme its credibility. Band Aid also dealt directly with the rebel aid agencies; spending US$10 million on the purchase and transport of food, medical supplies, and other relief items for ERA, and US$1.8 million for REST, from 1985 to 1990.[320]

Despite the needs of Tigray and Eritrea, many of the international organisations working in government-controlled areas, including UNICEF and CARE, chose not to become involved in cross-border provisioning in order to protect their work elsewhere.[321] In UNICEF's case, this stemmed from a rigid application of UN respect for sovereignty, perhaps because Addis Ababa, as the home of the UN Economic Commission on Africa (ECA) and the Organisation of African Unity, 'was of unusual importance to the UN system'.[322] CARE appears to have been driven by fears over staff being expelled from the country. Approached informally by USAID to consider getting involved in cross-border work, CARE Ethiopia's representative threatened to request an immediate transfer if the New York headquarters approved this plan, assuring headquarters he was 'not trying to be melodramatic'.[323] Reporting back from her visit to Ethiopia in April 1985, a representative from CARE headquarters agreed that involvement in such a scheme would jeopardise its work by 'politically tainting us'. By that time, CARE lobbyists were seeking to persuade the US government that both the cross-border and 'mercy-corridor' schemes should take lower priority than food for Gonder, Wollo, Showa, and Sidama in Ethiopia.[324] In the UK, Save the Children was concerned that Christian Aid's public support for Eritrea and Tigray might damage the organisation by association in the eyes of Ethiopian officials.[325] World Vision

---

[317] Bax to Raison, 4 Feb. 1985, CA 4/A/26/3.
[318] Duffield and Prendergast, *Without Troops,* xii.   [319] Gill, *Year in the Death,* 133–9.
[320] Band Aid, *With Love,* 16–17.
[321] Duffield and Prendergast, *Without Troops,* 87–8; de Waal, *Famine Crimes,* 131.
[322] Borton, *Changing Role,* 43.   [323] Dunn to Johnson, 13 Mar. 1985, CARE 1217/3.
[324] Levinger, Trip Report, 5–10 Apr. 1985, CARE 1217/3.
[325] Duffield and Prendergast, *Without Troops,* 87–8.

had at first refused to help Eritrea for fear of provoking the displeasure of Ethiopian authorities; but its leadership had a change of heart, stating that 'We had to make a choice and we tried to serve the most people in the best way.'[326]

After the media storm of October 1984, key donor governments, while still maintaining their official neutrality, were drawn into supporting a clandestine cross-border feeding operation in a move that quietly disregarded Ethiopian sovereignty.[327] The Ethiopian government was prepared to turn a blind eye to some food and relief supplies entering via Sudan on the condition that the agencies involved give no publicity to their work.[328] Responsibility for this cross-border operation was shared between the ERD, the Catholic Secretariat (an umbrella body of Catholic relief agencies), and the ICRC. In early 1985, the ICRC was the only agency consistently able to reach people in the so-called grey areas of the north that neither side controlled. Drawing heavily on US government funding, the ICRC set up feeding stations in Tigray, Eritrea, and in provinces bordering those regions; distributing 2,000 t of food a month in 1985. Consciously avoiding publicity, the ERD was for donor governments a 'quiet buffer' that was seen as legitimate, if unorthodox.[329] Oxfam and Oxfam America channelled large amounts of food aid through REST on a strictly 'off the record' basis.[330] Most organisations adopted a pragmatic approach, preferring to settle for 'low key, ad hoc arrangements' rather than force the issue with the Derg and risk jeopardising their operations. In fact, the ICRC rejected the British government's offer of raising the issue of safe passage with its Ethiopian counterpart. The ICRC's ties with the Ethiopian Red Cross also enabled it to circumvent the RRC in other ways.[331]

In the summer of 1985, supplies began flowing to the contested regions via the 'Food for the North' agreement signed between US and Ethiopian officials. Funded by USAID and channelled by CRS in Eritrea and by World Vision in Tigray, 36,000 t of aid were distributed in Eritrea and 15,000 t in Tigray from August 1985 to December 1986. Critics, however, argued that the supplies were supporting a pacification programme. Thus, USAID assistance flowed to these contested regions both through the ERD cross-border scheme and the Food for the North initiative, an apparently contradictory position that has been interpreted as giving humanitarian concerns priority over diplomatic

---

[326] John McMillan, as cited in the *New York Times*, 17 Dec. 1984.

[327] Duffield and Prendergast, *Without Troops*, 12.

[328] Briefing of Senator Edward Kennedy on Ethiopia at US Embassy London, 17 Dec. 1984, MS Oxfam, PGR 2/3/1/8; Jansson, 'Emergency Relief', 50.

[329] USAID, *Final Disaster Report*, 9; Poster, 'Gentle War', 417; Duffield and Prendergast, *Without Troops*, 6.

[330] Briefing of Senator Edward Kennedy on Ethiopia; Rob Buchanan, 'Reflections on Working with Rebel Movements in the Horn of Africa', in *Change Not Charity: Essays on Oxfam America's First 40 Years*, ed. Laura Roper (Boston: Oxfam America, 2010), 253.

[331] Rifkind to Bax, 1 Feb. 1985, CA 4/A/26/3; Poster, 'Gentle War', 417.

ones. However, the Derg's willingness to tolerate aid reaching rebel-held areas fluctuated over the course of relief operations from 1984 to 1986, sometimes yielding to diplomatic pressure before hardening its stance again. There were also immense practical difficulties involved in cross-border relief, as the Ethiopian air force considered aid convoys legitimate military targets. As a result, it might take five-times longer for relief to reach the hungry than it would have in peacetime.[332] In return, rebel groups sometimes attacked aid convoys; both CRS and Red Cross shipments were periodically targets of TPLF guerrillas.[333]

Food and Feeding

From 1984 to 1986, approximately 1.5 million tonnes of emergency food aid reached Ethiopia. Most came from bilateral and multilateral donors. Privately funded shipments by voluntary organisations accounted for only about 6 per cent of food aid in 1985–6.[334] However, the initiative and symbolism of sending food was important. In August 1984, frustrated by the lack of an official response from any major donor nation or UN agency, Oxfam, in partnership with Norwegian Church Aid and Redd Barna (Norway's Save the Children), took the unusual step of privately funding a grain shipment to Ethiopia, hoping to thereby shame international donors into taking action.[335] Similarly, an important and well-publicised aspect of the international response, when it came, was the launching of a food airlift to remote regions. By December 1984, 5,000 t of supplies had been airlifted.[336] This commitment was reflected in the language of expressive relief, such as the 'Feed the World' refrain of Band Aid.

Overall, the proportion of food aid distributed by voluntary organisations grew from approximately half of the total food aid at the start of the crisis to over 80 per cent by the end of 1985. Most of this aid was distributed in the form of dry rations to families registered through peasant associations. Individuals reported to a distribution centre once a month, returning to their homes on foot bearing their parcels.[337] In addition, rehabilitation programmes provided other gifts-in-kind, including seeds, tools, and livestock, and some longer-term development aid was also undertaken as a response to the famine. The CDAA consortium, for example, operated 100 distribution centres under its Nutrition Intervention Programme, allocating monthly rations of oil, cereal, and dried milk to families with children under five. The Red Cross JRO

[332] Peberdy, *Tigray*, 22.   [333] Poster, 'Gentle War', 421.   [334] Borton, *Changing Role*, 49.
[335] Penrose, 'Before and After', 151; Black, *Cause for Our Times*, 260.
[336] Penrose, 'Before and After', 154.
[337] Banga, *Reducing People's Vulnerability*, 7; USAID, *Final Disaster Report*, 36.

administered monthly rations of oil, flour, and beans through seventeen distribution points in Eritrea, twelve in Tigray, and nine in Wollo in government-controlled Ethiopia, accounting for about 8 per cent of all food aid distributed.[338] Oxfam's Tony Vaux later reflected that in some areas such as Tigray where grain was available for purchase, monetary disbursements would have been a more effective way to increase people's entitlements, but that aid agencies went to extraordinary lengths to ensure that food was distributed instead of cash.[339]

In addition to these feeding programmes, which were designed to keep people in their homes and villages, other food and medical care was provided via a network of camps (so-called relief shelters) across Ethiopia, Eritrea, and Tigray (see Figure 4.9). At the height of the relief efforts in April 1985, over half a million people were receiving aid at shelters – once again mainly as dry rations, while the same number continued to gather in unofficial camps in the vicinity of these shelters.[340] The shelters were supplied with Oxfam's specialised child feeding kits and prefabricated water tanks. Oxfam had also recently worked with scientists at Oxford Polytechnic and Fox's Biscuits to develop and manufacture a high energy child feeding product; the 'Oxfam biscuit', and the famine in Ethiopia was its first widespread test.[341] Migration to shelters was a last resort for famine-stricken people and reflected the failure of other distribution methods. Women and children were disproportionately represented there. Supplementary feeding and medical care programmes that targeted severely malnourished groups, mainly children and nursing mothers, were run by agencies including Oxfam, Save the Children, MSF, and the Red Cross JRO.[342]

However, the food provided by aid programmes was not always compatible with the tastes or usual diets of recipients. This point was raised by Manu Dibango, a musician from Cameroon who was featured on the Tam Tam pour l'Ethiopie record, after a visit to Korem in January 1985. African newspapers also warned that there was a danger that recipients of food aid might develop foreign tastes and become a market for Western surpluses after the danger of famine was over.[343] This concern, however, was not held in the West, and contrasted with the widespread desire of the European public to see the EEC's mountains of stockpiled food used to alleviate hunger in Africa. All agencies routinely received and rejected offers of food donations, such as the several tonnes of a 'macaroni/rice product' that a New Jersey company wished to

---

[338] Borton, *Changing Role.*   [339] Vaux, *Selfish Altruist,* 54–5.
[340] Borton, *Changing Role,* 29.
[341] IIED, *African Emergency,* 239; Black, *Cause for Our Times,* 262.
[342] Pankhurst, *Resettlement and Famine,* 40; Penrose, 'Before and After', 177; Jansson, 'Emergency Relief', 24.
[343] Hébert, 'Feed the World', 91.

Figure 4.9 Kurt Jansson, UN assistant secretary-general for emergency relief operations in Ethiopia, visiting a camp in Mekelle, Tigray province, where famine victims are receiving food and medical care, 11 Nov. 1984.
Courtesy of UN Photo by John Isaac

donate to CARE; it was politely declined.[344] CARE's field officer in Ethiopia was conscious that whatever the benefits of a collection of goods-in-kind for positive public relations in the USA, these were likely to be offset by negative publicity in the international press about 'white elephant aid', as well as the possibility of outright rejection by recipients.[345]

Vaux has suggested that Oxfam's early response was 'characterized by an inappropriate "refugee camp" ideology'.[346] An issue with supplementary feeding was that effective aid operations were geared to the distribution of basic rations. Many observers have stated that food and transport resources intended for humanitarian purposes were diverted from famine relief to resettlement,[347] as in areas where there was no major food distributing agency, like in Wollo. Visiting northern Ethiopia in July 1985, Vaux examined UN records that showed most relief grain was being earmarked for resettlers.[348]

---

[344] Cowan to Owsley, 26 Nov. 1984, CARE 199.
[345] Bernuth to Levinger, n.d. (late 1984), ibid.   [346] Vaux, *Selfish Altruist*, 57.
[347] Davey, 'Famine, Aid and Ideology', 547; Discussion Document prepared by Oxfam/Save the Children, Feb. 1985.
[348] Vaux, *Selfish Altruist*, 60.

This meant that supplementary food intended for children was diverted to families, creating an incentive for families to keep children in the low-weight category that qualified them for help. Accordingly, Oxfam's work in the region of Wollo shifted from supplementary nutritional feeding to distributing basic rations as well.

As the immediate famine crisis came under control, numbers in the relief camps gradually declined to approximately 15,000 by the end of 1985. Shelters were phased out as the transportation situation improved.[349] However, the closure of the camps was problematic for several reasons. There is evidence that the Mengistu regime sought to reduce the numbers of those in relief camps as part of a strategy to swell the population available for resettlement. For example, the premature closing of the famine relief camp at Ibenat in April 1985 that led to the forced expulsion of 36,000 people was rare in that it made headlines around the world and resulted in strong protests to the Ethiopian government. In an unusual move, the government responded by reopening the camp, claiming that a 'mistake' had been made.[350] As the relief camps in Ethiopia grew smaller, such protests ensured that UN monitors would be present at future closures.[351] Scenes from the relief camps also made for good television, serving as a public relations opportunity for aid agencies concerned with promoting their activities and soliciting additional funds. Oxfam's medical adviser was reluctant to shut down its supplementary feeding programme in Wollo because the operation had the positive effect 'of putting Oxfam nurses in the front line, and thus satisfied a public relations need'.[352]

Resettlement

The Ethiopian policy of emergency resettlement was the most controversial aspect of famine relief in 1984–5, causing aid agencies to face a moral and economic dilemma. Was it better to speak out about abuses of aid and jeopardise the wider relief effort, or remain silent and appear to condone the government's actions? Should one aid those forcibly resettled and appear complicit in the government's action or turn one's back and leave vulnerable migrants without support? Journalist Peter Gill notes that this question 'divided the international aid community down the middle'.[353] The movement of people from drought-prone and ecologically degraded regions in the north to more fertile areas in the south-west of the country had long been advocated by agricultural experts and the World Bank, and small-scale initiatives of this

---

[349] Penrose, 'Before and After', 158.
[350] François Jean, *Du Bon Usage du Famine* (Paris: Médecins Sans Frontières, 1986), 56.
[351] Jansson, 'Emergency Relief', 63.   [352] Vaux, *Selfish Altruist*, 58.
[353] Gill, *Year in the Death*, 142.

kind had been developed in the 1970s.[354] However, the resettlement scheme that the Derg launched in November 1984 as its major response to the famine was also a political strategy aimed at depriving rebel forces of their support base. Although ostensibly voluntary, the programme was, in fact, coercive, as officials were required to meet high quotas. Moreover, the preference for relocating able-bodied men resulted in the separation of families.[355] Prospective settlers might also register voluntarily, but if they changed their minds, they were unable to withdraw from the programme. Settlers who were interviewed likened the reception centres to which they had been initially lured, to 'rat traps' where food was used to ensnare people, rendering the 'concept of individual will almost meaningless'.[356]

By January 1986, almost 600,000 people had been relocated, largely by means of Soviet transport. Resettlement was hampered by a serious lack of preparation at the receiving sites. By 1985, the programme was coming under sustained criticism from abroad.[357] The figures are disputed, but as many as 300,000 people may have died in the process of resettlement, often because the forced migrants were too weak from famine to travel, and because of inadequate support at their destination. Despite the ICRC's requests that it be allowed to investigate humanitarian conditions and trace missing persons, the agency was repeatedly denied access to resettlement camps in 1985 and 1986.[358]

Most large donors, including the British, West German, and US governments, refused to support resettlement. Publicly, USAID declared the scheme a development programme rather than relief work, but in private officials went further and expressed concern about human rights.[359] Neighbouring African governments were more supportive, apparently prepared to accept the claim that resettlement was the only alternative to long-term food aid dependency.[360] The resettlement programme was largely suspended between June and September of 1985, but in November of that year the Italian and Canadian governments announced that they would support resettlement, although Canada provided only a small financial contribution. Italy gave US$150 million over the next few years, as part of its wider, controversial programme of aid to the Horn of Africa.

Resettlement placed huge pressure on the moral economy of aid, with most voluntary organisations preferring a policy of discretion and behind-the-scenes lobbying to public protests over abuses. However, a range of organisations investigated the realities of resettlement and sought to raise global awareness

---

[354] Jansson, 'Emergency Relief', 64.   [355] Gill, *Famine and Foreigners*, 45–62.
[356] Pankhurst, *Resettlement and Famine*, 46, 60.   [357] Penrose, 'Before and After', 172.
[358] ICRC, *Annual Report 1986* (Geneva: ICRC, 1987), 23.
[359] Sennett to Johnston on 'Ethiopia Emergency Interaction Meeting', 13 Nov. 1984, CARE 199.
[360] Hébert, 'Feed the World', 35.

of the manipulation of aid by the Ethiopian regime. They included Cultural Survival (USA), Survival International (UK), Berliner Missionswerk (West Germany), and MSF (France), as well as the ICRC.[361] Cultural Survival, a research organisation founded by social scientists at Harvard University, produced a study based on interviews with 270 refugees in six camps in Sudan. Their report was widely cited as evidence of abuse by organisations such as MSF, although it was loudly discredited by others, including Ethiopian researcher Richard Pankhurst, who dismissed it as based on 'hearsay'.[362] There was some coverage in broadsheet newspapers, but the story did not make it on to the television networks because footage of settlers being abused was lacking.[363]

The major operational aid organisations also remained sceptical of some human rights research, seeing it as politically motivated, but were in turn criticised for downplaying the difficulties that they faced in allocating aid in the field. Survival International, for example, accused British aid agencies of boycotting meetings organised in London to discuss the research into resettlement in order 'to avoid confronting the issue'.[364] Alula Pankhurst argued that the campaign against resettlement had created unwarranted comparisons between what was happening in Ethiopia and emotive examples from history, including Stalinist deportations, Nazi persecution, and Khmer Rouge atrocities in Cambodia, while the polarised depictions of resettlement as either a voluntary famine relief measure, or a systematic forced relocation scheme, were equally misleading.[365]

A concern of most international aid workers was not to jeopardise relief work elsewhere by open confrontation. In Ethiopia, CRDA members were reluctant to either fully support or outright condemn resettlement. In February 1985, CRDA's O'Keefe briefed Christian Aid in London, claiming that while he had heard rumours about forced resettlement, he had also witnessed people voluntarily walking to relocation depots.[366] By May, CRDA members decided that although they would refuse to provide transportation, they would consider humanitarian requests in support of resettled people.[367]

In addition, there were concerns that airing doubts would negatively affect support for Ethiopian relief among the donating public in the West. The British

---

[361] See Jason Clay and Bonnie Holcomb, *Politics and the Ethiopian Famine, 1984–85* (Cambridge, MA: Cultural Survival, 1985); Peter Niggli, *Ethiopia: Deportations and Forced-Labour Camps* (Berlin: Berliner Missionswerk, 1986); Survival International, *Ethiopia Resettlement: The Evidence* (London: Survival International, 1985).
[362] Pankhurst, 'Ethiopian Famine'. See also Vaux, *Selfish Altruist*, 64.
[363] Kaplan, *Surrender or Starve*, 112.   [364] Survival International, *Ethiopia Resettlement*, 11.
[365] Pankhurst, *Resettlement and Famine*, 65–6.
[366] Visit from O'Keefe, 14 Feb. 1985, CA 5/5/358.
[367] Visit to CRDA, 3 May 1985, CA 5/5/358.

ambassador in Addis Ababa warned a television journalist that drawing attention to the problems of resettlement could be detrimental to public attitudes
and contrary to her goal of keeping the cause in the headlines.[368] Critics
accused aid organisations like Oxfam, whose contributions had doubled
because of the famine, of being driven by financial considerations. The human
rights organisation Article 19 later claimed that in order to maintain their
increased levels of funding 'it was necessary for relief agencies to remain
active in Ethiopia, and therefore not to risk expulsion'.[369]

Behind the scenes, however, major aid agencies were worried about the
implementation of the resettlement programme. In February 1985, Oxfam and
Save the Children sent a joint statement to Jansson expressing their concern
that resources were being misappropriated.[370] Later that year, the two organisations discovered that their trucks were being forcibly commandeered on a
number of occasions to transport settlers. Rather than comment publicly, they
protested informally to the RRC. Oxfam felt that 'representations rather than
public protest are more effective'.[371] Similarly, in a private meeting of Western
ambassadors and aid organisations in Addis Ababa in September 1985, Jack
Finucane of Concern spoke of the 'horrible' conditions of resettlement, the
widespread failure to prepare the sites, and the estimated mortality rate of
15–20 per cent. He later denied these claims and refused to go on record with
the declaration.[372] In May 1985, Christian Aid admitted 'hard thinking' about
its policy in the face of the 500,000 people who were living in resettlement
areas, and the fact that several local church groups had already begun helping
those in need.[373] Similarly, in September, CRDA issued a statement that
rejected compulsory population movement, but suggested that it was dedicated
to assisting the Ethiopian people wherever they are in need, and could 'achieve
more by involvement rather than by boycotting' the resettlement in general.[374]

For MSF, however, refusal to take part in the silence that other organisations
considered expedient was integral to its commitment to '*témoignage* over
discretion' established since the Biafra crisis. MSF volunteers in Ethiopia
sought to expose the tactics of using food to lure famine victims to transit
camps. One MSF method was to work with the Western press when no other
aid agencies were prepared to go on the record. In November 1985, Michel
Fizsbin, the representative of MSF in Ethiopia, was the only member of a
voluntary organisation willing to be cited in a *Sunday Times* exposé about the

---

[368] Barder to FCO, 21 Feb. 1985, TNA(UK), FCO 31/4615.
[369] Article 19, *Starving in Silence*, 114.
[370] Discussion document prepared by Oxfam/Save the Children, Feb. 1985.
[371] 'Oxfam Position Paper on Resettlement', 9 Dec. 1985, MS Oxfam COM 2/6/11, 2; Article 19,
Starving in Silence, 114.
[372] Kaplan, *Surrender or Starve*, 110–11.   [373] Visit to CRDA, 3 May 1985, CA 5/5/358.
[374] CRDA Members Statement on Re-settlement, 19 Sept. 1985, CA 5/5/358.

abuses of resettlement.[375] Rony Brauman, then president of MSF, continued to repeat these allegations, stating at a press conference in Paris, 'Aid is not being used to save, but to oppress.'[376] Matters came to a head when the RRC sent a letter terminating the Ethiopian operations of MSF France immediately. It cited 'politically motivated false allegations' and refusal to follow norms and procedures like other voluntary organisations. Approximately thirty expatriate workers from MSF France were forced to leave; all MSF assets were frozen, and local staff found themselves without a job and fearing for their safety.[377]

While MSF's moral stance on resettlement put pressure on other organisations to defend their positions, few agreed with MSF, and they saw the dire consequences of speaking out. A copy of an open letter sent by MSF to all aid organisations working in Ethiopia was telexed to New York by CARE's Ethiopia representative as an example of 'the perils of error'.[378] British aid organisations held an emergency meeting in London to discuss the crisis. Their conclusion was that MSF had taken their protest too far.[379] Oxfam urged the need to keep the issue in perspective, since the resettlement programme was only affecting about 5 per cent of the population. Moreover, Oxfam felt it had to 'tread carefully' to protect its other projects in Ethiopia, which it concluded were not worth sacrificing to 'an issue of great emotional appeal'.[380] In a communication to the Ethiopian ambassador in December 1985, Oxfam expressed concern over forcible resettlement in Wollo, but generally limited its criticism to the 'haste, scale and timing' of the latest phase.[381]

Historian Eleanor Davey suggests that the French model of *sans frontiérisme*, with its emphasis on crisis relief, stood in contrast to a British model of development.[382] While MSF dedicated itself to the twin principles of providing aid and speaking out, most other organisations, including Oxfam, prioritised the humanitarian objective and saw principles as 'a hindrance rather than a help'.[383] There was also no support from UN agencies or donor governments. Jansson was dismissive of the MSF protest, characterising those taking part as young, immature, and 'highly excitable, reacting emotionally'

---

[375] Davey, 'Famine, Aid and Ideology', 549–50; Rony Brauman, *Rapport Moral 1985/86* (Paris: Médecins Sans Frontières, 1986); 'Resettling Ethiopians as Deadly as Famine, Says Banned Agency', *Times*, 3 Dec. 1985; Laurence Binet, *Famine and Forced Relocations in Ethiopia, 1984–1986* (Paris: Médecins Sans Frontières, 2013).

[376] Brauman, as cited in Binet, *Famine and Forced Relocations*, 80.

[377] Ahmed Ali to Desmoulins, 2 Dec. 1985, in Binet, *Famine and Forced Relocations*, 78.

[378] Dunn to Ramp, 23 Dec. 1985, CARE 1220/17.

[379] Hoult, 'Note of a meeting held at Save the Children Fund, 4 Dec. 1985, to discuss the Ethiopian Resettlement Programme', TNA(UK), FCO 31/4610, Part B.

[380] Hugh Goyder, 'Resettlement and Villagisation: Oxfam's Experience and Recommended Policy', Oxfam PRG/5/5/26; Tony Vaux, 'A Public Relations Disaster', *New Internationalist* 148, June 1985.

[381] 'Oxfam Position Paper on Resettlement', 9 Dec. 1985, MS Oxfam COM2/6/11, 2.

[382] Davey, 'Famine, Aid and Ideology', 550.   [383] Vaux, *Selfish Altruist*, 63.

to events.[384] While donors, including the US government, were wary of Mengistu's manipulation of aid and opposed to resettlement, they would have had difficulties withholding famine relief on political grounds because 'the newly fashionable post-Band Aid humanitarianism demanded action in Ethiopia'.[385]

Moreover, the crisis exacerbated a growing rift between MSF France and MSF Belgium. The Belgian section made a unanimous decision to continue working in Ethiopia, some members considering their French colleagues to have exaggerated their claims.[386] This dispute stemmed in part from the strong anti-communist stance taken at the time by MSF leaders that resulted in the formation of its short-lived political arm, Liberté Sans Frontières. The abuses of power by the Mengistu administration typified the form of government this think tank was created to combat: a totalitarian regime hiding behind a Third World façade. In France, the president of Action Internationale Contre la Faim (AICF) condemned MSF for abandoning the people of Ethiopia, arguing that it was harder to stay than leave and watch the tragedy 'play out in silence'.[387]

In an internal report aimed at rebutting the accusations of abuse, CARE noted that it preferred to work towards 'solving problems and resolving difficulties' with the government of Ethiopia, rather than 'publicly airing these and endangering the lives and future of poor Ethiopians' – an apparent rebuke of MSF's course of action. CARE and several other agencies sought to reclaim the moral high ground from those who preferred the tactic of 'public excoriation of the Marxist government', while at the same time downplaying the extent of the contradictions their organisations faced working in Ethiopia. Thus, CARE concluded that its famine relief and development activities had been carried out 'without compromising CARE's principles'.[388] Similarly, InterAction later issued a statement on behalf of a number of its members calling the MSF claims 'affrontery to truth'.[389]

While most organisations preferred to avoid working in such a situation, others believed the needs of the resettled peoples outweighed their own misgivings over the way the displaced population had been moved. Ethiopian churches and missions were among the first to become involved, followed in May 1985 by Secours Populaire Français and Menschen für Menschen. Although USAID had issued a prohibition on relief to government-run resettlement camps, CRS defied this and operated US-funded feeding programmes in some locations.[390] Concern Worldwide began working in resettlement areas in

---

[384] Jansson, 'Emergency Relief', 24; Kaplan, *Surrender or Starve*, 112, notes that the UN gave the 'kiss of death' to MSF's presence.

[385] Article 19, *Starving in Silence*, 116.   [386] Binet, *Famine and Forced Relocations*.

[387] Davey, 'Famine, Aid and Ideology', 552.   [388] 'Care Programs in Ethiopia', 5–6.

[389] Jansson, 'Emergency Relief', 77.   [390] Poster, 'Gentle War', 422.

November 1985. Band Aid was initially sceptical about funding such work, fearing its involvement would be interpreted as condoning resettlement. However, it came to see participation as a way of persuading other donor agencies to engage in rehabilitation and development in resettled communities. In 1986–90, Band Aid funded an RRC–Concern project supporting people in twenty villages who had been resettled from Wollo.[391]

Rehabilitation and Newcomers to Aid

The second half of 1985 marked a shift in the allocation priorities of some voluntary organisations and major donors from emergency feeding to rehabilitation. In March of that year, a UN donor conference held in Geneva made it clear that there was considerable reluctance to meet Ethiopia's development needs. However, one month later the Canadian government announced a CA$25 million fund for 'recovery' in Africa, earmarking CA$18 million for voluntary organisations.[392] CRDA successfully appealed to international donors for a rehabilitation programme that eventually distributed over 8,000 tonnes of seed, 100,000 tools, and 2,400 oxen through member agencies.[393] Nevertheless, the provision of seed, tools, and fertiliser proved to be inadequate, often arriving too late to make a difference. Thus, while harvests in 1985 were greater than 1984, they were still below normal.

There have been numerous attempts to historicise celebrity humanitarianism as a cultural phenomenon. However, analysis and discussion of the grant-making policy of the newcomers to humanitarian activity, Band Aid and USA for Africa, is limited. The new trusts attempted to shape the wider humanitarian sector in their own image through aid allocation, prioritising collaboration, and consensus, while integrating rehabilitation, research, and long-term development work.

By summer 1985, many of those involved with USA for Africa began to recognise that their efforts were too late to contribute much to the emergency feeding phase of the relief operation. In June, Harry Belafonte and the USA for Africa team embarked on a fact-finding mission to Ethiopia. They arrived with a planeload of supplies on a tour carefully stage-managed by Derg officials.[394] The US visitors were not told that instead of famine victims, the patients they were taken to see in a hospital were casualties of the civil war. Their subsequent tour of Tanzania, Sudan, and Kenya was well-received by the local

---

[391] Pankhurst, *Resettlement and Famine*, 79; Banga, *Reducing People's Vulnerability*, 162.

[392] IIED, *African Emergency*, 250.

[393] *CRDA Biannual Review 1985–6*, 9, CA 5/5/358; CRDA Rehabilitation Programme, 1 Aug. 1985, ibid.

[394] Giorgis, *Red Tears*, 217–19; USA for Africa, *Memories and Reflections*, 8–9.

press. Belafonte and the other (predominantly black) performers were welcomed and commended, but their African hosts maintained a detached attitude to US relief more broadly.[395]

USA for Africa shifted its activities towards providing medical supplies, implementing vehicle repair systems, and allocating funds for long-term recovery. Its board apportioned 35 per cent of its funds for emergency relief, 55 per cent for development, and 10 per cent for hunger in the USA. Director Marty Rogol recalled that 'what [we] did not want to get into was the traditional foundation game where we sort of sat up there on Mount Olympus and people would come and beg us for money and do the traditional proposals'.[396] USA for Africa expected organisations working in countries where it had programmes to jointly decide on relief and rehabilitation priorities.[397] A liaison agency appointed in each country collected individual proposals, ranked and rated them, and submitted recommendations to the umbrella body, InterAction. The effectiveness of the system varied greatly, and it may have created more interagency dissention than it avoided. In Ethiopia, concern was raised that USA for Africa threatened the fragile relationship between foreign organisations and the RRC by circumventing the government in the grant allocation process.[398] A problem was the lack of a USA for Africa representative in Ethiopia, which contrasted unfavourably with the Band Aid position, whose staff member in Addis Ababa was said to have an excellent relationship with the RRC.[399]

In October 1985, Geldof and Kevin Jenden embarked on a two-week tour, paid for by the London *Times*, across the Sahel region of Africa. Their goal was to identify funding priorities and see how Band Aid money had been spent in Ethiopia and Sudan.[400] There was growing unrest about Band Aid's management at the time, with a widespread sense among aid organisations that it was 'ludicrous for Geldof and his group of amateurs to set up a network of complex programmes from scratch'.[401] The British government had privately sounded out agencies for their views of Band Aid. The results were described as 'fairly horrific'.[402] Geldof was apparently not an easy man for the aid agencies to work

[395] Hébert, 'Feed the World', 106.
[396] Rogol as cited in USA for Africa, *Memories and Reflections*, 8.
[397] Programmes were run in Sudan, Ethiopia, Burkina Faso, Chad, Mali, Niger, Mozambique, and Mauritania.
[398] USA for Africa – Notes from a joint meeting of Interaction and OEOA, 14 Feb. 1986, CARE 1241/4.
[399] Jacqz to Davies and Neu, 10 Feb. 1986, CARE; Giorgis, *Red Tears*, 218–19.
[400] See the account of this trip in David Blundy and Paul Vallely, *With Geldof in Africa: Confronting the Famine Crisis* (London: Times Books, 1985), 9.
[401] Geoffrey Levy, 'Is It Time for Saint Bob to Call the Experts?', *Daily Express*, 5 Sept. 1985.
[402] Buist, 'Band Aid: Involvement with Other Agencies', 1 Oct. 1985, TNA(UK), Overseas Development (OD) 53/98; Browning, 'Band Aid Relations with ODA', 17 Sept. 1985, OD 53/97.

with, and they were not impressed by the red-tape cutting, 'rock 'n' roll' attitude of the Band Aid Trust, which was 'both envied and suspect'.[403]

Nonetheless, building personal relationships with Band Aid staff was a conscious strategy on the part of voluntary organisations keen to get a share of this money. One of the last actions of outgoing Oxfam director Guy Stringer in July 1985 was to write to Geldof, praising his 'superb initiative, brilliantly carried through' and stating that Oxfam was at Band Aid's service.[404] CARE's New York headquarters sent an urgent telex to its field offices ahead of the Africa tour, alerting its staff to this new 'VIP donor organisation' and requesting they 'extend all courtesies' to Geldof.[405] Some aid personnel were reluctant to be pulled away from their work to be lectured at by a rock star – even one with lots of money to spend. Still more controversial was the request that one voluntary organisation in each country in which Band Aid operated should chair a committee of their peers to prioritise proposals by consensus.[406] Although wary of voluntary organisations, Band Aid distrusted donor governments and UN agencies even more.

Repeated calls for Band Aid to set up 'appropriate administrative structures' were heeded when Penny Jenden, Band Aid's director, appointed an advisory board that Geldof boasted was the most 'over-qualified' body ever assembled.[407] Headed by Brian Walker, a former executive director of Oxfam, it consisted of leading academics and development experts.[408] This action marked the start of greater co-operation between Geldof's staff and certain agencies, notably Oxfam. Moreover, Band Aid began to reach out to a wider group of voluntary aid organisations, including Concern, CARE, War on Want, ERA, and the Disasters Emergency Committee.[409] By summer 1986, Band Aid's advisory board had reviewed over 700 applications for funding. Many were ill-thought-out schemes or poorly prepared applications, and 450 were rejected outright. There was apparently an assumption that the newcomers to aid would be something of 'a soft touch', as Walker put it.[410]

---

[403] Ure, 'My Live Aid Nightmare'; 'Band Aid's Band Wagon', *Development Report*, Feb. 1986.

[404] Stringer to Geldof, 16 July 1985, MS Oxfam PGR2/3/1/8.

[405] Piccione to Steinkrauss, 3 Oct. 1985, CARE 1241/2.

[406] Blundy and Vallely, *With Geldof in Africa*, 20; Paul Vallely, 'Bob Rocks the Boat in Africa', *Times*, 22 Oct. 1985; Geldof with Vallely, *Is That It?*, 352; Turnbull to Needham, 21 Dec. 1985, CARE 1241/2.

[407] Band Aid, *With Love*, 40.

[408] The board members were Robert Chambers (Institute of Development Studies, Sussex), Anthony Ellman (Commonwealth Development Corporation), Paul Richards (University College London), Lloyd Timberlake (Earthscan), Jeremy Swift (Institute of Development Studies), Stephanie Simmonds (Overseas Development Agency Health Advisory for Southern Africa), and David Ross (Overseas Development Agency and London School of Hygiene and Tropical Medicine).

[409] Band Aid, 'Minutes of Meetings with Coordinating Agencies on 23 September 1985'.

[410] Alastair Campbell, 'Live and Caring', *Daily Mirror*, 14 July 1986.

The focus on long-term development goals was welcomed, but Band Aid continued to be criticised for the length of time it was taking to vet proposals. Successful projects included small-scale water-well schemes, micro-dams, market gardens, grain banks, grinding mills, training programmes, and support for village-level agriculture or industry, particularly for women. A significant proportion of the grants awarded went to African-based voluntary groups.[411]

International food aid became a moral economic battleground in Ethiopia in 1984–6. Government and rebel forces alike sought to manipulate food aid for political and military gain, forcing donors to adapt allocation strategies that included earmarking relief for distribution via voluntary organisations and creating consortia to interpose additional administrative layers between donor and recipient. Aid organisations already working in Ethiopia were protective of their areas of operation, looking with suspicion on newcomers to aid and previously non-operational bodies that expanded their reach during the crisis. Targeting decisions were also influenced by considerations of what would be seen as newsworthy by the media covering the famine. Thus, feeding shelters, supplementary nutrition programmes, and dramatic air drops were more camera-friendly than the distribution of monthly rations or cash disbursements. In addition, organisations had to balance responding to the needs of famine-affected communities, on the one hand, against appearing to condone the abuses of aid, on the other. Most of the larger voluntary organisations were unwilling to compromise their programmes on moral or economic grounds, preferring discretion with regard to the Ethiopian government – or, as some would have put it, complicity – over defiance.

4.5   Targeting Aid: Realities on the Ground across Two Centuries

Delivering relief and allocating aid to Ireland, Soviet Russia, and Ethiopia posed major moral, economic, and logistic challenges to the voluntary organisations involved. While historians of humanitarianism rarely examine relief on the ground in detail, doing so allows us to identify commonalities over time, moments of change, and present a nuanced understanding of aid.[412] Soup kitchens and camps operated under trying conditions may dominate the public's image of famine relief, but over two centuries the reality has involved a great deal of routine bureaucratic administration: calculations of dry rations and scientific calorie counting; compiling and checking lists of recipients; mapping networks of distribution points and arranging transport; negotiating with other organisations, governments, and local partners; and monitoring, evaluating, and writing project reports.

---

[411] Band Aid, *With Love*, 17–39; IIED, *African Emergency*, 214.
[412] Taithe and Borton, 'History, Memory', 210–11.

Suspicious Minds

While philanthropy played a significant role in all three cases we examined, the bulk of food aid was derived from government stores of grain or largely financed by the public sector, even when it was delivered or allocated by voluntary agencies. In Ireland, the BRA acted as a proxy for UK government relief, with freight costs and other overhead expenses covered by Britain. During the famine in Soviet Russia, allocations by the US Congress through the ARA accounted for the major part of foodstuffs delivered. In Ethiopia, the US government was again the largest donor of aid, followed by the EEC and its member nations, although both had been slow to react to reports of the impending crisis, and there were significant time lapses between pledges of aid and the delivery of the goods.

In each instance studied, famine allocation decisions took place in a climate of suspicion and mistrust. Across our cases, aid agencies faced allegations that their services did more harm than good. Relief during the Great Irish Famine was influenced by the crude racial stereotyping of Irish recipients on the part of the British quasi-colonial government and underpinned by an inflexible political economy that saw dependency as the inevitable outcome of generous aid. The need for collaboration between Soviet authorities and major donors, particularly the USA, was likewise complicated by ideological tensions and criticism that aid would reinforce the Russian Revolution. The ARA was able to ensure a great degree of control in negotiations with the Bolshevik regime; other organisations, however, were less successful in this regard. In Ethiopia, two-thirds of all international aid was earmarked for distribution to beneficiaries by voluntary agencies, bypassing the widely reviled Mengistu regime. Here, the administration of relief took place against a backdrop of frequent press reports of the diversion of food aid. Different relief programmes were accused of helping the Derg and its hurtful resettlement scheme, or undermining the sovereignty of Ethiopia and bolstering the civil war.

Recipient authorities also viewed aid motives with suspicion. US donors to Ireland felt the British sometimes questioned their intentions, while parts of the Catholic establishment in Ireland, who were dubious of the aims of Protestant 'soupers', felt it their duty to provide aid as a means to prevent renunciation of the Catholic faith and win back apostates. In both Soviet Russia and communist-aligned Ethiopia, the authorities remained distrustful of Western relief organisations, viewing them, not without cause, as using aid to sway the hearts and minds of the hungry population. In addition, the Soviet regime was concerned that ARA-supplied food parcels might privilege those with anti-communist tendencies or the minority Jewish population. In Ethiopia, food aid became a proxy battle of the Cold War. Aid from left-wing voluntary groups and nations more ideologically aligned with the local administration was highly valued as an expression of solidarity, even if it was materially far less significant than aid from Western governments. In all cases, relationships relied on the creation of a range of umbrella bodies that could act as intermediaries or neutral screens, whereas idealistically conceived aid depended on the ability to turn a blind eye to the political circumstances.[413] High-profile figures who combined celebrity, fundraising, and administration such as Hoover and Nansen in Russia, or Jansson and Geldof in Ethiopia, helped facilitate a more positive relationship between donor governments and recipients.

Cash versus In-Kind Relief

In all three periods of famine that we investigated, relief organisations prioritised in-kind relief over giving money to recipients. While absolute shortages meant that food provisions were sometimes the only option, as in Soviet Russia, organisations generally avoided giving monetary aid, even where grain was available for purchase on the local market. This tendency was shaped by deep-seated suspicions about how cash allocations were subject to abuse. Much recent research, however, building on Sen's understanding of entitlements, argues for the advantages of cash relief. Increasing the purchasing power of recipients through disbursal of small sums of money can help prevent the movement of foodstuffs out of famine zones, limit population shifting, and restrict the growth of relief camps. It can also reduce inefficiencies in the transport and distribution of aid. Nevertheless, in Ireland, the BRA believed that cash allocations would cause inflation, although it did eventually grant its agents some flexibility in that area. Small sums were also occasionally doled out directly to recipients through the Catholic hierarchy.

For the most part, allocation-in-kind remained the norm. The recipient of a food parcel during the famine in Soviet Russia had to pledge not to sell any of its contents, while several aid organisations insisted that children targeted by feeding programmes had to consume their rations in the agency's kitchen. This also had the advantage of enabling medical care to be provided. Expressive humanitarianism continued to be greatly concerned about abuse, but a preference for forms of relief that would play well with audiences at home greatly influenced allocation decisions. Any disquiet over television footage of children dying in shelters or queuing up to be fed – reminiscent of the nineteenth-century spectacle of paying to watch paupers eat their soup – was supressed on the premise that the money raised through the humiliation of victims was worth it.

A strong preference for gifts-in-kind was also driven by the desire of donor governments to offload surplus foodstuffs from their domestic markets as relief goods, sometimes complicating the feeding schemes of aid organisations.

---

[413] Kaplan, *Surrender or Starve*, 30.

The Ethiopian famine occurred against a backdrop of bumper harvests in the Global North. Tensions existed between the need to provide rations that proved acceptable to local diets and customs, while at the same time taking advantage of what was available to the humanitarian market. The challenge of unfamiliar food – such as corn in Ireland and white bread in Soviet Russia – was a common perplexity. The need to balance nutritional requirements with available funds and distribution networks can be seen in the discussions of soup recipes in the 1840s. By the 1980s, such considerations evolved into the height/weight ratios that determined which children should be admitted to supplementary feeding programmes. As the twentieth century ended, aid agencies had developed special fortified foods in familiar formats, such as the high-energy 'Oxfam biscuit' that was appealing to donors, cheap to manufacture, and easy to transport. The focus on the innocent child as the paramount beneficiary of aid throughout the twentieth century, although traceable back to the 1840s, likewise favoured the provision of prepared food.

Other forms of in-kind aid, often unsolicited, were collected and distributed during famine relief. Blankets and clothing were especially valued, even if sometimes inappropriate for recipients, such as the men's suits that were given out in Ethiopian famine camps. Moreover, local purchasing might have proved more efficient than shipping goods from abroad. The ARA, for example, dismissed as naïveté the willingness of smaller aid organisations to accept all forms of gifts-in-kind during the Russian famine. In the 1980s, similar reservations were expressed by Oxfam and other established aid organisations about the contents of Band Aid shipments or aid convoys arranged by media organisations. The archival record shows that agencies sometimes put disproportionate amounts of time and effort into fielding offers of donated goods. In Ethiopia, at least, a strong emphasis on rehabilitation after the famine was supported by the distribution of donated seeds, tools, and livestock. In contrast to its public image to 'feed the world', a significant proportion of funds raised through celebrity humanitarianism was allocated to long-term development assistance that ranged from irrigation projects to market gardens.

Claiming credit for delivering aid is also a common, if contentious, theme. It ranges from the BRA's urgent press releases setting the record straight about who had funded relief ships sent to Ireland, to the extensive branding of ships, planes, and sacks of grain with 'With Love from Band Aid'. The symbolism and publicity given to food deliveries, whether the arrival of sailing vessels with relief goods, or airdrops by military planes and helicopters, is significant.

Aid Agencies, Personnel, and Logistics

Earmarking aid for specific recipient groups or affected regions is a hallmark of the moral economy of voluntary famine relief. In many cases, it is intended to make allocation more effective on the ground, while attracting and retaining donor interest. In practice, earmarking has not always been practical to implement. The BRA mentioned such special requests in its documentation of contributions, but did not let them take effect in the overall allocation for Ireland. The ARA's promise to provide impartial relief led to conflicts, as many affiliated organisations with a specific donor base had to account for in-group feelings, previously exploited during fundraising. In Ethiopia, aid agencies concentrating on the secessionist regions of Tigray and Eritrea viewed this as a political decision that went along with solidarity campaigns highlighting the needs of those areas. The tendency for relief agencies to divide up territories into spheres of influence was routine, but could sometimes create or exacerbate gaps in the provision of aid. Transport systems that were at best barely adequate were worsened by the disruptions of civil war, adverse weather, the strain of population movements, fuel shortages, and the lack of spare parts. In both Ethiopia and Russia, transportation difficulties dominated the initial period of relief operations, with port capacity a particular concern. It took some time before more agile arrangements could be put in place. In Ireland, as later in Russia, the immature railway network meant reliance on river and canal transport.

One key difference between the age of ad hoc relief and the expressive era is the relatively small number of external relief committees operating in Ireland, as compared to the more than sixty humanitarian organisations that rushed to Ethiopia. Moreover, disasters of great magnitude have seen the emergence of significant 'newcomers to aid', like Save the Children in the 1920s or Band Aid in the 1980s. These organisations arrived onto the international stage with much fanfare, and in time have become semi-permanent features of the humanitarian landscape.

Claims to legitimacy by different organisations are also a feature that bridges past and present. Examples are the challenges faced by the FSR in Russia or REST and the ERA in the 1980s in demonstrating to outsiders that they were reputable aid organisations. The increase in the number of parties involved has compounded earlier issues of communication and information management in the field. Despite advances in technology since the 1920s, the ARA's telegraph and carrier system was perhaps more successful in sharing and processing accurate information about food distribution during the Russian Famine than the UN office for Ethiopia. While soup kitchens were significant delivery points of relief during the Irish and the Russian famines, an increasing share of the aid in the case of Ethiopia was distributed as dry rations, often on a monthly basis.

The actual registration of recipients usually took place at the lowest possible level, that is, by local relief committees in Ireland and Soviet Russia, and peasant associations in Ethiopia. Here, the ad hoc humanitarianism of the mid-nineteenth century anticipated aspects of organised humanitarianism. The final targeting of aid by more privileged members of the community capitalised on local knowledge, but also opened the way to possible discrimination on the grounds of religion, ethnicity, language, political affiliation, or even personal animosities.

Relationships between foreign aid workers on the ground and beneficiaries were usually distant, but such information is largely undocumented. Recent scandals, notably the case of Oxfam, have begun to uncover widespread abuses during humanitarian crises. In Russia, the examples of relationships and marriages between US relief workers and local women hint at the possibility of greater abuses of power. In the Irish and Ethiopian case studies, the almost complete lack of archival evidence does not rule out various degrees of sexual exploitation.

The famine in Soviet Russia provided opportunities for aid workers to purchase valuable goods at low cost. In Ethiopia, despite government attempts to limit the numbers of expatriate staff, the concept of 'cars, compounds and hotels' may well reflect the physical and material experience of the many hundreds of overseas aid workers – at least those based in the capital, Addis Ababa. It marks a considerable shift from the lice-infested trains that aid workers in Russia complained about.[414]

Nonetheless, there was also a strong yearning among aid workers on the ground to do something themselves to relieve the hunger that they encountered, whether through the small amounts of cash they received as voluntary agents and officials with funds from the BRA in Ireland, aid parcels distributed by local ARA officers in Soviet Russia, or the high-energy biscuits and water bottles handed out by journalists and celebrities visiting relief camps in Ethiopia.

The tendency of famine-afflicted people to migrate in search of food is another shared feature of crises and raises questions about the voluntary nature of such migration. In Russia, decentralised distribution systems served to reduce migration, unlike in Ireland, which saw huge population shifts within the country and on to Britain and the New World. As in the case of resettled populations who moved from the north of Ethiopia to the south, reception areas at their destination were often ill-equipped to receive the newcomers. Their arrival increased mortality and strained resources that might otherwise have gone to famine-afflicted areas.

---

[414] Lisa Smirl, *Spaces of Aid: How Cars, Compounds and Hotels Shape Humanitarianism* (London: Zed, 2015).

5   Accounting

5.1   Humanitarian Accountability

Accountability is a moral precept that holds people answerable for their deeds, either to themselves, to someone else, or to a principle. A broad definition sees it as 'the giving and demanding of reasons for conduct', usually encompassing the possibility of sanctions.[1] While it is a ubiquitous standard, accountability is particularly critical for organisations that pursue a moral cause and are founded on trust.[2] The various accountability obligations that guide the work of aid providers encompass hierarchical principal–agent relationships, introspection and contractual ties, and voluntary patronage. Hence, a basic classification distinguishes vertical (upwards), horizontal, and diagonal (downwards, or social) accountability.[3]

While accountability is a universal principle arising from the dependence of human action on conscious decisions, it is also a hallmark of neo-liberal governance and the notion of 'rational choice' that has increasingly permeated the language and culture of humanitarian affairs.[4] However, the provenance of accountability goes beyond any particular school of thought and has been strongly in evidence over the past half-century. As early as the 1970s, there was a growing interest in social accounting,[5] and Médecins Sans Frontières (MSF) gave it a deliberately expressive twist with the propagation of its philosophy of *témoignage*, or, speaking out.

---

[1] John Roberts and Robert Scapens, 'Accounting Systems and Systems of Accountability: Understanding Accounting Practices in Their Organisational Contexts', *Accounting, Organizations and Society* 10, no. 4 (1985): 447 (quotation), 449.

[2] Friberg, 'Accounts', 247.

[3] Mark Bovens, 'Two Concepts of Accountability: Accountability as a Virtue and as a Mechanism', *West European Politics* 33, no. 5 (2010): 953–4.

[4] See Janice Gross Stein, 'Humanitarian Organizations: Accountable – Why, to Whom, for What, and How?', in *Humanitarianism in Question: Politics, Power, Ethics*, eds Michael Barnett and Thomas G. Weiss (Ithaca, NY: Cornell University Press, 2008), 124–42.

[5] Rob Gray, 'Thirty Years of Social Accounting, Reporting and Auditing: What (If Anything) Have We Learnt?', *Business Ethics* 10, no. 1 (2001): 9.

Moral Bookkeeping

Accountability is a prominent concept today – so much so that it is at risk of becoming a buzzword – and has always been a prerequisite for the legitimacy of aid efforts. A rare study analysing the emergence of the British charity market in the late nineteenth century argues that self-regulation and the establishment of accountability mechanisms were crucial for this development.[6] In its affinity with history, accounting provides a normative framework for reporting and bookkeeping practices.[7] However, few studies have mapped humanitarian accounting in a historical perspective. This absence aligns with the observation that 'the history of NGOs as businesses has yet to be written', and with the call for an alternative narrative of humanitarianism based on its 'capitalist logic'.[8] Moreover, it coincides with the widespread ignorance of how calculative routines foster legitimacy, something Herbert Hoover cited in a statistical overview of his Commission for Relief in Belgium (CRB) during the First World War:

> The multitude had but little concern for the bookkeepers in the back rooms of the offices of the relief organization. But the work of these men was of the utmost importance to those in official direction, not only that the relief undertaking might be effectively performed and presented to the world, but that our honor and the honor of our country in this trusteeship should never be challenged.[9]

Accounts as *lieux de mémoire* of their relief efforts are enduring monuments for philanthropic organisations, encompassing both economic and symbolic confirmation of their power. They are documents of altruistic accomplishment, similar to those that furnish individual donors – apart from a sense of pride – with their 'warm glow' of inner goodness. Reports of how their gifts are delivered, what such gifts mean to the distributors and beneficiaries, and the gratitude that they produce give donors an emotional return on their investment. At the same time, gratitude is a confirmation of the donor's role and may trigger societal, economic, and political transformation. Aid agencies are, therefore, eager to receive and document their share of moral credit. While some donors may display a lack of interest in a formal accounting, once a concern for impropriety or fraud is raised, the documentation of proper agency and the responsible administration of donations become essential. As the

---

[6] Roddy, Strange, and Taithe, *Charity Market*, 81.

[7] Geoffrey Whittington, 'Accounting and Economics', in *The New Palgrave: A Dictionary of Economics, vol. 1: A to D*, eds John Eatwell, Murray Milgate, and Peter Newman (London: Macmillan, 1987), 11–14.

[8] Taithe and Borton, 'History, Memory', 215; Dal Lago and O'Sullivan, 'Introduction', 7.

[9] Herbert Hoover, 'Foreword', in *Statistical Review of Relief Operations*, ed. George I. Gay (Stanford, CA: Stanford University Press, 1925), vi.

willingness to donate presupposes a belief in the appropriate distribution of aid, so accounting for revenues and allocations is a critical element of the moral economy.[10]

All of these issues reveal characteristic differences between humanitarian accounting and that of for-profit businesses. Apart from efficiency, the moral economy of the former is also bound up with legitimacy, governance, and justice. For example, humanitarian gifts may be earmarked and subject to restriction, in which case their use for overhead expenditures or additional fundraising becomes problematic. Moreover, humanitarian organisations are generally expected to put their funds to work immediately, even at the expense of utility. Their notions of distributive justice are, thus, closely linked to procedures of accounting.[11] At the same time, donations can be badges of social status, relational aspirations, and communalisation. The representation of prominent people on 'rolls of honour' and other donor lists may garner attention, as may lack of charity be reputation-damaging (a phenomenon that seems to have decreased over the past century).[12] Although the economic power of donations is life-saving in absolute terms, its significance is frequently judged according to the circumstances of the individual contributor. The attention devoted to the humble gifts of poor people; donations from marginal or disadvantaged groups; and the pocket money contributed by children illustrate a 'moral' bookkeeping notion that may have its roots in religious tradition.

The documentation of material sacrifices affects the quality humanitarian causes acquire when adopted by a mass movement, and in turn reflects back on the movement and its surrounding society as moral high ground. A national effort thus becomes a catalyst of purification and cohesion. Moreover, the fact and spirit of giving may appear more momentous than the actual sum raised, even to beneficiaries: although the means of alleviation are commonly inadequate, the recognition of those who are suffering, the experience of solidarity and the provision of partial relief may serve to energise and raise the hopes of vulnerable populations.

Moral Economic Priorities

Viewing events from a moral economy perspective offers a partial remedy to the absence of business scripts and accounting practices in humanitarian studies. Ebrahim's taxonomy of accountability mechanisms includes reporting,

---

[10] Lichtenberg, 'Absence and the Unfond Heart', 85.
[11] See Warwick Funnell, 'Accounting for Justice: Entitlement, Want and the Irish Famine of 1845–7', *Accounting Historians Journal* 28, no. 2 (2001): 187–206.
[12] Viviana A. Zelizer, *The Social Meaning of Money* (New York: Basic Books, 1994), 22, 200; Brewis, 'Fill Full', 899; Bekkers and Wiepking, 'Literature Review', 937.

evaluations, participation, self-regulation, and social auditing.[13] Sources for investigating these dimensions include financial disclosures, annual reports, and other publications that document ideas, actions, and circumstances. Such accounting material shows how aid agencies pursued governance, justice, effectiveness, and legitimacy. The existing records supply detailed information on particular relief efforts. At the same time, any analysis of aid provision should be mindful of Giddens's observation that the power of actors lies in their capability 'to make certain "accounts count" and to enact or resist sanctioning processes'.[14]

Accounting has been interpreted as a tool for handling 'the tensions that surround moral-economic experience' through an evaluation of the suitability of human choices and actions.[15] The abundance of human suffering and the consequential need of an efficient application of resources and a plausible selection among humanitarian causes are strong motives of accountability.[16] More specifically, the arena of ethical options between the donor and beneficiary commitment of relief agencies has been qualified as 'accounting's moral economy'.[17] This entails the prioritisation of certain stakeholders over others and, thus, encompasses needs assessment and the mechanics of triage.[18] However, the choice is generally not discretionary. Observers agree that an organisation's upward accountability 'for itself' generally overshadows its social accountability 'for the other'. The voluntary surrender of money and power disparities suggest a paternalistic moral compass that requires humanitarian agencies to be financially accountable to their funders, overriding broader normative postulates of social accountability. Much of the available literature deplores the donor-affinity of aid agencies compared to what frequently appears to be lip service to beneficiaries.[19]

---

[13] Alnoor Ebrahim, 'Accountability in Practice: Mechanisms for NGOs', *World Development* 31, no. 5 (2003): 813–29.

[14] Anthony Giddens, *Central Problems in Social Theory: Action, Structure and Contradiction in Social Analysis* (London: Macmillan, 1979), 83.

[15] C. Edward Arrington and Jere R. Francis, 'Giving Economic Accounts: Accounting as a Cultural Practice', *Accounting, Organizations and Society* 18, nos 2–3 (1993): 108 (quotation), 112.

[16] Austen Davis, *Concerning Accountability of Humanitarian Action* (London: Overseas Development Institute, 2007), 1; Jeff Everett and Constance Friesen, 'Humanitarian Accountability and Performance in the Théâtre de l'Absurde', *Critical Perspectives on Accounting* 21, no. 6 (2010): 474.

[17] Massimo Sargiacomo, Luca Ianni, and Jeff Everett, 'Accounting for Suffering: Calculative Practices in the Field of Disaster Relief', *Critical Perspectives on Accounting* 25, no. 7 (2014): 667.

[18] Gray, 'Thirty Years', 12; Friberg, 'Accounts', 250.

[19] Teri Shearer, 'Ethics and Accountability: From the For-Itself to the For-the-Other', *Accounting, Organizations and Society* 27, no. 6 (2002): 541–73; Bayard Roberts, 'Accountability', in *Humanitarianism: A Dictionary of Concepts*, eds Tim Allen, Anna Macdonald, and Henry Radice (London: Routledge, 2018), 4; Adil Najam, 'NGO Accountability: A Conceptual Framework', *Development Policy Review* 13, no. 4 (1996): 351.

Thus, the moral economy in question is shaped, on the one hand, by an asymmetry of tangible material stewardship, and on the other, by the more elusive commitment that ideally accompanies a gift. The difficulty of imagining a reversed transfer of resources or compelling social accountability mechanisms is 'the uncomfortable reality of charity', which explains why the broadly advocated revaluation of beneficiaries makes little progress.[20] Principals may be weak, agents strong, and professional humanitarianism may have its intrinsic logic. However, this does not ultimately provide support to recipients or make ethical imperatives on their behalf coercive. As long as social accounting remains voluntary and confronts unequitable recipient societies that are hard-pressed by an emergency, it cannot advance accountability or raise critical issues effectively.[21] Rather, accountability continues to presuppose subordination under the post facto scrutiny of a legitimate superior. The basic model remains that of an agent liable to a principal who provides resources for a specific purpose. Transfers entail an understanding of the right to expect material improvement and accounts of how means have been used.[22] As an internalisation of moral claims held by an external authority, accountability frequently emphasises the asymmetry between donors and recipients.[23]

Accountability is thus enmeshed with power, and at best may be a display of goodwill when exercised downwards.[24] Rather than 'multiple accountabilities disorder' (MAD) or agency loss through obstinate humanitarian organisations, the main problems remain the principal's (i.e., donor's) exercise of authority and the agent's 'over-accountability'.[25] Fraud and abuse are a particular concern in such an idealistic field as humanitarianism, making reliable books a necessity. However, an obsession with accountability and administrative integrity can foster proceduralism and risk aversion that may undermine relief work in emergencies – and the effectiveness and efficiency of collective action in general.[26] At the same time, visible downward accountability may serve the

---

[20] Davis, *Concerning Accountability*, 10.   [21] Ibid., 17–18; Gray, 'Thirty Years', 14.

[22] John Richard Edwards, *A History of Financial Accounting* (London: Routledge, 1989), 8; Vassili Joannidès de Lautour, *Accounting, Capitalism and the Revealed Religions: A Study of Christianity, Judaism and Islam* (Cham: Palgrave Macmillan, 2017), 4–5; Richard Laughlin, 'Principals and Higher Principals: Accounting for Accountability in the Caring Professions', in *Accountability: Power, Ethos and the Technologies of Managing*, eds Rolland Munro and Jan Mouritsen (London: Thomson, 1996), 227.

[23] Rob Skinner and Alan Lester, 'Humanitarianism and Empire: New Research Agendas', *Journal of Imperial and Commonwealth History* 40, no. 5 (2012): 741.

[24] See Roberts and Scapens, 'Accounting Systems', 449.

[25] Najam, 'NGO Accountability', 344; Jonathan G. S. Koppell, 'Pathologies of Accountability: ICANN and the Challenge of "Multiple Accountabilities Disorder"', *Public Administration Review* 65, no. 1 (2005): 94–108.

[26] Bovens, 'Two Concepts', 956; Stein, 'Humanitarian Organizations', 138; Friberg, 'Accounts', 253–4.

purpose of satisfying donors, that is, it may be a function of upward account-ability, or it might entrench local inequalities.[27]

5.2   Figures, Narratives, and Omissions: Ireland

Aid providers accounted for their efforts at the time of the Great Irish Famine in ways that varied greatly. Accounting was generally a tool for apportioning and keeping track of donations, satisfying donors and partners, and creating legitimacy for the aid approach chosen. In the mid-nineteenth century, there was a general expectation that relief efforts would be publicly accounted for in the press. Double-entry bookkeeping was widely practiced, but there was no overall model of accounting, and each organisation chose its own way of public disclosure. Table 5.1 presents an overview of major organisations that distributed relief in Ireland between 1846 and 1850. Many smaller-scale channels also received donations. These included local committees whose distribution need not be in compliance with government rules (and therefore not systematically registered), various community charities and churches whose social work took on the task of famine relief, and private money that was passed from individual to individual. The total sum of voluntary contribu-tions might thus have amounted to £1.5 million (the real price equivalent of £135 million in 2018[28]).

At the time, the famine was considered an internal Irish matter by the British. However, others saw it as the internal administrative and moral responsibility of the UK, which at the time was the wealthiest, most powerful country in the world, with an efficient government apparatus and a strong culture of voluntary action. By contrast, foreign countries lacked the bond of a joint body politic with the Irish, commanded humbler means, and could not easily imagine the extent to which unmitigated market forces and laissez faire policies were allowed to prevail in Ireland.[29] A disaggregation of the accounts of various organisations, tracking the geographic point of origin of Irish relief donations, shows that contributions from outside Ireland comprised less than one million pounds (Table 5.2). Ireland's own share of voluntary famine relief was probably higher than that of any external country, but is difficult to approximate; outside contributions were more systematically recorded. Irish famine relief in the 1840s was a worldwide endeavour, but our mapping shows considerable variations in the degree of responsiveness.

---

[27] Dennis Taylor, Meredith Tharapos, and Shannon Sidaway, 'Downward Accountability for a Natural Disaster Recovery Effort: Evidence and Issues from Australia's Black Saturday', *Critical Perspectives on Accounting* 25, no. 7 (2014): 649; Davis, *Concerning Accountability*, 12.

[28] See www.measuringworth.com/ (accessed 29 June 2019).

[29] Nally, *Human Encumbrances*, 10–11.

Table 5.1 *Distributors of contributions for Irish relief, 1846–9.*[30]

Organisation	Main collection areas	Period	Sum (£)
British Relief Association (BRA)*	England, colonies, worldwide	1847	376,397
Local Irish committees	Ireland	1846–7	314,259
Society of Friends	USA, England	1846–7	201,982
General Central Relief Committee for All Ireland (GCRC)	England, colonies (Canada, India), Ireland, USA, worldwide	1847–9	83,935
Protestant Relief Societies (Wesleyan, National Club, Spiritual Exigencies, Evangelical, Baptist)	England	1846–8	70,391
Catholic Church (estimation of contributions from outside Ireland only)	England, France, Italy, worldwide	1847	65,000
Irish Relief Association for the Destitute Peasantry	England, Ireland, colonies, worldwide	1846–8	42,346
Ladies' Relief Societies for Ireland	Ireland, England		23,835
Society of St Vincent de Paul	Ireland, France, the Netherlands, Europe	1846–50	22,895
Trustees of the Indian Relief Fund**	India	1846	13,920
General Relief Committee of the Royal Exchange	Ireland	1849	5,485
Total			1,220,445

*BRA's income destined for Ireland: £391,701 (of which £20,190 passed on to GCRC). In addition to £2,606 cash documented in its report, BRA distributed £4,886 in provisions for a Bristol committee ('Irish and Scotch Relief Committee-Room', *Bristol Mercury*, 20 Nov. 1847).
**From 1847 on, revenues of the Indian Relief Fund (£9,063) were transferred to the GCRC.

The geographical perspective is informative in some ways and misleading in others. There is insufficient data for estimating the amount individuals of Irish descent contributed to English and imperial collections, but there is evidence that they were over-represented, in particular when considering the distribution of wealth. Moreover, expatriate UK citizens were often the ones to organise donations from distant parts of the empire and other locations worldwide.

Although most donations from abroad came from England, the Irish were looked upon in Britain as an unruly and backward people, in a way we recognise from Orientalist discourse. As a people, the Irish lacked the goodwill that they enjoyed in places like the USA, France, or Italy. Irish landlords largely shared the image problem of their tenant farmers, and only in the north and east of Ireland was there a conspicuous middle class. In fact, the final

[30] The compilation is based on *Transactions*, 46, and various final reports and accounts.

Table 5.2 *Voluntary contributions for Irish relief 1845–9 by region (approximation).*

Country/region	Major collectors	Sum (£)
Ireland*	Local committees, General Central Relief Committee for All Ireland (GCRC), Ladies' associations, Society of St Vincent de Paul (SVP), Irish Relief Association for the Destitute Peasantry (IRA), Society of Friends (SoF)	380,000
Britain	British Relief Association (BRA), Protestant societies, SoF, Catholic Church, IRA, GCRC	525,000
India/Indian Ocean	Indian Relief Fund, BRA, GCRC	50,000
Canada	GCRC, BRA	22,000
West Indies	BRA	17,000
Australia	BRA, GCRC, IRA	9,000
South Africa	GCRC	4,000
Other British dependencies	BRA	2,000
USA	Local committees, GCRC, SoF, Catholic Church	170,000
France	Comité de secours pour l'Irlande (Catholic Church), SVP	26,000
Italy	Catholic Church, IRA, BRA	13,000
The Netherlands, Belgium, Denmark	SVP, BRA	5,000
Germany, Switzerland	BRA, IRA, GCRC, Catholic Church	4,500
Latin America	Catholic Church, BRA	3,500
Russia	BRA	2,500
The Ottoman Empire	BRA, SVP	2,000
Spain, Portugal	BRA	1,000

*Does not include unofficial charity not meeting government standards, the work of existing charities, informal local acts of charity, or domestic Irish donations to the Catholic Church used for famine relief.

report of the BRA claimed that the failure of the staple food crop in western Scotland had been as severe as in Ireland, but praised 'the prompt and systematic exertions which were made by the resident landowners and others in Scotland'. The BRA had placed its funds for Scottish relief at the disposal of two local committees. The approach towards Ireland, where there were few reliable agents, differed, and the Irish crop failure reportedly resulted in disproportionate suffering. Therefore, rather than local civil society, a government agency for military supplies, the Commissariat, was given primary responsibility for the distribution of relief.[31]

Despite prejudice towards Irish beneficiaries, the sum raised by the BRA during the Great Famine exceeded that of any other campaign at the time.

[31] *Report of the British Association*, 11–13.

It included substantial contributions from Catholics, Irish, the British Colonial Empire, and foreigners of various nations. Nonetheless, English Protestants donated more than any other source outside of Ireland.[32] Apart from reflecting geographic proximity and financial means, it illustrates that the commitment emanating from political association, although still inadequate, was greater than that resulting from ethnic or spiritual ties. Alternative means of voluntary aid, such as government relief measures, denominational prayers, and private remittances, contextualise rather than change this picture.

An analysis of the accounting message of different organisations shows both similarities and varying approaches. Most fundraisers were eager to emphasise the broad background of their donors, including those from the establishment, celebrities, and also common people and groups whose donations represented a sacrifice. Thus, contributions by convicts, slaves, and Native Americans received special attention in the press. For example, an Irish newspaper exclaimed: "'Lo! the poor Indian'' – he stretches his red hand in honest kindness to his poor Celtic brother across the sea.'[33] The first advertisement by the BRA set a precedent, listing a few humble donations among prominent and comparatively high ones, including a collection from a family's children and servants.[34]

British accounting, both governmental and voluntary, stressed the extent of relief efforts and the discharge of one's duty; it was geared to declare the end of famine and justify the cessation of aid. By contrast, the accounts of the Irish Quakers, who distributed most US and some British relief, tended to reveal the insufficiency of aid efforts, being both critical of the British government and self-critical, while conveying a sense of Quaker leadership in the humanitarian sector. US accounts emphasised rallying around Irish relief as a manifestation of national unity and an acknowledgement of essential humanitarian values. For the USA, supporting the Irish was both a goal in itself and a challenge to British primacy in this field (even when Britain touted their unpolitical engagement in an integral part of the UK). Finally, while the Catholic Church proper accounted for its aid sporadically, Catholic newspapers and civil society organisations like the Society of St Vincent de Paul (SVP) offered some of the most transparent accounts of aid and moral economic calculations at the time.

British Relief

'Were no accounts kept? Some people think that figures only tend to obscure (smiling).' This sardonic remark and gesture of the Lord Lieutenant of Ireland rebuffed the Reverend Townsend, a member of a deputation to Dublin, in

---

[32] *Report of the British Association*, 193–236.   [33] *Pilot*, 18 June 1847.
[34] *Times*, 6 Jan. 1847.

November 1847. Townsend, who had been one of the deputies from Skibbereen to London a year earlier, had voiced the 'belief' that not much money collected during the previous winter was left, if any.[35] On another occasion, while documenting the use of funds in a letter to a major donor, Townsend pointed to the expense of having to account for the daily expenditure of the many small sums he received.[36]

Accounting technologies were as crucial for British voluntary aid (see Figure 5.1) as they were for the government's struggle to keep entitlements for official relief at bay – principally by excluding the purportedly 'undeserving poor' and by depressing benefits to an uncomfortably low level.[37] The general suspicion was expressed by a *Times* journalist who told the Skibbereen ministers in December 1846, during their fundraising mission to London, 'that if the people of England were satisfied they would not be abused and laughed at by the Irish, it was not one million, but millions would be subscribed'.[38]

Despite the safeguards they took against fraud and their blunt communication during the fundraising campaign, the BRA was not even the limited success some researchers have claimed. Rather than creating trust, prejudices were perpetuated against Ireland by the way money was spent, which may in turn have tempered donations as much as the perceived Irish lack of gratitude.[39] The contribution of one guinea by an anonymous 'Saxon, who loves his brother Pat with all his faults', and the tenuous documentation of gratitude in the final report of the BRA (which had a technical section headed by an address to the Ottoman sultan but without a reference to the queen) illustrates this ambiguity.[40] One-sixth of the £470,041 collected was reserved for Scotland, reducing the Irish share to £391,700. Although celebrated as an achievement, this amount barely exceeded the funds raised during the partial Irish famine of 1822, and represents a fraction of what the *Times* journalist had estimated would be raised if English confidence in the cause of Ireland could be inspired.

One of the functions of public accounting was the circulation of what Roddy, Strange, and Taithe call 'a consistent tale of social hierarchies of giving'.[41] Suggested 'appropriate' contributions were solicited by establishing donor categories and subscription levels, and unlike later contributions, early ones were listed in order of status, rather than chronologically. Even before the

---

[35] 'Deputation from Skibbereen to the Lord Lieutenant', *Cork Examiner*, 10 Nov. 1847.
[36] Townsend to Dufferin, 1 May 1847, PRONI, D1071/H/B/T/252.
[37] Funnell, 'Accounting for Justice'; Philip O'Regan, '"A Dense Mass of Petty Accountability": Accounting in the Service of Cultural Imperialism during the Irish Famine, 1846–1847', *Accounting, Organizations and Society* 35, no. 4 (2010): 416–30.
[38] 'Skibbereen Relief Committee: The Deputation to England', *Southern Reporter*, 2 Jan. 1847.
[39] On perceived ingratitude, see Gray, 'National Humiliation', 214.
[40] *Report of the British Association*, 195, 181–91.
[41] Roddy, Strange, and Taithe, *Charity Market*, 133.

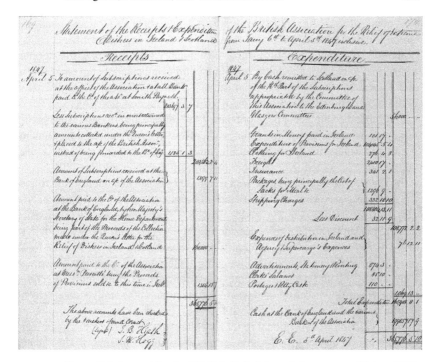

Figure 5.1 Account book of British Relief Association, entry of 5 Apr. 1847.
This image is reproduced courtesy of the National Library of Ireland (Ms 5218)

first subscriber list had been published, Queen Victoria was persuaded to raise the amount of her initial subscription. Prime Minister Lord Russell also increased his contribution, giving himself precedence over the home secretary. It was not publicly acknowledged at the time that the Quaker banker Samuel Gurney made the first pledge of money, setting a benchmark of £1,000 for donations of comparable firms.[42]

The official narrative started with the queen's prompt donation and request to have her name placed at the head of the list. In light of her promise 'of such further amount as the exigency might demand', the queen's failure to increase her initial subscription of £2,000 (apart from a £500 contribution to the Ladies' Clothing Fund) signalled a lack of desire to support a greater relief effort.[43] Along with other members of the royal family, the archbishops of Canterbury and York (the latter made two donations, indicating another adjustment), the

---

[42] 'Skibbereen Relief Committee: The Deputation to England', *Southern Reporter*, 2 Jan. 1847; see also Spring Rice's enveloped subscriber list, NLI, MP, 13, 396/11.
[43] *Report of the British Association*, 10. On the £500 donation, see Trevelyan, *Irish Crisis*, 117.

lord chancellor, and eventually his imperial majesty the Ottoman sultan, the queen's name headed some two dozen lists of ordinary subscribers, collections, and colonial bodies, furnishing the voluntary subscription with examples of national duty among officials (within the limits indicated by the sums given) and lending the campaign exotic prestige.[44] The contributions were discussed in the press, along with rumours about a trifling royal donation of a mere £5; or a report that the sultan had been prevented, for reasons of protocol, from giving ten times as much or sending relief ships. Thus, money was seen by contemporary observers as symbolising humanitarian commitment and as a way authorities discharged their paternal and maternal responsibilities.[45]

In 1846/7, the famine was viewed as a unique seasonal calamity (the role of the preceding government's interventionist policy that had prevented excess mortality in 1845/6 was not widely known).[46] The food shortage persisted after the calamities of 1846/7, and the blight returned with full force in 1848 and 1849. Years of extreme mortality were to continue, but by autumn 1847, the UK government treated the famine as having come to an end. There was little suspicion abroad that this negation reflected wishful thinking and a preconceived downscaling of relief, rather than an authoritative statement by public servants accountable to those that they governed.

The cessation of exceptional relief measures funded by the UK government and the turn to a solely Irish-supported poor law in the autumn of 1847 marks the beginning of an ideologically motivated famine denial. Trevelyan's quasi-official treatise, *The Irish Crisis*, published in January 1848, introduced a development image that attributed governmental and voluntary aid to Ireland back to 'the potato system' of an accounted for past. Selected data on funding, supplies, and policies corroborated the claim of an unparalleled relief effort that included a variety of experimental features. The reported figures demonstrated goodwill for the spiritual and temporal record, while claims that the Irish had been 'saved from a prolonged and horrible state of famine, pestilence, and anarchy', and that their case was 'at last understood' served to legitimise the status quo. At the same time, Trevelyan's apologia celebrated the restrictive management of aid, including timely accounting techniques, as having laid the groundwork for a moral (and thus sustainable) improvement of Irish society that reliance on aid from outside could not undermine. As Trevelyan saw it, 'great sacrifices' were still required, as the Irish had been forced to

---

[44] Newspapers published at least twenty-one subscriber lists. See *Times*, 23 Aug. 1847.

[45] 'Observations on the Most Remarkable Contributions to the British Relief Association', *Hereford Times*, 13 Nov. 1847 (adopted from *Morning Chronicle*); Kinealy, *Charity and the Great Hunger*, 11; Çelik, 'Between History of Humanitarianism', 17.

[46] On British belief in the one-season exceptionalism of the Irish Famine, see Peter Gray, 'Ideology and the Famine', in *The Great Irish Famine*, ed. Cathal Póirtéir (Cork: Mercier, 1995), 97.

realise 'that the plan of depending on external assistance has been tried to the utmost and has failed ... and that the experiment ought now to be made of what independent exertion will do'. Buttressed by conclusions drawn from recent experiences with Ireland, the underlying moral economic supposition was that relief, while occasionally a necessary evil, should exert pressure on the conscience of the local upper class and be distasteful to the pride of the lower classes in order to be properly contained.[47]

With his early 1848 account of Irish misery, relief, and improvement, Trevelyan made the British government's dismissive position on the Irish famine difficult to reverse, although those involved knew better. By 1849, the Treasury projected an outline of distressed areas of Ireland onto a railroad development plan, thus producing a contemporaneous famine map (Figure 2.1). Three colours were used to highlight (a) counties designated as 'distressed' by the Board of Works in May 1849 (the westernmost 60 per cent of the country); (b) areas bordering on the former that 'should have been included' in that category in the light of subsequent experience (10 per cent); and (c) areas that appeared 'to be unable, under present circumstances, to provide from their own resources adequate employment for their population' (10 per cent). However, the image of the distressed areas served as a depiction of the state of the country for internal administrative purposes only; there was no public acknowledgement of the needs depicted.[48]

Against the background of generalised reluctance to provide aid, the 1847 BRA campaign demonstrated to the English, the Irish, and to the world-at-large (and even to the Almighty) that the UK lived up to a standard of civilised Christian solicitude for the well-being of fellow-citizens and supplemented government support with supererogatory voluntary action. Public accounting was a legitimising tool towards this end. At the same time, the voluntary campaign did not require the detail and frequency of governmental accounting reports. This decreased the workload on relief workers and resulted in more aid to beneficiaries.[49]

Advertisements had already informed the public of some of the philosophy behind the use of funds when the BRA published its final report by early 1849. It included extracts of correspondence with agents, samples of working documents, resolutions of thanks, a balance sheet, tables of provisions, and a

---

[47] Trevelyan, *Irish Crisis*, 5, 107, 113, 151, 185–7, 193, 198 (originally published in the *Edinburgh Review* 87, no. 175 (1848): 229–320). On Trevelyan's official narrative's approval by the ministers, see Peter Gray, 'Charles Trevelyan', in *Atlas of the Great Irish Famine*, eds John Crowley, William J. Smyth, and Mike Murphy (New York: New York University Press, 2012), 85–6.

[48] TNA(UK), T 64/368A; map template taken from *Atlas to Accompany 2d Report of the Railway Commissioners Ireland 1838* (London, 1838).

[49] Routh to Trevelyan, 22 and 23 Feb. 1847, TNA(UK), T 64/362A.

complete list of donors and ancillary collections. The report reveals the voluntary campaign's dependence on official policy, but also includes one example in which public funding took over a measure instituted during the famine for some time after voluntary funds were exhausted. The issue was the feeding of school children, a major form of relief provided by the BRA from late 1847 to mid-1848, and which the BRA described as particularly satisfactory. The report viewed children as innocent victims of moral degradation who, by attending school, could be bearers of educational progress to society. The BRA chose poor law commissioners for Ireland as trustees of its remaining balance and by their actions endorsed the official denial that there was any continuation of the famine. It saw its own mission as having been accomplished and did not acknowledge the winter of 1848–9 as a period of repeated mass mortality.[50]

Quaker Relief

Presuming that 'evils of greater or less degree must attend every system of gratuitous relief', the BRA report announced its confidence in having shown that any such evil had been 'more than counterbalanced by the great benefits' of its work for 'starving fellow-countrymen'.[51] The Central Relief Committee (CRC) of the Society of Friends (SoF) in Dublin – the main broker of aid from the USA, and also an organisation supported by English Quakers and independent Irish and English donations – published its report in autumn 1852 in a different spirit. The committee explained the discontinuance of most of its efforts in the winter of 1847/8 as due to the exhaustion of relief workers (some helpers themselves having become 'fit objects' for aid and others dying), rather than because the situation had improved. When in the summer of 1849 Trevelyan, on behalf of the British prime minister, asked the CRC to resume its work (indirectly admitting governance failure and the premature nature of his own account), he was told that voluntary aid had necessarily been seasonal and that only the government commanded means to adequately address the prevailing distress.[52] Even the Irish Quakers admitted, 'We have made mistakes of judgment in the selection of the means of relief, and committed errors in the details of administration; so that the means placed at our disposal have perhaps been less useful than they might have proved in other hands.'[53]

The Quakers acknowledged that it was questionable for them to have used parts of the relief funds for a development project (a 'permanent object'). While justifying an investment in their 'model farm', rather than in aid to the destitute, as having the greater benefit of wages compared to gratuitous relief,

---

[50] *Report of the British Association*, 36–7, 46–7, 159.   [51] Ibid., 47–8.
[52] *Transactions*, 68, 452–4.   [53] Ibid., 5–6. For abuse, see 98.

they showed that they had lost confidence in the profitability of their industrial experiment. Likewise, they described various fisheries projects as 'failures as commercial undertakings'. They also discussed cash support versus relief-in-kind, anticipating much of Sen's argument.[54]

The CRC report totalled almost 500 pages. It accounted for £198,327, excluding 642 packages of clothing, the value of which remained undetermined. Of the total sum, £15,977 in cash and £133,847 worth of provisions (as its value was assessed in Ireland) had come from the USA in ninety-one shipments. The CRC discussed shifting public policy and what this meant for the liberality with which it offered its own relief. In addition, the report contained statistics on other organisations and pointed to a vast number of untraceable contributions there, estimating that the total sum of voluntary donations must have approached £1.5 million. The authors emphasised their close contact with fundraisers in the USA and fellow aid workers in Ireland. However, the voices of actual recipients were not heard in the report, and gratitude remained a minor issue in the documentation. Due to their meticulous accounting, the CRC occupied a special role among humanitarian organisations. They stressed their own reputation, including their capacity for self-criticism, which further increased the moral capital of the SoF. Moreover, they used their influence to advance the political argument that the problem of Ireland was a dysfunctional land law, rather than an improvident people.[55]

US Accounts

Despite an early attempt at coordination, no joint campaign for Irish relief was launched in the USA. Regional hubs aggregated collections from areas near and distant, while Quakers, Catholics, and a number of small towns took independent action. The major regional committees were initially based in New York and New Orleans, with Washington, Boston, Baltimore, Philadelphia, and Charleston as supplementary centres.[56] The committees in New York, Philadelphia, and Charleston put out their own reports, and the Boston-based New England Committee published documentation of their field mission. Other committees probably accounted for themselves by notifying local newspapers.[57] US committees generally used their funds for the purchase of food for shipment to Ireland. In 1847, the British government defrayed freight expenses in the amount of £42,674, which was applauded in the USA.

---

[54] Ibid., 105–7, 101–2.   [55] Ibid., 45–6, 60, 110, 334, 478–80.
[56] 'Public Meeting for the Relief of the Suffering Poor in Ireland', *National Era*, 18 Feb. 1847.
[57] The documentation of final accounts by the New England Committee exemplifies this. See *Boston Daily Advertiser*, 7 Jan. 1848.

Overhead was thus significantly reduced, leading the head office of the Irish Quakers to announce, 'The food put on board at New York, may be considered as laid down almost at the doors of the sufferers for whom it was intended.'[58] The fact that most US relief consisted of provisions-in-kind increased its value to the Irish and was so entered on the accounts of local Quakers. However, this effect seems to have been modest as famine prices rose to their highest level in Ireland before large US food shipments arrived.[59]

The New York Committee, which administered cash and provisions valued at a total of US$242,043 (£50,531), tasked a subcommittee with preparing a report to satisfy contributors. It considered extensive documentation necessary because external donors could not be expected to follow account notes in the New York press. Another motivation was correcting 'erroneous impressions that have obtained to some extent in Great Britain, in regard to the character and motives of the popular movement in America in behalf of the poor of Ireland'. The report was to show 'an act of hearty popular benevolence, unconfined in its locality, disconnected with party, creed or sect, and coupled with no selfish end or aim'.[60] The statement also hinted at the suspicion that the USA had interfered in British–Irish affairs and had disparaged UK relief efforts, perhaps also alluding to US sympathies for the repeal of the union between Great Britain and Ireland, and UK–US rivalry over the Oregon territory.[61] While admitting that US donations were small in comparison to the country's great wealth, the New York Committee maintained that the relief it provided had saved thousands from starvation, created ties across the ocean, and presented an example to the world. However, the committee devoted most of its space to lauding the campaign for its cohesiveness and promotion of Christian values among US citizens.[62]

The Philadelphia Committee, citing the difficulty of estimating the value of the charitable acts made possible by its US$75,600 (£15,783) contribution, presented a simpler moral economic balance sheet: in Ireland, it claimed, the

---

[58] *Aid to Ireland*, 11, 186, 124 (quotation).

[59] The value of cornmeal loaded onto the USS *Jamestown* in Boston, for example, was US$5 per barrel upon departure from the US, i.e., 21 s, calculating an average exchange rate of US$4.79 = £1 at the time (see www.measuringworth.com/datasets/exchangepound) and 25 s upon distribution in Cork (one barrel of cornmeal corresponding to 200 lbs or 0.0893 tons). For prices, see Robert Bennet Forbes, *The Voyage of the* Jamestown *on Her Errand of Mercy* (Boston: Eastburn, 1847), cxxxiii; 'Cork Corn Exchange', *Cork Examiner*, 26 Apr. 1847. Two months earlier, the price at government depots in Ireland ranged from 33 s up to 39 s (see *Correspondence* II, 129, 153, 188). In the USA, then and later, the price was approximately US$5 (see 'Review of the Market', *American Agriculturist* (1847): 101). The price in the west of Ireland was up to 48 s at the end of Feb. 1847. See MacHale, letter, dated 1 Mar., *Tablet*, 6 Mar. 1847.

[60] *Aid to Ireland*, 3–7, 65.

[61] Geary, 'Noblest Offering', 111, 118; Kinealy, *Charity and the Great Hunger*, 251, 254.

[62] *Aid to Ireland*, 7, 15.

lives of thousands were saved, while in the USA, the hearts of thousands 'were made to beat with pleasure, in the consciousness of good performed'. The report also suggested the enhanced positive relationship between nations as a permanent reward. Narrower in scope than the New York report, and without a list of subscribers or a full balance sheet, the Philadelphia summary presented a narrative into which key documents were integrated. It estimated that overall contributions channelled through Philadelphia had amounted to half a million US dollars, including separate collections from Quakers, Episcopalians, and Catholics, and more than US\$300,000 in private remittances.[63]

Boston's first relief ship to Ireland became iconic. The USS *Jamestown* was a decommissioned battleship that the US government provided for a peace mission. With marked symbolism, loading began on St Patrick's Day, and the ship's reception in Cork was ecstatic. In place of a full account of activities and fundraising, the Boston Committee published a narrative of the voyage of the *Jamestown* written by its captain, Robert Bennet Forbes.

The report adhered to genre conventions with its extensive appendices of documents and economic accounts, but differed in several respects. It was more graphic than was common at the time, including a lithograph showing the ship's departure from Boston harbour on 28 March 1847 (Figure 5.2). It also had poems of thanks that referenced the Bible: 'A cup of water given ... is registered in Heaven.' The report's brief first-hand accounts described scenes of horror with an accompanying comment that, considering the gravity of the situation, little more could be expected than to preserve the bare lives of the starving – with food that American hogs would reject. The report also suggested that Americans pay back a debt for relief that the Irish had provided to New England during the devastating war against Native Americans in 1676, including interest – the equivalent, it was said, of roughly US\$200,000. Although the Boston Committee eventually managed to raise three-quarters of that sum (US\$151,007, i.e., £31,525), in addition to receiving donations from New England through other channels, Captain Forbes wrote that Irish relief was 'partly for the payment of an old debt and partly to plant in Irish hearts a debt which will, in future days, come back to us bearing fruit crowned with peace and good will'. Finally, while observing that England was 'not deaf to the call of suffering Ireland' and that the Irish expected too much, he noted their complaints of want of sympathy from the government and trusted that England would learn a charitable lesson and do more than she was doing in the future.[64]

---

[63] *Report of the General Executive Committee*, 35–8.
[64] Forbes, *Voyage of the Jamestown*, v, 13, 21–2. For the extent of the Boston subscription, see 'The New England Committee', *Boston Daily Advertiser*, 7 Jan. 1848.

Figure 5.2 Departure of the USS *Jamestown* for Cork, Ireland, Boston,
28 Mar. 1847. Lithograph by Fritz Henry Lane.
This image is reproduced courtesy of the American Antiquarian Society

Accounting Practices among Catholics

Within the Catholic Church, donations were processed in a hierarchical,
parish-based context; accountability was practiced through individual correspondence, epistles, and verbal communications to congregants. By the middle
of the nineteenth century, these communal practices of the clergy were supplemented by such Catholic branches of civil society as voluntary associations
and the religious press. While the bookkeeping practices of the Church tended
to be lax, the SVP and the newspaper the *Tablet* represented a modernised
moral economy with higher accounting standards.

Collections among Boston Catholics illustrate the poor documentation of
most relief administered by bodies of the Church, reflecting the trust-base of
their system. A study of Boston Catholicism, while conceding the difficulty of
getting a clear picture of donated money and provisions, nevertheless estimates
that Catholic charities in America conveyed US$1 million to the Irish clergy –
a sum forty times the amount collected by Boston Catholics, and so highly
improbable.[65]

In New York, Catholics mostly transferred collections to the general city
fund for forwarding to the Dublin Quaker committee in a display of

---

[65] O'Connor, *Fitzpatrick's Boston 1846–1866*, 79.

ecumenical spirit. By contrast, the Catholic Church in Boston maintained their own separate fund. The documentation that has been preserved consists of correspondence between the bishop of Boston and his Irish colleague, Crolly, the archbishop of Armagh, in addition to scattered notes in a handwritten diocesan journal. These notes speak of various collection results, of an early interim 'report to the people' during a mass with a tally up to that point in time, and of the bishop's estimate that the collection would amount to US$25,000 (plus private remittances by Catholics, which he believed had totalled US$125,000 for the first half of 1847). While the overall extent of the collection is evident, the only clear detail is that the bishop forwarded a total of £4,917 11 s 8 d to Crolly (US$23,550) to be distributed among the other archbishops of Ireland. But the calculation was left to the reader, and the final remittance was a round sum that must have been an approximation of a collection in US dollars.[66] At the same time, in a letter to Ireland that he read to his congregation, the bishop accurately noted that the Catholic solicitation had taken place before the general fund drive and therefore attracted early donations by Protestants; thus need, rather than faith, should determine the distribution.[67]

Crolly stated that the archbishops had apportioned the distribution without distinction of creed, but did not specify the outcome of the division or the dispensation further down the aid chain.[68] Such lack of transparency was not a solitary case. Archbishop Murray of Dublin was reluctant to publicise how he distributed donations – his fear, according to one commentator, being that open accounting 'might generate expectations which he would not be able to meet'.[69]

By contrast, a nineteenth-century biography portrayed Archbishop MacHale of Tuam as a meticulous accountant and relief administrator. The writer (who lost the documents on which his book was based) claimed that MacHale did the whole work of receiving, acknowledging, and distributing donations unaided. However, MacHale's interest in public accounting seems to have primarily emanated from the opportunity for political messaging. For example, in one acknowledgement of donations, he stated that it was a pity private charity was 'rendered almost inoperative by the cruel and merciless theories of political economy; or, what is worse than theories, the cruel and merciless practical policy that has been adopted by our incapable rulers'. Elsewhere, he warned the government of the moral economy of hungry masses who would

---

[66] Diocesan Archives, Boston (DAB), Memoranda of the Diocese of Boston, vol. III, 260–3, 267, 269, 275, 294.
[67] Draft Fitzpatrick to Crolly, 27 Feb. 1847, DAB, Fitzpatrick Papers (FP).
[68] Crolly to Fitzpatrick, 22 Mar. and 21 May 1847, DAB, FP.
[69] Cullen, *Thomas L. Synnott*, 43.

'prowl for food wherever they can find any to appease the cravings of hunger, which no argument of terror or persuasion, short of food, can appease'.[70]

Vatican archives contain many details about Italian collections, and some records concerning the distribution of funds among Irish clerics; but attempts to aggregate this information have been limited and only sporadically published. A handwritten distribution chart for the second quarter of 1847 lists monies submitted to various Irish bishops and (to a lesser degree) monasteries. The total amount is £3,305, although due to a calculation error, the record underestimates the actual sum by £100.[71] In all, the Vatican sent approximately £10,000 to Ireland, £7,000 of which was collected in Italy.[72]

Unlike the Holy See, the French committee for Irish relief published a concise tabulation of their accounts for the greater part of 1847, in accordance with the civil society standards to which the committee declared its adherence. However, it listed revenues per diocese, revealing its de-emphasised ecclesiastical perspective.[73] The French raised and distributed £15,917 among the Irish clergy in 1847, and an additional £4,000 in 1848 and 1849, when other relief efforts had slackened. They also published letters of thanks from the Irish clergy and a final report with an overall accounting. The report speculated that the French effort might have saved 60,000 lives directly and, as a foreign encouragement, might have produced additional 'interest' by stimulating the charity of the local middle and upper classes.[74]

By contrast, the Catholics of England and Wales accounted for their relief work in a fragmentary manner. Proper balance sheets have come down to us only from the Lancashire District Catholic Fund, which brought in the highest proceeds of £4,921, and from the Northern District. In both cases, most of the revenue resulted from church collections. Whereas the northern distribution was scattered, the Lancashire fund was divided equally between the two archbishops in the most distressed southern and western parts of Ireland. This account also specified a minimum that Catholics from Lancashire had

---

[70] Bernard O'Reilly, *John MacHale, Archbishop of Tuam: His Life, Times, and Correspondence, vol. 1* (New York: Pustet, 1890), 653. We owe some critical details to a conversation with Archbishop Michael Neary of Tuam, 11 Jan. 2018. For MacHale's accounting in the press and the quotations, see 'To John Gray, Esq.', *Freeman's Journal*, 3 Mar. 1847; 'Donations for the Western Poor', *Freeman's Journal*, 21 Apr. 1847.

[71] 'Distribuzione', HAC, SC, First series, Ireland, vol. 29, f. 224–6.

[72] HAC, SC, First series, Ireland, vol. 29. For a detailed study of church fundraising in Italy, see Zavatti, 'Appealing Locally'.

[73] 'Comité de secours pour l'Irlande', *L'Ami de la religion*, 30 Dec. 1847.

[74] *Rapport a messeigneurs les archevêques et évêques de France et à messieurs les membres du Comité de l'Irlande* (Paris: Jules-Judeau, 1849). For letters of thanks, see *Oeuvre de Pie IX: Extraits de quelque lettres de NN. SS. les archevêques et évêques d'Irlande, a Monsieur O'Carroll, correspondent de Comité de Secours* (Paris: Sirou et Desquers, 1847).

submitted through other channels.[75] A similar balance sheet for the district of York reported episcopal collections and donations by Yorkshire Catholics to alternative funds. The cases of York and of the Eastern District indicate that the way of publicising such accounts was as an attachment to pastoral letters delivered orally to the parishes, and only incidentally reprinted for a wider audience.[76]

No other final accounts survive for dioceses in England and Wales, although some accumulated sums were published in the press at various points in time – principally in the *Tablet*. Thus, London reported £2,380 in early February 1847, and Wales approximately £422 in March.[77] No aggregated results are known for the Central District, but a church collection was reported from Birmingham, where relief efforts were concentrated on meeting the influx of Irish paupers to that city. As the London and the Central Districts passed their collections on to the GCRC via Murray, their overall totals may be approximated by studying the list of donations to that committee (£2,598 and £849, respectively).[78] The bishop of the Western district gave £5 to that fund out of his own pocket and published an impassioned plea for famine relief to his clergy, but his departure to Rome during the critical period seems to have preempted a coordinated effort at home. Instead, some Catholic churches of Bristol are recorded as having contributed to the city fund.[79]

Not only did the *Tablet*'s modern approach to publicity make it the best source for information on English Catholicism and the Irish famine, but it became a channel for relief in its own right. After Fredric Lucas had issued an early call for aid, donations started coming in, and a collection began that raised more than £3,000 by the beginning of July 1847. The collection continued to amass scattered donations until 1852, the final year of the famine. No overall balance is known, but the *Tablet* published weekly accounts during the initial months of its drive, and an occasional summary or ad hoc notifications

---

[75] 'Receipts and Disbursements', UshCL, UC/P32/105; 'An Account of Subscriptions', ibid., UC/P32/235.

[76] 'English Subscriptions for the Relief of Irish Distress', *Tablet*, 11 Dec. 1847; 'List of Contributions', Diocesan Archives, Westminster, London, Griffiths Papers, 1847 Pastorals.

[77] 'The London Catholic Collections', *Tablet*, 6 Feb. 1847; 'English Subscriptions for Irish Distress', *Tablet*, 13 Mar. 1847.

[78] 'General Central Relief Committee for All Ireland', *Freeman's Journal*, 30 Jan. 1847; General Central Relief Committee for All Ireland, *Alphabetical List of Subscribers, Commencing 29th December 1849, and Ending 24th September 1849* [GCRC 1850] (Dublin: Browne & Nolan, 1850), 7, 15, 27, 30, 33, 40–1. There was at least one more Catholic collection in the Central District (£30, see *Galway Vindicator*, 17 Apr. 1847), and there may have been further collections and additional church-oriented distribution channels.

[79] Ullathorne to Murray, 21 Jan. 1847, DAD, MP, 32/3/72; 'Irish and Scotch Distress', *Bristol Mercury*, 6 Feb. 1847.

after June 1847. Later contributions were sometimes announced under the heading 'Irish Poor' and thereby merged with charity in general.[80]

The amount received by the *Tablet* in the second week of January 1847 remained unsurpassed; the total for the last days of December and January was £1,202; the sum for February was approximately one-half of that; for March one-third; for April and May one-quarter; for June one-fifth. Contributions rapidly decreased after that. In general, donations were modest, and in many cases represented local collections taken among church congregations or solicited from the Irish community in England. 'A few workmen' sent five shillings, the smallest joint contribution, while the smallest individual subscription, given by 'a poor English labourer', was half a shilling. However, many individuals and groups donated several times over, or organised weekly collections. Some donors gave gold watches, silver cutlery, or precious textiles, which Lucas had to turn into cash. While this complicated the process of aid provision, it also conveyed a sense of the urgency of the aid cause.

Although the *Tablet* primarily solicited funds from Catholic residents of England, and engaged Catholic prelates and Catholic institutions for field distribution, some Protestants and people from abroad were among the *Tablet*'s contributors. Lucas mainly spread his relief throughout the severely afflicted western and southern parts of Ireland. Responding to appeals and correspondence published in his paper, and considering occasional requests by donors, he frequently indicated how he believed funds should be directed. To correspondents who faulted him for not sending money directly to local clerics, Lucas explained that the administrative burden of such a model would have been too high.[81]

The *Tablet*, with its long-lasting documentation of first-hand reports on the famine, appeals for aid, and letters of gratitude, also stimulated and recorded many direct transfers by individuals or local groups of donors to Irish clerics: the aggregate sum would require a detailed analysis.[82] The most comprehensive private investment may have been made by E. V. Paul, a retired merchant from Bristol who, after having donated £5 through the *Tablet*, canvassed his home town for four and a half months, reportedly going several miles per day from door-to-door to solicit 1 s for the relief of sufferers in Ireland. The result of this 'labour of love', which he claimed made him feel ten years older, was another £115, partly submitted through the *Tablet*, and partly sent directly to

---

[80] The analysis of the *Tablet* collection is based on a study of the years 1847 and 1848 and quarterly samples of the years that followed.

[81] 'To the Recipients of English Subscriptions', *Tablet*, 8 May 1847.

[82] Scattered documentation in the *Tablet* suggests that independent transactions may have been as high as those administered by Lucas, but it remains unclear how many English Catholic donations went without notice.

various Irish clerics.[83] The fact that Paul suggested in the local press that he forwarded contributions directly to the neediest places, without mentioning his distribution through the Catholic Church, raises the issue of transparency.[84]

In all, Catholic donations from England and Wales represented at least £20,000 out of the total of £525,000. This is double what might have been expected of a group which then comprised approximately 2 per cent of the population. The sum is even more remarkable since their numbers included many poorer individuals (frequently of Irish origin) and virtually excluded high society.

The Catholic institution that most systematically and openly accounted for its activities was the SVP. Despite consisting of a network of autonomous local branches, each of which was required to pay an overhead fee to the head office in Paris, the organisation granted the Cork 'conference' an extraordinary start-up gift of 100 francs (£4) in 1846. This gesture was meant to demonstrate the 'spirit of fraternity' among all Vincentians, and also illustrates the humble circumstances of the head office. In addition, the president and vice-president of the SVP gave a personal gift – eighteen copies of a lithograph that, when sold in Cork, brought in £25 (see Figure 5.3). Among other details and examples of field work, this event was extensively documented in the annual reports of the conference in Cork and the national council in Dublin.[85] Conferences held quarterly meetings on the local level, providing information that would 'allow the members generally to judge of the mode in which the affairs of the society are conducted, and to do this by laying before them all the details of its usual operations', including non-material aid such as sanitary measures and counselling.[86] By 1848, the Paris head office published the *Bulletin de la Société de Saint-Vincent de Paul*, with reports and financial summaries of the entire organisation's activities, including selected details from Irish communiques.

In 1847, the SVP's extraordinary appeal for Irish relief raised £6,141 among its affiliates in France, Belgium, Italy, Turkey, Algiers, Mexico, England, and especially the Netherlands – the latter contributing almost half of the total sum. As an exception to general transparency, and apart from the separately transferred and reported English contribution, the aggregate sum was not broken

---

[83] Letters Paul to Lucas, published in the *Tablet*, 6 Mar., 19 June, and 17 July 1847 (quotation from the July letter).

[84] Letter to the Editor, 6 Apr. 1847, published in *Bristol Mercury*, 10 Apr. 1847.

[85] *First Annual Report*, 10–11; *Report of the Society of Saint Vincent de Paul, for the Year 1846* (Dublin: Clarke, 1847), 24. For a reconstruction of the sum the engravings were sold for, see also *Report of the Society of St. Vincent de Paul, in Ireland, for the Year 1847* [SVP 1847] (Dublin: Wyer, 1848), 27. Reports by the Cork auxiliary, including a financial overview of the famine years, were regularly documented in the *Cork Examiner*.

[86] 'Society of St. Vincent de Paul', *Cork Examiner*, 26 Apr. 1847. For comprehensive statistical coverage, see 'Annual Meeting', *Cork Examiner*, 15 Dec. 1847.

Figure 5.3 *Moïse sauvé des eaux* (*Moses Saved from the Water*). Engraving by Henri Laurent after Nicolas Poussin, eighteen copies of which were a gift to Society of St Vincent de Paul Cork for fundraising purposes, 1846.
Courtesy of Harvard Art Museums/Fogg Museum, Gift of Belinda L. Randall from the collection of John Witt Randall

down in the accounts and cannot be reconstructed in full detail. This levelling was intended to avoid methodological nationalism and emphasise the unity of the SVP. By contrast, the French Bulletin expected donors to read the table of distribution among Irish conferences with interest. In addition to this, the SVP chapter in Constantinople submitted £284 to the BRA.[87] The establishment of new local branches throughout Ireland was of particular concern in the matter of using additional funds from abroad. In 1847, international donations rose almost to the level of domestic contributions. However, collections from abroad tended to dry up over time and amounted to only £6,628 of the

---

[87] SVP 1847, 39–40; 'Revue de la correspondence et faits divers', *Bulletin de la Société de Saint-Vincent de Paul* 1, no. 2 (1848): 43–4; 'Revue de la correspondence et faits divers', *Bulletin de la Société de Saint-Vincent de Paul* 1, no. 3 (1848): 72; 'Rapport général pour l'année 1847: Suite et fin', *Bulletin de la Société de Saint-Vincent de Paul* 1, no. 4 (1848): 93. On Algiers, see 'Correspondance particulière', *L'Ami de la religion*, 20 Mar. 1847; *Report of the British Association*, 202.

£22,895 in total funds raised between 1846 and 1850. This development can partly be attributed to the cautious financial management, reticence, and desire for reciprocity among the Irish, but also to the SVP's aid philosophy, which favoured long-term expansion and commitment to a limited number of cases rather than indiscriminate all-around distribution. Only £2,410 of the funds from abroad were distributed by the end of 1847, facilitating sustained organisational growth over the following years.[88]

In 1848, when there was still the prospect of a good harvest, the Irish SVP returned £300 for relieving the poor of Paris. The Irish branch was later convinced by the president general to retain a second instalment in order to benefit needier sufferers from the famine. This sum was invested in countering the Protestant mission in Dingle.[89] A SVP report included statistics suggesting that its work had reduced the number of converts to Protestantism ('Soupers') in the West Schull area, near Skibbereen, from 1,500 to 60, while the number of established Protestants had also declined from 600 to 300.[90]

The SVP believed that face-to-face contact between volunteers and beneficiaries was the best means of offering assistance. For example, the Cork chapter commended itself as a powerful instrument for wealthier locals to alleviate the misery surrounding them with little cost or trouble to themselves. Unable to relieve suffering everywhere, the organisation made it clear that it needed to select its clients after the 'likelihood of our being able to do most good'. This meant providing continuous relief, but in small increments, and preferably in kind, in order to guide clients towards self-help. Thereby, assistance could be provided to greater numbers. A particular concern was bridging periods of illness among breadwinners in order to prevent the degradation of whole families.[91] The national head office regarded such practices of triage as an economic service to the community, counteracting the increase of poorhouse inmates.[92]

SVP Cork pointed out that it also attended needy Protestant families, although it did so reluctantly in order not to look like proselytisers (SVP also considered Catholics more afflicted and Protestant clergymen better equipped to provide relief). Moreover, SVP Cork maintained that its Christian charity blessed both the volunteer and the recipient, in contrast to mere almsgiving, which tended to degrade the latter.[93] They explained the shared 'moral blessings' of their work as follows: while the rich visitor enlarged 'his' mind in the encounter with a less favoured 'fellow-creature' and came closer to achieving salvation through

---

[88] SVP Ireland, reports for the years 1846–50; SVP Cork 1846.   [89] SVP 1848, 5–7.

[90] *Report of the Proceedings of the Society of St. Vincent de Paul, in Ireland, during the Year 1849* [SVP 1849] (Dublin: Wyer, 1850), 25.

[91] *First Annual Report*, 28, 16 (quotations), 17, 31.   [92] SVP 1849, 7.

[93] 'Society of St. Vincent de Paul', *Cork Examiner*, 26 Apr. 1847.

charitable work, the poor counterpart experienced compassion and 'his heart expands to the best influences of that divine Religion, which he must recognise as the principle that prompts the disinterested benevolence of which he is the object'. Ultimately, the subaltern elite who engaged in Irish SVP work stated their aim of downward accountability ambigiously as 'raising tens of thousands of our fellow-countrymen from a state of abject misery, which makes the social condition of Ireland a disgraceful anomaly in modern civilization'.[94]

Accounts as Explicit and Implicit Disclosure

Not all organisations were as bold as one Irish relief committee that claimed, in 1849, it had saved 'probably 100,000 human beings' with the sum of £5,485 it had raised.[95]

The broadest adoption of accounting practices took place among Catholic institutions. The Church continued to utilise occasional letters circulated within its hierarchy, while contact with parishioners would take place from the pulpit. However, by the mid-nineteenth century, print media, on the one hand, and voluntary associations such as the SVP, on the other, represented an emergent culture of continuous reporting and transparency. Collaborative undertakings also enhanced open bookkeeping. Thus, while traditional trust-based modes of select accounting for charity persisted, they were (a) qualified by individual office holders; (b) supplemented by the contemporary review-based procedures of civil society; and (c) modernised by double-entry book-keeping. Modern Church-affiliated organs and organisations also played a major role in documenting the voices of recipients and first-hand observers.

As various secular US relief campaigns show, even within civil society, there were marked differences in accounting for relief efforts. Notes posted in newspapers were standard, but some of the more significant regional organisa-tions also published final reports or field mission documentation. The infor-mation presented varied considerably across cases. The report of the Dublin Quaker Committee appeared at a time when the famine had drawn to an end, in contrast to other final reports that were issued after the relief effort had prematurely ended. As most US relief was distributed by the Dublin Quaker Committee, their extensive documentation provides considerable insight into how resources and monies were deployed in practice.

While in a formal sense the BRA was a part of civil society, in reality it was a non-governmental organisation (NGO) commissioned by the UK government and intended to function as a form of quasi-colonial rule in

---

[94] *First Annual Report*, 24, 29.
[95] *Report and Proceedings of the General Relief Committee of the Royal Exchange, from 3rd May to 3rd September, 1849* (Dublin: Shea, 1849), 34, 51.

Ireland.[96] The BRA thus illustrates the striking discrepancy between meticulous British public or semi-public accounting for relief (including solid and multifaceted statistical aggregates), and the complete absence of official or otherwise reliable mortality statistics of more than a fragmentary character. Among providers of relief, the BRA was also unique for its total exclusion of recipient voices and the degree to which its appeals relied on accounting – including advertising its auditors' functions and names. The emphasis on reliable procedures, rather than compassion, reflected the a priori absence of trust in British–Irish relations. For Trevelyan, who was the acknowledged mastermind of official and semi-official famine relief, accounting for the provision of aid also became a means of relinquishing it in the future, with all due civilisational and Christian honours preserved. In the case of the BRA, morality became a de-humanised abstraction exclusively invested in the prevailing ultraliberal market economy, rather than in an equalising force that would uphold the dignity of human life.

5.3   The Power of Numbers: Soviet Russia

Supporters as well as critics of relief to Russia regularly demanded detailed information about incomes and expenses, purchasing practises, overhead costs, and the like. The lack of trust in Russian authorities and the promise of businesslike relief, but also the competition between different aid organisations, made professional bookkeeping a necessity. Accordingly, in the spirit of organised humanitarianism, relief workers were exhorted to rather 'not … issue supplies than to issue them and be unable to account for them'.[97]

Accounting was hampered by the difficulty of finding Russian personnel who were qualified for this task according to Western standards, and many local relief districts proved incapable of supplying central offices with adequate commodity reports, or they prioritised other tasks that they considered more urgent.[98] The steep currency depreciation in Russia – adding machines were soon unable to handle the high figures – led to further complications.[99] The Russian division of the American Relief Administration (ARA), which exchanged approximately US$650,000 for Russian roubles between 1921 and 1923, rejected the rates offered by the Russian government, saying that they would 'practically amount to the confiscation of a part of our

---

[96] NGO is here used as an analytical term for 'a private body in its capacity of being … used by a government'. See Götz, 'Reframing NGOs', 250.

[97] Circular letter to all districts and ports, no. 97, 5 June 1922, ARA, reel 55.

[98] Charles Telford, 'Accounting for Relief', Report of 17 Mar. 1923, ARA, reel 55; Circular letter to all districts and ports no. 97, 5 June 1922, ibid.

[99] Ramsey, 22 Aug. 1922, ARA, reel 55. The dollar–rouble exchange rate was 1:145,000 in Oct. 1921 and 1:41,000,000 in Feb. 1923.

money'.[100] Until Russian banks agreed to extend market prices, the ARA bought the roubles needed to cover operating expenses from private individuals who happily accepted dollars or pounds in their foreign accounts.[101]

Statistics regarding foreign relief provided under Hoover's direction from 1914 to 1923 shows that the Russian operation was a minor endeavour, standing for 1.2 per cent of the total budget.[102] Belgium received nine times that share between 1914 and 1919, and after the war the former enemy Germany received nearly twice as much. Excluding the massive supplies sent to France, Great Britain, and Italy, and taking into account only the so-called reconstruction period between August 1919 and July 1923, the ARA's aid for Soviet Russia comprised little more than one-third of the total tonnage.[103] Nevertheless, the ARA was the dominant force among those organisations providing Russian relief. It distributed 740,000 t under its umbrella, whereas the International Committee for Russian Relief (ICRR) and its affiliated organisations, according to its own reports distributed up to 90,000 t, and the Workers' Relief International (WIR) claimed to have distributed 30,000 t (see Table 5.3). At the same time, the relatively limited magnitude of relief for Soviet Russia does not diminish its practical and symbolic significance as a major instance of enemy aid, and as an engagement that facilitated a working relationship between the West and the victors of the Russian revolution in the early interwar period.

Organisations all desired to keep costs for personnel and administration low. The ARA instituted a hire-and-fire policy whereby staff could be laid off with one month's notice when their services were no longer needed.[104] Overhead costs – especially their public relations aspect – were a sensitive topic that led to heated debate and controversy. Relief organisations faced the difficult task of justifying their practices and expenditures, such as placing advertisements.

The sources and effectiveness of famine relief were also contentious matters and involved ideological pride, particularly between the ARA and Soviet authorities. In the resulting information war, both sides resorted to arguments partly based on 'creative accounting'. The political circumstances of enemy aid, combined with social expectations that both the public and individual donors held in connection with transnational aid, made gratitude an important element of the accounting genre.[105] Evidence in the form of reports, photos,

---

[100] Telford, 'Accounting for Relief'.   [101] Haskell to Brown, 21 Dec. 1921, ARA, reel 55.

[102] However, far less than 10 per cent of the $5 billion budget consisted of benevolent gifts; more than 80 per cent were credits. Noyes, 'American Relief of Famine'.

[103] Frank M. Surface and Raymond Bland, *American Food in the World War and Reconstruction Period: Operations of the Organizations under the Direction of Herbert Hoover, 1914 to 1924* (Stanford, CA: Stanford University Press, 1931), 7, 11, 9, 263.

[104] Memorandum to Page, 30 Dec. 1921, ARA, reel 548.

[105] Elisabeth Piller, 'The Frustrations of Giving: "Ingratitude", Public Outrage and German–American Relations in the Era of the Great War, 1914–24', unpublished paper, available at www.academia.edu/34414999 (accessed 29 June 2019).

Table 5.3 *Quantity of relief goods distributed, and available budget during the Russian Famine, 1921–3.*[106]

	Relief goods, tonnes	Total budget (incl. overhead and gifts in kind), US$
International Committee for Russian Relief and affiliated organisations	90,000 (of which c. 40 per cent was distributed by SCF and 20 per cent by FEWVRC)	7,100,000
(Save the Children Fund (SCF), International Save the Children Union, Friends' Emergency and War Victims Relief Committee (FEWVRC), various national Red Cross organisations, various smaller groups)		
Workers' Relief International/Internationale Arbeiterhilfe	30,000	2,500,000
(nearly a dozen national organisations, Friends of Soviet Russia (USA) raising more than half the budget)		
Relief under American Relief Administration direction	740,000	63,000,000
By source:		
American Relief Administration		10,200,000
Congressional Fund/Medical Fund		22,660,000
Food remittances		9,300,000
Jewish Joint Distribution Committee		5,000,000
American Red Cross Medical Fund		3,800,000
Laura Spelman Rockefeller Memorial		1,300,000
Soviet gold		11,300,000
Other contributors include: Catholic Welfare Council, Lutheran Council, American Friends Service Committee, Young Men's Christian Association/Young Women's Christian Association, Mennonite Central Committee, Volga Relief Society		
Estimated Russian contribution in form of transport, infrastructure, etc.	–	14,000,000
Total	**860,000**	**86,600,000**

films, gifts, and letters of thanks became an alternative return currency within the humanitarian moral economy. Different organisations, and even countries, struggled to receive their share – something that often led to conflict.

[106] League of Nations, *Report*, 104–5; Surface and Bland, *American Food Aid*, 245–64; Kelly, *British Humanitarian Activity*, 189; 'Nineteenth Session', *Bulletin of the IV Congress of the Communist International*, 1 Dec. 1922; Fisher, *Famine in Soviet Russia*. Fisher estimates that an additional US$4,750,000 not included in the ARA budget was separately administered by organizations affiliated with the ARA (553, n. 2).

Hoover attached paramount importance to securing the 'national portion' of gratitude. Even when co-operating with foreign organisations, the ARA considered it a 'fundamental principle' that relief coming from the USA had to be 'distributed as American food', and that recipients needed to understand its origin, which caused some problems. For example, the American Friends Service Committee (AFSC) used to co-operate closely with the British Quakers and had initially appointed one of them as its head of mission. The ARA did not understand the Friends' 'reluctance and opposition to letting it be known that the relief which they give emanates from America'.[107] At the end of the relief campaign, the ARA proudly stressed that relief given by its affiliated organisation to Russia 'outside the resources of the ARA, has amounted to over twice the total relief given to Russia by all other foreign relief organizations'.[108] In an interim report, Hoover even listed the contribution of US communist organisations.[109]

The British Save the Children Fund (SCF) also increasingly emphasised the national origin of relief aid. Unlike the previous Budapest effort in which International Save the Children Union (ISCU) money was pooled, in Russia it was determined 'that separate kitchens shall be maintained with the money received from different countries'. Each national group 'should reap the full credit which its sacrifices and generosity deserve', an article in *The Record* proclaimed.[110] Consequently, despite the ISCU's involvement and the contributions of chapters from other nations, the provision of food in Saratov was often described as the 'generous effort of the British people'.[111]

Considering the circumstances under which relief was provided, official statistics seem to understate losses and damages. The ARA claimed that the cargo shortage reported at the five main Soviet ports of Petrograd, Batumi, Novorossiysk, Odessa, and Theodosia was less than 0.5 per cent, while financial losses from damaged goods made up an average of 1 per cent of the value. During transit via trains, trucks, and interior shipment another 0.5 per cent of the cargo (less than 4,000 t) was reported as loss.[112] The British relief expert Robertson came to a similar conclusion during his trip through Russia in early 1922, estimating that losses during train transport amounted to approximately 0.5 per cent.[113]

According to §11 of the Riga agreement, the Soviet government was to reimburse the ARA for 'any misused relief supply', including shortages during transport.[114] By March 1923, the ARA had made 1,429 such claims,

[107] Rickard to Farrand (ARC chair), 23 Dec. 1921, ARA, reel 389.
[108] The Cooperating Organization, undated ARA report (probably mid-1923), ARA, reel 115.
[109] Interim Report on the Russian Relief Situation, ARA Bulletin 2, no. 27, Aug. 1922, 1–5.
[110] 'Co-operation True and False', *The Record* 2, no. 3 (1921).
[111] 'Of Giving Way to Others'.   [112] Telford, 'Accounting for Relief'.
[113] Robertson, 'Descriptive notes'.   [114] Printed in Patenaude, *Big Show*, 745–8.

'supported by copies of ten thousand protocols', totalling a sum of roughly US$300,000. Although there was no similar formulation included in the agreement Nansen had signed on behalf of the ICRR, British organisations assumed that Soviet authorities would compensate them for any shortage and submitted demand notes accordingly. Thus, the Soviet government was held responsible for losses on its territory, if not always financially, then morally and politically, and therefore found it in their own interest to prevent such incidents as far as possible. Many trains were under military protection, trucks and rail cars were sealed, and convoys partly accompanied by a special 'ARA regiment' of the Red Army. Warehouses in the cities 'were kept under continuous guard and under lock and seal when closed'. The feared secret police, Cheka, succeeded in February 1922 by the State Political Directorate (GPU), proceeded with rigor against any suspicion of theft, embezzlement, or diversion. For example, Cheka officers took samples of relief goods and made sure similar items were not being sold in local markets. By early 1922, the SCF had reported only four attempts to break into one of their 400 warehouses. The ARA likewise mentioned 'only few robberies of much importance' during the whole course of their operation, and blamed 'petty pilferage and leakage' for the major part of their losses.[115]

Businesslike Relief and Overhead Costs

In December 1921, Hoover's associate Rickard, like Hoover a mining engineer, stated that the ARA's 'governing principles' were the same as those of US engineering companies.[116] In the Riga negotiations, the ARA stipulated such conditions to the Russian government as had been given to countries that had previously received aid. This meant that the only costs for the ARA in Russia were the maintenance of US staff and the expenses related to the Food Remittance Division (including salaries for native personnel), as the latter was considered an enterprise–charity hybrid.[117] The Soviet government covered all internal costs connected with the child and adult feeding operations, such as the salaries of personnel cited earlier, travel expenses, kitchen and office equipment, and transport.[118]

---

[115] Telford, 'Accounting for Relief' (quotations); Robertson, 'Descriptive notes'.

[116] Patenaude, *Big Show*, 637.

[117] ARA Finance and Accounting Division, Summary of duties and responsibilities, 18 Mar. 1922, ARA, reel 55.

[118] However, in many cases foreign relief organisations covered at least part of such costs, sometimes indirectly. The ARA, for example, granted many of its local employees a so-called *paiok*, that is, a payment in the form of food, which altogether accounted for US$375,000 (Surface and Bland, *American Food*, 920–1).

In addition, the ARA staff remained small, comprising some 200 members at a time, supervising a body of about 125,000 local workers.[119] This kept administrative overhead costs low and was intended to stimulate self-initiative and responsibility, crucial elements of the ARA relief philosophy.[120] When smaller affiliated organisations wished to send their own representatives to Russia, it was regarded as a waste of money. Haskell cabled that the 'maximum amount of good could be accomplished' if unnecessary expenses like this were avoided.[121] The ARA considered the performance of other organisations inefficient, with few exceptions. A letter to potential donors stated that contributions were best invested in the ARA relief operation, as most other agencies worked in 'uneconomical' ways. At best, they were 'well-intended and wasteful', at worst, 'dishonest and wasteful'.[122]

For the SCF, nineteen British citizens supervised a native workforce of 5,000.[123] The SCF also stressed professionalism and formulated three aims for its relief work: '1. To get the food to the children; 2. To feed the children as economically as we can; 3. To feed as many children as we can.' Thus, they mirrored the ARA's goal of making every dollar provide the maximum relief. Compared with such goals, spontaneous charity appeared as an outdated model. Given the enormity of the Russian famine, the SCF stressed that there was 'little room for the amateur philanthropist'. For this reason, they discouraged potential donors from giving their money to other organisations: 'We are better fitted to deal with child relief than anybody else... It would be false modesty if we did not claim to have expert knowledge and to assert that charity if it is to be of any use at all must be conducted on efficient businesslike lines.'[124]

The examples show how accounting for aid and fundraising were intertwined. Low overhead and minimal purchase costs were extensively used in public relations work. The ARA proudly claimed that 'not one cent ... has been expended for internal overhead'; the AFSC promised that every dollar 'will be turned over without one cent deducted by us'; and the communist Friends of Soviet Russia (FSR) assured donors that 'experts in purchasing and shipping' will 'make every cent you give buy its utmost in value' by purchasing food 'at rock-bottom prices'.[125] Meanwhile, the SCF was 'carefully watching the world's markets' and 'buying on very large scale'.[126]

---

[119] 'The ARA Russian Operation at Glance', paper by Communication Division, 9 June 1923, ARA, reel 548.
[120] Patenaude, *Big Show*, 31.   [121] Haskell to London, 20 Mar. 1922, ARA, reel 115.
[122] Page to Sterret, 12 Dec. 1921, ARA, reel 504.
[123] 'The Save the Children Fund in Russia', *The Record* 3, no. 1 (1922).
[124] 'Of Giving Way to Others'.
[125] Appeal 'The World's Most Desperate Emergency' by General Relief Committee of the AFSC, ARA, reel 499; FSR 'Nation-Wide Holiday Drive'.
[126] 'Of Giving Way to Others'.

However, even businesslike practices made humanitarian organisations vulnerable to criticism. Its countrywide advertisements caused the SCF to face allegations that it was spending a great deal of the donated money it received on public relations instead of famine relief.[127] A lengthy article in *The Record* addressed this issue and informed readers that the aim of the SCF was 'to collect and distribute the largest possible amount at the smallest expense'. Old-fashioned fundraising based on personal contact and a network of regular donors was no longer adequate. In the face of urgent need, the SCF took 'the bold step of advertising on a large scale, proclaiming to the world what it was doing and why it was asking for help'. Readers were assured that 'advertising pays' and that experience had shown 'money drops off' without advertising.[128]

In December 1921, £10,998 spent on advertising yielded £61,115 in donations.[129] While the net profit in this example may appear impressive, 18 per cent overhead costs for public relations may appear less acceptable within a moral economy context, especially if compared to costs incurred by smaller organisations. In justification of the SCF position, Treasurer Watson later argued 'that the larger the sum which a society sets itself out to raise, the greater must be the proportional expenditure'. It was easy, he continued, to raise £1,000 by spending £100, but to achieve the same ratio when raising £500,000 was practically impossible.[130] However, the question remained as to what degree the increase of total relief was legitimate in the eyes of a critical public, if it caused a disproportionate rise in overhead costs.

This Achilles' heel of businesslike humanitarianism was soon attacked by adversaries of the SCF. Among them, the *Daily Express,* with its wide circulation, fought an aggressive campaign against the SCF's Russian operations. After unsuccessfully spreading doubts about the existence of the famine, its journalists began criticising SCF's overhead. One of the newspaper's first headlines read, 'One Pound in Three Goes in Expenses'. Although this statement was factually wrong, it touched a sore point.[131]

To cope with such accusations, the SCF adopted an offensive strategy and allowed the *Daily Express* to access its documents. The investigative journalists could only report that in the course of the two and a half years of its existence, the SCF had collected £1,115,000 and spent £204,000 on expenses, that is a moderate overhead rate of slightly more than 18 per cent.[132]

---

[127] Mahood and Satzewich, 'Save the Children Fund'; Breen, 'Saving Enemy Children'.
[128] 'Cheap Publicity', *The Record* 2, no. 5 (1921).   [129] Breen, 'Saving Enemy Children', 229.
[130] Letter by Watson, 19 Sept. 1922, SCF, reel 30.
[131] *Daily Express,* 26 Nov. 1921. The headline linked SCF's expenses to costs incurred for food and distribution, rather than revenue. See Weardale to Plender, 26 Nov. 1921, SCF, reel 30; letter draft by Jebb, 14 Feb. 1922, ibid.
[132] *Daily Express,* 10 Feb. 1922.

Furthermore, the SCF tried to demonstrate how reasonable its overhead was by drawing comparisons with other British relief organisations. As articles critical of the SCF often referred to the Quakers as shining examples, the Friends' Emergency and War Victims Relief Committee (FEWVRC) was involuntary drawn into the conflict. SCF representatives analysed their balance sheets and pointed out that the Friends' overhead rate was 19.5 per cent for the period September 1918 to September 1920 – higher than that of the SCF.[133] Chairwoman Ruth Fry, in turn, protested against such publicity and justified the Friends' overhead costs by explaining that they administered the distribution of many goods supplied by other organisations. While such distribution involved overhead costs, the relief goods themselves did not necessarily enter the credit side of the Quakers' accounts. For this reason, Fry claimed, and because of their service-intensive programme of medical aid, 'any comparison of the overhead expenditure of the two Societies must of necessity be fallacious and misleading'.[134] Watson replied that he was not criticising the Quakers' expenditure, but simply wanted to show 'that no big charitable work can be carried on nowadays except on very considerable costs'.[135] In a second letter, he pointed out that 'we did not start these comparisons and would not have troubled to make them had it not been for widespread criticisms of our work which are largely based on an alleged extravagance in our overhead expenditure and, on the other hand, underestimates yours'.[136]

While the SCF successfully repelled the first wave of attacks, the *Daily Express* raised another criticism, once again connected to the professionalism the SCF claimed to have embraced. Similar to profit-making companies, SCF's public relations campaigns were partly conducted on a commission basis, something that became public when journalists scrutinising SCF accounts noticed that an unnamed agent had received £10,000 as a commission fee. SCF representatives defended the sum by referring to the conditions under which that person had led the fundraising campaign: £8,000 per month were to be raised free-of-charge; everything beyond that earned the agent a 1.5 per cent commission. SCF argued that the fee was high because the campaign was effective and justified the bonus system: 'We distinctly do not believe, as many people do, that such business can safely be entrusted to amateurs with no business experience.' For this purpose, 'first-class business people' were engaged to bear the responsibility of organising a fund exceeding one million pounds. These people were said to earn far less than they would elsewhere.[137]

---

[133] Balance Sheet Notes on SCF, FEWVRC, and Imperial War Relief Fund (IWRF), undated (probably Nov. 1921), SCF, reel 33.
[134] Fry to Watson, 24 Nov. 1921, SCF, reel 33.
[135] Watson to Fry, 18 Nov. 1921, SCF, reel 33.   [136] Watson to Fry, 5 Dec. 1921, SCF 33.
[137] 'Saving the Children: Lord Weardale on Contracts Made by the Fund', *Daily Express*, 17 Feb. 1922; Weardale to *Daily Express*, 10 Feb. 1922, SCF, reel 30.

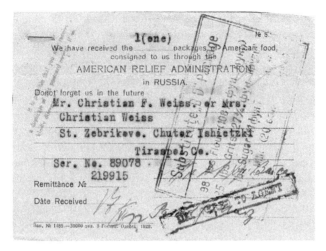

Figure 5.4 Receipt of Frederick Roesch, South Dakota, for a US$10
American Relief Administration remittance delivery to the Weiss family in
St Zebrikowa, 1922. The stamp indicates the content of the package. Note
also the renewed appeal 'Don't forget us in the future'.
Courtesy of Annie Roesch Larson Collection, Archives & Special Collections,
Northern State University, Aberdeen, SD, USA

Nevertheless, local SFC fundraisers were also upset, demanded explanations,
and some threatened to stop working unless such commissions were made
public.[138]

The ARA took a different approach towards publicity. Here, too, professionals were hired to work on public relations. However, Baker, their chief,
warned that 'the moment we get into paid advertising, we will be driven into
the position of a commercial enterprise'. Should this happen, Baker feared,
newspapers and magazines would start to ask for their share of the donations.[139] Instead of paying for advertisements, the ARA press department had
used its contacts with journalists and editors to produce articles and photo
spread themselves.[140] These 'mat releases' proved successful, especially in the
local press, and according to an analyst, the advertising space obtained in this
way would have cost US$500,000 for the food remittance programme alone, if
it had been purchased at display advertisement rates.[141] The FSR also provided
a 'matrix service' and allowed periodicals to publish famine pictures at no cost,
if they mentioned the FSR in the captions.[142]

---

[138] Emson to Watson, 1 Oct. 1922, and Emson to Jebb 8 Oct. 1922, SCF, reel 30.
[139] Baker to Hoover, 20 Oct. 1921, ARA, reel 549.
[140] Wilkinson to Baker, 2 June 1922, ARA, reel 549.
[141] Mayer to Baker, 10 Apr. 1922, ARA, reel 549.   [142] FSR, *Matrix Service*.

The total overhead costs of the ARA remain opaque, as concrete lists of expenditures do not exist. The rate of 3 per cent mentioned in several letters to donors may have referred to central administrative costs only, as other organisations claimed similar rates for such narrowly defined overhead.[143] Other documents merely state that the Russian government was responsible for the respective costs.[144] When the operation concluded, Haskell boasted that the margin established by the ARA in the sale of food packages earned enough money 'to balance the entire overhead expenses... Therefore, there has been no costs to the American contributor or taxpayer for administration of the Congressional or other funds.'[145] However, most expenditures were simply added to the value of relief provided. ARA historian Fisher mentions in passing that shipping costs were about US$6.5 per ton.[146] Based on the 740,000 t of relief goods the ARA was responsible for, this amounts to nearly US$5 million. A later report indicates that in many cases, up to one-fifth of the budget was consumed by costs for freight, insurance, and related expenses.[147] One aspect of donor-driven aid is that benefits also accrue to producers and suppliers in the donor nation. For example, US farmers, shipping companies, and other businesses profitted from ARA contracts.[148] Some used political influence to obtain them.[149] Others criticised the whole operation as incompatible with free-market capitalism. A letter to a newspaper blamed the ARA for 'selling food drafts on a profit basis, thereby interfering with the regular trade of American exporters'.[150]

In general, organisations depending on private money were faced with a proportional increase in overhead costs from mid-1922 on because donations began to decrease. As people became weary of giving, more effort was needed to motivate them. SCF treasurer Watson remarked that matters grow more difficult 'when the novelty of the appeal has worn off'.[151] Moreover, staff and infrastructure that had been established as donations peaked were not easily scaled back when less money was available. The FSR provides a particularly telling example. More than three-quarters of all cash donations the

---

[143] Page to Sterret, 12 Dec. 1921, ARA, reel 504. See Barringer to Kelton, 25 Jan. 1922, ARA, reel 502, and Page to Richards, 1 Oct. 1921, ibid. On other organisations, see Fry to Watson, 24 Nov. 1921, SCF, reel 33.

[144] Hoover to Harding, 16 July 1922, in Fisher, *Famine in Soviet Russia*, 547–51.

[145] Haskell to Hoover, 27 Aug. 1923, in *Documents of the American Relief Administration, Russian Operations 1921–1923, vol. 1: Organization and Administration* (Stanford, CA: Stanford University Press, 1931), 649.

[146] Fisher, *Famine in Soviet Russia*, 169.   [147] Surface and Bland, *American Food*, 899.

[148] Schaefer to Hoover, 25 Nov. 1921, ARA, reel 552; Jackson to Balpin, 2 Dec. 1921, ibid.; Fisher, *Famine in Soviet Russia*, 169.

[149] Baker to Brown, 10 Oct. 1921, ARA, reel 549.

[150] Copy of Letter to the Editor, *New York Times*, Dec. 1921, ARA, reel 566.

[151] Letter by Watson, 19 Sep. 1922, SCF, reel 30.

organisation collected came in the first fiscal year of the relief effort (August 1921 to July 1922). Overhead that year was 17.5 per cent. While FSR's absolute overhead costs remained about the same in the following year, the radical drop in donations nearly quadrupled their relative overhead to a staggering 69 per cent.[152]

Two Genres of (Creative) Accounting

During the famine, Nansen allegedly travelled second class in order to save £5, despite his status and age. This sum was reportedly used to prevent five Russians from starving.[153] A widespread feature of organisational articles, appeals, and accounting reports was stating the cost of one meal or of feeding a single recipient, often for a specific period of time. Such figures were supposed to convey a vivid impression of how efficiently the respective organisation worked. Conversely, potential donors could see how little was needed to save a child's life (children usually served as the reference point). The message was simple: any donation, no matter how small, is a meaningful contribution. At the same time, moral pressure was increased because a life could be portrayed against a trivial expenditure. Also, a donor could easily calculate how many children's' lives his or her money could save. Similar messages were directly communicated to donors by relief organisations: 'It may be of satisfaction to you to know that this check will be sufficient to provide food, clothing and medical attention to about seven children ... until next harvest. These seven children, in all probability, would perish had this aid not been given by you.'[154] Rounded figures were used, and costs given as a rough estimate. Only in a few cases was the cost calculation described in detail. However, whether or not overhead costs were taken into account made a significant difference in the calculation.

Throughout the campaign, the SCF consistently claimed that they kept a child alive for one week with 1 s. They did so in *The Record*, in advertisements, and in debates if challenged for allegedly excessive overhead costs.[155] When necessary, the ratio was projected onto larger groups, higher sums, or longer periods. For example, when the SCF appealed for £100 donations for their kitchen programme, the organisation maintained that 100 children could

---

[152] First year: income US$735,000, overhead approximately US$130,000; second year: income US$210,000, overhead approximately US$140,000. Calculation based on monthly financial statements published in each issue of *Soviet Russia* (since 1923 *Soviet Russia Pictorial*), covering the period 9 Aug. 1921 to 31 July 1923

[153] Mulley, *Woman Who Saved*, 293.   [154] Page to Morden, 29 Dec. 1921, ARA, reel 504.

[155] 'Millions of Children in Immediate Peril of Death', *Daily Telegraph*, 25 Nov. 1921; 'News from Relief Areas', *The Record* 2, no. 5 (1921); 'Cheap Publicity', ibid.; Weardale to *Daily Mirror* editor, 10 Feb. 1922, SCF, reel 30.

be fed for twenty weeks for that sum.[156] It was also pointed out that £1 covered the costs for a child for five months.[157] In a simplified version, the time span was not stated and the slogan went: 'Twenty shilling will save a life'. The SCF described itself in this context as unique in humanitarian history for being able to operate effectively with such an 'amazingly low sum'.[158] Critics, however, doubted this assertation. Based on the previous figures, the *Daily Express* calculated the amount per child at 1½ pence per day after overhead costs, and asked sardonically, 'How much food can be provided for this sum?'.[159] The ARA also doubted the SCF figures (at least internally) and assumed that considerably fewer children were being fed than officially claimed.[160]

Nevertheless, SCF and ARA figures were similar, the latter claiming that 'one dollar will feed a child for a month' (about 5 s in 1922).[161] This figure was rarely made public, as the ARA did not launch fundraising campaigns. Previous research has not questioned the amount; both the SCF and the ARA figures appear roughly adequate.[162]

Minor groups, especially those not affiliated with an umbrella organisation, had more difficulty keeping their expenditures per saved person low. In an appeal, the Federation for Ukrainian Jews (FUJ) promised that 'the sum of £2. 6s will keep a Jewish soul alive for one month'.[163] The FSR could only promise to feed a child for US$2 per month, calculating in other appeal contexts 10 ¢ per meal, which would amount to US$3 per month on a diet of one ration daily.[164] Donations to the FSR were accordingly only one-half (or one-third) as cost-effective as donations to the SCF or ARA, if one solely considers the stated money-per-life ratio. For many organisations and committees, the most efficient alternative to undertaking relief work themselves, therefore, was to buy ARA remittance packages (see Figure 5.4).[165] For political reasons, this was not an option for the FSR.

While organisations advertised low per capita costs, they boasted of impressively high total figures in their intermediate and final reports.[166] However,

[156] 'Links with Saratov – The Hundred Pound Roll of Honour', *The Record* 2, no. 8 (1922) and *The Record* 2, no. 10 (1922); 'A Suggestion to Public Schools', *The Record* 2, no. 9 (1922); 'SCF Kitchen Contact Scheme', *Daily Telegraph*, 25 Nov. 1921.
[157] Article from *De Telegraaf*, 22 Feb. 1922, SCF, reel 30.
[158] 'The Famine Film and the Future of Europe', *The Record* 2, no. 12 (1922).
[159] *Daily Express*, 17 Feb. 1922.
[160] Quinn to London office, 11 Mar. 1922, ARA, reel 115, and district supervisor Kinne to Haskell, 19 Nov. 1921, ibid.
[161] Cablegram by Baker, 14 Dec. 1921, ARA, reel 11.   [162] Patenaude, *Big Show*, 362.
[163] Advertisement 'Food or Death', *Jewish Chronicle*, 4 Aug. 1922, ARA, reel 115.
[164] 'Soviet Russia Calls'; 'A Million Meals for a Million Russian Orphans this Christmas', *Soviet Russia* 7, no. 11 (1922).
[165] Gay to Brown, 3 Jan. 1923, ARA, reel 115; Page to Brown, 17 Jan. 1923, ibid.
[166] 'The ARA Russian Operation at Glance', paper by Communication Division, 9 June 1923, ARA, reel 548.

terms like 'handled relief' or 'administered relief' in such reports indicate that organisations also distributing relief on behalf of others (like the SCF, the Quakers, or the ARA) often included those contributions as part of their own accounts. In the ARA's final statistics, the total tonnage was stated as 740,000 t.[167] This included not only contributions from organisations affiliated with the ARA, but approximately 170,000 t (almost one-quarter) paid for by the Soviet government as well. The SCF's final report was exemplary for its meticulous bookkeeping in support of the claim to have 'administered' 35,476 long tons of food worth £687,518 12 s 1 d.[168] This exceeded their £400,000–500,000 budget (inclusive of overhead expenditures) for Russian relief, as estimated earlier. The term 'administered' explains the gap: it included food that was contributed by Nansen's ICRR and by the British Russian Famine Relief Fund (RFRF). Nearly two-fifths of the tonnage came from the two organisations cited (see Table 5.4) and accounted for the more than thirty-five million adult rations listed in the report. As the ICRR likewise included relief goods 'administered by the SCF' in its own statistics (under the category 'despatched by ICRR'), this double accounting makes it difficult to obtain an accurate picture of the total relief purchased, administered, and distributed.[169]

In point of fact, the SCF had not provided the 121,339,834 children's rations all by itself that it claimed, as this figure included contributions by various non-British organisations affiliated with the ISCU, as well as donations from Commonwealth countries.[170] Non-British ISCU members and affiliates funded more than 10 per cent of the child feeding programme. Canada's contribution exceeded that of other Commonwealth nations, comprising goods worth more than £100,000 (or nearly 25 per cent of the children's food).[171]

Based on SCF's report, as shown in Table 5.4, less than one-third of the listed goods were purchased with private donations made directly to the SCF. If one excludes adult feeding from the calculation, the number rises to 47 per cent. Lists of donations for the kitchen programme up to July 1922 indicate a corresponding rate of approximately one-half for overseas and ISCU contributions.[172]

---

[167] Surface and Bland, *American Food*, 248. Fisher gives the figure of 718,000 t as the total tonnage (including the Soviet part), see *Famine in Soviet Russia*, 554.

[168] Report on Russia, undated (after summer 1923), SCF, reel 30. One long (or imperial) ton, is equal to 1.016 metric tonnes.

[169] 'Feeding of the Starving Russian Population on August 1st 1922: Organisations Working under the Nansen Agreement', *International Committee for Russian Relief – Information* 30 (30 Aug. 1922), 20. The same problem can be observed regarding US figures, as funds for ARA remitttance or bulk sales, for example, were booked in both the ARA and the buying organisation's account.

[170] This concerns not only national SCF branches, but the Danish, Bulgarian, French, Luxembourgian, Serbo-Croatian, and Belgian Red Cross, and several other organisations.

[171] 'Canada and the Children', *The Record* 2, no. 17 (1922).

[172] Total Money Received for Kitchens, list nos 11, 12, and 13, summer 1922, SCF, reel 30.

Table 5.4 *Origin of donations for food 'administered' by Save the Children Fund.*[173]

	Goods worth (£)	Percentage
Value of goods British Save the Children Fund (SCF) purchased with its own donations (including money collected from dominions and overseas total approx. £50,000)	201,921	29.4
Purchased by SCF with donations from other ISCU national committees for child feeding	75,465	11.0
Contribution of Canadian Committee of SCF for child feeding (purchased in Canada; excluding cash donations from Canada to British SCF)	105,456	15.3
British gifts for child feeding (including government stores and All British Appeal allocation)	42,389	6.2
Australian gifts for child feeding (excluding cash donations)	6,444	0.9
Received from International Committee for Russian Relief for adult feeding	135,077	19.6
Received from Russian Famine Relief Fund for adult feeding	120,764	17.6
Total 'administered' by the SCF	**687,518**	**100**

Figures were also used to illustrate successes. In order not to appear dry or boring, statistics were presented in a way that was intended to be easy to understand. The SCF, for example, compared the quantity of goods it distributed with a 'train 11,135 miles long'. The Communication Division of the ARA used considerable creativity to describe what had been accomplished. The final report informed readers that the American food delivered to Russia was enough to sustain 'every living soul in the British Empire ... for four days, still leaving enough over to give a meal to every inhabitant ... of China'. The milk cans shipped to Russia, if lined up, would 'encircle the earth at the equator', and the tea supplied could 'provide a large-sized cup for every man, woman, and child in the United States and England, still leaving enough in the samovars to give Romania a drink'.[174]

All Aid Is Relative

Most organisations saw voluntary food aid not only as saving recipients from starvation, but bringing emotional relief as well. Ruth Fry of the FEWVRC wrote to her American fellow-believer, Wilbur Thomas, that 'the value of our

[173] Report on Russia, undated (after summer 1923), SCF, reel 30.
[174] 'The ARA Russian Operation at Glance', paper by Communication Division, 9 June 1923, ARA, reel 548.

work is not measured purely by its size'.[175] The ARA claimed that food parcels 'have an immense moral value', and the SCF stated that 'every gift given in love is a talisman that awakes kind feelings'.[176] The SCF further suggested that gifts from people who themselves were in difficult straights would convey a moral uplift beyond the cash value of their contributions.[177]

The paradigm of those-who-do-not-have-but-give-anyway was widespread. Stories of self-sacrifice reached newspaper readers in the form of children who sold juice, collected mushrooms, or did gardening work to obtain money to donate. A little boy wanted to give his teddy bear or his bike to a hungry child in Russia. An inmate wished to donate a year's salary.[178] Sick, poor, and elderly people also were among disadvantaged groups who contributed. Their stories suggested that the value of a gift could not only be calculated in monetary terms, but determined by the circumstances of the donor as well. Even ARA officials, who normally dismissed small-scale campaigns as an ineffective 'drop in the bucket',[179] acknowledged that the moral capital certain kinds of fundraising and relief accrued might sometimes outweigh economic inefficiency. An example are the travels of the 'Russian Rag Doll Vera' – a handmade toy that the Central Institute for the Dumb and Deaf in Petrograd had given 'to the children of America' as an expression of gratitude. After extensive preparations, Vera toured the USA for one year, bringing in contributions totalling US$245, or roughly the same amount it cost to send her around.[180]

Organisations that depended on a large number of private contributions, rather than major donors and governmental aid, were especially inclined to motivate their audiences by assigning a moral, emotional, or even political value to the gifts they received. The WIR campaign in Germany, for example, claimed that 'every Mark from a worker carried more political weight than half a million from the bourgeoisie' (see also Figure 5.5).[181] Such meta-value was sometimes also ascribed to aid by the receiving parties. In a speech to high-

[175] Fry to Thomas, 31 Aug. 1921, cited in Daniel Roger Maul, 'Selling "Red" Relief: American Quakers and Famine Relief in the Soviet Union 1921–1923'. Paper presented at the workshop Brokers of Aid: Humanitarian Organizations between Donors and Recipients, Södertörn University, 12–13 June 2014.

[176] Committee of Russian representatives to ARA, asking to continue food remittance programme, 9 May 1922, ARA, reel 11. Russian Financial, Industrial and Commercial Association Paris to Hoover, 15 May 1922, ibid.; 'Every Loving Gift a Talisman', The Record 2, no. 4 (1921).

[177] 'The Lure of the Suffering Child', The Record 3, no. 1 (1922): 57.

[178] 'Bright Ideas', The Record 2, no. 4 (1921); 'National Office Notes', Soviet Russia 6, no. 3 (1922); 'State Salaries Go to Russian Relief', Soviet Russia 6, no. 10 (1922).

[179] Haskel to Brown, 29 Nov. 1921, ARA, reel 115.

[180] Murphy (Communication Division) to ARA New York, 16 Mar. 1922, ARA, reel 498; Walker to Dailey, 25 May 1923, ARA, reel 499; Direction for Vera's Travel, undated draft, ARA, reel 499; ARA to Deaf and Dumb Institute NY, 10 Apr. 1922, ARA, reel 498.

[181] Braskén, International Workers' Relief, 53.

Figure 5.5 Workers' Relief International (WIR) poster from 1922, printed in
Kazan. Inscription reads 'The workers of the world will save the vanguard of
the proletarian revolution from hunger – The working population of the
Russian Soviet Republic!'. Note, WIR/Internationale Arbeiterhilfe flag and
translation in Tatar language, using Arabic letters.
Poster collection, RU/SU 1304, Hoover Institution Archives, https://digitalcollections
.hoover.org/objects/22843

ranking Turkish officials in Ankara, the representative of the Crimean Socialist
Soviet Republic maintained that the Crimean population would 'prefer a
morsel of Turkey to a sack of flour from the Entente', as the 'flour of the
Entente will poison us, while Turkey's smallest relief is our remedy'.[182]

Some organisations magnified their own achievements and depreciated
those of others by not only taking the absolute sums that they collected into
account, but also circumstances such as national wealth, population size, or
political agenda. FSR and WIR, for example, systematically devalued famine
relief from competing non-communist workers' organisations in their public

---

[182] Cited in Kirimli, 'Famine of 1921–22', 57.

statements. WIR organiser Willi Münzenberg pointed out that the few thousand belonging to the communist party in the Netherlands had collected half a million Dutch guilders, while the Amsterdam International, with its 20 million members, only raised 1.4 million.[183] Such comparisons were also used to motivate an organisation's constituents to greater exertions. In early 1922, the FSR announced that US workers' contributions amounted to more than one-third of the combined WIR collection. However, the text continues, if they 'had done equally well as European workers, they would have donated one and a half million dollars', since in Europe wages were lower and unemployment higher.[184] Similarly, in late 1920, Jebb responded to the apology of a French delegate for her country's small contribution in these words: 'It's entirely right ... that England should give far more than France, for her sufferings in the war have been far less; and France by raising a Fund of this nature has lent to the movement a moral support which is of incalculated value.'[185]

The relativity of aid was also maintained by Russian authorities, who kept detailed accounts of imported relief goods. Such a report on the activities of foreign relief agencies registered the import of 540,600 t by those organisations up to August 1922.[186] According to this account, the ARA contributed 81.3 per cent of all imports, and the Nansen mission (including the SCF and British Quakers) 14.2 per cent, figures roughly corresponding with the Western data. However, the Russian accounting went further in listing the percentages of imported goods with regard to their value. In all, 68 per cent of food imports were corn and flour worth 25.8 per cent of the total value, whereas canned milk constituted 5.8 per cent of the total weight, but made up 40 per cent of the value. The account concludes that the composition of items in an average ton of goods from a relief organisation determined its value. Compared in this way, an average ton of food from the ARA was worth only 77 per cent of a ton from the Nansen mission.[187] A Russian newspaper article even claimed that, while ARA relief exceeded that of the communist WIR by far, it differed in quality because the ARA used this 'splendid occasion for throwing away all the defective and rotten goods that have been lying for years in the stores'.[188]

---

[183] 'Eighteenth Session', *Bulletin of the IV Congress of the Communist International*, 28 Nov. 1922. See also 'Famine Relief by the Workers'.

[184] FSR, *Forty Facts*, 3; 'Famine Relief by the Workers'.

[185] Hubert D. Watson, 'Three Days in Geneva', *The Record* 1, no. 2 (1920).

[186] Data in the original are given in the Russian unit of weight *pood*, often transcribed as *poud*, which equals about 16.3 kg.

[187] Report of the representative plenipotentiary on the activities of the foreign relief organizations from beginning of campaign to 1 Aug. 1922, ARA, reel 12.

[188] 'On the Volga', translation of an article in *Izvestia*, 11 Aug. 1922, ARA, reel 14.

Accounting for Gratitude

Just as the moral economy of food aid could not be handled by a business attitude alone, it was insufficient from a relief organisation's perspective to report credit and debit like an ordinary company. As the SCF pointed out, modern humanitarian work required a 'combination of spirit and method'.[189] The donating public expected more than figures of distributed food and numbers of saved children. The ARA informed donors that its food was also carrying American ideals to Russia, engendering gratitude and 'the reward of friendship for generations to come'.[190] The FSR argued similarly, although less subtly, that the names of donors would be 'kept in the archives of the Soviet government, as a testimonial of their active sympathy at an hour of need'.[191] Appeals from Russian individuals and groups likewise often started with expressions of gratitude or descriptions of how a donor changed their lives – before asking for more food.

Sometimes it was the humanitarian agents who conveyed the feelings of recipients to the donors. A Mennonite relief worker put it this way:

Oh, so often I wished that the kind donors in far away America could have been present when the packages arrived, that they might see the beaming faces, and the sparkling eyes of the children, and the tears of gratitude in the eyes of the parents. They would have been richer by one of the purest and most beautiful joys of their whole life.[192]

A representative of a village that received food from the Jewish-American Joint Distribution Committee (JDC) wrote that 'people kiss each other in the streets and tears of joy are flowing'.[193] Europeans and Americans who could not see this with their own eyes depended on such reports in order to feel the 'warm glow', causing many similar descriptions to appear in publications of the major organisations and in the media.

Relief organisations found themselves under a certain amount of pressure to solicit expressions of gratitude and convey them to donors (see Figure 5.6). Contributors were often promised that they could expect letters of thanks and acknowledgement.[194] During its adoption campaign in Germany and Central Europe, the SCF prompted children in camps to write thank you letters to donors.[195] The same request was made to children fed in SCF kitchens. In the Russian case, naming a kitchen after its sponsor strengthened the bond even more.

---

[189] 'The Skill of Love', *The Record* 1, no. 19 (1921).
[190] Stutesman to Sutter, 1 June 1922, ARA, reel 502; Stutesman to Rev. Batt, 31 Aug. 1922, ibid.
[191] FSR, *One Year of Relief Work*, 4.   [192] Hiebert and Miller, *Feeding the Hungry*, 285.
[193] Translation of undated letter by Rabbi Telushkin, Minsk, ARA, reel 569.
[194] Milan (American Library Association) to ARA New York, 1 Aug. 1922, ARA, reel 498; Page to Milan, 4 Aug. 1922, ibid.
[195] Mahood, *Feminsm and Voluntary Action*, 177.

Figure 5.6 Letter of gratitude to the American Relief Administration, depicting a life preserver with the Russian inscription 'Thank you, ARA'. In the middle, a girl leaps across the Atlantic from Russia to the USA to deliver her letter. The drawing appears to have been inspired by a popular advertisement by the Einem Chocolate Factory.
American Relief Administration Russian operational records, Reel 622, Box 521, Hoover Institution Archives

When the ARA's New York office made an applicant–donor match, they wrote to their colleagues in London and Moscow, 'We presume that you will have letters of thanks forwarded to us.'[196] Such requests for upward accountability were also passed on to recipients of aid, causing some irritation. For example, a Russian engineer who had received a food parcel complained, in a letter 'to the Chief of the ARA' about being asked to formulate a letter of thanks, maintaining that it was 'inadmissible to compel anyone to express their gratitude'.[197] The ARA replied that while they indeed had requested their delivery clerks to let recipients know that a letter of gratitude would be

---

[196] Arthur T. Dailey to ARA London office, 6 July 1922, ARA, reel 498.
[197] Zeliksen to ARA, undated (probably June 1922), ARA, reel 58.

appreciated, no one was compelled to do so. Had the delivery clerk shown 'excessive zeal' in this case, they apologised.[198]

Organisations working under the aegis of the ARA regularly demanded proof of gratitude from local supervisors. When the JDC's Strauss received a box full of letters of thanks that the ARA had collected, he found a note inside saying, 'I think your publicity department can get some pretty good stories out of them.'[199]

The JDC initially agreed to a non-sectarian distribution of its contributions (altogether amounting to US$5–6 million).[200] Large amounts were used for general relief, although preferably in regions and cities with a large Jewish population. The JDC hoped that at least half of the food it distributed would reach Jewish children, and that public knowledge about the generosity of the American Jewry would make 'the lot of Jews happier' locally.[201] The JDC leadership also was concerned about receiving 'a reasonable share' of credit for the aid that they were providing. In addition, they saw themselves as owing it to their constituency 'to take every possible step to insure that a fair share of our contribution reaches those for whom our funds are collected'.[202] The ARA promised to only use JDC funds in urban areas, and agreed on measures like placards to make sure the JDC received its 'full credit'.[203] The ARA also pointed out that much of its own general relief had reached the Jewish population.[204]

Smaller organisations that were not able to purchase or distribute relief goods on their own thought it particularly important that they receive a share of appreciation and gratitude for their activities, which took three forms: they could buy aid supplies in bulk sales (US$500 or more) to be distributed by the ARA according to the directives of the purchasing organisation; they could purchase drafts at US$10 each; or they could engage in so-called Eurelcon sales (European Relief Council), that is, buy food at cost from the ARA and distribute it themselves. Bulk and Eurelcon sales were the preferred methods as they provided a record of the food distribution. Members of communities or ethnic groups who bought individual remittance parcels left no systematic trace in the accounts, as their donations were aggregated and assigned to the ARA. For this reason, the Volga Relief Society (VRS) asked the members of German-Russian communities in the USA to notify the VRS of each food draft

[198] Renshaw to Zelikson, 10 July 1922, ARA, reel 58.
[199] Page to Strauss, 10 Apr. 1922, ARA, reel 569.
[200] Acct. Dept. Financial Reports, 4/29/23-3/31/26, JDC Archives, NY AR192132/1/1/7/68a.
[201] Rosenberg/JDC cable, 26 May 1922, ARA, reel 404.
[202] Ibid.; Rosenberg to Lyman Brown, 14 Sep. 1922, JDC Archives, NY AR192132/4/30/3/489. See also Lewis to Rickard, 21 Aug. 1922, ARA, reel 404.
[203] Agreement between ARA and JDC, 4 Aug. 1922, JDC Archives, NY AR192132/4/30/3/489.
[204] Minutes of Meeting between ARA and JDC, 20 Dec. 1922, JDC Archives, NY AR192132/4/30/3/489.

that they had purchased. The ARA, approving this strategy, requested that local branches mention their parent organisation when purchasing in bulk (something apparently often neglected).[205]

At the end of the relief operation, the ARA claimed that its relief was a 'miracle of God' for the 'Russian common people', coming to them 'under the stars and stripes'. The ARA not only brought food, but 'demonstrated that at least one organisation could exist and succeed in Russia without submission to dictation'.[206] Another report praised the 'excellence of the organization machinery of the ARA', which was said to have singly 'wiped out famine'.[207]

Not everyone agreed with this assessment. Throughout the operation, the ARA struggled against Soviet authorities who tried to make sure that the Russian people's gratitude towards the USA remained limited. There were some communists, especially at the end of the operation, who were eager to expose 'the wolf of capitalism under the sheepskin of charity'.[208] The consequence was an information war between the ARA and Soviet authorities, during which both groups vyed for the hearts and minds of the Russian population.[209] The Soviet press claimed, for example, that political pressure by the US proletariat had forced the ARA to help Russia, and that the class solidarity of farmers was what stood behind the donations of corn.[210] Münzenberg even suggested that most of the help for the starving actually came from Russia itself.[211] Although this was hardly the case, his claim was not without merit. ARA historian Fisher estimated Russia's contribution to the relief effort in cash, services, and facilities at US$14 million.[212] Together with the US$11 million in gold that was shipped to the USA, the Russian government was responsible for US$25 million – almost one-third of the total budget of the relief operation (see Table 5.3).

In addition, Nansen's role was exaggerated, by Russians and Europeans alike, during and after the famine. ARA officers complained that Nansen was

---

[205] *Newsletter Volga Relief Society*, 3 Oct. 1922; *Newsletter Volga Relief Society*, 13 May 1922.
[206] Haskell to Hoover, 27 Aug. 1923, in *Documents of the American Relief Administration*, 650.
[207] 'The ARA Russian Operation at Glance', paper by Communication Division, 9 May 1923, ARA, reel 548.
[208] Patenaude, *Big Show*, 676.
[209] Ibid., 644–53. When, for example, an ARA anti-cholera campaign was announced on Soviet posters in a way that disguised the programme's main donor, the ARA took countermeasures by printing its own posters (District Supervisor Coleman to Moscow, 13 July 1922, ARA, reel 14).
[210] Translation of article 'October, Nansen and the ARA', *Saratov Isvesta*, attached to a letter by District Supervisor Kinne to Moscow office, 10 Oct. 1921, ARA, reel 14; Coleman to Moscow office, 5 May 1922, ibid.; Patenaude, *Big Show*, 645. See also Vogt, *Nansens kamp*, 302–3.
[211] Eighteenth Session, *Bulletin of the IV Congress of the Communist International*, 28 Nov. 1922.
[212] Fisher, *Famine in Soviet Russia*, 553 (table I, footnote 1). This sum includes dock workers, transportation, electricity, water, gasoline, housing, travel costs, telephone, telegraph, and the like.

'helping the British with one hand and the Soviets with the other, and slapping the ARA with the back of both hands'.[213] Despite the fact that the ICRR and its affiliated organisations were responsible for little more than 10 per cent of the international relief programme, Nansen received more credit for his engagement than Hoover, not the least in the form of a Nobel Peace Prize.[214] The literature, both in Europe and in the Soviet Union, has overstated Nansen's role for decades.[215]

5.4   More than 'Dollars' and 'Per Cent': Ethiopia

Media and political interest placed extensive accountability requirements on organisations delivering famine relief to Ethiopia, Eritrea, and Tigray after October 1984. The scale of the disaster, coupled with growing public outrage about delayed international action in the face of abundance elsewhere, presented all parties with the challenge of proving that money pledged would be spent not only in an appropriate manner, but also as speedily as possible. Therefore, 'the rush was *to be seen* to deliver food', as the public, the media, and politicians came to demand visible action to salve their consciences over the earlier inadequate response.[216] However, despite vocal proclamations about public accountability, two newcomers to humanitarian aid, Band Aid and USA for Africa, resisted compliance with established accounting standards and charity regulators. At the same time, the 1980s was the decade in which evaluation became part of the toolbox of aid agencies. The United Nations (UN) World Food Programme (WFP), for example, conducted its first self-evaluation in 1985 in connection with the African Food Crisis.[217] While the suspicion with which major donors held the Ethiopian government and the rebel forces alike increased pressure for more rigorous accounting criteria than in other disasters, the political situation meant that many donor governments remained reluctant to enquire too closely into the potential effect of the resettlement programme or what might result from failure to ensure adequate aid to Tigray and Eritrea.

The difficulties of allocating famine relief in a country divided by civil war created the space for new auditors of aid, as most Western donors eschewed the Ethiopian government's distribution channels in favour of provision through voluntary organisations. At the same time, the work of aid agencies was subjected to extensive monitoring by the Ethiopian Relief and

---

[213] Wilkinson to Baker, 30 Aug. 1921, ARA, reel 549.   [214] Vogt, *Nansens kamp*, 256–62.
[215] For a brief historiographical overview, see Carl Emil Vogt, 'Fridtjof Nansen og kampen mot hungersnøden i Russland 1921–23', *Nordisk Øst-forum* 16, no. 2 (2002), 183–93.
[216] de Waal, 'Humanitarian Carnival', 52. Italics in original.
[217] Shaw, *World's Largest Humanitarian Agency*, 66.

Rehabilitation Commission (RRC). Each organisation was required to submit plans, budgets, quarterly and annual reports for scrutiny, and had to grant the RRC the right to review and verify its accounts.[218] However, the RRC itself had no procedure for accounting to international donors on how it had used the food aid it received.[219] Therefore, Jansson's UN Office for Emergency Operations in Ethiopia (OEOE) was described as the international community's 'auditor', a final check that the receipt and distribution of pledged grain and relief goods was, to the extent possible, as donors intended.[220] Similarly, consortia working with the liberation fronts, like the Emergency Relief Desk (ERD), conducted extensive monitoring, assessment, and evaluation work that proved more acceptable to donors than the reassurances of the Eritrean Relief Association (ERA) or the Relief Society of Tigray (REST) themselves.[221]

Such assurances were given without the major donors ever having questioned the fundamental assumptions of the wider effort. MSF, for example, argued in a 1986 report that 'donors have shown hardly any curiosity' about the use of food aid in Ethiopia, and responded to accusations of abuse by only superficial investigations.[222] Cultural Survival similarly lamented the 'subtle yet highly effective silence that surrounded the transfer of unprecedented amounts of relief supplies into Ethiopia'.[223] Only a small group of agencies that were mostly non-operational was committed to raising awareness of the manipulation of aid by the Ethiopian regime. Their goal was to promote greater accountability to aid recipients. The majority of aid providers preferred to focus on the job of delivering relief. In Italy, where corruption and political considerations influenced the state allocation of famine relief, some voluntary organisations tried unsuccessfully to take on a supervisory role and hold government spending to account on behalf of the public.[224]

Accounting for aid to Ethiopia in 1984–5 was a 'demanding task', as commentators noted at the time. As a result, total figures were highly unreliable. In the mid-1980s, a 'harmonised' system of accounting remained a low priority, even for organisations within a single legal jurisdiction.[225] Overall, USAID calculated that the total cost of international emergency assistance supplied by private and government donations came to more than US$2 billion (see Table 5.5). USAID's final disaster report is also one of the few sources

---

[218] 'General Agreement for Undertaking Relief and/or Rehabilitation Activities in Ethiopia by Non-governmental Organisations', Nov. 1984, CARE 1220/16.
[219] Gill, *Year in the Death*, 141.   [220] IIED, *African Emergency*, 37.
[221] Duffield and Prendergast, *Without Troops*, 8.   [222] Jean, *Bon Usage*, 36.
[223] Clay and Holcomb, *Politics and the Ethiopian Famine*, 6.
[224] 'La Cartias è disposta a collaborare con Forte', *La Repubblica*, 7 June 1985; Pietro Veronese, 'Forte dà 400 miliardi all Somalia', *La Repubblica*, 21 Jan. 1986.
[225] IIED, African Emergency, 296–8.

Table 5.5 *Food aid commodities allocated via the Ethiopian Relief and Rehabilitation Commission and voluntary agencies, 1985–6 (tonnes).*[226]

Donor	Food aid commodities allocated via RRC, fiscal years 1985 and 1986	Food aid commodities allocated via voluntary organisations, fiscal years 1985 and 1986	Grand total	Percentage of total food aid
US government	50,000	729,748	779,748	41
European Economic Community (EEC) and member states				30
EEC	245,603	109,541	355,144	
Belgium	24	15,033	15,057	
Denmark	–	1,852	1,852	
France	9,230	8,043	17,273	
Federal Republic of Germany	6,938	64,107	71,045	
Greece	7,540	–	7,540	
Ireland	–	1,543	1,543	
Italy	9,477	14,888	24,365	
Netherlands	282	10,556	10,838	
Spain	358	5,279	5,637	
UK	25,338	21,576	46,914	
Canada	75,472	55,922	131,394	7
Other Organisation for Economic Co-operation and Development states				6
Australia	6,934	28,468	35,402	
Austria	8,000	4,821	12,821	
Finland	–	4,958	4,958	
Iceland	–	64	64	
Japan	–	10,063	10,063	
New Zealand	–	140	140	
Norway	9,500	513	10,013	
Sweden	23,000	11,323	34,323	
Switzerland	–	4,196	4,196	
Warsaw Pact countries	24,003	930	24,933	1
Other governments	57,315	15,145	72,460	4
World Food Programme	61,558	39,439	100,997	5
Private donors	17,340	89,679	107,019	6

to acknowledge the significant contributions raised by Ethiopian-based organisations, including churches, police and army units, peasant associations, and overseas embassy staff, although the report was unable to arrive at an

[226] Compiled from data in USAID, *Final Disaster Report*, 38-38A.

overall amount for such aid.[227] The RRC itself calculated such home-grown aid at 2.6 million birr in cash and 32 million birr in kind, raised between December 1984 and August 1985 (in all US$17 million, according to the official exchange rate).[228] In fact, apart from the USAID report, which does not include accurate figures on private donations, it is rare to find accounting tallies that relate solely to aid for Ethiopia. It is difficult to separate the Horn of Africa, or Africa-at-large, from the rest of an organisation's global activities. In part, this may be due to accounting standards that did not require a geographical breakdown of expenditures, lingering colonial attitudes towards the continent of 'Africa', and a preference for unrestricted fundraising income. In addition, organisations operated with different fiscal years, making year-to-year comparisons difficult, and rarely distinguished between relief, rehabilitation, and development activities. As in earlier crises, the determination of commodity values is also especially problematic when seeking to make comparisons.

The best set of sources on famine relief income and expenditure in the 1980s are (a) the annual reports of individual voluntary organisations; (b) data collected by national umbrella bodies (e.g., InterAction in the USA or the Disasters Emergency Committee (DEC) in the UK); (c) evaluations published by various governmental or inter-governmental bodies (including USAID and the UN); and (d) retrospective histories of key consortia or partnerships.[229] Newspapers and magazines have also examined spending as part of their wider investigations into relief campaigns. In the summer of 1985, for example, the development weekly, *New Internationalist*, conducted a survey into accounting practices of UK voluntary organisations, noting that 'allocating of spending between budget headings can be very arbitrary'.[230] In the USA, the *Los Angeles Times* sought to hold the so-called pop charities to account for poor financial reporting.[231]

Impact of the Response on Voluntary Organisations

The international response to famine in Ethiopia is part of a long tradition of public generosity during major emergencies. In the 1980s, however, aid agencies were ready to presume donor fatigue after a succession of high-profile appeals in the previous decade (including campaigns for Ethiopia and Cambodia) and were surprised at the magnitude of public contributions

---

[227] USAID, *Final Disaster Report*, 9.   [228] Clarke, *Resettlement and Rehabilitation*, 33.
[229] For example, Solberg, *Miracle in Ethiopia;* Duffield and Prendergast, *Without Troops.*
[230] 'Accounting for Aid', *New Internationalist*, June 1985, 10–11.
[231] Dennis McDougal, 'Two Years Old and Still Accounting', *Los Angeles Times*, 4 Jan. 1987; Dennis McDougal, 'LA to Seek Accounting from Three Pop Charities', *Los Angeles Times*, 26 Mar. 1987.

prompted by media coverage in October 1984.[232] Commentators suggested that the potential for even greater involvement on the part of some donor publics, such as in Sweden, was missed because of a prevailing discourse of negativity towards fundraising for disasters.[233] The UN's own evaluation of the relief operation in Africa concluded that the cynical attitude of certain officials led many to dismiss what was in fact 'outstanding' public generosity.[234] Jansson himself expressed an official's ambivalence towards money raised by the public around the world, which he regarded as having little impact on the overall aid programme in 1984–5. He felt it was wrong to give the general public the impression that the responsibility for emergency aid lay with individuals or private groups 'when it should be mainly with governments'. However, his assertion that the amount raised by efforts like Band Aid represented only a 'tiny fraction' of the more than US$1 billion worth of relief funded by governments in 1984–5 is questionable.[235]

USAID judged that it was not possible to produce an accurate estimate of privately raised funds, but estimated that 'it is undoubtedly in the tens of millions of dollars'.[236] This is a conservative figure as the total donated to existing voluntary organisations by the public around the world, and through special campaigns like Band Aid, while hard to calculate, amounts to hundreds of millions of dollars. In the UK, for example, the public had donated almost £100 million by September 1985.[237] InterAction estimated that private donations in the USA totalled US$250 million, excluding all government relief grants and goods. Band Aid had raised US$144 million by 1991. Canada similarly experienced a very high level of public engagement: a poll conducted in February 1986 found that 56 per cent of all respondents had donated something to African famine relief over the previous year, and 10 per cent had been directly involved in the fundraising.[238] In our calculation, funds raised through expressive and participatory methods such as telethons, charity single recordings, and benefit concerts alone totalled over US$270 million (see Table 5.6), not counting sums remitted directly to voluntary organisations or umbrella collections like the DEC.

In 1984–5, all voluntary organisations working on famine in Africa saw rapid and impressive growth in income, with significant contributions coming

---

[232] Dodd, 'Oxfam's Response', 37.

[233] Eva Häggman, 'Varför fick inte vi också ge pengar?', *Aftonbladet*, 17 July 1985.

[234] IIED, *African Emergency*, 22.   [235] Jansson, 'Emergency Relief', 27.

[236] USAID, *Final Disaster Report*, 20.

[237] Charities Aid Foundation, *Charity Statistics 1984/5* (Tonbridge: Charities Aid Foundation, 1985), 9; DEC, 'Fundraising for Famine in Africa by British Public Channelled through Voluntary Relief and Development Agencies', Dec. 1985, CA 4/A/16.

[238] IIED, *African Emergency*, 251, 260.

Table 5.6 *Expressive fundraising, mid-1980s.*[239]

Event/activity	Time	Sum raised in original currency	Equivalent US$ (1985)
Live Aid concerts and associated income, not including the USA	July 1985–early 1986	Reported in US$	80,000,000
USA for Africa (single sales and associated activities)	Across period 1985–7	Reported in US$	58,000,000
Tag für Afrika telethon	Jan. 1985	125 million DM	39,500,711
Sport Aid	Apr. 1986–Jan. 1987	Reported in US$	32,000,000
Live Aid Foundation (Live Aid concerts and associated income raised in the USA)	July–Jan. 1987	Reported in US$	27,300,000
One for Africa, day of action in the Netherlands	Nov. 1984	81 million guilders	23,990,759
'Do They Know It's Christmas?' single	Nov. 1984–June 1985	Reported in US$	8,000,000
Chanteurs sans Frontières	To Nov. 1985	10 million francs*	1,114,107
'Tears Are Not Enough' charity single in Canada	1985	Can$ 3.2 million	2,343,979
Tam Tam pour L'Ethiopie	To Nov. 1985	1.6 million francs	178,257
'People Who Care' telethon event in Sweden	Nov. 1984	500,000 SEK	58,237
Total			**272,486,050**

*10 million francs remitted to Médecins Sans Frontières by November 1985, although overall income for Chanteurs sans Frontières widely reported as approx. 23 million francs (unverified).

from outside their traditional support base.[240] This influx of funds resulted in challenges of accounting to the new donor constituencies for aid. The largely unsolicited donations can best be understood in relation to the size of an organisation's normal operating budget.[241] In the UK and the USA,

---

[239] Conversion at month average rates for relevant month, or yearly average. Efforts to verify the sums mentioned have not always been successful; where exact figures are missing, estimates are reported. Band Aid, *With Love*; 'Tears Are Still Not Enough: 30 Years Later', available at www.cbc.ca/news/politics/tears-still-are-not-enough-30-years-later-1.2949836 (accessed 29 June 2019); USA for Africa, *Memories and Reflections;* Letter to Lady Marre, 17 Jan. 1985; BBC Written Archives; 'Stau und Rückstau', *Der Spiegel*, 8 Apr. 1985, 28–9; Anders Medin, 'Ricky spolar julen – startar jätteinsamling för Etiopien', *Aftonbladet*, 23 Dec. 1984; 'Bilan Financier', *Médecins Sans Frontières Special Ethiopie*, Dec. 1985, 7; McDougal, 'Two Years Old'.

[240] Joseph Berger, 'Offers of Aid for Stricken Ethiopia Are Pouring into Relief Agencies: Thousands Offer Aid to Ethiopian Famine Victims', *New York Times*, 28 Oct. 1984; Lutherhjälpen, *Utmaningen från Afrika: Lutherhjälpens årsbok 1985* (Uppsala: Lutherhjälpen, 1985), 47–8.

[241] IIED, *African Emergency*, 260.

organisations saw their income increase two- or three-fold, meaning many, like Oxfam, moved into 'an entirely different financial league'.[242] In the USA, Catholic Relief Services (CRS) received US$37 million in private donations in 1984, growing to US$50 million in 1985.[243] CARE had to employ a double shift to issue receipts to donors. In January 1985, it reported holding record sums in its bank account that were largely collected even before signing an agreement with the RRC to undertake relief work in Ethiopia. New donors were recruited and existing supporters increased their contributions; the average single donation to CARE more than doubled from US$11 to US$25 during the famine crisis.[244]

The dramatic rise in donations also had a great impact on smaller agencies. In the UK, War on Want's income grew from £1.7 million in fiscal year 1983/4 to £5.8 million in 1984/5, and its membership doubled (see Figure 5.7).[245] Save the Children's receipts grew from £16.5 million to £42.5 million over the same period, and its donors also doubled.[246] The growth was less spectacular in Sweden, where the income of Rädda Barnen (Save the Children, Sweden) climbed from 129 million kronor in 1983 to 145 million in 1984. However, more significant changes were seen in a 'wave of compassion' that resulted in increased donations from individuals.[247] Rädda Barnen had collected over 20 million kronor for Ethiopia by February 1985. The aid organisation of the Swedish Church, Lutherhjälpen, raised approximately 50 per cent more from July to December 1984 compared with the same period twelve months earlier.[248] Regular donations also increased alongside one-off sums given to the famine campaign.[249] Although the public response to the African crisis was more muted in France, MSF France and MSF Belgium also raised two to three times more from private donations than ever before.[250] This growth in income presented organisations with challenges on how to spend what were often restricted funds. Donations were sometimes earmarked for feeding programmes that the agency did not even operate, and difficulties arose in meeting donor expectations of how rapidly funds could be put to work and make a difference.[251]

By the 1980s, the trend in charity annual reports was to produce short, easy-to-digest, illustrated formats. They often contained photographs of

[242] Black, *Cause for Our Times*, 264.   [243] IIED, *African Emergency*, 231.

[244] Minutes of the Board of Directors for CARE, 9 Jan. 1985, 5, CARE 1174; Minutes of the Board of Directors for CARE, 13 Nov. 1985, 3, CARE 1174.

[245] *War on Want Annual Report 1984–85*, 1.

[246] *Save the Children Annual Report, 1984–1985*, 24.

[247] 'Rädda Barnens Årsrapport 1984', *Barnen & Vi* 24, no. 2, 1985, 21.

[248] Lutherhjälpen, *Utmaningen från Afrika*, 47.

[249] Lutherhjälpen, *Låt rätten flöda fram! Lutherhjälpens årsbok 1986* (Uppsala: Lutherhjälpen, 1986), 61.

[250] Binet, *Famine and Forced Relocations*, 108.   [251] IIED, African Emergency, 270.

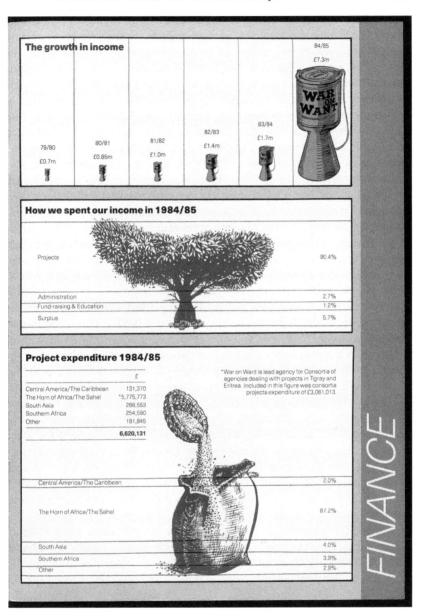

The growth in income

79/80	80/81	81/82	82/83	83/84	84/85
£0.7m	£0.85m	£1.0m	£1.4m	£1.7m	£7.3m

How we spent our income in 1984/85

Projects	90.4%
Administration	2.7%
Fund-raising & Education	1.2%
Surplus	5.7%

Project expenditure 1984/85

	£
Central America/The Caribbean	131,370
The Horn of Africa/The Sahel	*5,775,773
South Asia	266,553
Southern Africa	254,590
Other	191,845
	6,620,131

*War on Want is lead agency for Consortia of agencies dealing with projects in Tigray and Eritrea. Included in this figure was consortia projects expenditure of £3,081,013.

Central America/The Caribbean	2.0%
The Horn of Africa/The Sahel	87.2%
South Asia	4.0%
Southern Africa	3.9%
Other	2.9%

FINANCE

Figure 5.7 Explaining income and expenditure, War on Want Annual Report 1984–5.
Reproduced courtesy of War on Want

development and aid workers in action, alongside maps and tables listing relief goods. Reflecting the language used in appeals, annual reports sought to account for each pound, dollar, or krona entrusted to the organisation by donors. However, since few supporters were likely to seek out audited accounts with their full breakdowns, the short-form accounts utilised simple graphics (such as images of piles of coins) to explain spending. Sources of income become opaque in such quasi-accounts, enabling organisations to blur public donations, legacy income, government grants, joint appeals, and trading revenue. Oxfam, for example, highlighted income from its charity shops and downplayed government grants. This kind of accounting presentation also allows organisations to selectively illustrate areas of spending by giving them their own budget line. Oxfam regularly included 'blankets and clothing' as a separate type of expenditure, even though the amount was negligible compared to such a catch-all as 'grants to overseas programmes', which were not broken down further.[252] Established organisations also made use of the media to help report on their work, collaborating with broadcasters eager for stories, particularly in the wake of Live Aid. Feeding shelters, for example, provided 'accessible, visible evidence' of an organisation's work.[253] The International Committee of the Red Cross produced a film called *Strategy for Salvation* about its operation in Ethiopia and intended for distribution to the public via its national societies.[254]

Accounts can thus conceal as much as they reveal. In a typical instance, the British government in August 1985 granted £1.47 million to Christian Aid for the purchase and distribution of 5,600 t of wheat to rebel-held areas of Eritrea and Tigray. As this was against official diplomatic policy, Christian Aid agreed that the donation would receive no publicity and the purpose would not be mentioned in its annual report. While the sum would have to be listed in the accounts, there would be no reference to its use for cross-border aid supplies.[255] Similarly, War on Want's failure to make a clear distinction between its own funds and those of the Tigray Transport and Agriculture Consortium in its reporting was one reason behind the 1988 decision of the other consortium members to revoke its lead agency status.[256]

Although organisations were not required to provide a breakdown of expenditures by geographical region, the prominence of income for disaster relief in the mid-1980s meant that most groups were concerned to account for spending on famine relief in Ethiopia and elsewhere in greater detail. Table 5.7

[252] *Oxfam Review 1985/6*, back cover, MS Oxfam COM 1/1/2/1.
[253] William Shawcross, 'Report from Ethiopia: An Update on the African Nation's Catastrophic Famine', *Rolling Stone*, 15 Aug. 1985.
[254] ICRC, *Annual Report 1985* (Geneva: ICRC, 1986), 24.
[255] 'Food Aid for Eritrea and Tigray: Meeting with Christian Aid', 1 Aug. 1985, FCO 31/4614, 2.
[256] Borton, *Changing Role*, 82.

Table 5.7 *Expenditures of selected voluntary organisations on famine relief in Ethiopia.*[257]

Organisation	Time period covered	Total expenditure on relief for Ethiopia (including Eritrea and Tigray)	Equivalent in US$
International Committee of the Red Cross	1 Jan. 1984–31 Dec. 1985	131,852,379 SF	53,733,955
Oxfam*	1 Apr. 1984–31 Mar. 1986	£21,700,000	27,877,698
Band Aid	1 Jan. 1985–late 1986	US$25,611,437	25,611,437
Save the Children (UK)	1 Apr. 1984–31 Mar. 1986	£13,629042	17,509,047
War on Want**	1 Apr. 1984–31 Mar. 1986	£10,291,648	13,221,542
Lutherhjälpen	1 July 1984–31 Dec. 1985	61,626,050 SEK	7,168,570
Médecins Sans Frontières	1 Apr. 1984–30 Nov. 1985	52,406,910 francs	5,838,690
Rädda Barnen	1 Jan. 1984–31 Dec. 1985	41,105,900 SEK	4,781,591

*Oxfam's expenditure here also includes work in Sudan.
**War on Want's expenditure includes funds of the Eritrean Inter-Agency Agricultural
  Consortium and Tigray Transport and Agricultural Consortium, for which it was a lead agency.

shows expenditures in Ethiopia, Eritrea, and Tigray (and in some cases in Sudan) by selected voluntary organisations. These funds derived from a variety of sources, including public donations and grants from national governments or the European Economic Community (EEC). Techniques were developed to manage donors' expectations about what impact their contributions would make. Language used to convey the scale and complexity of the emergency reflected that of the original appeals.[258]

Voluntary organisations believed subsequent giving depended on an understanding of impact, and so agencies evolved different strategies for accounting to diverse groups of donors. Organisations primarily known for their development work, rather than emergency assistance, used annual reports and direct mailings to justify an apparent shift in priorities, while at the same time seeking to reassure long-term supporters.[259] Oxfam noted it had been 'compelled' to spend 69 per cent of its income in 1984/5 on emergency relief (compared to 33 per cent in 1983/4 and 20 per cent in 1982/3), but argued that an overall increase in income would mean more money for development.[260]

---

[257] Sources: Organisational annual reports; Band Aid, *With Love*. Currency converted to USD at yearly average for 1985.
[258] *Save the Children Annual Report 1984–1985*, 3.
[259] Ibid.; Lutherhjälpen, *Utmaningen från Afrika*, 33.
[260] *Oxfam Review 1984/5*, 1; *Oxfam Review 1982/3*; *Oxfam Review 1983/4*, MS Oxfam COM 1/1/2/1.

Newsletters sent to regular subscribers focused on long-term development projects, but communications with new donors presented more simplistic 'before' and 'after' stories. In one leaflet that was part appeal, part narrative, Oxfam used photographs of the same mother and child three weeks apart, after they had benefitted from a feeding programme in Bora, Ethiopia.[261] Similarly, providing lists of donated goods was an easy way to suggest impact. Oxfam's annual report for 1985/6 included a table of items sent to Ethiopia and Sudan. It listed 321 t of its branded 'Oxfam biscuits', 102 feeding kits, 10 Land Rovers, 75,000 identity bracelets, 16,000 t of wheat, and 700 rolls of plastic sheeting.[262]

While often described as a post-1945 phenomenon, the adoption of businesslike administrative, banking, marketing, and fundraising practices across voluntary organisations has its roots in the nineteenth century.[263] It was a notable feature of humanitarian organisations that emerged during and after the First World War, and was further propelled at a time of expressive humanitarianism by the enhanced resources of the 1984–5 famine. The growth in income in the 1980s enabled the recruitment of additional highly skilled staff with expertise in accountancy, marketing, and computer use – particularly in European organisations, which lagged behind the USA in this respect. Band Aid sought to 'bring unrelated business acumen to the problem of relief aid' by appointing a board of trustees composed of television executives, media professionals, and lawyers, and by recruiting volunteers with public relations skills to help run the operation.[264] George Harrison's main advice was that Band Aid should hire 'proper' accountants.[265]

As a relatively small organisation, War on Want was able to employ full-time professional fundraisers for the first time and engaged a high-profile external advertising agency.[266] War on Want's increased activity enabled a headquarters move to larger premises and the establishment of local offices across England and Wales.[267] MSF's fundraising department grew from two to five paid staff members, and a marketing director was employed.[268] Oxfam and others computerised their donor records to increase efficiency and avoid

---

[261] Oxfam, 'People in Crisis' leaflet, MS Oxfam APL 3/6/6.

[262] *Oxfam Review 1985/6*, MS Oxfam COM 1/1/2/1.

[263] For more on this topic, see Roddy, Strange, and Taithe, *Charity Market*; Jones, 'Band Aid Revisited', 195–6; Gabriele Lingelbach, 'Charitable Giving between the State and the Market: West Germany from 1945 to the 1980s', in *German Philanthropy in Transatlantic Perspective: Perceptions, Exchanges and Transfers since the Early Twentieth Century*, eds Gregory R. Witkowski and Arnd Bauerkämper (Cham: Springer, 2016), 160–1.

[264] Band Aid, *With Love*, 40.   [265] Ure, *If I Was*, 156.

[266] 'Fundraising', *War on Want News* 1 (1986); Luetchford and Burns, *Waging the War on Want*, 141.

[267] Luetchford and Burns, *Waging the War on Want*, 141.

[268] Binet, *Famine and Forced Relocations*, 108.

communication errors with supporters.[269] At the same time, CARE was nearing the end of a five-year plan to upgrade its administration systems, including 'office automation', which required new computer hardware, and specialist software packages for fundraising and accounting.[270]

A related development was the move by many organisations to greater monitoring and analysis of the effectiveness of fundraising campaigns. By February 1985, CARE had spent US$400,000 on advertising and direct marketing. It yielded US$5 million of funds earmarked for Ethiopia, an impressive 12.5 return on investment.[271] There was also a rise in the strategic use of magazine and newspaper inserts. From 1984 to 1985, Oxfam raised £1 million for Ethiopia through a selective mailing campaign. At the same time, it carried out its largest ever distribution of appeal inserts in magazines, resulting in nearly 17,000 new covenanters. In the second half of 1985, these Oxfam inserts generated an almost five-fold return on investment.[272] Save the Children worked closely with sponsors and the postal union to secure low-cost delivery of 20 million leaflets and 3 million envelopes, netting £1.5 million in donations.[273] In France, MSF sent a press kit to 1,500 newspapers, of which 150 took up the offer of an insert by March 1985.[274] The significant contribution to famine relief income derived from charitable trading arms and charity shops helped organisations to move towards more professional management.[275] In 1985, Oxfam had such 706 shops across the UK that generated a profit of £14 million that year.[276]

The scale of the response to the famine in Ethiopia also led to renewed attempts at coordination between voluntary aid agencies, both in the field and in donor countries. It was part of a wider goal of demonstrating the humanitarian sector's effectiveness, legitimacy, and accountability to donors. The umbrella group, InterAction, representing 121 US-based organisations, seized the opportunity presented by the African emergency to increase its influence with both the US government and UN agencies. Government endorsement consolidated InterAction's position as a 'legitimate, accountable

[269] Direct mail to Mrs Butterworth, 3 Dec. 1984, MS Oxfam COM 1/1/2/1.
[270] Minutes of the Board of Directors for CARE, 14 Nov. 1984, CARE 1174.
[271] Minutes Joint Meeting of the CARE USA Executive Committee and the Medico Advisory Board, 13 Mar. 1985, 5, CARE 1174.
[272] *Oxfam Review 1984/5*, 4, MS Oxfam COM 1/1/2/1; 'Oxfam: Cold Mailing', 'Oxfam Press Advertising', MS Oxfam APL/2/2/4.
[273] *Save the Children Annual Report, 1984–1985*, 25.
[274] Binet, *Famine and Forced Relocations*, 33.
[275] *Save the Children Annual Report, 1984–1985*, 27; Luetchford and Burns, *Waging the War on Want*, 140. See also Suzanne Horne, 'Charity Shops in the UK', *International Journal of Retail & Distribution Management* 26, no. 4 (1998): 155–61; Field, 'Consumption *in lieu* of Membership'.
[276] *Oxfam Annual Review 1984/5*; Black, *Cause for Our Times*, 261.

organization'.[277] It collected intelligence and convened regular meetings of organisations working in Ethiopia, pushed for greater co-operation between US and European aid agencies, and was widely regarded as having played an effective coordinating role.[278] In Canada, aid organisations formed a coalition called 'Africa Emergency Aid' to unify their response to the crisis. It marked the first time voluntary organisations played an active role in decision-making regarding spending by the Canadian International Development Agency (CIDA).[279] The six self-styled 'Ethiopia organisations' in Sweden came together in a fundraising campaign that explained how their contacts in the field and years of experience justified the support of the public.[280]

While co-operation was not always easy, overcoming differences between agencies increased legitimacy and accountability. Emergency Relief Desk (ERD), for example, celebrated working together 'often against all odds'.[281] In the UK, the DEC also framed itself as an accountable body that took very seriously the task of ensuring donations were spent 'wisely'.[282] In 1985, a conflict arose between the DEC's five members and the wider pool of UK aid organisations over perceived unfair access to the broadcast media, government ministers, and donors. The chairman of Action Aid suggested that having only a small number of agencies involved was 'inefficient as well as unjust' because it did not maximise the response of the British public to emergency appeals.[283] Such claims were rejected because broadcasters preferred working with one body that could 'provide the public with all reasonable guarantees of effective and responsible action'.[284]

Expressive Accounting

The self-styled newcomers to relief, Band Aid and USA for Africa, declared that their work faced greater media and public scrutiny than other agencies, repeatedly stressing this 'unique position' in the aid world. Band Aid also argued that because its income resulted from participatory fundraising activities, its donations held a greater value than would be recognised in the accounts. Thus, the Band Aid Trust suggested an alternative balance sheet when it stated that its contribution could not 'be measured simply in terms of

---

[277] 'Activities of Interaction's Public Outreach Unit', 3, CARE 199.
[278] 'Summary Notes, Meeting Ethiopian Emergency Relief, November 9, 1984', 4; 'Activities of Interaction's Public Outreach Unit', 1–3, CARE 199; IIED, *African Emergency*, 9.
[279] Morrison, *Aid and Ebb Tide*, 234–5.
[280] Ethiopia organisations advertisement in *Expressen*, 3 Nov. 1984, 17.
[281] Duffield and Prendergast, *Without Troops*, xi.
[282] *DEC Handbook*, 1984, no page information; Folder 'Emergency Appeals Policy', BBC Written Archives.
[283] Lees to Young, 29 May 1985, Folder 'Emergency Appeals Policy'.
[284] Young to Lees, 17 Jun. 1985, Folder 'Emergency Appeals Policy'.

Figure 5.8 School pupils at Saladine Nook School, Huddersfield, with their collections of food for School Aid, Oct. 1985.
Image by Mirrorpix, courtesy of Getty Images

the %'s or dollars in the charity's account'.[285] Such moral accounting was a hallmark of the Band Aid Trust, which labelled every plane, ship, and sack of relief goods: 'With love from Band Aid' (see Figure 5.8). In a report that listed the total income from all Band Aid, Live Aid, and Sport Aid fundraising activities from 1984 to 1991 as US$144 million, Geldof asked those who had participated to remember the emotional legacy of their involvement: 'Will you ever forget the gift of a small plastic record in the cold dark Christmas of '84? Will you ever forget singing on a bright summer day in '85? Will your legs not ache in sympathy with the memory of running in the spring of '86?'[286]

Discussions of Band Aid and Live Aid have tended to focus on fundraising rather than expenditure; researchers have noted only the impressive sums *raised* without analysing how funds were *spent*.[287] In part, this reflects Band Aid's reluctance to conform to traditional methods of accounting to donors, or its refusal to comply with charity watchdogs in favour of press releases. Other

---

[285] Band Aid, 'Band Aid Trust/Live Aid Foundation: A Statement of General Policy', CARE 1426.

[286] Band Aid, *With Love*, 3.

[287] Franks, *Reporting Disasters*, 75; Jones, 'Band Aid Revisited', 190; Müller, '"The Ethiopian Famine" Revisited', 67; Philo, 'From Buerk to Band Aid', 122.

participatory fundraisers in the era of expressive humanitarianism, including the UK children's television programme Blue Peter, have acted similarly. Since the 1960s, Blue Peter has developed innovative methods of reporting to its audience such as keeping a visual tally of funds raised via its hallmark 'totaliser'. A Blue Peter broadcast in January 1985, for example, acted as a form of 'annual report', providing viewers with physical evidence of what donations for Ethiopia had bought by filling the television studio with trucks, seeds, tools, and well-digging equipment.[288] Presenter Simon Groom's impassioned voice-over during his visit to Ethiopian relief camps was also a form of emotional accounting to the audience: 'As long as I live, I will never forget the sights and sounds of that feeding centre.'[289]

Similarly, the Band Aid Trust's early press releases containing detailed lists of goods sent on emergency flights and ships served as reports of its work to the public.[290] After Live Aid, a commemorative photo album was published. Like all Band Aid merchandise, its object was to generate income (it was labelled 'This book saves lives'), but it also gave an account of relief undertaken to date.[291] In early 1987, accountant Philip Rusted, responding to criticism that the Band Aid Trust had not filed any returns with the UK Charity Commission since July 1985, promised that a full report of spending would be forthcoming.[292] In fact, it was not until 1992 that 'With Love from Band Aid' was published as a report on grants that Band Aid had made to other organisations since 1985, although once again Band Aid stated that it was 'not a set of accounts'. In the introduction to the report, Geldof stressed Band Aid's focus on achievements, rather than spreadsheets: 'Seven years. You can count them now in trees and dams and fields and cows and camels and trucks and schools and health clinics, medicines, tents, blankets, clothes, toys, ships, planes.'[293]

Both Band Aid and USA for Africa, as organisations rooted in celebrity culture, produced documentaries that took the place of annual reports. They included details on how aid was distributed, facts and figures about sums raised and relief goods supplied, and information on administrative structures and personnel.[294] The Band Aid film *Food and Trucks and Rock 'n' Roll*, was first screened by the BBC in July 1985 as part of the Live Aid concert, although a section discussing the effects of African debt repayments to the West was omitted; following controversy, it was reinstated in a broadcast a

---

[288] Richard Marson, *Blue Peter: Inside the Archives* (Dudley: Kaleidoscope, 2008), 232–3.

[289] Ethiopia III Dubbing Script, Jan. 1985, Blue Peter Production File, 1984–5, no. 17, BBC Written Archives.

[290] Band Aid, 'Total Goods Sent by Band Aid as of 26 June 1985', Press release, 1985.

[291] Peter Hillmore, *The Greatest Show on Earth: Live Aid* (London: Sidgwick and Jackson, 1985).

[292] McDougal, 'Two Years Old'.   [293] Band Aid, *With Love*, 2, 4.

[294] See *Food and Trucks and Rock 'n' Roll*; 'We Are the World'.

year later.[295] The film was also sent to UK schools as part of a School Aid information pack. One question that the film addressed was Geldof's establishment of what appeared to be a permanent new aid agency, despite his highly publicised distrust of voluntary organisations. The Band Aid Trust, Geldof responded, was created to 'enable us to spend the money, the trustees to protect the money in people's interest and the volunteers to act in spending the money'.[296] While the film did discuss some of the media criticism of Band Aid – notably its Sudan trucking operation – it was silent on issues of allocation or monitoring.

In its communications with the public, Band Aid was quick to point out that, in contrast to the established aid world, its organisational overhead was kept to a minimum through the use of free office space and equipment, sponsorship, unpaid staff, and interest income from bank deposits.[297] This was part of keeping a promise made to famine-affected regions that 'every penny would go there'.[298] As Oxfam's Tony Vaux recalled, Geldof had an 'obsession with cost: nothing was to be wasted'.[299] Thus, CARE's initial applications to Band Aid for funding were turned down largely on the grounds of cost, including high salaries and overhead. Reporting to New York, CARE Britain's director judged Band Aid important, but 'unlike other donors... BA [is] very conscious of media attention and cannot be seen to be paying admin costs and high (by UK standards) salaries'.[300] This was frustrating for established organisations with fixed field expenditures in country and costly headquarters to maintain at home.

Band Aid's initial lack of investment in administration and its failure to employ professional staff 'hampered the efficiency of the organisation's spending' and resulted in 'naïve' mistakes, according to a UN evaluation of relief efforts. The report recommended that full overhead should be charged and 'proper explanations' given to the donating public to account for this.[301] Concerns about the Band Aid Trust's ability to manage its finances also caused discontent among its trustees, who were constantly being asked to make spending decisions far outside their areas of expertise: they were 'lamentably short of regular and systematic financial information', as one frustrated board member wrote to Geldof.[302] A set of management accounts was finally circulated to trustees in early September 1985, revealing an unallocated surplus

---

[295] 'In the Air', *Listener*, 3 July 1986; 'In the Air' *Listener*, 12 June 1986. Listener Historical Archive, 1929–91, available at http://tinyurl.galegroup.com/tinyurl/6jHW89 (accessed 29 June 2019).

[296] *Food and Trucks and Rock 'n' Roll.*   [297] Geldof with Vallely, *Is That It?*, 257.

[298] Band Aid, *With Love*, 2.   [299] Vaux, *Selfish Altruist*, 53.

[300] Needham to CARE New York, 26 Dec. 1985, CARE 1241/2.

[301] IIED, *African Emergency*, 215, 220.

[302] Grade to Geldof, 27 Aug. 1985, BBC Written Archives.

of £23.7 million. By late 1985, the scale of the enterprise compelled Band Aid to employ paid field directors and establish a computerised accounting system. However, concerns over poor accounting standards persisted and an independent evaluation of Band Aid's spending was later commissioned.

During the period for which figures are available (1985–91), Band Aid spent US$71.3 million on short-term relief and US$70.2 million on development projects across six African countries. Overheads came to US$2.5 million, but was covered by interest generated from large bank deposits.[303] The greatest beneficiary of aid was Ethiopia, receiving two-fifths (41 per cent) of relief spending and one-third (34 per cent) of development spending. However, against the aid allocated for Ethiopia, Eritrea, and Tigray alone in 1985 and 1986, the overall expenditure (US$25.6 million) is smaller than might have been imagined from the headlines it generated. Band Aid's direct spending in the main crisis year of 1985 included US$6.7 million for thirty-three voyages that brought food, medical supplies, shelter materials, and vehicles to Ethiopia, and US$5.4 million in food aid and additional equipment channelled via the Christian Relief and Development Association (CRDA). Behind the simplistic refrain of 'feed the world' lay the reality that money was spent not so much on food aid, as on a more ambitious programme of rehabilitation, development, and research projects, the last named accounting for US$3.4 million of the long-term spending.

USA for Africa set itself apart from Band Aid by 'the caution, the planning, the (albeit modest) bureaucracy, the hob-nobbing with the great'.[304] With offices in Los Angeles and New York, it maintained close relations with the UN and InterAction. By January 1986, USA for Africa had allocated US$19 million to direct relief, US$24.5 million to long-term recovery and development projects, and US$900,000 to domestic charity programmes in the USA. Many projects aimed at the rehabilitation of those affected by famine and at boosting the resilience of the country by digging wells, improving food storage, and creating horticulture schemes.

Like Band Aid, USA for Africa's grant-making programme became increasingly professionalised and from summer 1986 on, it employed consultants to inspect each initiative its board decided to fund.[305] The African press welcomed the decision to commit significant amounts for rehabilitation and long-term development.[306] However, the first round of grants was criticised by US activists because of the proportion of funding (44 per cent) which had gone to

[303] Figures cited from Band Aid, *With Love*, 10.
[304] Andrew Lycett, 'Songs for Africa with Another Tune', *Times*, 12 July 1985, 10.
[305] USA for Africa, *Memories and Reflections*; USA for Africa Press Release, 5 Mar. 1986, CARE 1241/4; 'Planned Expenditure of USA for Africa', ibid.; Gordon to Davies, 19 June 1986, CARE 1190/24.
[306] Hébert, 'Feed the World', 105.

UN agencies, with only 31 per cent to US-based voluntary organisations and 25 per cent to other parties. A poll commissioned by Save the Children USA found that 56 per cent of those interviewed had assumed all the money raised through the sale of a charity single would go to US-based voluntary organisations. The presumption was that USA for Africa's priority ought to be accountability to those who had bought the recording, or even to the US public-at-large, rather than to the recipients of its funded programmes. The poll results were considered a 'trump card' that could be used to influence USA for Africa's future spending patterns.[307] The organisation also came under greater scrutiny from US charity watchdogs than Band Aid: it was found to be non-compliant with seven voluntary standards for reporting financial information, and faced a potential state law suit for failing to file a financial disclosure statement for 1985.[308]

Voluntary organisations were frustrated by the grant-making practices of USA for Africa, Band Aid, and the Live Aid Foundation because some felt these newcomers had siphoned off money that otherwise would have gone to existing agencies.[309] However, this probably underestimates the capacity of celebrity organisations to stimulate giving by new constituencies and in sustaining interest in the famine over a longer period than might otherwise have been the case.[310] Moreover, the evidence available does not corrobate the speculation that the new trusts 'took all the money'.[311] Although in 1984/5 Band Aid's reported fundraising income of £56.5 million led the UK 'charities league table', a list compiled annually by the Charities Aid Foundation, overall donations to other international aid agencies were also up 163 per cent over the previous year's total. In fact, it was domestic charities in the fields of cancer, older people, youth, and the arts that appear to have suffered the most.[312]

Accountability and Abuse

After October 1984, both the public and the media demanded rapid, visible action in feeding Ethiopia. From 1984 through 1987 and beyond, a continuous preoccupation of the media was that money donated by the public was not being spent quickly enough.[313] This presented a major challenge to many organisations. In April 1985, television and magazines in West Germany

---

[307] Neu to Davies, re: 'USA for Africa', 22 Nov. 1985, CARE 1241/4.
[308] McDougal, 'Two Years Old'.
[309] Neu to Davies, re: 'USA for Africa', 22 Nov. 1985, CARE 1241/4.   [310] Ure, *If I Was*, 157.
[311] 'Oxfam and Band Aid', 1985, MS Oxfam PGR 2/3/10/8.
[312] Charities Aid Foundation, *Charity Statistics 1984/5*, 9.
[313] McDougal, 'Two Years Old'; Steve Coil, 'Live Aid and the Swirl of Criticism', *Washington Post*, 22 Nov. 1985.

raised questions about delays in spending the money raised in January by the Tag für Afrika event, with *Der Spiegel* criticising the often ambiguous nature of charity reporting.[314] In the USA, CRS faced heavy criticism in the summer of 1985 when the *New York Times* accused it of spending less than US$9 million of over US$50 million donated by the US public since the previous October, and of spending too much on administration.[315] The National Conference of Catholic Bishops was forced to appoint a special commission to investigate these charges, and to engage the services of high-profile accountants and lawyers.[316]

The Band Aid Trust faced similar accusations in the UK. A September 1985 article asserted that Live Aid money was 'resting in a high interest rate account'. It also reported the frustrations of voluntary organisations that Band Aid 'will not pass the cash around'.[317] The fear of trial-by-media for misallocated or delayed aid was strong, and some organisations chose to turn down donations rather than face such risks. Others stuck back. In a 1986 press release, USA for Africa answered its critics by stating 'it is our belief that the money can either be spent wisely or spent fast'.[318] The increased pressure to spend funds quickly could contribute to 'genuine moral and management problems' in already overburdened voluntary organisations. However, few such organisations could be held publicly accountable for their mistakes, for only a small number were willing to conduct external evaluations or report openly to donors. According to the UN's assessment of relief work across Africa, a lack of transparency lowered 'confidence in the integrity of NGO operations'.[319]

In Italy, the government's Fondo Aiuti Italani (FAI) came under scrutiny from the media and voluntary organisations. Caritas in Italy, for example, suspected political manipulation of aid and taking bribes, while the media was once again concerned over delays in spending the donated money.[320]

After MSF's expulsion from Ethiopia in December 1985, an event that made headlines around the world, the organisation needed to communicate urgently with its donors. It immediately issued a special edition of its newsletter explaining the reasons for speaking out, and seeking to retain its supporters'

---

[314] 'Stau und Rückstau', *Der Spiegel*, 8 Apr. 1985, 28–9
[315] Ralph Blumenthal, 'Catholic Relief Services Involved in Dispute over Spending of Ethiopia Aid', *New York Times*, 7 Aug. 1985.
[316] Solberg, *Miracle in Ethiopia*, 131.
[317] Geoffrey Levy, 'Is It Time for Saint Bob to Call the Experts?' *Daily Express*, 5 Sept. 1985. Geldof's reply was published the following week under the heading, 'I'm not Wasting Live Aid Money Says Geldof', *Daily Express*, 9 Sept. 1985. See also Gerald Kemp and Hugh Kilmurray, 'Live Aid Cash Still in Bank', *Sunday Express*, 28 Aug. 1985.
[318] USA for Africa Press Release, 5 Mar. 1986.
[319] IIED, *African Emergency*, 270, 16; Vaux, 'The Ethiopian Famine 1984', 37.
[320] 'La Caritas è disposta a collaborare con Forte', *La Repubblica*, 7 June 1985.

trust. The 'Special Ethiopie' issue published a full set of accounts of income and expenditures relating to its work in Ethiopia, Eritrea, and on the Sudanese border (see Figure 5.9). Enabled by a 'huge movement of solidarity' from April 1984 to the end of November 1985, MSF had earmarked just over 52 million francs (US$5.8 million) for this work (see Table 5.6). This included 19 million francs from private donations, 11.5 million francs from the sale of charity records, and 15.5 million francs from the EEC. Expenditures were broken down by salary for staff, medicine/nutrition, and transport costs, while

Figure 5.9 Médecins Sans Frontières special bulletin, Dec. 1985.
Courtesty of Médecins Sans Frontières

administrative costs were listed at 3 per cent.[321] The French organisation, Cimade, had republished the Ethiopian government's criticisms of MSF, notably that the organisation was 'known to waste money'. MSF strongly denied such accusations, pointing out that its work was subject to strict financial control, that its fully audited accounts were available to all, and that it had 'never been the subject of the least criticism'.[322] So confident in MSF's accounting was its president Brauman that he defiantly challenged critics to send their own accountants in to audit MSF's books within forty-eight hours, or face legal action for slander. This dramatic gesture, typical of the hunger for publicity of expressive humanitarianism, reportedly caused the financial director of MSF to 'nearly faint' when she heard of it.[323]

A second major concern was the potential for diversion of aid by the government of Ethiopia (to feed its soldiers and supply forced resettlement programmes) or by the rebel forces. Suspicion of the Marxist government fuelled ongoing media speculation, with some newspapers putting the diversion at about 30,000 t a month.[324] Such claims had a negative impact on fundraising. Vaux maintained that every such news article, however ill-founded, would lead indignant donors to call in and threaten to withdraw their support.[325] Concern that the RRC would not be able to resist political pressure in selecting recipients for relief led the US government to contract CARE to monitor the 'entire process of receipt and distribution of the food' for the small share of relief grain that it allocated to the RRC directly. CARE reported back that the RRC had 'performed commendably'.[326] Another strategy was the deployment of Western observers on aid convoys and at local grain transactions.[327] Max Peberdy, one such observer, pointed out that the need for voluntary organisations 'to show that the "money really does get there"' was for 'the benefit of us in Europe, not for the benefit of those in Tigray'.[328]

Band Aid's director, Penny Jenden, later recalled that the organisation's accounting and monitoring procedures were what she called 'doubly strict' when working with the rebel fronts.[329] Complicated 'switch arrangements' between relief grain and other goods that aimed to ensure timely supply and

[321] 'Bilan Fiancier', *Médecins Sans Frontières Special Ethiopie*, Dec. 1985, 7.
[322] Rony Brauman, 'Expulsion de MSF d'Ethiopie: Réponse à la CIMADE', 1 Jan. 1986, available at www.msf-crash.org/fr/publications/acteurs-et-pratiques-humanitaires/expulsion-de-msf-dethiopie-reponse-la-cimade (accessed 29 June 2019).
[323] Brauman interview, as cited in Binet, *Famine and Forced Relocations*, 99.
[324] Jacques de Barrin, 'Détournements, discriminations et fausses statistiques', *Le Monde*, 23 May 1985; Jean, *Bon Usage*, 37; 'Food Aid Hijacked', *Observer*, 16 Sept. 1984; Anne Dumas and Marcel Olivier, 'Food Aid Resold to Rebel Areas', *Guardian*, 10 Nov. 1984.
[325] Vaux, 'Public Relations Disaster', 24.   [326] USAID, *Final Disaster Report*, 7.
[327] Vaux, *Selfish Altruist*, 55.   [328] Peberdy, *Tigray*, 27.
[329] Jenden, as cited in Paul Vallely, 'Rebels with a Grudge and the Anatomy of a Damning Smear', *Independent Online*, 6 Mar. 2011.

save on transportation costs, and the use of military barracks to store grain, added fuel to allegations of abuse, but investigations by the EEC and the UN failed to find evidence of any large-scale diversion.[330] A Central Intelligence Agency (CIA) report from April 1985 noted that it had been impossible to substantiate the frequent rumours that aid was being intercepted by the Ethiopian government for military needs, although the report assumed that the regime would do so if shortages became critical. At the same time, the CIA did claim that some of the money raised by the Tigray People's Liberation Front (TPLF) for relief was 'almost certainly' being redirected for military purposes.[331] This statement was used as evidence for a 2010 BBC investigative report, although the BBC was later forced to retract it.[332]

In public, voluntary organisations have consistently rebutted claims that a sizeable proportion of aid for Ethiopia, Eritrea, and Tigray was ever misused by rebels or by the government. However, aid workers claim that, realistically, a certain proportion of aid will be diverted in any emergency, and losing some 10 per cent of food provisions may be the price to be paid for delivering 90 per cent.[333] While performing such calculations is a routine aspect of the moral economy of aid, this is a difficult message to convey to donors, and one that does not fit in with the simplistic media view of aid. In a discussion on this topic in Swedish newspapers in early 1985, Rädda Barnen and the Swedish Red Cross noted that even with the best monitoring systems, the nature of emergency relief meant that 'full proof that guarantees every krona reaches its target cannot be given'.[334] This speaks to a long-standing paradox: on the one hand, public displeasure at large sums being spent on administration or management, and, on the other, expectations that aid allocations should be thoroughly accounted for and monitored.

Voluntary organisations involved in relief to rebel forces pragmatically assessed the risk of a portion of the aid not reaching its intended destination, since 'there was no practical way to provide food aid to families without some of it going to feed soldiers in the rebel movements'.[335] However, throughout the 1980s, a good deal of ERA, REST, and ERD activity 'was consumed in furnishing monitoring reports and accounts' to prove to international donors

---

[330] Gill, *Year in the Death*, 72–5.   [331] CIA, *Ethiopia*, 4–6.

[332] 'BBC Apologises over Band Aid Money Reports', BBC News website, 24 Nov. 2010, available at www.bbc.com/news/av/uk-11691530 (accessed 29 June 2019).

[333] Jenden, as cited in Paul Vallely, 'Rebels with a Grudge and the Anatomy of a Damning Smear', *Independent*, 6 Mar. 2011.

[334] Claes-Göran Kjellander, 'Röda kors-chefen: Svinnet i Etiopien mycket begränsat', *Svenska Dagbladet*, 2 Jan. 1985. See also Per Stenbeck, 'Aldrig rätt att låta ett barn dö', *Svenska Dagbladet*, 13 Jan. 1985; Maria Torshall, '50 Miljoner till Etiopien: Insamlingarna i Sverige slår alla rekord', *Aftonbladet*, 3 Jan. 1985.

[335] Buchanan, 'Reflections on Working with Rebel Movements', 253.

that aid was not falling into the wrong hands.[336] In the case of Tigray in particular, this concern may have been misplaced. The 'TPLF was not a conventional army diverting relief grain, rather it was a political front mobilising a classic "people's war"'.[337] International food aid helped the liberation fronts in both Eritrea and Tigray to stabilise populations and expand their resource base, thus indirectly allowing them to enhance their military capability.[338] According to its official history, War on Want saw its role as channelling aid to ERA and REST as 'explicit support' for these wars of secession.[339] This support was not something addressed explicitly in War on Want annual reports at the time.

For many organisations, the famine in Ethiopia was a period of internal reflection over their policies and practices on the ground, but rarely was the challenging nature of the relief effort admitted to supporters. Oxfam's 1984/5 annual review reassured contributors that its 'programme is well managed despite immense political and logistical difficulties', while Save the Children sought to convince the public that its response had been 'prompt and appropriate'.[340] Vaux later recalled the widespread feeling among aid agencies 'that we must not frighten the donors' by asking difficult questions about an organisation's response.[341] Oxfam did, however, conduct several self-critical assessments of its decision-making.[342]

In general, commentators have upheld the view of the UN, CIA, and EEC that diversion of international food aid by the Derg, while likely to have taken place, was below that of similar emergencies elsewhere.[343] In 1985, Jansson and colleagues estimated no more than 5 per cent of aid was being diverted. They considered reported instances of hijacking or robbery, appropriation by military units, and food aid being offered for sale at markets 'insignificant in terms of food supplies lost'.[344] USAID reported a loss of 4.3 per cent, commenting that, once voluntary organisations took delivery of food at the ports, the reported loss was less than 0.5 per cent.[345] There is broad agreement, however, that the Mengistu regime manipulated international aid more fundamentally by prioritising grain for the resettlement scheme and by ensuring urban centres were well supplied.[346] The provision of international aid effectively allowed the government to transfer all of its own resources to its resettlement schemes. De Waal

---

[336] Duffield and Predergast, *Without Troops*, 28.   [337] de Waal, *Famine Crimes*, 130.

[338] Duffield and Predergast, *Without Troops*, 29.

[339] Luetchford and Burns, *Waging the War on Want*, 127.

[340] *Oxfam Review 1984/5*, Oxfam MS COM 1/1/2/1, 3; *Save the Children Annual Report, 1984–1985*, 4.

[341] Vaux, *Selfish Altruist*, 44.   [342] Gill, *Famine and Foreigners*, 42.

[343] Penrose, 'Before and After', 150.   [344] Jansson, 'Emergency Relief', 56–7.

[345] USAID, *Final Disaster Report*, 91.

[346] Theodore M. Vestal, 'Famine in Ethiopia: Crisis of Many Dimensions', *Africa Today* 32, no. 4 (1985): 19.

further argues that the main way that the Ethiopian government benefitted from international famine relief efforts may have been through exchange rates. By exchanging foreign currency at the official rate of 2.07 birr to the dollar, despite the fact that the market exchange rate was two to three times higher, the regime effectively taxed all monetary relief transactions, including port charges, transport, and local salaries, by 100–150 per cent.[347]

Overall, it has been estimated that the supply of aid prolonged the civil war in Ethiopia by at least a year.[348] There was continued reluctance to fully acknowledge the moral economic complexities of aid, and these were discussed only to a limited extent in the media in 1984 and 1985. A *Wall Street Journal* article argued the public understood that 'Ethiopia's rulers were no Mr Nice Guys', but that it was not prepared to hear that their own money might be doing more harm than good.[349]

In their concern to hold organisations to account over programming decisions and the speed with which aid was allocated, most critics, including journalists and researchers, focused on the needs of donors rather than recipients. Moral outrage was sparked at the thought of hard-earned public money held in bank accounts rather than being spent on food for the hungry, but rarely did one question whether the aid to Ethiopia could be harming the country. Critics noted that many donors expressed a lack of interest in how the food sent was distributed on the ground. In late 1984, Cultural Survival proposed a study to examine issues such as resettlement that might assist organisational planning. No operational agency was prepared to help fund this study; organisations said that they could not take part in compiling such information 'or even be seen to support its collection without jeopardizing our relief efforts in Ethiopia'.[350]

Privately, many agencies were uncomfortable with the Ethiopian government's approach to resettlement, but only MSF declared this publicly – and was expelled from the country by the Ethiopian government. After its expulsion, MSF issued an open letter to NGOs, explaining that its decision to speak out was based on concern that aid was being

diverted from its intended purpose towards ends that deny the interests of the drought victims... We believe that donors must be informed of the ways their contributions are to be used so that, aware of the facts, they may decide what they will support and what they will not.[351]

---

[347] de Waal, *Evil Days*, 193.   [348] de Waal, 'Humanitarian Carnival', 52.

[349] Suzanne Garment, 'West's Live Aid Digs Graves in Ethiopia', *Wall Street Journal*, 24 Jan. 1986.

[350] Clay and Holcomb, *Politics and the Ethiopian Famine*, 6.

[351] Desmoulins, Bertrand and Michael Fiszbin, 'An Open Letter to NGOs in Ethiopia', 13 Dec. 1985, CARE 1220, File 17.

MSF thus sought to put accountability towards famine-affected people back on the agenda. Speaking at the MSF general assembly meeting in 1986, Brauman denounced the way other humanitarian organisations were being complicit in the abuses of aid by their silence.[352] Interviewed fifteen years later, Vasset suggested that while many other aid agencies agreed privately with some of MSF's findings, they apparently 'found it easy to turn a blind eye to what was going on. They just focused on the little dying child.'[353] For such reasons, some critics looked upon aid organisations as largely driven by financial considerations.[354] Similarly, ongoing support for the aid effort had become a matter of course for Western donor governments whose voters demanded it. In contrast to MSF's stance, the concentration on the innocent victim allowed most voluntary organisations to comply with enhanced accounting and accountability requirements regarding their own operations, without having to engage with the wider question of whether the overall aid programme was being manipulated for ends outside of their knowledge.

Humanitarianism in the 1980s

In 1984–5, concern to keep the public and the media informed on how famine relief funds were spent tended to privilege short-term, expressive methods of accounting, such as press releases and television documentaries, over formal accounting procedures and compliance with national charity regulators. Given their much-vaunted commitment to ensuring every penny reached beneficiaries, the newcomers to aid were surprisingly reluctant to publish audited accounts or full expenditure reports. Both USA for Africa and Band Aid missed key deadlines for reporting income and expenditures, failing to adhere to conventions such as fiscal or calendar years in a manner that established organisations would not have dared to ignore. The two young agencies reported their income and expenditure over much longer time periods than was usual in the humanitarian sector, making comparisons with other organisations difficult, and leading subsequent researchers to focus on fundraising, rather than expenditure. Thus, expressive humanitarianism was characterised by low overall transparency. De Waal argues that the intense pressure unleashed on other organisations by Band Aid spending the enormous amounts of money it raised 'debased the currency of humanitarianism' because it meant 'high profile but less effective programs flourished at the expense of lower profile but more professional ones'.[355]

---

[352] Brauman, 'Rapport Moral 1985/86', 7.
[353] Vasset interview, 2000, as cited in Binet, *Famine and Forced Relocations*, 92.
[354] Gill, *Famine and Foreigners*, 51–2.   [355] De Waal, 'Humanitarian Carnival', 52.

Climbing income levels led to unanticipated growth for many established organisations involved in the relief effort, accelerating the adoption of businesslike practices in marketing, communications, fundraising, and administration across the humanitarian aid sector. There was a substantial increase in private giving. Although totals donated fell in 1986 from their 1984–5 peak, contributions in the UK were still double what they were on average at the beginning of the 1980s. One analysis of trends in giving to organisations involved in aid and development from 1978 to 2004 cites the increase between 1982 and 1985 as 'the surge'.[356] The realisation that the Band Aid organisers had tapped into a whole new constituency of givers was eye-opening, and many groups sought to learn lessons from them. Research conducted by Oxfam as part of an international study in 1987 found that aid and development had become 'legitimate areas of concern to the image-conscious youth of Britain', although the public still tended to hold simplistic, negative views about Ethiopia and Africa.[357] While disaster relief had remained at the periphery of USAID's mission in the 1960s and 1970s, it took prominence with the Ethiopian famine and marked the first time USAID donated over US$100 million to an international relief campaign, and created 'a blueprint for future policymakers to follow'.[358]

5.5 Keeping the Record: A Bicentennial Perspective

Our case studies illustrate the variety of aid documentation over time and across organisations. They also show the correlation of accounting practices with the logic of efficiency that has shaped the 'distinctive morality for modernity'.[359] Broader issues of governance, legitimacy, and equity, while informing humanitarian efforts, remained secondary to the principle of efficiency. Thus, the humanitarian record presents the entangled moral and economic choices made, while rarely addressing the dilemmas faced. At the same time, aid efforts turned the prevailing notion of moral economy upside down. While material supplies were delivered, the moral demand for accountability was primarily raised by or ascribed to donors. Accounting practices were directed at satisfying aid patrons and demonstrating the efficiency of

---

[356] Anthony B. Atkinson, Peter G. Backus, John Micklewright, et al., 'Charitable Giving for Overseas Development: UK Trends over a Quarter Century', *Journal of the Royal Statistical Society Series A* 175, no. 1 (2012): 167–90.

[357] Nikki van der Gaag and Cathy Nash, *Images of Africa: The UK Report* (Oxford: Oxfam, 1987), 43.

[358] Poster, 'Gentle War', 424.

[359] Peter Miller and Christopher Napier, 'Genealogies of Calculation', *Accounting, Organizations and Society* 18, no. 7/8 (1993): 645.

humanitarian efforts, but at the same time consumed resources that could have helped the needy.

Seen through the lens of Ebrahim's taxonomy of accountability mechanisms,[360] transnational famine relief throughout the 1840s, 1920s, and 1980s placed great emphasis on reports. These included some participatory and evaluative frames, such as co-operation with local relief committees in Ireland, similar low-key interactions in Russia and Ethiopia, and UN and other evaluative studies of famine relief in the 1980s. However, involvement schemes did not address power disparities, nor did self-regulation or social auditing play a significant role in any of the cases considered (the informal self-regulation of MSF when withdrawing from Ethiopia being perhaps the only exception). Thus, downward accountability was negligible.

Accounting as the means by which providers of relief documented their conduct and achievements was a process that accompanied the provision of aid. The information generated was frequently used in other fundraising drives. When an effort had come to an end, the final report produced would often combine mission statements and contributions received with selected descriptions of recipients and the relief operation. Such accounting sought to shape rather than reflect reality. Apart from serving the self-aggrandisement of the elites who issued them, they functioned as a 'technology of domination in-itself'.[361] This general conclusion of critical accounting research is illustrated by British accounting for famine relief in Ireland; by the attribution 'battles' in connection with aid to Soviet Russia; and by various aspects of reporting relief efforts in Ethiopia, including the conditionality of the regime's permission to work in the country.

Throughout the cases we studied, we encountered critical discussions about overhead costs and the diversion of relief. In each case, governments receiving aid contributed significant funds and services that supplemented bilateral and voluntary efforts. At the same time, both the Russian and Ethiopian government attempted to profit from the manipulation of exchange rates. The dependence of relief organisations on the government with jurisdiction over the emergency area, in addition to their material contribution, made SCF co-founder Jebb admit that humanitarian efforts (not to be confused with 'humanitarian interventions') stabilise any existing order.[362] While this order was represented by the governments in London and Moscow in the 1840s and 1920s, the Ethiopian case was more complex, with competing power holders in government- and rebel-held areas. At the outset, relief efforts stabilised them

---

[360] Ebrahim, 'Accountability in Practice', 819, 825.
[361] James Alfred Aho, *Confession and Bookkeeping: The Religious, Moral, and Rhetorical Roots of Modern Accounting* (Albany: State University of New York Press, 2005), xi.
[362] Mulley, *Woman Who Saved*, 291.

both, but indirect support for the liberation fronts through famine relief eventually contributed to the downfall of Addis Ababa's Derg regime in 1991.

The visibility of aid efforts was generally a major moral economic objective in itself, at times seeming to override that of making a difference on the ground. Such an inverted priority hampered British relief for Ireland, united communist and other foreign aid agencies in Russia, and was a common criticism of Band Aid and organisations working in Ethiopia. It was the beginning of what has become a neo-liberal obsession with metrics, benchmarks, and figures. However, the risk that accounting gimmicks result in a mere display of activity, and perhaps a concomitant misallocation, has been evident throughout our cases, paralleled by distortions linked to the quest for media visibility.[363] Conversely, statistical indicators, news items, and publicity images may all have enhanced the 'return on investment' for aid providers, making donors open their purses once again.

Shape of Accounts

Across our case studies, we noted a trajectory from prosaic and businesslike accounts to glossier publications by aid agencies, and from occasional to annual reports, even continuing on to opinionated storytelling or coffee table products, such as the commemorative photo book issued after Live Aid. These trends are broadly correlated to different periods of humanitarian action.

The era of nineteenth-century ad hoc humanitarianism was characterised by irregular (although in some cases frequent) accounts in the press and through campaign brochures. Not all relief efforts during the Great Irish Famine were systematically recorded. The Catholic Church in particular lacked a culture of written documentation. However, larger efforts often concluded with a major publication that became an organisation's public repository. These accounts, referred to a single aid cause and were narrowly focused. Public relations were conducted by amateurs who may have had some business background. Reports assumed an educated readership and, as they aimed at putting an ephemeral drive on the historical record, they often included copies of original documents, sometimes several hundred pages long. Trevelyan's semi-official summary was conspicuous with its broad polemic narrative, and the SVP reports were also noteworthy with their seriality and sweeping coverage of what was the first permanent transnational charity organisation.[364]

The SVP disclosures were a forerunner of the periodical reports that have become the standard for organised humanitarianism in the twentieth century. The SCF regularly published accounts of various kinds in its journal, *The*

---

[363] See also Terry, *Condemned to Repeat?*, 51–4.   [364] Götz, 'Emergence of NGOs', 25.

Record, including total figures, origin of donations, and lists of donors. Limited operations, such as Hoover's CRB and ARA, were reminiscent of the BRA of seventy years earlier, although on a grander scale and more dependent on government support. While the final reports issued by these organisations have much in common with some of the most comprehensive 'memorial publications' of the previous age, the government involvement in these aid initiatives assured the archival preservation of operational records.

Forms of popular accounting typical of the age of expressive humanitarianism (for example, showing how many times donated provisions would circle the earth) were already being employed by public relations experts at the beginning of the twentieth century. They became important tools to attract public attention for organisations delivering aid to Ethiopia in the 1980s. Film documentaries are another innovation that can be traced back to the aid efforts of the 1920s. By 1985, they were the vehicle for what amounted to Band Aid's annual report. Even the expressive gesture by which MSF announced that they would open their books for auditors sent by their critics had its predecessor in the conflict between SCF and the *Daily Express* in the 1920s.

One might expect that advances in computerised bookkeeping would have made relief efforts at the end of the twentieth century more transparent. Instead, one is struck by the poor shape of humanitarian accounting and the lack of improvement over time. We have probably a better estimate of the value of combined relief efforts during the Irish and Soviet famines than we do in the Ethiopian case.

When Band Aid finally released a report on its activities, it took the form of a simple list of achievements. Similarly, data provided by organisations active in the 1980s was generally fragmented, often consisting of sporadic figures documenting certain fiscal years, and sometimes arbitrary pieces of emergency infotainment. The multi-purpose organisations active at the time usually invested little effort in singling out particular aid causes, either geographically or with respect to their emergency or development nature, making inter-agency comparison and cross-agency aggregation of figures difficlt. However, on occasion, a need to create trust might facilitate good practice. For example, the relief societies associated with the liberation fronts in Tigray and Eritrea made a concerted effort to produce accurate accounts and monitoring reports of famine relief in order to establish their international credibility.[365]

Impersonalisation and Relativity of Aid

A specific feature of the age of ad hoc humanitarianism was the public use of donor lists to award individuals and groups (particularly church congregations)

---

[365] Duffield and Prendergast, *Without Troops*, 28.

recognition and permanent commemoration. Their names, aliases, and chosen descriptions, the sums given, and sometimes their earmarking were a means of moral economic communication and helped to shape a meaningful fundraising objective and hierarchy. In the mass society of the twentieth century, such tables became unfeasible, but during the famine of 1921–3, both SCF and FSR continued to publish lists of individual donors, local committees, church congregations, factory staff, and union groups. Moreover, the FSR promised its contributors that their names would be perpetuated in Russian archives. Today, the identity of celebrities and major philanthropists continue to be given prominence in humanitarian accounts. Nevertheless, the disappearance of donors' names, statuses, and contributions, and the disclosure of fundraisers' debits at a highly aggregated level only, are a significant development in twentieth-century humanitarian accounting. While obscuring the identity of individual donors and amounts contributed has decreased donor competition and status climbing, it may have enhanced the 'warm glow' experienced in private. Community and national pledges of support remain relevant as a public source of pride.

A parallel trend has been the increased anonymity of recipients and the declining interest in evidence of their gratitude. In the nineteenth century, the precarious relationship between the British Isles made gratitude a delicate issue, and its absence was a major cause for the paucity of English contributions. However, while subaltern reservations and the belief in entitlements prevailed among many Irish, gratitude depended on the aid giver's own perception of beneficiaries and vice versa. Gratitude, in most cases, was both expected and offered. Despite the rational economics of scale prevalent in the organised humanitarianism of the 1920s, evidence of gratitude remained significant for the legitimacy of aid to Soviet Russia among organisations and donor publics.

By the end of the twentieth century, Band Aid's Christmas single preempted the need for expressions of gratitude on the part of recipients by assuring donors, 'We can spread a smile of joy.' For most participants in the fundraising drive, with love to and from Band Aid, or some other organisation, sufficed as emotional recompense. Aid for Ethiopia illustrates that the self-contained donor and 'ironic spectator' of the late twentieth century appreciated self-celebratory and mediated narratives of relief operations without needing to hear the testimony of recipients, that is, sentimental feedback. In earlier times, some of those 'responses' had anyway been fabricated by aid workers. Although a wish that beneficiaries know to whom they owed their relief has always existed, a shift has taken place from expecting personal acknowledgement to simply being involved in greater enterprises of doing good. The most significant collective frame of reference has always been the nation, but various organisations (and their brands) have likewise been prominent.

Growing anonymity may be seen as a consequence of the increasing cultural distance between donors and recipients that is noted in our case studies. Like the difference between imaginations of the Orient proper and the demi-oriental perception of Eastern Europe,[366] the Irish and Russians were perceived as somewhat ambiguous cases in a civilisational matrix, with greater similarity to the majority of donors than the Ethiopians. As a result, the Irish and Russian population had some chance of reaching out to aid providers in the nineteenth and early twentieth century, while Indians or Chinese struck by famine at the time lacked such an opportunity. Therefore, they more closely resembled the later Ethiopian case. However, our selection of cases was made on the basis of major voluntary relief efforts; 'Oriental famines' outside the British imperial world were not met by major international responses until the second half of the twentieth century. In fact, the increasing self-centredness of donors and their indifference to the nationality or race of the recipients may have facilitated providing aid to culturally and politically diverse groups of people.

The increasing anonymity of benefactors and beneficiaries in the twentieth century has been accompanied by less and less interest in having a variety of donors. During the Great Irish Famine, the contributions of celebrities, along with collections among convicts, slaves, and Native Americans, received special publicity, and the biblical 'widow's mite' was a frequently used trope. The SCF summarised the relief efforts for Russia in a similar way, pointing to children, older people, and the poor, and concluding that its budget like 'a coral island grew from a multitude of minute creatures'.[367] By the 1980s, there was less reference to marginal groups among donors, although local fundraisers and school children were routinely singled out for praise in annual charity reports. Organisations also encouraged a community spirit among an active constituency of donors, members of local branches, and buyers of charity merchandise. Moreover, media commentary focused on the mobilisation of youth and the role of Band Aid in making aid to Africa popular among previously uninterested people. As a result, the particular moral value of contributions by lower classes and disadvantaged groups has been a declining narrative over the past century, mostly as a result of raised standards of living and the emergence of a distanced, 'ironic' spectatorship among donors. Nonetheless, a broad donor base continues to lend legitimacy to humanitarian accounting.

The motif of beggars, children, and poor people sharing the little they have belongs to a view that some donations are more valuable than others of equal size. The quality of the donor and the circumstances of giving are frequently

---

[366] Larry Wolff, *Inventing Eastern Europe: The Map of Civilization on the Mind of the Enlightenment* (Stanford, CA: Stanford University Press, 1994).
[367] 'The Lure of the Suffering Child'.

regarded to be of greater significance for overall accounting than the bare sum recorded in the books. In the Irish case, such a moral dimension caused many to esteem the pope's donation more highly than the queen's, although the latter was almost ten-fold as great. In Russia, Crimean Tatars allegedly favoured a few bushels of corn from Turkish fellow-believers over tonnes of grain from the USA. Even a major contributor to Ethiopian relief such as Band Aid claimed a surplus of moral capital that exceeded the purely monetary value of its relief.

Conclusion

The Moral Economy of Humanitarianism

After a fire partially destroyed Notre Dame Cathedral on 15 April 2019, more than one billion euros were pledged in two days to rebuild it. The support came from French business leaders and philanthropists, as might be expected; but other prominent individuals around the world, such as the chief executive of Apple, also rushed to publicly announce their contributions. In the days after the fire, stories circulated in the media of schoolchildren sending their spare change from abroad to repair Notre Dame, along with other small bequests, following a familiar pattern.[1]

Philosopher Peter Singer was one of many commentators who rebuked this outpouring of charity in support of a landmark building.[2] Academic critics and humanitarians were quickly joined by a transnational digital outcry on social media that described the huge corporate contributions as a sign of the exorbitant profits made by those businesses and pointed out the unsuitability of their immediate pledges of aid while children were dying of hunger in Yemen. Despite the famine there being qualified by United Nations (UN) officials as rapidly becoming the worst in living memory, the international response to this catastrophe has been muted.[3]

Making and publicising donations, whether large or small, as opposed to questioning their propriety, or weighing more pressing concerns, reflects alternative moral economies. All are within the wider landscape of charity, of which humanitarianism forms a part. However, actual commitment may work at cross purpose to another cause's claim to greater urgency as long as the concrete circumstances of the alternative remain vague. In the case of

---

[1] 'Notre Dame Fire: Tycoons and Citizens Pledge Hundreds of Millions', *Times*, 16 Apr. 2019; 'British Schoolgirl, Nine, Sends €3 to the Fund to Rebuild Notre Dame', *Daily Mail*, 26 Apr. 2019.

[2] Peter Singer and Michael Plant, 'How Many Lives Is Notre Dame Worth?', available at www .project-syndicate.org/commentary/notre-dame-restoration-opportunity-costs-by-peter-singer-and-michael-plant-2019-05 (accessed 29 June 2019).

[3] 'UN and Partners to Hold Conference Seeking Urgently Needed Funds to Save Millions in Yemen from "Horrific" Plight', UN News, 24 Feb. 2019, available at https://news.un.org/en/ story/2019/02/1033401 (accessed 29 June 2019).

Notre Dame, the logic of an earlier thought experiment by Singer (that was supposed to illustrate the lunacy of channelling donations in aid of museums rather than reducing human suffering) was subverted by the wave of private donations.[4] The emotional connection people worldwide feel for Paris and Notre Dame, a building that receives fifteen million visitors every year, evoked for many a greater moral obligation to assist than did the famine then raging in war-ridden Yemen.

Apart from the perceived distance, the religious background and conflict-related character of the crisis in Yemen, the thinly veiled support of one party by the US president, and the questionable impact of humanitarian action under extremely difficult conditions all remained an obstacle to any large-scale relief effort. In accordance with their current advertising strategy, Save the Children's fundraising slogan for Yemen was open in calling for contributors to focus on the afflicted, not the context: 'See the Child. Not the War.'[5] However, donors are generally not content to ignore facts on the ground, and donations tend to dry up as moral dilemmas mount. The lack of a humanitarian space in which transparent aid allocation is plausible is as discouraging for moral economic reckoning as turmoil is for calculations in the economy proper. Although obstacles to compassion were present during the famines in Ireland, Russia, and Ethiopia, donors weighed the moral economic variables involved and responded, at least temporarily, with considerable support.

Moral Economic Structures

Historian Cormac Ó Gráda, who has written extensively on famines, begins a recent book with the observation that 'no two famines are the same, yet, superficially at least, most have a lot in common'.[6] Similarly, the historical parallels we identify in Irish, Russian, and Ethiopian famine relief are neither incidental nor trivial. Understanding them may be clearer if one views humanitarian efforts as an outcome of moral economic considerations. This approach is consistent with the recent recognition of the links between humanitarianism and capitalism. It can be traced back to Thomas L. Haskell's influential argument that the rise of the modern market economy in the late eighteenth century went along with a shift in cognitive styles and perceptions of moral responsibility. These forces, in turn, shaped a new sensibility and readiness to lend assistance to distant people.[7] Others have suggested that humanitarian

---

[4] Peter Singer, 'Good Charity, Bad Charity', *New York Times*, 10 Aug. 2013, available at www.nytimes.com/2013/08/11/opinion/sunday/good-charity-bad-charity.html (accessed 29 June 2019).
[5] Save the Children, 'Fundraising for Yemen and Syria', available at www.savethechildren.org.uk/how-you-can-help/events-and-fundraising/fundraising-for-the-syria-and-yemen-crisis-appeals (accessed 29 June 2019).
[6] Ó Gráda, *Eating People*, 1.   [7] Haskell, 'Capitalism and the Origins'.

action is driven by economic rather than moral interests, although they concede that such action may be altruistic 'in the sense that the people who are involved in this work believe ... that their actions are moral'.[8]

There appears to be a substantial overlap between economic and moral motivation beyond what is commonly acknowledged and beyond what we conceive more narrowly as the moral economy of aid. Hence, the popular as well as academic notion that the economy is a zone devoid of moral foundation and content (the myth by which modern economics has established a techno-cratic hegemony) may be open to question. At the same time, rather than considering the moral idealistically, as that which is right and good, it may be more useful to see it in its social context, as a means of persuasion correlated to tangible interests. Along such lines, humanitarianism may be an expedient supplement to capitalism. It offers identity and a sense of community that can disperse international tensions. Despite its affinity to modern society, humani-tarianism is a force that targets the blind spots of capitalism. Therefore, it cannot operate according to the principles of regular markets and prices, but needs to attract the voluntary contributions of a gift economy, develop its own criteria for the allocation of goods and services, and account for its actions with a focus on human interest and equitable disbursal in place of income and economic profit. For all of its parallels, a charity business across borders is based on discretionary spending, although partly influenced by codes of triage (i.e., humanitarian prioritisation and selection); it is, therefore, not quite business as usual.

This perspective may be best epitomised by the term 'moral economy', which E. P. Thompson has defined as an agreement on subsistence rights, underpinned by the threat of popular riots. Hence, we turn the term 'moral economy' on its head and broaden its perspective to address the moral subjectivity and altruistically clothed interests of donors. As interpreted by Marcel Mauss, gift giving is not the innocent endeavour it superficially appears to be; rather, it is full of moral implications. The case studies presented here, and humanitarian efforts-at-large, are characterised by an asymmetry that clearly delineates donors, as superiors, from beneficiaries, as subalterns, who are hardly expected to return what they receive.[9] Even when aid has been framed as the redemption of a debt or awarded as a loan, gratitude was most often the sole currency of return. It was not always forthcoming, especially when aid was given to ideological enemies, or when it sufficed for donors to simply presume such appreciation.

Donors and their organisations, therefore, have always dominated the moral agenda and economic practice of humanitarianism. They are the ones who shape aid appeals, who are accountable for humanitarian efforts, whose actions

[8] Dal Lago and O'Sullivan, 'Introduction', 7–8.   [9] Mauss, *Gift*, 72.

cause aid to materialise, and on whose terms aid is allocated.[10] The voices of recipients, who have their own moral economic concerns and claims, may sometimes enter this arena, and are sometimes amplified, but this only happens at the discretion of donors and as they see fit. There are many less prominent donors who do not exercise much power. Nevertheless, like citizen tax payers, donors have an important place in the humanitarian structure, and differences in their status are minimised by the moral quality ascribed to their support (or the 'sacrifice' that they have made). Thus, all contributions are valued, great or small, relative to the contributor's means. The term 'donor community', although overused, can designate all those who support a particular moral economic cause.

While the moral economy of ordinary people is generally confined to their local area, charitable giving has frequently extended beyond the borders of the nation-state. The result, at times, has been conflicts of interest between the 'home crowd' and their representatives, on the one hand, and humanitarian organisations and their preferred beneficiaries abroad, on the other. An example is the fund to rebuild three historically black churches in Louisiana that were destroyed by racially motivated arson in the spring of 2019. The building fund had difficulty getting started, but grew dramatically after journalists, celebrities, and politicians compared it to the huge outpouring of donations for Notre Dame that same week, urging donors not to forget their 'neighbours'.[11]

However, the moral economy of the crowd at home can also work in reverse and encourage aid for distant strangers. In 1847, public pressure forced the Catholic bishop of London to revise an appeal that at first combined Irish relief with local charity, to one exclusively benefitting Ireland. Rising standards of living and the mechanisms of expressive humanitarianism have probably increased this willingness to extend one's compassion beyond borders, as efforts during the Biafran War or the famine in Ethiopia suggest. Public opinion put humanitarian organisations and national governments, as well as the UN and the European Economic Community, under considerable pressure to become engaged in long-distance charity.

Diachronic Perspectives

We have outlined how nineteenth-century ad hoc humanitarianism was superseded by organised humanitarianism around 1900, which was in turn followed by expressive humanitarianism after 1970, and how this affected the moral rationale of humanitarian efforts. Our reference to distinct periods is based on a

[10] Malkki, *Need to Help*.
[11] Katie Gagliano, 'Fundraiser for Burned St. Landry Churches Hits $1.8 Million Goal after 36-Hour Push', *Acadiana Advocate*, 17 Apr. 2019.

holistic interpretation of historical data, rather than on any formula. It may be understood by analogy to Max Weber's triad of tradition, bureaucracy, and charisma. The major trends that shape the moral economies of their time are not unique features of their respective periods. Spontaneity and status-orientation were especially prominent in the era of ad hoc humanitarianism; scale and efficiency typified organised humanitarianism; and self-reference and spectacle characterised expressive humanitarianism. Nevertheless, these different aspects of humanitarian action were always intertwined.

The humanitarian field has been characterised by such remarkable diversity that it defies easy generalisations, even within the periods we have identified. There were forerunners, latecomers, and hybrid efforts incorporating the logic of other sectors of society, such as the state or business; there were co-operation and competition; there were headquarters, facilitators, teams, and individual fieldworkers on the ground; there was advocacy, interference with long-term development, and overlapping with other issues; there was uncertainty, risk-taking, and bias; there were competing worldviews, languages, and iconographies. All these factors influenced the moral economic considerations that shaped humanitarian efforts in unique ways.

The basic structure of a disproportionate gift economy permeates all humanitarian causes, engendering many parallels, despite the rapid socio-economic and technological transformations of the past 200 years. The asymmetry in the benefactor–beneficiary relationship, and the symbolic status recognition and tacit strings attached to 'gifts' were already realised by commentators at the time. Suspicions regarding the 'true' intentions of aid organisations and their donors are as present in our case studies as are misgivings concerning the diversion of funds or resources and the negative effects of aid. Integrity and creativity on the part of recipients, and trust and control on that of donors, were crucial for establishing a positive working partnership, even though relations often remained strained.

Efficiency, another central issue, may have found its best expression in the Taylor-inspired approach typical of the early and mid-twentieth century. The same applies to the persistent tension between deontological and utilitarian understandings of humanitarianism, that is, the difficulty of finding a balance between 'doing the right thing' and 'doing things right'. Such conflicts, especially regarding advertising and allocation, are noticeable on different levels of the aid chain in all three cases we have examined. However, the businesslike provision of relief in the era of organised humanitarianism made such dilemmas more obvious.

Despite the prevalence of a universalistic humanitarian rhetoric, by the mid-nineteenth century, ad hoc humanitarianism was dominated by the moral implications of special relations, such as imperial hierarchies, kinship ties, and religious affiliations. The alleged entitlement of beneficiaries was often derived from their previous conduct, feelings of belonging to a group, and the idea of reciprocity. Elements of such a moral economy based on in-group mechanisms have survived. For example, Hoover's Commission for Relief in Belgium aided allies; the Near East Relief supported fellow Christians; and the Workers' Relief International was based on class solidarity. However, organised humanitarianism tended to broaden its clientele beyond the confines of such connections, establishing an effective altruism based on accessibility, business principles, and economies of scale. Still, the legitimacy of providing aid to distant strangers had to be defended regularly, and the credibility of beneficiaries, whose entitlement was not always evident to the 'home crowd', was a controversial topic.

Expressive humanitarianism maintained many features of its predecessors, but put increased emphasis on donors, celebrity fundraising, and voluntary organisations as morally and materially involved agents who buy and sell humanitarianism as part of a lifestyle or brand. Asserting historical or future reciprocity was no longer part of this moral economy, nor was the idea of reconciliation (although there were, at times, tinges of postcolonial guilt at play, and a sense of ecological liability for the plight of others has been a rising concern since the 1970s). Paradoxically, while the overall tendency towards greater universality widened the circle of beneficiaries, it made the same beneficiaries matter less, and limited their agency in the moral economy of aid. As philosopher Alain Finkielkraut has put it, 'Save lives: that is the global mission of the global doctor. He is too busy feeding rice to hungry mouths to listen to what these mouths are saying.'[12]

Whither Expressive Humanitarianism?

Since the 1980s, expressive humanitarianism has evolved in numerous ways. By the 2000s, the celebrity-endorsed methods of participatory fundraising embodied by Band Aid had emerged as the standard response to major humanitarian crises around the world – and to domestic incidents, too.[13] Those who cloned this model, however, have had to contend with its reduced impact. It has almost become more newsworthy when a major disaster does not herald a new charity record. Geldof himself organised re-recordings of 'Do They Know It's Christmas?' on three occasions, each time mobilising the latest generation of pop stars alongside some of the original cast. In 1989, he did this for a recurrence of famine in the Horn of Africa, in 2004, for the crisis in the

---

[12] Finkielkraut, *Name of Humanity*, 89.
[13] See, e.g., the charity single 'Lieber Gott' (Dear God) for the victims of the 2002 flooding in Germany or the cover version of 'Bridge over Troubled Water' for residents affected by the Grenfell Tower fire in the UK in 2017.

Darfur region of Sudan, and in 2014, for the Ebola epidemic. While all the recordings were commercially successful, undercurrents of criticism about intentions and outcomes grew ever louder. In 2014, the recording was dismissed by journalists, academics, and musicians as 'insulting' to Africans and epitomising the 'white saviour' complex; several celebrities publicly turned down the chance to appear on the single.[14] In similar ways, as charity television broadcasts became more commonplace, coupled with the rise of commercial television and, later, on-demand viewing platforms, telethons have struggled with reduced relevance and declining income.[15]

Humanitarianism's cultural imprint and mechanisms have remained relatively stable over the past decades, but political changes since the end of the Cold War have had a significant impact. The new latitude of the UN Security Council and the amplified power of the USA have reinforced an already ascendant human rights discourse, promoting 'military humanitarianism' and a UN-endorsed 'responsibility to protect' (R2P).[16] The area in which the expressiveness of humanitarianism has advanced the most, therefore, is the resort to power, and the bold disposition to intervene on behalf of others. However, waiting for powerful governments to take responsible action rather than conjuring up humanitarian arguments to justify the USA's and UN's own agendas – as in the Iraq War of 2003 or the 2011 intervention in Libya – may be futile.[17] The lack of duty-bound action in favour of the population of Yemen at the time this book is being published also raises doubts about the validity of any 'R2P', as does the degeneration of much of the discourse from the responsibility to protect to the coining of obscure acronyms.

Humanitarian action today tends to take place in the shadow of armed conflicts and political oppression, whereby aid organisations become the 'force multipliers' and 'trash collectors' of belligerent powers. The example of Yemen illustrates how large-scale food insecurity and famine conditions tend to be a direct consequence of aggression. Such was also the case in the most severe famine of recent decades: Somalia in 2011–12, although food shortages due to drought did play a role. Despite effective monitoring

---

[14] Robtel Neajai, Pailey Interview BBC Radio 4, 18 Nov. 2004; Haroon Siddique, 'Lily Allen: Band Aid Is Smug', *Guardian*, 23 Nov. 2014.

[15] Bettina Kreusel, 'Das Fernsehen als Spendengenerator: Eine Bestandsaufnahme auf der Angebotsebene', in *Massenmedien und Spendenkampagnen: Vom 17. Jahrhundert bis in die Gegenwart*, ed. Jürgen Wilke (Cologne: Böhlau, 2008), 311.

[16] Thomas G. Weiss and Karl M. Campbell, 'Military Humanitarianism', *Survival* 33, no. 5 (1991): 451–65; International Commission on Intervention and State Sovereignty, *The Responsibility to Protect* (Ottawa: International Development Research Centre, 2001).

[17] Jeremy Moses, Babak Bahadorand, and Tessa Wright, 'The Iraq War and the Responsibility to Protect: Uses, Abuses and Consequences for the Future of Humanitarian Intervention', *Journal of Intervention and Statebuilding* 5, no. 4 (2011): 347–67; Debora Valentina Malito, 'The Responsibility to Protect What in Libya?', *Peace Review* 29, no. 3 (2017): 289–98.

mechanisms, up to one-quarter of a million people died from famine. Because of the difficulty of operating in a failed state and having to deal with terrorist-affiliated authorities, the catastrophe did not receive a timely, coordinated response of the magnitude required.[18] A study of Swedish fundraising for Somalia found that aid organisations made only limited efforts either to praise donors or to entitle beneficiaries. These organisations set themselves up as branded enterprises that offered donors something beyond individual acclaim, namely, shareholding in larger efforts of doing good.[19] Nonetheless, their overall impact remained limited.

Although the present era is typified by warfare enveloping current humanitarian crises, there have been other cases, such as the famine in North Korea in the mid-1990s that resulted in a death toll of 250,000–400,000 people (other estimates claim the number is closer to three million). The UN World Food Programme played a key role in alleviating that emergency, which was a consequence of economic mismanagement. Due to North Korea's policy of secrecy and the lack of natural explanations for the famine, this did not become a popular cause, and international donors were forced to yield control over the relief that they provided to the North Korean regime. A number of organisations, including Médecins Sans Frontières (MSF), eventually withdrew from the effort rather than continue to 'collaborate with Kim Jong-il in his triage between those worthy of food and those who were not'. The exploitation of aid for political purposes, which made North Korea 'the site of the most manipulated aid programme in the world', was mutual, however. Foreign agencies who chose to stay on pursued goals such as peace and geopolitical stability that went beyond the humanitarian agenda.[20]

Humanitarian efforts can take many forms. 'Consumer aid' or 'brand aid' continue to be on the rise, relief agencies have moved further towards storytelling, and journalists in the field concoct their own personal 'trade marks'.[21] Social media as a tool of humanitarian communication can bring ordinary voices and user-created content to the fore. However, the peculiar celebrity culture of social media – such as the ubiquitous 'influencers' – tends to reinforce the expressive character of contemporary humanitarianism. The entrenching of stereotypes about the Global South as a result of

[18] Daniel Maxwell and Nisar Majid, *Famine in Somalia: Competing Imperatives, Collective Failures, 2011–12* (New York: Oxford University Press, 2016), 4–5; Cormac Ó Gráda, 'Famine Is Not', *Eating People*, 180–4.

[19] Lindström, *Moral Economy of Aid*.

[20] Fiona Terry, 'North Korea: Feeding Totalitarianism', in *In the Shadow of 'Just War': Violence, Politics and Humanitarian Action*, ed. Fabrice Weissman (Ithaca, NY: Cornell University Press, 2004), 100, 96–7 (quotations), 101–7; Ó Gráda, 'Famine Is Not', 199–205.

[21] Glenda Cooper and Simon Cottle, 'Humanitarianism, Communications, and Change: Final Reflections', in *Humanitarianism, Communications and Change*, eds Simon Cottle and Glenda Cooper (New York: Lang, 2015), 251, 257–8.

celebrity-mediated disaster relief will persist – and there is little reason to expect an improvement in online humanitarianism. The scandal resulting from Oxfam's attempt to cover-up sexual abuse by relief workers in the aftermath of the 2011 Haiti earthquake revealed a disturbing trend of similar transgressions and sexual exploitation across global humanitarian agencies, including MSF, Save the Children, the Red Cross, and UN agencies.[22] Overall, a 'terrible paradox' emerges, for well-intentioned attempts to relieve distant suffering may not be enough, and may even bring about more harm where least expected.[23] Recipients around the world have long been suspicious of donor motivations and are now perhaps increasingly so, even to the extent of rejecting international aid.[24]

Throughout the history of humanitarianism, donors have preferred to provide in-kind relief to recipients of aid. Conversely, direct cash transfer has been regarded as an exception, to be cautiously applied as circumstances require. However, over the past twenty years, a remarkable shift has taken place, with 'monetisation' as the new mantra of humanitarianism. While this sea change may appear as a breakthrough of Amartya Sen's theory on effective entitlements and preference for 'pulling' rather than 'pushing' food for reasons of efficiency, we see it primarily as a sign of how neo-liberal economics has profoundly recast entrenched patterns in present-day society, not sparing the liberal dogmas of old. The new esteem for cash transfer programmes, although as yet far from being the dominant form of aid, correlates with the designation of beneficiaries as humanitarian 'customers', and reliance on the latter's digital equipment for the transactions. Rather than the intervention of organisations from abroad, what Sen had in mind was a substantial commitment on the part of the welfare state to its own population. Nevertheless, cash or vouchers are often appreciated by those who receive them. Such an exchange can externalise and marketise logistic problems of humanitarian organisations.[25]

Against a backdrop of growing doubts about the sustainability of our prevailing economic system, the progress of political demagogy, and the rise of artificial intelligence, as well as increasing evidence of compassion for animals and the imagination of an inanimate world's subjectivity, posthumanism has become a trend in academia. Parallel to this, a notion of

---

[22] *Inquiry Report Summary Findings and Conclusions – Oxfam* (London: Charity Commission, 2019).

[23] Franks, *Reporting Disasters*, 178.

[24] Jaspars, *Food Aid*, 86–7; Dalia Hatuqa, 'Why Some Palestinians are Shunning Foreign Aid', *New Humanitarian*, 14 May 2019, available at www.thenewhumanitarian.org/analysis/2019/05/14/why-some-palestinians-are-shunning-foreign-aid (accessed 29 June 2019).

[25] Graham Heaslip, Gyöngyi Kovács, and Ira Haavisto, 'Cash-Based Response in Relief: The Impact for Humanitarian Logistics', *Journal of Humanitarian Logistics and Supply Chain Management* 8, no. 1 (2018): 87–106.

posthumanitarianism has started to take hold, something Lilie Chouliaraki describes as a move 'from an ethics of a "common humanity" towards a morality of "the self" as the main motivation for action'.[26] As a tendency that has prevailed for some decades, this development is a part of our concept of expressive humanitarianism. However, an analysis that tries to contrast current *practices* with past *ideals* – which is an impossible comparison – will fail to notice that the self of the donor has, in fact, been a significant driver since the beginnings of humanitarianism.

By contrast, the application of remote sensing, mobile phone technology, and crisis informatics, as well as humanitarian drones, biometrical systems, and distance management, may mark the beginning of a genuinely new, technologically fortified system of identifying needs and delivering humanitarian services. In addition, voluntary so-called digital humanitarians offer to support emergency aid on the ground, providing technological expertise and big data analysis. These trends, alongside an increasing 'bunkerization of the aid industry', are consistent with the request that greater responsibility be taken on behalf of victims and their local institutions in finding ways to cope with food insecurity.[27] Such a resilience-oriented approach 'walks a thin line between support and abandonment, between enabling the self-reliance of crisis-affected populations and refugees, and depriving them of basic protection'.[28] Abandonment may well be the major outcome, in particular for groups facing governments with adverse moral economies.[29] Mark Duffield suggests that, rather than marking the beginning of a new era, all this may be the 'long anticipated arrival' of a system of techno-governance facilitated by decades of cybernetic behaviourism.[30] Nevertheless, a novel kind of defensive humanitarianism with roots in the expressive age, with automated interfaces, and with thick 'firewalls' between donors and recipients may be in the making.

Towards a New History of Humanitarianism

In a recent essay, Bertrand Taithe suggests that revealing the uses of humanitarian history may be a rewarding academic endeavour, whereas attempting to

---

[26] Lilie Chouliaraki, 'Post-humanitarianism', in *Humanitarianism: A Dictionary of Concepts*, eds Tim Allen, Anna Macdonald, and Henry Radice (London: Routledge, 2018), 253.

[27] Mark Duffield, *Post-humanitarianism: Governing Precarity in the Digital World* (Cambridge: Polity, 2019), 89. See also Kristin Bergtora Sandvik and Kjersti Lohne, 'The Rise of the Humanitarian Drone: Giving Content to an Emerging Concept', *Millennium* 43, no. 1 (2014): 145–64.

[28] Dorothea Hilhorst, 'Classical Humanitarianism and Resilience Humanitarianism: Making Sense of Two Brands of Humanitarian Action', *Journal of International Humanitarian Action* 3, no. 15 (2018): 10 (quotation), 5–6.

[29] Jaspars, *Food Aid*, 2.   [30] Duffield, *Post-humanitarianism*, 149.

write the history of humanitarianism as such 'may prove foolhardy'.[31] This assessment refers to the amorphous character of a quasi-ideology with blurred delimitations regarding a wide range of phenomena. At the same time, one may suspect that any history of humanitarianism might devolve into a grand narrative, that is, a use of history, a piece of ideology, rather than providing the critical account that would advance our understanding of humanitarian history and practice. The near total lack of comprehensive histories of humanitarianism warns us of the difficulty of coming to terms with global action for more than two centuries because the field is often characterised by a paucity of distinctions, unintended consequences, disputable achievements, and poor archival records.

Nonetheless, during the course of this project, the history of humanitarian action has flourished and valuable research has been published covering a wide range of emergencies and aid protagonists. There is also an emerging self-reflexive discussion on the approaches that have created new knowledge in the field, and what is needed in the future.[32] In part, this historical interest is driven by the new source material that has become available through the opening of voluntary organisations' archives; but there is also a reappraisal of existing material as traditional celebratory histories written by insiders and supporters appear increasingly outdated. It is promising that leading aid organisations like Oxfam, CARE, and Save the Children have begun to recognise that their archives are strategic assets for analysing the evolution of humanitarianism in a changing political landscape. Academic attention has also benefitted from the momentum that transnational history and studies of civil society have shown at the beginning of the twenty-first century.

Most research pertains to relief efforts originating in the Global North, although there are some pioneering studies of Southern humanitarianism.[33] Regularly lamented is a lack of recipient perspectives. Moreover, the history of humanitarian or voluntary organisations as businesses is still in its infancy.[34] By following charity money from income generation, via the deployment of resources, to bookkeeping and documentation, the present volume hopes to

---

[31] Taithe, 'Humanitarian History?', 62.
[32] Matthew Hilton, Emily Baughan, Eleanor Davey, et al., 'History and Humanitarianism: A Conversation', *Past and Present* 241, no. 1 (2018): e1–e38.
[33] Maria Framke and Ester Möller, *From Local Philanthropy to Political Humanitarianism: South Asian and Egyptian Humanitarian Aid during the Period of Decolonisation* (Berlin: Leibniz-Zentrum Moderner Orient, 2019); Maria Framke, 'Political Humanitarianism in the 1930s: Indian Aid for Republican Spain', *European Review of History* 23, nos 1–2 (2016): 63–81; Pichamon Yeophantong, *Understanding Humanitarian Action in East and Southeast Asia: A Historical Perspective* (London: Overseas Development Institute, 2014).
[34] Exceptions are Roddy, Strange, and Taithe, *Charity Market*; Heike Wieters, 'Reinventing the Firm: From Post-war Relief to International Humanitarian Agency', *European Review of History* 23, nos 1–2 (2016): 116–35.

shed light on key economic dimensions, although from a viewpoint broader than that of business history. While some attention is given to diasporic relief, indigenous aid, and the agency of beneficiaries, these are not at the centre of our narrative. The focus on humanitarianism as a donor-driven endeavour derives from our readjusted 'moral economy' perspective, which begins with the fundamental question of why and under what conditions one would voluntarily want to share assets with a distant stranger, rather than follow Thompson and examine the desire and methods of the 'crowd' to appease their own hunger. In each of the case studies, we provincialise aid efforts, examining the biases of their 'universalism'. We attempt to highlight the agency of beneficiaries while continuing to focus on facilitating elites. The reaction and agency of recipients in the last mile; their creative appropriation of what is offered to them; their wounds and recalcitrance – all these deserve further attention. Whereas our work underscores the role of the diaspora more strongly than previous research, domestic giving is beyond the scope of our transnational inquiry.

Humanitarians have been content to apply academic evidence from disciplines like social psychology, nutritional science, and more recently logistics studies when shaping their practice, but they rarely draw on empirical historical research. The prevailing ahistoricism of relief agencies and aid workers is not only due to a lack of time and resources, but also to humanitarianism's ingrained focus on emergencies and action under apparently exceptional circumstances. Therefore, as John Borton puts it, the humanitarian sector is 'locked in a "perpetual present"' in which historical analysis is perceived as having little to contribute, especially if it goes beyond the immediate past.[35] There have been notable attempts by academics to enable humanitarians to better understand their history and vice versa: to convince historians to present their material and narratives in a way that professionals in the humanitarian sector would consider accessible and engaging.[36]

Our moral economy approach sees practice as central to humanitarian history. Such a history is a transdisciplinary endeavour, informed by a wide range of debates and observations, including donor psychology, humanitarian logistics, and critical accounting. We believe that such a perspective, with a

---

[35] Borton, 'Improving the Use', 195, 199.
[36] For example, the Overseas Development Institute's 'Global History of Modern Humanitarian Action', the Canadian Network on Humanitarian History, and MSF's many publications on 'MSF Speaking Out', available at http://speakingout.msf.org (accessed 14 Feb. 2020). See also Eleanor Davey and John Borton, 'History and Practitioners: The Use of History by Humanitarians and the Potential Benefits of History to the Humanitarian Sector', in *The Impact of History? Histories at the Beginning of the Twenty-First Century*, eds Pedro Ramos Pinto and Bertrand Taithe (Abingdon: Routledge, 2015), 153–68; Borton, 'Improving the Use'; Taithe and Borton, 'History, Memory'.

focus on fundraising appeals, allocation, and accounting, is of relevance to current humanitarian policy and practice, and will inspire future research. We acknowledge that a synthesis of two centuries of famine relief may not provide present-day humanitarian workers with concrete 'lessons' and blueprints for action. Yet, as with humanitarian relief itself, its historical study 'is not an exact science but an art'.[37] We hope that this book, by presenting 'an alternative perspective on familiar challenges',[38] will not only be read by our colleagues, but also furnish some of those working in the field with critical historical insight – perhaps even 'Aha!' moments – and stimulate them to peer beyond what is obvious in the present. There is a time to look backwards, as we have done, but there is also a time to look forwards, transcend the present, and put evidence of the past to use for imagining alternative futures.

---

[37] Allié, 'Introduction', 10.

[38] Eleonor Davey and Kim Scriven, 'Humanitarian Aid in the Archives: Introduction', *Disasters* 39, no. s2 (2015): 119.

References

Archives

BBC Written Archives, Reading
Bodleian Library, Oxford University
Oxfam Archive
Borthwick Institute, University of York
Cadbury Research Library, University of Birmingham
Save the Children Fund Archives (SCF)
Diocesan Archives, Birmingham
Diocesan Archives, Boston (DAB)
Fitzpatrick Papers (FP)
Memoranda of the Diocese of Boston
Diocesan Archives, Brixen
Consistorial Records
Diocesan Archives, Dublin (DAD)
Murray Papers (MP)
Diocesan Archives, Westminster, London
Griffiths Papers
Historical Archives of the Congregation for the Evangelisation of Peoples
    (HAC), Rome
Documents referred to in the weekly meetings (SC)
Hoover Institution Library and Archives, Stanford University
ARA Russian operational records (ARA)
JDC (American Joint Distribution Committee) Archives, New York
Library of the Society of Friends, London
Friends Emergency and War Victims Relief Committee (FEWVRC) Archive
Listener Historical Archive, 1929–91, available at http://tinyurl.galegroup
    .com/tinyurl/6jHW89
National Library of Ireland (NLI), Dublin
Manuscripts
Monteagle Papers (MP)
Slattery Papers (SP, microfilm from Diocesan Archives, Cashel (DAC))
New York Public Library
CARE Archives
Pontifical Irish College (PIC) Archive, Rome
Cullen Papers (CUL)

Public Record Office of Northern Ireland (PRONI), Belfast
Dufferin and Ava Papers (D1071)
The Robinson Library, Newcastle University (RLN)
Trevelyan Papers (TP)
Rothschild Archive, London
Private Correspondence Sundry, 1814–1913 (XI/109)
School of Oriental and African Studies (SOAS), University of London
Christian Aid (CA) Archive
War on Want (WOW) Archive
The National Archives, London (TNA(UK))
Foreign and Commonwealth Office (FCO)
Home Office (HO)
Treasury (T)
Overseas Development (OD)
The National Archives of Ireland, Dublin (TNA(IRL))
Relief Commission (RLFC)
Ushaw College Library (UshCL), Durham
Vicariate/Diocesan Papers (UC/P32)
Vatican Secret Archives (VSA), Rome
Secretary of State (SoS)
Vincentian Archives, Raheny
Minutes of the Provincial Council

Primary and Secondary Literature

Aaltola, Mika, 'Theoretical Departures to Disasters and Emergencies', in *The Politics and Policies of Relief, Aid and Reconstruction: Contrasting Approaches to Disasters and Emergencies*, ed. Fulvio Attina (Houndmills: Palgrave, 2012), 57–75.

Adam, Thomas, *Buying Respectability: Philanthropy and Urban Society in Transnational Perspective, 1840s to 1930s* (Bloomington: Indiana University Press, 2009).

Agamben, Giorgio, *Homo Sacer: Sovereign Power and Bare Life* (Stanford, CA: Stanford University Press, 1998).

Agné, Hans, 'Does Global Democracy Matter? Hypotheses on Famine and War', in *Transnational Actors in Global Governance: Patterns, Explanations, and Implications*, eds Christer Jönsson and Jonas Tallberg (Basingstoke: Palgrave Macmillan, 2010), 177–96.

Aho, James Alfred, *Confession and Bookkeeping: The Religious, Moral, and Rhetorical Roots of Modern Accounting* (Albany: State University of New York Press, 2005).

Aid to Ireland: Report of the General Relief Committee of the City of New York, Organized February 10th, 1847 (New York: General Irish Relief Committee, 1848).

Aiken, William, 'The Right to Be Saved from Starvation', in *World Hunger and Moral Obligation*, eds William Aiken and Hugh La Follette (Englewood Cliffs, NJ: Prentice-Hall, 1977), 115–23.

Alfani, Guido, and Cormac Ó Gráda, 'Famines in Europe: An Overview', in *Famine in European History*, eds Guido Alfani and Cormac Ó Gráda (Cambridge: Cambridge University Press, 2017), 1–24.

Allié, Marie-Pierre, 'Introduction: Acting at Any Price?', in *Humanitarian Negotiations Revealed: The MSF Experience*, eds Claire Magone, Michaël Neuman, and Fabrice Weissman (London: Hurst, 2011), 1–11.

Andreoni, James, 'Philanthropy', in *Handbook of the Economics of Giving, Altruism and Reciprocity, vol. 2: Applications*, eds Serge-Christophe Kolm and Jean Mercier Ythier (Amsterdam: North Holland, 2006), 1201–69.

Arnold, David, *Famine: Social Crisis and Historical Change* (Oxford: Blackwell, 1988).

Arrington, C. Edward, and Jere R. Francis, 'Giving Economic Accounts: Accounting as a Cultural Practice', *Accounting, Organizations and Society* 18, nos 2–3 (1993): 107–24.

Arsan, Andrew, Su Lin Lewis, and Anne-Isabelle Richard, 'Editorial: The Roots of Global Civil Society and the Interwar Moment', *Journal of Global History* 7, no. 2 (2012): 157–65.

Article 19, *Starving in Silence: Report on Famine and Censorship* (London: Article 19, 1990).

Athenian Letters, or, The Epistolary Correspondence of an Agent of the King of Persia, Residing at Athens during the Peloponnesian War, vol. 2 (Dublin: Archer, 1792).

Atkinson, Anthony B., Peter G. Backus, John Micklewright, Cathy Pharoah, and Sylke V. Schnepf, 'Charitable Giving for Overseas Development: UK Trends over a Quarter Century', *Journal of the Royal Statistical Society Series A* 175, no. 1 (2012): 167–90.

Atlas to Accompany 2d Report of the Railway Commissioners Ireland 1838 (London, 1838).

Baker, Robert, and Martin Strosberg, 'Triage and Equality: An Historical Reassessment of Utilitarian Analyses of Triage', *Kennedy Institute of Ethics Journal* 2, no. 2 (1992): 103–23.

Balcik, Burcu, Benita M. Beamon, and Karen Smilowitz, 'Last Mile Distribution in Humanitarian Relief', *Journal of Intelligent Transportation Systems* 12, no. 2 (2008): 51–63.

Band Aid, *With Love from Band Aid: Report of 7 Years Work* (London: Band Aid Trust, 1992).

Banga, Luther, *Reducing People's Vulnerability to Famine: An Evaluation of Band Aid and Live Aid Financed Projects in Africa Final Report* (Douala: PAID, 1991).

Banik, Dan, 'Is Democracy the Answer? Famine Prevention in Two Indian States', in *The New Famines: Why Famines Persist in an Era of Globalization*, ed. Stephen Devereux (London: Routledge, 2007), 290–311.

Barnett, Michael, 'Humanitarianism as a Scholarly Vocation', in *Humanitarianism in Question: Politics, Power, Ethics*, eds Michael Barnett and Thomas G. Weiss (Ithaca, NY: Cornell University Press, 2008), 235–63.

Empire of Humanity: A History of Humanitarianism (Ithaca, NY: Cornell University Press, 2011).

Bartels, Daniel M., 'Principled Moral Sentiment and the Flexibility of Moral Judgment and Decision Making', *Cognition* 108, no. 2 (2008): 381–417.

Bass, Gary J., *Freedom's Battle: The Origins of Humanitarian Intervention* (New York: Knopf, 2008).

Baughan, Emily, 'The Imperial War Relief Fund and the All British Appeal: Commonwealth, Conflict and Conservatism within the British Humanitarian Movement, 1920–25', *Journal of Imperial and Commonwealth History* 40, no. 5 (2012): 845–61.

Beaumont, Joan, 'Starving for Democracy: Britain's Blockade of and Relief for Occupied Europe, 1939–1945', *War & Society* 8, no. 2 (1990): 57–82.

Bechhofer, C. E., *Through Starving Russia, Being a Record of a Journey to Moscow and the Volga Provinces, in August and September, 1921* (London: Menthuen, 1921).

Bekkers, René, and Pamala Wiepking, 'A Literature Review of Empirical Studies of Philanthropy: Eight Mechanisms That Drive Charitable Giving', *Nonprofit and Voluntary Sector Quarterly* 40, no. 5 (2011): 924–73.

Belhoste, Bruno, *Augustin-Louis Cauchy: A Biography* (New York: Springer, 1991).

Benthall, Jonathan, *Disasters, Relief and the Media* (London: Tauris, 1993).

Benz, Wigbert, *Der Hungerplan im 'Unternehmen Barbarossa' 1941* (Berlin: Wissenschaftlicher Verlag, 2011).

Bew, John, '"From an Umpire to a Competitor": Castlereagh, Canning and the Issue of International Intervention in the Wake of the Napoleonic Wars', in *Humanitarian Intervention: A History*, eds Brendan Simms and D. J. B. Trim (Cambridge: Cambridge University Press, 2011), 117–38.

Bhatia, Vijay K., 'Generic Patterns in Fundraising Discourse', *New Direction for Philanthropic Fundraising* no. 22 (1998): 95–110.

Bienz, Marguerite E., ed., *Für unsere kleinen russischen Brüder! Gaben westeuropäischer Schriftsteller und Künstler für die notleidenden Kinder in den Hungersnotdistrikten Russlands* (Geneva: Hohes Kommissariat, 1922).

Binet, Laurence, *Famine and Forced Relocations in Ethiopia, 1984–1986* (Paris: Médecins Sans Frontières, 2013).

Black, Maggie, *A Cause for Our Times: Oxfam: The First 50 Years* (Oxford: Oxfam, 1992).

Bloodworth, Jeff, 'A Complicated Kindness: The Iowa Famine Relief Movement and the Myth of Midwestern (and American) Isolationism', *Historian* 73, no. 3 (2011): 480–502.

Bloom, Paul, *Against Empathy: The Case for Rational Compassion* (New York: Ecco, 2016).

Blundy, David, and Paul Vallely, *With Geldof in Africa: Confronting the Famine Crisis* (London: Times Books, 1985).

Bocking-Welch, Anna, *British Civic Society at the End of Empire: Decolonisation, Globalisation, and International Responsibility* (Manchester: Manchester University Press, 2019).

Bollina, Paola, and Michael R. Reich, 'The Italian Fight against World Hunger: A Critical Analysis of Italian Aid for Development in the 1980s', *Social Science of Medicine* 39, no, 5 (1994): 607–20.

Boltanski, Luc, *Distant Suffering: Morality, Media and Politics* (Cambridge: Cambridge University Press, 1999 [1993]).

Boltanski, Luc, and Eve Chiapello, *The New Spirit of Capitalism* (London: Verso, 2005).

Borstelmann, Thomas, *The 1970s: A New Global History from Civil Rights to Economic Inequality* (Princeton, NJ: Princeton University Press, 2012).

Borton, John, *The Changing Role of NGOs in the Provision of Relief and Rehabilitation Assistance: Case Study 3 – Northern Ethiopia and Eritrea* (London: Overseas Development Institute, 1994).

'Improving the Use of History in the International Humanitarian Sector', *European Review of History* 23, nos 1–2 (2016): 193–209.

Bovens, Mark, 'Two Concepts of Accountability: Accountability as a Virtue and as a Mechanism', *West European Politics* 33, no. 5 (2010): 946–67.

Bradol, Jean-Hervé, and Jacky Mamou, 'La commémoration amnésique des humanitaires', *Humanitaire*, no. 10 (2004): 12–28.

Braskén, Kasper, *The International Workers' Relief, Communism, and Transnational Solidarity: Willi Münzenberg in Weimar Germany* (Basingstoke: Palgrave Macmillan, 2015).

Brauman, Rony, *Rapport Moral 1985/86* (Paris: Médecins Sans Frontières, 1986).

'Global Media and the Myths of Humanitarian Relief: The Case of the 2004 Tsunami', in *Humanitarianism and Suffering: The Mobilization of Empathy*, eds Richard Ashby Wilson and Richard D. Brown (Cambridge: Cambridge University Press, 2009), 108–17.

Breen, Rodney, 'Saving Enemy Children: Save the Children's Russian Relief Operation, 1921–1923', *Disasters* 18, no. 3 (1994): 221–38.

Breeze, Beth, and Wendy A. Scaife, 'Encouraging Generosity: The Practice and Organization of Fundraising across Nations', in *Palgrave Handbook of Global Philanthropy*, eds Pamala Wiepking and Femida Handy (Houndmills: Palgrave Macmillan, 2015), 570–96.

Breve notizia dell' attuale carestia in Irlanda (Rome: Menicanti, 1847).

Brewis, Georgina, '"Fill Full the Mouth of Famine": Voluntary Action in Famine Relief in India 1896–1901', *Modern Asian Studies* 44, no. 4 (2010): 887–918.

A Social History of Student Volunteering: Britain and Beyond, 1880–1980 (New York: Palgrave Macmillan, 2014).

Brown, Ford K., *Fathers of the Victorians: The Age of Wilberforce* (Cambridge: Cambridge University Press, 1961).

Buchanan, Rob 'Reflections on Working with Rebel Movements in the Horn of Africa', in *Change Not Charity: Essays on Oxfam America's First 40 Years*, ed. Laura Roper (Boston: Oxfam America, 2010), 251–63.

Burritt, Elihu, *A Journal of a Visit of Three Days to Skibbereen, and Its Neighbourhood* (London: Gilpin, 1847).

Cabanes, Bruno, *The Great War and the Origins of Humanitarianism, 1918–1924* (Cambridge: Cambridge University Press, 2014).

Calhoun, Craig, 'The Imperative to Reduce Suffering: Charity, Progress, and Emergencies in the Field of Humanitarian Action', in *Humanitarianism in Question: Politics, Power, Ethics*, eds Michael Barnett and Thomas G. Weiss (Ithaca, NY: Cornell University Press, 2008), 73–97.

Campbell, John H., *History of the Friendly Sons of St. Patrick and of the Hibernian Society for the Relief of Emigrants from Ireland* (Philadelphia: Hibernian Society, 1892).

Carbonnier, Gilles, *Humanitarian Economics: War, Disaster and the Global Aid Market* (London: Hurst, 2015).

Carlson, Claire Elizabeth, Paul A. Isihara, Roger Sandberg, et al., 'Introducing PEARL: A Gini-like Index and Reporting Tool for Public Accountability and Equity in Disaster Response', *Journal of Humanitarian Logistics and Supply Chain Management* 6, no. 2 (2016): 202–21.

Cater, Nick, 'The Hungry Media', *Ten·8*, 10 (1985): 2–4.

Çelik, Semih, 'Between History of Humanitarianism and Humanitarianization of History: A Discussion on Ottoman Help for the Victims of the Great Irish Famine, 1845–1852', *Werkstatt Geschichte* no. 68 (2015): 13–27.

Charbonneau, André, and Doris Drolet-Dubé, *A Register of Deceased Persons at Sea and on Grosse Île in 1847* (Ottawa: Canadian Heritage, 1997).

Charities Aid Foundation, *Charity Statistics 1984/5* (Tonbridge: Charities Aid Foundation, 1985).

'Charity Souphouse at Skibbereen, 1846', *Journal of the Cork Historical and Archaeological Society* 51, no. 174 (1946): 189–90.

Chouliaraki, Lilie, 'The Theatricality of Humanitarianism: A Critique of Celebrity Advocacy', *Communication and Critical/Cultural Studies* 9, no. 1 (2012): 1–21.

    The Ironic Spectator: Solidarity in the Age of Post-Humanitarianism (Cambridge: Polity, 2013).

    'Post-humanitarianism', in *Humanitarianism: A Dictionary of Concepts*, eds Tim Allen, Anna Macdonald, and Henry Radice (London: Routledge, 2018), 253–68.

CIA, *Ethiopia: A Political and Security Impact of the Drought*, Apr. 1985, available at www.cia.gov/library/readingroom/docs/CIA-RDP86T00589R000200160004-5 .pdf (accessed 29 June 2019).

The Circular of the President General of the 21st November, 1846, to which is appended the Letter of the President of the Council of Ireland of 9th February, 1847 (Dublin: Clarke, 1847).

Clark, Jeffrey, *Civil Society, NGOs, and Development in Ethiopia: A Snapshot View* (Washington, DC: World Bank, 2000).

Clarke, John, *Resettlement and Rehabilitation: Ethiopia's Campaign against Famine* (London: Harney and Jones, 1987).

Clay, Henry, 'Appeal for Ireland', in *The American Common-School Reader and Speaker*, eds John Goldsbury and William Russell (Boston: Tappan, Whittemore, and Mason, 1850), 350–1.

Clay, Jason, and Bonnie Holcomb, *Politics and the Ethiopian Famine, 1984–85* (Cambridge, MA: Cultural Survival, 1985).

Cleary, Patrick, and Philip O'Regan, eds, *Dear Old Skibbereen* (Skibbereen: Skibbereen Printers Ltd, 1995).

Clements, Kendrick Alling, *The Life of Herbert Hoover, vol. 4: Imperfect Visionary 1918–1928* (New York: Palgrave Macmillan, 2010).

Coleman, Ann Mary Chapman, ed., *The Life of John J. Crittenden, with Selections from His Correspondence and Speeches, vol. 1* (Philadelphia: Lippincott, 1871).

Collet, Dominik, 'Mitleid machen: Die Nutzung von Emotionen in der Hungersnot 1770–1772', *Historische Anthropologie* 23, no. 1 (2015): 54–69.

Collingham, Lizzie, *The Taste of War: World War Two and the Battle for Food* (London: Allen Lane, 2011).

Comité de secours pour l'Irlande (Paris: A. Sirou et Desquers, 1847).

Coogan, Tim Pat, *The Famine Plot: England's Role in Ireland's Greatest Tragedy* (New York: Palgrave Macmillan, 2012).

Cooper, Glenda, and Simon Cottle, 'Humanitarianism, Communications, and Change: Final Reflections', in *Humanitarianism, Communications and Change*, eds Simon Cottle and Glenda Cooper (New York: Lang, 2015), 251–64.

Corni, Gustavo, and Horst Gies, *Brot – Butter – Kanonen: Die Ernährungswirtschaft in Deutschland unter der Diktatur Hitlers* (Berlin: Akademie, 1997).

Correspondence from January to March, 1847, Relating to the Measures Adopted for the Relief of Distress in Ireland (London: Clowes and Sons, 1847).

Correspondence from July, 1846, to January, 1847, Relating to the Measures Adopted for the Relief of Distress in Ireland (London: Clowes and Sons, 1847).

Cox, Mary Elisabeth, 'Hunger Games: Or How the Allied Blockade in the First World War Deprived German Children of Nutrition, and Allied Food Aid Subsequently Saved Them', *Economic History Review* 68, no. 2 (2015): 600–31.

Crossgove, William, David Egilman, Peter Heywood, et al., 'Colonialism, International Trade, and the Nation-state', in *Hunger in History: Food Shortage, Poverty, and Deprivation*, ed. Lucile F. Newman (Oxford: Blackwell, 1990), 215–40.

Cullen, Bob, *Thomas L. Synnott: The Career of a Dublin Catholic 1830–70* (Dublin: Irish Academic Press, 1997).

Curti, Merle, *American Philanthropy Abroad: A History* (New Brunswick, NJ: Rutgers University Press, 1963).

Curtis, Heather, 'Depicting Distant Suffering: Evangelicals and the Politics of Pictorial Humanitarianism in the Age of American Empire', *Material Religion* 8, no. 2 (2012): 153–82.

Cushing, Luther S., ed., 'Patrick Murray & Another vs. Terence McHugh [etc.]', in *Reports of Cases Argued and Determined in the Supreme Judicial Court of Massachusetts, vol. 9* (Boston: Little, Brown, 1858), 158–63.

D'Alton, Edward Alfred, *History of the Archdiocese of Tuam, vol. 2* (Dublin: Phoenix, 1928).

Dal Lago, Enrico, and Kevin O'Sullivan, 'Introduction: Toward a New History of Humanitarianism', *Moving the Social* no. 57 (2017): 5–20.

Darwen, Lewis, Donald Macraild, Brian Gurrin, and Liam Kennedy, '"Unhappy and Wretched Creatures": Charity, Poor Relief and Pauper Removal in Britain and Ireland during the Great Famine', *The English Historical Review* 134, no. 568 (2019): 589–619.

Davey, Eleanor, 'Famine, Aid, and Ideology: The Political Activism of Médicins sans Frontières in the 1980s', *French Historical Studies* 34, no. 3 (2011): 531–58.

Idealism beyond Borders: The French Revolutionary Left and the Rise of Humanitarianism, 1954–1988 (Cambridge: Cambridge University Press, 2015).

Davey, Eleanor, and John Borton, 'History and Practitioners: The Use of History by Humanitarians and the Potential Benefits of History to the Humanitarian Sector', in *The Impact of History? Histories at the Beginning of the Twenty-First Century*, eds Pedro Ramos Pinto and Bertrand Taithe (Abingdon: Routledge, 2015), 153–68.

Davey, Eleanor, John Borton, and Matthew Foley, *A History of the Humanitarian System: Western Origins and Foundations* (London: Overseas Development Institute, 2013).

318   References

Davey, Eleonor, and Kim Scriven, 'Humanitarian Aid in the Archives: Introduction', *Disasters* 39, no. s2 (2015): 113–28.
Davies, Thomas, *NGOs: A New History of Transnational Civil Society* (London: Hurst, 2013).
Davis, Austen, *Concerning Accountability of Humanitarian Action* (London: Overseas Development Institute, 2007).
Davis, Mike, *Late Victorian Holocausts: El Nino Famines and the Making of the Third World* (London: Verso, 2001).
de Waal, Alex, 'A Re-assessment of Entitlement Theory in the Light of the Recent Famines in Africa', *Development and Change* 21, no. 3 (1990): 469–90.
    Evil Days: 30 Years of War and Famine (New York: Human Rights Watch, 1991).
    Famine Crimes: Politics and the Disaster Relief Industry in Africa (Oxford: Currey, 1997).
    'The Humanitarian Carnival: A Celebrity Vogue', *World Affairs* 171, no. 2 (2008): 43–55.
    Mass Starvation: The History and Future of Famine (Cambridge: Polity, 2018), 94.
Deane, Seamus, 'Catholicism, Republicanism and Race: Ireland in Nineteenth-century French Thought', in *Paris – Capital of Irish Culture: France, Ireland and the Republic, 1798–1916*, eds Pierre Joannon and Kevin Whelan (Dublin: Four Courts, 2017), 110–29.
Delaney, Enda, 'Ireland's Great Famine: A Transnational History', in *Transnational Perspectives in Modern Irish History*, ed. Niall Whelehan (New York: Routledge, 2015).
Denzel, Markus A., *Handbook of World Exchange Rates, 1590–1914* (Farnham: Ashgate, 2010).
Desgrandchamps, Marie-Luce, '"Organising the Unpredictable": The Nigeria–Biafra War and Its Impact on the ICRC', *International Review of the Red Cross* 94, no. 888 (2012): 1409–32.
Devereux, Stephen, 'Sen's Entitlement Approach: Critiques and Counter-Critiques', in *The New Famines: Why Famines Persist in an Era of Globalization*, ed. Stephen Devereux (London: Routledge, 2007), 66–89.
    'Introduction: From "Old Famines" to "New Famines"', in *The New Famines: Why Famines Persist in an Era of Globalization*, ed. Stephen Devereux (London: Routledge, 2007), 1–26.
    ed., *The New Famines: Why Famines Persist in an Era of Globalization* (London: Routledge, 2007).
Devereux, Stephen, and Zoltan Tiba, 'Malawi's First Famine, 2001–2002', in *The New Famines: Why Famines Persist in an Era of Globalization*, ed. Stephen Devereux (London: Routledge, 2007), 143–77.
Diaz, Efrain M., 'Friends of Soviet Russia: The Friendly Front Survives the Famine', *Perspectives* 34 (2007/8): 41–58.
Dickens, Charles, *Bleak House* (London: Bradbury and Evans, 1853).
Distress in Ireland: Report of the Trustees of the Indian Relief Fund, Shewing the Distribution of the Sum of £13, 919 14s. 2d., Commencing the 24th April, and Ending the 31st December, 1846 (Dublin: Browne, 1847).
Documents of the American Relief Administration, Russian Operations 1921–1923, vol. 1: Organization and Administration (Stanford, CA: Stanford University Press, 1931).

Doering-Manteuffel, Anselm, and Lutz Raphael, *Nach dem Boom: Perspektiven auf die Zeitgeschichte seit 1970* (Göttingen: Vandenhoeck & Ruprecht, 2010).

Dolezal, Rudi, *Die Geschichte des Austropop in 20 Songs* (Salzburg: Servus, 2016).

Donnelly, James S., *The Land and the People of Nineteenth-Century Cork: The Rural Economy and the Land Question* (London: Routledge, 1975).

'The Administration of Relief, 1846–7', in *A New History of Ireland, vol. 5: Ireland under the Union, 1801–70*, ed. W. E. Vaughan (Oxford: Clarendon, 1989), 294–306.

'The Soup Kitchens', in *A New History of Ireland, vol. 5: Ireland under the Union, 1801–70*, ed. W. E. Vaughan (Oxford: Clarendon, 1989), 307–15.

Donovan, Daniel, 'Observations on the Peculiar Diseases to which the Famine of Last Year Gave Origin, and on the Morbid Effects of Insufficient Nourishment', *Dublin Medical Press* 19 (1848): 67–8, 129–32, 275–8.

Dufferin, Frederick, and George Boyle, *Narrative of a Journey from Oxford to Skibbereen during the Year of the Irish Famine* (Oxford: Parker, 1847).

Duffield, Mark, 'NGOs, Disaster Relief and Asset Transfer in the Horn: Political Survival in a Permanent Emergency', *Development and Change* 24, no. 1 (1993): 131–58.

'From Protection to Disaster Resilience', in *The Routledge Companion to Humanitarian Action*, eds Roger Mac Ginty and Jenny H. Peterson (London: Routledge, 2015), 26–37.

Post-humanitarianism: Governing Precarity in the Digital World (Cambridge: Polity, 2019).

Duffield, Mark, and John Prendergast, *Without Troops and Tanks: Humanitarian Intervention in Ethiopia and Eritrea* (Lawrenceville, NJ: Red Sea Press, 1994).

Ebrahim, Alnoor, 'Accountability in Practice: Mechanisms for NGOs', *World Development* 31, no. 5 (2003): 813–29.

Eckart, Wolfgang U., 'Nach bestem Vermögen tatkräftige Hilfe leisten', *Ruperto Carola* 3 (1999).

Von Kommissaren und Kamelen: Heinrich Zeiss – Arzt und Kundschafter in der Sowjetunion 1921–1931 (Paderborn: Schöningh, 2016).

Edkins, Jenny, *Whose Hunger? Concepts of Famine, Practices of Aid* (Minneapolis: University of Minnesota Press, 2000).

'The Criminalization of Mass Starvation: From Natural Disaster to Crime against Humanity', in *The New Famines: Why Famines Persist in an Era of Globalization*, ed. Stephen Devereux (London: Routledge, 2007), 50–65.

Edwards, John Richard, *A History of Financial Accounting* (London: Routledge, 1989).

Ein-Gar, Danit, and Liat Levontin, 'Giving from a Distance: Putting the Charitable Organization at the Center of the Donation Appeal', *Journal of Consumer Psychology* 23, no. 2 (2013): 197–211.

Einarsdóttir, Jónína, and Geir Gunnlaugsson, 'Applied Ethics and Allocation of Foreign Aid: Disparity in Pretensions and Practice', *Development Policy Review* 34, no. 3 (2016): 345–63.

Epstein, Keith, 'Crisis Mentality', *Stanford Social Innovation Review* 4, no. 1 (2006): 48–57.

Erlandsson, Arvid, Frederik Björklund, and Martin Bäckström, 'Emotional Reactions, Perceived Impact and Perceived Responsibility Mediate the Identifiable Victim

Effect, Proportion Dominance Effect and In-Group Effect, Respectively',
Organizational Behavior and Human Decision Processes 127 (2015): 1–14.

Everett, Jeff, and Constance Friesen, 'Humanitarian Accountability and Performance in
the Théâtre de l'Absurde', *Critical Perspectives on Accounting* 21, no. 6 (2010):
468–85.

Farmer, Paul, *Haiti after the Earthquake* (New York: Public Affairs, 2011).

Fassin, Didier, 'Les économies morales revisitées', *Annales: Histoire, Sciences sociales*
64, no. 6 (2009): 1237–66.

'Heart of Humaneness: The Moral Economy of Humanitarian Intervention', in
*Contemporary States of Emergency: Anthropology of Military and Humanitarian
Intervention*, eds Didier Fassin and Mariella Pandolfi (New York: Zone, 2010),
269–93.

Humanitarian Reason: A Moral History of the Present (Berkeley: University of
California Press, 2012).

'Feeding of the Starving Russian Population on August 1st 1922: Organisations
Working under the Nansen Agreement', *International Committee for Russian
Relief – Information* 30 (30 Aug. 1922).

Fegan, Melissa, *Literature and the Irish Famine 1845–1919* (Oxford: Clarendon,
2002).

Fehrenbach, Heide, 'Children and Other Civilians: Photography and the Politics of
Humanitarian Image-Making', in *Humanitarian Photography: A History*, eds
Heide Fehrenbach and Davide Rodogno (Cambridge: Cambridge University Press,
2015), 165–99.

Fehrenbach, Heide, and Davide Rodogno, 'Introduction: The Morality of Sight:
Humanitarian Photography in History', in *Humanitarian Photography: A History*,
eds Heide Fehrenbach and Davide Rodogno (Cambridge: Cambridge University
Press, 2015), 1–21.

eds, *Humanitarian Photography: A History* (New York: Cambridge University
Press, 2015).

Fetherstonhaugh, David, Paul Slovic, Stephen Johnson, and James Friedrich,
'Insensitivity to the Value of Human Life: A Study of Psychophysical Numbing',
Journal of Risk and Uncertainty 14, no. 3 (1997): 283–300.

Field, Jessica, 'Consumption *in lieu* of Membership: Reconfiguring Popular Charitable
Action in Post–World War II Britain', *Voluntas* 27, no. 2 (2016): 979–97.

Finkielkraut, Alain, *In the Name of Humanity: Reflections on the Twentieth Century*
(New York: Columbia University Press, 2000).

First Annual Report of the Society of Saint Vincent de Paul, Cork (Cork: O'Brien, 1846).

First Report of the Commissioners of Public Instruction, Ireland (London: Clowes and
Sons, 1835).

Fisher, Harold Henry, *The Famine in Soviet Russia, 1919–1923: The Operations of the
American Relief Administration* (New York: Macmillan, 1927).

Flint, James P., *Great Britain and the Holy See: The Diplomatic Relations Question
1846–1852* (Washington, DC: Catholic University of America Press, 2003).

Flynn, Jeffrey, 'Philosophers, Historians, and Suffering Strangers', *Moving the Social*
no. 57 (2017): 137–58.

Forbes, Henry A. Crosby, and Henry Lee, *Massachusetts Help to Ireland during the
Great Famine* (Milton: Captain Robert Bennet Forbes House, 1967).

Forbes, Robert Bennet, *The Voyage of the Jamestown on Her Errand of Mercy* (Boston: Eastburn, 1847).

Personal Reminiscences (Boston: Little, Brown, 1878).

Forstorp, Per-Anders, 'Fundraising Discourse and the Commodification of the Other', *Business Ethics* 16, no. 3 (2007): 286–301.

Framke, Maria, 'Political Humanitarianism in the 1930s: Indian Aid for Republican Spain', *European Review of History* 23, nos 1–2 (2016): 63–81.

Framke, Maria, and Ester Möller, *From Local Philanthropy to Political Humanitarianism: South Asian and Egyptian Humanitarian Aid during the Period of Decolonisation* (Berlin: Leibniz-Zentrum Moderner Orient, 2019).

Framke, Maria, and Joël Glasman, 'Editorial', *Werkstatt Geschichte*, no. 68 (2015): 3–12.

Franks, Susanne, *Reporting Disasters: Famine, Aid, Politics and the Media* (London: Hurst, 2013).

Fredrichsen, Kim, and Asger Pedersen, 'Dansk-Russisk Forenings tidlige historie', in *Dansk-russiske mellemfolkelige kontakter før og nu* (s.l.: Dansk-Russisk Forening, 2015), 2–5.

Friberg, Katarina, 'Accounts along the Aid Chain: Administering a Moral Economy', *Journal of Global Ethics* 11, no. 2 (2015): 246–56.

'Fridtjof Nansens Rede vor dem Völkerbund (24 Sept. 1921)' (in English), in *Themenportal Europäische Geschichte* (Berlin: Humboldt Universität, 2011), available at www.europa.clio-online.de/quelle/id/artikel-3535 (accessed 29 June 2019).

Fry, Ruth, 'The Relation of Relief to Propaganda', *Friends' Quarterly Examiner* 57 (1923): 322–35.

FSR, *Matrix Service* (New York: FSR, c. 1922).

Productive Relief for Soviet Russia (New York: FSR, c. 1922).

The Russian Famine: Forty Facts (New York: FSR, c. 1922).

The Russian Famine: One Year of Relief Work (New York: FSR, c. 1922).

The Russian Famine [Pictures – Appeals] (New York: FSR, c. 1922).

Fuller, Lisa, 'Justified Commitments? Considering Resource Allocation and Fairness in Médecins Sans Frontières-Holland', *Developing World Bioethics* 6, no. 2 (2006): 59–70.

'Priority-setting in International Non-governmental Organizations: It Is Not as Easy as ABCD', *Journal of Global Ethics* 8, no. 1 (2012): 5–17.

Funnell, Warwick, 'Accounting for Justice: Entitlement, Want and the Irish Famine of 1845–7', *Accounting Historians Journal* 28, no. 2 (2001): 187–206.

Gay, George I., *The Commission for Relief in Belgium: Statistical Review of Relief Operations* (Stanford, CA: Stanford University Press, 1925).

Gay, George I., and H. H. Fisher, eds, *Public Relations of the Commission for Relief in Belgium: Documents, vol. 1* (Stanford, CA: Stanford University Press, 1929).

Gazdar, Haris, 'Pre-modern, Modern and Post-modern Famine in Iraq, 1990–2003', in *The New Famines: Why Famines Persist in an Era of Globalization*, ed. Stephen Devereux (London: Routledge, 2007), 127–42.

Geary, Laurence M., '"The Noblest Offering That Nation Ever Made to Nation": American Philanthropy and the Great Famine in Ireland', *Éire-Ireland* 48, nos 3–4 (2013): 103–28.

Geldof, Bob, with Paul Vallely, *Is That It?* (London: Sidgwick and Jackson, 1986).

General Central Relief Committee for All Ireland, *Alphabetical List of Subscribers, Commencing 29th December 1849, and Ending 24th September 1849* [GCRC 1850] (Dublin: Browne & Nolan, 1850).

Giddens, Anthony, *Central Problems in Social Theory: Action, Structure and Contradiction in Social Analysis* (London: Macmillan, 1979).

Gill, Peter, *A Year in the Death of Africa: Politics, Bureaucracy and the Famine* (London: Palladin, 1986).

  Famine and Foreigners: Ethiopia since Live Aid (Oxford: Oxford University Press, 2010).

Gill, Rebecca, 'The Rational Administration of Compassion: The Origins of British Relief in War', *Le mouvement social* 227, no. 1 (2009): 9–26.

  Calculating Compassion: Humanity and Relief in War, Britain 1870–1914 (Manchester: Manchester University Press, 2013).

Giorgis, Dawit Wolde, *Red Tears: War, Famine and Revolution in Ethiopia* (Trenton, NJ: Red Sea Press, 1989).

Glasman, Joël, 'Measuring Malnutrition: The History of the MUAC Tape and the Commensurability of Human Needs', *Humanity* 9, no. 1 (2018): 19–44.

Gore, Charles, 'Entitlement Relations and "Unruly" Social Practices: A Comment on the Work of Amartya Sen', *Journal of Development Studies* 29, no. 3 (1993): 429–60.

Gorin, Valérie, 'L'enfance comme figure compassionnelle: Étude transversale de l'iconographie de la famine aux dix-neuvième et vingtième siècles', *European Review of History* 2, no. 6 (2015): 940–62.

Gossin, Eugène, *Vie de M. Jules Gossin* (Paris: Oudin, 1907).

Götz, Norbert, 'Reframing NGOs: The Identity of an International Relations Non-starter', *European Journal of International Relations* 14, no. 2 (2008): 231–58.

  'Rationales of Humanitarianism: The Case of British Relief to Germany, 1805–1815', *Journal of Modern European History* 12, no. 2 (2014): 186–99.

  '"Moral Economy": Its Conceptual History and Analytical Prospects', *Journal of Global Ethics* 11, no. 2 (2015): 147–62.

  'The Good Plumpuddings' Belief: British Voluntary Aid to Sweden during the Napoleonic Wars', *International History Review* 37, no. 3 (2015): 519–39.

  'The Emergence of NGOs as Actors on the World Stage', in *Routledge Handbook of NGOs and International Relations*, ed. Thomas Davies (London: Routledge, 2019), 19–31.

Götz, Norbert, Georgina Brewis, and Steffen Werther, 'Humanitäre Hilfe: Eine Braudel'sche Perspektive', in *Freiwilligenarbeit und gemeinnützige Organisationen im Wandel: Neue Perspektiven auf das 19. und 20. Jahrhundert*, eds Nicole Kramer and Christine G. Krüger (Berlin: DeGruyter, 2019), 89–119.

Götz, Norbert, and Frank Palmowski, 'Humanitäre Hilfe im Zeitalter Napoleons: Bürgerliche Gesellschaft und transnationale Ressourcen am Beispiel Erfurts', *Historische Zeitschrift* 305, no. 2 (2017): 362–92.

Gray, Peter, 'Ideology and the Famine', in *The Great Irish Famine*, ed. Cathal Póirtéir (Cork: Mercier, 1995), 86–103.

  Famine, Land and Politics: British Government and Irish Society, 1843–50 (Dublin: Irish Academic Press, 1999).

'National Humiliation and the Great Hunger: Fast and Famine in 1847', *Irish Historical Studies* 32, no. 126 (2000): 193–216.

'The European Food Crisis and the Relief of Irish Famine, 1845–1850', in *When the Potato Failed: Causes and Effects of the 'Last' European Subsistence Crisis, 1845–1850*, eds Cormac Ó Gráda, Richard Paping, and Eric Vanhaute (Turnhout: Brepols, 2007), 95–107.

'British Relief Measures', in *Atlas of the Great Irish Famine*, eds John Crowley, William J. Smyth, and Mike Murphy (New York: New York University Press, 2012), 75–84.

'Charles Trevelyan', in *Atlas of the Great Irish Famine*, eds John Crowley, William J. Smyth, and Mike Murphy (New York: New York University Press, 2012), 85–6.

'"The Great British Famine of 1845 to 1850"? Ireland, the UK and Peripherality in Famine Relief and Philanthropy', in *Famines in European Economic History: The Last Great European Famines Reconsidered*, eds Declan Curran, Lubomyr Luciuk, and Andrew G. Newby (Abingdon: Routledge, 2015), 83–96.

Gray, Rob, 'Thirty Years of Social Accounting, Reporting and Auditing: What (If Anything) Have We Learnt?', *Business Ethics* 10, no. 1 (2001): 9–15.

Graziosi, Andrea, 'Political Famines in the USSR and China: A Comparative Analysis', *Journal of Cold War Studies* 19, no. 3 (2017): 42–103.

Green, Abigail, 'Humanitarianism in Nineteenth Century Context: Religious, Gendered, National', *Historical Journal* 57, no. 4 (2014): 1157–75.

Greenwood, Ormerod John, *Quaker Encounters, vol. 1: Friends and Relief* (York: Sessions, 1975).

Gribble, Richard, 'Cooperation and Conflict between Church and State: The Russian Famine of 1921–1923', *Journal of Church and State* 51, no. 4 (2009): 634–62.

Grünewald, Guido, ed., *'Organisiert die Welt!': Der Friedensnobelpreisträger Alfred Hermann Fried (1864–1921) – Leben, Werk und bleibende Impulse* (Bremen: Donat, 2016).

Guillermand, Jean, 'The Historical Foundations of Humanitarian Action, vol. 1: The Religious Influence, vol. 2: Humanism and Philosophical Thought', *International Review of the Red Cross* 34, nos 298–9 (1994): 42–55, 194–216.

Hall, Stuart, with Martin Jacques, 'People Aid: A New Politics Sweeps the Land', in *The Hard Road to Renewal: Thatcherism and the Crisis of the Left*, ed. Stuart Hall (London: Verso, 1988), 251–8.

Halttunen, Karen, 'Humanitarianism and the Pornography of Pain in Anglo-American Culture', *American Historical Review* 100, no. 2 (1995): 303–34.

Hannig, Florian, 'The Biafra Crisis and the Establishment of Humanitarian Aid in West Germany as a New Philanthropic Field', in *German Philanthropy in Transatlantic Perspective: Perceptions, Exchanges and Transfers since the Early Twentieth Century*, eds Gregory R. Witkowski and Arnd Bauerkämper (Cham: Springer, 2016), 205–25.

Harvey, Charles, Mairi Maclean, and Suddaby Roy, 'Historical Perspectives on Entrepreneurship and Philanthropy', *Business History Review* 93, no. 3 (2019): 443–71.

Haskell, Thomas L., 'Capitalism and the Origins of the Humanitarian Sensibility, Part 1', *American Historical Review* 90, no. 2 (1985): 339–61.

Hatton, Helen E., *The Largest Amount of Good: Quaker Relief in Ireland, 1654–1921* (Kingston: McGill-Queen's University Press, 1993).

Heaslip, Graham, Gyöngyi Kovács, and David B. Grant, 'Servitization as a Competitive Difference in Humanitarian Logistics', *Journal of Humanitarian Logistics and Supply Chain Management* 8, no. 4 (2018): 497–517.

Heaslip, Graham, Gyöngyi Kovács, and Ira Haavisto, 'Cash-Based Response in Relief: The Impact for Humanitarian Logistics', *Journal of Humanitarian Logistics and Supply Chain Management* 8, no. 1 (2018): 87–106.

Heerten, Lasse, *The Biafran War and Postcolonial Humanitarianism: Spectacles of Suffering* (Cambridge: Cambridge University Press, 2017).

Henckaerts, Jean-Marie, and Louise Doswald-Beck, *Customary International Humanitarian Law, vol. 1: Rules* (Cambridge: Cambridge University Press, 2005).

'Hibernian Benevolent Emigrant Society (Chicago)', in *Irish American Voluntary Organizations*, ed. Michael F. Funchion (Westport, CT: Greenwood Press, 1983), 135–6.

Hickey, Patrick, 'The Famine in the Skibbereen Union (1845–51)', in *The Great Irish Famine*, ed. Cathal Póirtéir (Cork: Mercier, 1995), 185–203.

Famine in West Cork: The Mizen Peninsula Land and People, 1800–1852: A Local Study of Pre-famine and Famine Ireland (Cork: Mercier, 2002).

Hiebert, P. C., and Orie O. Miller, *Feeding the Hungry: Russian Famine 1919–1925, American Mennonite Relief Operations under the Auspices of Mennonite Central Committee* (Scottdale, PA: Mennonite Central Committee, 1929).

Hilhorst, Dorothea, 'Classical Humanitarianism and Resilience Humanitarianism: Making Sense of Two Brands of Humanitarian Action', *Journal of International Humanitarian Action* 3, no. 15 (2018): 1–12.

Hillmore, Peter, *The Greatest Show on Earth: Live Aid* (London: Sidgwick and Jackson, 1985).

Hilton, Matthew, Emily Baughan, Eleanor Davey, et al., 'History and Humanitarianism: A Conversation', *Past and Present* 241, no. 1 (2018): e1–e38.

Hilton, Matthew, James McKay, Nicholas Crowson, and Jean-Francois Mouhot, *The Politics of Expertise: How NGOs Shaped Modern Britain* (Oxford: Oxford University Press, 2013).

Himmelfarb, Gertrude, *Poverty and Compassion: The Moral Imagination of the Late Victorians* (New York: Knopf, 1991).

Hinds, Stuart W., 'On the Relations of Medical Triage to World Famine: An Historical Survey', in *Lifeboat Ethics: The Moral Dilemmas of World Hunger*, eds George R. Lucas and Thomas W. Ogletree (New York: Harper & Row, 1976), 29–51.

Hirota, Hidetaka, *Expelling the Poor: Atlantic Seaboard States and the Nineteenth-Century Origins of American Immigration Policy* (New York: Oxford University Press, 2017).

Hogan, Neil, *The Cry of the Famishing: Ireland, Connecticut and the Potato Famine* (East Haven: Connecticut Irish-American Historical Society, 1998).

Holguín-Veras, José, Noel Pérez, Miguel Jaller, Luk N. van Wassenhove, and Felipe Aros-Vera, 'On the Appropriate Objective Function for Post-Disaster Humanitarian Logistics Models', *Journal of Operations Management* 31, no. 5 (2013): 262–80.

Hong, Young-Sun, *Cold War Germany, the Third World, and the Global Humanitarian Regime* (Cambridge: Cambridge University Press, 2015).

Hoover, Herbert, 'Foreword', in *Statistical Review of Relief Operations*, ed. George I. Gay (Stanford, CA: Stanford University Press, 1925), v–vi.

Horne, Suzanne, 'Charity Shops in the UK', *International Journal of Retail & Distribution Management* 26, no. 4 (1998): 155–61.

Hourihan, Kevin, 'The Cities and Towns of Ireland, 1841–51', in *Atlas of the Great Irish Famine*, eds John Crowley, William J. Smyth, and Mike Murphy (New York: New York University Press, 2012), 228–39.

Howe, Paul, 'Priority Regimes and Famine', in *The New Famines: Why Famines Persist in an Era of Globalization*, ed. Stephen Devereux (London: Routledge, 2007), 336–62.

Hughes, Sarah Forbes, ed., *Letters and Recollections of John Murray Forbes, vol. 1* (Boston: Houghton, Mifflin, 1899).

Hurst, Samia A., Nathalie Mezger, and Alex Mauron, 'Allocating Resources in Humanitarian Medicine', *Public Health Ethics* 2, no. 1 (2009): 89–99.

Hysenbelli, Dorina, Enrico Rubaltelli, and Rino Rumiati, 'Others' Opinions Count, but Not All of Them: Anchoring to Ingroup versus Outgroup Members' Behavior in Charitable Giving', *Judgment and Decision Making* 8, no. 6 (2013): 678–90.

ICRC, *Annual Report 1985* (Geneva: ICRC, 1986).

Annual Report 1986 (Geneva: ICRC, 1987).

IIED, *Report on the African Emergency Relief Operation 1984–1986 with Particular Reference to the Contributions of Non Governmental Organisations, and at the Request of the UN Office for Emergency Operations in Africa* (London: International Institute for Environment and Development, 1986).

Inquiry Report Summary Findings and Conclusions – Oxfam (London: Charity Commission, 2019).

Interim Report of European Relief Council, Including Statement of Contributions by States, and Auditors' Preliminary Report on Accounts (New York: Brown, 1921).

International Commission on Intervention and State Sovereignty, *The Responsibility to Protect* (Ottawa: International Development Research Centre, 2001).

Iriye, Akira, *Global Community: The Role of International Organizations in the Making of the Contemporary World* (Berkeley: University of California Press, 2002).

Iserson, Kenneth V., and John C. Moskop, 'Triage in Medicine, Part I: Concept, History, and Types, Part II: Underlying Values and Principles', *Annals of Emergency Medicine* 49, no. 3 (2007): 275–87.

Ivarsson, Carolina Holgersson, 'Moral Economy Reconfigured: Philanthropic Engagement in Post-tsunami Sri Lanka', *Journal of Global Ethics* 11, no. 2 (2015): 233–45.

James, Trevor, and Hanna Zagefka, 'The Effects of Group Memberships of Victims and Perpetrators in Humanly Caused Disasters on Charitable Donations to Victims', *Journal Applied Social Psychology* 47, no. 8 (2017): 446–458.

Jansson, Kurt, 'The Emergency Relief Operation: An Inside View', in *The Ethiopian Famine: The Story of the Emergency Relief Operation*, eds Kurt Jansson, Michael Harris, and Angela Penrose (London: Zed Books, 1987), 1–77.

Jaspars, Susanne, *Food Aid in Sudan: A History of Power, Politics and Profit* (London: Zed, 2018).

Jaspars, Susanne, Tom Scott-Smith, and Elizabeth Hull, *Contested Evolution of Nutrition for Humanitarian and Development Ends: Report of an International Workshop* (Oxford: Refugee Studies Centre, 2018).

Jean, François, *Du Bon Usage du Famine* (Paris: Médecins Sans Frontières, 1986).

Joannidès de Lautour, Vassili, *Accounting, Capitalism and the Revealed Religions: A Study of Christianity, Judaism and Islam* (Cham: Palgrave Macmillan, 2017).

Johns, Alessa, 'Introduction', in *Dreadful Visitations: Confronting Natural Catastrophe in the Age of Enlightenment*, ed. Alessa Johns (New York: Routledge, 1999), xi–xxv.

Johnston, Don, 'An Examination of the Principles-Based Ethics by which Red Cross Personnel Evaluate Private Donor Suitability', in *Conscience, Leadership and the Problem of 'Dirty Hands'*, eds Matthew Beard and Sandra Lynch (Bingley: Emerald, 2015), 119–37.

Jones, Andrew, 'The Disasters Emergency Committee (DEC) and the Humanitarian Industry in Britain, 1963–85', *Twentieth Century British History* 26, no. 4 (2015): 573–601.

'Band Aid Revisited: Humanitarianism, Consumption and Philanthropy in the 1980s', *Contemporary British History* 31, no. 2 (2017): 189–209.

'The Unknown Famine: Television and the Politics of British Humanitarianism', in *Global Humanitarianism and Media Culture*, eds Michael Lawrence and Rachel Tavernor (Manchester: Manchester University Press, 2019), 122–44.

Jones, Marian Moser, *The American Red Cross from Clara Barton to the New Deal* (Baltimore: Johns Hopkins University Press, 2013).

Kane, John, *The Politics of Moral Capital* (Cambridge: Cambridge University Press, 2001).

Kaplan, Robert D., *Surrender or Starve: The Wars behind the Famine* (London: Westview Press, 1988).

Käpylä, Juha, and Denis Kennedy, 'Cruel to Care? Investigating the Governance of Compassion in the Humanitarian Imaginary', *International Theory* 6, no. 2 (2014): 255–92.

Kay, Alex J., 'Germany's Staatssekretäre, Mass Starvation and the Meeting of 2 May 1941', *Journal of Contemporary History* 41, no. 4 (2006): 685–700.

Kearney, Terri, and Philip O'Regan, *Skibbereen: The Famine Story* (Skibbereen: Macalla, 2015).

Keen, David, *The Benefits of Famine: A Political Economy of Famine and Relief in Southwestern Sudan, 1983–1989* (Princeton, NJ: Princeton University Press, 1994).

Keleman, Paul, *The Politics of the Famine in Ethiopia and Eritrea* (Manchester: Manchester University Press, 1985).

Kelly, James, *Food Rioting in Ireland in the Eighteenth and Nineteenth Centuries: The 'Moral Economy' and the Irish Crowd* (Dublin: Four Courts, 2017).

Kelly, Luke 'British Humanitarianism and the Russian Famine, 1891–2', *Historical Research* 89, no. 246 (2016): 824–45.

British Humanitarian Activity in Russia, 1890–1923 (Cham: Springer, 2018).

Kennedy, Thomas C., *British Quakerism 1860–1920: The Transformation of a Religious Community* (Oxford: Oxford University Press, 2001).

Kent, Randolph C., *Anatomy of Disaster Relief: The International Network in Action* (London: Pinter, 1987).

Kerr, Donal A., *A Nation of Beggars? Priests, People, and Politics in Famine Ireland, 1846–1852* (Oxford: Clarendon, 1994).

The Catholic Church and the Famine (Blackrock: Columba, 1996).

Kilby, Patrick, *NGOs and Political Change: History of the Australian Council for International Development* (Canberra: Australian National University Press, 2015).

Kind-Kovács, Friederike, 'The Great War, the Child's Body and the American Red Cross', *European Review of History* 23, nos 1–2 (2016): 33–62.

Kinealy, Christine, *The Great Irish Famine: Impact, Ideology and Rebellion* (Basingstoke: Palgrave Macmillan, 2002).

'The Operation of the Poor Law during the Famine', in *Atlas of the Great Irish Famine*, eds John Crowley, William J. Smyth, and Mike Murphy (New York: New York University Press, 2012), 87–95.

Charity and the Great Hunger in Ireland: The Kindness of Strangers (London: Bloomsbury, 2013).

Kirimli, Hakan, 'The Famine of 1921–22 in the Crimea and the Volga Basin and the Relief from Turkey', *Middle Eastern Studies* 39, no. 1 (2003): 37–88.

Kissi, Edward, 'Beneath International Famine Relief in Ethiopia: The United States, Ethiopia, and the Debate over Relief Aid, Development Assistance, and Human Rights', *African Studies Review* 48, no. 2 (2005): 111–32.

Klein, Natalie, *'L'humanité, le christianisme, et la liberte?' Die internationale philhellenische Vereinsbewegung der 1820er Jahre* (Mainz: Zabern, 2000).

Kogut, Tehila, and Ilana Ritov, 'The "Identified Victim Effect": An Identified Group, or Just a Single Individual?', *Journal of Behavioral Decision Making* 18, no. 3 (2005): 157–67.

Koppell, Jonathan G. S., 'Pathologies of Accountability: ICANN and the Challenge of "Multiple Accountabilities Disorder"', *Public Administration Review* 65, no. 1 (2005): 94–108.

Krause, Monika, *The Good Project: Humanitarian Relief NGOs and the Fragmentation of Reason* (Chicago: University of Chicago Press, 2014).

Kreusel, Bettina, 'Das Fernsehen als Spendengenerator: Eine Bestandsaufnahme auf der Angebotsebene', in *Massenmedien und Spendenkampagnen: Vom 17. Jahrhundert bis in die Gegenwart*, ed. Jürgen Wilke (Cologne: Böhlau, 2008), 233–335.

Kuhnert, Matthias, *Humanitäre Kommunikation: Entwicklung und Emotionen bei britischen NGOs 1945–1990* (Berlin: de Gruyter, 2017).

Kurasawa, Fuyuki, 'The Making of Humanitarian Visual Icons: On the 1921–1923 Russian Famine as Foundational Event', in *Iconic Power: Materiality and Meaning in Social Life*, eds Jeffrey Alexander, Dominik Bartmanski, and Bernhard Giesen (New York: Palgrave Macmillan, 2012), 67–84.

Lancaster, Carol, *Aid to Africa: So Much to Do, So Little Done* (Chicago: University of Chicago Press, 1999).

Laqua, Daniel, 'Inside the Humanitarian Cloud: Causes and Motivations to Help Friends and Strangers', *Journal of Modern European History* 12, no. 2 (2014): 175–85.

Laughlin, Richard, 'Principals and Higher Principals: Accounting for Accountability in the Caring Professions', in *Accountability: Power, Ethos and the Technologies of Managing*, eds Rolland Munro and Jan Mouritsen (London: Thomson, 1996), 225–244.

League of Nations, *Report on Economic Conditions in Russia: With Special Reference to the Famine of 1921–1922 and the State of Agriculture* (Geneva, League of Nations, 1922).

Lee, Seyoung, and Thomas Hugh Feeley, 'The Identifiable Victim Effect: A Meta-analytic Review', *Social Influence* 11, no. 3 (2016): 199–215.

Lewin, Rebecca, Maria Besiou, Jean-Baptiste Lamarche, Stephen Cahill, and Sara Guerrero-Garcia, 'Delivering in a Moving World ... : Looking to Our Supply Chains to Meet the Increasing Scale, Cost and Complexity of Humanitarian Needs', *Journal of Humanitarian Logistics and Supply Chain Management* 8, no. 4 (2018): 518–32.

Lichtenberg, Judith, 'Absence and the Unfond Heart: Why People Are Less Giving than They Might Be', in *The Ethics of Assistance: Morality and the Distant Needy*, ed. Deen K. Chatterjee (Cambridge: Cambridge University Press, 2004), 75–97.

'Altruism', in *The Routledge Companion to Humanitarian Action*, eds Roger Mac Ginty and Jenny H. Peterson (London: Routledge, 2015), 131–40.

Lindström, Julia, *The Moral Economy of Aid: Discourse Analysis of Swedish Fundraising for the Somalia Famine of 2011–2012* (Huddinge: Södertörn University, 2016).

Lingelbach, Gabriele, 'Charitable Giving between the State and the Market: West Germany from 1945 to the 1980s', in *German Philanthropy in Transatlantic Perspective: Perceptions, Exchanges and Transfers since the Early Twentieth Century*, eds Gregory R. Witkowski and Arnd Bauerkämper (Cham: Springer, 2016), 157–69.

Little, Branden, 'An Explosion of New Endeavours: Global Humanitarian Responses to Industrialized Warfare in the First World War Era', *First World War Studies* 5, no. 1 (2014): 1–16.

Long, Douglas C., and Donald F. Wood, 'The Logistics of Famine Relief', *Journal of Business Logistics* 16, no. 1 (1995): 213–29.

Lousley, Cheryl, '"With Love from Band Aid": Sentimental Exchange, Affective Economies, and Popular Globalism', *Emotion, Space, and Society* 10 (2014): 7–17.

Luetchford, Mark, and Peter Burns, *Waging the War on Want* (London: War on Want, 2003).

Lutherhjälpen, *I God Jord: Lutherhjälpens årsbok 1984* (Uppsala: Lutherhjälpen, 1984).

Utmaningen från Afrika: Lutherhjälpens årsbok 1985 (Uppsala: Lutherhjälpen, 1985).

Låt rätten flöda fram! Lutherhjälpens årsbok 1986 (Uppsala: Lutherhjälpen, 1986).

MacAskill, William, *Doing Good Better: How Effective Altruism Can Help You Make a Difference* (New York: Gotham, 2015).

Macdonagh, Oliver, 'Introduction: Ireland and the Union, 1801–70', in *A New History of Ireland, vol. 5: Ireland under the Union, 1801–70*, ed. W. E. Vaughan (Oxford: Clarendon, 1989), xlvii–lxv.

MacSuibhne, Peadar, *Paul Cullen and His Contemporaries, vol. 1* (Naas: Leinster Leader, 1961).

Magone, Claire, Michaël Neuman, and Fabrice Weissman, eds, *Humanitarian Negotiations Revealed: The MSF Experience* (London: Hurst, 2011).

Mahood, Linda, *Feminism and Voluntary Action: Eglantyne Jebb and Save the Children, 1876–1928* (Basingstoke: Palgrave, 2009).

Mahood, Linda, and Vic Satzewich, 'The Save the Children Fund and the Russian Famine of 1921–23: Claims and Counter-claims about Feeding "Bolshevik" Children', *Journal of Historical Sociology* 22, no. 1 (2009): 55–83.

Maibom, Heidi L., ed., *Empathy and Morality* (Oxford: Oxford University Press, 2014).

Malito, Debora Valentina, 'The Responsibility to Protect What in Libya?', *Peace Review* 29, no. 3 (2017): 289–98.

Malkki, Liisa H., *The Need to Help: The Domestic Arts of International Humanitarianism* (Durham, NC: Duke University Press, 2015).

Malthus, Thomas Robert, *An Essay on the Principle of Population, as It Affects the Future Improvement of Society: With Remarks on the Speculations of W. Godwin, M. Condorcet and Other Writers* (London: Johnson, 1798).

Marcus, Harold G., *A History of Ethiopia*, 3rd ed. (Berkeley: University of California Press, 2002).

Marshall, Dominique, 'The Construction of Children as an Object of International Relations: The Declaration of Children's Rights and the Child Welfare Committee of League of Nations, 1900–1924', *International Journal of Children's Rights* 7, no. 2 (1999): 103–47.

'Children's Rights from Below: Canadian and Transnational Actions, Beliefs, and Discourses, 1900–1989', in *Taking Liberties: A History of Human Rights in Canada*, eds David Goutor and Stephen Heathorn (Oxford: Oxford University Press, 2013), 189–212.

'International Child Saving', in *The Routledge History of Childhood in the Western World*, ed. Paula Fass (London: Routledge, 2013), 469–89.

Marson, Richard, *Blue Peter: Inside the Archives* (Dudley: Kaleidoscope, 2008).

Martin, James Gerard, 'The Society of St. Vincent de Paul as an Emerging Social Phenomenon in Mid-Nineteenth Century Ireland' (MA thesis, National College of Industrial Relations, 1993).

Maul, Daniel, 'Appell an das Gewissen: Fridtjof Nansen und die Russische Hungerhilfe 1921–23', in *Themenportal Europäische Geschichte* (Berlin: Humboldt Universität, 2011), available at www.europa.clio-online.de/essay/id/artikel-3604 (accessed 29 June 2019).

'American Quakers, the Emergence of International Humanitarianism, and the Foundation of the American Friends Service Committee, 1890–1920', in *Dilemmas of Humanitarian Aid in the Twentieth Century*, ed. Johannes Paulmann (Oxford: Oxford University Press, 2016), 63–87.

Mauss, Marcel, *The Gift: Forms and Functions of Exchange in Archaic Societies* (London: Cohen & West, 1954).

Maxwell, Daniel, and Nisar Majid, *Famine in Somalia: Competing Imperatives, Collective Failures, 2011–12* (New York: Oxford University Press, 2016).

McFadden, David, and Claire Gorfinkel, *Constructive Spirit: Quakers in Revolutionary Russia* (Pasadena, CA: International Productions, 2004).

McGowan, Mark, 'Grosse Île, Quebec', in *Atlas of the Great Irish Famine*, eds John Crowley, William J. Smyth, and Mike Murphy (New York: New York University Press, 2012), 532–5.

McLean, David, 'Famine on the Coast: The Royal Navy and the Relief of Ireland, 1846–1847', *English Historical Review* 134, no. 566 (2019): 92–120.

Measures Adopted in Boston, Massachusetts, for the Relief of the Suffering Scotch and Irish (Boston: Eastburn, 1847), 14–15.

Melkas, Helinä, *Humanitarian Emergencies: Indicators, Measurements, and Data Considerations* (Helsinki: UNU/WIDER, 1996).

Miles, James E., and Meaburn Tatham, *The Ambulance Unit, 1914–1919: A Record* (London: Swarthmore Press, 1919).

Mill, John Stuart, *Principles of Political Economy: With Some of Their Applications to Social Philosophy, vol. 2* (London: Parker, 1848).

Miller, Ian, 'The Chemistry of Famine: Nutritional Controversies and the Irish Famine, c.1845–7', *Medical History* 56, no. 4 (2012): 444–62.

Miller, Peter, and Christopher Napier, 'Genealogies of Calculation', *Accounting, Organizations and Society* 18, no. 7/8 (1993): 631–47.

Moeller, Susan D., *Compassion Fatigue: How the Media Sell Disease, Famine, War and Death* (New York: Routledge, 1999).

Moniz, Amanda B., *From Empire to Humanity: The American Revolution and the Origins of Humanitarianism* (New York: Oxford University Press, 2016).

Morgan, John Minter, *A Tour through Switzerland and Italy in the Years 1846–47: In Letters to a Clergyman* (London: Longman, 1851).

Morrison, D. R., *Aid and Ebb Tide: A History of CIDA and Canadian Development Assistance* (Waterloo: Wilfrid Laurier University Press, 2011).

Moses, Jeremy, Babak Bahadorand, and Tessa Wright, 'The Iraq War and the Responsibility to Protect: Uses, Abuses and Consequences for the Future of Humanitarian Intervention', *Journal of Intervention and Statebuilding* 5, no. 4 (2011): 347–67.

Mühlens, Peter, *Die Russische Hunger- und Seuchenkatastrophe in den Jahren 1921–22* (Springer: Berlin, 1923).

Mulcahy, Matthew, *Hurricanes and Society in the British Greater Caribbean, 1624–1783* (Baltimore: Johns Hopkins University Press, 2006).

Müller, Tanja R., '"The Ethiopian Famine" Revisited: Band Aid and the Antipolitics of Celebrity Humanitarian Action', *Disasters* 37, no. 1 (2013): 61–79.

Mulley, Clare, *The Woman Who Saved the Children: A Biography of Eglantyne Jebb, Founder of Save the Children* (Oxford: Oneworld, 2009).

Najam, Adil, 'NGO Accountability: A Conceptual Framework', *Development Policy Review* 13, no. 4 (1996): 339–53.

Nally, David, *Human Encumbrances: Political Violence and the Great Famine* (Notre Dame, IN: University of Notre Dame Press, 2011).

'The Colonial Dimensions of the Great Irish Famine', in *Atlas of the Great Irish Famine*, eds John Crowley, William J. Smyth, and Mike Murphy (New York: New York University Press, 2012), 64–74.

Nathanson, Janice, 'The Pornography of Poverty: Reframing the Discourse of International Aid's Representations of Starving Children', *Canadian Journal of Communication* 38, no. 1 (2013): 103–20.

Neal, Frank, *Black'47: Britain and the Famine Irish* (Houndmills: Palgrave Macmillan, 1998).

Neville, Grace, "'Il y a des larmes dans leurs chiffres": French Famine Relief for Ireland, 1847–84', *Revue Française de Civilisation Britannique* 19, no. 2 (2014): 67–87.

"'Le pays classique de la faim": France and the Great Irish Famine', in *Atlas of the Great Irish Famine*, eds John Crowley, William J. Smyth, and Mike Murphy (New York: New York University Press, 2012), 487–91.

Newby, Andrew G., 'The Society of Friends and Famine in Ireland and Finland, c. 1845–68', in *Irish Hunger and Migration Myth, Memory and Memorialization*, eds Christine Kinealy, Patrick Fitzgerald, and Gerard Moran (Quinnipiac: Quinnipiac University Press, 2015), 107–19, 190.

Niggli, Peter, *Ethiopia: Deportations and Forced-Labour Camps* (Berlin: Berliner Missionswerk, 1986).

Nilsson, Martin, 'Svensk nödhjälp', in *Svälten på Afrikas horn*, eds Lars Adaktusson and Allan Hofgren (Uppsala: EFS-förlaget, 1986), 72–9.

Noyes, Charles E., 'American Relief of Famine in Europe', in *Editorial Research Reports, vol. 2* (Washington, DC: CQ Press, 1940), 53–68.

Nussbaum, Heinrich von, 'Das Medienspektakel: "Ein Tag für Afrika"', *Medium* no. 2 (1985): 5–7.

Nussbaum, Martha C., *Upheavals of Thought: The Intelligence of Emotions* (Cambridge: Cambridge University Press, 2001).

Ó Gráda, Cormac, 'Ireland's Great Famine: An Overview', in *When the Potato Failed: Causes and Effects of the 'Last' European Subsistence Crisis, 1845–1850*, eds Cormac Ó Gráda, Richard Paping, and Eric Vanhaute (Turnhout: Brepols, 2007), 43–57.

Famine: A Short History (Princeton, NJ: Princteon University Press, 2009).

'Mortality and the Great Famine', in *Atlas of the Great Irish Famine*, eds John Crowley, William J. Smyth, and Mike Murphy (New York: New York University Press, 2012), 170–9.

Eating People Is Wrong, and Other Essays on Famine, Its Past, and Its Future (Princeton, NJ: Princteon University Press, 2015).

'Ireland', in *Famine in European History*, eds Guido Alfani and Cormac Ó Gráda (Cambridge: Cambridge University Press, 2017), 166–84.

O'Connor, Thomas H., *Fitzpatrick's Boston 1846–1866* (Boston: Northeastern University Press, 1984).

O'Neill, Onora, 'Lifeboat Earth', *Philosophy and Public Affairs* 4, no. 3 (1975): 273–92.

O'Regan, Philip, "'A dense mass of petty accountability": Accounting in the Service of Cultural Imperialism during the Irish Famine, 1846–1847', *Accounting, Organizations and Society* 35, no. 4 (2010): 416–30.

O'Reilly, Bernard, *John MacHale, Archbishop of Tuam: His Life, Times, and Correspondence, vol. 1* (New York: Pustet, 1890).

O'Rourke, John, *The History of the Great Irish Famine of 1847, with Notices of Earlier Irish Famines* (Dublin: McGlashan and Gill, 1875).

O'Sullivan, Kevin, 'A "Global Nervous System": The Rise and Rise of European Humanitarian NGOs, 1945–1985', in *International Organisations and Development, 1945–1990*, eds Marc Frey, Sönke Kunkel, and Corinna R. Unger (New York: Macmillan, 2014), 196–219.

'Humanitarian Encounters: Biafra, NGOs and Imaginings of the Third World in Britain and Ireland, 1967–1970', *Journal of Genocide Research* 16, no. 2/3 (2014): 299–315.

'Biafra's Legacy: NGO Humanitarianism and the Nigerian Civil War', in *Learning from the Past to Shape the Future: Lessons from the History of Humanitarian Action in Africa* (London: Overseas Development Institute, 2016), 5–13.

O'Sullivan, Kevin, Matthew Hilton, and Juliano Fiori, 'Humanitarianism in Context', *European Review of History* 23, no. 1–2 (2016): 1–15.

Ockwell, Ron, *Recurring Challenges in the Provision of Food Assistance in Complex Emergencies: The Problems and Dilemmas Faced by WFP and Its Partners* (Rome: World Food Programme, 1999).

Oeuvre de Pie IX: Extraits de quelque lettres de NN. SS. les archevêques et évêques d'Irlande, a Monsieur O'Carroll, correspondent de Comité de Secours (Paris: Sirou et Desquers, 1847).

Omaka, Arua Oko, *The Biafran Humanitarian Crisis, 1967–1970: International Human Rights and Joint Church Aid* (Madison: Fairleigh Dickinson University Press, 2016).

Orbinski, James, 'Médecins Sans Frontières: Nobel Lecture', Nobelprize.org (10 Dec. 1999), available at www.nobelprize.org/prizes/peace/1999/msf/lecture/ (accessed 29 June 2019).

Özpolat, Koray, Juanita Rilling, Nezih Altay, and Eric Chavez, 'Engaging Donors in Smart Compassion: USAID CIDI's Greatest Good Donation Calculator', *Journal of Humanitarian Logistics and Supply Chain Management* 5, no. 1 (2015): 95–112.

Palmieri, Daniel, 'Humanitarianism on the Screen: The ICRC Films, 1921–1965', in *Humanitarianism & Media, 1900 to the Present*, ed. Johannes Paulmann (New York: Berghahn, 2019), 90–106.

Pankhurst, Alula, *Resettlement and Famine in Ethiopia: The Villagers' Experience* (Manchester: Manchester University Press, 1992).

Pankhurst, Richard, 'The Ethiopian Famine: Cultural Survival's New Report', *Anthropology Today* 2, no. 3 (1986): 4–5.

Pantti, Mervi, and Minttu Tikka, 'Cosmopolitan Empathy and User-Generated Disaster Appeal Videos on YouTube', in *Internet and Emotions*, eds Tova Benski and Eran Fisher (New York: Routledge, 2014), 178–92.

Paras, Andrea, *Moral Obligations and Sovereignty in International Relations: A Genealogy of Humanitarianism* (Abingdon: Routledge, 2019).

Parfitt, Tudor, *Operation Moses: The Story of the Exodus of the Falasha Jews from Ethiopia* (London: Wiedenfield and Nicolson, 1985).

Parker, Ben, 'Famine and the Machine: Can Big Money and Big Data Make Famine a Thing of the Past?', *The New Humanitarian* (12 Oct. 2018), available at www.thenewhumanitarian.org/analysis/2018/10/12/famine-and-machine-funding-prevention-data (accessed 29 June 2019).

Parker, Evan C., *Altruism, Empathy and Efficacy: The Science behind Engaging Your Supporters* (Washington, DC: Georgetown University, 2018), available at http://csic.georgetown.edu/wp-content/uploads/2018/01/Altruism-Empathy-and-Efficacy-The-Science-Behind-Engaging-Supporters-1.29.18.pdf (accessed 29 June 2019).

Patenaude, Bertrand M., *Big Show in Bololand: The American Relief Expedition to Soviet Russia in the Famine of 1921* (Stanford, CA: Stanford University Press, 2002).

Paulmann, Johannes, 'Conjunctures in the History of International Humanitarian Aid during the Twentieth Century', *Humanity* 4, no. 2 (2013): 215–38.

'The Dilemmas of Humanitarian Aid: Historical Perspectives', in *Dilemmas of Humanitarian Aid in the Twentieth Century*, ed. Johannes Paulmann (Oxford: Oxford University Press, 2016), 1–31.

Peberdy, Max, *Tigray: Ethiopia's Untold Story* (London: Relief Society of Tigray UK Support Committee, 1985).

Penrose, Angela, 'Before and After', in *The Ethiopian Famine*, eds Kurt Jansson, Michael Harris, and Angela Penrose (London: Zed Books, 1987), 79–189.

Philo, Greg, 'From Buerk to Band Aid: The Media and the 1984 Ethiopian Famine', in *Getting the Message: News, Truth and Power*, ed. John Eldridge (London: Routledge, 1993), 104–25.

Pictet, Jean, *The Fundamental Principles of the Red Cross Proclaimed by the Twentieth International Conference of the Red Cross, Vienna, 1965: Commentary* (Geneva: Henry Dunant Institute, 1979).

Development and Principles of International Humanitarian Law (Dordrecht: Nijhoff, 1985).

Pius IX, 'Praedecessores nostros', in *The Papal Encyclicals, vol. 1: 1740–1878*, ed. Claudia Carlen (Raleigh: Pierian, 1990), 285–6.

Pogge, Thomas, 'Moral Priorities for International Human Rights NGOs', in *Ethics in Action: The Ethical Challenges of International Human Rights Nongovernmental Organizations*, eds Daniel Bell and Jean-Marc Coicaud (Cambridge: Cambridge University Press, 2007), 218–56.

Ponte, Stefano, and Lisa Ann Richey, 'Buying into Development? Brand Aid Forms of Cause-Related Marketing', *Third World Quarterly* 35, no. 1 (2014): 65–87.

Poster, Alexander, 'The Gentle War: Famine Relief, Politics and Privatization in Ethiopia, 1938–86', *Diplomatic History* 26, no. 2 (2012): 399–425.

Potter, George, *To the Golden Door: The Story of the Irish in Ireland and America* (Boston: Little, Brown, 1960).

Prochaska, Frank, *The Voluntary Impulse: Philanthropy in Modern Britain* (London: Faber and Faber, 1988).

Rangasami, Amrita, '"Failure of Exchange Entitlements" Theory of Famine: A Response', *Economic and Political Weekly* 20, nos 41–2 (1985): 1747–52, 1797–801.

Raponi, Sandra, 'A Defense of the Human Right to Adequate Food', *Res Publica* 23, no. 1 (2017): 99–115.

Rapport a messeigneurs les archevêques et évêques de France et à messieurs les membres du Comité de l'Irlande (Paris: Jules-Judeau, 1849).

Ravallion, Martin, 'Famines and Economics', *Journal of Economic Literature* 35, no. 3 (1997): 1205–42.

Redfield, Peter, 'Doctors without Borders and the Moral Economy of Pharmaceuticals', in *Human Rights in Crisis*, ed. Alice Bullard (Aldershot: Ashgate, 2008), 129–44.

'Sacrifice, Triage, and Global Humanitarianism', in *Humanitarianism in Question: Politics, Power, Ethics*, eds Michael Barnett and Thomas G. Weiss (Ithaca, NY: Cornell University Press, 2008), 196–214.

Life in Crisis: The Ethical Journey of Doctors without Borders (Berkeley: University of California Press, 2013).

Reiter, Stanley, 'Efficient Allocation', in *The New Palgrave: A Dictionary of Economics, vol. 2: E to J*, eds John Eatwell, Murray Milgate, and Peter Newman (London: Macmillan, 1987), 107–20.

Report and Proceedings of the General Relief Committee of the Royal Exchange, from 3rd May to 3rd September, 1849 (Dublin: Shea, 1849).

Report of the British Association for the Relief of the Extreme Distress in Ireland and Scotland (London: Clay, 1849).

Report of the General Executive Committee of the City and County of Philadelphia ... to Provide Means to Relieve the Sufferings in Ireland (Philadelphia: Crissy and Markley, 1847).

Report of the Proceedings of the General Central Relief Committee for All Ireland from Its Formation on the 29th December, 1846, to the 31st December, 1847 (Dublin: Browne, 1848).

Report of the Proceedings of the Society of St. Vincent de Paul, in Ireland, during the Year 1848 [SVP 1848] (Dublin: Wyer, 1849).

Report of the Proceedings of the Society of St. Vincent de Paul, in Ireland, during the Year 1849 [SVP 1849] (Dublin: Wyer, 1850).

Report of the Society of Saint Vincent de Paul, for the Year 1846 (Dublin: Clarke, 1847).

Report of the Society of St. Vincent de Paul, in Ireland, for the Year 1847 [SVP 1847] (Dublin: Wyer, 1848).

Ridge, John, 'The Great Hunger in New York', *New York Irish History* 9 (1995): 5–12.

Rieff, David, *A Bed for the Night: Humanitarianism in Crisis* (New York: Simon and Schuster, 2002).

Rietzler, Katharina, 'From Peace Advocacy to International Relations Research: The Transformation of Transatlantic Philanthropic Networks, 1900–1930', in *Shaping the Transnational Sphere: Experts, Networks, Issues, 1850–1930*, eds Davide Rodogno, Bernhard Struck, and Jakob Vogel (New York: Berghahn, 2015), 173–95.

Riley, Barry, *The Political History of American Food Aid: An Uneasy Benevolance* (Oxford: Oxford University Press, 2017).

Ritov, Ilana, and Tehila Kogut, 'Ally or Adversary: The Effect of Identifiability in Intergroup Conflict Situations', *Organizational Behavior and Human Decision Processes* 116, no. 1 (2011): 96–103.

Roberts, Bayard, 'Accountability', in *Humanitarianism: A Dictionary of Concepts*, eds Tim Allen, Anna Macdonald, and Henry Radice (London: Routledge, 2018), 1–15.

Roberts, John, and Robert Scapens, 'Accounting Systems and Systems of Accountability: Understanding Accounting Practices in Their Organisational Contexts', *Accounting, Organizations and Society* 10, no. 4 (1985): 443–56.

Robertson, Benjamin, *The Famine in Russia: Report* (London: The Russian Famine Relief Fund, 1922).

Robinson, Lucy, 'Putting the Charity Back into Charity Singles: Charity Singles in Britain 1984–1995', *Contemporary British History* 26, no.3 (2012): 405–25.

Roddy, Sarah, Julie-Marie Strange, and Bertrand Taithe, 'The Charity-Mongers of Modern Babylon: Bureaucracy, Scandal, and the Transformation of the

Philanthropic Marketplace, c. 1870–1912', *Journal of British Studies* 54, no. 1 (2015): 118–37.

The Charity Market and Humanitarianism in Britain, 1870–1912 (London: Bloomsbury, 2019).

Rodogno, Davide, 'Beyond Relief: A Sketch of the Near East Relief's Humanitarian Operations, 1918–1929', *monde(s)* 6, no. 2 (2014): 45–64.

Rodogno, Davide, Francesca Piana, and Shaloma Gauthier, 'Shaping Poland: Relief and Rehabilitation Programs by Foreign Organizations 1918–1922', in *Shaping the Transnational Sphere: Experts, Networks, and Issues from the 1840s to the 1930s*, eds David Rodogno, Bernhard Struck, and Jakob Vogel (Oxford: Berghahn, 2014), 259–78.

Rorty, Richard, 'Who Are We? Moral Universalism and Economic Triage', *Diogenes* 44, no. 173 (1996): 5–15.

Rosmini-Serbati, Antonio, *Opere: Epistolario, part 1, vol. 2* (Turin: Paravia, 1857).

Roy, Parama, *Alimentary Tracts: Appetites, Aversions, and the Postcolonial* (Durham, NC: Duke University Press, 2010).

Rubenstein, Jennifer C., *Between Samaritans and States: The Political Ethics of Humanitarian INGOs* (Oxford: Oxford University Press, 2015).

Rubenstein, Richard L., *The Age of Triage: Fear and Hope in an Overcrowded World* (Boston: Beacon, 1983).

Ryfman, Philippe, *Une Histoire de l'humanitaire*, 2nd ed. (Paris: La Découverte, 2016).

Salvatici, Silvia, *A History of Humanitarianism, 1755–1989: In the Name of Others* (Manchester: Manchester University Press, 2019 [2015]).

Sandvik, Kristin Bergtora, and Kjersti Lohne, 'The Rise of the Humanitarian Drone: Giving Content to an Emerging Concept', *Millennium* 43, no. 1 (2014): 145–64.

Sargeant, Adrian, and Stephen Lee, 'Trust and Relationship Commitment in the United Kingdom Voluntary Sector: Determinants of Donor Behavior', *Psychology & Marketing* 21, no. 8 (2004): 613–35.

Sargiacomo, Massimo, Luca Ianni, and Jeff Everett, 'Accounting for Suffering: Calculative Practices in the Field of Disaster Relief', *Critical Perspectives on Accounting* 25, no. 7 (2014): 652–69.

Sasson, Tehila, 'From Empire to Humanity: The Russian Famine and the Imperial Origins of International Humanitarianism', *Journal of British Studies* 53, no. 3 (2016): 519–37.

Sasson, Tehila, and James Vernon, 'Practising the British Way of Famine: Technologies of Relief, 1770–1985', *European Review of History* 22, no. 6 (2015), 860–872.

Save the Children Annual Report, 1984–1985 (London: Save the Children, 1985).

Save the Children Annual Report 1986 (London: Save the Children, 1986).

Schlesinger, Arthur M., 'Biography of a Nation of Joiners', *American Historical Review* 50, no. 1 (1944): 1–25.

Scott-Smith, Tom, *On an Empty Stomach: The Humanitarian Approach to Hunger* (Ithaca, NY: Cornell University Press, forthcoming 2020).

Sen, Amartya, *Poverty and Famines: An Essay on Entitlements and Deprivation* (Oxford: Clarendon, 1981).

'Food Entitlements and Economic Chains', in *Hunger in History: Food Shortage, Poverty, and Deprivation*, ed. Lucile F. Newman (Oxford: Blackwell, 1990), 374–86.

Development as Freedom (Oxford: Oxford University Press, 1999).

'Human Rights and Development', in *Development as a Human Right: Legal, Political, and Economic Dimensions*, eds Bård A. Andreassen and Stephen P. Marks (Cambridge, MA: Harvard School of Public Health, 2006), 1–8.

Shah, Ami V., Bruce Hall, and Edward R. Carr, 'Bono, Band Aid, and Before: Celebrity Humanitarianism, Music and the Objects of Its Action', in *Soundscapes of Wellbeing in Popular Music*, eds Gavin Andrews, Paul Kingsbury, and Robin Kearns (Farnham: Ashgate, 2014), 269–88.

Shaw, D. John, *The World's Largest Humanitarian Agency: The Transformation of the UN World Food Programme and of Food Aid* (Houndmills: Palgrave Macmillan, 2011).

Shearer, Teri, 'Ethics and Accountability: From the For-Itself to the For-the-Other', *Accounting, Organizations and Society* 27, no. 6 (2002): 541–73.

Sheehy, David C., 'Archbishop Murray of Dublin and the Great Famine in Mayo', *Cathair na Mart* 11 (1991): 118–28.

Shrout, Anelise Hanson, '"Distressing News from Ireland": The Famine, the News and International Philanthropy' (PhD dissertation, New York University, 2013).

Shue, Henry, 'Morality, Politics, and Humanitarian Assistance', in *The Moral Nation: Humanitarianism and U.S. Foreign Policy Today*, eds Bruce Nichols and Gil Loescher (Notre Dame, IN: University of Notre Dame Press, 1989), 12–40.

Siméant, Johanna, 'Three Bodies of Moral Economy: The Diffusion of a Concept', *Journal of Global Ethics* 11, no. 2 (2015): 163–75.

Singer, Peter, 'Famine, Affluence, and Morality', *Philosophy and Public Affairs* 1, no. 3 (1972): 229–43.

'Reconsidering the Famine Relief Argument', in *Food Policy: The Responsibility of the United States in the Life and Death Choices*, eds Peter G. Brown and Henry Shue (New York: Free Press, 1977), 36–53.

'The Singer Solution to World Poverty', *New York Times Magazine* (5 Sept. 1999).

'Outsiders: Our Obligations to Those beyond Our Borders', in *The Ethics of Assistance: Morality and the Distant Needy*, ed. Deen K. Chatterjee (Cambridge: Cambridge University Press, 2004), 11–32.

'Preface', in *Famine, Affluence, and Morality* (Oxford: Oxford University Press, 2016), ix–xxix.

Skinner, Rob, and Alan Lester, 'Humanitarianism and Empire: New Research Agendas', *Journal of Imperial and Commonwealth History* 40, no. 5 (2012): 729–47.

Slim, Hugo, 'Wonderful Work: Globalizing the Ethics of Humanitarian Action', in *The Routledge Companion to Humanitarian Action*, eds Roger Mac Ginty and Jenny H. Peterson (London: Routledge, 2015), 13–25.

Humanitarian Ethics: A Guide to the Morality of Aid in War and Disaster (London: Hurst, 2015).

Slovic, Paul, 'If I Look at the Mass I Will Never Act: Psychic Numbing and Genocide', in *Emotions and Risky Technologies*, ed. Sabine Roeser (Dordrecht: Springer, 2010), 37–59.

Sluga, Glenda, *Internationalism in the Age of Nationalism* (Philadelphia: University of Pennsylvania Press, 2013).

Small, Deborah, and George Loewenstein, 'Helping a Victim or Helping the Victim: Altruism and Identifiability', *Journal of Risk and Uncertainty* 26, no. 1 (2003): 5–16.

Small, Deborah A., George Loewenstein, and Paul Slovic, 'Sympathy and Callousness: The Impact of Deliberative Thought on Donations to Identifiable and Statistical Victims', *Organizational Behavior and Human Decision Processes* 102, no. 2 (2007): 143–53.

Smirl, Lisa, *Spaces of Aid: How Cars, Compounds and Hotels Shape Humanitarianism* (London: Zed, 2015).

Smyth, William J., 'The Story of the Great Irish Famine 1845–52: A Geographical Perspective', in *Atlas of the Great Irish Famine*, eds John Crowley, William J. Smyth, and Mike Murphy (New York: New York University Press, 2012), 4–12.

'The Creation of the Workhouse System', in *Atlas of the Great Irish Famine*, eds John Crowley, William J. Smyth, and Mike Murphy (New York: New York University Press, 2012), 120–7.

Solberg, Richard W., *Miracle in Ethiopia: A Partnership Response to Famine* (New York: Friendship Press, 1991).

Soyer, Alexis, *Soyer's Charitable Cookery, or the Poor Man's Regenerator* (Dublin: Hodges and Smith, 1847).

Stamatov, Peter, *The Origins of Global Humanitarianism: Religion, Empires, and Advocacy* (New York: Cambridge University Press, 2013).

Stegemann, Lea, and Jonas Stumpf, *Supply Chain Expenditure and Preparedness Investment Opportunities* (Schindellegi: HELP Logistics, 2018).

Stein, Janice Gross, 'Humanitarian Organizations: Accountable – Why, to Whom, for What, and How?', in *Humanitarianism in Question: Politics, Power, Ethics*, eds Michael Barnett and Thomas G. Weiss (Ithaca, NY: Cornell University Press, 2008), 124–42.

Strang, Julian, and Joyce Toomre, 'Alexis Soyer and the Irish Famine: "Splendid Promises and Abortive Measures"', in *The Great Famine and the Irish Diaspora in America*, ed. Arthur Gribben (Amherst: University of Massachusetts Press, 1999), 66–84.

Strum, Harvey, 'South Carolina and Irish Famine Relief, 1846–47', *South Carolina Historical Magazine* 103, no. 2 (2002): 130–52.

'Famine Relief from an Ancient Dutch City', *Hudson River Valley Review* 22, no. 2 (2006): 54–78.

'A Jersey Ship for Ireland', in *Ireland's Great Hunger: Relief, Representation, and Remembrance, vol. 2*, ed. David Valone (Lanham, MD: University Press of America, 2010), 3–20.

'Pennsylvania and Irish Famine Relief, 1846–1847', *Pennsylvania History* 81, no. 3 (2014): 277–99.

Surface, Frank M., and Raymond Bland, *American Food in the World War and Reconstruction Period: Operations of the Organizations under the Direction of Herbert Hoover, 1914 to 1924* (Stanford, CA: Stanford University Press, 1931).

Survival International, *Ethiopia Resettlement: The Evidence* (London: Survival International, 1985).

Suski, Laura, 'Children, Suffering, and the Humanitarian Appeal', in *Humanitarianism and Suffering: The Mobilization of Empathy*, eds Richard Ashby Wilson and Richard D. Brown (Cambridge: Cambridge University Press, 2009), 202–22.

Svenska röda korsets Årsbok 1984 (Stockholm: Svenska röda korset, 1985).

Taithe, Bertrand, 'Reinventing (French) Universalism: Religion, Humanitarianism and the "French doctors"', *Modern & Contemporary France* 12, no. 2 (2004): 147–58.

——— '"Cold Calculation in the Face of Horrors?" Pity, Compassion and the Making of Humanitarian Protocols', in *Medicine, Emotion and Disease, 1700–1950*, ed. Fay Bound Alberti (New York: Palgrave Macmillan, 2006), 79–99.

——— 'Humanitarian History?', in *The Routledge Companion to Humanitarian Action*, eds Roger Mac Ginty and Jenny H. Peterson (London: Routledge, 2015), 62–73.

Taithe, Bertrand, and John Borton, 'History, Memory and "Lessons Learnt" for Humanitarian Practitioners', *European Review of History* 23, nos 1–2 (2016): 210–24.

Tatham, Peter, and Martin Christopher, 'Introduction', in *Humanitarian Logistics: Meeting the Challenges of Preparing for and Responding to Disasters*, 3rd ed. (London: Kogan Page, 2018), 1–18.

Taylor, A. J. P., 'Genocide', in *From Napoleon to the Second International: Essays on Nineteenth-Century Europe* (London: Hamish Hamilton, 1993 [1962]), 152–7.

Taylor, Dennis, Meredith Tharapos, and Shannon Sidaway, 'Downward Accountability for a Natural Disaster Recovery Effort: Evidence and Issues from Australia's Black Saturday', *Critical Perspectives on Accounting* 25, no. 7 (2014): 633–51.

'Tears Are Still Not Enough: 30 Years Later', available at www.cbc.ca/news/politics/tears-still-are-not-enough-30-years-later-1.2949836 (accessed 29 June 2019).

ten Have, Henk, 'Macro-triage in Disaster Planning', in *Disaster Bioethics: Normative Issues When Nothing Is Normal*, eds Dónal P. O'Mathúna, Bert Gordijn, and Mike Clarke (Dordrecht: Springer, 2014), 13–32.

Terry, Fiona, *Condemned to Repeat? The Paradox of Humanitarian Action* (Ithaca, NY: Cornell University Press, 2002).

——— 'North Korea: Feeding Totalitarianism', in *In the Shadow of 'Just War': Violence, Politics and Humanitarian Action*, ed. Fabrice Weissman (Ithaca, NY: Cornell University Press, 2004), 88–108.

Thieme, Sebastian, 'Thirteenth General Report of the Colonial Land and Emigration Commissioners', *Justice of the Peace, and County, Borough, Poor Law Union, and Parish Law Recorder* no. 17 (1853): 582.

——— *Das Subsistenzrecht: Begriff, ökonomische Traditionen und Konsequenzen* (Marburg: Metropolis, 2012).

Thompson, E. P., 'The Moral Economy of the English Crowd in the Eighteenth Century', *Past and Present* no. 50 (1971): 76–136.

——— 'The Moral Economy Reviewed', in *Customs in Common* (London: Merlin, 1991), 259–351.

Tierney, Kathleen, *The Social Roots of Risk: Producing Disasters, Promoting Resilience* (Stanford, CA: Stanford University Press, 2014).

Tomkins, Stephen, *The Clapham Sect: How Wilberforce's Circle Transformed Britain* (Oxford: Lion, 2010).

Tönsmeyer, Tatjana, Peter Haslinger, and Agnes Laba, eds, *Coping with Hunger and Shortage under German Occupation in World War II* (London: Palgrave Macmillan, 2018).

Touré-Tillery, Maferima, and Aleyet Fishbach, 'Too Far to Help: The Effect of Perceived Distance on the Expected Impact and Likelihood of Charitable Action', *Journal of Personality and Social Psychology* 112, no. 6 (2017): 860–76.

Transactions of the Central Relief Committee of the Society of Friends during the Famine in Ireland in 1846 and 1847 (Dublin: Hodges and Smith, 1852).

Trevelyan, Charles Edward, *The Irish Crisis* (London: Longman, Brown, Green & Longmans, 1848).

Trythall, Marisa Patulli, '"Russia's Misfortune Offers Humanitarians a Splendid Opportunity": Jesuits, Communism, and the Russian Famine', *Journal of Jesuit Studies* 5, no. 1 (2018), 71–96.

Twomey, Christina, 'Framing Atrocity: Photography and Humanitarianism,' *History of Photography* 36, no. 3 (2012): 255–64.

Tyrrell, Ian, *Reforming the World: The Creation of America's Moral Empire* (Princeton, NJ: Princeton University Press, 2010).

Ure, Midge, *If I Was . . . : The Autobiography* (London: Virgin Books, 2005).

USA for Africa, *Memories and Reflections: USA for Africa's Experiences and Practice: The First 20 Years* (s.l.: USA for Africa, 2005).

USAID, *Final Disaster Report Ethiopia Drought/Famine FY 1985 1986* (Washington, DC: USAID, 1987), available at http://pdf.usaid.gov/pdf_docs/PNABG233.pdf (accessed 29 June 2019).

van der Gaag, Nikki, and Cathy Nash, *Images of Africa: The UK Report* (Oxford: Oxfam, 1987).

van Wassenhove, Luk N., 'Humanitarian Aid Logistics: Supply Chain Management in High Gear', *Journal of the Operational Research Society* 57, no. 5 (2006): 475–89.

Vanhaute, Eric, Richard Paping, and Cormac Ó Gráda, 'The European Subsistence Crisis of 1845–1850: A Comparative Perspective', in *When the Potato Failed: Causes and Effects of the 'Last' European Subsistence Crisis, 1845–1850*, eds Cormac Ó Gráda, Richard Paping, and Eric Vanhaute (Turnhout: Brepols, 2007), 15–40.

Vaux, Tony, *The Selfish Altruist: Relief Work in Famine and War* (London: Earthscan, 2001).

Vernon, James, *Hunger: A Modern History* (Cambridge, MA: Belknap, 2007).

Vestal, Theodore M., 'Famine in Ethiopia: Crisis of Many Dimensions', *Africa Today* 32, no. 4 (1985): 7–28.

Vestergaard, Anne, 'Humanitarian Appeal and the Paradox of Power', *Critical Discourse Studies* 10, no. 4 (2013): 444–67.

Vincent, C. Paul, *The Politics of Hunger: The Allied Blockade of Germany, 1915–1919* (Athens: Ohio University Press, 1985).

Vinyard, JoEllen McNergney, 'Irish Emigrant Society (Detroit)', in *Irish American Voluntary Organizations*, ed. Michael F. Funchion (Westport, CT: Greenwood Press, 1983), 168–71.

Vogt, Carl Emil, 'Fridtjof Nansen og kampen mot hungersnøden i Russland 1921–23', *Nordisk Øst-forum* 16, no. 2 (2002), 183–93.

Nansens Kamp mot Hungersnøden i Russland 1921–23 (Oslo: Aschehoug, 2007).

'"Først vore egne!" Da Aftenposten saboterte Nansens nødhjelp til Russland', *Historisk Tidsskrift* 108, no. 1 (2008): 29–59.

'Fridtjof Nansen and European Food Aid to Russia and the Ukraine 1921–1923', *Dvacáté století* 1, no. 2 (2009): 40–50.

Walzer, Michael, 'On Humanitarianism: Is Helping Others Charity, or Duty, or Both?', *Foreign Affairs* 90, no. 4 (2011): 69–80.

Watenpaugh, Keith David, *Bread from Stones: The Middle East and the Making of Modern Humanitarianism* (Oakland: University of California Press, 2015).

Watson, Brad, 'Origins of Child Sponsorship: Save the Children Fund in the 1920s', in *Child Sponsorship: Exploring Pathways to a Brighter Future*, eds Brad Watson and Matthew Clarke (New York: Palgrave Macmillan, 2014), 18–40.

Weidling, Paul, 'From Sentiment to Science: Children's Relief Organisations and the Problem of Malnutrition in Inter-war Europe', *Disasters* 18, no. 3 (1994): 203–12.

Weindling, Paul, *Epidemics and Genocide in Eastern Europe, 1890–1945* (Oxford: Oxford University Press, 2000).

Weiss, Thomas G., and Karl M. Campbell, 'Military Humanitarianism', *Survival* 33, no. 5 (1991): 451–65.

Weissman, Benjamin M., *Herbert Hoover and Famine Relief to Soviet Russia, 1921–1923* (Stanford, CA: Stanford University Press, 1974).

Werth, Nicolas, 'Déni, connaissance, responsabilité: Le régime stalinien et la grande famine ukrainienne de 1932–3', *European Review of History* 22, no. 6 (2015): 900–16.

Westley, Frances, 'Bob Geldof and Live Aid: The Affective Side of Global Social Innovation', *Human Relations* 40, no. 10 (1991): 1011–36.

Whittington, Geoffrey, 'Accounting and Economics', in *The New Palgrave: A Dictionary of Economics, vol. 1: A to D*, eds John Eatwell, Murray Milgate, and Peter Newman (London: Macmillan, 1987), 11–14.

Wieters, Heike, 'Reinventing the Firm: From Post-war Relief to International Humanitarian Agency', *European Review of History* 23, nos 1–2 (2016): 116–35.

The NGO CARE and Food Aid from America, 1945–80: 'Showered with Kindness'? (Manchester: Manchester University Press, 2017).

Wilkens, Ann, 'Katastrofbiståndsutredningen: Fallstudie Etiopien. Svältkatastrofen i Etiopien 1984/85, en dokumentation av nödhjälpsoperationen', in *Katastrofbistånd för utveckling: Några fakta och synpunkter. Fallstudier av Etiopien och Bangladesh*, ed. Sture Linnér (Stockholm: SIDA, 1986).

Williams, David, 'Review Article: Aid as Autobiography', *Journal of the International African Institute* 72, no. 1 (2002): 150–63.

Winkler, Heinrich August, ed., *Organisierter Kapitalismus: Voraussetzungen und Anfänge* (Göttingen: Vandenhoeck & Ruprecht, 1974).

Wisor, Scott, 'How Should INGOs Allocate Resources?', *Ethics & Global Politics* 5, no. 1 (2012): 27–48.

Wolff, Larry, *Inventing Eastern Europe: The Map of Civilization on the Mind of the Enlightenment* (Stanford, CA: Stanford University Press, 1994).

Woodham-Smith, Cecil, *The Great Hunger: Ireland 1845–9* (London: Hamish Hamilton, 1962).

'Work of the International Russian Relief Committee', *International Committee for Russian Relief – Information* no. 26 (10 July 1922).

Yeophantong, Pichamon, *Understanding Humanitarian Action in East and Southeast Asia: A Historical Perspective* (London: Overseas Development Institute, 2014).

Yordanov, Radoslav A., *The Soviet Union and the Horn of Africa during the Cold War: Between Ideology and Pragmatism* (Lanham, MD: Lexington Books, 2016).

Zagefka, Hanna, and Trevor James, 'The Psychology of Charitable Donations to Disaster Victims and Beyond', *Social Issues and Policy Review* 9, no. 1 (2015): 155–92.

Zavatti, Francesco, 'Appealing Locally for Transnational Humanitarian Aid: Italian Bishops and the Great Irish Famine', *Quellen und Forschungen aus italienischen Archiven und Bibliotheken* 99 (2019): 313–39.

Zelizer, Viviana A., *The Social Meaning of Money* (New York: Basic Books, 1994).

Index

Abdulmejid I (Ottoman Sultan), 34
absence of humanitarian action, 13
abuse of aid, *see* misappropriation of aid
academics, aid appeals by, 114
accountability of aid, 219–24, 291–4
  Ethiopian famine relief, 266–91
  Irish famine relief, 224–45
  moral economy of, 221–4
  Soviet famine relief, 245–66
ad hoc humanitarianism, 4, 24, 28, 33, 302
  accountability of aid in, 293–4
  limitations of, 170
Addis Ababa, 192
adoption of children, symbolic, 48, 112
adult feeding programmes, 180–1
advertisements, use of, 116, 121
  in accountability of aid, 123, 231, 263
  criticism on costs of, 250–3
Africa, Western conceptions of, 129, 137
Aftonbladet (newspaper, Sweden), 120
AFSC (American Friends Service Committee, USA), 49
  Soviet famine relief by, 51, 96
  conflicts with ARA, 188, 190, 248
aggression, famines resulting from, 304
agricultural machinery, as famine relief, 186–7
aid workers
  expatriate
    in Ethiopian famine relief, 193
    in Soviet famine relief, 249–50
  on gratitude of aid beneficiaries, 262
  idealism of, 218
  in-group solidarity of, 15
  local, hiring of, 246
  on misappropriation of aid, 287
  sexual abuse by, 167, 175, 218, 306
  working conditions of, 171
aid-in-kind, *see* in-kind relief
airlifting of aid, for Ethiopian Famine, 191–2, 201
allocation of aid, 144–5
  decision-making on, 145–7, 213–15

earmarking, 217
  Ethiopian famine relief, 133, 191–213
  Irish famine relief, 149–70
  priority regimes in, 19–22
  Soviet famine relief, 170–91
American Philanthropy Abroad (Curti), 25
Amin, Mohamed, 63, 116–18, 137
AMR (American Mennonite Relief), 189
Anglican Church humanitarianism, 77
anonymity of aid beneficiaries, 295–6
anti-communism, Soviet famine relief affected by, 50, 96–8, 214
anti-famine contracts, 11
ARA (American Relief Administration), 29, 51
  child-focused charity by, 48
  professionalisation of, 55–6
  Soviet famine relief by, 52–3, 56, 95–7, 109, 179, 265
  accountability of, 245–50, 256–7, 261–5
  allocation of aid, 172–3, 177, 183–4
  conflicts with other organisations, 188–90
  food remittance programme, 46, 113–16, 173–5, 180, 183, 185, 249
  fundraising strategies, 100–2, 105
  medical aid, 182
  overhead costs, 253–4
  Special Funds for the Relief of Individual Cases of Suffering, 185
ARC (American Red Cross), 28, 121
  fundraising campaigns by, 125
  Soviet famine relief by, 182
archives of relief organisations, 308
Article 19 (human rights organisation), 207
Assab (Ethiopia), 191
asymmetric power relations, between donors and beneficiaries of aid, 222–4, 300–1
attacks on aid convoys, in famine relief for Tigray and Eritrea, 201
'Austria für Afrika' (song), 132
authoritarian regimes, and famine, 9

342

Lightning Source UK Ltd.
Milton Keynes UK
UKHW022216221022
410945UK00023B/412